D1614188

DWDM

Books of Related Interest from IEEE Press

FAULT DETECTABILITY IN DWDM: Toward Higher Signal Quality & System Reliability
Stamatios V. Kartalopoulos
2001   Hardcover   156 pp   ISBN 0-7803-6044-3

INTRODUCTION TO DWDM TECHNOLOGY: Data in a Rainbow
Stamatios V. Kartalopoulos
2000   Hardcover   274 pp   ISBN 0-7803-5399-4

UNDERSTANDING SONET/SDH AND ATM: Communications Networks for the Next Millennium
Stamatios V. Kartalopoulos
A volume in the IEEE Press Understanding Science & Technology Series
1999   Softcover   288 pp   ISBN 0-7803-4745-5

DWDM
NETWORKS, DEVICES, AND TECHNOLOGY

Stamatios V. Kartalopoulos, Ph.D.

IEEE Communications Society, Sponsor

IEEE PRESS

WILEY-INTERSCIENCE

A JOHN WILEY & SONS, INC., PUBLICATION

For general information on our other products and services please contact our Customer Care Department within the U.S. at 877-762-2974, outside the U.S. at 317-572-3993 or fax 317-572-4002.

Library of Congress Cataloging-in-Publication Data Is Available.

ISBN 0-471-26905-0

Printed in the United States of America

10 9 8 7 6 5 4 3 2 1

To the enlightened mind that is sparked by curiosity
To curiosity that stimulates research
To research that seeks the truth
To the truth that enlightens the mind

CONTENTS

2 Optical Components   93

PREFACE

DWDM, dense wavelength division multiplexing, is a new technology that, with the help of photonic components, "bootstraps" many individually modulated optical wavelengths in a single fiber and enables bandwidth scalability to levels not possible before. A parallel to this is many differently colored threads brought together to construct a thin rope, where each thread corresponds to a wavelength. The receiving end performs the reverse function; it unravels the rope to its constituent colored threads.

In legacy systems, increasing the bandwidth of transported information by a few tens of Mbps was considered remarkable and was "big news." In DWDM, only if the increase is by a few hundreds of Gbps does it become noticeable. In DWDM, the race for unprecedented bandwidths is on and as soon as 800 Gbps was announced, it was soon followed by another at 1,600 Gbps; currently, aggregate bandwidths at Peta-bits per second (Pbps) are discussed (1 Pbps = 1,000 Tbps = 1,000,000 Gbps). DWDM technology, systems and networks enable aggregate data rates per fiber at several Tb/s and long fiber spans (1,000 Km or more) without amplification. The significance of this becomes clear if one considers that a SONET repeater may cost thousands of dollars per signal and per 40 Km of fiber.

An information channel, when realized with a modulated optical frequency or wavelength, is termed an *optical channel*. A binary data rate modulates the optical wavelength. Most optical components in DWDM are insensitive to bit rate and all are insensitive to the content of data, with the exception of a long stream of ZEROs (or absence of light) that may affect the receiver synchronizing function. Thus, since DWDM optical components are insensitive to bit rate, in theory, each DWDM optical channel may have different information content as well as a different bit rate. The latter, along with an extremely high aggregate bandwidth, is what makes DWDM a highly attractive technology that is used in all levels and layers of future communications networks.

In communications, *multiplexing* can be accomplished at different levels. When in electronic form, many signals may be multiplexed in the time domain using time compression (or bit rate upping), such as time division multiplexing (TDM), by bit interleaving as in VTs of SONET/SDH, or by packet interleaving. In DWDM, multiplexing means many wavelengths modulated, coupled, and transmitted over the same fiber medium. The term *DWDM* has been expanded to include not only an optical multiplexing technology but also a whole suite of functions such as optical amplification, optical switching, optical equalization, optical filtering, and so on. In the acronym DWDM, D stands for *dense* (wavelengths), in CWDM, C stands for *course*, and in UDWDM, UD stands for ultradense. The term *dense* is relative and it indicates a large number of wavelengths in a given spectral bandwidth (e.g., C-band) and thus tighter specifications (channel width, channel spacing, etc.), in contrast to few optical channels with very relaxed specifications in the same bandwidth. However, it is expected that soon, what we now call dense will be tomorrow's coarse and ultra-dense will be the true dense.

Thus, based on this technology, new optical systems are being designed and new networks are being architected. And as new systems and networks are on the drawing board and new software is developed, new issues emerge, new standards are drafted, new services emerge, and new consumer devices are offered. These new systems and networks can offer more bandwidth at less cost, and soon bandwidth will become from premium a commodity item.

This is the third book in the series on DWDM. The first book, *Introduction to DWDM Technology: Data in a Rainbow* (IEEE Press, 2000) provides a high-level introduction to DWDM technology. The second, *Fault Detection in DWDM: Towards Signal Quality and System Robustness* (IEEE Press, 2001), provides a treatise in fault mechanisms of DWDM components, systems, and networks, how they correlate, and how they are detected. This book provides a comprehensive treatment of DWDM, its technology, systems and networks, and engineering design aspects. In all, it provides an A-to-Z approach to DWDM, how it works, how it is used in system design, how optical network architecture can benefit from DWDM, and what the design issues are. Optical components are described in detail supported by useful equations and tables but avoiding complex mathematical derivations. DWDM systems and networks are supported by telecommunications fundamentals and legacy systems. New areas pertinent to DWDM (such as wavelength diversity), network and service survivability are explained. Failure modes in the DWDM optical regime are identified and correlated as they impact the quality of optical signal, quality of service, system reliability, and network and service survivability to aid in engineering more robust DWDM components, systems, and networks. Finally, open issues and future trends are identified and discussed, as well as emerging technologies applicable to DWDM communications systems and networks. A fourth book provides a treatment on *SONET/SDH and ATM: Communications Networks for the Next Millennium* (IEEE Press, 1999).

It is my hope that this book will raise many questions to DWDM technologists; will excite and stimulate many communications engineers, system designers and network architects; and will aid in the design of robust, efficient, and cost-effective systems and networks. I wish you happy and easy reading.

STAMATIOS V. KARTALOPOULOS, Ph.D.

ACKNOWLEDGMENTS

To my wife Anita, son William, and daughter Stephanie for their consistent patience and encouragement. To my publisher's staff for their collaboration, enthusiasm, and project management. To all the technical reviewers for their useful comments and constructive criticism. And to all those who worked diligently on all phases of this production.

LIST OF PHYSICAL CONSTANTS

c	velocity of light	2.99792458×10^8 m/sec
e	electron charge	1.60218×10^{-19} Coulomb
m_e	mass of electron	9.1085×10^{-28} gram
m_p	mass of proton	1.67243×10^{-24} gram
m_n	mass of neutron	1.67474×10^{-24} gram
m_E	mass of earth	5.983×10^{27} gram
E_e	rest energy of electron	0.51098 MeV
ε_0	permitivity of free space	8.8542×10^{-12} Farad/m
μ_0	permeability of free space	$4\pi \times 10^{-7}$ Henry/m
h	Plank's constant	$6.6260755 \times 10^{-34}$ Joule-second
k	Boltzmann's constant	1.38×10^{-23} Joule/$^\circ$K
N_A	Avogadro's number	6.0221×10^{23}/mol
Zo (μ_0/ε_0)	impedance of free space	376.731 Ohm (Ω)
g	acceleration due to gravity	980.665 cm/sec^2
π	dimensionless number, pi	$3.141593+$
e	base of natural logarithm	$2.7182818+$

Other Constants

Density of pure water at 3.98°C	1 g/ml
Density of air (at 0°C and 760 mmHg)	1.293×10^{-3} g/cm^3
Velocity of sound in air (at 0°C and 760 mmHg)	331.7 m/sec
Velocity of sound in water (at 20°C)	1470 m/sec
dn/dT of PMMA acrylic	$-8.0 \times 10^5/^\circ$C
dn/dT of polystyrene	$-12.0 \times 10^{-5}/^\circ$C
Linear expansion coefficient of PMMA acrylic	6.74×10^5/cm/$^\circ$C
Linear expansion of coefficient of polystyrene	8.0×10^{-5}/cm/$^\circ$C

Useful Conversions

1° of angle $= 60$ minutes $= 3600$ seconds $= 1.7453$ rads
$\qquad = 2.778 \times 10^{-3}$ circumference

1 circumference $= 360^\circ$

1 rad $= 360^\circ/2\pi = 0.1592$ circumference $= 57.296^\circ$

1 meter $= 100$ cm $= 1000$ mm $= 10^6$ μm $=$ **39.37 in.** $= 3.280833$ ft $= 1.09361$ yd

1 km = 3300 ft

1 μm = 0.04 mils

1 nm = 10 angstroms (Å)

1 inch = 2.540005 cm

1 liter = 1000.027 cm^3 = 33.8147 fl oz = 0.26418 gal

1 ounce = 28.34953 grams

1 atmosphere = 1.0133 bar = 14.696 lb/in^2

$0°C$ = 273 K = $32°F$

1 Joule (abs) = 1 Newton-meter = 1 Watt-second = 1×10^7 ergs
$\qquad\qquad$ = 1 V-Coulomb = 9.4805×10^{-4} Btu

1 HP (electrical) = 746.00 W

1 HP (mechanical) = 745.70 W = 0.70696 Btu/sec

1 eV = 1.6×10^{-12} erg = 1.60218×10^{-19} Joule

1 wavelength (red) = 632.8 nm

1 wavelength (green) = 546.07 nm

1 wavelength (blue) = 488 nm

10 wavelengths (red) = 0.00025 inches

INTRODUCTION

Advancements in communications technology and communications services have triggered a global *voracious appetite* for bandwidth. Yesterday, downloading an image over the Internet, even if it took several minutes, was exciting; today, one or two mere seconds are annoying. Yesterday, accessing scanty news from a distant country by clicking the "mouse" was a challenge; today, broadcasting the "news" as it happens with real-time video, is expected, even in remote and ragged areas. Contrasting today's and yesterday's advancements can go on and on. Yet, today's advancements are made possible because of ever-shrinking electronics, increasing processing power at lower cost (Figure i), making it possible new services to emerge allowing for mobility and easy access and because of optical technology that enables networks to transport over a single strand of fiber a huge aggregate bandwidth.

In fact, the bandwidth explosion is so rapid that all predictions on today's bandwidth needs that were made one or two years ago, despite a temporary pause due to market and economic pressures, have missed the mark. Exciting and previously unimaginable end-user devices and services have been forecasted, which under different circumstances would be considered science fiction. However, we should keep in mind that *"today is yesterday's future and tomorrow's past."*

Yet, what we see today in terms of communication services is but the tip of an iceberg, an iceberg that is made of imagination, innovation, and determination and is founded on "bandwidth availability" that only optical technology can offer (Figure ii).

Glass-based fiber as the transmission medium and many novel optical components have fueled the bandwidth appetite. Glass-based fiber is very thin, immune to

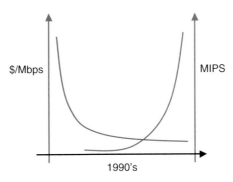

Figure i In the 1990s, denser and faster electronics and at lower cost, paved the way for an unprecedented bandwidth demand.

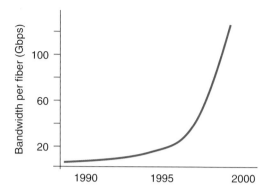

Figure ii   Since the 1990s, the available bandwidth follows an explosive trend, largely due to DWDM technology.

electromagnetic interference allows light to travel for very long distances (thousands of kilometers) without significant loss, and it is almost independent of bit rate. In addition, the cost of fiber is affordable and comparable to that of copper. Therefore, fiber has been the transmission medium of choice for several years for long-haul (long distances) as well as for metropolitan area networks (MAN) in inner city and inner campus applications. And, based on end-customer demand for higher bandwidth, fiber penetration in the loop plant is becoming noticeable. In particular, SONET/SDH technology, based on the time division multiplexing (TDM) approach, has paved the fiber-way for ultra-high bit rates and ultra-bandwidths. And, many thousands of kilometers of fiber are installed each year around the world.

With respect to optical components, there is a full range of functions that take advantage of the physical properties of materials; such as optical multiplexing and demultiplexing, optical filtering, optical switching, optical amplification, and more (Figure iii). On going research and development keep improving their performance,

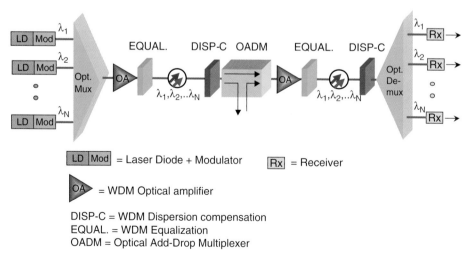

Figure iii   A broad range of optical components has made it possible for WDM networks to transport several Terabits per second.

make them more compact, and increase the level of integration to offer optical components with more complex functionality at lower cost. As a result, the penetration of optical functionality (as opposed to electronic) in systems and in networks keeps increasing. Optical cross-connecting units are replacing electronic units, optical amplifiers are replacing opto-electronic transponders and regenerators, and optical add-drop multiplexers are replacing electronic ones. At the same time, lasers and modulators have pushed the bit rate envelope from 2.5 Gb/s to 40 Gb/s, and researchers are announcing 160 Gb/s and beyond.

However, as communications systems and networks become more "optical" and the aggregate bandwidth keeps increasing, certain values cannot be compromised, such as quality of signal and availability of quality service. Therefore, network architectures must demonstrate redundancy, intelligence, reliability, and service survivability. For this, systems must have sophisticated optical monitoring mechanisms and intelligent communications protocols to identify severe degradations and failures that affect optical signal quality and service, and be able to quickly reroute traffic. Monitoring mechanisms, in conjunction with fault management and smart network protocols can preempt catastrophic failures that impact the optical signal and in certain cases the network.

IN THIS BOOK

This Book Is Organized in Three Parts.

Part I describes the DWDM technology underlying physics and concepts upon which DWDM optical components, systems, and networks work, and it also provides a thorough description supported by equations and tables of most key optical components used in DWDM system design. It also provides a thorough treatment of bit error rate, how it is affected by the nonlinearities and linearities of the transmission medium and other optical components and what the penalty is at the receiver.

Part II consists of three chapters. Chapter 4 provides a comprehensive description of the design aspects of various building blocks that are used to design DWDM systems, their interfaces, management strategies, and description of DWDM systems by network layer, access, metro, add-drop multiplexers, cross-connects, short-haul and long-haul systems. It also describes protection and interoperability aspects and it provides engineering design examples. Chapter 4 is preceded by a brief yet comprehensive description of the fundamental communications concepts (such as TDM, SONET, IP, Ethernet, DSL) that have set the foundation and trends of modern communications systems and networks as well as certain limitations.

Part III provides a treatment of DWDM networks. Chapter 5 provides a description of network topologies, network layers and domains, inter-networking, network reconfigurability, elasticity and scalability, bandwidth and wavelength management, network protection and survivability strategies, and engineering aspects of the DWDM network. It also provides a brief description of wireless and free-space optical DWDM networks. Chapter 6 provides a general overview of emerging technologies and the future of optical DWDM systems and networks.

It is my hope that this book will stimulate thinking and generate more questions leading to innovation and that it will accelerate the process of reaching the future communications network sooner and in a cost-effective manner.

All three parts are supported by a plethora of examples, illustrations, tables, exercises, and research references, as well as supporting standards.

Notice: This book contains device specifications for illustrative and educational purposes. Because specifications are continuously changing, no responsibility is assumed for correctness. The reader is encouraged to consult the latest versions of standards as well as the most current manufacturer's data sheets.

THE PHYSICS OF OPTICAL COMPONENTS

1.1 INTRODUCTION

The study of optical components requires knowledge of two disciplines, the physics of light and the physics of matter (mostly solid-state). Not to underestimate them, other disciplines such as metallurgy, chemistry, and crystallography are equally critical, but for the purpose of this book they are of secondary importance. Here we focus on that part of the physics of light and matter that helps one to understand how optical components work and what their issues are so that we can better appreciate how optical communications systems and networks are built, and how they can be built better, more efficiently, and at lower cost.

The study of light is not new. In antiquity, light intrigued many cultures and religions, and at least one ancient religion worshiped light. However, some ancient scientists realized that although light had wonderful and unexplained properties, particularly as it passed through colorful crystals, these properties were not caused by divine intervention, but they were real and therefore they could be scientifically explained. This curiosity finally demystified the properties of light. Perhaps the mythological story of Prometheus is an attempt to convey in lay language the message that light is for people to use and understand.

Once light was demystified, people used it in a number of applications, including the earliest optical communications network, which was constructed with light towers and used torches to signal a message from one tower to another (as Aeschylus wrote in his play *Agamemnon*). This optical network proved effective but vulnerable to interception, and Aeneas Takitos (a 4th c. B.C. military scientist from the town of Stymphalos) developed encoding techniques to transmit coded optical messages securely. The applications with light continued, and although today ancient applications sound trivial and

This chapter contains device specifications for illustrative and educational purposes. Because specifications are continuously changing, no responsibility is assumed for correctness. The reader is encouraged to consult the most current manufacturers' data sheets.

elementary, at the time they were considered marvelous and state-of-the-art, exactly as our state-of-the-art achievements will be considered by future generations. In that regard, *today is yesterday's future, and today is tomorrow's past.*

In the pursuit of explaining the properties of light, scientists discovered that both visible and invisible light truly consist of a continuum of components and many scientists tried to decompose it. Of course, nature did it in a natural way when light passed through a prismatic crystal. From this research effort, it was discovered that even the chlorine yellow line can be split into two lines by using a strong magnetic field. Soon it was proven that light was electromagnetic energy, but it also was discovered that light consists of quantized particles called photons. This discovery raised many eyebrows and created some animosity. Similarly, the propagation properties of light in transparent materials and in optical waveguides were studied. And this is history.

Today many interesting materials have been developed, and glass-fiber is the chosen transmission medium for high-speed, high-reliability, and long-distance terrestrial and submarine communications. Currently, bit rates at 40 Gbps are used in a single fiber. With *dense wavelength division multiplexing* (DWDM), the aggregate bandwidth has exceeded one terabit per second. DWDM systems with 160 wavelengths have been announced, and 1000 wavelengths have been on the experimenter's workbench for some time. What does this mean? A 40-wavelength DWDM system at 40 Gbps per wavelength has an aggregate bandwidth of 1.6 Tbps, a bandwidth that can transport in a single fiber the contents of about 45,000 volumes of an encyclopedia in 1 second.

Table 1.1   Units and site in decimal

Number	10^N	Name	Time Unit	Bit Rate	Length Unit
1,000,000,000,000,000	10^{15}	1 quadrillion	(see note 1)	Peta-bps (Pbps)	
1,000,000,000,000	10^{12}	1 trillion		Tera-bps (Tbps)	
1,000,000,000	10^9	1 billion		Giga-bps (Gbps)	
1,000,000	10^6	1 million		Mega-bps (Mbps)	
1,000	10^3	1 thousand		Kilo-bps (Kbps) (see note 3)	Kilometer (km)
100	10^2	1 hundred			
10	10^1	Ten			
1	10^0	One	Second (s) (see note 2)	Bit-per-second (bps)	Meter (m)
0.1	10^{-1}	One-tenth			Decameter (dm)
0.01	10^{-2}	One-hundredth			Centimeter (cm)
0.001	10^{-3}	One-thousandth	Millisecond (ms)		Millimeter (mm)
0.000 001	10^{-6}	One-millionth	Microsecond (μs)		Micrometer (μm)
0.000 000 001	10^{-9}	One-billionth	Nanosecond (ns)		Nanometer (nm) (see note 4)
0.000 000 000 001	10^{-12}	One-trillionth	Picosecond (ps)		Picometer (pm)
0.000 000 000 000 001	10^{-15}	One-quadrillionth	Femtosecond (fs)		

[1]Blank entries signify an uncommon unit.
[2]One day has 86,400 seconds; light travels at about 10^{10} cm/sec or 30 cm/ns.
[3]The bit rate of uncompressed PCM voice is 64 Kbps.
[4]3.4 nm is the length of one helical turn of a DNA strand.

If a file of 1 terabit was transmitted using a 56-Kbps modem, it would take about 7 months (i.e., without interruption); at 40 Gbps it would take just 25 seconds!

Denser DWDM systems are currently a trend that increases not only both the number of wavelength density per fiber and the aggregate bit rate, but also the length of fiber without signal amplification (Fig. 1.1).

Certain numbers mentioned in this book may seem very small or very large. Table 1.1 puts into perspective what these number mean, such as a picosecond (ps) or a terabit per second (Tbps):

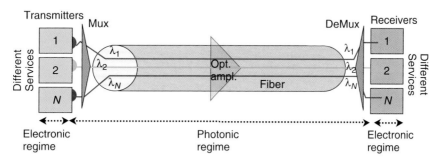

Figure 1.1   A conceptual DWDM path with many wavelength-channels in the same fiber.

1.2   THE NATURE OF LIGHT

The surprising dual nature property of light a couple or so centuries ago, which sounded like a contradiction, is accepted and well understood (well, we think so): one nature is (electromagnetic) wave and the other nature is particle.

1.2.1   The Wave Nature of Light

The wave nature of light is the same as that of radio waves and X-ray waves. As such, it is subject to reflection, refraction, diffraction, interference, polarization, fading, loss, and so on. Thus, being an electromagnetic wave, light interacts with any charges that may be present in the neighboring space. Therefore, to measure the force (magnitude and direction) of the electric field of light at any point in space, a theoretical positive charge is introduced at that point. Similarly, to measure the force (magnitude and direction) of the magnetic field, a theoretical elemental magnetic dipole is introduced at that point.

An electromagnetic wave, and thus light, is characterized by frequency and wavelength, as well as by phase and propagation speed with respect to a reference point.

- Frequency is the number of peak waves in a second, and wavelength is the traveled distance of a complete wave (e.g., peak-to-peak) in free space or in a medium. The unit for frequency is cycles per second or hertz, and the unit for wavelength is nanometer (nm) or micrometer (mm). An older unit that is also encountered is the angstrom; one angstrom is equal to 10^{-10} meters.

- Phase with respect to a reference point is the phase angle difference between the peaks of the wave with that point.

- Propagation speed is the distance traveled by a peak of a wave within the unit of time.

Monochromatic light, or single color light, is light that consists of waves that are all of exactly the same "single" frequency. Waves that propagate in space have a spherical front. However, to simplify the mathematical analysis, electromagnetic waves are considered planar. Thus, light is described by the Maxwell's electromagnetic plane wave equations:

$$\nabla^2 E = (1/v^2)(\eta^2 E/\eta t^2)$$

$$\nabla^2 H = (1/v^2)(\eta^2 H/\eta t^2)$$

$$\nabla D = \rho$$

and

$$\nabla B = 0$$

where ∇ is the Laplacian operator; u is the speed of the wave in a medium; E and H are the electric and magnetic fields, respectively; D is the electric displacement vector (its gradient is the charge density ρ); and B is the magnetic induction vector. These four vectors are interrelated as

$$D = \varepsilon_0 E + P$$

$$B = \mu_0 H + M$$

where ε_0 and μ_0 are the dielectric permittivity and permeability, respectively, both constants of free space, and P and M are the electric polarization and the magnetic polarization of the wave, respectively.

When an electromagnetic wave propagates in a linear (e.g., noncrystalline) medium, the electric polarization is expressed as

$$P = \varepsilon_0 \chi E$$

where χ is the electric susceptibility of the medium (in a nonlinear medium, this is expressed as a tensor); note that in a nonlinear medium, the latter relationship includes higher-order terms.

Moreover, the dielectric constant of the material, ε, is connected with the susceptibility as

$$\varepsilon = \varepsilon_0(1 + \chi)$$

The propagation of a plane wave (Fig. 1.2) is described by the two relationships:

$$E(r, t) = E_0 e^{-j(\omega t - k \cdot r)}$$

and

$$H(r, t) = H_0 e^{-j(\omega t - k \cdot r)}$$

where ω is the angular frequency, r is the directional vector, and k is the wave vector, which is connected with the dielectric constant by the relationship

$$k = |k| = \omega \theta (\mu_0 \varepsilon)$$

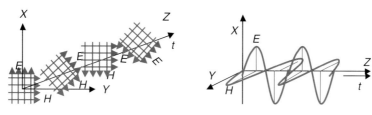

For an observer on the wave   For an observer at the origin

Figure 1.2   Graphical representation of an *E*-*H* plane wave evolution.

The aforementioned two wave relationships are complex numbers, and they consist of a real term, $\cos(x)$, and an imaginary term, $\sin(x)$. However, since the measurable quantity is the only real part, they are simplified as

$$E(r, t) = E_{o} \cos(\omega t - k \cdot r)$$

and

$$H(r, t) = H_{o} \cos(\omega t - k \cdot r)$$

Finally, when the (monochromatic) plane wave travels in free space, it travels at a maximum and constant speed (since μ_{o} and ε_{o} are constant quantities):

$$c = \omega/k = 1/[\sqrt{(\mu_{o}\varepsilon_{o})}]$$

where $c = 2.99792458 \times 10^{10}$ cm/sec, or $\sim$30 cm/nsec
    When light travels in a medium (other than free space), its velocity u is expressed by

$$u = \omega/k = 1/[\sqrt{(\mu\varepsilon)}]$$

The speed of light, *u*, in a medium is always smaller than *c* because $\mu > \mu_{o}$ and $\varepsilon > \varepsilon_{o}$.

1.2.1.1 *Photometric Terms*
Comparing two light sources or two illuminated objects, one can tell which one is brighter. Such comparisons are useful, but they do not provide precisely the absolute value of light brightness. As a consequence, certain measurable units must be introduced.

- (Total) *luminous flux*, Φ, is the rate of optical energy flow (or number of photons per second) emitted by a point light source in all directions; it is measured in lumens (lm). In radiometric terms, this is known as optical power and is measured in watts.

- *Luminous* (or *candle*) *intensity*, *I*, is the rate emitted in a solid angle of a spherical surface area equal to its radius (e.g., radius = 1 m, surface area = 1 m^2). Luminous intensity is measured in *candelas* or *candles* (cd). The luminous intensity of a sphere is $\Phi/4\pi$.

- *Illuminance*, *E*, is the flux density at an area *A* (m^2), or the luminous flux per unit area; it is measured in *lux* (lx). The illuminance at a point of a spherical

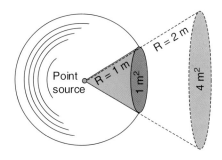

Figure 1.3   Definition of luminous (or candle) intensity and the law of inverse square.

surface is $E = \Phi/4\pi R^2$. Illuminance refers to light received by a surface. Since the luminous intensity I of the sphere is $\Phi/4\pi$, then $E = I/R^2$. This is known as *the law of inverse squares* (Fig. 1.3).

- *Luminance*, B, is the amount of optical energy emitted by a lighted surface per unit of time and per unit of solid angle and per unit of projected area. Luminance is measured in cd/m^2 and is also known as nit (nt).

Some examples of luminance are (in cd/m^2):

Clear blue sky:	10^4
Sun:	1.6×10^9
Candle:	2×10^6
Fluorescent lamp:	10^4

Table 1.2 summarizes the photometric units that are used in optics and optical communications, their measuring units, and their dimensions (M = mass, T = time, L = length):

Table 1.2   Photometric units (M = mass, T = time, L = length)

Definition	Photometric Unit	Dimensions
Energy	Luminous energy (talbot)	ML^2T^{-2}
Energy per unit area	Luminous density (talbot/m²)	MT^{-2}
Energy per unit time	Luminous flux (lumen)	ML^2T^{-3}
Flux per unit area	Luminous emittance (lumen/m² or lambert)	MT^{-3}
Flux per unit solid angle	Luminous intensity (lumen/steradian)	ML^2T^{-3}
Flux per unit solid angle per unit projected area	Luminance (candela/m²)	MT^{-3}
Flux input per unit area	Illuminance (meter-candela)	MT^{-3}
Ratio of reflected to		
incident flux	Luminous reflectance	
incident flux	Luminous transmittance	
Ratio of absorbed to		
incident flux	Luminous absorptance	

1.2.1.2 Radiometric Terms

Similar to photometric terms, radiometric terms are defined as follows:

- *Radiant power* (ϕ) or optical power is the rate of flow of radiant energy, and it is measured in watts (w).
- *Radiant energy* (Q) is the energy transferred by electromagnetic waves. It is the time integral of radiant power and is measured in joules (J).
- *Radiant intensity* (I) is the radiant power per unit solid angle, and it is measured in watts/steradiant (w/sr).
- *Radiance* (L) in a given direction is the radiant intensity per unit of projected area of the source as viewed from that direction, and it is measured in w/sr-m^2.
- *Spectral radiance* (L_λ) is the radiance per unit wavelength interval at a given wavelength, and it is measured in watts/steradiant-unit area-wavelength interval (w/sr·m^2·nm).
- *Irradiance* (E) or power density is the radiant power per unit area incident upon a surface, and it is measured in watts/square meter (w/m^2).
- *Spectral irradiance* (E_λ) is the irradiance per unit wavelength interval at a given wavelength, and it is measured in watts/unit area-unit wavelength interval (w/m^2·nm).

1.2.2 The Particle Nature of Light

Like all particles, light exerts pressure and causes a wheel to spin (Compton's experiment). Thus, light is described in terms of number of particles or *photons*, the smallest quantity of monochromatic light, described by the energy (E) equation

$$E = h\nu$$

where h is Planck's constant, $6.6260755 \times 10^{-34}$ (joule-second), and ν is the frequency of light.

Visible light (light that the human eye can see, such as light from an incandescent lightbulb) consists of a continuum of wavelengths that span the (visible) spectrum from deep red (700 nm) to deep violet-blue (400 nm) (Fig. 1.4).

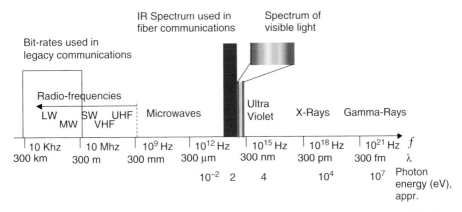

Figure 1.4 The visible spectrum is in the range from 0.7 μm (700 nm) to 0.4 μm (400 nm). The spectrum used in fiber communications is beyond the red.

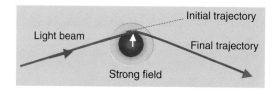

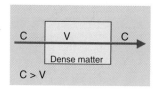

Figure 1.5 Light travels in a straight path but it "bends" when it crosses a strong field.

In free space, light (of all wavelengths) travels in a straight path at a constant maximum speed. However, the speed of light changes when it travels in a medium, and this change is not the same for all media or for all wavelengths. By free space it is meant space that is free from matter (vacuum) and/or free from electromagnetic fields. Thus, the speed of light in free space is defined by Einstein's equation:

$$E = mc^2$$

Frequency, v, speed of light in free space, c, and wavelength, λ, are interrelated by:

$$v = c/\lambda$$

From the energy relationships $E = mc^2 = hv$ and the last one, an interesting relationship is obtained, the equivalent mass of a photon (which is a controversial issue among scientists)

$$m = hv/c^2$$

When light is in the vicinity of a strong electromagnetic field, it interacts with it. From this interaction and other influences, its trajectory changes direction (Fig. 1.5). In fact, in the presence of gravitational fields of cosmic proportions, the trajectory change of light causes a phenomenon known as *gravitational lensing*, which is used in astrophysics to detect dark matter and distant galaxies.

1.2.3 Huygens–Fresnel Principle

When light from a monochromatic point source impinges on a screen having a small round hole on the order of the wavelength, the hole behaves like a light source of the same wavelength and phase (Fig. 1.6). This is known as the *Huygens–Fresnel principle*, and it is a key principle in the study of *interference of light*.

1.2.4 Interference

1.2.4.1 Classical Interference

Consider the optical setup of Figure 1.7 with a monochromatic light source, a screen with two pinholes equidistant from the axis of symmetry, and a second screen behind

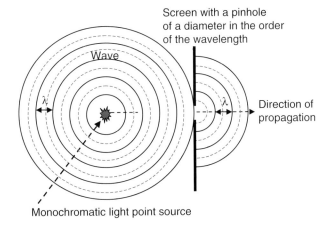

Figure 1.6 Principle of Huygens–Fressnel.

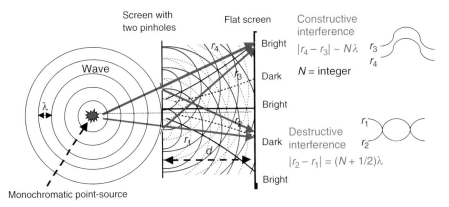

Figure 1.7 Interference of two coherent sources of the same wavelength.

the first and parallel to it. Based on the Huygens-Fresnel principle, the pinholes become two sources of coherent light. Then, alternating bright and dark zones, or fringes, are seen on the second screen. The bright or dark state of a fringe depends on the absolute difference of the optical paths, which is equal to the variation of the product $n \times r$, where n is the refractive index of the medium and r is a vector, the magnitude of which equals the travel distance. In the setup of Figure 1.7, the medium is free space and thus $n = 1$. Thus, the variation of the optical path is equal to the variation of the travel distance, which is closely related to wave phase difference between the rays r_1, r_2, r_3, and r_4:

$$\Delta = |r_2 - r_1| \quad \text{or} \quad \Delta = |r_4 - r_3|$$

Bright zones (*constructive interference*) are formed when the path difference is an integer multiple of λ (i.e., $k\lambda$, $k = 1,2,3\ldots$), and dark zones (*destructive interference*) are formed when the travel difference between the two rays is half-integer multiple of λ [i.e., $(k + 1/2)\lambda$, $k = 0,1,2,3\ldots$].

Interferometric fringes can easily be formed when a collimated laser beam impinges on a transparent plate. As monochromatic light reflects back and forth within the two surfaces of the plate, the emerging rays interfere among them to form zones of maxima and minima of light intensity, or fringes. The shape of fringes depends on the plate thickness and its refractive index. Thus, interferometry is also used to measure surface, thickness, and refractive index uniformity; when the plate is under stress, both thickness and refractive index change, and interferometric techniques measure nonintrusively and remotely the distribution of stress or temperature on plates. Typically, there are two well-known methods, the Fizeau method and the Twyman–Green method. Based on interferometric techniques, only surface variations up to $\lambda/40$ can be measurable; this determines the accuracy of the method and also its limits. For example, if red laser light ($\lambda = 600$ nm) is used, then accuracy is within 15 nm, and if ultraviolet (UV) light ($\lambda \sim 300$ nm) is used, then it is within approximately 7.5 nm. Clearly, the shorter the wavelength, the higher the accuracy, and the more complex the method. Consequently, as we move into the realm of subnanometer accuracy, more advanced technologies are needed with a fine subatomic scale resolution. In this category, the phase-shifting interferometric microscope (PSIM) provides a resolution of approximately a tenth of a nanometer and the Nomarski interferometric technique can be as good as 10 times that of the PSIM and of the atomic force microscope (AFM).

1.2.4.2 Quantum Interference

Consider an atom with only one electron at the outer orbit (e.g., Na), being at the ground energy level or state S_1. Then, when a photon of energy E_{12} is absorbed, the electron "jumps" to a higher energy level S_2. While at level S_2, the electron may absorb another photon of energy E_{23} to "jump" to energy level S_3.

Photon absorption by an electron (or an atom) implies that the atom is "opaque" for that frequency (or wavelength) to which the photon corresponds. Photons that are not absorbed travel through it, and thus the material is "transparent."

Thus, when the atom is at level S_1, it is transparent to energy E_{23} and opaque to E_{12}; and when the atom is at level S_2 it is transparent to energy E_{12} and opaque to E_{23}. At some random time, and while at energy level E3, the atom may jump down to ground energy level S_1, releasing photonic energy.

Consider a "cloud" of such atoms illuminated with both E_{12} and E_{23}. However, since all atoms in the cloud are not excited by photons at the same time and atoms are not synchronized, jumping from one state to another becomes a random process. Therefore, statistically there will be a time when a mix of both states will exist, S_1 and S_2. It turns out that, under a specific mix of states S_1 and S_2 and intensity of E_{12} and E_{23}, the "cloud" seems to be transparent to both photonic energies. Macroscopically, this seems like a destructive interferometric action at the quantum (atomic energy) level, hence quantum interferometry. Quantum interferometry is an area of current research. More findings and developments are expected to be announced in the near future.

1.2.5 Holography

Holography is an interferometric method by which, using coherent light (laser light), the phase and amplitude characteristics of diffracted light by a three-dimensional (3-D) object is captured on a two-dimensional photographic plate.

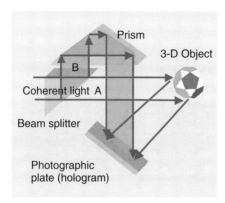

Figure 1.8   Principles of holography; generating a hologram.

Consider the following experiment illustrated in Figure 1.8: a monochromatic coherent light source is split into two beams, A and B. Beam A impinges on a three-dimensional object and is diffracted onto a photographic film. A prism reflects beam B such that it too impinges on the photographic plate. At the plate, beams A and B interfere and depending on the travel difference of each ray in the two beams, because of the three-dimensionality of the object, the amplitude and phase difference from each point of the object are recorded on the photographic plate. The end result is an incomprehensible image of dense stripes and whorls on the plate. This exposed plate is known as a *hologram*.

Based on "diffraction at infinity," the phase and amplitude information of a 3-D object have been recorded in a myriad of locations of a hologram. Thus, each small segment of the hologram contains all phase and amplitude information of the 3-D object.

To recreate an image of the 3-D object, the hologram must be illuminated with coherent light. The dense stripes and whorls in the plate (acting like a diffraction grating) interact with the incident coherent beam, decoding phase and amplitude, and recreate a replica image of the object (Fig. 1.9).

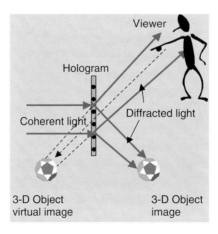

Figure 1.9   Principles of holography; creating a holographic image.

1.2.6   Optical Correlators and Storage

Among the applications that holography has found are optical storage, image recognition, and pattern correlation. When coherent light passes through a transparent plate with a set of images and then passes through the hologram of an object, if there is a match, two conjugate inverted images appear on a screen matching the one in the hologram; if there is no match, a blurred dot appears.

Thousands of holograms may be contained in a square millimeter of a holographic plate. Thus, many thousands of different images may be stored in few square millimeters of a holographic plate. The storage capacity of a hologram, C_{store}, is in the terabit range and is theoretically limited to the hologram volume, V_{hol}, divided by the cube of the source wavelength, λ:

$$C_{store} = V_{hol}/\lambda^3$$

It has been reported that 160,000 holograms have been stored and successfully reconstructed in a single crystal.

Optical correlators work by comparing the Fourier transform of two patterns or images that are combined with holographic methods to retrieve an optical pattern and recognize an image fast. Hence, holographic methods promise very large capacity optical storage applicable in many areas including communications.

Among these applications, Fe-doped $LiNbO_3$ crystals and organic photopolymers have been used in write once read many times (WORM) memories. The write capability is accomplished with high-power low-cost semiconductor lasers, and the read capability, or desired holographic frame, is selected by activating a micromirror in a matrix (see MEMS).

Among other applications, holography may be used in the creation of 3-D crystals. In this case, 3-D molds, such as photonics crystals, gratings, and integrated optics, may be rapidly designed and reproduced. It may also be used in 3-D spatiotemporal storage.

1.2.7   Light Attributes

The attributes of light and their significance, of interest in this book, are listed in Table 1.3.

Table 1.3   Attributes of light

Attribute	Significance
Dual nature	Electromagnetic wave and particle ($E = h\nu = mc^2$)
Consists of many λs	Wide and continuous spectrum
Polarization*	Circular, elliptic, linear (TE_{nm}, TM_{nm}); affected by fields and matter
Optical power	Wide range (from μW to MW); affected by matter
Propagation	In free space in straight path; in matter it is affected differently (absorbed, scattered, through); in optical waveguides (fiber) it follows its bends
Propagation speed	In free space $c \sim 10^{10}$ cm/sec, in matter c/n; different wavelengths travel at different speed
Phase	Affected by variations in fields and matter

*Polarization is discussed in subsequent sections.

1.3   OPTICAL MATERIALS

When light enters matter, its electromagnetic field interacts with localized electromagnetic fields. The result is a change in the characteristics of light and in certain cases a change in the properties of matter as well. The strength of the field of light, its wavelength, its polarization state, and matter determine how light will be affected. Moreover, external temperature, pressure, and fields (electrical, magnetic, and gravitational) influence the interaction of light with matter. Such interactions may degrade propagation of light, and thus they are undesirable but they are also used to advantage in the design of optical components.

1.3.1   Transparent Versus Opaque Matter

- Some matter allows most optical energy (all photons) to propagate through it and is called *optically transparent*. In contrast, some dense matter absorbs light within the first few atomic layers and is called *nonoptically transparent* or *opaque* matter (it scatters and/or absorbs it). **Example:** compare clear glass or water with a sheet of metal.

- Some matter passes a portion of optical energy through it and absorbs part of it (typically ~50%), and is called *semitransparent* matter. Such matter attenuates the optical power of light and may be used in optical devices known as *optical attenuators*. **Example:** most transparent matter, semitransparent mirrors.

- Some matter allows selected frequencies to propagate through and is called an *optical filter*. **Example:** red, green, yellow, or blue glass (each allows a selected range of frequencies to be propagated through it).

- Some matter in an ionized state absorbs selected frequencies and passes all others. **Example:** the sun's ionized surface or the hot vapors of sulfur.

- Some matter permits rays with certain polarization to propagate through and absorbs or reflects the others; it is called a *polarizing filter*. **Example:** polarizing sunglasses.

- Some matter emits photons when in intense electric field and some matter emits photons of specific wavelengths when it is illuminated with light of another shorter wavelength. **Example:** most minerals under UV light; fluorescent substances, erbium, and so on.

1.3.2   Homogeneity and Heterogeneity

A *homogeneous* optically transparent medium has the same consistency (chemical, mechanical, electrical, magnetic, or crystallographic) throughout its volume and in all directions. A *heterogeneous* optically transparent medium does not have the same consistency (chemical, mechanical, electrical, magnetic, or crystallographic) throughout its volume.

1.3.3   Isotropy and Anisotropy

Isotropic optically transparent materials have the same index of refraction, same polarization state, and same propagation constant in every direction throughout the

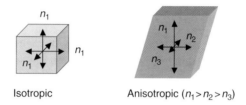

Isotropic   Anisotropic ($n_1 > n_2 > n_3$)

Figure 1.10 Principle of isotropic and anisotropic materials.

material. Materials that do not exhibit all these properties are known as *anisotropic* (Fig. 1.10).

Anisotropy is explained as follows: the electrons of certain crystals, such as calcite-$CaCO_3$, move with a different amount of freedom in selective directions of the crystal, and the dielectric constant as well as the refractive index of the crystal is different in these selective directions. As a result, as photons enter the crystal, their electromagnetic field interacts differently in one direction than in another and this affects their propagation pattern in the crystal.

1.3.4 Organic Materials

Besides inorganic compounds such as traditional crystals and oxides, there is a growing interest in organic compounds. Organics promise components that can be easily manufacturable in large quantities and thus at low cost. Certain compounds can be deposited to virtually any type of other material such as glass, plastic, and treated paper. For example, consider organic compounds that can be made into optical organic thin films (OTF). Then, based on fluorescence properties, when a voltage excites their molecular state, they emit light of a specific wavelength, known as *exciton*. The duration of light emission of such compounds is on the order of many microseconds. Among these compounds is *perylene*, which emits blue light; *coumarin-6*, which emits green light; and other compounds that emit different colors. These compounds have high luminescent efficiency at a wide angle. Thus, OTFs may find several optoelectric applications, such as flat thin displays with transparent electrical contacts made of titanium oxides or indium tin oxide (ITO) by deposition.

Other organic compounds, such as *pentacene*, have electrical properties that are suitable for producing field-effect transistors. Pentacene is a simple molecule made of five connected *benzene* rings that form crystals. These compounds may be applicable to portable devices, communications, electronic identification, and others.

In a different endeavor, organic matter is used to extract compounds that can be used in optical and semiconductor fields. For example, corn is used to extract compounds that can be turned into plastic films. Rice hull or coconuts are rich in silicon dioxide, or silica, which can be used for semiconductors or in devices with specific properties. Obviously, the world of organics holds many secrets for the near future.

1.3.5 Photochromaticity

Photochromaticity is the property of some clear materials, either in solution or in plastic film, or in organic crystals (e.g., diarylethene), to change their color upon irradiation with ultraviolet (UV) light. Photochromic materials return to their clear state upon exposure to visible light.

Of particular importance are certain organic crystals, such as diarylethene, that change not only their color but also their size. It has been found that when diarylethene molecules are irradiated with UV light, each molecule changes by a fraction of a nanometer. However, if several molecules comprise a layer, then the change in thickness of the layer is proportional to the number of molecules, and thus nanometer variation is easily achieved by manipulating the layer thickness.

1.4 LIGHT MEETS MATTER

When light meets matter, its electromagnetic field interacts with the near fields of ions and electrons, and depending on consistency and the structural details of matter interactions take place that may affect the light properties, the material properties, or both. In fact, in many cases light affects matter, which in turn affects light.

1.4.1 Reflection and Refraction: Snell's Law

When a ray impinges on an angle the planar interface of two homogeneous transparent media (e.g., free space and glass), a portion of it will be reflected and the remainder will be refracted (Fig. 1.11).

The index of refraction of a transparent medium (n_{med}) is defined as the ratio of the speed of monochromatic light in free space, c, over the speed of the same monochromatic light in a medium (v_{med}):

$$n_{med} = c/v_{med}$$

Then, between two mediums (1 and 2), the relationships are true:

$$n_2/n_1 = v_1/v_2$$

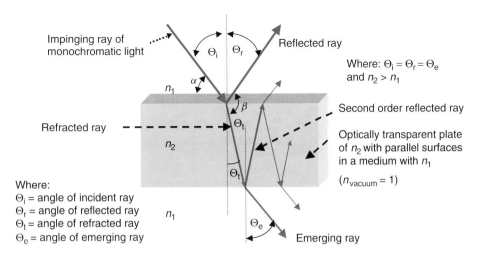

Figure 1.11 Reflection and refraction.

and

$$n_1 \cos \beta = n_2 \cos \alpha$$

where n_1, v_1, and n_2, v_2 are the index of refraction and the speed of light in the two media, and α and β are the angle of incidence and the angle of refraction with respect to the surface of incidence, respectively.

When the angle of incidence is very small, $\cos \alpha = 1 - \alpha^2/2$ and the cosine equation becomes

$$n_1(1 - \beta^2/2) = n_2(1 - \alpha^2/2)$$

The index of refraction, or *refractive index*, for free space has the numerical value of 1, whereas for other materials it is typically between 1 and 2, and in some cases it is greater than 2 or 3.

The reflected portion of monochromatic light is known as Fresnel reflection. The amount of reflected power and the polarization state of the reflected light depend on the polarization state of the incident light, the angle of incidence, and the refractive index difference.

For normal incidence on a single surface, the reflectivity, ρ, is given by the Fresnel equation

$$\rho = (n - 1)^2/(n + 1)^2$$

If the absorption of the material over a length d is A, which is calculated from the absorption coefficient (absorbed power per cm) α, then the internal material transmittance, τ_i, is defined as the inverse of the material absorption. For internal transmittance τ_i, the external input–output transmittance (taking into account the reflectivity, ρ by the surface) is given by

$$\tau = [(1 - \rho)^2 \tau_1]/[1 - \rho^2 \tau_1^2]$$

The following basic relationships are also useful:

Speed of light in free space:	$c = \lambda f$
Speed of light in medium:	$v_{med} = \lambda_{med} f$
Index of refraction:	$n_1/n_2 = \lambda_2/\lambda_1$

where f is the frequency of light and λ is its wavelength. Both the letter f and the Greek v are used for frequency. Here we use f to eliminate confusion between v (for speed) and ν (for frequency).

Snell's law relates the ratio of index of refraction with the angle of the incident (Θ_i) and with the refracted (Θ_t) rays (Fig. 1.11):

$$n_2/n_1 = \sin \Theta_i / \sin \Theta_t$$

1.4.2   Critical Angle

Critical angle, $\Theta_{critical}$, is the (maximum) angle of incidence of light (from a material with high to low refractive index) at which light stops being refracted and is totally reflected (Fig. 1.12). As the angle of incidence approaches the critical angle, the refracted ray becomes parallel to the surface (and without added phase shift) and

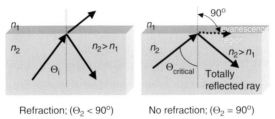

Refraction; ($\Theta_2 < 90°$)   No refraction; ($\Theta_2 = 90°$)

Figure 1.12   Definition of critical angle.

is termed *evanescent*. Beyond that point, there is no refracted ray. The critical angle depends on the refractive index and the wavelength of light.

$$\sin \Theta_{\text{critical}} = n_1/n_2$$

for $n_1 = 1$ (air), then

$$\sin \Theta_{\text{critical}} = 1/n_2$$

In certain cases, a gradual variation of refractive index may take place. When light rays enter from one side, rays are refracted such that they may emerge from the same side they entered. This is the case of the natural phenomenon known as a *mirage*.

Although to this day the index of refraction has been considered to be only positive and greater than $+1$, the value of vacuum, researchers and theoreticians have been trying to learn, what would have happen to light if there were materials with negative values. Materials with negative values would solve several issues in optics and would find several important applications in the optics and photonic areas.

1.4.3   Antireflection

In optical communications, it usually is desirable to have all optical power of a signal coupled in the fiber or an optical component and to have zero or minimal reflected power. This is accomplished by using *antireflection coatings* at the interface air–component.

Antireflection coatings consist of one or more thin layers (film) of material, each layer having a specific thickness and a specific refractive index. A transition from one layer to another represents an index of refraction discontinuity. Thus, as a beam of light travels through the layers, it is partially reflected by the refractive index discontinuities. These reflections, on their way back interfere destructively, canceling each other out, and thus no reflection emerges from the layers.

For example, to minimize the reflected optical power of incident light on glass, the layer that interfaces glass with air has a low refractive index.

In an arrangement of a single antireflection thin film, two requirements must be satisfied:

$$n_2 d_2 = m\lambda/4$$

and

$$n_2 = \text{sqrt}(n_1 \cdot n_3)$$

where d_2 is the film thickness and m is an odd integer $(1,3,5,\ldots)$.

In practice, it is very difficult to find materials with a refractive index n_2, as calculated by the last relationship; if n_1 is for air (=1) and n_3 is for standard glass (=1.52), then n_2 is calculated to be 1.23. However, it is very difficult to find a material with this exact value, and the closest to it is cryolite with a refractive index at 1.35; consequently, the cryolite film will also be partially reflective. As a result, complex structures with more layers are used (approximately 40–50 layers) to construct antireflective films.

As an example of an antireflecting film, consider the two-layer structure that consists of a first layer of MgF_2 ($n = 1.38$) and a second layer of PbF_2 ($n = 1.7$) deposited on a glass plate ($n = 1.5$). In this structure, each layer has a thickness of a quarter-wavelength such that rays reflected by each layer interfere destructively. As a consequence, the *extinction of reflection* at the designed wavelength is very high. This means that the antireflection coating is also wavelength-selective. Because of the wavelength selectivity of antireflecting films, they are also used as optical filters (see Filters).

1.4.4 Prisms and Superprisms

Consider that two planes of a plate intersect each other at an angle Θ_2 to form a *prism*. When a polychromatic narrow beam of light impinges on one of the prism surfaces, each frequency component is refracted at different angle. As each frequency reaches the other surface, it is also refracted at a different angle again. Thus, the output from the second surface of the prism consists of frequency components separated by a small angle.

The angle of each frequency component with the original composite beam is known as the *angle of deflection*, ε; that is, the angle of deflection varies with frequency (Fig. 1.13).

In Figure 1.13, note that when $n_1 = 1$, then

$$n_2 = \{\sin[(\Theta_2 + \varepsilon)/2]\}/\sin(\Theta_2/2)$$

The following prism laws hold (see figure 1.17 for Θ_λ):

- The angle Θ_λ increases as the index of refraction increases.
- The angle Θ_λ increases as the prism angle Θ_2 increases.

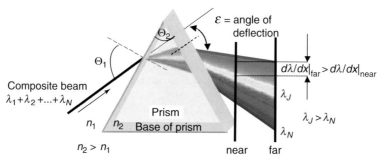

Figure 1.13 The angular deflection varies with optical frequency. With common prisms, an acceptable resolution is achieved only at impractical far distances.

- The angle Θ_λ increases as the angle of incidence Θ_1 increases.
- The angle Θ_λ increases as the frequency of light increases (or the wavelength decreases).

When the angle of incidence Θ_1 varies, so does the angle of deflection ε and in a nonlinear manner. For a given wavelength and prism, it is noted that (Fig. 1.14):

- There is a minimum angle of deflection below which no light emerges.
- The deflection angle ε is the same for two different values of angle of incidence Θ_1.

The angular separation of each frequency component is known as *angular dispersion* and is given by

$$d\theta/d\lambda = [(d\theta/dn)(dn/d\lambda)]$$

where n is the index of refraction and λ is the wavelength.

The first factor of the latter product depends on the geometry of the prism, whereas the second factor depends on the material.

Amici prisms are right-angle prisms that have an interesting property used in many optical instruments and experimental apparatus; they cause image inversion as in Figure 1.15.

The angular dispersion of common prisms is not substantial enough to be used to advantage in optical components for communications. However, certain artificial crystalline structures, known as *superprisms*, promise to remedy this. Superprisms consist of an artificial optic structure known as a *photonic crystalline* structure. Photonic crystalline optics, a relatively new field, is a periodic dielectric lattice structure fabricated

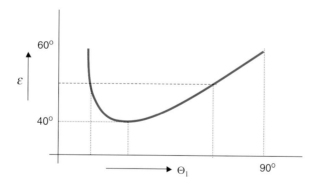

Figure 1.14   Variation of angle of deflection ε versus angle of incidence Θ_1.

Figure 1.15   Principles of the Amici prism.

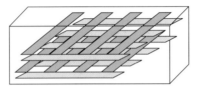

Figure 1.16 Photonic crystalline optics are based on three-dimensional periodic lattices. This lattice emulates the exoskeleton structure (and the iridescent properties) of certain fishes and butterflies.

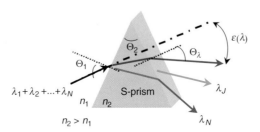

Figure 1.17 Prisms made with photonic crystalline optics exhibit angle of deflection 500 times that of ordinary prisms.

on Si using nanotechnology (Fig. 1.16). The periodicity of the crystalline lattice is three-dimensional and is several tens of nm (reported at 180 nm). This periodicity consists of three-dimensional periodically distributed bands and gaps. Depending on periodicity, an optical frequency range is defined within which optical frequencies (wavelengths) are or are not permitted to propagate.

Photonic crystalline structures may act as energy band-gap filters (i.e., filters that do not pass photons within certain energy range). They also may act as highly dispersive structures.

Photonic crystalline structures are solid-state grown epitaxially (such as SiO_2 on Si); they are very small and have superb diffraction properties. Formed like a prism, photonic crystalline structures exhibit an angular dispersion that is approximately 500 times that of conventional prisms (Fig. 1.17). Their structure is the result of close examination of the iridescent hairlike spines of the sea mouse (genus *Aphrodita*), as well as of certain butterflies and caterpillars. Therefore, even though we claim that photonic crystals are synthetic, in reality nature was first, millions of years ago.

In addition to solid-state materials, other materials such as block copolymers and polystyrene have been used on an experimental basis.

1.4.5 Propagation of Light

As already described, when light enters matter, it is reflected by its surface, it is refracted by the matter, and its velocity changes as well as its wavelength, but not its frequency. This is important to remember throughout this book.

1.4.5.1 Phase Velocity

A monochromatic (single ω or λ) wave that travels along the fiber axis is described by

$$E(t, x) = A \exp[j(\omega t - \beta x)]$$

where A is the amplitude of the field, $\omega = 2\pi f$, and β is the propagation constant.

Phase velocity, v_ϕ, is defined as the velocity of an observer that maintains constant phase with the traveling field (i.e., $\omega t - \beta x = $ constant).

Replacing the traveled distance x within time t, $x = v_\phi t$, the phase velocity of the monochromatic light in the medium is

$$v_\phi = \omega/\beta$$

1.4.5.2 *Group Velocity*

When a signal is transmitted in a dispersive medium, it is necessary to know its speed of propagation. A continuous sine wave does not provide any meaningful information because a real optical signal consists of a band of frequencies in a narrow spectrum. Moreover, each frequency component in the band travels (in the medium) at a slightly different phase. This is explained mathematically as follows:

Consider an amplitude-modulated optical signal, e_{AM}, traveling along the fiber

$$e_{AM}(t) = E[1 + m\cos(\omega_1 t)]\cos(\omega_c t)$$

where E is the electric field, m is the modulation depth, ω_1 is the modulation frequency, ω_c is the frequency of light (or carrier frequency), and $\omega_1 \ll \omega_c$.

Trigonometric expansion of this expression results in three frequency components with arguments:

$$\omega_c, \quad \omega_c - \omega_1, \quad \text{and } \omega_c + \omega_1$$

Each component travels along the fiber at a slightly different phase velocity (β_c, $\beta_c - \Delta\beta$, $\beta_c + \Delta\beta$, respectively) accruing a different phase shift. Eventually, all three components form a spreading envelope that travels along the fiber with a phase velocity

$$\beta(\omega) = \beta_c + (\eta\beta/\eta\omega \mid \omega = \omega_c)\Delta\omega = \beta_c + \beta'\Delta\omega$$

Group velocity, $v_g = c/n_g$, is defined as the velocity of an observer that maintains constant phase with the group traveling envelope (i.e., $\omega t - (\Delta\beta)x = $ constant).

Replacing x by $v_g t$, the group velocity is expressed by

$$v_g = \omega/\Delta\beta = \eta\omega/\eta\beta = 1/\beta'$$

where β is the propagation constant and β' is the first partial derivative with respect to ω (remember that in this case ω is not purely monochromatic, and thus the derivative of ω is not zero).

1.4.5.3 *Impact of Impurities*

Impurity is the presence of unwanted elements or compounds in matter. During the purification process of matter, certain undesired elements cannot be completely removed and traces remain. These undesired elements alter the optical characteristics of transparent materials, such as fiber, causing an absorptive or scattering effect that amounts to optical throughput loss.

A similar effect is caused by small fluctuations of the refractive index, which is on the order of the wavelength of light through it. This effect is known as *Rayleigh scattering*.

Iron, copper, cobalt, and oxides are some examples of impurities that affect optical absorption. For instance, blue glass is the result of cobalt or copper in glass (it looks blue because it absorbs all wavelengths except the blue). Another "impurity" is the OH^-, which is responsible for increased fiber absorption at approximately 1400 nm.

In special cases, specific elements are intentionally introduced to modify the optical propagation and/or excitation properties of matter, such as dispersive fibers, fiber amplifiers, and so on.

1.4.5.4   Impact of Microcracks

Microcracks may be viewed as abrupt discontinuities in the index of refraction of the material and with surfaces that are not necessarily plane or parallel. Microcracks in the crystallized matrix of matter or in amorphous solid matter are generated as a result of stresses (mechanical or thermal) or material aging.

Microcracks may have an adverse effect on the propagation of light as well as on the strength of the material. In fact, if the crack gap (the distance between the crack surfaces) increases because of tensile forces on the order of a wavelength ($\lambda/4$, $\lambda/2$), it may act as an uninvited filter, which may not be what light would expect to encounter.

1.4.5.5   Impact of Mechanical Pressure

When mechanical pressure is applied on matter, its internal microstructure is disturbed, which causes a variation of the refractive index with a distribution determined by the distribution of pressure. This variation affects the propagation of light in matter, and in general pressure points are undesirable points of optical disturbance. Similarly, when fiber is bent, the outer periphery experiences stretching and the inner periphery undergoes compression, and this also affects optical propagation. Thus, the safe bend radius recommended by ITU-T is 37.5 mm (ITU-T G.652, para. 5.5, note 2).

1.4.5.6   Impact of Temperature Variation

Temperature variations affect the properties of any material. They affect its physical, mechanical, electrical, magnetic, chemical, and crystalline (if any) properties. As a result, the index of refraction also is affected, which impacts the propagation characteristics of light. Clearly, temperature variations are undesirable in optical communications, although there are cases where they have been used productively to control the refractive index of optical devices.

1.4.6   Diffraction

Consider a screen having a small hole with sharp edges at the periphery and dimensions comparable to those of wavelength light (this may be an aperture, a slit, or a grating). Consider also a parallel (collimated) and monochromatic beam, known as *light from a source at infinity*, directed to this screen (or diaphragm) and a second screen behind it at distance d (Fig. 1.18). Since light travels straight in free space and a small round projection is expected, D_{EXP}, a wider projection is seen instead, D_{ACT}, with concentric rings around it. The smaller the diameter of the hole, the wider the projection. This phenomenon is attributed to interference at each edge point of the hole, which acts like a secondary source resulting in *diffraction*; this is also known as the *phenomenon of*

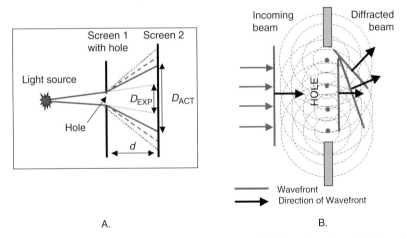

Figure 1.18 Diffraction by a hole in the order of wavelength; A. Experiment, and B. Based on the Huygens–Fresnel principle, secondary sources form a multiplicity of possible waveforms at specific angles.

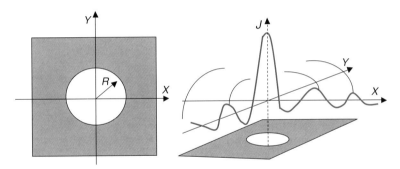

Figure 1.19 Intensity distribution of diffracted light by a round hole (the formed rings on a screen are known as "Airy rings").

Fresnel. Moreover, the intensity of rings, J, decreases with distance from the center of the projection (Fig. 1.19). This pattern is also known as *Fraunhoffer diffraction.*

According to Huygens's principle, the incident wave excites coherent secondary waves at each point of the wavefront. All these waves interfere with each other and cause the diffraction pattern. The pure mathematical analysis of diffraction is studied by approximating the scalar Helmholz equation in which the wavefront is a spherical function; this analysis is quite involved and it beyond the scope of this book. However, to illustrate this point, if a plane wave is incident on an aperture, then the radiant intensity per unit of projected area of the source viewed from that direction (i.e., the radiance, L), is described by

$$L(\alpha, \beta - \beta_0) = \gamma_0 (\lambda^2 / A)[F\{U(x, y, z = 0) \exp(i2\pi\beta_0 y)\}]^2 \, (\text{W/sr-m}^2)$$

where α, β, and γ are propagation vectors in the x, y, and z directions, respectively; A is the area of the diffracting aperture; λ is the wavelength; F is the Fourier transform; and U is the complex amplitude distribution emerging from the aperture (hence $z = 0$).

Integrating the above, invoking the conservation of energy theorem and using Parceval's (or Rayleigh's) theorem, which converts the integral of the squared modulus of a function $f(x)$ to the integral of the squared modulus of its Fourier transform $f(\omega)$,

$$\int |f(x)|^2 \, dx = (1/2\pi) \int |f(\omega)|^2 \, d\omega$$

where the integrals are from $-$ to $+$ infinity, then the radiance is expressed by

$$L(\alpha, \beta - \beta_0) = K\gamma_0(\lambda^2/A)|F\{U(x, y, z = 0)\exp(i2\pi\beta_0 y)\}|^2 \text{ for } a^2 + b^2 \leqq 1$$

$$L(\alpha, \beta - \beta_0) = 0 \text{ for } a^2 + b^2 > 1$$

where K is a normalization constant.

Now let us consider that the aperture is not round but a narrow rectangular slit of height h and width w. In this case, the monochromatic collimated beam passes through it and due to refraction, the projection on a screen is a rectangle rotated by $90°$; that is, the refracted pattern is narrow in the direction in which the aperture is wide. Moreover, because of two dimensional Fourier expansion, the refracted light forms many secondary rectangles in the X–Y plane of the screen, with intensity fading away from the axis of symmetry (Fig. 1.20). This is also known as *Fraunhoffer diffraction* of a rectangular aperture. The condition for these rectangles on the screen is

$$R(x, y) = \text{Rect}(x/w_0)\text{Rect}(y/h_0) = 1, \quad \text{for } |x| < w_0/2 \text{ and } |y| < h_0/2,$$

and

$$R(x, y) = 0 \text{ elsewhere.}$$

Theoretically speaking, when a diffracting aperture is illuminated by a uniform monochromatic plane wave, λ, the total radiant power, P_{TR}, emanating from the diffracting aperture is calculated using Rayleigh's theorem and Fourier transforms:

$$P_{\text{TR}} = \lambda^2 \iint |U_0(x, y; 0)\exp^{i2\pi\beta y}|^2 \, dx \, dy$$

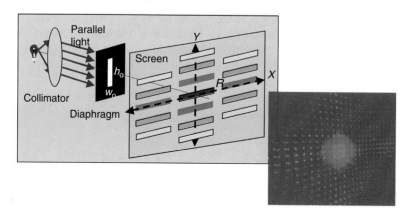

Figure 1.20 Diffraction at infinity.

where U_0 is the function of the complex amplitude distribution emerging from the diffracting aperture, β is the propagating vector, and $\{x, y\}$ are the Cartesian coordinates; both integrals are from $-$infinity to $+$infinity.

This discussion applies to monochromatic light. If light were polychromatic, then each color (frequency) component would be diffracted differently (i.e., at a different angle). Then, fringes on the screen would be of different color but overlapping. The corollary is that the angle of diffraction depends on the frequency (color) of light.

If in the preceding experiment, instead of one slit or hole there was an array of parallel slits, then light would be diffracted in certain angles due to interference among the slits. This diffraction of light is known as *diffraction by transmission*. Interesting phenomena take place when slits are positioned in a matrix configuration. Diffraction then takes place in a two-dimensional plane and the fringe pattern depends on the size, shape, density, and topological arrangement of the slits.

If in the preceding discussion, instead of slits in the diaphragm there are parallel grooves each at a width comparable to wavelength, then the above discussion of diffraction, as well as the same theory, applies. Instead, now light does not pass through but it diffracts back at certain angles that depend, among other factors, on the wavelength. All other factors being equal, each wavelength diffracts at different angles. This is known as *diffraction by reflection*.

We have discussed slits, holes, and grooves. What it really means to light when it encounters them is a periodic variation of the refractive index, in the case of a slit or hole the refractive index is 1 as opposed to the refractive index of the diaphragm, which is >1 or infinity. Having said that, one can then take a transparent plate and form on it parallel strips of another transparent material but of a different refractive index. A diffraction pattern is still observed. All these slotted, grooved, or stripped plates are known as gratings.

A simple, quick, and convincing experiment, which I often demonstrate in lectures, involves a CD-ROM. When light impinges in an angle on the CD-ROM surface, one sees many colors as a result of diffraction of ambient light in the visible spectrum by the "grooves" of the CD-ROM.

1.4.7 Polarization

Polarization Vector. If we examine the electrical state of matter on a microscopic level, we discover that it consists of charges, the distribution of which depends on the presence or absence of external fields. If we assume that for every positive charge there is a negative charge, then we may think that each positive–negative charge constitutes an electric dipole. The electric moment of a dipole at some distance is a function of distance and charge density. For a distribution of electric dipoles, *the electric dipole moment per unit volume is defined as the polarization vector* P.

Transverse Wave. Two relationships describe the propagation of light in nonconducting media:

$$E(r, t) = \varepsilon_1 E_0 \, e^{-j(\omega t - k \cdot r)}$$

and

$$H(r, t) = \varepsilon_2 H_0 \, e^{-j(\omega t - k \cdot r)}$$

where ε_1 and ε_2 are two constant unit vectors that define the direction of each field, k is the unit vector in the direction of propagation, and E_o and H_o are complex amplitudes, which are constant in space and time.

Assuming a wave propagating in a medium without charges, then $\nabla E = 0$ and $\nabla H = 0$. Based on this, the product of unit vectors is:

$$\varepsilon_1 \cdot k = 0 \quad \text{and} \quad \varepsilon_2 \cdot k = 0$$

That is, the electric (E) field and the magnetic (H) field are perpendicular to the direction of propagation k (Fig. 1.2). Such a wave is called a *transverse wave*.

Circular, Elliptical, and Linear Polarization. Polarization of electromagnetic waves is a complex subject, particularly when light propagates in a medium with a different refractive index in different directions. As light propagates through a medium, it enters the fields of nearby dipoles and field interaction takes place. This interaction may affect the strength of the electric and/or magnetic fields of light differently in certain directions so that the end result may be a complex field with an elliptical field distribution or a linear field distribution.

For example, the electric field E becomes the linear combination of two complex fields E_{ox} and E_{oy}, the two components in the x and y directions of a Cartesian coordinate system, such that

$$E(r, t) = (\varepsilon_x E_{ox} + \varepsilon_y E_{oy}) e^{-j(\omega t - k \cdot r)}$$

This relationship implies that the two components, E_{ox} and E_{oy}, vary sinusoidally; they are perpendicular to each other; and there may be a phase between them, ϕ. From this relationship, a vector is defined, which is known as the *Jones vector*; the Jones vector $J = [J_1, J_2]$ is related to the radiation aspects of the wave:

$$J = \begin{vmatrix} E_{ox} & e^{j\phi x} \\ E_{oy} & e^{j\phi y} \end{vmatrix}$$

In this case, the dielectric quantity ε is described by a tensor that generally has different values in the three axes:

$$\varepsilon = \begin{vmatrix} \varepsilon_x & 0 & 0 \\ 0 & \varepsilon_y & 0 \\ 0 & 0 & \varepsilon_z \end{vmatrix} = \varepsilon_o \begin{vmatrix} n_x^2 & 0 & 0 \\ 0 & n_y^2 & 0 \\ 0 & 0 & n_z^2 \end{vmatrix}$$

Now, from

$$\nabla^2 E = (1/v^2)(\theta^2 E / \theta t^2)$$

and

$$E(r, t) = \varepsilon E_o e^{-j(\omega t - k \cdot r)}$$

one obtains

$$k \times (k \times E_o) + \mu_o \varepsilon \omega^2 E_o = 0$$

or

$$[k \times (k \times I) + \mu_{\rm o}\varepsilon\omega^2][E_{\rm o}] = 0$$

where I is the identity matrix. The latter is a vector equation equivalent to a set of three homogeneous linear equations with unknowns the components of $E_{\rm o}$, $E_{\rm ox}$, $E_{\rm oy}$ and $E_{\rm oz}$. In a typical case, the component $E_{\rm oz}$ along the axis of propagation is equal to zero.

This vector equation determines a relationship between the vector k (k_x, k_y, k_z), the angular frequency ω, and the dielectric constant ε (ε_x, ε_y, ε_z), as well as the polarization state of the plane wave.

The term $[k \times (k \times I) + \mu_{\rm o}\varepsilon\omega^2]$ describes a three-dimensional surface. As the (complex) electric field is separated into its constituent components, each component may propagate in the medium at a different phase. The phase relationship as well as the magnitude of each vector define the *mode of polarization*.

If $E_{\rm ox}$ and $E_{\rm oy}$ have the same magnitude and are in phase, then the wave is called *linearly polarized*.

If $E_{\rm ox}$ and $E_{\rm oy}$ have a phase difference (other than $90°$), then the wave is called *elliptically polarized*.

If $E_{\rm ox}$ and $E_{\rm oy}$ have the same magnitude, but differ in phase by $90°$, then the wave is called *circularly polarized*.

For example, in circularly polarized light the wave equation (propagating in the z direction) becomes:

$$E(r, t) = E_{\rm o}(\varepsilon_x \pm j\varepsilon_y)\, e^{-j(\omega t - k \cdot r)}$$

Then, the two real components (in the x and in the y directions) are:

$$E_x(r, t) = E_{\rm o} \cos(k \cdot r - \omega t)$$

and

$$E_y(r, t) = \pm E_{\rm o} \cos(k \cdot r - \omega t)$$

These equations indicate that at a fixed point in space the fields are such that the electric vector is constant in magnitude but rotates in a circular motion at a frequency ω. The term $\varepsilon_x + j\varepsilon_y$ indicates a counterclockwise rotation (when facing the oncoming wave), and this wave is called a *left circularly polarized* wave or a wave with *positive helicity*. The term $\varepsilon_x - j\varepsilon_y$ indicates a clockwise rotation (when facing the oncoming wave), and this wave is called a *right circularly polarized* wave or a wave with *negative helicity*.

Using the notion of positive and negative helicity, E can be rewritten as

$$E(r, t) = (\varepsilon_+ E_+ + \varepsilon_- E_-)\, e^{-j(\omega t - k \cdot r)}$$

where E_+ and E_- are complex amplitudes denoting the direction of rotation.

If E_+ and E_- are in phase but have different amplitude, the last relationship represents an *elliptically polarized* wave with principal axes of the ellipse in the directions ε_x and ε_y.

Then, the ratio semimajor-to-semiminor axis is $(1 + r)/(1 - r)$, where $E_-/E_+ = r$.

If the amplitudes E_+ and E_- have a difference between them, $E_-/E_+ = r\, e^{j\alpha}$, then the ellipse traced out by the vector E has its axes rotated by an angle $\phi/2$.

When $E_-/E_+ = r = \pm 1$, the wave is *linearly polarized*.

Thus, we have come to the same definition of polarization modes. This discussion for the electric field E can also be repeated for the magnetic field H.

In a mathematical analysis, it is shown that the displacement vector yields a vector equation similar to the one above, which also yields a refractive index with an ellipsoidal distribution or an ellipsoid of revolution around the z axis (the axis of propagation). The ellipsoidal distribution is a mathematical result from the analysis of the displacement vector D and the electric field E that is related by

$$D = \varepsilon_0 \varepsilon E$$

where ε is a tensor (a 3×3 matrix with elements ε_{xx}, ε_{xy}, ε_{xz}, ε_{yx}, ε_{yy}, ε_{yz}, ε_{zx}, ε_{zy}, ε_{zz}). Because of the conservation of energy, the tensor is symmetric, that is, $\varepsilon_{xy} = \varepsilon_{yx}$, $\varepsilon_{xz} = \varepsilon_{zx}$, and $\varepsilon_{yz} = \varepsilon_{zy}$, which greatly simplifies the mathematical derivation of the tensor expression in the three displacement components:

$$D_x = \varepsilon_0 \varepsilon_x E_x, \; D_y = \varepsilon_0 \varepsilon_y E_y, \; \text{and} \; D_z = \varepsilon_0 \varepsilon_z E_z$$

Based on this, the energy, W, stored in the electric field is then expressed by

$$W = (1/2)DE = \varepsilon_0(D_x^2/\varepsilon_x + D_y^2/\varepsilon_y + D_z^2/\varepsilon_z)$$

In this relationship, the parenthesis is of the form $(x^2/a + y^2/b + z^2/c)$, which defines an ellipsoid, and hence the name of the ellipsoidal refractive index of nonlinear optical crystals. Remember that a cross section through the center of an ellipsoid can yield an ellipse or a circle. In addition, a sphere for which $a = b = c$ is a special case of an ellipsoid (this is also the definition of isotropy).

In simple terms, the electromagnetic wave nature of monochromatic light implies that the electric field and the magnetic field are in quadrature and time phase. When created light propagates in free space, the two fields change sinusoidally, and each one lies on one of two perpendicularly to each other planes, as in Figure 1.2. When light enters matter, then depending on the displacement vector distribution in matter (and hence the dielectric and the refractive index), light (its electric and/or magnetic field) will interact with it in different ways. If the two planes (of the electric or magnetic field) are in a Cartesian coordinate system and fixed, then light is *linearly polarized*. If on the other hand, the planes keep changing in a circular (corkscrew-like) motion and the (vectorial) fields remain at the same intensity, then light is *circularly polarized*. If in addition to it, the intensity of the field changes monotonically, then light is *elliptically polarized*. Figure 1.21 illustrates some polarization distributions around the axis of propagation of an electromagnetic plane wave.

If we consider that light is separated into two components, one linearly polarized, I_P, and one unpolarized, I_U, the degree of polarization, P, is defined as

$$P = I_P/(I_P + I_U)$$

Light may be polarized when it is reflected, refracted, or scattered. In polarization by reflection, the degree of polarization depends on the angle of incidence and the

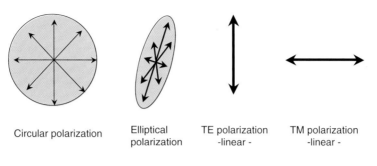

Figure 1.21 Examples of polarization modes of an *E-M* wave (direction of light is perpendicular to page).

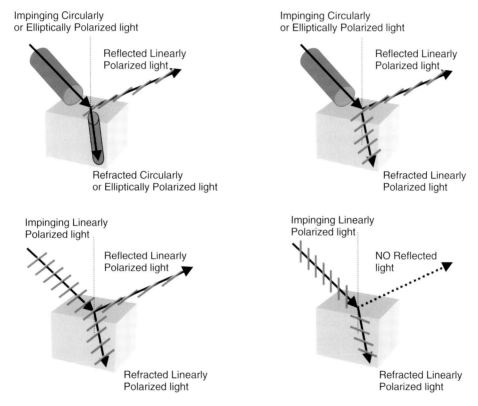

Figure 1.22 Four examples of polarization by reflection and refraction.

refractive index of the material, given by *Brewster's law*:

$$\tan(I_P) = n$$

where n is the refractive index and I_P is the polarizing angle. Figure 1.22 illustrates some examples of reflected and refracted polarization.

The Stokes Vector. The Jones vector describes the polarized radiation components of the *E*-*M* wave. However, in the general case, the propagating wave may consist of a polarized component and a nonpolarized component. This is described by the Stokes vector $S = [S_0, S_1, S_2, S_3]$ in which each of the four parameters is defined in terms of the two component fields E_{ox} and E_{oy} and the phase difference ϕ, as

$$S_0 = E_{ox}^2 + E_{oy}^2$$

$$S_1 = E_{ox}^2 - E_{oy}^2$$

$$S_2 = 2 E_{ox} E_{oy} \cos \phi$$

$$S_3 = 2 E_{ox} E_{oy} \sin \phi$$

and are related between them as

$$S_0^2 = S_1^2 + S_2^2 + S_3^2$$

Based on this definition, light intensity, degree of polarization, ellipticity, amplitude ratio of the field components in the *x* and *y* directions and their phase difference, and polarization azimuth are expressed in terms of the Stokes parameters as

I (intensity) $= S_0$
P (degree of polarization) $= \mathrm{sqrt}(S_1^2 + S_2^2 + S_3^2)/S_0$
ε (ellipticity) $= \frac{1}{2} \arctan S_3 / \mathrm{sqrt}(S_1^2 + S_2^2)$
E_{oy}/E_{ox} (amplitude ratio) $= \mathrm{sqrt}[(S_0 - S_1)/(S_0 + S_1)]$
ϕ (phase difference) $= \phi_y - \phi_x = \arccos[S_2/(S_0^2 - S_1^2)]$
α (azimuth) $= \frac{1}{2} \arctan(S_2/S_1)$

Relationship between Jones and Stokes Vectors. The relationship for specific polarization states of the Jones and Stokes vectors are:

Unpolarized light: $J = $ [not defined], $S = [1,0,0,0]$
Circular polarized right: $J = \mathrm{sqrt}(2)^{-1}[1, i]$, $S = [1,0,0,1]$
Circular polarized left: $J = \mathrm{sqrt}(2)^{-1}[1, -i]$, $S = [1,0,0,-1]$
Linear polarization horizontal: $J = [1,0]$, $S = [1,1,0,0]$
Linear polarization vertical: $J = [0,1]$, $S = [1,-1,0,0]$
Linear polarization $+45°$: $J = \mathrm{sqrt}(2)^{-1}[1, 1]$, $S = [1,0,1,0]$
Linear polarization $-45°$: $J = \mathrm{sqrt}(2)^{-1}[1, -1]$, $S = [1,0,-1,0]$

1.4.7.1 The Faraday Effect

Certain materials exhibit a particularly optical nonlinear behavior manifested by a polarization phenomenon known as *photorefraction*. Photorefraction is the phenomenon by which the polarization plane of light is caused to rotate (Fig. 1.23). This phenomenon is also known as the *Faraday effect*. Devices based on the Faraday effect are known as *rotators*. The rotation of polarization is also known as *polarization mode shift*, θ. This is explained as follows:

Plane-polarized light upon entrance in the *photorefractive* medium is decomposed in two circularly polarized waves rotating in opposite directions and traveling in the

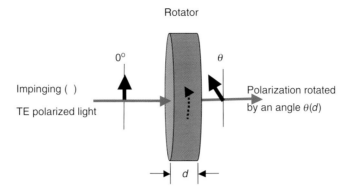

Figure 1.23   Principle of polarization rotator — The Faraday effect.

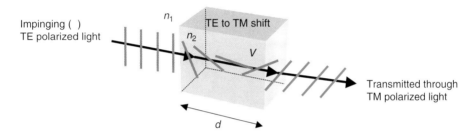

Figure 1.24   Polarization shift from TE to TM mode.

medium at different speeds. Thus, a phase between the two is created, increasing linearly the more it travels in the medium. The two waves recombine upon exiting the medium, producing a wave but with a polarization plane shifted (or rotated) by an angle relative to its polarization at the entrance. The amount of mode shift depends on the thickness of the medium, d (cm), on the magnetic field H (Oersted), and a material constant V, known as the *Verdet constant* (min/cm-Oe), expressed by:

$$\theta = VHd$$

Based on the above, devices of material with a large Verdet constant and a large thickness may be made such that when in a strong magnetic field can shift the polarization mode from TE to TM (Fig. 1.24).

Among solid photorefractive materials are the *α-quartz* and crystallized *sodium chlorate*. Among liquid photorefractive materials is the water solution of *cane sugar*, and among gaseous materials is *camphor* vapor.

1.4.7.2 The Poincare Sphere
The interaction of light with matter affects the state (or states) of polarization (SoP). In general, a state of polarization (SoP) with azimuth α and ellipticity ε is expressed by

$$\text{SoP} = \begin{vmatrix} 1 + \cos(2\alpha)\cos(2\varepsilon) \\ \cos(2\alpha)\sin(2\varepsilon) + i\sin(2\varepsilon) \end{vmatrix}$$

Under certain circumstances, the SoP of a wave changes (rotates) as it travels through a medium; such change is associated with delay. When the rotation is 90°, it results in two orthogonal SoPs (one before and one after the rotation). Two mutually orthogonal SoPs, both at equal intensity, result in a depolarized field.

Described in terms of the Stokes parameters, the unpolarized part $S_0 - \sqrt{(S_1^2 + S_2^2 + S_3^2)}$ in the Poincare sphere is left out and only the polarized part is considered. The three Stokes' parameters on terms of the azimuth ε and ellipticity α are expressed by:

$$S_1 = \cos(2\varepsilon)\cos(2a)$$

$$S_2 = \cos(2\varepsilon)\sin(2a)$$

$$S_3 = \sin 2\varepsilon$$

The Poincare sphere is a graphical representation of all possible SoPs; each point on the sphere's surface is a SoP defined by S. As the SoP changes, the point S on the surface defines a trajectory on the Poincare sphere; the trajectory is directly related to the retardation experienced by the field components. If the sphere is defined by the three axes x, y, and z, then a linear retardation without axis rotation moves S on a circle with plane perpendicular to the x-axis; the arc traveled on the circle due to polarization rotation equals the amount of linear retardation. A linear retardation with axis rotation by θ moves S on a circle with plane perpendicular to an axis x-axis, which is in an angle 2θ with the x-axis. Similarly, a circular retardation moves S along a circle on a plane perpendicular to the y-axis. In this case, the rotation angle is equal to the amount of circular retardation. In conclusion, think of the Poincare sphere as the sphere of the Earth; then the equator of the sphere represents linear polarizations states; the poles (north and south) represent the left and right circular polarizations states, respectively; and any other point on the sphere represents elliptical polarization states, Figure 1.25.

1.4.7.3 Polarization-Dependent Loss
When light travels through matter, it suffers loss of power. The contributors to power loss are many, one of them being polarization.

Virtually all optically transparent materials interact with light and affect to some degree its polarization state, some more and some less. In general, optically transparent

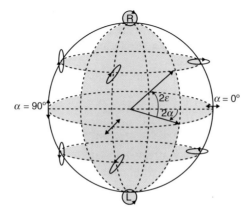

Figure 1.25 Poincare sphere.

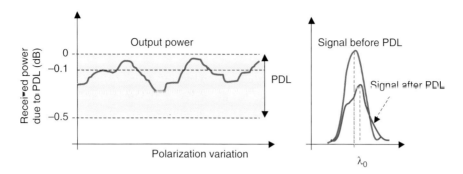

Figure 1.26 Polarization dependence loss.

materials exhibit a spatial polarization distribution. As an optical signal passes through it, due to spatial polarization interaction it suffers selective power reduction, or optical power loss, in specific directions; this power loss due to local polarization influencies is wavelength-dependent. This is known as *polarization-dependent loss* (PDL) and is measured in decibels (dB); that is, the polarization loss (L_{PDL}) has been calculated based on $10 \log(L_{PDL})$. Power loss affects system performance and therefore the power loss of all contributors should be considered.

At low data rates, PDL as compared to IL is a minor contributor to loss; at data rates of 10 Gb/s and above PDL becomes as important as IL. Therefore, when operating at high bit rates, PDL must be carefully examined. The surprising result here is that over a span there may be several contributors in PDL, so the total loss due to PDL is not the algebraic sum. To explain this, consider two cascaded PDL elements, A and B. Element A will attenuate the optical signal due to partial polarization rotation. This signal then will enter element B, which has a random polarization axis and properties with element A. Therefore, the partially polarized light exiting element A and entering element B undergoes another stage of polarization distortion and loss, which now depends on the polarization orientation and characteristics between the two elements A and B, as well as the polarization state of light at the entrances and exits. As a simple example, if the two elements have parallel orientations and similar characteristics, the total PDL is $L_{PDL,1-2} = [L_{PDL,1} + L_{PDL,2}]/[1 + L_{PDL,1}L_{PDL,2}]$.

The power loss due to polarization of the received signal may vary by approximately 0.5 dB (Fig. 1.26). In worst-case optical transmission design, the maximum loss level (as much as -0.5 dB) should be used, whereas in typical performance design an average level (typically at about -0.1 dB). This value does not change with respect to the center wavelength of the received signal. However, asymmetric spectral polarization loss causes asymmetric amplitude signal distortions, and the signal may appear with shifted center wavelength.

1.4.8 Extinction Ratio

Consider polarized light traveling through a polarizer. The maximum transmittance, T_1, is termed *major principal transmittance*, and the minimum transmittance, T_2, is termed *minor principal transmittance*. The ratio of major to minor is known as *principal transmittance*. The inverse, minimum to maximum, is known as the *extinction ratio*.

Consider two polarizers in tandem, one behind the other with parallel surfaces. Then, if their polarization axes are parallel, the transmittance is $T_1^2/2$. If their axes are crossed (perpendicular), the transmittance is $2T_2/T_1$. This is also (but erroneously) termed the *extinction ratio*.

In optical communications, the term *extinction ratio* is defined slightly differently. It describes the modulation efficiency in the optical medium, considering that the source (laser) is always continuous and it is externally modulated on–off (i.e., on–off keying modulation). In this case, the extinction ratio is defined as the ratio of the transmitted optical power of a logic 1 (ON), P_1, over the transmitted optical power of a logic 0, P_0, and it is measured in decibels,

$$\text{Extinction ratio} = 10 \times \log(P_1/P_0) \text{ (dB)}$$

Or, in percentage
$$\text{Extinction ratio} = (P_1/P_0) \times 100 \text{ (\%)}$$

1.4.9 Phase Shift

In contrast to polarization rotation some dielectric materials, shift the phase of transmitted light through it (Fig. 1.27). The amount of phase shift $\Delta\phi$ depends on the wavelength λ, the dielectric constant ε, the refractive index ratio n_1/n_2, and the optical path (thickness) of material.

1.4.10 Birefringence

Anisotropic materials have a different index of refraction in specific directions. As such, when a beam of monochromatic unpolarized light enters the material at a specific angle and travels through it, it is refracted differently in the directions of different indices (Fig. 1.28). That is, when an unpolarized ray enters the material, it is separated

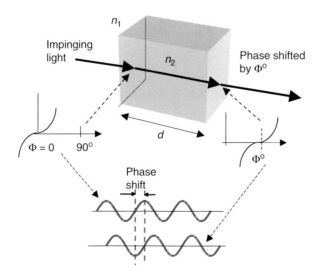

Figure 1.27 Principle of phase angle shift.

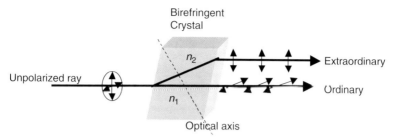

Figure 1.28 Birefringent materials split the incident beam in the ordinary and extraordinary rays, each with different polarization.

into two rays, each with a different polarization, a different direction, and a different propagation constant; one is called an *ordinary* ray (O) and the other is called an *extraordinary* ray (E). In these directions, the refracted index is similarly called *ordinary index*, n_o, and *extraordinary index*, n_e, respectively. This property of crystals is known as *birefringence*. In general, all optically transparent crystals have some degree of birefringence (some have more than others), unless they belong to the cubic system or they are amorphous.

Some birefringent crystals are:

- Calcite ($CaCO_3$) with $n_e = 1.477$ and $n_o = 1.644$ measured at 1,500 nm. Calcite has a spectral transmission range of 0.2 to 3.2 μm, is nonhydroscopic but is a soft crystal.

- Quartz (SiO_2) with $n_e = 1.537$ and $n_o = 1.529$ measured at 1,500 nm. Natural or synthetic quartz is used. Quartz has a spectral transmission range of approximately 0.2 to 2.6 μm.

- Titanium dioxide (rutile) has an index of refraction difference (index of birefringence) $n_o - n_e = 0.27$. The spectral transmission is in the range of 0.45 to 6.2 μm.

Certain optically transparent isotropic materials become anisotropic when under stress. Stress may be exerted due to mechanical forces (pulling, bending, twisting), thermal forces (ambient temperature variations), and electrical fields. Under such conditions, the index of refraction, polarization, and propagation characteristics become different in certain directions within the material. Figure 1.29 illustrates an unpolarized light ray traversing a birefringent plate, and Figure 1.30 shows the optical effect of a birefringent crystal plate.

Clearly, birefringence in fiber alters the polarization state of the characteristics of the propagating optical signal in an undesirable manner. Consequently, birefringence in fiber is highly undesirable. Therefore, several steps have been taken to minimize fiber birefringence. First, because the major contributor to fiber birefringence is due to geometry imperfections (core not exactly circular) and variations in the refractive index, serious manufacturing steps have been taken to resolve these issues. Additionally, several techniques are applied to minimize residual birefringence. One technique that monitors and controls the polarization at the receiver is accomplished by using polarization-maintaining fibers. Another technique uses transmitting and receiving strategies to "immunize" the system from fiber polarization

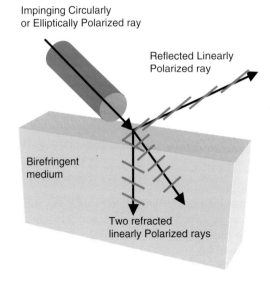

Figure 1.29   Example of birefringence on a nonpolarized beam before and after.

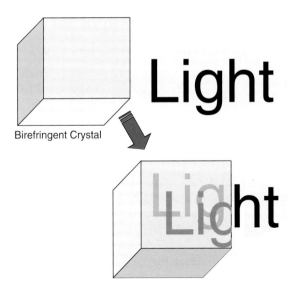

Figure 1.30   Effect of a birefringence crystal.

variations, such techniques are *polarization spreading* (polarization scrambling, data-induced polarization) or *polarization diversity*.

On the other side, birefringence has also been used to construct filters that function as wavelength multiplexers and as demultiplexers (see filters).

1.4.10.1   *Quarter-Wavelength Plates*

A birefringent plate of a quarter-wavelength ($\lambda/4$) thickness and with surfaces parallel to the optic axis has important effects on polarized light.

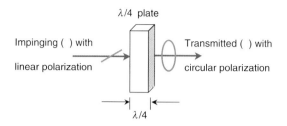

Figure 1.31   Effect of a quarter-wavelength plate.

If light is linearly polarized and at 45° to the fast optical axis, it is transformed into circularly polarized light and vice versa (Fig. 1.31).

If light is linearly polarized and parallel to the fast or slow axis, it remains unchanged.

If light is linearly polarized and is at any other angle to the optical axis, it is transformed into elliptical light and vice versa.

If the plate consists of quartz or mica, the thickness, d, is related to wavelength by the relationship

$$d = (R \cdot \lambda)/\Delta n$$

where $\Delta n = n_e - n_o$ is the refractive index difference of the extraordinary and ordinary paths and R is a constant real number.

The phase difference, δ, is related to R by

$$\delta = 2\pi R$$

For $\lambda/4$ plates, $R = \pm 0.25$.

1.4.10.2 Half-Wavelength Plate

A birefringent plate of a half-wavelength ($\lambda/2$) thickness and with the surfaces parallel to the optic axis has other important effects on polarized light than the quarter-wavelength plate.

If light is linear-polarized and at an angle θ with the fast optical axis, it remains linear but the orientation is rotated by 2θ degrees. Thus, if the angle is 45°, the linear polarization is rotated by 90° (Fig. 1.32).

For $\lambda/2$ plates, $R = \pm 0.5$.

1.4.11 Material Dispersion

The refractive index of matter is related to the dielectric coefficient and to the characteristic resonance frequency of its dipoles, which interact stronger with and

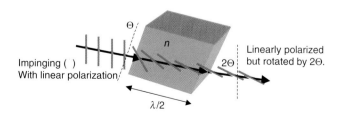

Figure 1.32   Effect of half-wavelength plate.

absorb more optical energy closer to their resonance frequency. Consequently, the refractive index $n(\omega)$ depends on the optical frequency ω. This dependency is termed *material dispersion* and is measured in ps/nm. Dispersion is easier to explain if one considers an optical signal that consists of a narrow band of frequencies. Then, dispersion represents a time delay difference per nanometer of frequency spectrally distributed in an optical signal. That is, a 100-nsecond delay over a 10-frequency spectrum is different from a 20-nsec delay over the same spectrum.

Silica, a key ingredient of optical fiber cable, has a refractive index that varies with optical frequency. Thus, dispersion plays a significant role in fiber-optic communications.

The polarization of an E-M wave, P, induced in the electric dipoles of a medium by an electric field, E, is proportional to susceptibility, χ:

$$P = \varepsilon_o[\chi^1 \cdot E + \chi^2 \cdot E \cdot E + \chi^3 \cdot E \cdot E \cdot E + \cdots]$$

where ε_o is the permittivity of free space.

For an isotropic medium, the first-order term expresses the linear behavior of matter. The second-order term is orthogonal and thus it vanishes; for anisotropic media the second order still holds. Higher order terms are negligible (in optical communications, this may not be true for long fiber lengths or for ultrahigh bit rates).

Thus, for an isotropic medium the above series relationship is simplified to $P = \varepsilon_o \chi \cdot E$. However, nature is not as simple, and most materials are either anisotropic or become anisotropic under certain conditions. In this case, higher-order terms should also be considered. In particular, the third-order term becomes significant and results in nonlinear effects that may affect and limit optical transmission.

The most influential nonlinear effects in optical transmission, particularly when many wavelengths at high optical power are transmitted over the same medium (e.g., DWDM), are *four-wave mixing* (FWM), *stimulated Raman scattering* (SRC), and *Brillouin scattering* (BS).

1.4.12   Electro-Optic Effects

Electro-optic effects refer to variation of material optical properties when in an electric field. When matter is in an electric field, it influences its electron motions in the atoms or molecules, or it influences the crystal structure and thus its refractive index distribution and its optical properties. For example, the application of an electric field may cause an isotropic crystal (e.g., GaAs) to become nonisotropic (birefringent). In general, the refractive index n^* (after a field is applied) is a function of the applied electric field and may be expanded in a series (similar arguments hold when a magnetic field, and in some cases a gravitational field, is applied):

$$n^* = n + a_1 E^1 + a_2 E^2 + \cdots$$

where n^* and n are the refractive indices after and before the application of the electric field, and a_1 and a_2 are known as the first-order and second-order electro-optic coefficients.

This expansion assumes an isotropic medium. In a general case, this expansion is very involved because the applied electric field on a crystal will yield different series expansions for each crystallographic axis, a problem that is studied with tensors having a matrix notation. Thus, if a crystal had three indices (n_1, n_2, n_3) in three directions, then the applied field would affect each one differently (thus adding a second subscript to keep track). Moreover, if the direction of the field changed, then this would be further complicated (thus adding a third subscript). Furthermore, if the field also changed in the time domain, then one realizes the complexities in studying the electro-optic effect of a complex crystal.

1.4.12.1 The Pockels Effect

In the previous expansion (repeated for convenience), consider only the first (linear) term:

$$n^* = n + a_1 E^1 + [a_2 E^2 + \cdots]$$

Then, the difference in refractive index is

$$\Delta n = n^* - n = a_1 E$$

This relationship characterizes the Pockels effect. However, the coefficient a_1 is not nonzero for all materials. In fact, it is zero ($a_1 = 0$) for all liquids and noncrystals, as well as for all crystals that have a symmetric structure. Thus, glasses and NaCl, exhibit no Pockels effect, but GaAs, LiNbO$_3$, and KDP (KH$_2$PO$_4$-potassium dihydrogen phosphate) do.

If an electric field E_a is applied to an isotropic crystal (n_0) with nonzero a_1 coefficient (e.g., GaAs), then birefringence is induced that changes the refractive index to two n_1 and n_2. The new refractive indices are given by

$$n_1 = n_0 + (1/2)n_0^3 r_{22} E_a$$

and

$$n_2 = n_0 - (1/2)n_0^3 r_{22} E_a$$

where the constant r_{22} is called the Pockels coefficient, measured in m/V, which depends on the material and the crystal structure. In fact, even the Pockels coefficient is not the same for all directions in the crystal; the Pockels coefficient along the propagation axis is denoted r_{13}.

Typical Pockels coefficient values of LiNbO$_3$ (measured at 500 nm) are $r_{13} = 8.6 \times 10^{-12}$ m/V, and $r_{22} = 3.4 \times 10^{-12}$ m/V.

As the electric field is applied and birefringence is induced, a propagating optical monochromatic beam through the crystal is polarized differently in two directions; two beams are formed, each propagating at a different speed, and thus they have a phase difference. As the electric field changes, so does the phase difference (Fig. 1.33). This is known as a phase modulator or a *Pockels cell*.

Consider that a voltage V is applied across a Pockels cell of thickness d and length L, and in a direction (y-axis) perpendicular to optical transmission (z-axis). Then, the field across the cell is $E = V/d$. Because of the induced birefringence, an optical beam is separated into two polarized beams. After length L, the first beam will have a phase ϕ_1 and the second beam ϕ_2:

$$\phi_1 = (2\pi n_1 L)/\lambda = [2\pi L/\lambda][n_0 + (1/2)n_0^3 r_{22} V/d]$$

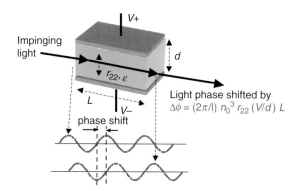

Figure 1.33   Principle of Pockels cell. In the Kerr cell the field is much stronger.

and

$$\phi_2 = (2\pi n_1 L)/\lambda = [2\pi L/\lambda][n_0 - (1/2)n_0^3 r_{22} V/d]$$

Thus, the phase difference is

$$\Delta\phi = \phi_1 - \phi_2 = (2\pi\lambda)n_0^3 r_{22}(V/d)\ L$$

This relationship indicates that the phase difference is proportional to the field (V/d) and to the length of the cell. Thus, if more phase difference is required, the length of the cell may be increased and the thickness d of the Pockels cell may be decreased. Pockels cells are applicable to phase modulators or polarization modulators.

1.4.12.2   Kerr Effect

In the refractive index expansion (repeated for convenience), consider only the second-order (nonlinear) term:

$$n^* = n + a_2 E^2$$

In this case, the refractive index difference is

$$\Delta n = n^* - n = a_2 E^2 = (\lambda K)E^2$$

where K is the Kerr coefficient, measured in m/V^2. It is noteworthy that K depends on the wavelength.

In contrast to the Pockels effect (according to which only some materials have a nonzero a_1 coefficient), all materials have a nonzero a_2 coefficient, and thus all materials, including glass exhibit the Kerr effect to some degree.

The Kerr effect is very similar to the Pockels effect in that it induces birefringence and thus causes two polarized optical beams and a phase difference. However, the Kerr effect is a second-order phenomenon and therefore it is significant when the applied field is strong. In addition, certain crystals exhibit a Kerr effect with a response time on the order of picoseconds or less, and this is what makes them suitable as ultrafast modulators at bit rates exceeding 10 Gbps. A typical value for the Kerr coefficient of glass is 3×10^{-15} m/V^2.

1.4.13 Material Attributes

The attributes of material and their significance, of interest in DWDM, are:

- Refractive index (n): is a function of molecular structure of matter;
  is a function of optical frequency $\{n(\omega)\}$,
  is a function of optical intensity;
  determines optical propagation properties of each λ;
  may not be distributed equally in all directions;
  is affected by external temperature, pressure, and fields;
- Reflectivity (R): it is a function of geometry, λ and n
  material surface reflects optical power;
  changes polarization of incident optical wave;
  changes phase of incident optical wave
- Transparency (T): depends on matter consistency;
- Scattering: due to molecular matrix disorders
- Absorption (A): due to ion presence in matrix
- Polarization (P): due to X–Y uneven E-M fields (light–matter interaction)
- Birefringence (B): due to nonuniform distribution of n in all directions.
- Phase shift ($\Delta\Phi$): due to wave propagation property of light through matter
- Ions act like dipoles: exhibit eigen frequencies;
  exhibit antenna characteristics (receiver/transmitter)

1.5 THE FIBER AS AN OPTICAL TRANSMISSION MEDIUM

The first work that dealt with the propagation of electromagnetic waves in dielectric rods was published in 1910. Since then, this seminal work evolved to take the form of optical transmission in dielectric fibers.

A single fiber strand consists of an ultrapure silica glass SiO_2 (70–95 wt%), several kilometers long, mixed with specific elements such as germanium, fluorine, phosphorus, and boron, which are known as *dopants*. Dopants are added to adjust the refractive index of fiber and its light propagation characteristics. The purity of glass fiber is measured by its very low loss, about 0.35 dB/Km at 1,310 nm and 0.25 dB at 1,550 nm.

The fiber strand consists of several concentric layers. The innermost layer is the silica *core*; in optical communications, this is where the photonic signal propagates. The core is covered by another layer of silica with a different mix of dopants, known as *cladding*; it has a lower refractive index than the core. The cladding is covered with a buffer *coating* to absorb mechanical stresses, and this is covered with a strong material such as Kevlar (Kevlar is a trademark of E.I. du Pont & Co.). Finally, an external layer of plastic material covers this. The final fiber including coating is standardized to 245 μm diameter for compatibility reasons. Fiber cables used in long-haul communications consist of a bundle of fiber strands, and depending on cable and manufacturer, they may incorporate 432 or even more than 1,000 strands.

Fiber is made by vertically drawing a cylindrical *preform* (also known as a *blank*), which is made of ultrapure SiO_2 and in which a number of dopants (e.g., GeO_2) have been added. Dopants are homogeneously distributed in a tubular fashion in controlled

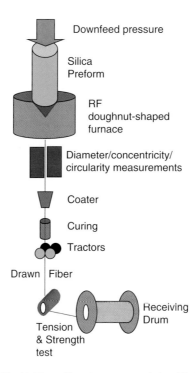

Downfeed pressure

Silica Preform

RF doughnut-shaped furnace

Diameter/concentricity/ circularity measurements

Coater

Curing

Tractors

Drawn | Fiber

Tension & Strength test

Receiving Drum

Figure 1.34 Making a fiber (a conceptual simplified diagram).

quantities to determine the distribution of the refractive index in the core or the fiber *refractive index profile*.

The preform blank has been immersed in a high-frequency doughnut-shaped furnace such that the base of the blank is heated at 2000 °C. At this temperature the base of the blank starts melting and becomes viscous (Fig. 1.34). Then the lower tip of the molten blank forms a *gob* that starts falling from the blank, thus pulling a thin fiber behind it. The gob is cutoff, and the fiber is threaded into a tractor assembly and is drawn. The diameter of the drawn fiber is continuously monitored, and minute adjustments are made (via an automatic control mechanism) to the drawing rate so that a produced fiber complies with the diameter tolerance specified by ITU-T standards. The various coatings are also applied during the drawing process.

The cylindrical preform is made with one of several proprietary methods. Such methods are the vapor-phase axial deposition (VAD); the outer vapor deposition (OVD); and the modified chemical deposition (MCVD), which was invented in 1970 by scientists at Bell Laboratories. The cylindrical preform starts with the manufacture of a hollow tube of highly pure silica. One of the methods to produce the tube is Lucent Technologies' *sol gel* method (described and illustrated in *http://www.bell-labs.com/org/physicalsciences/projects/solgel*, 1999).

Based on the MCVD method, the silica hollow tube is placed horizontally on a lathe and oxygen and vaporized ultrapure oxides (such as $SiCl_4$, $GeCl_4$) enter the rotating tube in a specified sequence. The rotating tube is kept at a high and constant temperature such that the inner walls of the silica tube chemically interact with the oxides in a controlled manner, evenly depositing elements such as Ge, P, B, and F. In

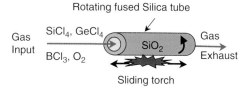

Figure 1.35   Making the preform.

this case, the chemical reaction of oxides with oxygen is

$$SiCl_4 \text{ (gas)} + O_2 \Longrightarrow SiO_2 \text{ (deposited solid)} + 2Cl_2 \text{ (gas)}$$

$$GeCl_4 \text{ (gas)} + O_2 \Longrightarrow GeO_2 \text{ (deposited solid)} + 2Cl_2 \text{ (gas)}$$

As deposition takes place, the opening of the tube is closing in (Fig. 1.35). The radial deposition of dopants in the preform determines the profile of the index of refraction of the fiber.

Application-specific optical fiber (ASOF) can be custom-made by modifying, with any of the methods mentioned, the sequence and concentration of dopants of the fiber core and/or the geometry of the fiber. According to this, fibers with specific properties for specific applications can be made.

One would think that glass fiber is fragile "like glass." However, what is important in communications fiber is the tensile strength of the fiber cable, which indeed is higher than that of copper. In fact, the tensile strength of copper is 100 pounds per square inch, whereas that of glass fiber is theoretically 2 million pounds per square inch. However, due to surface microcracks that exist in any glass fiber, it is about 800,000 pounds per square inch. In addition to high strength, glass fiber has a long service lifetime of well above 20 years.

ITU-T has defined parameters specific to many optical components but not to fiber. Here we provide a list of parameters that pertain to fibers; in the following sections, we elaborate on these parameters, and it will become evident that indeed the fiber is one of the most important components in optical communications.

- fiber type (multimode, single mode, dispersion-compensating)
- forward attenuation per kilometer
- backward attenuation per kilometer (if asymmetric)
- polarization mode dispersion
- polarization-dependent loss (PDL)
- birefringence
- dispersion (chromatic and material)
- zero-dispersion wavelength
- dispersion flatness over spectrum range
- birefringence
- cutoff wavelength

1.5.1 Composite Refractive Indices

Each element and each compound are characterized by their own refractive index. Certain compounds have a low index and some others high (Chalcogenides) and when combined they produce a different refractive index value. However, there is no exact relationship that predicts what the end refractive index value will be based on a specific mix of elements or compounds; the refractive index is merely measured after a new compound is produced. As such, the value of many diffractive indices has been derived experimentally, and experimental graphs may aid in predicting the refractive index.

Polymers (e.g., polysterene, vinyl) have a high index of refraction. As a consequence, polymers have started making inroads in applications ranging from optical components to ultra-short-haul (very short distance) fiber communication.

Some refractive indices of certain materials are listed in Table 1.4 (note that the refractive index is a function of the wavelength for which it is measured and thus the tabulated numbers are approximate, indicating only a relative degree of magnitude):

1.5.2 Fiber Modes

When monochromatic light travels in an optical waveguide, transmission takes place through specific guided modes. These modes are determined from the *eigenvalues* of second-order differential equations and their boundary conditions, a similar analysis to propagation of electromagnetic waves in cylindrical waveguides. The solution of these equations determines the modes of propagation in the waveguide, as well as the *cutoff frequency* beyond which the fiber does not support transmission.

The propagation characteristics of light in silica fiber depend on the chemical consistency (silica + dopants) and the cross-sectional dimensions of core and cladding.

Table 1.4 Approximate refractive index of certain materials

Material	Refractive Index
SiO_2 (0.8 wt% F)	1.65
CaF_2	1.56
CsBr	1.67
BaF_2	1.47
MgF_2	1.37
KBr	1.53
NaCl	1.52
GeO_2 (at 2 mol%)	1.46
P_2O_5 (at 2 mol%)	1.46
B_2O_3 (at 8 mol%)	1.46
CdTe	2.70
Diamond	2.40
Si	3.43
Fused silica	1.41
GaAs	3.31
Ge	4.02
Polyurethane	1.46
Polysterene	1.59
N-vinyl carbazol	1.68
PMMA aczylic (red)	1.49

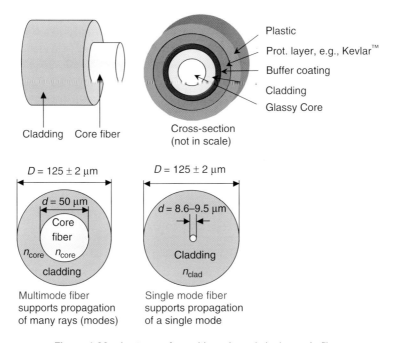

Plastic

Prot. layer, e.g., Kevlar™

Buffer coating

Cladding

Glassy Core

Cladding   Core fiber

Cross-section
(not in scale)

$D = 125 \pm 2$ μm

$d = 50$ μm

Core
fiber

n_{core} n_{core}

cladding

Multimode fiber
supports propagation
of many rays (modes)

$D = 125 \pm 2$ μm

$d = 8.6$–9.5 μm

Cladding

n_{clad}

Single mode fiber
supports propagation
of a single mode

Figure 1.36   Anatomy of a multi-mode and single-mode fiber.

Typically, core and cladding have a diameter of about 125 μm, but the core itself comes in two sizes, depending on the application for which the fiber is intended. Fiber with a core diameter of about 50 μm supports many modes of propagation, and thus it is known as *multimode* fiber, whereas fiber with a core diameter of about 8.6 to 9.5 μm (theoretically) supports one mode of propagation and is known as *single-mode* fiber (per ITU-T G.652) (Fig. 1.36).

1.5.2.1   Cutoff Wavelength

When electromagnetic waves propagate in a guided medium (i.e., fiber), the guide puts a limit on the shortest wavelength (highest frequency) that can pass through. Propagation in rectangular waveguides is studied using simple boundary conditions and Cartesian coordinates and is used in circular waveguides using Bessel functions.

The actual number of modes, M, supported by a fiber depends on fiber geometry (core diameter), the refractive index of core and cladding (or the numerical aperture), and the wavelength of the optical signal. These fiber parameters are combined in a normalized parameter known as the M number, expressed by

$$M = \tfrac{1}{2}\left\{(4\pi/\lambda)d\,\sqrt{(n_{\text{clad}}^2 - n_{\text{core}}^2)}\right\}^2$$

where λ is the wavelength and d is the core diameter. Note that a fiber supports fewer modes at shorter frequencies and more modes at higher frequencies.

The square root in this relationship is also known as the *numerical aperture*, NA, of the step index fiber, i.e.,

$$NA = \sqrt{(n_{\text{clad}}^2 - n_{\text{core}}^2)}$$

In optical fibers with complex refractive index profiles, the theoretical calculation of numerical aperture and cutoff wavelength is complex and is only determined using approximate models with acceptable accuracy. In general, if the wavelength at free space is λ, the wavelength in the guide is λ_g and the cutoff wavelength λ_c is provided by

$$(1/\lambda_c^2) = (1/\lambda^2) - (1/\lambda_g^2)$$

In terms of the M number, the condition for single mode transmission is

$$M </ = M_{\text{cutoff}} = \sim 2.4$$

The wavelength below which a single-mode fiber allows multiple modes is expressed as

$$\lambda >= \lambda_{\text{cutoff}} = \sim 2.6 r (NA)$$

where r is the core radius and NA is the numerical aperture of the fiber.

The cutoff wavelength, per ITU-T G.650, is defined as the wavelength that experiences by the waveguide a "fundamental mode power decrease to less than 0.1 dB." ITU-T G.650 also elaborates that in this case when many modes are equally excited "the second-order (LP_{11}) mode undergoes 19.3 dB more attenuation than the fundamental (LP_{01})" mode.

Propagation modes are labeled as TE_{MN} or TM_{MN} (where M and N are integers), depending on the magnitude of the *transverse electric* field ($E_Z = 0$) or the *transverse magnetic* field ($H_Z = 0$) at the surface of the fiber core (the boundary) in the transverse direction.

Figure 1.37 graphically illustrates certain modes of standard circular waveguides. The theoretical critical wavelengths for the three modes, and for a waveguide of diameter D, are provided by the relationship

$$\lambda_c = \pi D/s$$

where s is the Bessel function constant. The theoretical values are listed in Table 1.5.

Based on dielectric constant and dimensions, the optical fiber supports the fundamental mode TE_{11} (also known as HE_{11} or H_{11}) or higher modes. A fiber that supports many modes is known as a *multimode* fiber, and a fiber that supports only one mode

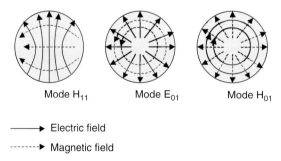

Mode H_{11} Mode E_{01} Mode H_{01}

———▶ Electric field

┄┄┄┄▶ Magnetic field

Figure 1.37 Graphical representation of the distribution of electro-magnetic fields in circular waveguide for certain modes (shown cross-section).

Table 1.5   Critical wavelengths for three modes

Mode	λ_c
H_{11}	1.71D
E_{01}	1.31D
H_{01}	0.82D

(the HE_{11}) is known as a *single-mode* fiber. A single-mode fiber supports transmission along its longitudinal axis (H_{11}).

Multimode fibers and single-mode fibers have different refractive index profiles, different cross-sectional dimensions, and therefore different transmission characteristics. Consequently, different fiber types are used in different network applications, such as multimode fibers in access communication and single-mode fibers in long-haul communication.

The propagation of light in matter is typically illustrated by using the ray technique. This is a graphical and visual technique that shows the paths of optical rays as they travel through matter and through the fiber, depicting diffraction, refraction, polarization, and birefringence. Figure 1.38 shows two cases of light propagating in a step index fiber and in a graded index fiber using the ray technique. This technique is used extensively throughout this book.

1.5.2.2 Multimode Fiber Graded Index Characteristics

A list of the salient characteristics of multimode fiber graded index (MMF GRIN) follows:

- It minimizes delay spread, but is still significant in long lengths.
- One percent index difference between core and cladding amounts to 1–5 ns/Km delay spread (compare with step index that has about 50 ns/Km)
- Easier to splice and easier to couple light into it
- Bit rate is limited; up to 100 Mb/s for lengths up to 40 Km; higher bit rates for shorter lengths

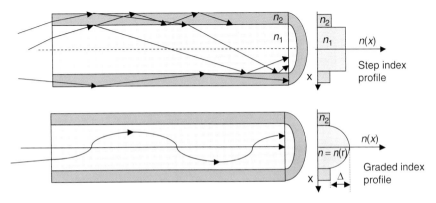

Figure 1.38 Propagation of light rays in step and in graded index fibers (shown cross-section along the axis).

- Fiber span without amplification is limited; up to 40 Km at 100 Mb/s (extended to Gbps for shorter distances for graded index)
- Dispersion effects for long lengths and high bit rates is a limiting factor

1.5.2.3 Single-Mode Characteristics

A list of the salient characteristics of standard single-mode fiber (SSMF) follows:

- It (almost) eliminates delay spread
- More difficult to splice (than multimode) due to critical core alignment requirements
- More difficult to couple all photonic energy from a source into it.
- Difficult to study propagation with ray theory; it requires Maxwell's equations
- Suitable for transmitting modulated signals at 40 Gb/s (or higher) and up to 200 km without amplification
- Long lengths and bit rates greater than 10 Gb/s bring forth a number of issues due to residual nonlinearity/birefringence of the fiber
- Fiber temperature for long lengths and bit rates greater than 10 Gb/s becomes significant

1.5.2.4 Critical Cone and Exit Cone

Critical cone, also known as *acceptance cone*, is a cone of an angle within which all rays that are launched into the core are reflected at the core–cladding interface at or beyond the critical angle (Fig. 1.39). The half angle of the critical cone, also known as *numerical aperture*, depends on the refractive index distribution function in the core and cladding and is independent of the core diameter. For a step index fiber, the numerical aperture is

$$NA = \sin \Theta_{NA} = \mathrm{sqrt}\,(n_1^2 - n_2^2)$$

where n_1 is for the core and n_2 is for the cladding.

When light emerges from the far end of the fiber, it does so in a cone, which is known as the *emerging cone* or the *exit cone*. In single-mode fiber, the exit cone is approximately the same as the acceptance cone. Clearly, for best coupling results, the acceptance cone and the exit cone should be as acute as possible.

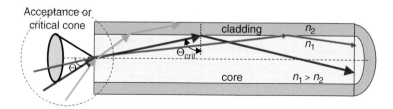

Figure 1.39 Illustrative definition of acceptance or critical cone (shown cross-section along the axis).

1.5.3   Fiber Attenuation and Power Loss

Fiber consists of optically transparent matter that, like any other matter, absorbs and scatters part of the optical power of light. This is termed *attenuation*. The more light travels in matter, the more it is attenuated. Fiber attenuation depends on scattering and fluctuations of the refractive index, on the imperfection in the fiber, and on impurities. Metal ions and OH radicals have a particular effect, particularly in the range of 1.4 μm, although fiber cable, almost free of OH radicals, has been successfully manufactured.

However, there are more mechanisms that contribute to optical power loss in the presence of matter. This sum of all power lost due to all contributors is clearly measured by subtracting the power out from the power in the fiber. This is termed *fiber loss* (many times used synonymously with *power attenuation*). Power loss is a very important transmission characteristic that imposes a limiting effect on the fiber length. Fiber loss, for a given optical power, $P(0)$, launched into fiber affects the total power arrived at the receiver, P_r. Based on this, fiber loss limits the fiber span, L_{max}, without amplification, and/or determines the required amplification gain.

For a fiber with optical power attenuation constant $\alpha(\lambda)$, the optical power attenuation at a length L is expressed as

$$P(L) = P(0)10^{-\alpha(\lambda)L/10}$$

In this relationship, if we replace $P(L)$ with the minimum acceptable power at the receiver, P_r, then the (ideal) maximum fiber length is

$$L_{max} = [10/\alpha(\lambda)]\log_{10}[P(0)/P_r]$$

In subsequent sections, we will see that there are additional limiting factors (e.g., dispersion and bit rate) that further limit the (ideal) maximum fiber length.

In general, the optical power attenuation constant, $\alpha(\lambda)$, is nonlinear and depends on the wavelength

$$\alpha(\lambda) = C_1/\lambda^4 + C_2 + A(\lambda)$$

where C_1 is a constant (due to Rayleigh scattering), C_2 is a constant due to fiber imperfections, and $A(\lambda)$ is a function that describes fiber impurity absorption as a function of wavelength.

The optical power attenuation constant of a fiber (measured in dB/km) is typically plotted as a function of the wavelength (Fig. 1.40).

Conventional single-mode fibers have two low attenuation ranges, one at about 1.3 μm and another at about 1.55 μm. Between these two ranges, and at about 1.4 nm, there is a high attenuation range (1,350–1,450 nm), due to the OH radical with a peak at 1,385 nm, known as the "fifth window."

If the OH radical could be eliminated from the fiber material, then the high attenuation region at about 1.4 nm also could be used in DWDM communications. The AllWave[TM] is a low water peak fiber (LWPF) with minimum attenuation over the entire spectrum between 1,310 nm and 1,625 nm, increasing the number of optical channels by over 50%, as compared with the conventional single mode fiber (CSMF); this corresponds to about 500 channels with 100 GHz channel spacing. This fiber is suitable for metropolitan area network applications.

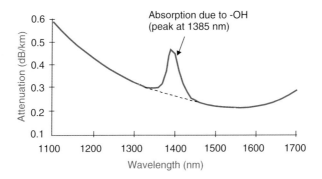

Figure 1.40   Attenuation as a function of wavelength for single mode fiber.

Fiber attenuation is measured in dB per kilometer. ITU-T G.652 recommends losses below 0.5 dB/km in the region 1,310 nm, and below 0.4 dB/km in the region 1,500 nm.

1.5.3.1 *The Decibel Unit*
Optical power, power attenuation, and optical loss are measured in decibel (dB) units. Power in dB units is defined as 10 times the logarithm (base 10) of power (in watts):

$$\text{Power (dB)} = 10 \log_{10}[P \text{ (watts)}]$$

In communications, the transmitted optical signal is at extremely low power, on the order of milliwatts. To denote that the reference power point is in milliwatts, the dB unit is expressed in dBm:

$$\text{Power (dBm)} = 10 \log[P \text{ (mWatts)}] = 10 \log[P \times 10^{-3} \text{ (W)}]$$

Here, a few properties of logarithms are recalled (Table 1.6), because they play a key role in the understanding of dos and don'ts when dealing with decibels.

When adding or subtracting dBs and dBms, certain cautions should be taken regarding the mix-and-match of units. Decibel units are additive if their argument

Table 1.6   Properties of logarithms

1. $\log(AB) = \log A + \log B$
2. $\log(A/B) = \log A - \log B$
3. $\log(A^N) = N \log A$
4. $\log\{N \text{ root } (A)\} = (1/N) \log A$
5. $\log 10 = 1$
6. $\log 1 = 0$
7. $\log A = \log(e)\ln A$
8. $\log(e) = \log(2.71828+) = 0.434294$
9. $\ln 10 = 2.30258+$
10. $\ln 2.71828 = 1$
11. $\log A = +\log A$, where $A > 1$
12. $\log A = -\log |A|$, where $0 < A < 1$
13. $\log(A + B)$ not equal to $\log A + \log B$

is multiplicative, and therefore, if the dB units are not handled correctly, one may make a serious erroneous calculation.

For example, 1 dBm $= 10 \log[10$ mW], but 1 dBm $+ 1$ dBm is *not* 2 dBm because this is not the result of $10 \log(10$ mW $\times 10$ mW), as a result of property #1 in Table 1.6. If it were, however, then 10 mW $\times 10$ mW is 100×10^{-6} W $= 10^{-4}$ W, and hence $10 \log 10^{-4} = -40$ dB! As a consequence:

- dBms cannot be added.
- dBms can be subtracted (as a result of property #2 in Table 1.6); the result is in dBs (not in dBms) since a dBm difference implies a power ratio.
- dBs can be added; the result is in dBm.
- a dB can be added to a dBm; the result is in dBm.

Power attenuation or power loss is also expressed in dB units. In this case, it is (10 times) the logarithm of the ratio of received power over transmitted power, both expressed in the same units, and thus the ratio is dimensionless. Hence, the attenuation over a fiber span is expressed in dB units, regardless of whether the power is in W or mW units):

$$\alpha\lambda = 10 \log P_1/P_2 \text{ (dB)}$$

For example, a power ratio of 1,000 is 30 dB, of 10 is 10 dB, of ~3 is 5 dB, of 2 is ~3 dB, and a ratio of 0.1 is -10 dB. To the untrained eye and mind, loss or gain in dBs is very abstract because we are trained to think of loss and gain in ratios, such as, for example, 100 times less or 100 times more versus 20 dB. However, a dB is a more convenient unit and is widely used in optical communications; Figure 1.41 illustrates how a 5-dB loss of a signal is seen at the receiver.

Besides decibels, power loss is provided as a percentage of power transmitted compared with that received, such as 60%, and so on. That is, if 100 units of power were transmitted and 60 units were received, the loss is $100 - 60 = 40$ and in percentage it is $(100 - 60)/100$. The correspondence of dB to percentage is easy to calculate. For example, 90% power loss corresponds to $10 \log\{(100 - 90)/100\} = -10$ dB, 50% corresponds to $10 \log 0.5 = -3$ dB and 2% to $10 \log 0.98 = -0.01$ dB. Table 1.7 lists a conversion table from dB loss to percentage loss and percentage loss to dB loss.

Another power ratio that is widely used in communications is the signal-to-noise ratio (SNR), which is also expressed in dB units.

Example #1: Convert -1 dBm optical power in mWatts.

From the definition of dB: -1 dBm $= 10 \log(0.1$ mW) dBm

$\Rightarrow$ The optical power is: $P = 0.1$ mW $= 10^{-4}$ W

Figure 1.41 Perceived 5 dB loss of optical signal.

Table 1.7   dB loss and percent loss

dB Loss	%Loss	%Loss	dB Loss
0	0	0	0
−0.1	−2.3	−0.5	−0.02
−0.5	−10.9	−1	−0.04
−1	−20.6	−5	−0.22
−2	−36.9	−10	−0.46
−5	−68.4	−40	−2.22
−10	−90.0	−90	−10.00
−20	−99.0	−99	−20.00

Example #2: Convert −1 dBm in optical power density (W/cm^2) if −1 dBm is launched in a fiber core with diameter $D = 10$ μm

⇒ The cross-sectional area of fiber is: $A = (\pi/4)D^2 = (3.14/4)[10 \times 10^{-4}]^2$ cm^2 $= 0.785 \times 10^{-6}$ cm^2

⇒ The optical power density is $P/A = 10^{-4}$ W/[0.785×10^{-6}] cm$^2 = 10^2/0.785$ (W/cm^2) $= 127$ (W/cm^2)

Example #3: Calculate the optical loss for a laser beam with a step intensity distribution and a diameter of 12 μm if the reflectivity of the fiber surface is 5%.

⇒ There are two loss contributions, A. due to cross-sectional area mismatch between beam and fiber core, and B. due to reflectivity.

⇒ A. the cross section of the beam is $A = (\pi/4)D_2^2 = (3.14/4)[12 \times 10^{-4}]^2$ cm$^2 = 0.785[1.44 \times 10^{-6}]$ cm$^2 = 1.130 \times 10^{-6}$ cm^2.
Thus, the part of optical power impinging on the core is calculated from:
$[D/D_2]P = [0.785 \times 10^{-6}/1.130 \times 10^{-6}]10^{-4}$ W $= 0.69 \times 10^{-4}$ W

⇒ B. From the optical power impinging on the fiber core 95% is coupled in and 5% is lost due to reflectivity. Thus, the power launched in the fiber is:

$$0.95 \times 0.69 \times 10^{-4} \text{ W} = 0.66 \times 10^{-4} \text{ W} = \underline{0.066 \text{ mW}}$$

The latter is expressed in dBm as follows:

$$10\log(0.066 \text{ mW}) = 10\log(0.066) \text{ dBm} = 10(-1.18) \text{ dBm} = \underline{-10.18 \text{ dBm}}$$

Here we have assumed a laser beam with circular and step distribution intensity. In practice, the beam has a distribution such as Gaussian, Poisson's, Maxwellian, and so on. In addition, the near-field or far-field positioning of the fiber from the beam source may be considered as well as any beam transformations (corrective and/or focusing lens).

1.5.3.2   Fiber Spectrum Utilization
The spectral low-loss of fiber has been distinguished in ranges such as:
   The S-band (also known as short wavelength or second window) is defined as the range 1,280 nm to 1,350 nm. The S-band was the first band to be used in high-speed

long-haul applications. The S-band and C-band have found applications in WDM metropolitan networks.

The "new band" (also known as the fifth window) is defined as the range from 1,350 nm to 1,450 nm; perhaps we should call it the N-band for new band, or the W-band for water band (from the well-known fiber water-peak absorption), or the M-band for middleband. The window in the range from 1,450 to 1,528 nm (also part of the fifth window) is used in single-mode fiber short-distance networks, such as MAN, that do not require erbium-doped fiber amplifiers (EDFA); perhaps we should call it the M-band for medium band.

The C-band (also known as the conventional or third window) is defined as the range from 1,528 nm to 1,565 nm. This is subdivided in to the "blue band" (1,528–1,545 nm), and the "red band" (1,545–1,561 nm).

The L-band (also known as the long wavelength or fourth window) is defined as the range from 1,561 nm to 1,660 nm. This band, in conjunction with dispersion shifted fiber (DSF) was first bands deployed in DWDM applications in Japan.

The C-bands and L-bands have found applications in ultra-high-speed (10–40 Gbps) DWDM communications. The C-band is currently popular in the United States and elsewhere, and the L-band is popular in Japan and elsewhere. The L-band takes advantage of the dispersion-compensating fiber. Recently, the L-band has been extended to 1,625 nm to a band known as UL (for ultra-L). In fact, the 1,650-nm wavelength is used for maintenance and testing.

Finally, the first window refers to the wavelength range from 820 nm to below 900 nm, which is popular in multimode-fiber applications. Ultraviolet wavelengths are not used in communications.

Table 1.8 summarizes the frequency bands, and Figure 1.42 illustrates the channel-grid in the C-band spectral range.

1.5.3.3 Limits of Optical Power in Fiber

The maximum acceptable optical power density is the amount of optical power that a fiber can support without being damaged. Power density is the ratio of laser beam

Table 1.8 Summary of frequency utilization for fiber applications

Window	Label	Range	Fiber-type	Applications
1st	—	820–900 nm	MMF	
2nd	S	1280–1350 nm	SMF	Single-λ
3rd	C	1528–1561 nm	SMF	DWDM
4th	L	1561–1620 nm	DSF	DWDM
5th	—	1350–1450 nm	SMF AllWave™	DWDM
5th	—	1450–1528 nm	SMF	DWDM/MAN

Note: Wavelengths are measured in free-space

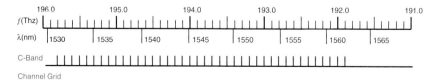

Figure 1.42 100 GHz channel grid in the C-band.

power over the cross-sectional area of the laser beam. Because the cross-sectional areas are very small, low powers may have large densities. For example, a 10-mW power beam with a 6-μm diameter produces a power density of

$$P/A = 10 \times 10^{-3}/\pi (3 \times 10^{-4})^2 \text{ W/cm}^2$$
$$= 10 \times 10^{-3}/28.26 \times 10^{-8} = 35 \text{ kW/cm}^2$$

In communications, the optical signal is modulated in the form of pulses. A pulse is typically characterized by duration (in psec or nsec) and energy per pulse in millijoules. In this case, to calculate the power density of the pulse, the energy over time must first be converted into power and then into power density. Thus, a pulse of 10 mJ for 1 nsec is equivalent to a power

$$P = 10 \times 10^{-3}/10^{-9} \text{ J/s}$$
$$= 10 \text{ megawatts}$$

1.5.4   Fiber Birefringence

The ideal single-mode fiber would support two orthogonally polarized modes or *states*, one along the x-axis and one along the y-axis (the z-axis is along the fiber). However, since there are only real fibers, they have a small amount of birefringence which in some applications is considered negligible, but in other applications (long spans and high bit rate) is significant. The *degree of fiber birefringence* is defined by

$$B = |n_x - n_y|$$

where n_x and n_y are indices for the polarized fiber modes in the axes x and y (z is the axis of propagation).

Fiber birefringence causes power exchange between the two polarization states in a continuous manner, changing the polarization from linear to elliptical, to circular, and finally back to linear. The length of birefringent fiber over which a complete revolution of polarization takes place is defined as *beat length* (Fig. 1.43). The beat length is given by

$$L_B = \lambda / B$$

For $\lambda = 1{,}550$ nm and $B \sim 10^{-7}$, $L_B \sim 15$ meters.

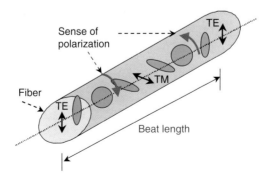

Figure 1.43   Polarization evolution and beat-length.

In optical communications, the receiver detects total photonic intensity directly, and fiber birefringence may not be a serious problem. However, in coherent communications, where a specific polarization at the receiver is expected, or when polarization-sensitive components are used, birefringence may be of concern.

Polarization-preserving fibers (PPF) is used to minimize the effects of fiber birefringence; polarization-preserving fibers exhibit a very strong degree of birefringence ($B \sim 10^{-4}$). Thus, when the signal enters the PPF, the birefringence induced by the fiber is so strong than it "overshadows" other sources of birefringence, which are negligible by comparison.

1.5.5 Dispersion

In an ideal world of propagating monochromatic signals chromatic dispersion has no meaning, with the exception of a dispersion type that depends on the geometry of the medium or its polarization state. Aside from this, in the real world there are no monochromatic signals, but polychromatic signals with a bundle of frequencies in a narrow band. This reality raises many issues, most of which are undesirable. In the following sections, we examine dispersion types, their issues, and their countermeasures.

1.5.5.1 *Modal Dispersion*

An optical signal launched into a fiber may be considered as a bundle of rays. Although a serious effort is made to launch all rays parallel into the fiber, due to imperfections of optical devices, rays are transmitted within a small cone. The nonparallelism of the rays in the fiber affects transmission.

Consider a modulated optical signal consisting of various rays of the same wavelength coupled into the fiber (Fig. 1.44); here we make a simplification of this effect by assuming ideal monochromaticity. Because the rays are not parallel they travel different paths along the fiber in different zigzag paths, as electromagnetic waves travel in waveguides; each zigzag path represents a different *mode*. Thus, ray A travels in a straight path along the core of the fiber (one mode), whereas ray B travels in an angle bouncing off the cladding (another mode). Thus, as each ray travels a different distance, it arrives at a distant point of the fiber at a different time. As a result, due to

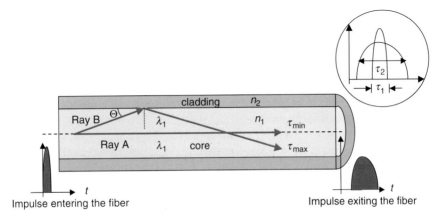

Figure 1.44 Modal dispersion causes a narrow pulse to widen.

modal delays the initial narrow pulse spreads out. This is known as *modal dispersion*; modal dispersion is particularly important in multimode fibers.

Thus, as a pulse spreads out, at some point it starts overlapping the pulse that follows it. Obviously, in ultrafast digital transmission where pulses are as narrow as a few tens of picoseconds, this is highly undesirable.

In digital transmission, a rule of thumb for acceptable dispersion (of any type) is

$$\Delta\tau < T/k$$

and the bit rate information limit is expressed by

$$R_b < 1/(k\Delta\tau)$$

where $\Delta\tau = \tau_2 - \tau_1$, R_b is the information (bit) rate, T is the bit period, k is the dispersion factor (a transmission design parameter, typically selected to $k = 4$). If $k = 5$, then less dispersion is acceptable, and if $k = 3$, then more dispersion is acceptable.

The travel time of the two rays is expressed as

$$\tau_{\min} = (Ln_1)/v$$

and

$$\tau_{\max} = (Ln_1)/v\cos\Theta$$

for $\Theta = \Theta_{\text{crit}}$ (total reflection) and from Snell's law

$$\cos\Theta_{\text{crit}} = n_1/n_2$$

The difference in travel time (assuming total reflection) is

$$\Delta\tau = \tau_{\max} - \tau_{\min} = \{(Ln_1)/v\}\Delta n/n_1$$

Hence, the maximum bit rate, R_b, is calculated from

$$R_b < 1/(4\Delta\tau) = (1/4)(v/Ln_1)(n_1/\Delta n)$$

Consider the case of two connected multimode fibers. Clearly, the connection point of the two fibers represents a perturbation or a discontinuity in the optical path. When light rays reach the end of the first fiber, they are launched into the second fiber. However, since there are many modes (i.e., different rays travel in different angles), each ray enters the second fiber at a different angle and thus is refracted differently, changing from one mode to another mode. This is known as *mode mixing*, and it occurs only in interconnected multimode fibers.

Mode mixing affects the actual transmitted bandwidth (BW_{act}) over the multimode fiber length (L), defining an effective bandwidth. To distinguish the effect of mode mixing on bandwidth, an empirical *scaling factor*, γ, has been devised, defining the effective bandwidth as

$$BW_{\text{eff}} = BW_{\text{act}}/L^\gamma$$

where γ is between 0.7 and 1.0.

The difference in travel time (assuming total reflection) is improved if a graded index fiber is used, with a graded index refraction profile $n(r)$. In this case, the fiber dispersion is improved if the condition holds:

$$R_b \doteq /<2v_g/(n_g L\Delta^2)$$

where n_g is the group refractive index, Δ is the maximum relative index between core and cladding, and v_g is the group velocity in the medium.

Fibers with various graded index profiles have been made. An example of a profile is:

$$n(r) = n_1\theta\{1 - 2\Delta(r/a)^\alpha\}, \quad \text{for} \quad r < a$$

1.5.5.2 Chromatic Dispersion

The refractive index and the propagation constant of the fiber medium are functions of wavelength. Thus, the travel time of each wavelength over a unit length of fiber depends on these two parameters. In addition, a real optical pulse is not purely monochromatic but consists of a narrow band of wavelengths. Thus, each wavelength in the band travels at a different speed, creating a relative delay among them. The end result of this is that the pulse broadens as it travels in the medium. This is termed *chromatic dispersion*. Thus, chromatic dispersion is the rate of change of the group delay with wavelength.

In terms of the propagation constant, β_o, if it is expanded in a Taylor series, then

$$\beta(\omega) = \beta_o + \beta_1(\omega - \omega_o) + 0.5\beta_2(\omega - \omega_o)^2 + \cdots$$

In the series, the term β_1 is the inverse of the group velocity and β_2 is the group velocity dispersion, which causes pulse broadening.

Chromatic dispersion consists of two contributions, *material dispersion* and *wavelength dispersion*; by some sources it is also termed *waveguide dispersion*. Dispersion is measured in ps/nm-Km (i.e., delay per wavelength variation and per fiber length).

In general, the photonic impulse response, $H(t)$, of a dispersive material can be expressed by

$$H(t) = \exp[(i\pi t^2)/(2\beta'' z)]$$

where z is the optical path distance in the dispersive medium, and β'' is the second derivative of the propagation constant with respect to frequency ϖ (or second-order dispersion coefficient).

Material dispersion is due to the dependence of the dielectric constant, ε, or the refractive index, n, on frequency, ω. Thus, the propagation characteristics of each wavelength in a fiber are different. Different wavelengths travel at different speeds in the fiber, which results in dispersion due to material.

Material dispersion is the most significant and is characterized by a parameter M, defined as the derivative of group index, N, with respect to wavelength, λ

$$M(\lambda) = -(1/c)(dN/d\lambda) = (\lambda/c)(d^2n/d\lambda^2)$$

where n is the refractive index, λ is the wavelength, c is the speed of light in free space, and $N = n - \lambda(dn/d\lambda)$.

Consider a medium with a region in which the distribution of n changes nonlinearly; then the group and phase velocity change accordingly. If a narrow light pulse that consists of a narrow range of wavelengths is launched in a medium, each individual wavelength arrives at the end of the fiber at a different time. The result is a dispersed pulse due to *material dispersion.*

Waveguide dispersion or *wavelength dispersion* is the contribution due to nonlinear dependence of the propagation constant on frequency, ω. Wavelength dispersion is explained as follows.

Assume a narrow optical impulse that consists of a narrow spectral range. Consider two wavelengths, λ_1 and λ_2, in the same impulse. We assume that both wavelengths travel (along the core of the fiber) in a straight path, but λ_1 travels faster than λ_2 ($\lambda_1 < \lambda_2$) because of nonlinear dependence of the propagation constant on frequency ω (and on wavelength).

Wavelength dispersion has different sign than material dispersion (Fig. 1.45), although material dispersion is the major contributor. The counteracting action of wavelength dispersion to material dispersion slightly ameliorates the combined effect. Negative dispersion implies that shorter wavelengths travel slower than longer wavelengths. As a consequence, fiber with negative dispersion can be used to compensate for positive dispersion (see Dispersion Compensation).

The travel time t for a group velocity v_g over a length of fiber L is

$$\tau = L/v_g$$

or

$$\tau = L\beta' = L\{\eta\beta/\eta\omega\}$$

where β is the propagation constant, β' is the first derivative with respect to ω, and η is the partial derivative.

The variation of τ with respect to ω, $(\eta\tau/\eta\omega)$, is

$$\eta\tau/\eta\omega = L\eta(1/v_g)/\eta\omega = L\eta^2(\beta)/\eta\omega^2 = L\beta''$$

where β'' is the second derivative with respect to ω.

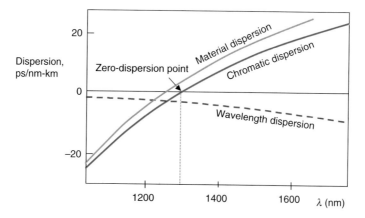

Figure 1.45   Chromatic dispersion components for single mode fiber.

For a signal with a spectral width $\Delta\omega$, then

$$\Delta\tau = (\beta'')L\Delta\omega$$

That is, the pulse spread $\Delta\tau$ (chromatic dispersion) depends on the second derivative with respect to ω, β'' and is proportional to the length of the fiber, L, and the spectral range, $\Delta\omega$.

Based on this, a *group velocity dispersion* (GVD) coefficient, D, is defined as the variation of travel time due to the wavelength variation per unit length of fiber, L

$$D = (1/L)(\eta\tau/\eta\lambda)$$

The coefficient D is also known as the *chromatic dispersion coefficient*; it gives a measure of the *group delay rate change* with wavelength. Consequently, in communications, the chromatic dispersion of a fiber can be found by measuring the time delay of wavelength components that constitute an optical pulse.

It follows that

$$D = (1/L)(\eta\tau/\eta\omega)(\eta\omega/\eta\lambda)$$

However,

$$\eta\tau/\eta\omega = L\beta''$$

and

$$\eta\omega/\eta\lambda = -2\pi v/\lambda^2$$

and thus

$$D = -(2\pi v/\lambda^2)\beta''$$

and

$$\Delta\tau = DL\{[-1/(2\pi v/\lambda^2)]\Delta\omega\}$$

Finally, the pulse spread, or chromatic dispersion (where η has been replaced by Δ) is expressed by

$$\Delta\tau = |D|L\Delta\lambda$$

where $\Delta\lambda$ is the optical spectral width of the signal (in nm units); occasionally, the chromatic dispersion is also denoted by the Greek letter σ.

Clearly, the pulse spread due to dispersion imposes a limitation on the maximum bit rate; this is also viewed as penalty due to dispersion, which is measured in dB. The dispersion penalty is related to the maximum allowable delay (a fraction ε of the bit period T) before severe signal degradation and unacceptable bit error rate (BER) occurs. From the definition of decibel, a 1-dB penalty corresponds to a bit period fraction approximately 0.5. At ultrahigh bit rates, 0.5T may be few picoseconds.

Figure 1.46 illustrates the various actions of chromatic dispersion.

1.5.5.3 *Chromatic Dispersion Limits: ITU-T*
The maximum *chromatic dispersion coefficient* (CDC), $D(\lambda)$, is specified by ITU-T G.652, G.653, and G.655.

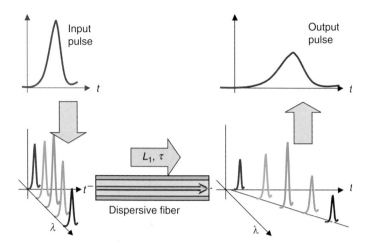

Figure 1.46   Chromatic dispersion: How it works.

ITU-T G.652 recommends the limits of CDC for single-mode fiber and for wavelengths in the range of 1,260 to 1,360 nm. In this case, the CDC limits are calculated by

$$D_1(\lambda) = (S_{0max}/4)[\lambda - (\lambda_{0min}^4/\lambda^3)]$$

and

$$D_2(\lambda) = (S_{0max}/4)[\lambda - (\lambda_{0max}^4/\lambda^3)]$$

where S_{0max} is the maximum *zero-dispersion slope* set at $S_{0max} = -0.093$ ps/(nm²·km), $\lambda_{0max} = 1,300$ nm, and $\lambda_{0max} = 1,324$ nm.

ITU-T G.653 recommends the chromatic dispersion coefficients for dispersion-shifted fiber cables. In this case, the CDC is calculated by

$$D(\lambda) = S_0(\lambda - \lambda_0)$$

where S_0 is the zero-dispersion slope [typically equal to or less than 0.085 ps/(nm²·km)], λ_0 is the zero-dispersion wavelength in nm, and λ is the wavelength of interest. Assuming a zero-dispersion fiber at $\lambda_0 = 1,550$ and λ within the range of 1,525 to 1,575 nm, then $D < 3.5$ ps/(nm·km).

ITU-T G.655 recommends the chromatic dispersion coefficients for nonzero dispersion-shifted fiber cables. In this case, the CDC should be within the range specified by

$$D_{min} =< |D_{min}(\lambda)| =< D_{max}, \quad \text{for} \quad \lambda_{min} =< \lambda =< \lambda_{max}$$

where 0.1 ps/(nm·km) $=< D_{min} =< D_{max} =< 6$ ps/(nm·km), and $1,530$ nm $=< \lambda_{min} =< \lambda_{max} =< 1,565$ nm.

Fiber cable manufacturers provide chromatic dispersion coefficients by wavelength regions and for each cable type.

The total dispersion over a fiber span is calculated assuming a linear dependence on length; that is, the coefficient is multiplied by the fiber length in Km.

1.5.5.4 Dispersion-Shifted Fibers and Dispersion-Flattened Fibers

The dependency of the refractive index of silica fiber is nonlinear. As such, at some wavelength, the derivative $d^2\{n(\omega)\}/d\lambda^2$ becomes zero, that is, the material dispersion parameter is given by

$$M(\lambda) = -(dN/d\lambda)/c = (\lambda/c)(d^2n/d\lambda^2)$$

The value λ_0 for which M becomes zero is known as the *zero-dispersion wavelength*. Then, for $\lambda > \lambda_0 M$ is positive and for $\lambda < \lambda_0 M$ is negative.

In certain cases, the wavelength dispersion and the chromatic dispersion within a spectral (wavelength) range may be of opposite sign, and they may either cancel each other or greatly minimize the net effect. In this case, the effective zero-dispersion wavelength moves to a longer wavelengths. The wavelength range over which this may take place depends on the dispersion slope, given by

$$dD(\lambda)/d\lambda =\sim (\lambda/c)(d^3n/d\lambda^3)$$

In general, the operating point on the dispersion curve is not exactly at the zero wave-length point. A small dispersion, enough to ensure that the overall pulse width is still acceptable, is desirable to minimize nonlinear interactions that result in pulse-shape distortion and thus noise generation. When the laser source is expected to increase in frequency, such as for example when the temperature rises (a phenomenon known as *positive chirping*), then the operating point is below the zero wavelength; that is, a small negative dispersion is desirable *as it starts at the outset with pulse compression.*

The amount of desirable dispersion is a function of both the data rate and the modulation method (return-to-zero versus nonreturn-to-zero). As the data rate increases, the pulse width narrows and pulse distortions become more pronounced. Similarly, reducing the optical power density (power per cm^2 of fiber core cross section) reduces nonlinear effects. Consequently, increasing the effective area of the fiber core is desirable as well.

A conventional single-mode fiber with a core diameter of about 8.3 μm and an index of refraction variation of about 0.37% has a zero-dispersion at about 1.3 μm. Below this point, wavelength dispersion is negative, and above this point it is positive.

A fiber with a zero-dispersion point shifted at 1,550 nm (1.55 μm) (i.e., where the minimum absorption for silica fiber is) is called a *dispersion-shifted fiber* (DSF). Such fibers are compatible with optical amplifiers that perform best at around 1,550 nm.

DSF with low loss in the L-band range (1,570–1,610 nm) provides a wide range of wavelengths, making it suitable for DWDM applications. For example, DSF fiber has been installed extensively in Japan.

Another fiber with near-zero dispersion in the range from 1.3 μm to 1.55 μm is called *dispersion-flattened fiber* (DFF). In this category, depending on the slope of the DFF, there is *positive DFF* and *negative DFF*.

To address dispersion effects and to improve optical transmission, a variety of specialty fibers have been engineered, such as the *dispersion-compensated fiber* (DCF), the *dispersion-flattened compensated fiber* (DFCF), the *dispersion-slope compensated fiber* (DSCF), the *dispersion-shift compensated fiber* (DSCF), the *nonzero-dispersion-shifted fiber* (NZDSF), and others. Figure 1.47 illustrates the relative zero-dispersion wavelength between standard single-mode fiber (SSMF), DSF, and NZDSF.

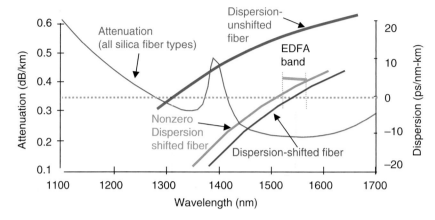

Figure 1.47 SSMF, DSF and NZDSF fibers.

Certain fibers with improved optical transmission characteristics bear tradenames such as *Large Effective Area Fiber* (LEAF™) and *MetroCor*™ by Corning Inc., *True-Wave*™ and *AllWave*™ by Lucent Technologies, Inc., and others. In general, although dispersion is undesirable, it turns out that operation at the zero-dispersion wavelength may seriously degrade certain channels. Therefore, it is recommended that frequencies passed the zero-dispersion point are used; that is, a small amount of positive or negative dispersion is desirable. Figure 1.48 illustrates the dispersion of several commercial fibers, also indicating the undesirable region ($+1$ to -1 ps/nm-km), and Table 1.9 tabulates their parameters.

For example: MetroCor™ is a negative-dispersion fiber designed for applications to transport 10 Gb/s C-band WDM signals generated by a distributed feedback laser and for spans in the range of 70 to 100 km. To explain the merits of this fiber, assume that a 1,550-nm signal in a positive dispersion fiber matches its dispersion zero-wavelength. However, assume that the laser source has a positive-frequency chirp (such as a DFB); that is, as the signal travels in the fiber, the wavelength

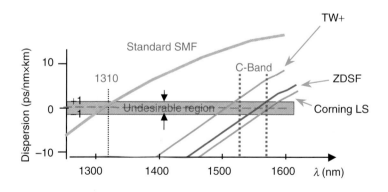

Figure 1.48 Chromatic dispersion (approximate) and zero-dispersion wavelength for different fibers types.

Table 1.9   Fiber parameters

Fiber	D (ps/nm-Km)	S (ps/nm^2-Km)	A_{eff} (μm^2)	Loss (dB/Km)
TWRS	4.4	0.045	55	0.21
TWRS+	4.4	0.030	55	0.21
LEAF	4.0	0.09	72	0.21
SSMF	17	0.056	80	0.21
TeraLight	8	0.058	65	0.21
DCF	-100	-0.33	20	0.5

D = chromatic dispersion coefficient
S = dispersion slope
A_{eff} = fiber core effective area

of the leading end of the signal shortens (shifts to the blue) and the wavelength of the trailing edge elongates (shifts to the red). As more wavelengths in the same band propagate in the fiber, nonlinear effects and chirp affect the quality of signal permitting reliable transmission over a fiber span to about 10 km. The MetroCor negative-dispersion fiber minimizes the chirp effect allowing for a fiber length in the range of 70 to 100 km.

TrueWave^{TM} is a two-member fiber family of nonzero-dispersion fibers optimized for WDM applications over long fiber spans (i.e., long haul). This type of fiber is made so that a segment of positive dispersion alternates with an equal length of negative dispersion. Thus, the total dispersion adds up to almost zero. TrueWave comes in different flavors. The TrueWave reduced slope or TW-RS member is optimized for minimal dispersion to minimize cross talk. It introduces only small dispersion (3–7 ps/nm-km) that over a broad spectrum including both the C-bands and L-bands, thus making it suitable for DWDM applications. In addition, the total dispersion over a span of 800 km has less residual dispersion than other fibers with competing specifications. The TrueWave XL is optimized for high-power DWDM signals suitable for undersea long spans and at rates up to 10 Gbps per wavelength.

For example, the TW-RS fiber is specified with:

- maximum noncabled fiber attenuation coefficient (loss) of less than or equal to 0.25 dB/km at 1,550 and 1,600 nm
- maximum attenuation fluctuation in the range of 1,525 to 1,625 nm is no more than 0.05 dB/km greater than the attenuation at 1,550 nm
- chromatic dispersion in
- the 3rd window (1,530–1,565 nm) is from 2.6 to 6.0 ps/nm-km
- the 4th window (1,565–1,625 nm) is from 4.0 to 8.9 ps/nm-km
- typical dispersion slope at 1,550 nm is equal to 0.045 ps/nm^2-km
- effective group index of refraction at 1,310, 1,550, and 1,625 nm is equal to 1.470
- cabled polarization mode dispersion at 1,550 nm is equal to or less than 0.05 ps/sqrt(km)
- fiber weight per km is 64 grams
- fiber can be cut at lengths of 6.4, 12.6, 19.2, 25, and 38.2 km

Some typical dispersion values, measured at 1,550 nm, are:

$$\text{Standard single-mode fiber (SSMF)} = 16.9$$

$$\text{TrueWave RS (TWRS)} = 4.41$$

$$\text{E-LEAF} = 4.32$$

Numerical Example: Single-Mode Chromatic Dispersion Calculations
The following is an approximate example of dispersion calculations over a fiber link.

Optical fiber manufacturer model:		"XYZ, Inc", model X-F145X
Bit rate:		1.2 Gb/s
Maximum allowable dispersion:		220 ps
Transmitter wavelength (nominal):	λ_{nom}	1,310 ($\pm$20) nm
Total fiber span length:	L	45 Km
Zero dispersion wavelength:	λ_0	1,310 nm
Dispersion slope at nominal wavelength:	S_0	0.1 ps/nm^2-km
Source spectral line width:	$\Delta\lambda$	0.5 nm
Chromatic dispersion coefficient @ λ_{max}:	$D(\lambda_{max})$	2.9 ps/nm-km
(provided by manufacturer or calculated		
by equation: $D(\lambda) = [S_0\lambda/4][1 - (\lambda_0^4/\lambda^4)])$		
Chromatic dispersion (calculated):	σ	$\Delta\lambda*D*L = 0.5*2.9*45$
		$= 65.25$ ps

Conclusion: The calculated chromatic dispersion 65.25 ps is within the system manufacturer's allowable dispersion of 200 ps.

1.5.5.5 *Chromatic Dispersion Compensation*
Dispersion was not a serious issue for bit rates up to 2.5 Gb/s over SMF fiber lengths less than 500 km. However, at higher bit rates, the bit period decreases and chromatic dispersion dramatically increases, having an adverse effect on the integrity of optical signal. It turns out that the bad effect dispersion has on the signal integrity increases as the square of the data rate.

For example, increasing the bit rate four times, from 2.5 to 10 Gb/s, the effect of chromatic dispersion increases 16 times, and increases by the same factor when increasing from 10 to 40 Gb/s. Similarly, over the same length of fiber the tolerable dispersion at 2.5 Gb/s is 16,000 ps, at 10 Gb/s it is 1000 ps, and at 40 Gb/s is only 60 ps. As another example, at 10 Gb/s a 33% return-to-zero (RZ) pulse has a width of ~33 ps, at 40 Gb/s a width of ~8 ps and at 160 Gb/s a width of ~2.1 ps. It is not difficult to calculate the maximum allowed dispersion before sequential pulses broaden and interfere among them (e.g., at 40 Gb/s it should be $\pm$12 ps from the center wavelength).

In fiber communications, an increase in dispersion means a decrease in fiber length, as dispersion is cumulative, and for all practical purposes linearly increasing over the length of SMF fiber (the dispersion coefficient is given in ps/nm-km and for SMF it is about 1 ps/nm-Km). Thus, due to dispersion, although at 2.5 Gb/s a fiber length of 500 km may be reasonable, at 10 Gbps it is not, and the length must be 80 km or less. One can easily extrapolate what the fiber length should be at 40 or 160 Gb/s. Nevertheless, the situation is not hopeless. There are dispersion-compensating methods that can spectrally shrink (compensate for) dispersed pulses and allow them to travel over longer fiber lengths.

Because of the sensitivity of the transmitted optical signal to dispersion, particularly at bit rates of 40 Gb/s and beyond, even temperature variations of the fiber must be considered, as the refractive index and hence dispersion are affected. For example, if the dispersion variation per degree Celsius is 0.0025 ps/nm-km-°C (for a NZ-DSF fiber type), for a span of 500 Km and for temperature variation of $\Delta T \sim 50\,°C$, the total dispersion is calculated to be about 50 ps. Such dispersion puts a limit on high bit rates greater than 10 Gb/s.

1.5.5.6 *Dispersion Compensation Methods and Figure of Merit*

Chromatic dispersion compensation may be achieved by several methods; we describe two.

A popular method is the *dispersion-compensating fiber* (DCF). A DCF is a fiber with a diffractive index profile that has an opposite dispersive effect than conventional fibers. For instance, because most of the SMF deployed have a positive dispersion effect, whereby longer wavelengths travel slower than shorter wavelengths, DCF is made with negative dispersion over a specific range of wavelengths (Fig. 1.49).

The core of a DCF fiber is heavily doped with germanium and the cladding with fluoride to control the difference of index of diffraction between cladding and core, and between silica and germanium, so that, with a proper geometry of index profile, a negative dispersion is achieved. In addition, the DCF's core has an effective aperture three to four times and a refractive index about five times than that of standard SMF. Figure 1.50 illustrates DCF's effect if it is placed after a dispersive fiber (SSMF).

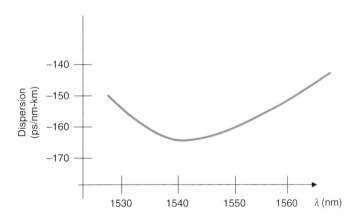

Figure 1.49 Dispersion for DCF (approximate).

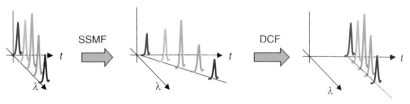

Longer wavelengths travel slower   Shorter wavelengths travel slower

Figure 1.50 Dispersion compensation action for an optical channel.

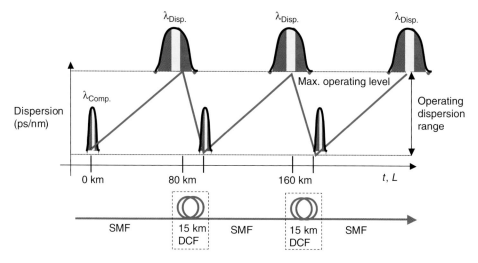

Figure 1.51 Dispersion compensation action for several fiber links (propagation from left to right).

Thus, if standard SMF and DCF fiber are alternating over the complete length, the dispersion induced by the SMF is undone by the DCF. In fact, every 80 km of SMF a spool of about 15 km DCF fiber is connected (this spool is in a central office or in a cabinet). Thus, when a DCF fiber is coupled to the transmitting (conventional) fiber, chromatic dispersion is compensated for the group of wavelengths the DCF is best designed for. DCFs are attractive for DWDM applications in the C-band (with zero dispersion at 1,550 nm), particularly when there are plans for EDFA optical amplification (Fig. 1.51).

However, although this method seems simplistic in its application, it has two "watch outs." First, it affects the optical transmission loss budget as DCF exhibits twice the loss of standard SMF (clearly this impacts the overall optical amplification plan as well). Second, SMF and DCF are not exactly spectrally balanced; that is, in DWDM whereas one wavelength (optical channel) is exactly compensated, the remaining wavelengths in the band are not, longer wavelengths have a negative residual dispersion and shorter wavelengths a positive, and thus there is a residual dispersion. The variation from positive to negative residual is known as *dispersion slope mismatch* (Fig. 1.52).

When the silica fiber is heavily doped with germanium and the cladding with fluoride to create negative dispersion slope (i.e., a DCF) at an operating wavelength, the doping creates an unpleasant and anomalous increase in optical loss. In DCFs, a figure of merit (FOM) is defined as the ratio of the absolute value of chromatic dispersion to transmission loss, at the wavelength of interest (e.g., 1,550 nm) (Fig. 1.53). Here, two additional parameters are of interest, the difference of the refractive index between cladding (in this case, fluorine-doped) and silica core (germanium-doped), Δ^-, and the difference of the refractive index of germanium and silica, Δ^+.

Chromatic dispersion is also compensated by using chirped in-fiber Bragg gratings. According to this, adjacent wavelengths in a channel are reflected at different depths of the FBG, thus compensating for the travel time variation. However, this type of arrangement accounts for single wavelength compensation; for a band of frequencies, an equal amount of gratings is required. Another method is to have several gratings

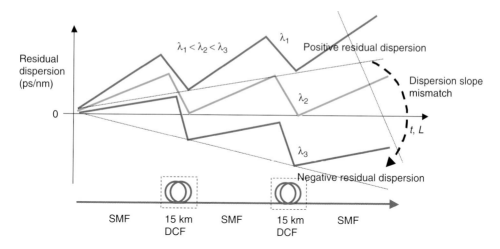

Figure 1.52   Residual dispersion in dispersion compensation.

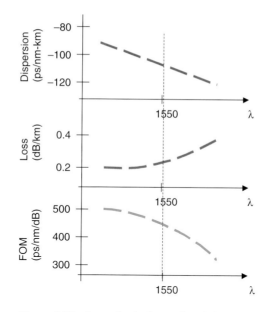

Figure 1.53   Approximate figure of merit for DCF.

written in a longer fiber (on the order of a meter), or having a pattern written in a shorter fiber (on the order of several centimeters) emanating from a sampling function. The Fourier transform of a sampling function results in many replicas, each at a different frequency. Thus, the sampling function creates different gratings with negative dispersion, each operating at different frequencies.

Another promising method for compensating dispersion is using an interferometer-based on *nonlinear optical loop mirrors* (NOLM). A NOLM is made with a 50/50 splitter and a loop of dispersion-shifted fiber (see Resonant Ring) to construct a two-port device, with each of the ports being a possible output. Typically, light is reflected

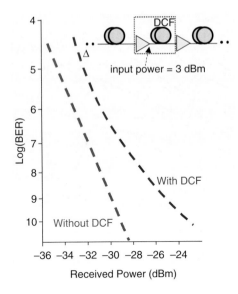

Figure 1.54   Improvement of BER using DCF.

back to the fiber input. However, because of self-phase modulation in the nonlinear fiber, a phase-shift occurs that causes an interference fringe shift that changes the direction of propagation and light propagates onward. Switching from one input to the other in a NOLM is a very fast process, on the order of picoseconds, and thus this technique is suitable in soliton transmission.

Compensation at very high bit rates is very critical. Hence, dispersion-compensating modules (DCM), that incorporate a dispersion-compensating technology have been developed to allow for dispersion management. As such, DCMs monitor the dispersion of each optical channel at a receiving terminal of a DWDM system and individually compensate each channel for dispersion. In general, DCMs improve dispersion and thus the bit error rate (BER) of the signal(s) allowing for longer fiber length (Fig. 1.54). Therefore, at high bit rates, and particularly in DWDM transmission, they provide a very important function.

The (ideal) salient characteristics of DCMs are:

- uniform dispersion compensation over the spectral range of interest
- uniform insertion loss over the spectral range of interest
- zero polarization
- zero birefringence
- small package and low cost

1.5.5.7   Polarization Mode Dispersion

All fibers have some degree of birefringence and have a core that is not perfectly circular over their entire length. Fiber birefringence and core noncircularity causes an optical (monochromatic) signal to be separated into two orthogonally polarized signals, or principal states of polarization (PSP), each traveling at different speed and phase. The same occurs to each pulse of a modulated optical signal; the pulse is

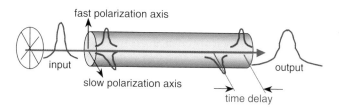

Figure 1.55 Polarization-mode dispersion.

separated into two pulses, each traveling at a different speed. Thus, when the two signals recombine, because of the variation in time of arrival, a pulse spreading occurs (Fig. 1.55). This phenomenon is particularly noticeable in single-mode fiber transmission at ultrahigh bit rates (above 2.5 Gbps) and is known as *polarization mode dispersion* (PMD).

By definition (see ITU-T G.650), PMD is measured by the average differential group delay time (DGD) over wavelength between two orthogonally polarized modes (measured in ps). PMD is maximized if both PSPs are equally and maximally excited resulting in maximum DGD and pulse spreading. Conversely, PMD vanishes or is greatly minimized if only one of the two states is excited. Similarly, the *polarization mode dispersion coefficient* is defined as the PMD divided by the square root of fiber length (measured in ps/$\sqrt{\text{km}}$). Optical fibers have a polarization mode dispersion coefficient of less than 0.5 ps/$\sqrt{\text{km}}$ (see ITU-T G.650, G.652, G.653, and G.655).

Another phenomenon, experimentally demonstrated but not fully explained theoretically, is also attributed to PMD. According to this phenomenon, when a stream of very narrow (few picoseconds) orthogonally polarized pulses with separation of few tens of picoseconds is transmitted in a fiber, then two sequential (orthogonally polarized) pulses interact and generate two pulses at lower amplitude and different polarization. Thus, two consecutive pulses, one polarized at +45 degrees and the other at −45 degrees produce a third linearly polarized signal at lower amplitude (Fig. 1.56). It has been shown that as the separation between the two pulses increases, this PMD generated signal decreases.

As a consequence of the DGD definition, if DGD is measured by the average difference of time arrival, $\Delta\tau$, between the two orthogonally polarized modes, and that the two polarized modes are related to the birefringence of the fiber, Δn_g, then DGD is measured by

$$Dt = (\Delta n_g L)/c$$

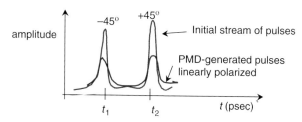

Figure 1.56 In polarization mode dispersion, sequential orthogonally polarized pulses interact to generate another stream of linearly polarized pulses.

where c is the speed of light, L is the length of the fiber, and Δn_g is the refractive index variation corresponding to the group velocity of the orthogonal polarization states.

PMD has been phenomenologically explained by extensive vectorial analysis that considers the propagation of principle states of polarization. In a graphical representation of polarization states, see Poincare' sphere (Figure 1.25), PSPs are located in diametrically opposite points on the sphere's surface; points on the equator of the sphere represent linear polarization, polar points represent circular, and points on the hemispheres represent elliptical polarizations states (the northern hemisphere represents right-handed and the southern hemisphere represents left-handed).

As the noncircularity of a fiber core causes PSPs, each polarization state at different speed and phase, an issue emerges at the connecting point of two fibers where in most practical cases core noncircularity is not matched. Hence, slow and fast states from one segment are coupled into another core with different orientations of polarization. Thus, at the interface as the polarization states from one fiber are coupled into the next, input PSPs are transformed into different output PSPs. This is known as *polarization mode coupling* (PMC). As a consequence, over a fiber span with several connections, PMC becomes a random event that affects DGD and PSPs randomly to further complicate PMD compensation.

In reality, the fiber core is not perfect (free from geometrical imperfections) but it varies between circular and elliptical and in a nonuniform manner. Moreover, the optical channel is not purely monochromatic. Therefore, as an optical channel propagates in the fiber core, PMD is the unavoidable result of fiber core birefringence and channel nonmonochromaticity. As a consequence, as two orthogonal (principle) states propagate in the fiber core, they reexperience a variability in polarization (due to nonuniform fluctuation of imperfections), known as Stokes noise, and due to optical channel wavelength content, known as chromatic jitter. In this case, the square of the relative DGD noise $(d(\Delta\tau)/\Delta\tau)$ is the sum of squares of each noise component (the Stokes-related and the jitter-related components):

$$[d(\Delta\tau)/\Delta\tau]^2 = [d(\Delta S)/\Delta S]^2 + [d(\Delta\varpi)/\Delta\varpi]^2$$

where $\Delta\varpi$ is the frequency (or wavelength), d is the differential operator, and ΔS is the polarization state variability at the output of the fiber; the inverse of the latter is also known as the "bandwidth efficiency factor," α:

$$\alpha = 1/d(\Delta S)$$

The bandwidth efficiency factor is characteristic of the measuring method (it may have a value from less than 1 to more than 200), and it is related to the signal-to-noise ratio (SNR) of the optical signal in the following sense:

$$SNR = <\alpha\Delta\tau\Delta\varpi$$

That is, given the value of α, and measuring $\Delta\tau$ and $\Delta\varpi$, the potential maximum SNR is calculated from which the potential amount of noise is determined.

In summary, the key fiber PMD parameters are the differential group delay, the beat length, and the correlation length. PMD adds to the fiber dispersion characteristics and puts additional limits on both fiber span and optical received power (Fig. 1.57).

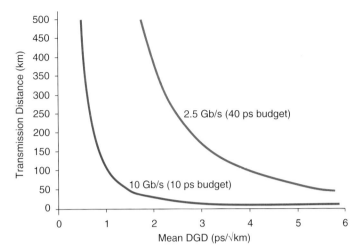

Figure 1.57 Transmission distance as a function of fiber differential group delay; at higher data rates PMD becomes more significant as it effectively shortens the fiber length (actual graph depends on fiber).

Currently, there are several methods under development aiming to compensate for PMD. For an STS-192/STM-64 signal (~10 Gbps), this PMD coefficient value limits the fiber length to 400 km.

1.5.5.8 Fiber Polarization-Dependent Loss

Virtually all optically transparent materials, including fiber, exhibit some degree of polarization sensitivity. That is, optical power passes without power reduction selectively in certain polarized sates while with reduced power in others. As a result, optical power suffers loss. This is termed fiber *polarization-dependent loss* (PDL), and it represents the peak-to-peak optical power variation measured in decibels (dB). Clearly, linear polarizers have strong PDL values (e.g. >30 dB), whereas SMF very little (<0.02 dB).

In DWDM, PDL becomes critical when the bit rate is high (greater than 10 Gb/s) and the number of optical channels (wavelengths) gets dense, with a narrow linewidth, at or less than 0.05 nm at full-width half maximum (FWHM); such narrow linewidths become highly polarized. Strong PDL adds to IL and cross talk. An issue with polarization dependence is that a source may change its polarization state randomly, and thus PDL, complicating power budget calculations, degrading the quality of signal and service and system performance.

PDL, like PMD, has been phenomenologically explained by extensive vectorial analysis and considering the propagation of principle states of polarization.

1.5.5.9 Polarization Mode Dispersion Compensation

Fibers are specified by an average *differential group delay* (DGD) in ps or a mean DGD coefficient in ps/$\sqrt{\text{km}}$. Thus, for a low PMD fiber, the mean DGD coefficient is less than 0.1 ps/$\sqrt{\text{km}}$, for a high PMD is ~2 ps/$\sqrt{\text{km}}$. Thus, for a fiber length of 625 km the average DGD for low PMD fiber is about 2.5 ps whereas for high PMD fiber is about 50 ps ($2 \times \sqrt{625} = 2 \times 25 = 50$). In terms of decibels, the receiver sensitivity penalty for avg DGD of 50 ps is less than 0.1 dB at 2.5 Gb/s, and greater than 4 dB at 10 Gb/s. Extrapolating to 40 Gb/s, the receiver penalty clearly becomes very severe.

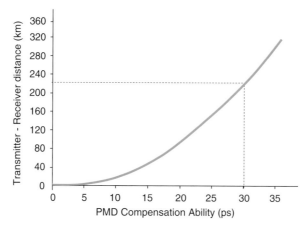

Figure 1.58 PMD compensation increases the transmitter-receiver fiber span; e.g., 30 ps compensation corresponds to more than 200 km (actual graph depends on fiber).

Consequently, PMD becomes a main contributor to dispersion as the bit rate approaches and exceeds 40 Gb/s, necessitating the need for PMD compensation. However, compared with chromatic dispersion, PMD is much more difficult to compensate for, and for the time being there are no easy and inexpensive solutions. Clearly, this presents an opportunity, and substantial research is being conducted in this area. As the bit rate keeps increasing,, and PMD compensation will improve the length of the fiber; the distance between transmitter and receiver versus the PMD compensation ability is illustrated in Figure 1.58 for a fiber with *polarization mode dispersion coefficient* ~2 ps/sqrt(km).

1.5.6 Spectral Broadening

The refractive index of many materials depends on the amplitude of the electrical field. Thus, as the electrical field changes, so does the refractive index. Thus, as an almost monochromatic light pulse travels in a transparent medium, its amplitude variation causes *phase change* and *spectral broadening*.

The *phase change* is given by

$$\Delta\Phi = [2\pi(\Delta n)L]/\lambda$$

where L is the fiber length and Δn is the refractive index variation,

$$\Delta n = n(\lambda, E) - n_1(\lambda)$$

Phase variations are equivalent to frequency modulation or to "chirping."

The *spectral broadening* is given by

$$\delta\omega = -d(\Delta\Phi)/dt$$

For a *Gaussian* shaped pulse, spectral broadening is

$$\delta\omega = 0.86\Delta\omega\Delta\Phi_m$$

where $\Delta\omega$ is the spectral width and $\Delta\Phi_m$ is the maximum phase shift in radians.

Spectral broadening appears as if one half of the pulse is frequency downshifted (known as *red shift*) and the other half is frequency upshifted (known as *blue shift*). Such shifts are also expected in pulses that consist of a narrow range of wavelengths that are centered on the zero-dispersion wavelength. Below the zero-dispersion point *wavelength dispersion is negative and above it positive*. Significant spectral broadening is observed when $\Delta\Phi_m$ is equal to or greater than 2.

1.5.7 Self-Phase Modulation

The dynamic characteristics of a propagating optical pulse in fiber, due to the Kerr effect of the medium, result in modulation of its own phase. This nonlinear phenomenon, which is known as *self-phase modulation*, causes spectral broadening, the principles of which are illustrated in Figure 1.59.

If the wavelength of the pulse is below the zero-dispersion point (known as *normal dispersion regime*), then spectral broadening causes temporal broadening of the pulse as it propagates. If the wavelength is above the zero-dispersion wavelength of the fiber (the *anomalous dispersion regime*), then chromatic dispersion compensates self-phase modulation reducing temporal broadening.

1.5.8 Self-Modulation or Modulation Instability

When a single pulse of an almost monochromatic light has a wavelength above the zero-dispersion wavelength of the fiber (known as the anomalous dispersion regime), another phenomenon occurs that degrades the width of the pulse. That is, two side lobes are symmetrically generated at either side of the pulse (Fig. 1.60), thus adding to the noise content of the signal. This is known as *self-modulation* or *modulation instability*.

Modulation instability depends on material dispersion, the optical traveled path (or fiber length) and the optical channel power. Modulation instability is considered a special four-wave mixing case that affects the signal-to-noise ratio.

Modulation instability is reduced by operating at low energy levels and/or at wavelengths below the zero-dispersion wavelength.

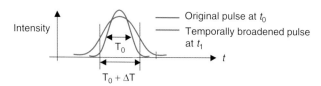

Figure 1.59 The dynamic propagating characteristics of a light-pulse in fiber result in modulating its own phase causing pulse broadening.

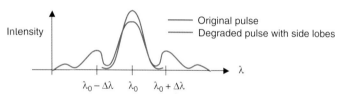

Figure 1.60 When an optical channel operates above the zero-dispersion point, two side lobes are symmetrically generated at a pulse, a phenomenon known as self-modulation or modulation instability.

1.5.9 Effect of Pulse Broadening on Bit Error Rate

The type of fiber used in optical communications is extremely important and different fiber type, based on standards (such as ITU-T G.652, G.653, and G.655) is selected for each application. As an example, according to Chinese officials (presented at the Asian-Pacific Optical Communications Conference in Beijing, November 2001) China will invest $300 billion in communications infrastructure in the period 2001–2005, becoming that "largest network in the world" with more than 400 million lines and more than 1259 million Km fiber; the average projected growth per year will be 60 million lines for the next five years (China with an excess of 1 billion people had only 10 million lines in 1990). This is a significant decision if one considers that the China optical network requires fiber with high dispersion point (G.652) only for currently existing systems, next generation fiber (G.655) with large Aeff, and improved dispersion and dispersion slope to be deployed in high-traffic density networks, whereas discontinuing the DSF (G.653) fiber.

The various forms of dispersion cause pulse broadening that degrades the quality of the signal and increases the *bit error rate* (BER); BER is a measure of the signal quality and is measured in number of errored bits in 1000 received bits. To counterbalance BER increase one needs to shorten the fiber span, which in long-haul communications is highly undesirable; in later sections we will also examine other methods such as the *forward error correction* (FEC). Notice that BER is not defined in the unit of time as this would not be a good metric if we consider that in communications there is a large variety of bit rates ranging from 64 Kb/s to 40 Gb/s; if the unit of time were used instead, then 5 errored bits in one second could be 5 of 64,000 or 5 of 40 billion bits, and clearly this is not a good-quality metric.

One of the factors that causes BERs is pulse broadening which may be the combined effect of many degradation mechanisms as already examined. As pulses broaden, they spread in adjacent bit periods. If in a bit period a logic "zero" should be, spreading of optical power may raise the level such that the receiver may "see" it as a logic "one" (Fig. 1.61). In Chapter 2 we examine how BER can be predicted and what defense mechanisms can be built to restore the degraded signal quality.

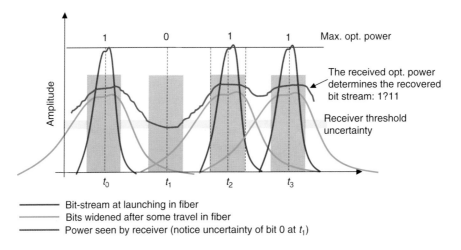

Figure 1.61 Effect of excessive pulse-widening on ISI and BER.

1.6   NONLINEAR PHENOMENA

When light enters matter, photons interact with atoms, and under certain circumstances photons may be absorbed by atoms and excite them to higher energy levels. Many atoms in an excited state become metastable (they cannot remain at that level for a short time, in the range of ns to μs). However, while in the excited state, certain photons may trigger them (or stimulate them) to come down to their initial lower energy level by releasing energy, *photons*, and/or *phonons* (acoustic quantum energy).

In addition to the phenomena from the photon–atom interaction, there are also photon–atom–photon interactions that result in some complex phenomena, some of which are not well understood yet. These interactions, known as nonlinear phenomena, are best described by quantum theory, and thus we provide only a quantitative description. They are distinguished in *forward scattering* and *backward scattering* (Raman and Brillouin scattering) as well as in *four-wave (or four-photon) mixing*. The direction (forward and backward) is with respect to the direction of the excitation light with respect to the direction of the stimulated light. Backward scattering is due mostly to reflected light at the end face (or other discontinuities) of the fiber.

In optical systems, nonlinear phenomena are viewed as both advantageous and degrading.

- *Advantageous* because lasers, optical amplifiers, and dispersion compensation are based on them.
- *Degrading* because signal losses, noise, cross talk, and pulse broadening are caused by them.

In general, the input–output relationship of a system is expressed by

$$O = k^1 \cdot I + k^2 \cdot I \cdot I + k^3 \cdot I \cdot I \cdot I + \cdots$$

where k^n is a higher-order system coefficient, O is the output, and I is the input vector.

The first term ($n = 1$) describes the linear behavior of the system, whereas other terms ($n > 1$) describe higher-order nonlinear behavior.

The response of any dielectric (such as glass fiber) to optical power is nonlinear; the behavior of dielectric to optical power is like that of a dipole. It is the dipole nature of dielectric that interacts harmonically with electromagnetic waves such as light.

When the optical power is low, it results in small oscillations, and the first term of the series approximates the photon–fiber system behavior (i.e., a linear system). However, when the optical power is large, the oscillations are such that higher-order terms (nonlinear behavior) become significant.

Similarly, the polarization of an electromagnetic wave, P, induced in the electric dipoles of a medium by an electric field, E, is proportional to *susceptibility*, χ:

$$P = e_0[\chi^1 \cdot E + \chi^2 \cdot E \cdot E + \chi^3 \cdot E \cdot E \cdot E + \cdots]$$

where e_0 is the permittivity of free space.

Here again, the first term ($n = 1$) describes the linear behavior of the system whereas other terms ($n > 1$) describe higher-order nonlinear behavior.

For an *isotropic* medium, the second-order is orthogonal and thus it vanishes (or is negligible). Zero second-order nonlinearity implies no second-order nonlinear processes or electro-optic variability (modulation). Silica glass, unlike quartz crystals, is amorphous with macroscopic inversion symmetry. Thus, it too has zero (or near zero) second-order nonlinearity. However, the third-order term produces nonlinear effects that may be significant. Among the nonlinearities, in the following, we examine four-wave mixing, stimulated Raman scattering, and stimulated Brillouin scattering.

If silica fiber with nonzero second-order could be made, and hence with a linear electro-optic coefficient, then it would be possible to manufacture active fibers that could be used as wavelength converters, parametric oscillators, electrically tunable Bragg gratings, optical switches, frequency doubling, optical storage, and so on. Currently, stoichiometric $LiNbO_3$ and $TiTaO_3$ with reportedly superior nonlinear and electro-optic coefficients than ordinary congruent crystals have been produced, and it is expected that they soon will be applicable to nonlinear parametric devices.

1.6.1 Stimulated Raman Scattering

Consider a short-wavelength intense source (source A) and a longer-wavelength (by about 80 nm) weak source (source B) propagating within the same medium.

The short-wavelength high-energy ($\sim$500 mW) source A (known as a pump) excites atoms to a high-energy level. Then, due to some weak nonlinear properties of the medium, excited atoms "drop" after some short time to an intermediate energy level releasing light energy at a wavelength longer than the pump source A. Eventually, all atoms at the intermediate level will "drop" to their initially low (or ground) energy level by releasing the remaining energy in the form of (optical) phonons (Fig. 1.62). This is known as *stimulated Raman scattering* (SRS). In general, when an ion falls from an energy level E_{high} to a lower energy level E_{low} the emitted photon frequency (or wavelength) is determined by the relationship $E = h\nu$:

$$\nu = [E_{high} - E_{low}]/h$$

If the excited atoms are stimulated by the photons of the weak source B, the stimulated atoms emit photons of the same wavelength with the stimulating source and under the right conditions signal B is amplified; this is known as *Raman amplification* (more

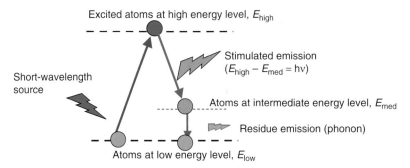

Figure 1.62 A short-wavelength source excites atoms to a higher-energy level. When the atom is stimulated, it releases photonic energy of a longer wavelength.

of this later). In theory, Raman lines are generated, known as Stokes lines) according to relationship $f - n\Delta f$, where for single mode fiber Δf is 70 nm at 1310 nm and 102 nm at 1550 nm.

Thus, because of Raman scattering, energy from the pump is transferred to atoms and it is downshifted (wavelength becomes longer) and it is transferred to the weak signal. Raman scattering occurs in either direction (forward or backward) with respect to the direction of the signal (see also Raman Amplification).

1.6.2   Stimulated Brillouin Scattering

Stimulated Brillouin scattering (SBS), in contrast to Raman scattering, produces stimulated emission while a photon–acoustic phonon interaction takes place. Although stimulated emission is in both directions, the part that is in the same direction with the original signal interacts with acoustical phonons and is scattered, and the part that is in the opposite direction is guided by the fiber. In this case, the stimulated light is at a shorter wavelength (downshifted by 11.1 GHz at 1550 nm, or 13.2 GHz at 1310 nm, although upshifting has also been predicted). If another optical signal at the downshifted wavelength propagates in the fiber in the direction opposite to the original signal, it will be mixed with the transferred energy. This may increase signal cross talk.

It has been experimentally determined that SBS is dominant when the spectral power (brightness) of the source is large and it abruptly increases when the launched power reaches a threshold value. Several factors determine the actual threshold value of launched power, such as the fiber material, the linewidth of the source light, the fiber length, the fiber-core effective cross-section area, and the bit rate of the signal.

Threshold values for SBS in fiber systems are in the range of 5 to 10 mW of launched power (for externally modulated narrow linewidths) and 20 to 30 mW for directly modulated lasers (ITU-T G.663).

Brillouin scattering, like Raman scattering, restricts the launched power per channel. However, SBS also may be advantageously used in optical amplification, where the backward signal may be the pump and the forward signal the one to be amplified.

1.6.3   Four-Wave Mixing

Consider three lightwave frequencies, f_1, f_2, and f_3, closely spaced (in terms of wavelength). Then, from the interaction of the three, a fourth lightwave frequency is generated, f_{fwm}, such that $f_{fwm} = f_1 + f_2 - f_3$. This is known as *four-wave mixing* (FWM) or *four-photon mixing*. The order of lightwave frequencies is f_1, f_{fwm}, f_3, and f_2 (Fig. 1.63). In fact, TU-T defines the generated FWM component as $f_{fwm} =$

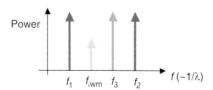

Figure 1.63   In four-wave mixing, three optical frequencies, f_1, f_2, and f_3 may interact to produce a fourth frequency, f_{fwm}, $f_{fwm} = f_1 + f_2 - f_3$.

$f_1 \pm f_2 \pm f_3$. FWM is a nonlinear effect that is described by a nonlinear equation. The FWM component, E_{FWM}, at the output of a fiber segment, L, generated by the three components E_1, E_2, and E_3, with angular frequency ω, refractive index n, nonlinear refractive index χ and loss α is described by

$$E_{\text{FWM}} = j[(2\pi\omega)/nc]d\chi\, E_1 E_2 E_3\, e^{-\alpha(L/2)} F(\alpha, L, \Delta\beta)$$

where $F(\alpha, L, \Delta\beta)$ is a function of fiber loss, fiber length, and propagation variation (phase mismatch) related to channel spacing and dispersion.

The output power of the f_{fwm} and the efficiency of four-wave mixing depend on several factors. These factors are:

- the wavelength mismatch or channel spacing, D_b, or Δf
- the power intensity of the contributing frequencies f_1, f_2, and f_3
- the chromatic dispersion of the fiber
- the refractive index
- the fiber length
- higher-order polarization properties of the material (nonlinear Kerr coefficient)

Four-wave mixing (FWM) may also occur with two signals at different wavelength if their intensity and wavelengths are in a specific relationship. In this case, the fiber refractive index is modulated at the beat frequency of the two wavelengths. The phase modulation in this case creates two sidebands (at frequencies given by this difference) the intensity of which is weak as compared with the intensity of the mixing products from three signals.

The effect of FWM on optical transmission and in single mode fiber is:

- cross talk, due to superposition of uncorrelated data from the contributing channels
- signal power depletion as a result of signal power sharing among the contributing channels to the FWM generated channel
- signal-to-noise degradation, due to superposition of noise and random data from the contributing frequencies

As the signal input power of f_1, f_2, and f_3 increases, or as the channel spacing decreases (due to more wavelength-channels in the same fiber), the FWM output term f_{fwm} increases. ITU-T (G.663) recommends that the critical optical power for FWM is greater than 10 mW, although this depends on channel spacing. At 200 GHz channel spacing, it has been experimentally verified that the FWM effect is drastically decreased as compared with 100 GHz or less spacing.

The current trend (caused by bandwidth demand) is to fit more channels into the same spectrum; as a result of this, the channel spacing decreases to less than 100 GHz (50 GHz for 80 channels in the C-band going down to 25 GHz) and thus FWM cross talk becomes more significant. A widely used formula for FWM-induced cross talk is given by

$$P_{ijk}(L) = (\eta/9)D^2\gamma^2 P_i P_j P_k\, e^{-\alpha L}\{[1 - \exp^{-\alpha L}]^2/\alpha^2\}$$

where P_i, P_j, and P_k are the input powers of the three input signals f_1, f_2, and f_3; L is the optical traveled length (i.e., fiber length); α is the attenuation coefficient; η is the FWM efficiency; D is a degenerative factor (equal to 3 for degenerative FWM or 6 for nondegenerative FWM); and γ is a nonlinear coefficient (for the fiber medium) given by

$$\gamma = (2\pi n_2)/(\lambda A_{\text{eff}})$$

where λ is the wavelength in free space, and A_{eff} and n_2 are the effective area and the nonlinear refractive index of the fiber, respectively.

The nonlinear refractive index is related to nonlinear susceptibility χ_{1111} of the optical medium and to the refractive index of the core n of the fiber given by

$$n_2 = [(48\pi^2)/(cn^2)]\chi_{1111}$$

The FWM efficiency factor depends, among other parameters, on a phase matching factor, which depends on fiber dispersion and channel spacing. In fact, at the zero-dispersion wavelength, FWM is at its best performance; this is one of the reasons that in DWDM communications the zero-dispersion wavelength is avoided and the wavelength operating point is preferably positive and slightly above the zero-dispersion wavelength. Thus, four-wave mixing, as opposed to Raman scattering, requires strong phase matching of coincident energy from all three wavelengths. Moreover, both chromatic dispersion and length of fiber reduce the intensity of the FWM product.

In short, the FWM efficiency depends on material dispersion, channel separation, optical traveled path (or fiber length) and on optical power level of each contributing channel. The resultant FWM component affects the quality of the signal in terms of cross talk and bit error rate and thus FWM limits the channel capacity of a fiber system.

As a side note, it is of interest to note that the same mechanism that causes FWM also causes modulation instability.

1.6.4 Temporal FWM, Near-End and Far-End

Consider a narrow light pulse at a wavelength traveling along a fiber segment. Think of the light pulse as a sliding window along the fiber with constant speed. As the light pulse slides along the fiber, it influences the electric dipoles of the fiber segment for as long as they are in it. If at the same time, there are two more pulses on adjacent wavelength channels, overlapping in time, then in this segment FWM occurs. Since the signal power at the *near-end* of the fiber (close to the source) is at its maximum, the FWM product also is at its highest intensity. This is a consequence from the discussion on the FWM efficiency factor and the strong phase matching required for FWM.

Similarly, when the three light pulses arrive at a *far-end* segment of a fiber that is several kilometers long, due to dispersion and attenuation of the pulses, the FWM product at that segment is at its lowest intensity. Figure 1.64 qualitatively illustrates the contribution of FWM at the near-end and at the far-end of a fiber. Clearly, FWM occurs in a time-continuous manner, and although at the near-end it has a maximum

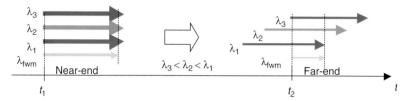

Figure 1.64 The effect of FWM is strongest at the near-end of synchronized channels, and it is diminished at the far-end where channels are weakest due to attenuation and dispersion.

effect, its cumulative strength diminishes as the pulses travel along the fiber. The study of FWM in the time domain is termed *temporal FWM* (tFWM).

1.6.5 Impact of FWM on DWDM Transmission Systems

As the density of wavelengths (channels) in DWDM systems increases, cross talk increases in importance.

- If the optical power of each channel is increased, FWM becomes more intense.
- If the launched optical power of each channel is lowered, then the actual fiber length is decreased to ensure that the arriving signal can be detected reliably. This may necessitate optical amplification to extend the fiber path (optical amplification increases the cost).
- If the channel (wavelength) density increases, or if the channels are spaced very close to each other, FWM becomes more intense.
- If the channels are spaced farther apart, then fewer wavelength channels can fit into the fiber.

1.6.6 Countermeasures to Reduce FWM

Four-wave mixing is a phenomenon that cannot be entirely eliminated. However, it can be greatly minimized so that its effect is not destructive. Several countermeasures and design approaches may aid to suppress the FWM contribution.

- Channels are spaced unevenly.
- Channel spacing is increased.
- The launched power into the fiber is reduced.
- Segments of fibers with opposing nonzero dispersion characteristics after long spans of standard fiber cable are used to maintain a near-zero net chromatic dispersion.

1.7 SOLITONS

Self-modulation (red shift and blue shift) depends on pulse shape. Under specific conditions (very short pulses with a specific power spectrum), spectral broadening due to self-modulation can be compensated for by fiber dispersion. In this case, assuming an ideal fiber, pulses preserve their input shape and are stable over the entire length of the fiber. Pulses that preserve their shape, amplitude, and width are known as *solitons*, and the conditions for generation and sustained propagation are known as the *soliton regime*.

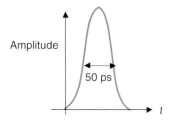

Figure 1.65 Self-modulation of very narrow pulses can be compensated for by fiber dispersion thus preserving the pulse shape; such pulses, known as solitons, have the ability to travel for thousands of kilometers.

The *soliton regime* involves parameters such as "input optical power" (derived from a *hyperbolic secant* function), "effective area and cross section of the fiber core," "dielectric constant" of fiber and of free space ($\varepsilon_0 = 8.854.10^{-12}$ F/m), and fiber type. Similarly, a rigorous theoretical analysis of soliton generation and propagation entails solving a homogeneous Shrödinger-type equation. Any optical pulse within an area of $A = \text{sqrt}(1.6)W^{1/2}$ ps ($\pm 50\%$) can reach the soliton regime in a typical single-mode fiber. Typical solitons are about 50 ps wide or less (Fig 1.65).

Solving Shrödinger's equation is beyond the scope of this book (many textbooks have dealt with this); it is more appropriate, however, to provide a qualitative description of the soliton.

When a narrow pulse is launched into a fiber, its initial pulse shape oscillates temporarily as two competing effects act on it, spectral broadening and compensation by dispersion. Finally, this oscillation, at some time later and after some fiber length, reaches an equilibrium compensating state and the soliton takes a shape very close to its initial form. However, the shape of a soliton is also affected by other effects, such as third-order dispersion effects may cause the soliton to change its velocity and thus its shape, and fiber losses that may cause the soliton to lose amplitude and broaden. For example, 15 Km travel in standard single-mode fiber doubles the soliton width, but a low-loss single mode fiber with low third-order dispersion characteristics enables solitons to travel much longer distances (on the order of a few thousand kilometers) without amplification and because of the narrowness of pulses allow for very high bit rates.

When solitons are used in DWDM systems collision among solitons that belong to different optical channels also may take place. Collision may take place over a fiber length for which solitons overlap; this length is known as the *collision length*, L_{coll}. The collision length depends on fiber parameters, channel spacing, channel wavelength, and the bit rate of the colliding channels; L_{coll} can be 10 Km or even 100 Km.

It has been shown that an exchange of energy takes place during soliton collision. As a result, there is a soliton frequency and temporal phase-shift that cause residual effects. At the receiver, because of the *collision-induced temporal shift* and because 1s and 0s in the bit stream are random (timing) *jitter* is induced. Only transitions from 1 to 0 or from 0 to 1 would cause this as a contiguous string of ones would cause the same shift from bit to bit and thus no jitter. When the collision length becomes comparable to the amplifier spacing, the residual shift (jitter) may be about 0.1 GHz, which is an unacceptable value since jitter is cumulative.

Soliton generation in long-haul and particularly transoceanic transmission systems using dispersion managed fibers promise a technology that exhibits reduced nonlinear effects, high spectral efficiency, RZ modulation, ultrahigh bit rates, and fiber spans at very long lengths (many hundreds of kilometers) without regeneration or amplification. Yet the soliton integrity must be maintained over a path despite path diversity, temperature variations, and the addition or removal of splices, connectors, and fiber type over time; and this is what slows down the soliton deployment in fiber paths that in practice cannot remain unchanged. Soliton applicability in medium-haul and short-haul land network is, for the time being, cost-prohibitive but they are promising in submarine cross-Atlantic deployment.

1.8 SUMMARY OF NONLINEAR PHENOMENA

Briefly, the most important nonlinear phenomena in optical communication are:

- Stimulated Raman scattering (SRS): OChs with optical power above a threshold may behave as a pump for longer wavelengths or cause photonic spontaneous emission in either direction that degrades the signal to noise ratio. There is no well-known controlling mechanism for SRS.
- Stimulated Brillouin scattering (SBS): Similar to SRS, dominant in the backward direction, and the threshold is from ~5 to 10 mW for external modulation, and from ~20 to 30 mW for direct modulation. SBS is controlled by lowering the signal intensity, or by making the source linewidth wider than the Brillouin bandwidth.
- Four-wave mixing (FWM): Created sidebands that deplete the optical power of contributing signals. Channel spacing and optical power management controls FWM.
- Modulation instability (MI): MI may degrades the signal to noise ratio due to created sidebands and thus decrease the optical power level.
- Self-phase modulation (SPM): Changes in optical intensity cause variation in the phase of the optical signal; this broadens the signal spectrum (and pulse width). Operating in the anomalous dispersion region, chromatic dispersion and SPM compensate each other. However, this may result in spontaneous formation of Solitons.
- Cross-phase modulation (XPM): Interacting adjacent optical channels induce phase changes and thus pulse broadening. This is controlled by channel spacing selection.

1.9 FACTORS THAT AFFECT MATTER AND LIGHT

We have discussed the parameters that influence light, the parameters that influence matter, and the interactions that take place when light meets matter. In this section, we summarize these effects, what causes them, and how they are measured. Table 1.10 tabulates the effects and what causes them, and Table 1.11 lists the parameters and the measuring methods.

For more details, see ITU-T recommendations G.650, G.652, G.653, and G.654.

Table 1.10   Cause and effect

Cause	Effect
λ interacts with λ	Interference
λs interact with matter	Linear and nonlinear effects: absorption, scattering, birefringence, phase shift, reflection, refraction, diffraction, polarization, polarization shift, PDL, modulation, self-phase modulation, etc.
$\lambda-$matter$-\lambda$ interaction	FWM, issues, SRS, SBS, OFA
Nonmonochromatic channel	Pulse broadening, finite number of channels within available band.
Refractive index variation (n)	Affects propagation of light
Transparency variation	Affects amount of light through matter;
Scattering	optical power loss (attenuation)
Reflectivity	Affects polarization of reflected optical wave; Affects phase of reflected optical wave
Ions in matter	Dipoles interacting selectively with λs; Energy absorption or exchange; Affect refractive index;

Table 1.11   Parameters and measuring methods

Parameter (Symbol, Unit)	Measuring Method
Attenuation $\{A(\lambda), \text{-dB}\}$	$A(\lambda) = 10\log[P_{\text{out}}(\lambda)/P_{\text{in}}(\lambda)]$, $P_{\text{in}} > P_{\text{out}}$
Attenuation coefficient $\{\alpha(\lambda), \text{dB/km}\}$	$\alpha(\lambda) = A(\lambda)/$
Insertion Loss, $(IL, \text{-dB})$ between port i and port j	$IL_{ij} = P_j - P_i$, or $IL_{ij} = -10\log_{10} t_{ij}$, (where $t_{ij} = I/O$ power transfer matrix)
Amplification gain (g, dB)	$g(\lambda) = 10\log[P_{\text{out}}(\lambda)/P_{\text{in}}(\lambda)]$, $P_{\text{in}} < P_{\text{out}}$
Birefringence	P_O/P_E; indirectly (BER, X-talk)
Extinction ratio	P_B/P_F; indirectly from IL & $A(\lambda)$
Pulse spreading (ps)	$\Delta\tau_{\text{OUT}} - \Delta\tau_{\text{IN}}$ (indirectly from BER, X-talk, eye diagram)
Group delay (ps)[+]	$\tau(\lambda) = \tau 0 + (S_0/2)\{\lambda - \lambda_0\}^2$ (see G.653)
Diff. group delay (DGD, ps)	(see ITU-T G.650 for procedure)
Chromatic disp. coeff. (D, psec/nm-km)	$D(\lambda) = S_0(\lambda - \lambda_0)^{**}$ (see G.653)
Chromatic disp. slope (S, psec/nm²-km)	it requires laboratory optical setup
Polarization mode dispersion (PMD, ps)	it requires laboratory optical setup
Phase shift $(\Delta\phi,^\circ, \text{rad})$:	it requires interferometric setup
Polarization mode shift $(\Theta,^\circ, \text{rad})$	it requires laboratory optical setup

1.10   REGARDING OPTICAL FIBER

Optical fiber is one of the most important parts of the communications network because it impacts the quality of signal, cost, and maintenance. Therefore, a tremendous effort is consumed to select the right fiber for the application at hand and to engineer the fiber span, because once the fiber type has been selected, the span has been engineered, and the cable has been installed, the cost to make changes is not trivial.

1.10.1 Ideal Fiber Versus Real Fiber

To design a fiber, one starts with a mathematical fiber model, which (in theory) is ideal. However, when the real fiber is manufactured, based on this model, it turns out that its theoretical model is only a good approximation. For example, the physical dimensions of fiber are not exact and uniform over its length, although they may be contained within the ITU-T–defined limits, its refractive index is not exactly uniform, and it is not absolutely stress-free (stress causes birefringence). As a consequence:

- The diameter of the core and of the cladding varies.
- The refractive distribution over length varies.
- The radial refractive distribution (refractive index profile) varies.
- The density of contaminants or dopants over length varies.
- Birefringence varies.
- Polarization varies.
- Many other parameters also vary.

These imperfections affect the quality of the signal and they are either manifested as power loss, polarization state variation, noise, and other linear and nonlinear effects. Fiber manufacturers are aware of these imperfections and strive to produce the most uniform fiber with the most desired propagation characteristics. In general, good fiber should have the same characteristics in every kilometer of its length.

1.10.2 The Evolving Bandwidth-Span Product

Although current fiber meets the bandwidth needs and spans in optical networking, it is clear that fiber is continuously evolving and improving in both transmission performance and cost. When the first SMF, optimized for 1310 nm, made its debut in 1983, announcing that it supports optical transmission at 2.5 Gb/s for up to 640 km without amplification (or 10 Gb/s up to ~100 km), it was in the news. Recent SMF transports the same optical signal (2.5 Gb/s) to over 4,400 km (or 10 Gb/s up to ~500 km) without amplification. With a simple extrapolation, it is reasonable to expect in the next decade that new fiber will further push the envelope to ~2,000 km for 10 Gb/s signals and to 500 km for 40 Gb/s, and 2.5 Gb/s will be used in lower network layers (Metro and Access) and not in long-haul applications.

Based on this data rate trend, for 2.5 Gb/s the transportable bandwidth-span product without amplification has increased (per channel) from 1600 to 11,000, and for 10 Gb/s it has increased from 1,000 to 5,000 and projected to approximately 20,000.

In DWDM, the aggregate bandwidth-span product is calculated by multiplying the bandwidth-span product by the number of optical channels; for 10 Gb/s and for 160 channels, this is projected to 3,200,000!

1.10.3 Fiber Amplifiers and Spectral Continuum

Transmitting photonic signals over very long fiber spans (tens or hundreds of kilometers) it requires optical signal amplification due to fiber loss (unless in the special case where optical transmission is in the soliton regime). Unfortunately, a single amplifier type does not perform over the entire 1,300 to 1,600 nm spectrum but only within a narrow band, as already discussed.

Although a more comprehensive presentation of optical fiber amplifiers is in the next chapter, here, it is important to identify some doped fiber amplifiers.

Praseodymium-doped fluoride fiber amplifiers (PDFFA) promise acceptable performance in the 1,310 nm range. Thorium-doped fiber amplifiers (ThDFA) promise to fill the need of photonic amplification in the 1,350 to 1,450 nm range and Thulium-doped fiber amplifiers (TmDFA) in the range 1,450–1,530 nm.

Erbium-doped fiber amplifiers (EDFA) have been extensively used for optical signal amplification. The 1,550 nm range is the first to be used extensively in DWDM applications, and for which standards have been drafted. In the L-band, modified tellurium-erbium-doped fluoride fiber amplifiers (Te-EDFA) extend this range from 1532 to 1608 nm, which is suitable for long-reach network applications.

Currently, Raman amplifiers have made inroads in fiber amplification as they efficiently address an extended spectrum using standard single-mode fiber. Other fiber amplifiers, better suited in short-wavelength ranges, take advantage of optical parametric properties of fibers. Figure 1.66 illustrates the diversity in optical amplification and the range that each covers.

1.10.4   New Fibers

New fiber types are a matter of intense research and development. Application-specific optical fiber (ASOF) is custom-made by modifying the sequence and concentration of dopants of the fiber core and/or the geometry of the fiber. According to this, fibers with specific properties for specific applications are made. A new type of fiber, currently in experimental phase, is known as *photonic crystal fiber* (PCF) promising improved propagation properties suitable to DWDM applications.

PCFs consist of a bundle of microscopic silica tubes, about one micrometer in diameter (Fig. 1.67). To construct this, one starts with filling a larger silica tube with many smaller silica tubes (like a bundle of thin spaghetti) about 1 millimeter in diameter. This is fused and drawn into long lengths with conventional fiber manufacturing techniques reducing the air hole of each tube to a micrometer scale. The end result is a fiber that when viewed under a microscope consists of microscopic hollow capillary tubes. Light coupled in PCF fiber is confined by the walls of capillary tubes, which guide it

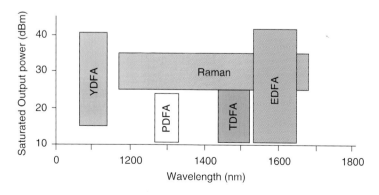

Figure 1.66   Optical amplifiers are many, each suitable for a different spectral range.

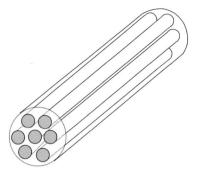

Figure 1.67 Hollow nano-tube optical waveguides (light may travel in each tube for ultra long distances, many hundreds of Km).

through the (photonic) air gap confinement of airholes. The (photonic) air gaps turn out to be in a specific relationship with particular wavelengths, and thus only certain of them are transmitted through the PCF. This implies that there is spectral selectivity or iridescence (a similar iridescence effect is observed in the fibrous feathers of birds and butterflies), and also that all propagating wavelengths in PCF have the same propagation characteristics. Moreover, since the tube is hollow (no dielectric) light propagates in air with virtually no loss, it does not suffer from dispersion and thus it can travel for ultralong distances (many hundreds of kilometers).

PCFs are still in the experimental phase, but they promise customization to guide multiwavelength light in single mode, with uniform characteristics and low attenuation. Thus, it is projected that PCFs will find a variety of applications in communication, amplifiers, sensors, and others.

1.10.5 How Strong Is Fiber?

In communications, it is important that cables are flexible as well as strong when they are pulled. One would think that glass fiber is fragile "like glass," yet it is flexible enough and its tensile strength is stronger than copper. In fact, the tensile strength of copper is 100 pounds per square inch, whereas that of glass fiber is theoretically 2 million pounds per square inch. However, due to surface microcracks, in practice it is about 800,000 pounds per square inch, still much stronger than copper. In addition to high strength, glass fiber does not corrode, is immune to external electromagnetic interference, is waterproof, and has a long service lifetime of well above 20 years.

1.11 FIBER CONNECTIVITY

Copper wire may be installed in segments, each segment connected with one or more segments by simply bringing the copper ends into physical contact by any means. Consequently, no special treatment of the two copper ends is required other than removing possible contaminants.

Unlike copper wire, fiber requires specialized treatment. Two fiber ends placed one next to the other represent a discontinuity and imperfections. For example, the two fibers may be of different type and different refractive index profile; each fiber may have been supplied by a different manufacturer or in a different time. Moreover, the glassy end-faces may be flat or not, parallel or not, of good optical quality (with minor imperfections on the faces) or not, and between the end-faces there may be a minute but finite air-gap. Thus, photons traveling from one fiber to the other must overcome this discontinuity and the imperfections with minimal loss. Consequently, certain special precautions must be taken to minimize power loss as photons travel through it.

- The two fiber ends to be connected should be treated so that the end-faces are flat, perpendicular to the fiber's longitudinal axis, and highly polished (or the faces may be formed into a spherical lens, a specialized operation that requires more specialized personnel and equipment).
- The two end-faces should be treated with antireflecting coatings.
- The two fiber-cores should be in perfect alignment.
- The two end-faces should be brought to close (small fraction of λ) proximity.
- In some cases, a refractive index matching fluid may be used.

The first two precautions are related to the treatment of fiber ends and it is accomplished with specialized abrasive materials and coatings. The third is related to how precisely the fiber circular core is at the center of the fiber and how precisely the interconnecting devices align the cores. Concerning A, the concentricity error of a single-mode fiber (based on ITU-T G.652) should be less than 1 μm, and concerning B, the cores are precisely aligned with biconical self-aligned connectors or with aligned groves. The fourth item is related to the flatness and perpendicularity of the two end-surfaces and on the accuracy of the connectors.

Another fiber interconnecting method does not use connectors, but it splices two fibers by fusing them permanently. This operation requires specialized splicing equipments with which the two fiber ends are first stripped from their cladding and then are fused together and re-treated to yield a continuous fiber. Clearly, this process does not require end-face treatment, antireflection coatings.

Splicing is preferred when fiber connectivity is permanent (i.e., repairing broken cables) and in the field (aerial or buried cable). Connectors are preferred in central offices, cabinets and huts where connectors are protected and disconnecting and reconnecting may be expected. However, core alignment of the two fibers and polarization issues are still relevant.

In either case, connector optical power loss is taken into serious account when estimating the overall power loss of an optical link, and it should be a small fraction of a dB per connector or splice. Because of stringent power loss budget, fibers preferably are installed in long (many km) segments to minimize a large number of interconnecting devices. However, unforeseen fiber breakage is reality and an estimated amount of loss due to future splices/connectors should be included in the power budget.

1.12 OPTICAL PWBs

As communications systems become more "optical," the optical transmission medium between system plug-in units also should be optical; today, this is accomplished by using connectorized fiber cables. The "old days," a similar approach was used with copper cables; individual cables interconnected the various plug-ins forming such a cable-clattered space that deservingly was known as the "rat nest." However, multilayered printed wiring boards (PWB) with vias and connectors eliminated this and greatly simplified the nightmare of cable management. Today, the optical cabling "rat nest" has once more revived, and an interim solution is given using flat ribbon fiber cables. However, the solution of a true "optical PWB" is still awaited (in this case, W stands for waveguide), although currently there is substantial research in this direction. Optical PWBs will provide a compact and cost-effective solution.

EXERCISES

1. Calculate the distance traveled by light in 10 picoseconds and in free space.

2. When monochromatic light of frequency f transverses the boundary from matter into free space, its speed changes but its energy is preserved. What does it change?

3. A stream of bits at 100 Gb/s propagate in free space. How many bits could fit in a distance of 1 meter (round off the number)?

4. Calculate the energy of a 157-nm wavelength photon (in eV). The electron charge is $e = 1.6 \times 10^{-19}$ coulomb.

5. Could n be smaller than 1?

6. Could n be negative?

7. If, in Figure 1.11, Θ_i is zero (i.e., ray is perpendicular to surface) then:

   a. would there be a reflected ray?

   b. would there be a refractive ray? If yes, what would the refractive angle be?

8. A coin lies on the bottom of a pond that appears to be 3 feet deep. We try to reach the coin with a 3.5-foot long stick, but we discover that we cannot reach it. Why?

9. A pulse of almost monochromatic light enters matter in which it propagates. If we compare the phase with the group velocity, which is faster? Or are they the same?

10. Two coherent light sources impinge on a screen as shown. Identify points of intensity maxima in the highlighted area.

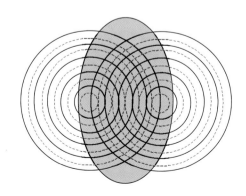

11. Could a moving photon in space be stopped, captured, and stored?

12. What happens when a photon interacts with an atom?

13. Consider two coherent sources (at the same long wavelength) interfering and forming fringes on a screen. The density of fringes on the screen depends on the distance and other factors. If we keep the distance fixed but change the wavelength to short, what can you tell about the fringe density?

14. Consider a fiber, 1 km long, with a refractive index $n = 1.5$. Consider also a source with a data rate at 10 Gbps. Calculate the number of bits at any time in the fiber, or the fiber bit capacity (approximate the group velocity by $v = c/n$).

15. In a step index fiber, the core has $n_1 = 1.48$ and the cladding $n_2 = 1.46$. Calculate the numerical aperture (NA) or the critical cone for the fiber.

16. An optical link consists of three fiber segments; the first is 10 km long, the second is 30 km, and the third is 20 km. The fiber attenuation is 0.1 dB/km. The segments are connected with connectors at 0.1 dB loss each. Calculate the total loss due to fiber and connectors over the link.

17. An amplifier of gain 8 amplifies an optical signal of 3 mW. Calculate the amplified signal in dBm units.

18. One source of 5 dBm and another source of 9 dBm combine. Is the total power 14 dBm? If not, explain why.

19. For an optical channel, the group delay is as shown in the following figure. With respect to chromatic dispersion and for λ_0 at the zero dispersion wavelength:

    a. what can you say for wavelengths λ_A and λ_B?

    b. what can you say for wavelengths λ_C and λ_D?

    c. what can you say for wavelengths λ_A and λ_D?

    d. after some travel time, what would the original pulse look like?

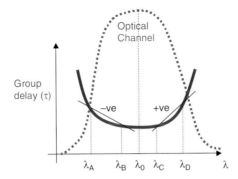

REFERENCES

1. S.V. Kartalopoulos, *Understanding Neural Networks and Fuzzy Logic: Basic Concepts and Applications*, IEEE Press, New York, 1995.

2. A. Kastler, *Optique*, 6th ed., Masson & Cie, Paris, 1965.

3. M.H. Freeman, *Optics*, 10th ed., Butterworths, London, 1990.

4. E.B. Brown, *Modern Optics*, Reinhold Publishing Corp., New York, 1965.

5. M. Francon, *Optique: Formation et Traitement des Images*, Masson & Cie, Paris, 1972.

6. D. Hondros and P. Debye, Electromagnetische wellen an dielektrischen drahten, *Ann. Phys.*, vol. 32, Leipzig, 1910, pp. 465–476.

7. S.V. Kartalopoulos and D. Raftopoulos, Interferometry for the evaluation of the dynamic optical and mechanical properties of transparent materials, *Eng. Fracture Mechanics*, vol. 19, no. 6, 1984, pp. 993–1003.

8. S.V. Kartalopoulos and D. Raftopoulos, The reflected and transmitted shadow methods for the study of sharp v-notched plates under pure bending, *Eng. Fracture Mechanics*, vol. 10, 1978, pp. 553–563.

9. S.V. Kartalopoulos and D. Raftopoulos, A novel optical method for the evaluation of the ratio of Poisson's ratio to the modulus of elasticity of optically transparent materials, *J. Phys. D: Appl. Phys.*, vol. 11, 1978, pp. 2083–2089.

10. S.V. Kartalopoulos and D. Raftopoulos, Simple interferometric instrument for evaluating the dynamic stress-optical coefficients and the ratio Poisson's ratio to modulus of elasticity, American Institute of Physics, v. *Sci. Instrum.* vol. 51, no. 6, June 1980, pp. 853–854.

11. S.V. Kartalopoulos and D. Raftopoulos, A Novel Electro-Optical Instrument for Measuring the Stress-Optical Coefficient, 10th Annual Electro Optics/Laser conference, 1978.

12. T. Vorburger, et al., *Beam Effects, Surface Topography, and Depth Profiling in Surface Analysis*, Czanderna et al., eds., Plenum Press, New York, 1998, pp. 275–354.

13. M. Francon, *Holographie*, Masson & Cie, Paris, 1969.

14. P.M. Duffieux, *L'Integrales de Fourier et ses Application a l'Optique*, Masson & Cie, Paris, 1970.

15. T. Wildi, *Units and Conversion Charts*, 2nd ed., IEEE Press, New York, 1995.

16. S.R. Nagle, Optical fiber—the expanding medium, *IEEE Circuits Devices Mag.*, vol. 5, no. 2, March 1989, pp. 36–45.

17. S.V. Kartalopoulos, Emerging technologies at the dawn of the millennium, *IEEE Comm. Mag.*, vol. 39, no. 11, pp. 22–26, Nov. 2001.

18. N. Araki, H. Izumita, N. Honda, and M. Nakamura, Extended optical fiber line testing system using L/U-band crossed optical waveguide coupler for L-band WDM transmission, Technical Digest OFC 2002, paper TuY-2, March 2002, pp. 165–166.

19. R.H. Stolen, Non-linear properties of optical fibers, in *Optical Fiber Telecommunications*, S.E. Miller and G. Chynoweth, eds., Academic Press, New York, 1979.

20. J.B. Eom, D.S. Moon, U.-C. Paek, and B.H. Lee, Fabrication and transmission characteristics of couplers using photonic crystal fibers, Technical Digest OFC 2002, paper ThK-2, March 2002, pp. 465–466.

21. C.D. Poole and R.E. Wagner, Phenomenological approach to polarization dispersion in long single-mode fibers, *Electron. Lett.*, vol. 22, no. 19, 1986, pp. 1029–1030.

22. P. Lu, L. Chen, and X. Bao, Polarization mode dispersion and polarization dependent loss for a pulse in single-mode fibers, *J. Lightwave Technol.*, vol. 19, no. 6, June 2001, pp. 856–860.

23. P. Lu, L. Chen, and X. Bao, Principal states of polarization for an optical pulse in the presence of polarization mode dispersion and polarization dependent loss, Proc. 2000 Int. Conf. Applicat. Photon. Technology (ICAPT'2000), QC, Canada, June 12–16, 2000.

24. N. Gisin, Statistics of polarization dependent losses, *Optics Comm.*, vol. 114, 1995, pp. 399–405.

25. D. Cotter, Stimulated Brillouin scattering in monomode optical fiber, *J. Opt. Commun.*, vol. 4, 1983, pp. 10–19.

26. G. Waarts and R.P. Braun, Crosstalk due to stimulated Brillouin scattering in monomode fibers, *Electron. Lett.*, vol. 24, 1988, pp. 78–80.

27. P.T. Thomas et al., Normal acoustic modes and Brillouin scattering in single-mode optical fibers, *Phys. Rev.*, vol. B19, 1979, pp. 4986–4998.

28. K. Inoue, Phase-mismatching characteristics of FWM in fiber lines with multi-stage optical amplifiers, *Opt. Lett.*, vol. 17, 1992, pp. 801–803.

29. K.O. Hill, D.C. Johnson, B.S. Kawasaki, and R.I. MacDonald, CW three-wave mixing in single-mode optical fibers, *J. Appl. Phys.*, vol. 49, 1978, pp. 5098–5106.

30. K. Inoue, Four-wave mixing in an optical fiber in the zero-dispersion wavelength region, *J. Lightwave Technol.*, vol. 10, no. 11, Nov. 1992, pp. 1553–1561.

31. S. Song, C.T. Allen, K.R. Demarest, and R. Hui, Intensity-dependant phase-matching effects on four-wave mixing in optical fibers, *J. Lightwave Technol.*, vol. 17, no. 11, Nov. 1999, pp. 2285–2290.

32. J. Hansryd, H. Sunnerud, P.A. Andrekson, and M. Karlsson, Impact of PMD on four-wave-mixing-induced crosstalk in WDM systems, *IEEE Photon. Tech. Lett.*, vol. 12, no. 9, Sept. 2000, pp. 1261–1263.

33. C.F. Buhrer, Four waveplate dual tuner for birefringent filters and multiplexers, *Appl. Optics*, vol. 26, no. 17, Sept. 1987, pp. 3628–3632.

34. A. Hasegawa, Soliton-based optical communications: an overview", *IEEE J. Select. Topics Quantum Electronics*, vol. 6, no. 6, Nov./Dec. 2000, pp. 1161–1172.

35. S.-Y. Lin and J.G. Fleming, A three-dimensional optical photonic crystals, *J. Lightwave Technol.*, vol. 17, no. 11, Nov. 1999, pp. 1944–1947.

36. H. Kosaka et al., Superprism phenomena in photonic crystals: toward microscale lightwave circuits, *J. Lightwave Technol.*, vol. 17, no. 11, Nov. 1999, pp. 2032–2038.

37. C. Palmer, *Diffraction Grating Handbook*, *www.thermorgl.com* April 2002.

STANDARDS

1. ANSI/IEEE 812-1984, "*Definition of terms relating to fiber optics*," 1984.

2. IEC Publication 793-2, Part 2, "*Optical fibres — Part 2: Product specifications*, 1992.

3. ITU-T Recommendation G.650, "*Definition and test methods for the relevant parameters of single-mode fibres*," 1997.

4. ITU-T Recommendation G.652, "*Characteristics of a single-mode optical fiber cable*," 1997.

5. ITU-T Recommendation G.653, "*Characteristics of a dispersion-shifted single-mode optical fibre cable*," 1997.

6. ITU-T Recommendation G.654, "*Characteristics of a cut-off shifted single-mode optical fibre cable*," 1997.

7. ITU-T Recommendation G.655, "*Characteristics of a nonzero-dispersion shifted single-mode optical fibre cable*," 1996.

8. ITU-T Recommendation G.671, "*Transmission characteristics of passive optical components*," 1996.

9. ITU-T Recommendation G.702, *"Digital hierarchy bit rates,"* 1988.

10. ITU-T Recommendation L.41, *"Maintenance wavelength on fibres carrying signals,"* May 2000.

11. Telcordia (previously Bellcore), TR-NWT-499, *"Transport systems generic requirements (TSGR): common requirements,"* issue 5, Dec. 1993.

2

OPTICAL COMPONENTS

DWDM systems require specialized optical and photonic components that are based on light–matter and light–matter–light interactions as well as on the propagation properties of light. The optical components deployed in communications systems provide an equivalent functionality of their electrical or electronic counterparts. Such components are transformers (Fourier lens), transmitters, receivers, filters, modulators, amplifiers, add-drop multiplexers, cross-connect, couplers, and so on. In this chapter we provide a thorough description of the critical optical components that are used in the design of DWDM systems.

2.1.1 Geometrical Optics

The earliest optical components used for scientific and commercial purposes were lenses and mirrors. Ancient mathematicians, geometers, and astronomers, such as Apollonios of Perga (3rd c. B.C.), Diocles of Carystos (3rd c. B.C.), Eudoxos of Cnidos (5th–4th c. B.C.), Hipparchos of Nicaea (2nd c. B.C.), Zenodoros of Athens (ca. 3rd–2nd c. B.C.) and others, studied the propagation and reflectivity of light and developed the theory of spherics; they also discovered the focusing imperfection of spherical mirrors and corrected them with parabolic mirrors. In the centuries that followed, these and new theories along with the development of purer glass and tribology made it possible to manufacture better lenses in various shapes and sizes, which led to the development of reading glasses, microscopes, telescopes, and other scientific optical instruments.

Depending on curvature, lenses are distinguished as plano-convex, convex-convex, plano-concave, concave-concave, convex-concave (or meniscus), and cylindrical (Fig. 2.1), as well as other specialized shapes.

This chapter contains device specifications for illustrative and educational purposes. Because specifications are continuously changing, no responsibility is assumed for correctness. The reader is encouraged to consult the most current manufacturers' data sheets.

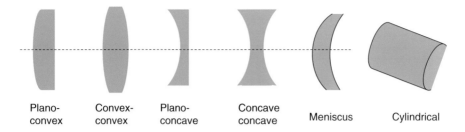

| Plano-convex | Convex-convex | Plano-concave | Concave concave | Meniscus | Cylindrical |

Figure 2.1   Types of lenses (shown cross-section perpendicular to axis).

Instruments rarely consist of a single lens; they typically, consist of lens systems. Lens systems, depending on the function they perform, may be comprised of one or more lens types. Thus, telescope or microscope eyepieces differ from telescope objectives in lens size and composition. Thus, some lenses utilize a large area (aperture), whereas others use only that portion that is near their axis. Some lens systems are complex in order to correct image distortions caused by lens imperfections and by interaction of lens material with light such as spherical aberration, astigmatism, coma, pincushion (positive) or barrel (negative) distortion, lateral color aberration, dichroism, and so on. All these aberration types degrade either the quality and/or the power level of the optical signal. Consequently, image distortion–free lens systems have been for many years a serious design effort that has led a number of notable lens arrangements such as for example the Gauss, the Tessar, the Petzval, the Dogmar/Aviar, the Augulon/Biogon, and others.

If we consider a common convex-convex lens (Fig. 2.2) of thickness T, two radii of curvature R_1 and R_2 (asymmetric lens), object to lens distance O, lens to image distance I, object to image distance D, refractive index of lens material n, refractive index of surrounding the image n_o (for air $n_o = 1$), focal length F, object size Y, and image size Y', then the most common relationships are

$$F = (D \times M)/(M + 1)^2$$

$$1/F = 1/O + 1/I = (n - 1)(1/R_1 - 1/R_2) \text{ (for thin lens } T \ll R)$$

$$1/F = (n - 1)[1/R_1 - 1/R_2 + T(n - 1)/nR_1R_2] \text{ (for thick lens)}$$

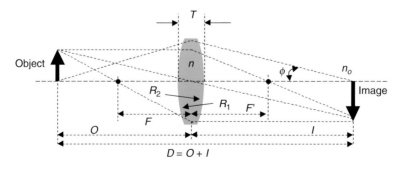

Figure 2.2   Common lens definitions.

Magnification $(M) = Y'/Y = I/O = F/(O - F) = (I - F)/F$

Clear aperture = lens diameter

Numerical aperture $(NA) = n_o \sin \phi$

Relative aperture $(F/\#) = F/$lens diameter $= 1/2$ (NA)

In nonimaging laser applications (such as communications), because of the monochromaticity of the beam and the narrow field of view, a simple miniature lens with one or two aspheric surfaces is used; aspheric lenses have a low relative aperture $(F/\#)$ and are intended for nonimaging applications. In fact, in communications where size is important, a new category of geometric optical components is developed, known as *micro-optics* and soon to be called *nano-optics*. These are passive geometric optical components of a microscale and in some cases nanoscale.

One should keep in mind that the optical frequencies used in DWDM communications are in the far infrared region (0.8–1.6 μm). Consequently, optical materials used in component design must be transparent to the working optical frequencies. In fact, infrared system design uses equations that have been corrected for the infrared frequencies of interest, and infrared design has become a specialized branch of optical systems design.

2.1.2 Insertion Loss and Isolation

At the outset of this chapter, two definitions pertaining to all optical components are made because they will be referred to repeatedly.

Insertion loss (IL) is defined as the optical power lost due to the intervention of an optical component or as the ratio of power-in to power-out. IL is measured in dB, and its mathematical definition is $-10 \log$ (Pin/Pout), where the photonic power is in milliwatts. Insertion loss reduces the optical signal amplitude and is additive. Over a complete path, many components, connectors, and splices remove some of the signal power due to IL which contributes to the overall power loss. If the total power loss exceeds the budgeted power, then amplification is required. Thus, the desirable value of insertion loss is near zero. In communications, lower insertion loss allows longer transmission distance before signal amplification and thus fewer amplifiers and reshapers, and consequently less maintenance and lower cost.

Isolation is defined as the degree of transmitted power through a component compared with the returned power. The desirable value of isolation is near infinity (or zero power returned through the component). In communications, lower isolation reduces both interference and potential second-order resonance.

Component isolation should not be confused with *optical channel isolation*. *Optical channel isolation* refers to the spectral gap between neighboring optical channels. In practice, it is required that channels be spectrally isolated; a better term would be *optical channel separation*. The maximum spectral width and the minimum optical channel separation determine the operating wavelength range of a channel; that is, they set the spectral boundaries within which a channel should be, spectrally speaking.

2.1.3 Parameters Common to All Components

A list of the most common parameters of all optical components, most of which were defined in Chapter 1, is:

- insertion loss (IL)
- optical reflectance
- operating wavelength range
- polarization-dependent loss (PDL)
- polarization-dependent wavelength (var.) (PDW)
- polarization-dependent reflectance
- isotropy/anisotropy of refracting material
- isotropy/anisotropy of diffracting material
- birefringence of optical material
- effects of temperature, pressure, and humidity on components
- effects of vibration (G_{max}) on components
- effects of E-M fields on components
- typical and min-max operating conditions
- mechanical (flex, twist, side and longitudinal pull, etc.)

2.2 OPTICAL FILTERS

The function of optical spectral filters is to recognize a narrow band of optical frequencies from a multiplicity and either pass or reject it, similar to the function of their
electrical counterparts. Optical spectral filters are based on *interference* or *absorption*
and they are distinguished as *fixed optical filters* or *tunable optical filters*.

Fixed optical filters are constructed for a specific application and for a specific and
narrow slice of the spectrum (hence fixed) with specific requirements. As such, although
they may have limited applicability, they are simpler and less expensive compared with
tunable optical filters.

When the electric field of light interacts with the atoms or molecules of matter,
absorption takes place. Thus, absorption is wavelength-dependent. For example, colored glass appears so because it absorbs some of the visible light passing through most
of the unabsorbed wavelengths. Thus, many optical filters are wavelength-selective
absorptive. Some filters that consist of metallic films (such as chromium, nickel, etc.)
are not selective for wavelength absorption.

The amount of light absorbed is proportional to the intensity of incident light. If α is
the absorption coefficient, c is the concentration of absorbing centers (atoms, molecules;
for solid matter $c = 1$), and x is the path traveled in matter, then a *transmittance*, T_x,
is defined as

$$T_x = 10^{-\alpha c x}$$

The total transmittance, T_T, of a stack of filters is the product of each filter's transmittance. Thus

$$T_T = T_1 \times T_2 \times \cdots \times T_N$$

The inverse of transmittance is known as *opacity*. Another term that is also used is the
logarithm of the inverse of transmittance, known as *optical density*, D:

$$D = \log(1/T)$$

The most common parameters specific to filters, in addition to the previously listed common parameters for all components, are (those with an asterix are not included in ITU-T G.650):

- backward loss
- polarization mode dispersion
- modulation depth (modulated light)
- output light intensity (optical power per optical channel)
- finesse (FP filter)
- spectral width
- line width
- cutoff λ
- extinction ratio
- line spacing

Tunable optical filters (TOFs) are constructed with passive or active optical components and provide the flexibility to "slide" on the optical spectrum in a controllable manner. Thus, the salient characteristic of TOFs is their ability to select a range of wavelengths. However, for TOFs to be useful in optical communications systems, they must satisfy certain requirements, such as:

- wide tuning range
- narrow bandwidth
- fast tuning
- flat gain
- low insertion loss
- low polarization-dependent loss
- low cross talk
- insensitivity to temperature

Certain of the common parameters pertaining to filters, such as center and peak wavelength, insertion loss, passband, 20-dB bandwidth, and others, are shown in Figure 2.3. Note that the bandwidth difference ΔBW = (20-dB bandwidth) − (1-dB bandwidth) is a measure of *steepness* and an indication of rejection of signals outside the filter passband; the smaller the difference, the better. In addition, *slope of the filter* in $\Delta\lambda$ is calculated from the wavelengths corresponding to 80% of the peak transmission and the 5% absolute transmission; the lower and higher (or left and right) slopes are not necessarily symmetric, yielding two different slope measurements. The slope is expressed as a percentage and is calculated by

$$\text{Slope} = [\{\lambda(80\% \text{ of peak}) - \lambda(5\% \text{ absolute})\}/\lambda(5\% \text{ absolute})] \times 100(\%)$$

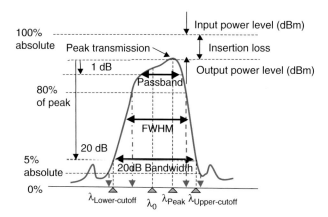

Figure 2.3   Filter parameter definition.

In this section, we examine the following filters:

- the Fabry–Perot and the liquid crystal Fabry–Perot
- the dielectric thin film
- the diffraction Bragg-grating and the fiber Bragg-grating
- the arrayed waveguide grating
- the Mach–Zehnder, fixed and tunable
- the birefringence
- the absorption
- the acousto-optic tunable
- the hybrid filter

2.2.1   Fabry–Perot Interferometer

A *Fabry–Perot resonator* is an arrangement of two parallel reflectors (semi-mirrors) at a distance d from each other, through which multiwavelength light travels but only few wavelengths are reflected back and forth (or resonate) by the two reflectors. Our interest in this arrangement is to formulate *the condition for resonance*.

2.2.1.1   Resonant Modes

Let R_1 and R_2 be reflector #1 and reflector #2 *power reflected coefficient*, respectively. In a general case, between the two plates may be a medium with attenuation α_s, perhaps with gain g (if the medium is active) and perhaps with modulating optical parameters (parameters that change in a controllable manner). All these variations have established this resonator as valuable in many optical and photonic devices.

Assume that there is a pulse of photons $E(t, x)$ entering the mirror assembly at reflector #2, $E(t = 0, x = 0)$ (Fig. 2.4). Then

$$E(t, x) = A \exp[(g - \alpha_s)x/2] \exp[j(\omega t - \beta x)]$$

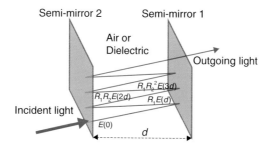

Semi-mirror 2

Semi-mirror 1

Air or
Dielectric

Outgoing light

$R_1R_2^2E(3d)$

$R_1R_2E(2d)$ $R_1E(d)$

Incident light

$E(0)$

d

Figure 2.4   Principles of a Fabry–Perot interferometer.

where g is the intensity gain coefficient, α_s is the intensity attenuation coefficient, β is the propagation constant, and ω is the light frequency. The first exponent is the propagation component and the second exponent is the phase component.

The field at mirror #2 ($x = 0$), after one reflection by mirrors #1 and #2, is

$$E(t, 0) = R_1 R_2 A \exp[(g - \alpha_s)d] \exp[j(\omega t - 2\beta d)]$$

For steady-state oscillations, the amplitude of the initial light pulse ($t = 0$, $x = 0$), must be equal to the amplitude after it has been reflected back and forth. This leads to two conditions.

The amplitude condition:

$$R_1 R_2 A \exp[(g - \alpha_s)d] = A$$

and the phase condition:

$$\exp(-j2\beta d) = 1$$

The phase condition is satisfied only if

$$2\beta d = 2\pi m$$

where

$$\beta = (2\pi n)/\lambda$$

where m is an integer, n is the refractive index, β is the propagation constant, and λ is the wavelength in free space.

The values of λ that satisfy the relationship

$$\lambda = (2dn)/m$$

provide the *resonant wavelengths* or *modes* of the Fabry–Perot resonator.

Examples: for $m = 1$ and $n = 1$, then $\lambda = 2d$; for $m = 2$ and $n = 1$, then $\lambda = d$

The frequency spacing Δf between consecutive (longitudinal) modes is obtained from

$$m - (m - 1) = (2dn/c)f_m - (2dn/c)f_{m-1}$$

or,

$$1 = (2dn/c)\Delta f$$

from which one derives the frequency spacing

$$\Delta f = c/2dn$$

and the wavelength spacing

$$\Delta \lambda = \lambda^2/2dn$$

The latter indicates that a multiplicity of frequencies (wavelengths) is transmitted through the Fabry–Perot resonator. A typical transmittance profile is shown in Figure 2.5.

Note (Fig. 2.5) that the distance between two adjacent peaks is known as free spectral range (FSR), and the spectral width at half amplitude is known as full-width half-minimum (FWHM); FWHM is not the same for all transmitted spectra.

2.2.1.2 Spectral Width, Linewidth, and Line Spacing

Spectral width is defined as the band of frequencies that a Fabry–Perot filter will pass through (Fig. 2.6). The spectral width is characterized by an upper frequency threshold

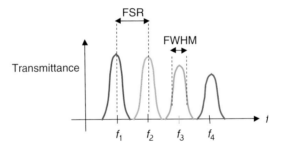

Figure 2.5   A typical transmittance profile of a Fabry–Perot resonator.

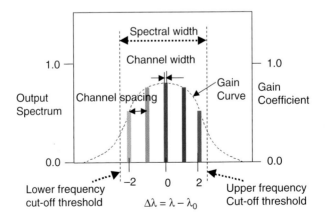

Figure 2.6   Definition of gain, spectral, channel and spacing width.

and a lower frequency (wavelength) threshold. In addition, it is characterized by a gain curve, which is a measure of the degree of flatness over the spectral width.

Line width or *channel width* is defined as the width of the frequency channel. An ideal channel would be monochromatic (i.e., a single wavelength). However, this is not possible, and thus the line width is a measure of how close to ideal a channel is, and also is an indication of the spectral content of the channel.

Line spacing is defined as the distance in wavelength units (nm) or in frequency units (GHz) between two channels.

These definitions are important in system design. They determine the number of channels that the system can support as well as the distance for error-free communication over a dispersive fiber.

2.2.1.3 Reflectivity
If the reflectivity of the surfaces is R, then the intensity between maxima is

$$I = (1 - R)^2/(1 + R)^2.$$

As the reflectivity of the surface increases, the intensity between maxima decreases, thus increasing the sharpness of the interferometer (Fig. 2.7).

2.2.1.4 Finesse
The number of wavelengths (or optical channels) that can simultaneously pass the Fabry–Perot (F–P) resonator without severe interference among them determines the *finesse* of the filter. Finesse is a measure of the energy of wavelengths within the cavity relative to the energy lost per cycle, and it is related to the channel resolution of the filter. Thus, the higher the finesse, the narrower the resonant line-width. Equivalent to finesse is the Q-factor of electrical filters. Finesse is defined as the ratio of successive wavelength peak separation (or the deviation x from the peak wavelength, λ_{max}) to full-width half-maximum (FWHM), as

$$x = (\lambda - \lambda_{max})/\text{FWHM}$$

Similarly, finesse is also expressed in terms of the FSR and FWHM as

$$F = \text{FSR}/\text{FWHM}$$

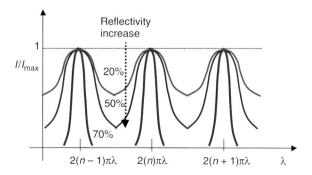

Figure 2.7   As reflectivity increases, the interferometer sharpness increases.

If mirrors were fully (100%) reflective they would not allow light in or out, and if they were only slightly reflective, the cavity would not sustain an adequate amount of optical power in it. In terms of reflectivity, R, and assuming the same reflectivity for both mirrors, the finesse, F, is expressed by

$$F = (\pi R)/[2(1 - R)]$$

Thus, high mirror reflectance results in high filter finesse (finesse values of 20–100 are typical).

Finesse is affected by:

- the angle of incidence of the light beam
- mirror insertion losses
- mirror reflectance
- mirror imperfections (e.g., flatness)
- cavity losses (or opacity of the medium)

It is concluded that a Fabry–Perot interferometer has at least two highly controlled requirements, exactly parallel mirrors and highly polished (high reflectivity) with surface imperfections smaller than $\lambda/100$ (surface imperfections are defined as a fraction of wavelength).

2.2.1.5 *Intensity Maxima*

Based on the Fabry–Perot resonator, a Fabry–Perot interferometer can be as simple as a thin transparent plate with parallel semireflecting surfaces (Fig. 2.8). Then the condition for maximum interference of a wavelength is

$$2dn_m \cos \Theta = m\lambda$$

where n_m is the refractive index of the medium (plate), d is the thickness of the plate, m is a nonzero positive integer, and θ is the internal angle of incidence (angle within the resonant plate). Since this is a trigonometric relationship, this condition is satisfied by a number of wavelengths multiple of 2π.

The maxima points of intensity are defined by

$$I_{\max} = E^2$$

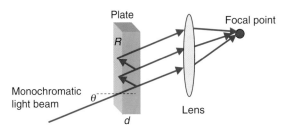

Figure 2.8 A thin transparent plate constructs a simple Fabry–Perot interferometer. This experiment is used to study the effect in Figure 2.7.

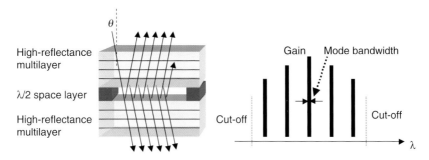

Figure 2.9 The Fabry–Perot interference filter as a band-pass filter.

If the angle of external incidence ϕ is small (in which case $\cos\theta \sim \theta$) and if the external refractive index is n_e, then the wavelength of peak transmittance is given by

$$\lambda = \lambda_{\max} \sqrt{\{1 - \{n_m/n_e)^2 \sin^2 \phi\}}$$

2.2.1.6 Bandpass Fabry–Perot Filters

Typical Fabry–Perot filters (FPF) consist of two high-reflectance multilayers (see Bragg Filter) separated by a $\lambda/2$ space layer (Fig. 2.9). Multiple interferences cause the filter output spectral characteristic to peak sharply over a narrow band of wavelengths that are a multiple of the $\lambda/2$ spacer layer. Thus, a Fabry–Perot interference filter is used exclusively as a bandpass filter.

In DWDM, a bandpass should be as accurate as one part in 10,000 (1‰$_{000}$) in wavelength. Some FPFs, when compared with a simple grating for comparable spectral resolution and spatial resolution, produce throughput more than 100 times. If the medium within the F–P resonator is active, it is excited by an external stimulus (electric or photonic) and is stimulated; it then produces coherent photons (i.e., a laser device). However, because the Fabry–Perot resonator supports a multiplicity of (periodic) wavelengths, the F–P laser device does so as well.

2.2.1.7 Tunable Fabry–Perot Filters

Tunability of Fabry–Perot filters is accomplished in different ways:

- An F–P interferometer (FPI) achieves tunability manually, typically by using a micrometer to move the position of one of the two mirrors. Although this may be suitable in a laboratory arrangement, it is far from usable in an automated communications system.

- An automated FPI has replaced the manual micropositioner by a piezoelectric actuator to cause movement of the mirror.

- Another FPI type uses an entirely different approach. Instead of moving mirrors to change their separation distance, a dielectric such as a liquid crystal is sandwiched between the two (Fig. 2.10). The premise here is that if the dielectric constant is controllable, then the refractive index is controllable, the effective optical path d between the two mirrors is controllable, and hence controllable resonance is achieved. Indeed, if in this case an electric voltage is applied to the dielectric, the electric field affects the dielectric constant, and so on. Because the medium used

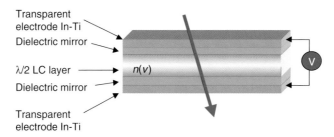

Transparent
electrode In-Ti

Dielectric mirror

$\lambda/2$ LC layer

Dielectric mirror

Transparent
electrode In-Ti

$n(v)$

V

Figure 2.10 Principles of the liquid-crystal tunable Fabry–Perot filter; the thickness of the L-C layer depends on the applied voltage.

in this is a liquid crystal, this is known as a liquid crystal FPI (LCFPI). However, the properties of liquid crystals are temperature-sensitive, and therefore accurate LCFPIs require stable temperature.

2.2.2 Dielectric Thin Film

Dielectric thin film (DTF) interference filters consist of alternate layers (50 to 200) of high refractive index (e.g., Ge, Si, Ta_2O_5) and low refractive index (e.g., GeF_3, SiO, SiO_2) in the wavelength range of interest films, each layer $\lambda/4$ thick. The selection of the actual material depends on several characteristics such as:

- absorption
- transmission loss
- durability
- adhesion
- stress
- thermal expansion
- material density
- stability
- evaporation behavior
- humidity
- solubility
- accuracy of thickness deposition (also depends on technique)
- abrasion
- threshold for laser-induced damage
- chemical interaction
- material compatibility
- others

Light reflected within the layers of high index does not shift its phase, whereas those within the low index shift by $180°$. Taking into account the travel difference (in multiples of $2 \times \lambda/4$), the successively reflections recombine constructively at the front face producing a highly reflected beam with wavelengths in a well-defined range (Fig. 2.11).

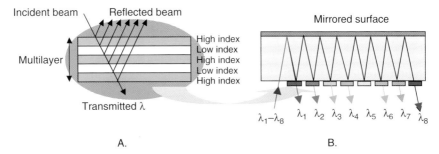

Figure 2.11 A dielectric interference filter is made with alternating layers of high/low refractive index, each l/4 thick, A. Using such filters at one side of a mirrored plate, a demultiplexer is built, B.

Outside this range the output wavelengths drop abruptly. Thus, such a stack comprises a highly reflective "mirror" for all wavelengths but one. At the other side, the transmitted beam contains only one wavelength.

In DWDM, a thin film would transmit only that wavelength (optical channel) the film was designed and would reflect all others in the DWDM signal.

The primary considerations in DTF design are:

- Low passband insertion loss (less than 0.3 dB). This is achieved with multilayer structures (~200 layers) that exceed 98% reflectance. However, as the number of layers increases, so does optical power loss due to scattering and absorption.
- Low selected band loss (less than 1 dB).
- Good channel spacing (better than 10 nm). This requires multilayer structures consisting of several hundred layers, currently a technological limitation. DWDM applications with 50 GHz channel separation (80 channels in C-band) are currently challenging thin-film technology.
- Low interchannel cross talk (better than −28 dB).

The stack of thin films is made using one of three methods: plasma-assisted deposition (PAD), ion beam sputtering (IBS), and ion beam–assisted deposition (IBAD). The common goal in any method is to deposit molecules of the material to construct a layer of highly controlled thickness without voids that might entrap water or other contaminants.

Thin films exhibit a very low temperature coefficient (~0.002 nm/°C), long stability, and minimal losses due to chromatic dispersion and polarization-related dispersion. Thin film packaged components are three-port devices, one input port and two output ports. The assembly usually contains three pigtail fibers, a focusing device (microlens, grated index lens), the thin film, and an adhesive.

The wavelength range at the output of the $\lambda/4$ stack depends on the ratio high to low refractive index. Thus, a DTF can be used as a high-pass filter, a low-pass filter, or a high-reflectance layer.

2.2.3 Diffraction Gratings

In Chapter 1 we described the physics of diffraction. Diffraction is used in a type of filter known as a *diffraction grating*. A diffraction grating is a passive optical device that diffracts incident parallel light in specific directions according to the angle of incidence on the grating, the optical wavelength of the incident light, and the design characteristics of the grating, *line spacing* a, and *blaze angle* Θ_B (Fig. 2.12). The number of strips per unit length is also known as *grating constant*.

The blaze angle, Θ_B, and the line spacing are connected with the wavelength λ, as

$$\Theta_B = \sin^{-1}(\lambda/2a)$$

In a simple implementation, a glass substrate with adjacent epoxy strips is blazed to form a (planar) *diffraction grating*.

There are two fundamental planar grating types, the *reflection* grating (Fig. 2.11) and the *pass-through* grating (Fig. 2.13).

In one implementation, a pass-through grating may be constructed using a transparent plate and in another, a liquid crystal sandwich. In nematic liquid crystals, molecules are arranged in an orientation and distance that depends on the applied voltage. Hence, the blaze angle of the sawtooth formation of the nematic liquid crystal is controllable (tunable) as the external voltage varies (Fig. 2.14).

A diffraction grating works as follows: incident rays are reflected by each groove. The reflected rays have a path difference that represents a delay or a phase difference, equal to $m\lambda$, where m is an integer and λ is the wavelength. These reflected rays

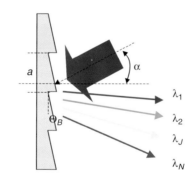

Figure 2.12   A diffraction grating.

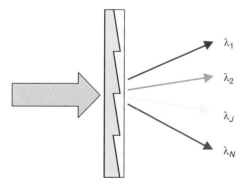

Figure 2.13   A pass-through grating diffracts each wavelength in different angle.

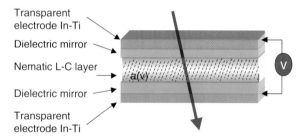

Transparent
electrode In-Ti

Dielectric mirror

Nematic L-C layer

a(v)

Dielectric mirror

Transparent
electrode In-Ti

V

Figure 2.14   Principles of the nematic liquid-crystal tunable Bragg grating filter; the grating constant depends on the applied voltage.

recombine and, depending on distance, geometry of grooves, and angle of incidence, constructive or destructive interference takes place according to the delay of each reflected ray by adjacent strips and its wavelength, and thus each wavelength component is diffracted at different angles, according to

$$d(\sin\alpha + \sin\beta) = m\lambda$$

where α is the angle of incidence, β is the angle of diffraction, and m is the diffraction order (or spectral order) that takes integer values $0, \pm 1, \pm 2, \ldots$. Simply stated, when a polychromatic light beam impinges on a diffraction grating, each wavelength component is diffracted at selected angles. According to the grating relationship $d(\sin\alpha + \sin\beta) = m\lambda$ and for different m values, a wavelength may be diffracted to more than one direction, positive or negative; the diffraction order m may be zero, positive or negative.

When $m = 0$, the diffraction grating acts like a mirror to the incident beam; that is, wavelengths are not separated. This is known as *zero-order diffraction* or *specular reflection*, and the grating acts like a mirror. This condition is known as *in Littrow*. Under this condition, $\alpha = \beta$, when the incident light beam is reflected back, the sinusoidal grating relationship is simplified to

$$2d \sin\alpha = m\lambda$$

The nonzero values of m define the diffracted angular direction of wavelengths. By definition, positive direction is the direction for which m has positive values, $\beta > -\alpha$, and with respect to the normal axis to the grating plane, the wavelengths are reflected at the same side of the normal (Fig. 2.15). Similarly, negative direction is the direction for which m has negative values, $\beta < -\alpha$, and with respect to the normal axis to the grating the wavelengths are reflected at the other side of the normal axis.

Gratings diffract a wavelength in both positive and negative orders, for which

$$-2d < m\lambda < 2d$$

When $\lambda/d \ll 1$, a large number of diffracted orders exist. Typically, few orders are desirable, and thus the grating spacing should be comparable to wavelength. For realizable gratings the empirical relationship is useful

$$|m\lambda/d| < 2$$

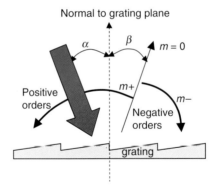

Figure 2.15 Definition of positive and negative diffraction modes.

The latter relationship, which is based on wavelength and grating spacing, limits the number of values or *orders* of the integer m.

Note that, in the grating relationship $d(\sin \alpha + \sin \beta) = m\lambda$ the parameter d is a constant. Thus, for a fixed angle of incidence α the grating relationship is satisfied by several wavelengths. In fact, two or more wavelengths can be diffracted in the same direction, each satisfying the grating relationship for a different value of m. This is an undesirable case of wavelength overlapping. However, it should also be noticed that in practice the angles α and β are smaller than $90°$. That is, $\sin \alpha < 1$ and $\sin \beta < 1$, hence $\sin \alpha + \sin \beta = <2$, and thus the grating relationship is valid only for those values of m for which $|m\lambda/d| < 2$.

The *angular dispersion*, D, between wavelengths for a given order m is obtained from the diffraction equation by differentiating β for λ. Doing so, it is obtained

$$D = d\beta/d\lambda = m/(d \cos \beta)$$

That is, the angular dispersion increases as d decreases.

Similarly, the *linear dispersion* of the grating provides an indication of how far apart in space two wavelengths are in the focal plane, that is:

$$D = dx/d\lambda$$

The inverse of this relationship, which is known as *spectral resolution*, R, indicates how many wavelengths per unit of distance in the focal plane are

$$R = d\lambda/dx$$

The *absolute efficiency* of a grating is defined as the energy flow (or power) of the diffracted monochromatic light of order m relative to the energy flow of the incident light. The efficiency of gratings depends on the:

- type of grating (reflective or transmission)
- grating material
- density of grooves

- uniform periodicity of grooves
- parallelity of grooves
- geometry of grooves
- type of coating of grooves
- reflection efficiency of grating
- conductivity of groove surface
- flatness of grating (unless concave gratings are examined)
- angle of incidence
- apodization
- spectral content of the beam
- order m for which efficiency is measured
- polarization of light

Clearly, the most desirable gratings are those with the highest efficiency. Consequently, grating efficiency per diffracted wavelength, bandpass, and wavelength resolution are the measurable quantities. Measurements of these quantities produce efficiency curves from the wavelength at which the maximum efficiency occurs.

Thus, having selected the most suitable grating for the application and knowing the wavelengths, the angle of incidence, and the specifications of the grating, then, the angle of diffraction for each wavelength is calculated and at the focal points receiving fibers are placed, a fiber for each wavelength (Fig. 2.16). Focusing the diffracted wavelengths may be achieved with a lens system or with a diffraction grating in a concave form.

Gratings are used in a variety of applications, such as:

- optical multiplexers/demultiplexers
- optical cross-connects (in conjunction with beam deflectors)
- optical channel add-drop
- filters
    narrow bandpass
    band rejection (including ASE noise suppression)
- dispersion compensation
- pulse reshaping (including pulse broadening compensation)

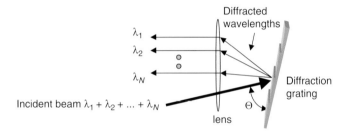

Figure 2.16   Operation of a diffraction gratings.

- optical taps
- short-wavelength sensor gratings
- mode and polarization converters
- distributed feedback laser wavelength stabilizers
- monochromators, spectrographs, and sensors

Typically, diffraction gratings are made by etching single silicon crystals (known as *ruled gratings*) or using holographic techniques (known as *holographic gratings*). In the first case, a master grating is replicated by a precision-ruling apparatus; in the second case, a holographic interference pattern is projected onto a photoresist plate, which is developed to produce the holographic grating. The first case produces gratings with excellent reflectivity and as accurate (or inaccurate) as the apparatus used. The second case produces more accurate gratings, but they have an inherent lower reflectivity and higher insertion loss.

2.2.4 Bragg Gratings

The *Bragg grating* is an arrangement of many parallel weakly reflecting plates, in contrast to the Fabry–Perot resonator, which has only two highly reflecting plates.

2.2.4.1 The Bragg Resonator

To examine how this arrangement functions, consider the following (Fig. 2.17):

- Let N plane parallel weak reflectors be separated by d (known as *Bragg spacing*).
- Let there be a medium with intensity attenuation coefficient α_s and gain g between the plates.
- Let R be the *power reflected coefficient*, such that $R \ll 1$, and T the *power transmitted coefficient*, such that $T \sim 1$.
- Let the propagation constant be β.
- Let a pulse of photons $E(t, x)$ enter through mirror 1, $E(t = 0, x = 0)$

The key question in this arrangement is *what is the condition for strong reflection?*

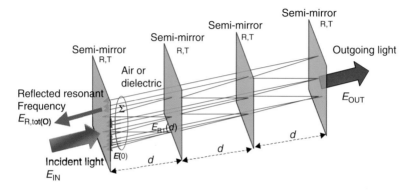

Figure 2.17 Principles of the Bragg grating.

Then

$$E(t, x) = A \exp\{g - \alpha_s x/2\} \exp[j(\omega t - \beta x)]$$

where ω is the light frequency.

Let the first light pulse at the first mirror be E_{IN}.

The reflected part of E_{IN} by the first semi-mirror is $E_{R1}(0) = E_{IN}(0)R$ and the transmitted part is $E_{T1}(0) = E_{IN}(0)T$.

The transmitted portion $E_{T1}(0)$ is again partially reflected

$$E_{R2}(d) = E_{T1}(0)R\, e^{-j\beta d}$$

and partially transmitted

$$E_{T2}(d) = E_{T1}(0)T\, e^{-j\beta d}$$

by the second mirror, and so on.

The reflected part at the Nth mirror is:

$$E_{RN}[(N - 1)d] = E_{T(N-1)}[(N - 2)d]R\, e^{-j\beta d}$$

and the transmitted part is:

$$E_{TN}[(N - 1)d] = E_{T(N-1)}[(N - 2)d]T\, e^{-j\beta d}$$

Thus, many reflected parts by all other mirrors will arrive at the first mirror. Taking into account the propagation constant, each part is expressed by the general relationship

$$E_{RN}[(N)d] = E_{T(N-1)}[(N - 1)d]R^{N-1}\, e^{(N-1)j\beta d}$$

The sum of all reflected components at the first mirror yields a geometric series from which it is obtained

$$E_{R,\mathrm{tot}}(0) = E_{IN}(0)R(1 - M^N)/(1 - M)$$

where

$$M = T^2\, e^{-2j\beta d}$$

That is, if N is sufficiently large, then the total reflected energy at the first mirror approximates the incident energy, even if the reflectivity R is small; this is in contrast to the Fabry–Perot resonant cavity, which requires strong reflectivity.

In the previous relationship, the phase angle of waves at each mirror was arbitrary. However, if the phase angle were a multiple of 2π, then a condition for strong reflection would be obtained. That is,

$$\arg(M) = 2\arg T - 2\beta d = 2\arg T - 2(2\pi/\lambda)d = m2\pi$$

where m is the order of the Bragg grating.

For simplicity, when the phase is equal to zero, or setting $\arg(\cdot) = 0$, then $-(2\pi/\lambda)d = n\pi$, from which the *condition for strong reflection*, also known as the

Bragg condition, is obtained (the negative sign denotes reflection):

$$d = -m\lambda_B/2$$

That is, the Bragg spacing (or grating period) should be an integer multiple of the half wavelength. When $m = 1$ (first order), $d = \lambda/2$, and when $m = 2$ (second order), $d = \lambda$.

In summary, a Bragg resonator functions as a wavelength-selective reflector or a reflecting filter. In this resonator, we may think of the first Bragg cavity as a Fabry–Perot resonator with weak reflectivity; the second cavity increases the reflectivity, the third increases it further, and so on. Thus, although each cavity has a weak reflectivity, the aggregate effect yields a highly reflective resonant cavity structure with very sharp spectral slopes, and although many wavelengths may enter the Bragg resonator, only the wavelength that satisfies the aforementioned condition is reflected back.

Bragg gratings are employed in distributed feedback (DFB) lasers. According to DFB, Bragg gratings are monolithically integrated to act as both reflectors and filters that support only the lasing mode the grating is designed for, and thus, among other factors, they also determine the frequency and threshold gain of the laser.

2.2.4.2 Fiber Bragg Gratings

The Bragg resonator consists of many parallel weak reflectors, or a periodic variation in reflectivity. One may also think of it in terms of propagation constant variation, or better in terms of refractive index variation.

A *fiber Bragg grating* (FBG) consists of a fiber segment whose index of refraction varies periodically along its core length. This periodic variation is formed by exposing the germano-silicate core of the fiber to an intense ultraviolet (UV) optical interference pattern that has a periodicity equal to the periodicity of the grating to be formed. Altering the refractive index by exposure to intense light is a property of germanium-doped silicate known as photosensitivity. Thus, when the fiber is exposed to an intense UV periodic uniform pattern, structural periodic defects are formed and thus a permanent variation of the refractive index with the periodicity intended for. The periodic variation of the grating may be made using a mask or producing an interference pattern. In either case, the grating pattern has a periodicity that depends on the wavelength band the FBG is designed to operate. For near-infrared wavelengths of about 1.55 μm, the grating is made with a periodicity d of 1 to 10 μm. Figure 2.18 illustrates a fiber Bragg grating using the UV method and also a monolithically made FBG with a corrugated $In_xGa_{1-x}As_yP_{1-y}$ over an InP substrate. Another method uses ion (such as helium) beam implantation in the fiber core. Since the refractive index varies with the dose of ions, the target refractive index is easily achieved. Gratings with a periodicity of 500 μm have been produced with this method. Fiber Bragg gratings incorporated in line with the transmitting fiber are also called *in-fiber Bragg gratings*.

The grating reflectivity for a given mode at center wavelength is given by

$$R = \tan h^2[\pi L \cdot \Delta n \cdot \eta(V)/\lambda_b]$$

where L is the length of the grating, Δn is the magnitude of index perturbation, and $\eta(V)$ is a function of the fiber parameter V, which represents the fraction of the integrated mode intensity contained in the core.

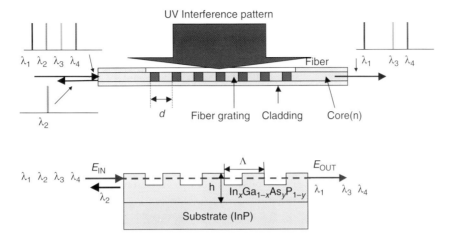

Figure 2.18 A fiber Bragg grating is made by exposing the core with a UV pattern and a monolithic one is made with corrugated InGaAsP over InP substrate.

This grating assumes a single-mode polarization-maintaining fiber with a circular core. However, when the core is (imperfectly) elliptical, the grating supports two propagation modes, with each polarization axis having different propagation constant.

The UV pattern is formed with one of several optical methods (diffraction or interferometric) that generate an interference pattern of alternating minima and maxima of light intensity. Regardless of method used, the interference pattern must be of high quality with uniform periodicity, high contrast, and sharp edges.

The UV source is provided by an excimer laser that operates at a wavelength in the range from 157 nm to 351 nm. The peak absorption of germanosilicate is at 240 nm, and thus this wavelength is the most efficient. Excimer lasers may produce hundreds of millijoules in a 10 to 40 nsec pulse and can create a grating pattern in fiber in a single high-energy shot, as the fiber is drawn. Continuous wave (cw) laser sources at 1-watt output may also be used.

The average UV power is typically 20 to 40 mW with a pulse repetition rate of 50 Hz. About half of this power is incident on the fiber with flux levels of 1 to 2 w/cm^2. At this flux level, the exposure is several minutes. A two-beam interferometer (each beam focused on the fiber at an angle θ where the interferogram on the fiber will be generated) generates an interference pattern on the side of a 10-mm section of a stripped fiber (i.e., a fiber whose plastic coating has been removed). Gratings 5 to 10 mm long with reflectivity of 76% and bandwidth of 20 GHz have been achieved.

Applying periodic pressure along the fiber may also form a FBG. Pressure also alters the structure of the fiber and the refractive index, thus creating a FBG. However, excessive pressure of sharp edges may also create microcracks that weaken the tensile strength of fiber.

Fiber Bragg gratings have many uses. A fiber Bragg grating placed at the output of a circulator reflects back only the wavelength it is designed for, thus constructing a bandstop filter. Placed at the output of a laser, it reflects back a portion of the power, which is monitored by a light-emitting diode (LED). When the laser ceases to function, the LED detects it and sends a message to the system controller. Other applications include the WDM narrow bandpass filter, band rejection filter, optical fiber amplifier spontaneous emission noise suppression filter, add-drop filter, optical tap, wavelength sensor, mode and polarization converter, and more.

A similar Bragg grating reflector is based on a stacked dielectric structure composed of quarter-wavelength thick layers, known as *photonic lattice*, each with a different refractive index. Photonic lattice reflectors have been found to reflect wavelengths selectively over all possible angles of incidence, and they do not absorb any of the incident energy, as mirror-based reflectors do.

2.2.4.3 Chirped Fiber Bragg Gratings
Fiber Bragg gratings with a variable pitch, which are known as chirped FBGs, are used both as filters and to compensate for chromatic dispersion (Fig. 2.19). In the latter case, because of the varying pitch (or chirp), different wavelengths within a channel are reflected back at different depths of the grating, thus compensating for the travel time variation of the wavelengths or for chromatic dispersion. Thus, chirped FBGs perform *chromatic compression* on a chromatically dispersed pulse.

2.2.4.4 Tunable Bragg Gratings
The wavelength at which the reflection is maximal is given by the Bragg condition

$$\lambda_B = 2d/n$$

To make the Bragg grating tunable (i.e., to control the reflected wavelength), the Bragg spacing (grating period) must be controllable. This is achieved by one of several methods. For example, application of a stretching force elongates the fiber and thus changes its period (*mechanical tuning*). Application of heat elongates the fiber and thus changes its period (*thermal tuning*).

FBGs may be used to compensate for fiber dispersion, gain flattening of erbium-doped fiber amplifiers, and in add-drop multiplexers or demultiplexers.

However, since a FBG depends on the quality of the fiber, the fiber should be free of macroscopic imperfections as well as of microscopic variations of the refractive index.

Some of the characteristics of tunable fiber gratings and desirable ranges are:

- Tuning range (ps/nm); wide range ($100 \times$ ps/nm)
- Tuning granularity (ps/nm); small increments (few ps/nm)
- Compensation responsiveness (sec); less than 1 sec per channel

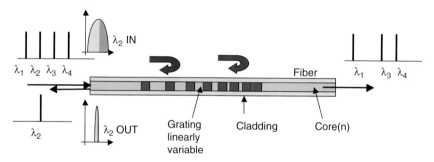

Figure 2.19 A fiber Bragg chirped grating reflects dispersed wavelengths of a channel at different depths, thus restoring the spectral width.

- Optical bandwidth (nm); wide range (several nm around λ_o)
- Insertion loss (dB); very small (<1 dB per channel)
- Group delay ripple (ps); small (few ps)
- Polarization mode dispersion (ps); very small ($\ll 1$ ps per channel)
- Polarization-dependent loss (dB); very small ($\ll 1$ ps per channel)

2.2.4.5 *Dependence of Gratings on Temperature*

A diffraction grating consists of matter, the optical parameters of which are affected by heat. As the grating is heated, matter expands, the grating constant (number of lines per unit length) changes, as do its diffraction specifications. In this example, we consider the reflected type grating (the transmitted and the blazed fiber type may equally be considered) as well as the fiber Bragg grating; for clarity we repeat some of the relationships already provided.

The blaze or Bragg angle Θ_B, the wavelength λ, and the line spacing a are related by

$$\Theta_B = 1/\sin(\lambda/2a)$$

The diffraction angle β is related to the incident angle α and the wavelength by

$$\sin\beta = \sin\alpha \pm (\lambda/n_0 a)$$

where $a = 2\pi/K$, K is the grating wave number.

For a fixed incident angle α, the variation of λ, $\Delta\lambda$, with respect to the Bragg angle is

$$\beta = \Theta_B + \Delta\lambda/(n_0 a \cos\Theta_B)$$

As the Bragg grating temperature changes as a result of the variation of the grating constant, a stationary observer sees a wavelength shift by $\Delta\lambda_o$ from the original wavelength λ_o. This change is given by

$$\Delta\lambda_o = \zeta\Delta T\lambda_o$$

where ζ is the thermal expansion coefficient for the grating material (for silica it is 0.55×10^{-6}). In the case of a fiber Bragg grating, this is modified as

$$\Delta\lambda_o/\lambda_o = (\zeta + \xi)\Delta T$$

where ξ is the thermo-optic coefficient ($\sim 8.3 \times 10^{-6}$ for germanium-doped silica core) of the fiber Bragg grating.

The effect of the thermal expansion on the Bragg spacing is

$$\Delta a = \zeta\Delta T$$

Thus, for a fixed λ, λ_{FIXED}, and for a fixed incident angle α, the variation of β, $\Delta\beta$, with respect to the Bragg spacing a is:

$$\sin\beta = \sin\alpha \pm (\lambda/n_0 a)$$

Applying perturbation theory:

$$\Delta\beta/\Delta T \cos\beta = \pm\Delta/(\lambda/n_0 a)\Delta T$$

or

$$\Delta\beta/\Delta T \cos\beta = \pm(\lambda/n_0)\Delta a/\Delta T$$

where the term a is constant and thus is eliminated.

For very small angles of diffraction β, this is simplified to

$$\Delta\beta/\Delta T = \pm\zeta\lambda/n_0$$

That is, the spatial distribution of wavelengths (or the angle of diffraction) depends on the Bragg grating temperature expansion coefficient.

2.2.4.6 Specifying a Grating

Gratings are important optical components in DWDM communications systems. There are certain parameters that characterize the Bragg gratings. However, a single grating does not fit all applications. Thus, the challenge of the system designer is to specify the grating spectral characteristics that best meet the specified performance of the system. Inversely, the challenge of the component manufacturer is to calculate the grating design parameters that best meet the specified grating spectral characteristics.

- *Lines/mm*: Gratings are characterized by the groove density that defines the spectral dispersion. In general, the greater the line or groove density, the better the optical resolution of the grating but the more truncated the spectral range.
- *Spectral range*: It is the wavelength dispersion of the grating across the linear array; it is also expressed as the "size" of the spectra on the array. When selecting gratings, one must choose a wavelength range with a width equal to the Spectral Range entry in the Spectrometer Grating Selection Chart. The spectral range (spectral response) is what is "seen" by the detector. The observed range scales inversely with the groove density (i.e., 600–650 nm for a 600 lines/mm grating, 300–325 nm for a 1,200 lines/mm grating, and so on). When one specifies a spectral range, the wavelength range should be equal to the spectral range of the grating for the highest grating efficiency. Although certain gratings have a wide spectral range, they diffract efficiently only a narrower band within it. This narrower band in which efficiency is greater than 30% is known as the "best" or "most efficient" region in the range.
- *Efficiency*: All ruled or holographically etched gratings are designed for optimum first-order spectra at a certain wavelength region. An efficiency of 30% or better is expected over the specified range. Intensity drops drastically beyond the optimum range.
- *Blaze wavelength*: This is the peak wavelength in the typical efficiency curve, which is the most efficient wavelength region of the grating.

2.2.5 Mach–Zehnder Interferometry

Consider that a coherent light source containing several wavelengths is split into two or more beams, each with the same wavelength content. Also, that the phase in each beam is altered in a controllable manner. Then, all beams are recombined to interfere. Then, because of interference, the minima and maxima for each wavelength, corresponding to destructive and constructive interference, respectively, differ, and the min-max spatial locations for each wavelength can be calculated from the wavelength, phase difference, and index of refraction. Thus, a mix of wavelengths in an optical beam is separated to its component wavelengths. This method is known as Mach–Zehnder interferometer (MZI), based on which the Mach–Zehnder filters (MZF or MZ) are made.

The attractiveness of Mach–Zehnder filters is that they can separate (or filter out) many wavelengths simultaneously and can be monolithically integrated with other components on substrates such as silica. The latter is accomplished by combining flame hydrolysis deposition and conventional photolithography followed by ion etching.

2.2.5.1 Mach–Zehnder Filters

In fiber-optic systems, a phase difference between two optical paths may be artificially constructed to take advantage of Mach–Zehnder interferometry. For simplicity, consider an input fiber with two wavelengths, λ_1 and λ_2. The optical power of both wavelengths is equally split and each half is coupled into two waveguides of unequal length, with a length difference ΔL (Fig. 2.20). Since each half travels a different distance, the two halves arrive at an interference recombiner with a phase difference

$$\Delta\Phi = 2\pi f(\Delta L)n/c$$

where n is the refractive index of the waveguide.

Then, based on the phase variation, each wavelength interferes constructively on two different specific points and interferes destructively elsewhere. At the two points where constructive interference takes place, two output fibers have been positioned. In this example, wavelength λ_1 interferes constructively on the first fiber and wavelength λ_2 interferes on the second fiber. More specifically, wavelength λ_1 contributes maximally at output fiber #1 if the phase difference at the recombiner satisfies the conditions and the position of the output fiber,

$$\Delta\Phi_1 = (2m - 1)\pi$$

Similarly, wavelength, λ_2, contributes maximally at output fiber #2 if the phase difference satisfies the condition

$$\Delta\Phi_2 = 2m\pi$$

where m is a positive integer.

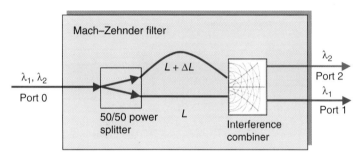

Figure 2.20 Principles of a Mach–Zehnder filter.

Then

$$2\pi f_1 \Delta Ln/c = (2m - 1)\pi$$

and

$$2\pi f_2 \Delta Ln/c = 2m\pi$$

Since these relationships are satisfied for a number of m values, the MZF supports a periodic passband. Then, from the last two relationships, the *optical channel spacing*, Δf, is derived as

$$\Delta f = c/[2n(\Delta L)]$$

2.2.5.2 Tunable Mach–Zehnder Filters

If the quantity ΔL can be controlled predictably, then the MZF can be tuned. Since the path difference ΔL introduces a phase shift at the recombiner or directional coupler #2, it is clear that by controlling the propagation delay of the path $L + \Delta L$ with respect to path L the phase shift is controlled. Thus, by controlling the refractive index of the path, wavelength selectability is accomplished, making the MZF a tunable *optical frequency discriminator* (OFD). Selectability is achieved by altering either the refractive index of the path (and thus the effective optical path) or its physical length (Fig. 2.21). For example,

- Mechanical compression, by means of a piezoelectric crystal, alters the physical length of the waveguide segment and its refractive index.
- Heat, by means of a thermoelectric thin film heater placed on the longer path, alters the refractive index of the waveguide segment and its refractive index. A polymer material known to change its refractive index when exposed to heat is perfluorocyclobutane (PFCB).
- Electric field, by applying an electric voltage, also alters the refractive index of certain optical materials, such as $LiNbO_3$.

2.2.6 Arrayed Waveguide Grating Filters

Arrayed waveguide gratings (AWGs) are based on the principle of Mach–Zehnder interferometry. AWGs belong to the category of phased-array gratings (PHASARS) and waveguide grating routers (WGR). Consider a fiber, F, carrying a multiplicity of

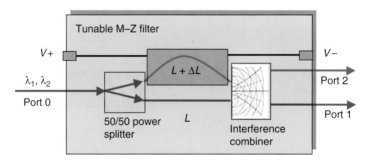

Figure 2.21 Principles of a thermo-tunable Mach–Zehnder filter.

wavelengths, $\lambda_1, \lambda_2, \ldots, \lambda_N$. Let the power of all wavelengths from F be split equally into N parts in cavity S_1, and each part be coupled in one of the waveguides in an array, $w_1, \ldots, w_N$. These waveguides are separated from each other by a distance d_1. These waveguides have a length difference ΔL among them. At the other end, all waveguides terminate at a combiner S_2. However, because of the optical path difference, each wavelength from each waveguide arrives in the cavity S_2 with a phase difference or a phase delay. According to the phase relationship among the same wavelengths from the N waveguides, each wavelength interferes constructively in a specified location in S_2 and interferes destructively elsewhere; this implies that the phase difference should be an integer multiple of 2π, and thus the location of constructive interference depends on the wavelength. Clearly, the constructive interference locations also depend on the geometry and propagation constants β_1 and β_2 of the materials of the splitter S_1 and the combiner S_2. Having placed fibers where each wavelength contributes maximally, each wavelength is coupled in separate output fibers (Fig. 2.22).

If the order of the AWG is N and the central frequency is f_0, then a free spectral range (FSR) is defined, given by

$$\text{FSR} = f_0/N$$

and the passband spectrum, $P(\lambda)$, is described by

$$P(\lambda) = |I(\lambda)|^2 = \left| \sum h_N \exp\{-i(2x/\lambda)nL_N\} \right|^2$$

where n is the refractive index, h_N is the normalized field amplitude at the Nth waveguide of optical path length L_N; the sum is over all N waveguides.

AWGs are typically made using a process known as *flame hydrolysis deposition* (FHD). Using FHD, silica-glass layers are deposited onto planar silicon or quartz substrate. Deposition of silica onto quartz or silica onto silicon provides a reliable composition. Then, waveguide layers are etched into circuit patterns and they are isolated between them by embedding a glass-cladding layer. Thus, AWGs are monolithic compact devices. SiO$_2$ AWGs for 128 channels (wavelengths) with 25 GHz channel spacing have been reported as well as InP AWGs for 64 channels with 50 GHz channel spacing.

In addition to this, polymers have also been used to construct low-cost and acceptable performance AWGs. However, polymers have a thermo-optic coefficient 10 times that of silica and have a thermal expansion coefficient of 80 ppm/$^\circ$K. This means that

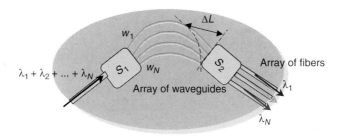

Figure 2.22   Principles of an arrayed waveguide grating.

polymer AWGs are very sensitive to temperature and thus cannot be used reliably. However, some experiments have demonstrated that if polymers with matching positive and negative coefficients are used, then athermal devices comparable to silica may be made.

The salient characteristics of AWGs are:

- AWGs are polarization-dependent, but means to overcome this dependency have been reported.
- Insertion loss is low, less than 0.1 dB/cm (and <0.2 dB/connection)
- Typical AWGs have a Gaussian transfer function and very low side lobes
- Low cross talk due to random optical phase errors in the arrayed waveguides. Typical cross talk is better than −35 dB.
- AWGs exhibit good flat spectral response over many optical channels (some over 400 channels with 25 nm spacing in the $C + L$ ranges. Flat spectral response eases wavelength control.
- AWGs are suitable for integration with photodetectors.
- AWGs are temperature-sensitive. To eliminate thermal drift, thermoelectric coolers have been used. In addition, athermal AWGs have been made using SiO_2 AWGs that use silicon adhesives with a negative thermal coefficient; 32-channel athermal AWGs have demonstrated temperature insensitivity over the range 0 to 60 °C, thus making them suitable in low-cost Metro applications.
- AWGs operate in a wide temperature range, reportedly from 0° to 85 °C.

2.2.7 Polarizing Filters

Polarizing filters are based on the birefringence properties of crystals and stretched films. In general, when light travels through a polarizing film, only that polarization component (vector) that is in the direction of polarization with the film passes through (Fig. 2.23). Similarly, birefringent crystals split the incoming optical power into two parts and with orthogonal polarization states (see Chapter 1).

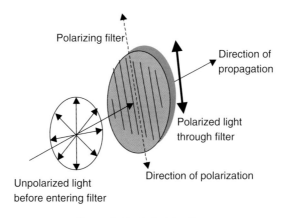

Figure 2.23 Polarizing filter.

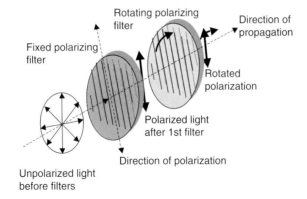

Figure 2.24 An assembly of a fixed and a rotating polarizing filter to rotate the polarization direction.

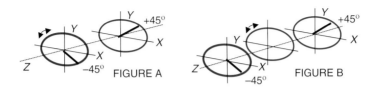

Figure 2.25 Birefringent plates construct fixed optical filters, A, or tunable filters, B.

The properties of birefringent crystals and films may be employed in both fixed or tunable optical filters. Consider two quarter-wave birefringent disks positioned in parallel such that the first disk has its fast axis at $+45°$ and the second disk at $-45°$. Based on this, the retardation to a monochromatic beam propagating in the z-axis is summed up to zero because one disk accelerates as much as the other disk decelerates. If one of the two disks is rotated by an angle $45° + \rho$, then an acceleration or deceleration proportional to the angle ρ is introduced and a phase controlling mechanism is constructed (Fig. 2.24).

However, in this two-disk structure, as one of the two disks rotates, it also rotates the polarization of the beam. This is rectified by placing a rotating disk between the two $45°$ fixed disks. This arrangement constructs a single tuning stage (Fig. 2.25). Now, if the beam, prior to entering the first disk, is split by a birefringent crystal in two rays (the ordinary and extraordinary), then, one ray can be controlled differently than the other and a tunable filter is constructed as they recombine at the output. This type of filter can be constructed to include more levels of tuning stages.

2.2.8 Absorption Filters

Absorption filters allow a specific narrow spectral band to pass through while they heavily absorb the others bands, thus exhibiting sharp rejection edges (i.e., high absorption) at the boundaries of the passband (Fig. 2.26). *Absorption filters* depend heavily on material properties (e.g., germanium) and thus there is little flexibility in modifying the absorption characteristics of this filter. However, a filter with both sharp rejection edges and interference filter flexibility can be constructed when absorption materials are used in combination with interference filters (DTF, Fabry–Perot).

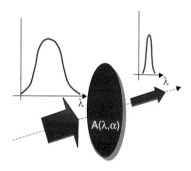

Figure 2.26 Absorption filter.

2.2.9 Acousto-Optic Tunable Filters

Acousto-optic tunable optical filters (AOTF) are based on the Bragg principle, according to which only those wavelengths that comply with the Bragg condition pass through it. Periodic fluctuation of the refractive index is achieved by applying a radio frequency (RF) signal to an optically transparent waveguide. The applied frequency disturbs the molecular structure of the waveguide and causes a disturbance in the distribution of strain, and hence birefringence, throughout the material. If the dimensions of the material and the applied RF are properly selected, then a standing wave is created and thus a periodic fluctuation in the index of refraction. As the optical frequency passes through the material (and in the same direction as the fluctuation), the optical frequency that is in phase with the fluctuating refractive index interact. As a result, the Bragg effect takes place and the polarization state of the optical wavelength that complies with the Bragg condition is rotated from TE to TM.

An acousto-optic tunable filter consists of an acousto-optic TE-to-TM converter [a surface acoustic wave (SAW) device on which the acoustic signal is applied], two crossed polarizers, and two optical waveguides that are in very close proximity so that light is coupled from one waveguide to the other (Fig. 2.27).

The selected λ is related to the applied acoustic frequency f_a (in MHz) by

$$\lambda = (\Delta n) V_a / f_a$$

where Δn is the medium birefringence ($n_{TE} - n_{TM}$) for the selected λ, and V_a is the acoustic velocity in the waveguide medium.

Similarly, the optical wavelength, λ, and the wavelength of the acoustic wave, Λ, are interrelated by

$$\lambda = \Lambda (\Delta n)$$

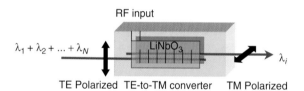

Figure 2.27 A conceptual acousto-optic tunable filter.

The required applied acoustic power P_a for 100% polarization rotation of the selected λ is approximated to

$$P_a = (\lambda^2 A)/(2L^2 M_2) \text{ (mW)}$$

where A is the acoustic transducer cross-sectional area, L is the transducer width (or interaction length), and M_2 is the acoustic figure of merit of the medium determined by the parameters of the crystal (refractive indices in both *TE* and *TM*, elasto-optic constant p, acoustic speed V_a, and crystal density ρ),

$$M = [(n_{TE} n_{TM})^3 p^2]/(\rho V_a^3)$$

Typically, P_a is expressed in 100s of milliwatts.

When the acoustic wave is considered to be a Raleigh wave, by a good approximation, the acoustic energy is confined in a waveguide that is formed at the surface of the crystal and about one acoustic wavelength deep, Λ. This is important in determining the thickness of the crystal and the optical coupling in the device. Thus, for a waveguide width W, the cross-sectional area is

$$A = W\Lambda \ (\mu m^2)$$

The filter passband $\Delta\lambda$, which determines the number of optical channels through the filter, is approximated by

$$\Delta\lambda = (0.8\lambda^2)/(L\Delta n) \ (\mu m)$$

and the full-width half-maximum (FWHM) is approximated by

$$\Delta\lambda = (0.8\lambda\Lambda/L) \ (\mu m)$$

This relationship is true for a single-stage acousto-optic device. However, single-stage devices have certain drawbacks, such as for example TE-to-TM and TM-to-TE conversions and frequency shifting for each conversion. These drawbacks are alleviated with more complex devices, such as a double-stage device which is a TE–TM–TE converter. In this case, the latter relationship is adjusted (according to a mathematical analysis that is beyond our scope) to

$$\Delta\lambda = (0.6\Lambda\lambda/L) \ (\mu m)$$

Finally, since for an acoustic wave to propagate through the crystal it takes time to set up the Bragg grating, the access time τ is estimated by

$$\tau = L/V_a \ (\mu s)$$

The TE-to-TM converter of an AOTF filter is constructed with Ti:LiNbO$_3$, on which the remaining components may also be integrated to produce a single compact component.

AOTFs are distinguished as *collinear* and *noncollinear*. Collinear AOTFs are those in which the optical signal propagates and interacts collinearly with the acoustic wave. Otherwise, they are noncollinear.

Another AOTF type is *polarization-independent*. This device consists of a more complex acousto-optic structure that is able to select a wavelength regardless of its polarization state.

The salient characteristics of AOTF filters (typically of the collinear type) are:

- broad tuning range, from 1.2 to 1.6 μm
- narrow filter bandwidth, less than 1 nm
- fast tunability, about 10 μs
- acceptable insertion loss, less than 5 dB
- low cross talk, less than −20 dB
- one to many wavelengths selection
- possible wavelength broadcast
- easy wavelength registration and stabilization

AOTF filters are used as:

- Single-wavelength tunable receivers
- Multiwavelength tunable receivers
- Wavelength selective space-switch (demultiplexers)

A disadvantage of typical AOTFs is the misalignment of the polarization state of incoming light. Although the direction of the polarizer is known, the polarization state of incoming light is hard to maintain in a single-mode fiber and thus is hard to control. Polarization mismatch results in coupling loss.

Another disadvantage of typical AOTFs is a frequency shift of the light by an amount equal to the acoustical frequency due to Doppler effect. However, devices have been constructed that counterbalance the Doppler effect.

2.2.10 Hybrid Filters

Hybrid filters consist of a structure that combines different filter types and other optical components, such as, for example, a DTF and a grating, and other optical components. Hybrid filters take advantage of the grating filter's ability to separate closely spaced optical wavelengths and the ability of the DTF filter to separate widely spaced optical wavelengths.

2.2.11 Comparing Tunable Filters

Each tunable filter has its own performance characteristics. Therefore, depending on the application, the filter type that best matches the performance requirements should be used.

If a *large number of channels* (∼100 s) is required, then Fabry–Perot and acousto-optic filters are better suited, as compared with electro-optic and semiconductor filters that can process fewer channels (∼10 s).

If *fast tuning* (∼ ns) is required, then electro-optic and semiconductor filters are better suited, as opposed to acousto-optic devices (∼ μs) and Fabry–Perot filters (ms), although Fabry–Perot filters that employ liquid crystals, known as liquid crystal FPI (LCFPI), may also tune quickly (in the ms range).

Mechanical tuning is slow (1–10 ms), but mechanical tuners have a wide tuning range (~500 nm), as compared with acousto-optic tuners (tuning range of about 250 nm) and electro-optic tuners (tuning range of about 16 nm).

If *low loss* is required, then semiconductor filters exhibit negligible loss, as compared with other types that exhibit a loss on the order of 3 to 5 dB.

Based on this, the selection of the filter type in communications depends on the application and service for which the system is designed. In applications with a large number of channels but relatively slow switching speeds (e.g., video broadcasting), the Fabry–Perot filter seems to be better suited. In applications with few but very fast switching times (circuit switch of a few channels), the electro-optic or semiconductor types are better suited. In addition, the tuning range and the cost of each type should be taken into account, particularly in systems that require many components or are cost-sensitive.

2.3 OPTICAL DIRECTIONAL COUPLERS

The main function of optical directional couplers is to transfer the maximum possible power from one input to another. For instance, optical power transfer may be from a light source into a fiber, from a fiber to a fiber, from a fiber to an optical device, or from an optical device to a fiber.

Single-mode waveguide directional couplers are based on the evanescence property of light guides by which when the light guides are in close proximity, on the order of the wavelength, optical power is transferred from one guide to the other. This is somewhat hard to visualize in classical mechanics; its justification lies in quantum mechanics. For example, an electron of velocity v is associated with a wavelength according to $E = h\nu = mv^2$, or $\lambda = (2\pi h/e)$ sqrt (r/m); where e is the electron charge, m is the electron mass, and r is the atomic radius. Substituting in the latter the values for m (10^{-27} gr), for e (4.8×10^{-10} CGSE or 1.6×10^{-19} Coulomb) and h ($6.6260755 \times 10^{-34}$ Joule-second), the wavelength is approximately six times the atomic radius r, or three times its diameter. In terms of quantum mechanics, this means that when the electron (although it is a charged particle) has a wavelength comparable to the dimensions of an atom, the motion of the electron in the atom is described purely by wave mechanics. Similarly, when light (a wave) propagates in a waveguide interacts and another waveguide is at a distance comparable to the wavelength (the evanescence region), it interacts with the second waveguide and its optical power is transferred from one waveguide to the other (this property of waves is also applicable in diffraction as well as in quantum-well lasers).

The amount of transferred optical power depends on the wavelength, λ; the separation distance between waveguides, d; the length of the evanescence region, L_0; the dielectric material in the evanescence region separating the light guides; and the presence or absence of a field (Fig. 2.28). When a voltage, Vs, is applied across the evanescence region, the propagation characteristics of the material between light guides changes and this, along with other parameters (which are fixed) determine how much optical power is guided through the same guide.

For example, if there is no field $V = 0$, then power is transferred through the evanescent separation region to the adjacent guide. If a field $V = Vs$, is applied,

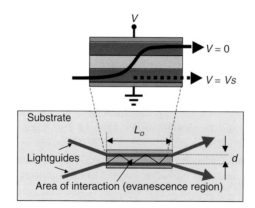

Figure 2.28 Solid-state optical directional couplers.

then the maximum optical power is transferred. Thus, if the voltage changes from 0 to Vs, a switching activity takes place. If the voltage changes between 0 and Vs, then intermediate quantities of optical power are transferred. In this case, the coupler behaves like an optical splitter.

For maximum power transfer from one light guide to another, end-faces are cut perpendicular to the longitudinal axis, they are highly polished, and they are coated with antireflective film to prevent reflections and optical feedback that may stimulate a laser effect. However, for maximum power transfer, certain conditions must exist:

- The two light guides are in close proximity, separated by a distance d comparable to the wavelength λ to be coupled. If the separation distance, d, between the two guides at the coupling length L_o increases, then optical coupling decreases and at some distance d there is no coupling at all.
- The two phase velocities are in perfect synchronization
- The refractive index of both light guides is the same. A mismatch between light guide refractive indexes results in power loss during power transfer.
- The interaction (or coupling) length, L_o, is precisely equal to a coupling length [which is proportional to $e^{(d/d0)}$].

Couplers are also characterized by a power loss, Γ. Power is lost as a result of:

- scattering and absorption by the bulk of the light guide material in the coupling length
- structure irregularities of the sidewalls
- epitaxial interface scattering at the interface with the substrate and at the edges (due to reflections and insertion loss)

Assuming two waveguides, a and b, the optical modes (in the direction z) $a(z)$ and $b(z)$ for each waveguide are obtained by solving Maxwell's wave equations. Then the optical coupling of the modes between the two waveguides is studied with a theory known as the coupled-mode theory (CMT), which involves a set of coupled differential equations of the interactive fields of the two waveguides and a coupling parameter k. The equations defining the coupled-mode amplitudes along the wave-guides are given by

$$d(a_z)/dz = i\beta_a a(z) + i k_{ab} b(z)$$

and

$$d(b_z)/dz = i\beta_b b(z) + i k_{ba} a(z)$$

where β is the propagating constant (in waveguide a and b) and k is a coupling constant (from a to b and from b to a). Note that for a single waveguide (without coupling, the k term vanishes and the two differential equations reduce to two independent equations).

The most desirable characteristics of optical couplers are:

- high isolation
- maximum power transfer and thus low coupling power loss, (in dB). A typical coupler power loss is about 3 dB at 1.5 μm.
- no signal reflectivity
- no signal absorption
- no through-phase shift
- no signal distortion over the entire wavelength range of interest
- no added dispersion effects
- no added polarization effects
- no added noise
- steady performance over a wide range of temperatures

An example of typical specifications is given in Table 2.1

Integrated couplers employ a variety of compounds, such as:

- GaAs doped (10^{15}) over a highly doped (10^{18}) GaAs substrate
- InP doped over a highly doped InP substrate
- GaAs over AlGaAs over a GaAs substrate

Table 2.1   Typical specifications of optical directional coupler

Center wavelengths (nm)	TBD (e.g., 1310, 1480, 1550)
Bandwidth (nm)	TBD
Maximum insertion loss (dB)	3.4
Coupling ratio	TBD
Coupling efficiency	TBD
Typical excess loss (dB)	0.1 max
PDL (dB)	0.1 max
Directivity (dB)	−55 max
Cross talk (dB)	TBD
Temperature coefficient (dB/°C)	0.002
Operating temperature (°C)	−40 to +85
Storage temperature (°C)	−40 to +85
Fiber length (m)	1

- InGaAsP over a InP substrate
- Ti-diffused over a lithium niobate ($LiNbO_3$) substrate, also abbreviated $Ti:LiNbO_3$

Among them, $Ti:LiNbO_3$ has the least loss, requires a relatively low voltage, and responds quickly. Thus, these devices are also suitable in photonic switching, whereas InP and GaAs are better suited to monolithic optoelectronic integration with laser sources and detectors.

Based on the operation of couplers, if the isolation between the two guides over the length L_o is controlled, then devices with different functionality, in addition to switching and splitting, may be constructed. In this venue, directional couplers may become programmable power attenuators, or they may become isolators with a measure of goodness based on the amount of power coupled in the desired direction with respect to the undesired (in dB). Finally, when the amount of transferred power can be controlled at high speed, they may become fast optical modulators.

2.4 OPTICAL POWER ATTENUATORS

Optical power attenuation is an impediment in optical transmission. Despite this, components with controlled attenuation, known as optical power attenuators, play an important role in the design of optical communication systems. The main function of optical power attenuators is to adjust the optical power of selected DWDM channels (wavelengths) at the input and/or output of optical amplifiers so that the power differential among all DWDM channels is minimal and the dynamic range of the receiver is matched. They also aid testing of optical system performance under varying optical power conditions.

Optical attenuators may be fixed or variable; variability is achieved either mechanically or electrically.

The desired characteristics of variable attenuators are:

- small size
- polarization insensitivity
- dynamic power attenuation range (1–40 dB)
- wide operating wavelength range (1200–1600 nm)
- resolution (0.1–0.2 dB)
- low optical return loss (>50 dB)
- repeatability
- stability
- wide operating temperature (0–65 °C)
- low cost

In addition to parameters common to all components in Section 3.1.2, key parameters specific to attenuators are:

- insertion loss tolerance
- attenuation range (specific to variable attenuators)

- incremental attenuation (specific to variable attenuators), and
- polarization shift

2.5   POLARIZERS AND ROTATORS

Materials that allow one polarization state of light to propagate through them are called
polarizers. Such materials are in the form of plates or prisms; birefringent plates can
be also be used as polarizers.

Certain materials rotate the polarization state by an angle, according to the Faraday
effect, and they are called *rotators*. Rotators can be plates or can be made with fibers
doped with elements or compounds that have a large Verdet constant, such as terbium
(Tb), YIG ($Y_3Fe_5O_{12}$)-yttrium-iron-garnet, and TbBiIG ($Tb_{3-x}Bi_xFe_5O_{12}$)-bismuth-
substituted terbium-iron-garnet. Some rotators, such as the YIGs may also require
a strong magnetic field.

Materials with a large Verdet value in strong magnetic field result in compact optical
rotators. For example, for $45°$ polarization rotation at $\lambda = 633$ nm, a terbium-doped
glass fiber would be around 108 mm long [for H = 1,000 Oe (Oersted) and a Verdet
constant of V = 0.25 min/cm-Oe]. On the other hand, for $45°$ polarization rotation at
$\lambda = 1300$ nm, YIG devices in strong (saturated) magnetic field are about 2 mm long.
TbBiIG devices have also been used in the $\lambda = 1500$ nm range.

2.6   BEAM SPLITTERS

Beam splitters are optical devices, passive or active, that divide the incoming optical
power into two or more parts, either all equal or in predetermined percentages. For
example, a transparent plate becomes a beam splitter when an optical beam impinges
the surface at an angle; part of the beam is reflected and the other part is refracted.

There are several technologies to construct a passive beam splitter, the cube, the
plate and the hybrid each with its own pros and cons.

The cube beam splitter consists of two matched right-angle prisms, all faces of
which have been treated with an antireflection coating and cemented at the hypotenuse
faces. Polarizing beam splitters, in general, are cube beam splitters, the hypotenuse of
which has a polarizing film. In this case, an incident circularly polarized or unpolarized
beam of light is separated into two linearly polarized beams, one reflected and the other
refracted, one in TE and the other in TM mode (Fig. 2.29). To minimize polarization,
the cube faces are coated with an all-dielectric nonpolarizing material. Cube beam
splitters are easy to mount and thus are widely used. However, to minimize aberrations,
the incident light beam should be collimated.

Plate beam splitters consist of a thin optical glass plate, on one side of which an
all-dielectric film has been deposited and on the other an antireflection coating. When
an incident beam is at $45°$ part of it is transmitted and part of it is reflected. Plate
beam splitters have negligible absorption and can withstand high levels of laser power
without damage, but their splitting performance depends on the angle of incidence.

Pellicle beam splitters are made with a high tensile-strength membrane stretched
and bonded over a black anodized frame; when stretched, the membrane is several
μm thin. The pellicle is then treated with a coating so that an incident beam at $45°$ is
partially reflected and partially transmitted.

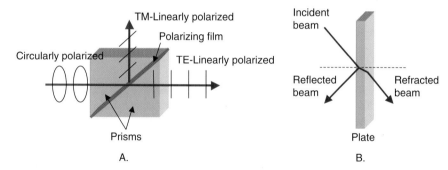

Figure 2.29 A polarizing beam splitter consisting of two prisms and a polarizing film, A, and a plate beam splitter, B.

Active beam splitters are made on the principle of couplers (or power dividers made with lithium niobate), as in Figure 3.27. When the applied voltage is in a range between the upper limit and the lower limit (for which the evanescence region supports optical power transfer at one or the other output), the incoming power is divided into two parts, the ratio of which depends on the voltage value.

Beam splitter manufacturers provide data that define the ratio reflectance over transmittance per wavelength and the variability with angle of incidence, as well as the variability with environmental parameters.

2.7   OPTICAL ISOLATORS AND CIRCULATORS

Optical isolators are two-port devices that allow optical power (of a spectral band) to flow unidirectionally from one terminal to the other, a function similar to the electrical diode.

Optical isolators (Fig. 2.30) are characterized by

- *insertion loss*, L, or the loss of optical power through it, and by
- *isolation*, I, or the ratio of transmitted power in the desired direction over the other.

Ideally, optical isolators should transmit all power in the desired direction and no power in the other; that is $L = 0$ and $I = $ infinite.

The quantities L and I are expressed by:

$$L(\text{dB}) = P_I(\text{dB}) - P_T(\text{dB})$$

and

$$I(\text{dB}) = P_I(\text{dB}) - P_R(\text{dB})$$

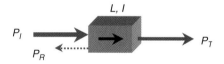

Figure 2.30   Model of an optical isolator.

where P_I, P_T, and P_R are the incident power, the transmitted power, and the reflected power, respectively, all expressed in decibel units.

Isolators may be constructed with polarizes and rotators. In such a structure, isolation is accomplished using a $\pi/4$ rotator sandwiched between two polarizers (Fig. 2.31).

Isolation may also be accomplished by combining a polarizer, an acousto-optic filter, and a beam splitter (Fig. 2.32). The acousto-optic filter is tuned to rotate the polarization of a selected wavelength (in this example, λ_2) by $90°$ (TE-to-TM) and to pass the remaining wavelengths unchanged.

More than one isolator may be connected to form a three-terminal device permitting unidirectional energy flow from terminal 1 to 2, from 2 to 3, and from 3 to 1 (Fig. 2.33). This device is known as a *circulator*. Other circulator configurations are possible, such as from 1 to 2 and from 2 to 3, or from 1 to 2 and 3 to 2, as well as four port circulators.

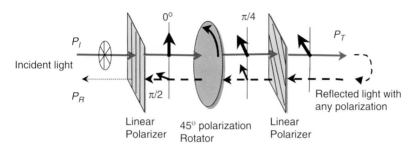

Figure 2.31   Polarizers and a $\pi/4$ rotator construct an isolator.

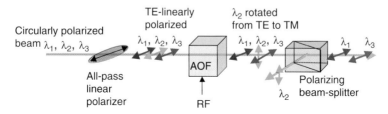

Figure 2.32   A wavelength isolator may be constructed by combining an all-pass polarizer, an acousto-optic filter and a polarizing beamsplitter.

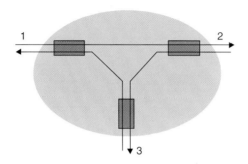

Figure 2.33   Model of a three-port optical circulator.

Among the desirable characteristics of circulators are small size, high isolation (>50 dB), low insertion loss (<1 dB), low return loss (>50 dB), directivity (≪−50 dB), low polarization sensitivity, low PDL loss (<0.05 dB), low PMD (<0.1 ps), high optical power (>300 mW), environmental stability over the specified wavelength range, and wide operating temperature range ($-20\,°C$ to $+60\,°C$). In addition, when one signal is transmitted from port 1 to port 2, a three-port circulator should not restrict another signal to pass from port 2 to port 3.

2.8 QUARTER-WAVELENGTH AND HALF-WAVELENGTH PLATES

Quarter-wavelength plates are made of birefringent material to convert linear polarized light to circular light, as already discussed. Conversely, *half-wavelength plates* rotate the orientation of linear polarized light at an angle θ by 2θ. Thus, linear polarized light at 45° is rotated by 90°, as also discussed in Sections 1.4.10.1 and 1.4.10.2.

2.9 OPTICAL MULTIPLEXERS AND DEMULTIPLEXERS

Optical demultiplexers receive a multiwavelength beam and separate it spatially into its wavelength components; that is, each wavelength appears at a different output. There are two classifications of optical demultiplexers, *passive* and *active*. Passive demultiplexers are based on prisms, diffraction gratings, and spectral (frequency) filters. Active demultiplexers are based on a combination of passive components and tunable detectors, each tuned to detect a specific frequency; however, active demultiplexers may not be suitable in certain applications (e.g., optical add-drop multiplexing/demultiplexing) as detectors may not be present.

Multiplexers perform the reverse functionality of demultiplexers; they receive several spatially separated wavelengths and form a single beam that consists of all these wavelengths.

Several demultiplexing technologies have been demonstrated today, but based on their merits (cost included), only a few have been commercially deployed. However, we mention several to point out the plethora of technologies; gratings, superprisms, Mach–Zehnder interferometer, four-wave mixing in dispersive fiber, cross-phase modulator, nonlinear optical loop mirrors, semiconductor optical amplifiers, Michelson interferometers, and others.

In addition to parameters common to all components in Section 2.1.2, key parameters specific to multiplexers and demultiplexers are:

- wavelength-dependent attenuation
- far-end cross talk
- near-end cross talk

2.9.1 Prisms and Superprisms

In Chapter 1 (Section 1.4.4), we examined the properties of prisms and superprisms. Accordingly, a collimated (parallel) beam of polychromatic light impinging on the prism surface is angularly dispersed in its component frequencies, each directed to a different point in space. Knowing the angle of incidence of the wavelength multiplexed beam, the wavelengths in the beam, and the specifications of the prism, the angular dispersion for each wavelength is known. A fiber for each wavelength is placed at the focal points of each wavelength. The result is a N-wavelength in (in single beam) to N individual wavelengths out, or a N-by-1 wavelength demultiplexer. Since prisms are passive nondirectional components, the reverse may also take place and hence a prism multiplexer.

However, although conventional prisms, in theory, perform the demultiplexing or multiplexing function, they do not provide the sufficient angular dispersion needed in optical devices for communications. With the advent of *photonic crystalline optics* and superprisms that exhibit a 500-fold angular dispersion than conventional prisms, prism deployment in demultiplexer or multiplexer functionality is reexamined and cost-effective well-performing devices may become available. In addition, since they are made with Si, they may be integrated with other devices to provide complex functionality.

2.9.2   Gratings

In Section 2.2.3, we examined the properties and conditions of gratings and described how a grating separated a polychromatic collimated light beam into its wavelength components, each directed to a different point in space. Knowing the angle of incidence of the wavelength-multiplexed beam, the wavelengths in the beam and the specifications of the grating, the angle of diffraction for each wavelength is known. A fiber for each wavelength is placed at the focal points of each wavelength. Focusing diffracted wavelengths to a focal point may be achieved either with a lens system or with a concave diffraction grating. The result is an N-wavelength in (in single beam) to N 1-wavelength out, or N-by-1 wavelength demultiplexer. Since gratings are passive nondirectional components, the reverse may also take place and hence a grating multiplexer.

2.9.3   Mach–Zehnder Demultiplexer

In Section 2.2.5, we studied the Mach–Zehnder interferometer and filter. Accordingly, two wavelengths from a single light guide were separated into two light guides; this inherently constitutes a demultiplexing function. Thus, several Mach–Zehnder filters may be cascaded to construct a demultiplexer. For example, eight wavelengths, λ_1 to λ_8 are separated by the first stage Mach–Zehnder filter into two groups (λ_1, λ_3, λ_5, λ_7) and (λ_2, λ_4, λ_6, λ_8); this is a (advantageous) consequence of the integer m in the Mach–Zehnder relationships (see Section 3.2.5). At the two-filter second stage, each group is separated into two subgroups yielding (λ_1, λ_5), (λ_3, λ_7), (λ_2, λ_6), and (λ_4, λ_8), and at the third stage (of four filters) all eight wavelengths are separately obtained (Fig. 2.34). Although cascaded MZFs appear to be attractive because they can be monolithically integrated with standard planar techniques, the insertion loss of each stage is additive, and this becomes an engineering challenge.

2.9.4   Arrayed Waveguide Grating Demultiplexers

Arrayed waveguide grating demultiplexers are considered an extension of the Mach–Zehnder interferometer (see Section 2.2.6). Accordingly, based on Mach–Zehnder interferometry a mix of wavelengths is spatially separated to its constituent wavelengths and each becomes available at specific points (outputs) of the device.

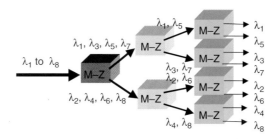

Figure 2.34 Cascaded Mach–Zehnder filters construct a multilevel demultiplexer.

2.9.5 Channel Interleavers and Channel Splitters

Channel interleavers perform the function of channel multiplexing. However, interleaving pertains more to multiplexing when two sets (or more) of channels are interleaved to obtain higher channel density and with closer channel spacing. For example, consider a set (set A) of 80 channels based on the ITU grid (with a separation of 50 GHz). Now, suppose we need to double the number to 160. We construct another set (set B) of 80 channels with 50 GHz separation, but each channel is wavelength-shifted by 25 GHz. The two sets could be interleaved to produce a superset of 160 channels with 25 GHz spacing. However, close spacing raises the FWM issue. To minimize FWM, consider that prior to interleaving the two sets, set A was polarized linearly in one direction and set B was polarized linearly but in the orthogonal direction. Then the interleaved output channels with have alternating polarized states (Fig. 2.35A), which have minimal FWM effect orthogonally polarized adjacent channels do not easily interact.

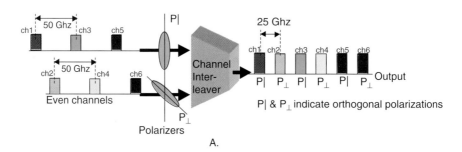

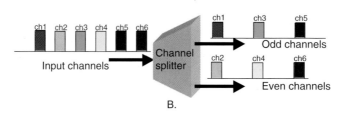

Figure 2.35 A. An interleaver performs the reverse function of a channel splitter. B. A channel splitter separates channels into odd and even.

In a different demultiplexing category is the function of channel "splitting." According to it, a number of optically multiplexed channels are separated into two groups, one consisting of odd channel numbers and the other of even channel numbers (Fig. 2.35B). Channel splitters may be constructed using birefringent or polarizing filters (this is obvious if we de-interleave the output of Figure 2.35A), dielectric filters, or all-fiber Mach–Zehnder filters.

2.10 OPTICAL CROSS-CONNECTS

Cross-connect is a key function in most communications systems. In electronic systems, the cross-connecting fabric is constructed with massively integrated circuitry and is able to interconnect thousands of input channels with thousands of output channels. The same interconnectivity function is also required in many optical communications systems.

Switching fabrics, based on switching speed and real-time aspects are distinguished in *static* or *semistatic switches* (or *cross-connects*), and in *dynamic switches*. Cross-connects interconnect any input to any output based on remote provisioning or a predetermined connectivity table; these switches are relatively slow, and once connectivity has been established it may not change for a long period (hours to days). *Dynamic switches* interconnect any input with any output, as determined upon execution of a protocol, dynamically and synchronously with the clock and sync of the system (connectivity may last from a few seconds to minutes). Typically, electronic cross-connects connect facilities bearing high bit rate (DS1 to OC-48), whereas dynamic switches connect facilities on a lower bit rate (DS0 to DS1). In DWDM, because of the high bit rate, switches are optical cross-connects (OXC), and currently dynamic switching is not a requirement other than fast provisioning. Nevertheless, fast and dynamically switching optical fabrics will enable new cost-effective features valuable to optical networking.

Switching fabrics are also distinguished as *non-blocking* and *blocking*. Blocking fabrics are not able to connect any input to any output all the times; based on statistical models indicating that not all subscribed channels will be requesting connectivity at the same time, they cross-connect only a percentage of channels (a case of oversubscription). In contrast, non-blocking channels are able to cross-connect any number of channels. Because statistical models are based on historical data, and because of the rapid growth of services and bandwidth expansion, statistical models do not provide accurate predictions; therefore we consider only nonblocking cross connecting optical fabrics.

Optical cross-connect may be accomplished in two ways:

- The *hybrid approach*: Convert the optical data stream into electronic, use electronic cross-connect technology, and then convert the electronic data stream into an optical data stream.
- *All-optical switching*: Cross-connect optical channels directly in the photonic domain.

The hybrid approach is currently popular in medium aggregate bandwidths due to existing expertise in designing high-bandwidth multichannel nonblocking electronic cross-connect fabrics. However, in high aggregate bandwidths on the order of several Tb/s, or in small add-drop optical rings, optical cross-connect becomes more efficient and cost-effective. However, as optical technology improves and cost becomes lower, it is expected that optical cross-connects will displace their electronic counterparts and electronic cross-connects will be deployed only in the low-end electronic regime of the network.

It should also be pointed out that although there is a race to produce the largest optical cross-connecting fabric (e.g., 1,000 × 1,000, 2,000 × 2,000 or larger), not all applications require such fabrics. In fact, the larger the fabric, the fewer the applications. For example, if a network node requires 3.2 Tb/s aggregate and a 1,000 × 1,000 fabric, and another nodes requires 100 Gb/s with a 100 × 100 fabric, which of the two is more widely deployed? Clearly, it is the latter. Similarly, as the fabric size increases, what can you tell about the switching speed of each switching element in the fabric? SONET requires a total 50 ms switching time for all elements in the fabric (regardless of size). Thus, the switching speed per element as the fabric size increases must be faster.

In DWDM, switching may be required on a different level. For example, it may be on the *fiber level* or on the *wavelength level*.

On the fiber level, all optical channels from one fiber are switched to another fiber; this is termed *fiber cross-connect* (FXC). This is useful during restoration and switching to protection fiber. In a similar implementation, each fiber (or waveguide) carries an individual wavelength, and each wavelength is directed to an output waveguide (see also Chapter 4).

On the wavelength level there are two subcategories: those fabrics that connect a wavelength from one fiber to another fiber without changing the wavelength, termed *wavelength selective cross-connect* (WSXC), and those fabrics that connect a wavelength from one fiber to another but require wavelength conversion, termed *wavelength interchanging cross-connect* (WIXC) (Fig. 2.36). WSXC implies that when a

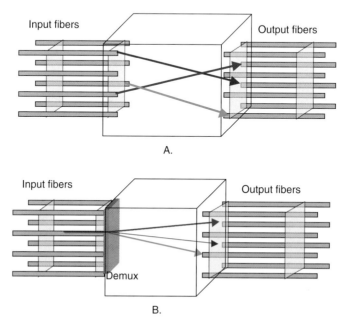

Figure 2.36 All optical cross-connect fabrics: A. On the fiber level and, B. Wavelength selective; notice the demultiplexing function at the switch input.

wavelength is moved from one fiber to another, that fiber does not already have an optical channel with the same wavelength; a case that required a priori knowledge of the wavelength grid on fibers. WIXC implies that the switch supports wavelength conversion and that the fiber and optical components (filters, etc.) support the new wavelength. Moreover, when switching wavelengths from one fiber to another, with a WSXC or WIXC, there are other technical issues to be addressed pertaining to quality of the optical signal (and hence quality of service), such as power level equalization, polarization states, and signal-to-noise ratio.

Currently, optical cross-connect fabrics are either free-space (MEMS, Mach–Zehnder, WGR), or solid-state (e.g., acousto-optic, electro-optic, and holographic), or polymer-based (including liquid crystals), or in combination of these technologies. In the following sections, the type of each switch will become obvious from its description.

2.10.1 Free-Space Optical Switching

Free-space optical switching implies that beams of light from a bundle of fibers, monochromatic or polychromatic, are steered into space so that from any fiber they are coupled into another fiber. In this category, steering a light beam electromechanically (e.g., moving mirrors) directs the beam to one of many fibers.

A technology has been developed, primarily for communications applications, by which beams from a bundle of fibers are focused on micromirrors (few tens of micrometers in diameter) that can tilt by electrostatic activation to deflect the beam. This technology, known as micro-electro-mechanical systems (MEMS), can produce many micromirrors on the same substrate (chip) using standard planar process (deposition, etching, and lithography), exactly the same with semiconductor integrated circuits. Based on it, a number of mirrors are integrated on the same substrate, on which small moveable platforms have been constructed and when they are electrostatically activated each one can be tilted in the range of 3 to 8 degrees (Fig. 2.37).

In a different configuration, many micro-cymbals are made and arranged in a matrix and in each one a micromirror has been embedded. One such MEMS device may be used with a fixed plane mirror to construct a large optical switch (or more correctly, a large optical cross-connect) (Fig. 2.38).

In another yet configuration, two MEMS devices, facing each other, are used to construct a large optical switch (Fig. 2.39).

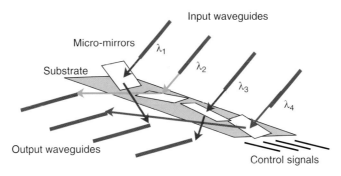

Figure 2.37 A MEMS array cross-connecting optical beams from input to output fibers.

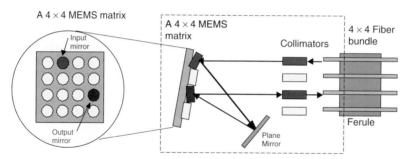

Figure 2.38 Single MEMS with plane mirror constructs an optical cross-connect.

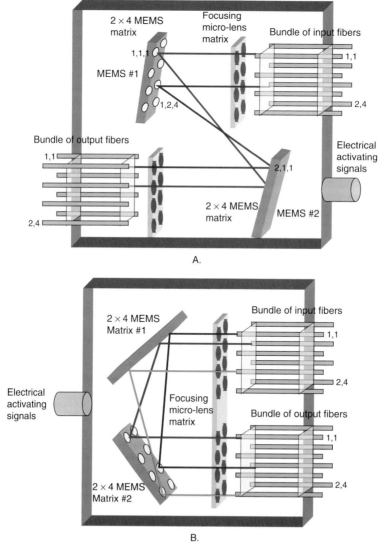

Figure 2.39 A. One arrangement of two MEMS 2 × 4 devices to construct an 8 × 8 optical space cross-connect switch. B. Another arrangement of two MEMS 2 × 4 devices to construct an 8 × 8 optical space cross-connect switch.

The latter can yield an optical cross-connecting fabric as large as $1,000 \times 1,000$ or larger. Because such mirrors are wavelength-independent and bit rate–independent, there is no limit or restriction on the number of optical channels in the beam, nor aggregate bandwidth per beam, the total aggregate bandwidth through such a cross-connect may be on the order of Petabit per second (1,000 beams, each at 1 Tb/s). MEMS have demonstrated low loss fiber-to-fiber insertion loss (a fraction of 1 dB), on-off contrast ratio better than 60 dB, low switching power (2 mW), very good cross talk (<-50 dB), compact design, but slower switching time (5–10 msec) than other technologies (LiNbO$_3$ $\sim$ nsec; see next section).

Although such large switching matrices ($1,000 \times 1,000$) are attractive, they nevertheless present a manufacturing challenge to produce mirrors with uniform properties across the matrix. For example, the insertion loss of a mirror to any output must be the same or at minimum within certain predetermined tolerances. Clearly, the path from the first mirror of the first MEMS (mirror 1,1,1) to the first mirror of the second MEMS (mirror 2,1,1) is not the same with the path of the mirror (1,1,1) to the mirror (2,1000,1000) (see Fig. 2.38), nor the deflection angles are. In practice, a two-dimensional insertion loss table is provided that tabulates IL values indicating the uniformity of the cross-connect (Table 2.2). Similar tables may also be constructed tabulating switching times, as the deflection angle of mirror (1,1,1) to any other mirror elements in the matrix requires different angles and thus different times.

In a different implementation, MEMS technology can be used in free-space switching, not with mirrors but with lasers. In this implementation, a high density of tiny tiltable platforms is constructed and a VCSEL laser source is embedded or grown on each. In this configuration, as each platform is tilted it directs the beam of each VCSEL to an output fiber (Fig. 2.40). Similarly, photodetectors may be embedded instead of VCSELs.

The generalized Mach–Zehnder waveguide grating router (WGR) is a free-space interferometric optical cross-connect that is able to connect one of many inputs with one of many output ports. With this device, a given wavelength at any input port appears at any specified output port (Fig. 2.41), according to an input-to-output connectivity map. This implementation is attractive from the standpoint that the fabric is integrated on the same substrate using standard planar monolithic methods. However, because

Table 2.2   IL example of a 4 × 4 (4 inputs, 4 outputs) cross-connect

		FIBER OUTPUT			
		1,1	1,2	2,1	2,2
FIBER INPUT	1,1	10.27	10.56	10.48	12.28
	1,2	11.78	10.50	11.59	11.01
	2,1	11.54	12.22	11.85	10.99
	2,2	12.61	11.83	10.54	10.57

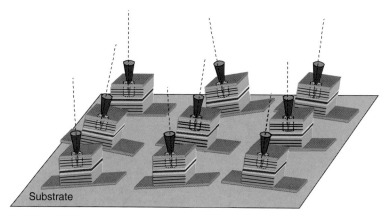

Figure 2.40   Many VCSEL lasers grown on a matrix of tiltable platforms and integrated on the same substrate direct each beam in different direction.

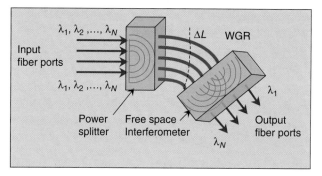

Figure 2.41   A WGR is an optical cross-connect that routes specific wavelengths to specified output fibers.

this device is based on interferometric principles, it is wavelength-dependent with a fixed relationship between wavelength and output port. A consequence of the latter is that the same wavelength cannot appear at more than one input.

2.10.2   Solid-State Cross-Connects

Solid-state optical cross-connecting devices are based on semiconductor directional couplers, as already discussed and illustrated in Figure 2.27. They are one-to-two or two-to-two port devices that selectively change one of their optical properties when a control signal is applied. The optical property that is controlled is:

- birefringence that causes change in the polarization state
- dielectric constant and index of refraction that causes change in the propagation constant and phase
- absorption, which causes a change in the amplitude of optical power
- the nonlinear parametric constants that cause change in the signal wavelength (this is a special case)

Depending on material and optical property to be controlled, one of the following may be applied: heat, light, mechanical pressure or tension, electric current, electric field (voltage), and in special cases magnetic field. As an example, current injection controls the refractive index of a semiconductor waveguide, whereas electric field controls the index of refraction of ferroelectric $LiNbO_3$ crystals. Thin-film heaters may also be applied to control the refractive index of waveguides.

The material type, the controlling mechanism and the controlled property impact the switching speed of the device as well as the number of ports of the switch. For example, switches made with $LiNbO_3$ crystal exhibit switching speeds on the order of nanoseconds whereas those made with SiO_2 on Si exhibit speeds on the order of less than 1 millisecond. However, $LiNbO_3$ switching elements are 2×2, and to construct a nonblocking $N \times N$ fabric (also known as a Benes switch), $(N \log_2 N - N/2)$ elements are required; that is a large number, which also affects the total insertion loss of the fabric.

In the solid-state category, an entirely different solid-state approach is used to record or store holographically a number of different gratings in crystals with specific properties, such as potassium lithium-tantalate niobate (KLTN). In this case, the charge distribution of KLTN crystals is distributed according to the pattern of incident light, thus generating an optically induced diffraction grating in the bulk of the crystal. By changing the incident light pattern, a different distribution is induced and thus a different grating. Interestingly, each holographic grating can be activated by the application of a specific voltage (see Section 2.2.3). Clearly, this can be used to construct optical cross-connects whereby an activated grating diffracts a particular wavelength and passes through others. If several such crystals are arranged in a symmetric configuration (e.g., a matrix), then a switching fabric may be constructed for many wavelengths (Fig. 2.42).

Solid-state optical cross-connects are characterized by a number of parameters. For example, (numbers in parentheses refer to a typical SiO_2 on Si device):

- size of switching matrix (2×2 to 64×64) and number of input-output ports
- insertion loss (typ. 1 dB)
- isolation (typ. 35 dB)
- cross talk (typ. -40 dB)
- switching speed (in the range of ms to ns)

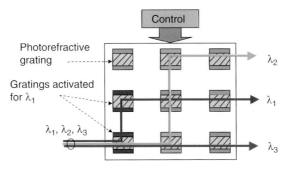

Figure 2.42 Para-electric photorefractive crystals store grating holograms. When in a matrix, they constitute an electro-holographic cross-connect with fast switching time.

- polarization dependent loss (fraction of dB)
- spectral flatness (typ. ±1 dB)
- operating temperature (0–70 °C)
- operating voltage (typ. +5 V)
- number of inputs and outputs (e.g., 2 × 2)
- whether they block or not an input
- multicasting capability
- low power consumption

In addition to these parameters, ITU-T G.650 recommendation defines parameters specific to all switching components. An enhanced list (those with an asterix are not included in G.650) follows:

- switching time matrix
- repeatability
- uniformity
- cross talk
- directivity
- extinction ratio*
- transfer matrix
- Doppler shift (in mechanical sw)*

2.10.3   Polymers and Inks

Polymers are by nature insulators and do not conduct electricity. However, when they are oxidized (p-type) or reduced (n-type), their conductivity increases by a factor of 10^9. In addition, thin layers (about 100 nm) of organic crystals, such as hydroxy-quinoline aluminum (AlQ) or poly-para-phenylene-vinylene (PPPV or PPV) luminesce when forward bias voltage is applied to them.

Luminescence is the product of migration along the polymer chain of charged cations and charged molecules, known as *polarons*. Adding fluorescent dyes and/or luminous synthetic chromophores (similar to those found in fluorescent jellyfish) determines the emitted color (wavelength) and increases the quantum efficiency of luminescence. Thus, making a three-layer sandwich of polymer materials, each with the proper concentration of additives, some interesting photonic devices may be formed, such as *organic light-emitting diodes* (OLED).

In general, polymers are not very suitable materials for optical communications for the following reasons:

- For the majority of polymers, a strong absorption takes place in the region 1.3 to 1.55 μm, which is the usable spectral range in fiber communications. This absorptive spectrum is due to overtones of carbon in the C–H bond. In particular, the 1.55 μm absorption is due to combination tones of the first C–H overtones and other vibration modes. However, the absorption peak may be shifted if H is replaced with heavier atoms such as deuterium, fluorine, or chlorine (as in deuterated-fluoromethacrylate), which at 1.3 μm has an absorption profile close to that of silica waveguide. Changing H to other atoms changes the refractive index to a higher or lower value.

- Their luminous efficiency (which is measured in candelas) is only a few percent.
- Switching speeds are comparatively slow.
- Polymers are sensitive to temperature.

However, because of their low cost and easy manufacturability attractiveness polymers have challenged researchers. Thus, organic crystals from which optical light-emitting diodes (OLED) and OLED displays with a very wide viewing angle have already been produced and deployed. And research continues with benzene organic crystals that exhibit low absorption and high conductivity, and with nonlinear electro-optic polymers such as amino-phenylene-isophorone-isoxazolone (APII) that promise switching speeds on the order of few picoseconds.

A different technology developed by Agilent Technologies Inc. capitalizes on inkjet printing to construct cross-connecting fabrics. According to this technology, tiny cavities on a transparent plate are filled with a liquid of low boiling point. If the liquid remains cool, a beam of monochromatic light passes through it unchanged. If the liquid is heated, it forms a bubble that reflects the beam. Thus, a number of beams aligned with the cavities on the plate construct a switching function.

2.10.4 Photochromic Materials

When certain materials absorb light, their color changes reversibly. Such materials are known as *photochromic*. Photochromic materials either block light at a specific wavelength or transmit light at a wavelength different from the one absorbed. For example, AgCl in a gel compound has been used to absorb light; in this case, Ag^+ changes to Ag^0 agglomeration, which changes its color. However, the response time in this application is on the order of several minutes, which currently makes it unsuitable to communications.

Photochromicity has been used in color photography for many years, but this process is not reversible; one would say that this application is write once read many times (WORM or ROM). Thus, photochromicity may be applied to a variety of applications, such as optical memories and slow switching devices.

2.10.5 Technologies and Switching Speeds

In DWDM, a number of different and interesting technologies have been developed to construct optical cross-connecting fabrics. Among them, lithium-niobate crystals, liquid crystals, bubbles, holograms, thermo- and acousto-optics, and tiny tilting mirrors integrated on the same substrate. More technologies and techniques are announced claiming that can switch light more efficiently or more inexpensively, or faster. Which is the best technology is a question that cannot be quickly answered, as each has its own merits that fit differently in a particular application. Here, we summarize some of these technologies:

- Lithium niobate are solid state fast switches but have a high insertion loss and comparatively small fabric.

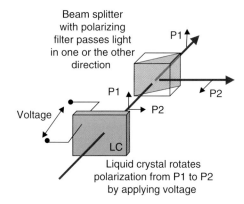

Beam splitter
with polarizing
filter passes light
in one or the other
direction

Voltage

Liquid crystal rotates
polarization from P1 to P2
by applying voltage

Figure 2.43   Model of a liquid crystal switching element.

- Liquid crystals change the transmissivity of light by applying an electric current, thus changing their polarization state and thus the pass/no-pass state (Fig. 2.43).

- Micro-electro-mechanical systems (MEMS) are based on standard planar monolithic silicon substrate etching techniques to produce many micrometer small mirrors on the same substrate; by applying an electrostatic field around them (it requires voltages in the range 100–200 V) their three-dimensional position changes.

- Small liquid bubbles formed by ink-jet printing techniques act like mirrors to reflect light.

- Holograms inside crystals can be activated to selectively diffract a wavelength.

- The refractive index of certain materials may be altered by heat and thus, thermo-optic switching is achieved by employing interferometry.

- Application of an acoustic RF wave produces a wavelength selective grating over a coupler to produce a wavelength selective switch (see Acousto-Optic Tunable Filters, Section 2.2.9).

The speed of optical switching devices depends on materials used to make the switch, the principle on which the switch operates, and technology. Switching speeds vary from seconds to nanoseconds. However, in addition to switching speed, there are many more parameters to be considered such as optical loss, dispersion, reliability, stability, switching-matrix size, external voltage (if any), temperature dependence, physical size, cost, and others.

Here is an example of some current switching speeds:

- Thermo-optic switching is on the order of milliseconds.

- Acousto-optic switching is on the order of microseconds.

- Electro-optic ceramic-compound switching is on the order of microseconds.

- MEMS switching is on the order of microseconds per mirror.

- SiO_2 on Si planar switching is on the order of msec to μsec.

- $LiNbO_3$ switching is on the order of nanosecond.

Table 2.3   Some switching technologies and approximate specifications

Swich Type	Switching Speed (Appr.)	Insertion Loss	PDL	Cross talk	λ-Flatness	Typical Size
Fiber-Bragg grating	$\sim$100 μs	$\sim$2 dB	0.5 dB/cm	-40 dB	N.A.	Up to 32 $\times$ 32
Acousto-optic	$\sim$5 μs	$\sim$8 dB	$\sim$8 dB	-25 dB	$\pm$10 dB	Up to 1 $\times$ 1024
MEMS	$\sim$10 ms	3–7 dB	$\sim$0.5 dB	-50 dB	$\sim$1 dB	Up to 1000 $\times$ 1000
Electrorefractive holograms	$\sim$ ns	$\sim$4 dB	$\sim$0.1 dB	-40 dB	$\sim$0 dB	Up to 16 $\times$ 16 and perhaps 64 $\times$ 64
LC	$\sim$5 ms	1 dB	$\sim$0.1 dB	-40 dB	$\sim$2 dB	Up to 16 $\times$ 16
Bubble-jet	$\sim$10 ms	5 dB	$\sim$0.2 dB	-50 dB	N.A.	Up to 32 $\times$ 32

- Potassium lithium tantalate-niobium electroholographic crystals are on the order of nanoseconds.
- Nonlinear electro-optic polymers (e.g., amino-phenylene-isophorone-isoxazolone) promise speeds on the order of a few picoseconds.

Table 2.3 lists some current technologies and switching speeds.

2.11   OPTICAL ADD-DROP MULTIPLEXERS

The function of dropping channels (i.e., rerouting channels from the main stream) and adding channels (in the main stream) is a well-established function in communications systems and networks. To visualize this, we describe the following parallel.

Imagine that in a transportation system, airplanes, trains, and buses did not make any interim stops to drop off passengers and board new ones but were going non-stop point-to-point. Clearly, the point-to-point route would not be cost-effective and efficient unless all passengers were going to the same destination and their number exceeded a threshold or percentage of occupancy. Thus, to provide efficient capacity utilization and service flexibility, transportation systems make several stops to drop off and add on, or *add-drop*, passengers. And although there is no limit on the number of those that drop off, the condition that must be satisfied to those that add-on is that they cannot exceed the available capacity of the vehicle. This cost-efficient function-ality is applicable to any type of transportation, regardless if it is for people, goods, or data.

In DWDM communications, the capacity of the plane is the bandwidth capacity of the node or the fiber, and the number of passengers is the number of wavelengths, or if wavelengths are time-shared with others, the number of time slots (as in the TDM case, see Chapter 3). In current DWDM systems, the main function of an *optical add-drop multiplexer* (OADM) is to selectively remove a wavelength from the fiber (the data content of which is rerouted to another fiber — the drop side), pass the remaining wavelengths through the OADM, and add the same wavelength but with different data content (from the add fiber) in the same direction.

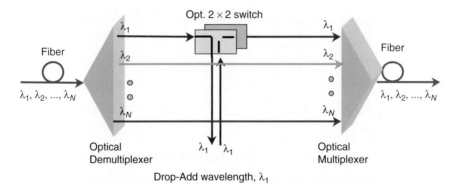

Figure 2.44 Model of a single wavelength optical add-drop multiplexer; shown are a demultiplexer, a multiplexer and a 2 × 2 switch to accomplish this function. More wavelengths can be added and dropped by adding more switches.

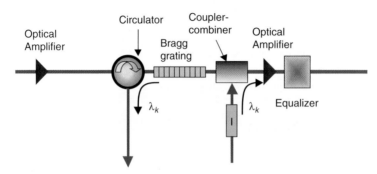

Figure 2.45 A single wavelength optical add-drop multiplexer using a Bragg grating, a circulator and a coupler; the amplifiers and the equalizer are optional.

Table 2.4 Typical specifications of optical add-drop multiplexers

Channel spacing (ITU-T Grid)	50, 100, or 200 GHz
Center wavelength	100 GHz nm ITU Grid
Min. channel passband	0.3–0.5 nm
Max. insertion loss (drop output)	1.5–3 dB
Max. insertion loss (channel through output)	0.6–2.5 dB
Max. PDL	0.1–0.2 dB
Channel isolation (add-drop)	25 dB
Channel isolation (channel through output)	20 dB
Min. directivity	50 dB
Max. center wavelength thermal stability	0.001–0.005 nm/°C
Maximum optical power	300 mW
Operating temperature	0 to +60 °C
Storage temperature	−40 to +85 °C
Max. tensile load	5 N
Fiber length	1 m

The model of an OADM for wavelength λ_1 is schematically shown in Figure 2.44, where F_1 signifies a filter selecting wavelength λ_1 while passing through all other wavelengths, and M1 signifies a multiplexer that multiplexes all wavelengths.

OADMs are classified as *fixed* wavelength or *dynamically* wavelength selectable OADMs. In fixed OADMs, one or more wavelengths have been chosen and remain the same until human intervention changes some settings to deselect and select others. In one configuration, fixed wavelength add-drop multiplexers may be implemented with a demultiplexer or multiplexer and a 2×2 switch (optical or lithium-niobate), or with fiber gratings and circulators (Fig. 2.45). In a dynamically selectable wavelength OADM, the wavelengths between the optical demultiplexer or multiplexer may be dynamically selected from the outputs of the demultiplexer to any of the inputs of the multiplexer. This may be accomplished, for example, with an array of micromirrors or tunable fiber gratings and circulators. Some typical specification ranges of fiber-type add-drop multiplexers are shown in Table 2.4.

2.12 OPTICAL EQUALIZERS

When wavelengths are generated by one or more optical sources, not all the wavelengths have the same amplitude (optical power). Moreover, as OADM takes place, those wavelengths added are not of the same optical power as they come from a different system or even network. However, when the added wavelengths join the other wavelengths, all of them must be within a tolerable range of the same power (as well as quality), so that the fiber transmission specifications are met and the variation does not exceed the acceptable dynamic specifications of receivers.

Another source of unevenness of power level across all optical channels is known as *spectral hole burning* (SHB) (Fig. 2.46). According to SHB, there is a localized wavelength depression in gain, which is *signal power–dependent*. For EDFA amplification and in the C-band the deepest hole with the narrowest width is in the 1,533 nm region. In the L-band SHB is not significant. Similarly, there is also *polarization hole burning* (PHB), which is also a localized wavelength depression in gain but it is *signal power and polarization dependent*. In fact, it has been established that the magnitude of PHB is proportional to the degree of polarization of the incoming signal. The polarization dependency of PHB is manifested as *polarization-dependent gain* (PDG); that is, the EDFA gain favors a particular states of polarization of signal to be amplified.

Equalization also improves the signal-to-noise ratio, and thus it enhances the performance of optical amplifiers in ultra-long-haul transmission. The latter allows for

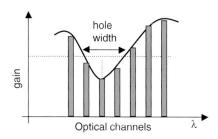

Figure 2.46 Spectral hole burning is a localized depression in the spectral band.

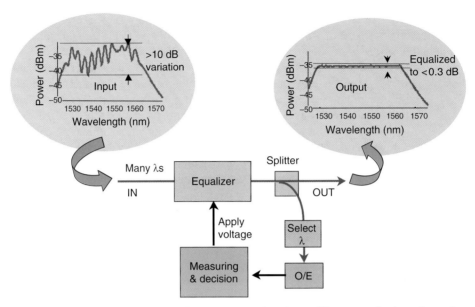

Figure 2.47 An optical equalizer receives many wavelengths at different amplitude and equalizes each one to the same level.

longer fiber spans (few thousands of kilometers) between amplifiers. Therefore, for proper transmission operation it is necessary to have a flat power spectrum at the output of any major device such as an add-drop multiplexer, a fabric switch, or a comb generator (a source of many wavelengths).

The component that equalizes all optical channels is known as an *optical equalizer*. *Optical equalizers* monitor the power level of each wavelength channel of a band of wavelengths and selectively make power level adjustments flattening the optical power of each channel within a prespecified power range; in one application, this is accomplished using VOAs (Fig. 2.47).

Optical equalizers that perform equalization on a dynamic basis are also called dynamic gain equalizers (DGE), dynamic wavelength equalizers (DWE), or dynamic gain equalization filters (DGEF).

Currently, optical equalizers are optoelectronic feedback control subsystems that incorporate several components, optical and electronic. Among them, there may be a silica-arrayed waveguide or a multiplexer and a demultiplexer; power splitters, per channel variable optical attenuators, an optical monitoring mechanism to measure wavelength and channel power, and a microprocessor which according to an algorithm performs per channel real-time gain management on the C-band and/or L-band. A compact, all-optical equalizer with fast dynamic range is a device of the future.

The desirable characteristics of optical equalizers are:

- broad wavelength range
- low ripple of the spectrum amplitude (small peak-to-peak variation)
- high dynamic range
- low loss

- polarization-independent
- fast acquisition

In a different implementation, DGEs are made using planar silica waveguide technology. This technology lends itself to monolithic integration with other Si-based components, both active and passive, such as dynamic filters, optical switches, and electronic components.

2.13 LIGHT SOURCES

One of the key components in optical communications systems is the transmitter, specifically the light source. In optical communications, light sources must be compact, monochromatic, stable, and long-lived (many years). Stability implies constant optical power level (over time, voltage, and temperature variations) and constant wavelength (at the desired wavelength and without drifts). In practice, there are no monochromatic light sources; there are merely light sources that generate light within a very narrow band of wavelengths with a Gaussian distribution.

Light sources are classified as *coherent* (photons are in phase) and *incoherent* (photons are random and out of phase). The first classification includes all lasers and the second includes light-emitting diodes (LED) and incandescent sources. Light sources are also classified as *continuous wave* (CW) and as *modulated* (light is encoded). In communications, CW sources require external modulators that are placed in the optical path. In this arrangement, an electrical signal representing a data stream acts upon the modulator, affecting the flow continuity of the light passing through (Fig. 2.48A). Modulated sources are affected by the application of a modulated voltage, current, or light so that the sourced light is directly modulated. In this classification, there are also sources that consist of two monolithically integrated sections; a continuous laser source the light of which is coupled in the modulation section (Fig. 2.48B).

Light sources are classified into four categories according to their driving optical power over a length of SSMF fiber (with no amplification):

- *Extended long reach* if the driving optical power is up to 80 km SMF (lasers)
- *Long reach* if the driving optical power is up to 40 km on SMF (lasers)
- *Intermediate reach* if the driving optical power is up to 15 km on MMF or SMF (lasers)

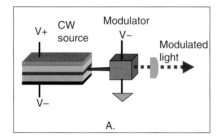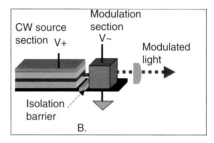

Figure 2.48 A. A continuous wave light source is externally modulated, and B. A monolithically integrated source and modulator.

- *Short reach* if the driving optical power is up to 2 km on MMF, and a fifth emerging classification (LEDs or lasers)
- *Very short reach* if the driving optical power is less than 1 km on glass MMF or even plastic fiber (LEDs)

Laser sources must satisfy Class I Laser Safety requirements according to the U.S. Food and Drug Administration (FDA/CDRH) and international IEC-825 standards.

ITU-T G.650 has defined parameters for many optical components. Here we add a list of parameters for light sources. These parameters are described in subsequent sections.

- optical channel output power
- optical channel center wavelength λ_0
- line spacing
- cutoff wavelength (tunable sources)
- spectral width (tunable sources)
- line width
- modulation depth (modulated sources)
- bit rate (max-min; modulated sources)
- source noise
- chirp
- dependency on bias
- dependency on temperature

2.13.1 Light-Emitting Diodes

A light-emitting-diode (LED) is a monolithically integrated p-n semiconductor device which when it is biased, and during the electron-hole recombination process at the junction of n- and p-doped semiconductors, energy is released in the form of light. As the recombination is a statistically random event, the LED light, in contrast to lasers, is not coherent. The output optical power emerges from the device edge in a relatively large cone and its amplitude depends on the current density, which depends on the electron concentration and the applied voltage. Electrically, LEDs exhibit the same I-V characteristics of common diodes. In addition, a threshold is defined, below which the optical power is negligible.

The *switching speed* of LEDs depends on the recombination rate, R, and is expressed by

$$R = J/(de)$$

where J is the current density (A/m^2), d is the thickness of the recombination region, and e is the electron charge.

The *output power* of LEDs is expressed by

$$P_{\text{out}} = \{(\eta hc)/(e\lambda)\}I$$

where I is the LED drive current (A), η is the quantum efficiency (relative recombination/total recombination), h is Planck's constant, e is the electron charge, and λ is the wavelength of light.

The output optical spectrum of LEDs is the range of emitted wavelengths. This depends on the absolute junction temperature (i.e., the range widens as temperature increases) and the emission wavelength λ:

$$\Delta\lambda = 3.3(kT/h)(\lambda^2/c)$$

where T is the absolute temperature at the junction, c is the speed of light, k is Boltzmann's constant, and h is Planck's constant.

Temperature has an adverse effect on the stability of an LED device. As temperature rises, its wavelength shifts and its intensity decreases (Fig. 2.49).

A decrease in intensity decreases the signal-to-noise ratio and the ability to transmit the signal to long fiber length, whereas wavelength shift may have an unpleasant effect on cross talk and bit error rate increase (Fig. 2.50).

The modulated current density J is expressed by

$$J = J_o + J_o m_j \exp(j\omega t)$$

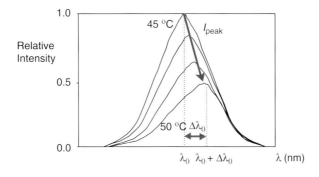

Figure 2.49   Effect of temperature on wavelength and optical intensity of solid state light sources.

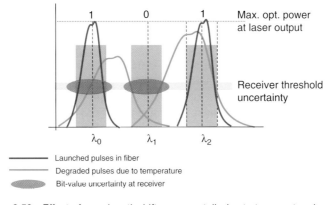

Figure 2.50   Effect of wavelength drift on cross talk due to temperature increase.

where J_0 is the steady-state current density, m_j is the modulation depth, and ω is the modulation frequency.

This current modulates the electron density difference through the junction, $\Delta n = n - n_o$ (n_o is the electron density at equilibrium with no bias current) as

$$\Delta n = N_o \{1 + M_N \exp[j(\omega t - \theta)]\}$$

where N_0 is the electron density at steady state, M_N is the electron modulation depth, and θ is the phase shift.

From the differential $d(\Delta n)/dt$, the output power modulation index, I_M, is derived in terms of the output modulation response, M_N:

$$I_M = M_N \exp(-j\theta) = m_j/(1 + j\omega\tau_r)$$

where τ_r is the electron-hole recombination time.

Comparing the modulation response with a first-order low-pass (LP) filter, it is concluded that their transfer functions are identical. Thus, the modulation response may be studied like an LP filter, from which the 3-dB modulation bandwidth is derived:

$$\omega_{3\ dB} = 1/\tau_r$$

Based on this analysis, the salient features of LEDs and their applicability are summarized as follows:

- Their bandwidth depends on device material.
- Their optical power depends on current density (i.e., on the operating V-I point).
- Optical power and spectrum depend on temperature.
- The emitted light is not coherent.
- They are relatively slow devices (<1 Gb/s); in communications they may be used only in low bit rates.
- They transmit light in a relatively wide cone; in communications they may be used only over MMF.
- They exhibit a relatively wide spectral range.
- They are inexpensive.

2.13.2 Lasers

LASER stands for light amplification by stimulated emission of radiation. Lasers are devices based on the property of some elements, which when in gaseous state (e.g., He-Ne) or doped in crystals (e.g., ruby with 0.05% chromium), absorb electrical or electromagnetic energy and remain in a semistable excited energy state. When in an excited state, other photons of a specific wavelength that travel through the material stimulate the excited atoms, which in turn release photonic energy.

The actual process of excitation and stimulation varies from element to element. Depending on the particular atom or ion, the excitation and stimulation mechanism may be simple or complex. It all depends on the quantum energy levels of particular electrons, the energy available to excite them, and the energy provided to stimulate

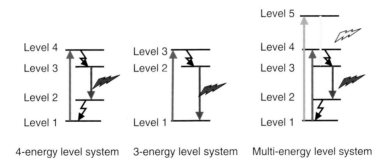

Figure 2.51   A four, three and multi-energy level system.

them. Electrons may absorb energy and "jump up" to a higher energy state. The excitation energy may be electrical or photonic. From the excited state, at an unspecified time (several microseconds or milliseconds) electrons may "jump down" stepwise to lower energy levels (by releasing photonic or acoustic energy) until they reach the energy level they came from (the ground state). However, when excited electrons are stimulated, they immediately release photonic or acoustic energy. Figure 2.51 illustrates two different transition systems, a 4-energy-level system and a 3-energy-level system.

In lasers, stimulated photons enter a region known as the resonant cavity to form a strong directional and *coherent* monochromatic beam; photons traveling in other directions are lost through the walls of the cavity and do not contribute to the laser beam. The resonant cavity has specific dimensions with polished ends or gratings to form reflectors forming a frequency-selective mechanism that produces an optical beam within a narrow spectrum. As energy is pumped in and the excitation and stimulation process continues, the optical gain reaches a threshold and the lasing process starts. Thus, depending on semiconductor composition, structure, pumped energy, and feedback mechanism, lasers exhibit a large positive gain.

Like all resonant cavities, the laser cavity may support a number of frequencies (wavelengths) that meet the condition $\lambda = (2 \times L)/N$, where N is an integer and L is the cavity length. However, the upper and lower bounds of wavelengths as well as the amplitude of each wavelength depend on the gain bandwidth of the laser (Fig. 2.52).

Ideally, the generated beam should have a symmetric intensity cross section, termed TEM_{00}. However, the resonant cavity determines the actual cross section, or transverse mode, of the beam, which can deviate from the ideal to yield cross sections such as TEM_{01}, TEM_{10}, TEM_{11}, etc. (Fig. 2.53) or a combination of them. Typically, the quality of the laser beam is specified as a percentage of TEM_{00} in the beam.

Semiconductor materials such as AlGaAs and InGaAsP generate photons with wavelengths compatible with the low loss regions of silica fiber and compatible with other optical components. The active layer of this structure, such as a straight channel of InGaAsP, is sandwiched between n- and p-type layers of InP, also known as *cladding layers*. When bias is applied, the recombination of holes and electrons in the active region releases light, the wavelength of which depends on the energy band-gap of the active material. The active layer has a much higher refractive index than the cladding layers and thus the cladding layers confine the electron-hole pairs and the photons in the

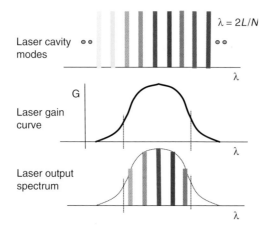

$\lambda = 2L/N$

Laser cavity modes

Laser gain curve

Laser output spectrum

Figure 2.52 Multimode output of a laser cavity.

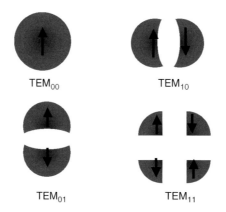

TEM_{00}

TEM_{10}

TEM_{01}

TEM_{11}

Figure 2.53 Output transverse modes of a laser.

active region. The active region forms a resonant cavity that supports coherent photons of a selected optical frequency (wavelength). These photons are coherent (because of the resonant cavity) and form a beam within a very narrow cone. In many lasers, the generated beam is guided so that about 95% is emitted at the front-face of the device and the remainder at the back-face for monitoring purposes. The ratio front-to-back of output power is known as the *tracking ratio*. A photodetector measures the back-face power and based on the tracking ratio the power at the front face is calculated as well as the wavelength of the generated light.

In addition, the beam may be directly or indirectly modulated. However, direct modulation at very high bit rates (10 Gb/s and higher) may cause lasers to optically chirp adding to wavelength jitter and noise. Optical chirping is observed as a spectral line that jitters about the central wavelength. Optical chirping occurs because the refractive index of the laser cavity depends on the drive current. As the drive current change from a logic ONE to a logic ZERO and vice versa, the refractive index changes dynamically and thus the resonant cavity characteristics; this causes a dynamic changes in wavelength which broadens dynamically the laser line width, and hence *optical chirping*. Chirping is avoided if external modulation is used in which case the laser emits a continuous wave (CW). When lasers and modulators (made with In + Ga + As + P) are monolithically integrated on InP substrates, electrically isolation is required to avoid chirping. Chirping is more easily tolerated at low bit rates.

Compactness is very important to communications, and several key optical functionality, such as lasers, filters, modulators, and others, are currently integrated using advanced monolithic methods to produce components with more functionality per cube unit that operates efficiently over a wide temperature range. Wavelength and signal amplitude stability of semiconductor lasers are important in all applications. Stability depends on materials, bias voltage, and temperature. In high bit rate applications, frequency and amplitude stabilization is achieved using thermoelectric cooling techniques to keep temperature stable within a fraction of a degree Celsius. However, this adds to the cost and power consumption of the device and developments are in progress to design "cooler" devices at higher optical powers and bit rates.

Lasers may support a *single transverse mode* (known as *single-mode lasers*), or both a *single transverse mode* and a *single longitudinal mode* (*single-frequency lasers*), or may oscillate at *several frequencies simultaneously*, longitudinal or transverse (*multifrequency lasers*). Moreover, lasers may have a single *fixed frequency* or they may be *tunable*.

Fixed wavelength CW lasers used in communications have a typical output power in the range of 10 to 30 mW, linewidth better than 10 MHz, single mode suppression ratio (SMSR) less than 50 dB, and wavelength stability 10 pm (± 1.25 GHz).

2.13.2.1   Fabry–Perot Lasers

Fabry–Perot semiconductor lasers have a cavity (or optical feedback) based on Fabry–Perot resonator principles. A simplified structure of a Fabry–Perot laser is shown in Figure 2.54; the actual laser structure is complex and varies among manufacturers. This consists of a semiconductor material in the form of a straight channel (p-type AlGaAs), which is both the active region (for stimulated emission) and the optical waveguide (to guide photons in one direction). Both ends of the channel are carefully cleaved to act as mirrors with a reflectivity:

$$R = \{(n-1)/(n+1)\}^2$$

where n is the refractive index of the active medium.

Since the Fabry–Perot resonator supports a multiplicity of wavelengths, so does the F–P laser device. Thus, Fabry–Perot lasers generate several longitudinal frequencies (modes) at once. The semiconductor laser material, the frequency spacing, and

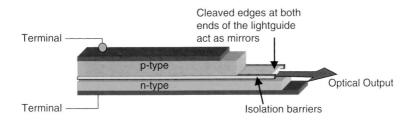

Figure 2.54   Fundamentals of a Fabry–Perot laser source.

the Fabry–Perot laser length determine the range of frequencies. The bias current determines the threshold frequency.

In a different configuration, the two reflectors of the Fabry–Perot resonator are external to the laser active region. Thus, any changes in the propagation properties between the two mirrors change the resonance characteristics of the cavity, and thus the produced wavelength. Thus, tunability of the F–P laser is achieved.

2.13.2.2 Bragg Lasers

The cleaved edges of a Fabry–Perot resonator (Fig. 2.55) consist of mirrors with reflectivity and flatness that may result in laser light that lacks the required spectral quality; employing Bragg gratings as reflectors a narrower spectrum is achieved. The Bragg grating is achieved by periodically varying the doping of the material (or the index of refraction, dark or light blue regions). Such lasers are known as distributed Bragg reflectors (DBR).

Distributed feedback (DFB) lasers are monolithic devices with an internal structure based on InGaAsP waveguide technology and internal grating, typically at the interface n-InP substrate and n-InGaAsP layers to provide optical feedback at a fixed wavelength that is determined by the grating pitch, hence DBR-DFB. The DFB structure may be combined with multiple quantum-well (MQW) structures to improve the linewidth of the produced laser light (make it as narrow as a few hundred kHz). MQWs have a similar structure with the diode structure but the active junction is few atomic layers thin; see next section).

Distributed feedback (DFB) tuned laser arrays have also been integrated to produce a range of desired wavelengths. In this arrangement, an independent filter, rather than a cavity with a waveguide grating, determines the wavelength of each individual DFB laser. All laser outputs have then been multiplexed and launched into the fiber. Reportedly, 20-channel selectable sources with 50 GHz separation and 0 dB output power and modulated at 2.5 Gb/s have produced devices with long-term reliability and low chirp.

DFB advantages:

- Lasers can be integrated on a small device.
- DFBs have a short cavity and are modulated at high speeds independently.
- Temperature variability is the same for all lasers in the device.

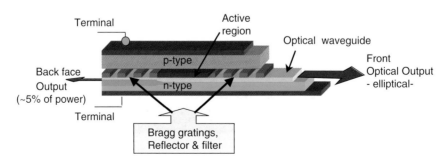

Figure 2.55 Fundamentals of a Bragg laser (notice the ∼5% laser light from the back face).

DFB disadvantages:

- Difficult to obtain precise channel spacing due to variability of individual filters.
- Frequency shift of lasers does not track each other and they may drift into each other.
- Difficult to integrate many channels due to intrinsic losses.
- DFBs require a fine period grating.
- Increased electrical cross talk due to close proximity of integrated amplifiers.
- Directly modulated DFBs exhibit positive frequency chirp; the spectral leading edge of a pulse is blue-shifted (wavelength shortens) and the trailing edge is red-shifted (wavelength is elongated).

2.13.2.3 *VCSEL Lasers*

Fabry–Perot, DFBs, and DBR lasers require electrical current on the order of tens of milliamperes. Moreover, their output beam has an elliptical cross section, typically an aspect ratio of 3:1, that does not match the cylindrical cross section of the fiber core. Thus, a noncylindrical beam may require additional optics to convert it to a cylindrical beam.

Semiconductor quantum-well lasers (QWL) are diode lasers, the active junction layer of which is 50 to 100 angstroms or 5 to 10 atomic layers thin; conventional diode lasers have a 10-fold or larger active layer. Very thin layers are typically grown with molecular beam epitaxy (MBE) or with metal organic chemical vapor deposition (MOCVD).

The active region is a layer doped with elements of the III-V semiconductor group. In one case, it consists of a quantum-well GaAs layer sandwiched between a p-type $Al_xGa_{1-x}As$ layer and n-type $Al_yGa_{1-y}As$ layer. In principle, a stack of 40 p- and n-type AlGaAs and quantum-well GaAs layers are grown on a thick n-type GaAs substrate, topped by a last p-type GaAs thick layer. That is, GaAs*/n-AlGaAs/GaAs/p-AlGaAs/GaAs/.../p-AlGaAs/GaAs* vertical structure, where GaAs* indicates substrate thick layers. This structure is again sandwiched between two metallic electrode layers for the bias voltage (ground is connected with the n-type GaAs* layer). The p-type and n-type multilayers (40–60 quarter-wavelength layers) comprise Bragg reflectors (DBR) that are made with In + Ga + As + (Al or P). More complex structures with multiple quantum wells produce what is termed *multiple quantum-well lasers* (MQWL or MQW). Other VCSEL structures are based on indium phosphide.

The extremely thin active QWL layer has some very interesting properties. A bias current excites the active region and generates electron-holes which produce photons when recombined. The generated electron-hole however are confined to move in an almost horizontal plane found in a narrow energy gap between the p- and n-layers. Although the generated electron-hole pairs represent a small current, nevertheless, they are confined in a small area, and thus the probability of recombination is high. Consequently, a small current produces a large amount of coherent photons within a narrow linewidth. In addition, these narrow layer guides released photons perpendicular to their surface and thus they are also called surface-emitting lasers (SEL). The vertical structure of SELs produces an almost cylindrical beam (TEM_{00}) emitted perpendicularly to the surface of the device, and thus it is commonly known as *vertical-cavity surface-emitting laser* (VCSEL) (Fig. 2.56).

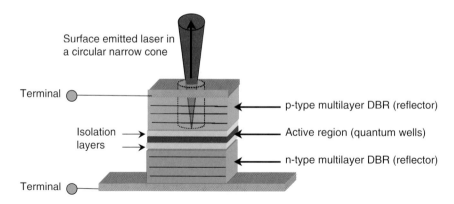

Surface emitted laser in
a circular narrow cone

Terminal

Isolation
layers

Terminal

p-type multilayer DBR (reflector)

Active region (quantum wells)

n-type multilayer DBR (reflector)

Figure 2.56 Fundamentals of a vertical-cavity surface-emitting lasers.

The active region sandwiched between the two Bragg reflector structures comprises a Fabry–Perot resonant cavity. A ridge waveguide structure around the active region or a buried heterostructure barrier confines lateral-mode emission. Thus, the thickness of the layers and the active region determine the wavelength desired. For example, In + Ga + As + P is used for lasers in the wavelength window from 1300 nm to 1550 nm. Other VCSELs are made to emit laser light in the 980 nm range, making them suitable for EDFA pump lasers, or to emit laser light in the 850 nm range, making them suitable for multimode fiber applications. Typical output optical power is in the range of 1 to 1.5 mW, and it depends on device structure, materials used, and manufacturer.

Another important characteristic of the VCSEL is that the produced beam is almost cylindrical with very small divergence (<3 mrad). Because the surface of the VCSEL can be larger than its edge emitting counterpart, the beam has more overall output power (reported to close to 500 mW) yet a lesser output power density. A power density below a catastrophic threshold may keep the device operational longer and thus make it more reliable. In addition, with a surface aperture in excess of 300 μm in diameter, the output power is more efficiently coupled into a single mode fiber.

Because the VCSEL structure is very compact (several micrometers wide), it lends itself to high integration; many VCSELs may be integrated on the same substrate in an array or matrix configuration, each at the same or different wavelength. When VCSELs are integrated with detectors and other optical components (such as modulators and filters) optical devices with more complex functionality may be made, such as space optical switches. An array configuration with VCSELs 125 μm apart may be directly coupled in an aligned array of fibers (such as a fiber ribbon) suitable to a number of communications and parallel computing applications. Moreover, clustering VCSELs and by varying the bias current creates a phenomenon known as thermal lensing by which the laser beam becomes steerable in space; this may lead to optical switching applications.

VCSELs are inherently more immune to chirping (an important issue at bit rates of 10 Gb/s and up) making them better suited to direct modulation in contrast to edge emitting DFBs that require external modulation, or complex monolithic integration with modulators.

Typical VCSELs sourcing wavelengths in the 800-nm range have a typical output power of 0.2 mW, 1 nm spectral linewidth, and they require a ball lens for beam focusing. VCSELs sourcing in the C-band have a typical output power in the neighborhood of 20 mW, and 50 kHz spectral linewidth. However, because of the tremendous interest in VCSELs and the effort in VCSEL R&D, improved specifications are announced frequently.

2.13.2.4   *Optical Comb Generators*

Consider an angle modulated optical signal $Y(t)$ described by

$$Y(t) = A_S \cos(\omega t + m \sin \Omega t)$$

where A_S is the signal amplitude, ω is the optical frequency, m is the modulation index, and Ω is the modulation frequency.

This relationship indicates that the power of the applied signal $Y(t)$ spreads among a spectrum that consists of the fundamental frequency and several sidebands, the amplitude of which is exponentially decreasing. The total number of components depends on the value of m. For example, for $m = 3$, there are seven terms, one fundamental and three sidebands on each side. Thus, $2K + 1$ distinct wavelengths with a predetermined spacing Ω may be generated by a device known as optical comb generator (Fig. 2.57).

The output spectrum of a comb generator is described by

$$S(f) = \Sigma A_k \delta(f - k\Omega), \quad -K < k < K$$

where A_k is the amplitude of the kth component and $\delta(f - k\Omega)$ is the frequency-member of the comb represented by a delta function.

Ideally, all A_k values should be identical; in reality, due to an amplitude modulation (filtering) effect they are not.

Multifrequency tunable lasers are comb generators. The Fabry–Perot laser may also be included in this category because it generates a multiplicity of frequencies (wavelengths), as already explained.

2.13.2.5   *Supercontinuum Spectrum-Slicing Sources*

One technique, known as *supercontinuum generator*, that generates a large number of wavelengths is based on a high-intensity light source, a fiber (about 4-Km long dispersion shifted fiber), and on self-modulation in a highly nonlinear medium (a lithium niobate-based waveguide or a polarization maintaining fiber).

This method employs a continuous wave source, S, which enters a highly nonlinear medium, the supercontinuum generator, SG, where the self-modulation phenomenon generates frequencies within the spectrum of the C-band. Subsequent to this, the

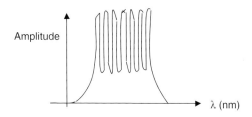

Figure 2.57   Comb generators have an spectral output reminding a comb.

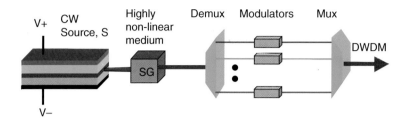

Figure 2.58   Principles of a super-continuum generator.

generated wavelengths enter a demultiplexer (such as a grating). Each wavelength obtained from the demultiplexer constitutes a continuous light source, and therefore each wavelength is individually modulated, and then all modulated sources are multiplexed and coupled into one fiber to construct a WDM signal (Fig. 2.58).

Similarly, a very narrow high-intensity pulse (a few femptoseconds wide), is coupled in a highly dispersive fiber from which a set of different wavelengths is generated; this method is known as chirped-pulse wavelength-division multiplexing (CPWDM).

Consider that the impulse response of the dispersive medium is expressed by

$$H(t) = \exp[j(\pi t^2)/(2\beta'' z)]$$

where z is the optical path distance in the dispersive medium, β'' is the propagation constant second derivative with respect to frequency ϖ (or second-order dispersion coefficient), t is time, and j is the imaginary quantity.

Due to dispersion, the narrow pulse undergoes a Fourier transform spreading the spectral frequency content of the impulse and generating many frequency components; the narrower and more intense the impulse, the more frequency components. If the frequency components are spatially separated, then a large set of individual wavelengths is obtained. This is known as the *chirped-pulse method*, or simply *chirping*.

The optical pulse Fourier expansion in the time domain is a function of the length of optical travel in the medium, the dispersion properties of the medium, and of the spectrum. If L is the optical path length, D is the dispersion coefficient, and $dD/d\lambda$ is the dispersion slope (the derivative of dispersion with respect to wavelength), then the travel time variation per wavelength is

$$\Delta t = DL\Delta\lambda + (1/2)L(\Delta\lambda)^2(dD/d\lambda)$$

The actual length of the dispersive medium plays an important role in the chirping method, as the Fourier transform is a progressive time–space process and it depends on the dispersion coefficient and propagation characteristics of light in the medium. Thus, for a pulse duration τ (in picoseconds) and for a β'' value (in ps^2/km), the dispersion length L_{disp} (in km) is expressed by:

$$L_{\text{disp}} = \pi\tau^2/\beta''$$

It turns out that the actual dispersive fiberlength is few times longer than L_{disp}, preferably three times. As an example, $L_{\text{disp}} = 0.3$ km for a dispersive fiber with

$\beta'' = 21.6$ ps^2/km (Corning SMF-28) and for $t = 1$ ps, then the preferred length is about 1 km.

To encapsulate this chirping method, consider a mode-locked laser source that emits a sequence of ultrashort pulses. Each pulse generates a set of pulsed frequencies in the time-spectrum continuum; each of these pulses is called a *slice*. Now, time-division multiplexed data (via a fast modulator) modulate the bits of every slice and thus each frequency channel is modulated with different data.

2.13.2.6 Chirped-Pulse Amplification

The chirped-pulse method may also be used to generate a high power pulse, a method known as *chirped-pulse amplification* (CPA). According to CPA, the initial pulse is chirped, as described in the previous section, to generate several wavelengths (optical channels); pulse energies are less than a joule. Now, consider that each chirped pulse is passed through an solid-state optical amplifier, such as a Ti:sapphire rod, and is amplified. Then all amplified chirped-pulses are coupled in a fiber of high negative dispersion. The latter retards the low frequencies and synthesizes the chirped frequency components to the original pulse, which in essence performs an inverse Fourier transform; experiments in the 1990s reported peak power at the PetaWatt (10^{15} W) range. Thus, although a single optical amplifier cannot amplify a pulse at such power level, the gain of several amplifiers is combined to yield a very large sum of gains. Current reports claim pulses as short as 24 femtoseconds with an average power of 13 W and a repetitious rate up to 10 KHz.

2.13.2.7 Multifrequency Cavity Lasers

Multifrequency cavity lasers (MFL) are complex devices that consist of a multifrequency laser, a K-input, an N-output port (KXN) waveguide grating router (WGR) possibly integrated with optical amplifiers at each output port, similar to that illustrated in Figure 2.40.

A WGR is a generalized Mach–Zehnder interferometer. The optical signal at each input port of a WGR consists of many wavelengths that are coupled via the first free-space region into the waveguide grating. The waveguide grating consists of waveguides each of different length and/or index of refraction. The optical path difference between neighboring waveguides ΔL causes a wavelength-dependent linear phase shift between them. It turns out that (because of constructive and destructive interference) light of a certain wavelength is coupled to only one output port. Then, each λ is modulated separately and all modulated OChs are multiplexed into one fiber again.

The number of ports N and the *free spectral range* (FSR) determine the optical channel spacing (CS):

$$CS = FSR/N$$

where the FSR is determined by (n_g is the group index of refraction and λ is the wavelength)

$$FSR = \lambda^2/(n_g \Delta L)$$

However, the actual number of channels is constrained by device technology (fiber type, resolution of transmitters and receivers, filter and amplifier characteristics), maximum bit rate, and optical power budget.

WGR advantages:

- Optical channel spacing is extremely accurate.
- Insertion loss is low.
- Simultaneous operation of all wavelengths.
- Fast tuned (<3 ns).
- WGRs are scalable (N × N).
- Temperature variation shifts all wavelengths (entire comb) but CS remains the same.
- Broadcast capability.

WGR disadvantages:

- WGRs are not fiber-based.
- They have a relative large physical size.
- Electrical cross talk increases due to proximity of integrated amplifiers.
- As number of channel increases, the optical channel spacing should be decreased, and thus, the size of the MFL increases, the intracavity loss increases and device performance decreases.

2.13.2.8 Tunable Lasers

Tunable lasers provide the flexibility to selectably generate a wavelength, among a multiplicity as defined by the ITU-T wavelength grid. Tunable lasers find numerous applications in medicine, chemistry, environmental monitoring, and agriculture. In DWDM communications networks, wavelength selectability is a highly desirable feature that facilitates network reconfigurability, survivability, and traffic management.

Tunable lasers can be *single-frequency* or *multifrequency*. Single-frequency lasers (such as DBR lasers) are tuned by controlling the resonant cavity characteristics (refractive index or dimensions). Multifrequency lasers can be *integrated cavity lasers* or *arrayed lasers*. In the former, the cavity is both a filter and a multiport optical power combiner (multiplexer). In the latter, an array of lasers is integrated of individually tuned-frequency lasers, the output of which is combined to produce a range of desired frequencies.

Laser tunability may be achieved electrically, mechanically (by trimming or constriction), or by controlling the temperature (a change of a few degrees is sufficient to tune the laser to another wavelength channel).

Tunability by controlling the temperature has two significant limitations, namely, the tunable range is narrow and as temperature increases, the power consumption of the laser increases and the output power decreases. Therefore, it is more common to achieve tunability by changing the current stepwise (from 1 to 100 mA) in the tuning stage of the device and based on a known relationship between wavelength and tuning current.

Tunability by constriction is achieved by electrorestrictive cantilever action on top of a VCSEL device, thus affecting the effective distance of the upper DBR reflector to the active region and hence the resonant characteristics of the device and the actual wavelength.

Currently, devices with 20 or 40 optical channel selectability on the ITU-T 50 GHz grid have a stability better than 20 pm (picometer), and chirp less than 1 angstrom. However, these devices are relatively slow in wavelength selection on the order of a second. Thus, although they are attractive in some applications, they are not suitable for dynamic selectability (required on the order of milliseconds or faster).

Monolithic multistage tunable lasers may be integrated on the same substrate with filters, amplifiers and modulators. In this case, the modulator is of the electroabsorption (EA) type and the filter of the Bragg type. However, integration may generate undesirable parasitic coupling that induces chirp, electrical cross talk, optical cross talk, and linewidth broadening that degrade the accuracy of the wavelength and the quality of the optical signal.

2.13.2.9 Nanolasers

A growing activity in the field of nanotechnology, a technology to produce devices with nanometer dimensions, is in making lasers with nanoscale dimensions. This activity is an offspring of an effort to grow nanowires needed to massively interconnect many very small devices with a wire density in the millions per square cm.

According to this technology, a metal oxide grows on a matching substrate to form high density whiskers that can be used as interconnecting nanowires. If ZnO whiskers are grown on a sapphire substrate, it turns out that the whiskers may lase when they are pumped up by light at a wavelength of 266 nm, emitting light at 386 nm.

In addition, if p and n dopants are introduced during the process of growing these whiskers, then a high-density nanolaser devices is formed, a density that can be in the range of many billions per square centimeter. Moreover, if instead of ZnO a different metal is used (such as cadmium for blue, magnesium for deep ultraviolet, or other metals well known in the glass industry for their vibrant colors), then the possibilities for a variety of colors including ultraviolet are many.

Nanolasers, when reliably manufactured, will find many applications in the fields of communications, medicine, biotechnology, analytic chemistry, optical computing, storage, displays, optical connectivity, and consumer products. In addition, they will miniaturize many optical devices which at low power will provide critical functionality in many systems.

Yet another activity uses semiconductor materials to produce lasers in the atomic scale (in the range of 100 to 10,000 atoms large), known as *quantum dots*. The benefits of quantum dot lasers is that they need very small current, the produce a narrow linewidth since the "few atoms" device is based on discrete (quantum) energy bands, compared with large devices operating on almost continuous energy bands, and that they have a high differential gain that is suitable for fast on–off switching. The light-emitting characteristics of quantum dots depend on their size, and thus they may find applications in optical switching and optical correlators. Currently, quantum dots in the visible spectrum as well as in the infrared (1.3 μm) spectrum have been produced.

2.13.2.10 Laser Comparison

There is a large range of different lasers meeting different needs and cost models. Lasers may be cooled or uncooled. They may be integrated with modulators or may be stand-alone. They may produce high or low power light. They may produce a very thin (almost) circular beam or an elliptical one. They may be tunable or fixed.

They may be suitable for long-haul or short-haul applications and so on. Therefore, a fair comparison between different types is not a simple process. However, there are certain characteristics that can be compared, assuming everything else remains the same.

For example, Fabry–Perot uncooled lasers, due to dispersion limitations, are suitable for Gigabit Ethernet applications (thus operated at 1.25 Gb/s) up to 10 km fiber-lengths (without amplification) and up to 1 km at 10 Gb/s; a DFB uncooled laser would extend the distance up to 50 km. However, because their cost models are different, selection between the two depends on the actual network characteristics. Similarly, cooled lasers (typically DFB) extend the fiber length to many tens of kilometers at bit rates in excess of 10 Gb/s at a premium (predominantly used in high bandwidth and long-haul applications).

VCSELs have a low emitted optical power (on the order of 5 mW for a device of aperture diameter of 5–10 μm). In comparison, edge emitting DFB lasers have a power density on the order of 5 mW/cm^2 or 200 mW output power from a facet of 1×4 μm, whereas that of a VCSEL may be on the order of 30 kW/cm^2, for a device aperture of 100 μm diameter. This translates to a VCSEL limitation over edge emitting DFB lasers in long-haul communications applications where long fiber length and high bit rate are very important. Although currently DFB lasers at 1.5 μm are suitable for about 800 km single-mode fiber at bit rates exceeding 10 Gb/s (i.e., long-haul applications), VCSELs at 1.3 μm can be used for about 200 km single-mode fiber at bit rates exceeding 1 Gb/s or at 10 Gb/s for about 50 km (suitable for large or medium metropolitan Gigabit Ethernet application), and also for about 50 km multimode fiber at bit rates exceeding 50 Mb/s (small metropolitan networks) or for 1 km at 1 Gb/s (small metropolitan and fiber-to-the-home access applications). This comparison is summarized in Table 2.5 (values are approximate and depend on type of fiber and optical quality of components).

In addition, VCSELs have found several other applications where continuous wave (CW) red, green, and blue lasers are needed, in LAN multimode applications, in printers, and so on. Because of the current interest in sources for communications, more potent VCSELs are expected to become commercially available and applicable in many applications, including single mode fiber and at or above 10 Gb/s. In a similar application, many VCSELs in a matrix configuration and on the same substrate are used to collectively produce a powerful laser beam (Fig. 2.59).

Table 2.5 A comparison between DFB and VCSEL lasers

Laser	Fiber	Distance	Bit Rate	Application
DFB-edge	SMF	40–800 km	~10 Gb/s	DWDM Ultra-long-haul
DFB-edge	SMF	40–200 km	~40 Gb/s	DWDM long-haul
DFB-edge	SMF	10–200 km	~10 Gb/s	Single-λ (1.3 μm) long-haul
DFB-edge	SMF	10–80 km	>10 Gb/s	Single-λ (1.3 μm) long-haul
VCSEL	SMF	10–200 km	~10 Gb/s	Single-λ (1.3 μm) long-haul
VCSEL	SMF	10–80 km	>10 Gb/s	Single-λ (1.3 μm) long-haul
VCSEL	MMF	1–30 km	~50 Mb/s	Single-λ (1.3 μm) Metro
VCSEL	MMF	1–30 km	~50 Mb/s	Single-λ (0.8 μm) Metro
VCSEL	MMF	1 km	~1 Gb/s	Single-λ (0.8 μm) Access
VCSEL	MMF	0.1–0.5 km	~10 Gb/s	Single-λ (0.8 μm) Access

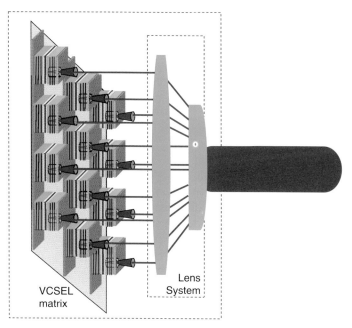

Figure 2.59 Many VCSELs on the same substrate collectively increase the total output power to high intensity.

2.13.2.11 Laser Modules

Laser modules are hermetically sealed packages that contain several individual devices that are required for frequency and power stabilization over a wide range of temperature and over time (due to device aging). Such components are:

- A laser (such as multiquantum wells and DFBs)

- A Fabry–Perot etalon or a Bragg filter

- A modulator (internal or external)

- An internal optical isolator or antireflecting filter to suppress laser reflections (optical feedback)

- A thermistor, a thermoelectric cooler or heat pump (TEC), and a heatsink. The thermistor monitors the package temperature, and a microprocessor acquisition circuit controls the TEC to a constant level, typically $25\,°C$

- A photodiode (PIN or APD) at the back-face of the laser monitors the laser power and an electronic circuit controls the laser bias and thus the forward output optical power

- A connectorized fiber pigtail guides the laser output outside the hermetically sealed package to be coupled with the transmitting fiber. The pigtail may (or may not) be a polarization-maintaining fiber (PMF).

- Finally, the package may include a semiconductor optical amplifier (SOA).

In general, laser modules may operate in one of the wavelength ranges (e.g., about 1,310 nm, or 1,555 nm, etc.) over the temperature range -40 to $65\,°C$, and at bit rates up to 40 Gb/s. They may have an optical power up to 40 mW or higher, and they require a single voltage (+5 V), or one voltage for the laser (+3.7 V), another for the modulator (depending on type), and yet another for the thermoelectric heat-pump (+5 V). Depending on type, the typical physical size of a laser module is approximately 50 mm × 15 mm × 5 mm and for larger assemblies the footprint may be approximately 120 mm × 100 mm.

2.14 LASER BEAMS

Up to this point we have assumed that laser beams have a uniform cross sectional distribution of intensity, they are monochromatic and they are coherent. In reality, most beams have a radial intensity distribution, more intense in the center of the beam reducing radially away from the center, closely matching a Gaussian distribution. Moreover, "monochromatic" beams are not exactly monochromatic, but they also have a Gaussian spectral distribution around a center frequency, ω_o, or wavelength, λ_0. Such beams are known as Gaussian. For a pulse of width τ_0, the Gaussian spectral distribution is expressed as:

$$\Psi(\omega) = (2\tau_0^2/\pi)^{1/4} \cdot \exp[-\tau_0^2(\omega - \omega_o)^2]$$

In the above expression, the frequency ω is set to the angular units rad/s (1 Hz = 2π rad/s); for example, a wavelength of 1.55 μm corresponds to 1.215×10^{15} rad/s.

2.14.1 Gaussian Beams

As the laser beam emerges from the device, the intensity distribution of its cross section is not uniform, but it usually has a Gaussian distribution. Consequently, even if the beam emerges exactly parallel, it does not remain so because spatial diffraction causes the beam to first narrow at a point known as the waist, w_0, and then to diverge at an angle, Θ. As the Gaussian distribution widens, and for all practical purposes, the center area of the beam may be considered almost uniform. The beam radius, w, is defined as the distance from the center or peak intensity of the beam to the point where the intensity has dropped at $1/e^2$, or 13.5% of its peak value. Figure 2.60 depicts the characteristics of a Gaussian beam (Figure 2.60A). In practical beams, the intensity distribution may be neither Gaussian nor circular (Figure 2.60B); noncircular cross-section reduces the coupling efficiency of the beam in fiber. The noncircularity of the beam is corrected with cylindrical microlens (Fig. 2.60C).

The optimum waist, $w_{0,\text{optimum}}$, for a wavelength λ at a distance z from the source is defined as:

$$w_{0,\text{optimum}} = [\lambda z/\pi]^{1/2}$$

Similarly, the distance at which the radius spreads by a factor sqrt2 is called Rayleigh range, z_R, defined by:

$$z_R = \pi w_0^2/\lambda$$

In practice, not all beams are Gaussian. The deviation from a Gaussian beam is indicated by a M-square factor, M^2. For example, pure Gaussian beams have a value of

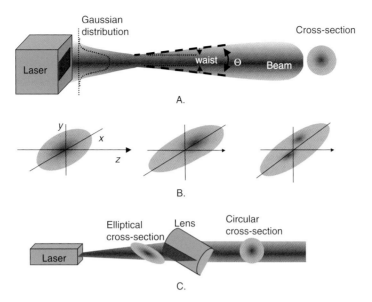

Figure 2.60 Characteristics of a Gaussian beam, A, cross-sectional distributions of practical beams, B, and corrective action, C.

M = 1, the He-Ne is very close to Gaussian with M < 1.1, and diode laser beams have M ranging from 1.1 to 1.7.

Divergent beams are corrected to parallel with a lens system known as a *collimator*.

2.14.2 Near-Field and Far-Field Distribution

The beam generated by a laser device is neither perfectly narrow, nor cylindrical, nor centered. Thus, the almost Gaussian distribution in the x-axis may differ from the distribution in the y-axis. Moreover, the intensity distribution at the "edge" or the output facet of the laser device (also known as the aperture of the source) is not the same with the distribution at some distance. At a short distance from the source aperture, the intensity distribution is known as *near-field*, and at a far distance, where the intensity distribution seems to remain almost unchanged, it is known as *far-field* (Fig. 2.61).

The near-field is that region where light rays exhibit disordered phase fronts. This region is also known as the Fresnel zone. The far-field is that region where fronts have become ordered and the beam propagation characteristics have been stabilized. This region is also known as the Fraunhofer zone.

Because the terms near and far are fuzzy and subjective, a metric has been developed to distinguish between the two. Thus, the near-field distance, D_{nf}, and the far-field distance, D_{ff}, have been expressed in terms of the source aperture (the area of the laser waveguide at the edge) and to the wavelength of the laser light, as:

$$D_{ff} \gg \pi d^2 / \lambda$$

and

$$D_{nf} \ll \pi d^2 / \lambda$$

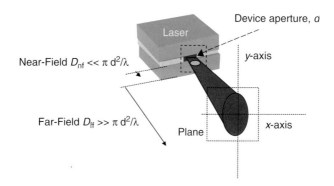

Figure 2.61 Definition of near field and far field.

Which of the two parameters (D_{ff} or D_{nf}) is more suitable depends on the optical design specifications. For monochromatic light, and if focusing lens are incorporated into the design, then the far-field is better suited. In addition, the far-field angular dispersion is superior to that of the near-field. If, however, the laser light needs to be coupled in another waveguide in the vicinity of the laser, the near-field may be better suited. For laser diodes with divergent beams, the near-field is few microns from the output facet. If the far-field divergence angle is θ and the near-field width is w, a beam parameter for a given wavelength λ, K, is defined as

$$K = 4\lambda/\pi w\theta$$

Occasionally, a similar parameter M is used, defined as $M = 1/\text{sqrt}\,K$. Typically, laser manufacturers provide near-field and far-field data for their devices.

2.14.3 Peak Wavelength

Photonic sources do not source a purely monochromatic beam. In practice, they source a continuum of wavelengths in a narrow spectral range with a near-Gaussian distribution. The wavelength with the highest radiant intensity of the source is known as the *peak wavelength*. The wavelength spread at either side of the peak is measured in nm; e.g., 1550 ± 20 nm indicates that 1550 is the peak wavelength with a Gaussian spread at either side of 20 nm. A *monochromator* is a narrow bandpass filtering device that allows a very narrow spectral portion to pass through it.

2.14.4 Degree of Coherence

Laser beams, by definition are considered coherent; that is, the wavefronts of all rays departing the laser device are in phase. However, this is not absolutely true, as it is verified with a simple interference experiment (see Interference by Two Point Sources in Chapter 2). According to this experiment, when the intensity minima and maxima of the fringes in the interference pattern are well defined, the beam is considered *coherent*, and when they are not (the pattern appears blurry), the beam is *incoherent*. In fact, because coherency is not absolute and in order to remove subjectiveness, a *degree of coherence* has been defined to indicate the percentage of rays in phase. Thus, if in such experiment the minimum and maximum intensities of the fringed pattern are I_{min} and I_{max}, respectively, then the degree of coherence is defined as

$$\text{Degree of coherence} = (I_{max} - I_{min})/(I_{max} + I_{min})$$

As a rule of thumb, a beam is considered coherent when the degree of coherence is above 0.88, partially coherent if it is less than 0.88, and incoherent if it is very small (<0.5).

It is worth noting that, although at the output of a source a beam may be considered coherent, as the beam travels through matter and because the propagation constant is not uniform for all wavelengths in the beam, coherency (or the in-phase state) may change. Thus, the length of travel during which the beam remains coherent (>0.88) is known as the *coherence length*, and, correspondingly, the travel time along this length is known as the *coherence time*.

When coherency of two beams varies with time and the two beams interfere, a time-varying interferogram is produced, which is known as a *speckle pattern*.

2.14.5 Laser Safety

Safety cannot be stressed enough or overlooked. The spectrum used in communications is invisible light to human eyes, an oxymoron but true. Therefore, it is very risky to look straight into a laser beam or into a fiber with bare eyes to check if there is any light in it; this invisible light may be at a power level or at an irradiance that can permanently damage the *cornea* and/or the *retinal sensors*. Retinal sensors do not regenerate, and once they are damaged they remain so.

The eye physiology is such that light is focused on the *retina*, where there are about 130 millions of light sensors, rods and cones, the axons of which send elec-trochemical signals to other retinal neurons where image preprocessing takes place and from where more signals are sent via the optic nerve to the brain for final post-processing (Fig. 2.62).

Rods are very sensitive and need only a few photons to be activated, and they mediate black-and-white (and gray-scale) vision. Cones need many photons to be activated, and they mediate color vision. The highest concentration of cones is in the *fovea*, that part of the retina, which is on the visual axis of the lens. However, both rods

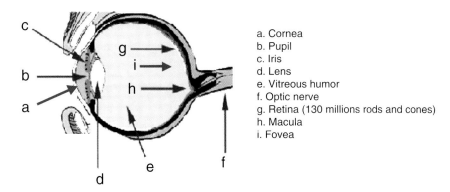

a. Cornea
b. Pupil
c. Iris
d. Lens
e. Vitreous humor
f. Optic nerve
g. Retina (130 millions rods and cones)
h. Macula
i. Fovea

Figure 2.62   Physiology of the eye.

and cones have a very narrow spectral response, from red to violet and they cannot "see" wavelengths below red (infrared) that are used in communications, or beyond violet (ultraviolet) that are used in manufacturing and photochemistry. Because of the lens-focusing action, a beam with a cross section of 1 cm^2 on the lens is concentrated to less than 20 μm^2 on the fovea. This represents an enormous power density factor, such that 1 W/cm^2 on the lens becomes many kW/cm^2 on the fovea. Thus, laser light may permanently damage the retina and particularly the cornea.

There are two factors to consider in retinal damage, radiance of the beam and time of exposure (of a continuous or pulsed beam), and one safety rule, use laser eye protectors. A source is considered continuous if it emits light continuously from 0.25 to 30,000 seconds; below 0.25 sec, it is considered pulsed, and ordinary eye protectors made with polycarbonate can withstand irradiances up to 100 W/cm^2 (1 mW/m^2) at 10.6 μm for several seconds.

Federal law mandates to have the classification of the laser source affixed on the device. The most common classifications are:

- Class I: Laser sources that do not impose any hazard.
- Class II: Low-power laser sources that do not impose hazard due to the blinking of the eye. However, prolonged exposure may cause damage.
- Class IIIa: Laser sources that are not hazardous when viewed for <0.25 seconds. However, they may be hazardous if the exposure is prolonged or if the laser beam is focused by a lens.
- Class IIIb: Laser sources that may cause damage if viewed directly or through specular reflections but do not produce hazardous reflections.
- Class IV: Laser sources that cause damage if viewed directly or through specular reflections and produce hazardous reflections.

In general, laser sources in fiber communications are of Class I with Hazard Level 3A, and this may lead us to underestimate the danger; what if there is also a pump laser at 1 W? As a consequence, system designers and fiber connector designers take precautions so that there is automatic power laser shutdown (APSD) as soon as a fiber is disconnected from the source, particularly where laser power radiation exposure is greater than 50 mW (17 dBm).

APSD on the system site accomplished with "smart" fiber connectors, or connectors that when are optically disconnected they are also electrically disconnected. However, smart connectors do not address the outside plant in case of laser exposure due to fiber cut. This is addressed by IEC, which has defined the "Probability of Potential Exposure" when APSD fails to function but has not issued recommendations yet.

The safety issue is so serious that standards bodies have issued certain recommendations. For example:

- The ITU-T recommendation G.664 provides optical safety procedures.
- The American National Standard Institute (ANSI Z136.1–2,000) provides maximum permissible exposure (MPE) limits and exposure durations, from 100 fsec to 8 hours.
- Similarly, the American Conference of Governmental Industrial Hygienists (ACGIH) provides the threshold limit values (TLV) and biological exposure indices (BEI).

- Both ANSI and ACGIH have become the basis for the U.S. Federal Product Performance Standard (21 CFR 1,040).

The APSD response time needs to be fast, the speed of which is calculated from eye safety exposure requirements. Thus, an output optical power of 500 mW (27 dBm) requires an APSD response time of about 2 seconds. However, as the total optical power in the fiber may be the sum of optical amplifiers and optical signals, the sum of power is greater than 500 mW, and therefore the response time should be decreased to less than 500 msecs.

2.15 MODULATORS

Certain optical materials exhibit properties that significantly affect at least one of the characteristics of (monochromatic) light when it traverses them, namely, frequency, phase, polarization, or optical intensity. Such materials are used as optical modulator devices to affect one of the light characteristics in a controllable and timely manner.

This type of modulation is indirect. That is, the modulator is positioned in line with the optical path of a continuous wave (CW) laser beam, and as the beam traverses the device, it affects one of the light characteristics by applying a modulated electrical signal to it. Modulators may be either *external* to the laser source or *monolithically integrated* with it.

In certain cases, modulation of the optical signal is *direct*. That is, the laser source is directly modulated in amplitude by varying the applied voltage to it (i.e., bias plus data).

External modulation is more suitable to extremely high bit rates (>10 Gb/s) and long fiber spans and direct modulation to lower bit rates (<10 Gb/s) and shorter fiber spans for the following reason:

> The dielectric constant and refractive index of the active region of the laser depend on the applied field. In direct modulation, as the modulating voltage is directly applied to the laser device, at the transitions of the voltage from high to low value and vice versa, the optical parameters of the active region temporarily vary and so does the tuning of the resonant ability of the cavity. Thus, the optical pulse that is generated by the laser has a spectral frequency that consists of the center wavelength but also of shorter and longer wavelengths. This is known as the *chirping effect*. Now, as the chirped signal travels in a dispersive medium (the fiber), dispersion puts a limit on the bit rate and/or the transmission distance source-detector.

Consequently, *external modulators* have negligible chirp (phase jitter) because the modulating voltage is applied on them only, while the laser source remains at constant voltage; this is in contrast to direct modulated lasers. In addition, external modulators can modulate high optical power CW beam with depth greater than 20 dB. On the other hand, external modulation requires more than one component. This is addressed with *monolithically integrated* modulators and laser sources that yield a compact single component design. However, there are several applications (up to 10 Gb/s and short-span of few kilometers) for which direct modulated laser sources are suitable and attractive because of their low cost (compared to external or *monolithically integrated*), such as coarse WDM and Metro applications.

The parameters that characterize the performance of optical modulators are *modulation depth*, η, *bandwidth*, *insertion loss*, *degree of isolation*, and *power*.

For **intensity modulators**: The *modulation depth*, η, is

$$\eta = (I_0 - I)/I_0$$

The *extinction ratio* is the maximum value of η, η_{max}, when the intensity of the transmitted beam is a minimum, I_{min}, and it is given by:

$$\eta_{max} = \eta(I_{min})$$

In intensity modulation, the terms *modulation depth* and *extinction ratio* (measured in dB) determine the intensity of the optical signal after modulation corresponding to logic "one" bit and to logic "zero" bit; that is, extinction ratio is the ratio of peak optical intensity for logic "1" to peak for logic "0". The extinction ratio of the signal impacts the quality and integrity of the optical signal and thus the BER at the receiver; an extinction ratio of 8 dB corresponds to a BER of 10^{-15}. A similar term to extinction ratio is the *contrast ratio*. This indicates the peak to minimum value of a return to zero (RZ) pulse, and not the ratio of peak of logic "one" to the peak of logic "zero."

The extinction ratio is also related to the *modulation voltage* of the modulator; that is, to the maximum and minimum voltage required to modulate a continuous optical signal to logic "one" and to logic "zero."

For **phase modulators**: The *modulation depth*, η, is defined similarly provided that the intensity is related to phase ($I = I(\phi)$).

For **frequency modulators**: A figure of merit is used known as the maximum frequency deviation D_{max}, defined by:

$$D_{max} = |f_m - f_0|/f_0$$

where f_m is the maximum frequency shift of the carrier f_0.

The *degree of isolation*, in decibels, represents the maximum optical change produced by the modulator and is related to the extinction ratio ($10\log(\eta)$) or to the max. frequency deviation ($10\log D_{max}$).

Additional parameters are:

- Modulator sensitivity on polarization refers to modulator's transmissivity and performance based on the polarization state of the modulated optical beam; it is also known as *polarization sensitivity*.

- Frequency response refers to the frequency at which the output optical power falls at half its maximum value; it is also known as 3 dB modulation bandwidth.

- Chirp refers to the amount and amplitude of added or enhanced frequency side-lobes to the center frequency of the optical signal.

- Insertion loss refers to the loss of the optical signal.

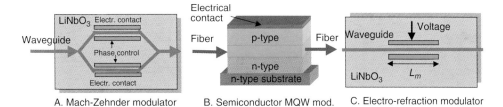

A. Mach-Zehnder modulator   B. Semiconductor MQW mod.   C. Electro-refraction modulator

Figure 2.63 Shown are three types of optical modulators, a Mach–Zehnder, a multi-quantum well (MQW), and an electro-refraction modulator.

2.15.1 Types of Modulators

Among the various modulators, the semiconductor type is most interesting because it may be integrated with laser devices. Among them are the lithium niobate (LiNbO$_3$) Mach–Zehnder (M–Z), the indium phosphide (InP) electroabsorption, the electroabsorption multiquantum well (MQW), and the electrorefraction (Fig. 2.63).

The Mach–Zehnder (MZ) modulators consist of a Y-splitter junction, one or two phase-modulators (typically made with diffused titanium or hydrogen in LiNbO$_3$ or with InGaAsP), two waveguides and a Y-combiner junction (Fig. 2.63A); however, these materials are not the only ones as other materials, such as polymers, may also be used. Thus, the incoming optical power is split by the first Y-junction into two equal paths (of the waveguide segments). The application of a field (voltage) on one of the paths causes a refractive index change and thus a shift in the relative phase between the two paths. Then, the two parts recombine. Based on the degree of phase-shift, light from the two segments interferes at the recombining Y-junction destructively or constructively and the continuous signal is modulated. For best destructive interference, the induced phase shift must be 180° at the recombination junction yielding a logic "zero." Constructive interference yields a logic "one." If the voltage required to cause 180° shift is V_{180}, then any applied voltage V (other than V_{180}) causes a phase shift:

$$\Delta\Phi = k\,180°\,(V/V_{180})$$

where k is a general function that compensates for possible nonlinear material behavior; in a typical case and for small voltage variations, k is linear and constant almost equal to one.

When the applied voltage V is less than V_{180}, destructive interference is partial and the modulation depth is not the deepest (the deepest modulation depth possible is the most desirable). To keep the applied voltage relatively small, the length of the device short, and yet further increase the modulation depth, a separate voltages is applied simultaneously at each waveguide segment but with opposite polarities. Thus, the index of refraction of both paths is affected but in opposite direction and hence the phase difference between the two paths is maximized to nearly 180°. In this case, the phase difference $\Delta\Phi$ is

$$\Delta\Phi = 180°\,(|V_1/V_{180}| + |V_2/V_{180}|)$$

Note that because the applied voltages are smaller, the operating voltage points at each path are within the linear behavior of the material and thus the linearity assumption holds.

The modulation depth is directly related to the extinction ratio of the modulator, or the optical power of logic "one" over the optical power of logic "zero." Similarly, the quadrature bias of the modulator is also directly related to its dynamic range. Thus, the extinction ratio of the modulator is closely linked with the received BER of the signal.

Electroabsorption (EA) modulators are on–off optical devices made with InGaAsP and the percent of absorbed photons depends on the strength of the applied field. They are compact and stable devices easily integrated with other optical devices (e.g., DFB lasers). EAs have an almost logarithmic attenuation of optical power that depends on a reverse voltage applied to them, as opposed to laser devices that require forward bias. With no voltage applied, EA modulators are transparent and when a voltage is applied they absorb light at the laser wavelength they are designed for. Thus, they cause a modulation depth in excess of 45 dB. They are fast devices and therefore they can modulate a continuous laser power and become sources of short optical pulses (and small duty cycle) and at bit rates in excess of 40 Gb/s. However, the integrated structure should be electrically isolated from the laser device to avoid parasitic influences.

Electroabsorption multiquantum-well (EA-MQW) modulators are directional couplers with light-absorption properties that are based on semiconductor structures known as multi-quantum-wells. In this case, light is absorbed based on the voltage applied. MQWs act as fast shutters and may be integrated with DFB lasers.

Electrorefraction modulators (ER) are based on the Pockels effect to directly control the phase of an optical wave upon the application of a voltage. These modulators consist of a Ti diffused waveguide (to increase the refractive index) in a $LiNbO_3$ substrate. Deposited at either side of the waveguide are strip electrodes to apply a transverse field across the waveguide. The applied voltage for $180°$ shift depends on the length of the waveguide immersed in the field and on the plane orientation with respect of the field and the optical propagation for which the $LiNbO_3$ crystal is cut.

Modulators have a transfer function which describes the optical output power versus applied field or voltage and based on which a bias for optimum modulation is determined and must be maintained.

2.15.2   A Case: Amplitude Modulation

An analysis of amplitude (intensity) modulation of an optical channel yields some interesting results that explain certain degradations observed during experimentation with very fast bit rates (>10 Gb/s). Here, we present a simple modulation case to identify these results; the reader may expand this discussion with more comprehensive cases.

Consider a monochromatic signal, ω_c, which is amplitude modulated by a function $g(t)$, and described by

$$m(t) = g(t) \cos \omega_c t$$

The amplitude modulating function $g(t)$ is described in general by

$$g(t) = [g_0 + mv(t)]$$

and thus

$$m(t) = [g_0 + mv(t)] \cos \omega_c t$$

where m is the modulation index (equal to 1 for 100% modulation), g_0 is a DC component that for simplicity can be set to 1, and $v(t)$ is the modulating function.

Now, depending on the trigonometric function of $v(t)$, the modulated signal $m(t)$ may be expanded in three terms:

$$m(t) = g_0 \cos \omega_c t + (m/2)[g_m \cos(\omega_c - \omega_m)t] + (m/2)[g_m \cos(\omega_c + \omega_m)t]$$

Here we have assumed a simple case where $v(t) = g_m \cos \omega_m t$; in more complex cases, trigonometric expansion becomes more elaborate, yet more interesting. The above expansion yields three terms, the main frequency (first term) and two sidebands, each ω_m far from ω_c.

In a vectorial representation, the latter relationship is written as

$$m(t) = \text{Re}[e^{j\omega ct} + (m/2)e^{j(\omega c - \omega m)t} + (m/2)e^{j(\omega c - \omega m)t}]$$

where Re denotes the real part of the complex exponential notation. If the e^{xt} terms are viewed as phasors, then $m(t)$ consists of three terms, one stationary and two counter-rotating terms, the sum of which yields the modulation signal. If the amplitude of the carrier is unity, then each sideband has a power of $m^2/4$ and both $m^2/2$.

Based on this analysis and under certain worst-case conditions, an interesting degradation may take place; if the lower sideband frequency $(\omega_c - \omega_m)$ is shifted clockwise by θ degrees and the upper sideband $(\omega_c + \omega_m)$ is shifted clockwise by 180-θ degrees, the resultant vector represents a phase-modulated wave the amplitude modulation of which is largely canceled, or the modulation index becomes zero. Clearly, in cases in between, the degradation of the modulation index is partial.

In fiber transmission, the two sidebands represent different wavelengths, one at λ_1 corresponding to $(\omega_c - \omega_m)$ and another at λ_2 corresponding to $(\omega_c + \omega_m)$ which, because of dispersion phenomena, travel at different speeds, and thus at different phases. Consequently, on–off keying (OOK) modulation, under certain conditions, is expected to trigger certain interesting phenomena.

2.15.3 Modulation and Bit Error Probabilities

Noise in communications causes erroneous bits with a probability of occurrence related to the distribution of noise (Gaussian), the signal-to-noise ratio, and the modulation method.

Consider electrical bipolar modulation. Consider a noise content in the signal with a root mean square (RMS) voltage value V_n (to simplify this discussion, we disregard noise added by the receiver), and an arriving at the receiver pulse with peak voltage $|V_p|$. Consider also that there is a decision voltage, b, based on which a determination is made whether the received pulse is logic "one" or logic "zero." Typically, the decision voltage is selected such that is well above the RMS noise for a positive pulse and well below it for a negative pulse; thus, in the bipolar case, the threshold may be set at the zero level, $b = 0$. Depending on the actual relative difference of the received amplitudes for V_p and V_n, and on the expected signal voltage, the probability of an errored "one" is P_{MARK} $(V_p - V_n < 0)$, or noise is more negative than the received positive signal and therefore the decision threshold, b, perceives it as a "zero." Similarly, the probability for an errored "zero" is P_{SP} $(-V_p + V_n > 0)$. Thus, assuming that the probability of an errored "one" and an errored "zero" is equal (which is a good assumption for a long string of bits), then the total probability that an error will occur, P_ε, is

$$P_\varepsilon = \tfrac{1}{2} P(V_p - V_n < 0) + \tfrac{1}{2} P(-V_p + V_n > 0)$$

When the probabilities are worked out analytically, the total probability is expressed in terms of the RMS value of the Gaussian standard deviation noise σ_n and the error complementary function erfc(.), as

$$P_\varepsilon = \tfrac{1}{2} \, \text{erfc}(V_p / \sqrt{(2\sigma_n)})$$

where the function erfc(.) is a complementary error function provided by tables and is expressed as

$$\text{erfc}(x) = \{1/[x \sqrt{(2\pi)}]\} \, e[\exp(-x^2/2)]$$

and the standard deviation σ is expressed in terms of the number of samples n, the observations x_i, and the mean value x_{mean} of the n observations, as

$$\sigma = \sqrt{\left\{[1/(n-1)] \sum (x_i - x_{\text{mean}})^2\right\}}$$

The square of the standard deviation, σ^2, is also known as the variance. The variance of a discrete random variable (or variate) x with mean x_{mean} is by definition

$$\text{Var}(x) = \sum (x_i - x_{\text{mean}})^2 P_x(i) \text{ over all samples } i \text{ of the variate } x$$

where P is the probability function for the discrete case and the mean is

$$x_{\text{mean}} = \sum i P_x(i) \text{ for all } i$$

In this case, the ratio of peak signal voltage to RMS noise is the SNR.

From this relationship of probability for errored bits, a bit error rate (BER) relationship may be obtained. In practice, the BER relationship is expressed in measurable terms of the means (μ_0 and μ_1 for space and mark, respectively), the standard deviations (σ_0 and σ_1 for space and mark, respectively), and decision threshold voltage V_d:

$$\text{BER} = \tfrac{1}{2} \, \text{erfc}\{(|\mu_1 - V_d|)/\sigma_1\} + \tfrac{1}{2} \, \text{erfc}\{(|\mu_0 - V_d|)/\sigma_0\}$$

The same measurable terms also derive the signal to ratio Q-factor as:

$$Q = (|\mu_1 - \mu_0|)/(|\sigma_1 - \sigma_0|)$$

In traditional communications, it has been established that in order to achieve a probability of one errored symbol in 10^{10} symbols, then a SNR of more than 15 dB is needed. In fact, because the probability of error decreases rapidly with small increases in SNR above 15 dB, the region above 15 dB is known as the *cliff*.

A similar analysis follows for optical signals; the difference is that electrical power is now expressed as optical power. Thus, the probability of bit error for the ASK (coherent or synchronous detection) modulation method, and for the OOK are given by the formulas are estimated using the same logic as previously, but now the unipolar

Table 2.6   Corresponding BER values with SNR

BER-Pe	SNR (dB)
10^{-10}	19.4
10^{-9}	18.6
10^{-8}	18
10^{-7}	17.3
10^{-6}	16.4
10^{-5}	15.3

signal varies between a zero level and a positive peak level V, and therefore the threshold, b, is positive (and not zero as we assumed in the bipolar case):

$$\text{ASK (coherent): } P_e = \frac{1}{2}\,\text{erfc}\sqrt{\frac{S}{4N}}$$

and

$$\text{OOK: } P_e = \frac{1}{2}\,\text{erfc}\sqrt{\frac{S}{N}}$$

where the function erfc is the complementary error function, which is a rather complicated function the value of which is obtained from mathematical tables. Table 2.6 lists some BER and corresponding SNR approximate values.

Example 1: A random discrete variable x has the following probability function:

$P_x(i) = 1/10$ for $i = 2$, $P_x(i) = 2/10$ for $i = 3$,

$P_x(i) = 4/10$ for $i = 4$, $P_x(i) = 2/10$ for $i = 5$, $P_x(i) = 1/10$ for $i = 6$.

Calculate: a. the mean value, b. the standard deviation.

A. From the relationship $x_{\text{mean}} = \sum i\,P_x(i)$ for all i, the mean value is calculated:

$$x_{\text{mean}} = (1/10)(2) + (2/10)(3) + (4/10)(4) + (2/10)(5) + (1/10)(6)$$
$$= (40/10) = 4$$

B. From the relationship $\sigma = \text{sqrt}\{[1/(n-1)]\sum(x_i - x_{\text{mean}})^2\}$, the standard deviation is calculated:

$$\sigma = \text{sqrt}\,1/5[\{(1/10) - 4\}^2 + \{(2/10) - 4\}^2 + \{(4/10) - 4\}^2$$
$$+ \{(2/10) - 4\}^2 + \{(1/10) - 4\}^2]$$
$$= \text{sqrt}\,1/5[15.21 + 14.44 + 12.96 + 14.44 + 15.21] = \text{sqrt}\,[14.45] = 3.80$$

Example 2: Calculate the probability error in the ASK (coherent) case if the S/N ratio is 18 dB. The S/N power ratio is calculated from $18(\text{dB}) = 10\log x$ as $x = 63.36$. Based on this, the probability error is calculated:

$$P_e = (1/2)\,\text{erfc}(\text{sqrt}[63.36/4]) = (1/2)\,\text{erfc}(\text{sqrt}(15.84)) = (1/2)\,\text{erfc}\,(3.98)$$
$$= (1/2)[1.8 \times 10^{-8}] = 9 \times 10^{-9}.$$

2.16   PHOTODETECTORS AND RECEIVERS

Optical detectors, or *photodetectors*, are transducers that alter one of their parameters according to the amount of photons impinging on them. Thus, light may affect conductivity (photoresistors), electrochemical properties (rods and cones of retina), or the amount of electron-hole pairs generated (photodiodes); in semiconductor materials, when a photon interacts with it (is absorbed), an electron is excited from the valence to the conduction band, leaving in the valence band a positive hole. However, the response time is very different for each case. In communications, fast response is very critical for multimegabit rates, and thus photodetectors that convert photonic pulses to electrical are more suitable. In particular, photodetectors with high optical power sensitivity, very fast response time (fast rise and fall time), and a desirable response to a range of wavelengths that matches the range of transmitted wavelengths are desirable. Such photodetectors are the semiconductor *positive intrinsic negative* (PIN) photodiode and the *avalanche photo diode* (APD) (Fig. 2.64).

The principles of photodetectors are based on the p–n junction electrical potential structure and the optical wavelength that penetrates it. For example, when a p-type and an n-type semiconductor material come in electrical contact, the Fermi level of the two lign up, and as a consequence the conduction and valence levels of the two are not lined up at the same level (the p is higher) and a potential difference (or drift space) between the two is created, also known as *depletion layer*. The Fermi level of a p-type semiconductor material is between the conduction layer and valence layer but closer to the latter; for an n-type, it is closer to the conduction layer. The energy difference between valence and conduction energy bands is known as the *band gap*, and for different crystals it has different values; for example, Ge has 0.67 eV, Si 1.12 eV, InP 1.35, and GaAs 1.42 eV. Thus, when an electron is excited in the p-conduction level, it drifts down to the n-conduction level as a result of the potential difference. The two levels may be better aligned by an externally applied forward bias (voltage), or be further separated by a reverse bias.

Now, in certain p–n junctions, electrons are excited by photons from the valence to the conduction level. Clearly, the energy of the photon must be equal or greater than

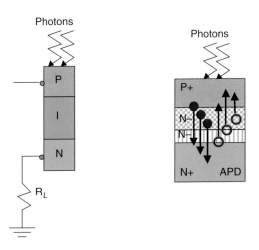

Figure 2.64   A PIN and an APD conceptual photodiode structure.

the energy between the valence and conduction bands, or *energy gap Eg*. This defines the minimum energy of photons, or the longest wavelength (also known as *critical* or *cutoff wavelength*), above which neither excitation nor absorption takes place; in such case the junction appears transparent to the photon. Thus, thee longest wavelength that establishes the critical wavelength for a particular junction is derived from the well-known relationship $Eg = h\nu = hc/\lambda$, where $hc = 1.24$ eV·μm and conduction levels and λ is the critical wavelength. Since Eg is not the same for all materials (Ge, In, P, As, Ga, etc.), the critical wavelength depends on the type of materials that comprise the p–n junction. There are several compound materials that can absorb light and thus be used as photodetecting materials, such as ZnSe, GaAs, CdS, InP, InAs, etc. However, in fiber communications only those materials that absorb photons of wavelength between 0.8 and 1.65 μm are usable, and among them are GaAs and InP. As an example, Eg for GaAs is approximately 1.42 eV, then the cutoff wavelength is at 1.24 (eVμm)/1.42 (eV) = 0.87 μm, which indicates that GaAs is transparent to wavelengths greater than 0.87 μm, and thus they cannot be detected and thus better matching compounds are used such as InGaAs.

As electrons are excited to the conduction level, they drift into the depletion layer. However, these electrons travel at a speed that depends on both the potential difference across the drift space (or depletion layer) and the physical length of the junction (based on a lattice constant determined by the atomic arrangement of the compound); these electrons constitute a photocurrent.

Based on the above, certain key parameters characterize the photodetectors used in communications; *spectral response*, *photosensitivity*, *quantum efficiency*, *dark current*, *forward biased noise*, *noise equivalent power*, *terminal capacitance*, *timing response* (rise time and fall time), *frequency bandwidth*, and *cutoff frequency*.

- *Spectral response* relates the amount of current produced with the wavelengths of impinging light. Different materials respond differently to electromagnetic radiation. Si detectors respond well to short wavelengths (0.5–1.2 μm), they are compatible with integrated Si devices and inexpensive, but they fall short in DWDM applications (1.3–1.6 μm). Similarly, InSb responds to a spectrum about three times as wide as that of Si (0.5–5.1 μm).

- *Photosensitivity* is the ratio of optical power (in watts) incident on the device to the resulting current (in amperes); also known as *responsivity* (measured in A/W).

- *Absolute spectral power responsivity* is the ratio of the output photocurrent (in amperes) from the photodetector to the spectral radiant flux (in watts) at the input of the photodetector.

- *Sensitivity* (in dBm) is the minimum input optical power detected by the receiver (at a certain BER).

- At a specific high bit rate, the output photocurrent swing falls at half its maximum; this maximum bandwidth is known as *3-dB bandwidth*.

- *Quantum efficiency* is the number of generated electron-hole pairs (i.e., current) divided by the number of photons.

- *Dark current* is the amount of current that flows through the photodiode at the absence of any light (hence, dark), when the diode is reverse biased. This is a source of noise under reversed bias conditions.

- *Forward biased noise* is a (current) source of noise that is related to the shunt resistance of the device. The shunt resistance is defined as the ratio voltage (near 0 V) over the amount of current generated. This is also called *shunt resistance noise*.

- *Noise equivalent power* is defined as the amount of light (at a given wavelength) that is equivalent to the noise level of the device.

- *Timing response* of the photodetector is defined as the time lapsed for the output signal to reach from 10% to 90% its amplitude (also known as rise time) and from 90% to 10% (also known as fall time).

- *Terminal capacitance* is the capacitance from the p–n junction of the diode to the connectors of the device; it limits the response time of the photodetector.

- *Frequency bandwidth* is defined as the frequency (or wavelength) range in which the photodetector is sensitive. The frequency sensitivity boundaries are found from the wavelength with maximum power level and at a power drop measured in decibels, such as 3 dB down, or measured in percentage, such as 10% down.

- *Cutoff frequency* is the highest frequency (longest wavelength) to which the photodetector is (meaningfully) sensitive.

Based on these definitions, the shot noise current I_{S-N} from a photodetector is then provided by the relationship

$$I_{S-N} = [2e(I_{dark} + I_{ph})B]^{1/2}$$

where, I_{dark} is the current that flows at the absence of the photonic signal, hence *dark current*, I_{ph} is the photocurrent generated by the photonic signal, and B is the bandwidth of the photodetector (in MHz).

Similarly, when the generated current flows through a load resistor, thermal noise current is generated, I_{Th-N}, the mean value of which is expressed by:

$$I_{Th-N} = [4\,kTB/R]^{1/2}$$

where, T is the temperature (in degrees Kelvin), B is the bandwidth of the photodetector, k is Boltzmann's constant, and R is the load resistance.

If the signal power is expressed in terms of the photocurrent and the load resistor, then the signal to noise ratio, SNR, is expressed by:

$$\text{SNR} = 10\log\,[\text{Signal power/(Total noise power)}] = 10\log[I^2_{Th-N}/(I^2_{S-N} + I^2_{ThN})]\ (\text{dB})$$

One word of caution: the latter relationship assumes an incoming signal free from noise. In reality, the incoming photonic signal already contains optical noise generated by several sources. As a result, the optical noise needs be evaluated and included in the Total noise power to calculate a realistic SNR.

ITU-T recommendation G.650 has defined parameters specific to many optical components. Here we add the parameters specific to receivers. These parameters are described in subsequent sections.

- minimum threshold optical power
- center wavelength λ_0

- wavelength discrimination
- receiver bit rate (max-min)
- min-max threshold level (one-zero)
- dependency on one's density
- dependence on polarization
- demodulation
- receiver noise
- dependency on bias
- dependency on temperature

2.16.1   The PIN Photodiode

The PIN semiconductor photodiode consists of an intrinsic (lightly doped) region sandwiched between a p-type and an n-type. When it is reversed biased, its internal impedance is almost infinite (such as an open circuit) and its output current is proportional to the input optical power.

The input-output relationships that define the *responsivity*, R, and the *quantum efficiency*, η, of the photodiode are:

$$R = (\text{output current } I)/(\text{input optical power } P) \text{ (amperes/watts)}$$

and

$$\eta = (\text{number of output electrons})/(\text{number of input photons})$$

The quantities R and η are related through the relationship

$$R = (e\eta)/(h\nu)$$

where, e is the electron charge, h is Planck's constant, and ν is the light frequency.

When a photon creates an electron-hole pair, the PIN produces a current pulse with duration and shape that depends on the R-C time constant of the PIN device. The capacitance of the reversed biased PIN photodiode is a limiting factor to its response (and switching speed). At low bit rates ($<$ Gb/s), and thus switching speeds, the parasitic inductance of the PIN may be neglected. However, as the bit rate becomes very high (well exceeding Gb/s), parasitic inductance becomes significant and causes "shot noise."

2.16.2   The APD Photodiode

The avalanche photodiode (APD) is a semiconductor device that is in operation is equivalent to a photomultiplier. It consists of a two-layer semiconductor sandwich where the upper layer is n-doped and the lower layer is heavily p-doped. At the junction, charge migration (electrons from the n and holes from the p) creates a depletion region and from the distribution of charges a field is created in the direction of the p-layer. When reverse biased is applied and no light impinges on the device, then due to thermal generation of electrons a current is produced, known as "dark current," which is manifested as noise. If the reversed bias device is exposed to light, then photons reach the p-layer and cause electron-hole pairs. However, because of the strong field in the APD junction, the pair flows through the junction in an accelerated mode. In fact, electrons gain enough energy to cause secondary electron-hole pairs, which in turn cause more. Thus, a multiplication or *avalanche* process takes place (hence its name), similar to photomultipliers, and a substantial current is generated from just few initial photons. Now, the generated electrons build up a charge and if the bias voltage is below the breakdown point, the built-up charge creates a potential that counteracts the avalanche mechanism and thus the avalanche ceases. If the bias is above the breakdown voltage, then the avalanche process continues and a large current is obtained from a single photon.

APD structures come in different types:

- The *deep-diffusion* type has a deep n-layer, compared with the p-layer, and such resistivity so that the breakdown voltage is high at about 2 kV. Thus, a wide depletion layer is created, and more electrons than holes, thus reducing the dark current. In general, this type has high gain at wavelengths shorter than 900 nm and switching speed no faster than 10 ns. At longer wavelength, the speed increases but the gain decreases.

- The *reach-through* type has a narrow junction and thus photons travel a very short distance until they are absorbed by the p-type to generate electron-hole pairs. These devices have uniform gain, low noise and fast response.

- The *superionization* type is similar to reach-through with a structure so that accelerating field is gradually increasing. As a result, a low ionization number of holes to electrons ratio (for a certain amount of incident light) is achieved, thus increasing gain and carrier mobility (electrons are faster than holes) and switching speed.

During this multiplication (avalanche) process, shot noise is also multiplied, estimated as:

$$\text{Shot noise} = 2eIG^2F$$

where F is the APD noise factor and G is the APD gain expressed as:

$$G = I_{\text{APD}}/I_{\text{primary}}$$

I_{APD} is the APD output current and I_{primary} is the current due to photon-electron conversion.

If τ is the effective transit time through the avalanche region, the APD bandwidth is approximated to:

$$B_{\text{APD}} = 1/(2pG\tau)$$

APDs may be made with silicon, germanium, or indium-gallium-arsenide. However, all types do not have the same performance and characteristics. The type of material determines, among others, the responsivity, gain, noise characteristics? and switching speed of the device. Thus, although indium-gallium-arsenide responds well in the range of 900 to 1700 nm, has low noise, has fast switching speeds, and is relatively expensive, silicon responds in the range of 400 to 1100 nm, is very inexpensive and is easily integrable with other silicon devices; germanium is a compromise between these two.

2.16.3   Photodetector Figure of Merit

The following is a summary of three figures of merit (FOM) that are important in the performance evaluation of photodetectors. Additional specific figures of merit may also be provided by photodetector manufacturers.

- Responsivity $(R) = V_s/(HA_d)$ (VW^{-1})
- Noise equivalent power (NEP) $= HA_d\{V_n/V_s\}$ (W)
- Detectivity $(D) = 1/(\text{NEP})$ (W^{-1})

where V_s is the root mean square (rms) signal voltage (V), V_n is the rms noise voltage (V), A_d is the detector area (cm^2), and H is irradiance (Wcm^{-2}).

In general, APD photodetectors have a much higher gain than PIN photodetectors, but PINs have a much faster switching speed, and thus they have been largely deployed in high bit rate (40 Gb/s) detection, particularly the waveguide PIN detectors. However, APDs keep improving, and it is possible to combine their high gain advantage with fast switching speeds.

2.16.4   ITU-T Nominal Center Frequencies

For WDM system interoperability, the operating nominal frequencies (wavelengths) of lasers, filters, and other optical components must be the same. Presently, ITU-T (standards) has recommended 81 channels (wavelengths) in the C-band starting from 1528.77 nm and incrementing in multiples of 50 GHz (or 0.39 nm).

According to this, starting with the first center frequency at 196.10 THz (or 1528.77 nm) and decrementing by 50 GHz (or incrementing by 0.39 nm), a table with all center frequencies (wavelengths) is constructed. These are the center frequencies (wavelengths) of the channels that are recommendation in ITU-T G.692 (October 1998). Thus, the first of the 81 channels in the C-band is at frequency 196.10 GHz or a wavelength 1528.77 nm, the second channel is at frequency 196.05 GHz or wavelength 1529.16 nm, and so on, and the last frequency is at 192.10 GHz or wavelength 1560.61 nm. However, as fiber technology evolves and optical components improve, more channels in the L-band may be appended to this table.

For channel spacing of 100 GHz, one starts with the first center frequency (wavelength) and continues with every other one. Similarly, for channel spacing of 200 GHz or 400 GHz, one starts with the first center frequency (wavelength) and continues accordingly.

Note that in ITU-T the frequency (and not the wavelength) is used as a reference. The reason is that certain materials emit specific well-known optical frequencies, which can be used as accurate reference points, and also that the frequency remains the same as light travels through matter but not the wavelength as it is influenced by the refractive index of the material.

2.17   OPTICAL AMPLIFIERS

Optical signals experience attenuation as they propagate in a medium they. In communications, any transmission medium, be it wire, wireless, or optical (at the exception of purely free space), is characterized by certain amount of attenuation per unit length. Thus, as the source transmits a known optical power level and the receiver at the other end of the path expects a lower power level because of attenuation, the received optical power must be at a measurable level such that the signal is detected reliably and at an expected low bit error rate ($\sim 10^{-9}$ to $\sim 10^{-11}$).

Optical media (such as fiber) are characterized by *attenuation per kilometer*, or attenuation coefficient, α, provided in db/km. Consequently, knowing the power level at the source, P_S, and the expected power level at the receiver, P_R, one can easily calculate the total attenuation and translate it into an acceptable fiber length. If for simplicity we neglect other types of losses (due to dispersion, polarization, etc.), the fiber length is calculated as:

$$L = (P_S - P_R/\alpha) \text{ (km)}$$

Thus, attenuation puts a limit on fiber length between source and receiver unless the optical power of the signal is amplified, typically every 40 to 80 km, compensating for losses and extending the source–receiver distance.

Amplification of optical signals is a multistep process. The traditional state of the art, would first convert the optical signal to an electronic signal; the electronic signal would be retimed, reshaped, and amplified (an operation known as 3R); and then it was converted back to an optical signal. This function is known as *regeneration*. Typically, a regenerator consists of three major functional blocks, the optical receiver, the electronic amplifier, and the optical transmitter. Figure 2.65 illustrates the transfer function of a regenerator and three major functions; timing, error recovery, and pulse shaping are not shown.

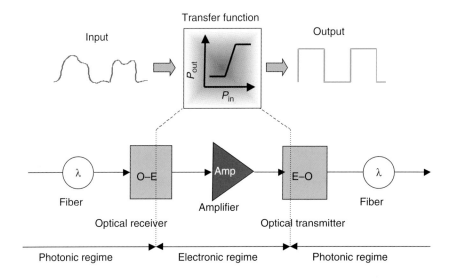

Figure 2.65 The model of a regenerator and the three major functions, optical receiver, electronic amplifier, and optical transmitter.

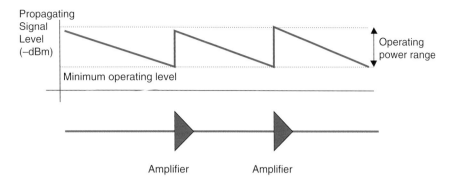

Figure 2.66 Signal attenuation and amplification action.

A regenerator performs the three Rs on a per-wavelength basis. Consequently, in DWDM and over the span of a fiber link, a great number of regenerators are required to maintain the signal at a sufficient power level (Fig. 2.66). As the number of regenerators increases, it collectively adds to material, provisioning, and maintenance cost of the network. In addition, the probability of regenerator failure increases, and thus the probability for transmission interruptions; this necessitates complex counter measure (service and network survivability) strategies that add another level of complexity to optical communications and a severe penalty cost.

Recently, direct amplification technologies have been developed and used, known as *optical amplifiers* (OA), to directly amplify a weak optical signal. To date, the best known are three, *semiconductor optical amplifiers* (SOA), *optical fiber amplifiers* (OFA), and *Raman amplifiers*.

The key common characteristics of optical amplifiers are *gain*, *gain efficiency*, *gain bandwidth*, the *gain saturation* and *noise*, *polarization sensitivity* and *output saturation power*. Other characteristics are *sensitivity (gain and spectral response) to temperature* and other environmental conditions, *dynamic range*, *cross talk*, *noise figure*, *physical size*, and others.

- *Gain* is the ratio of output power to input power (measured in dB).
- *Gain efficiency* is the gain as a function of input power (dB/mW).
- *Bandwidth* is a function of frequency, and as such *gain bandwidth* is the range of frequencies over which the amplifier is effective.
- *Gain saturation* is the maximum output power of the amplifier, beyond which it cannot increase despite the input power increase.
- *Noise* is an inherent characteristic of amplifiers. In electronic amplifiers noise is due to (random) spontaneous recombination of electron-hole pairs that produces an undesired signal added to the information signal to be amplified. In optical amplifiers, it is due to spontaneous light emission of excited ions, which we will further explore.
- *Polarization sensitivity* is the gain dependence of optical amplifiers on the polarization of the signal.
- *Output saturation power* is defined as the output power level for which the amplifier gain has dropped by 3 dB.

Based on principle, OAs are distinguished as:

- semiconductor optical amplifiers
- optical fiber amplifiers
- stimulated Raman amplifiers
- stimulated Brillouin amplifiers

Depending on application, each structure has its own advantages and disadvantages.

Optical amplifiers introduce noise that contaminates the optical signal and thus decreases the signal-to-noise ratio (SNR) and influences the overall system performance. Therefore, it is important that the noise characteristics of any amplifier be specified.

The noise figure (NF) of an amplifier is the dimensionless ratio of input SNR to output SNR of an amplifier

$$NF = SNR_{in}/SNR_{out}$$

Amplifiers are distinguished as *single wavelength*, *multiwavelength* (or multichannel), and *analog amplifiers* used in applications such as CATV.

2.17.1 Semiconductor Optical Amplifiers

Semiconductor optical amplifiers (SOA) are based on conventional laser principles; an active waveguide region is sandwiched between a p-region and an n-region. A bias voltage is applied to excite ions in the region and create electron-hole pairs. Then, as light of a specific wavelength is coupled in the active waveguide, stimulation takes place and causes electron-hole pairs to recombine and generate more photons (of the same wavelength as the optical signal), and hence optical amplification is achieved. In a different implementation, the active region is illuminated with photonic energy to cause the necessary excitation in the active region. For best coupling efficiency of the optical signal in the active region, the SOA end walls have been coated with an antireflecting material (Fig. 2.67).

The excitation and recombination of the electron-hole process is described by rate equations, the mathematical analysis of which is beyond our scope. However, the rate of electron-hole generation and the rate of recombination must be balanced for sustained amplification. This depends on many parameters, largely by the active region and bias as well as density and lifetime of carriers. In addition, in the presence of a photonic signal, the number of recombined electron-holes per stimulating photon provides a

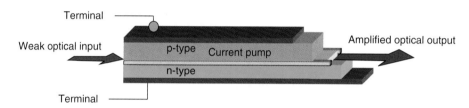

Figure 2.67 Semiconductor optical amplifiers (SOA) are devices based on conventional laser principles.

direct measure of the spectral response, the optical power, and thus the spectral gain of the SOA.

The amplifier gain, G, is approximated as

$$G = -12[(\lambda - \lambda_p)/\Delta\lambda]^2 + G_p$$

where G_p is the peak gain at the corresponding wavelength λ_p, $\Delta\lambda$ is the full-width half-maximum (FWHM) gain bandwidth, and the factor 12 is a result of the definition of $\Delta\lambda$.

The 3-dB saturation output power, P_s, is described as a function of λ by

$$P_s = q_s(\lambda - \lambda_p) + P_{s-p}$$

where q_s is a linear coefficient and P_{s-p} is the 3-dB saturation output at the peak gain wavelength λ_p.

Depending on the actual structure, SOAs are distinguished as:

- semiconductor traveling wave laser optical amplifiers
- Fabry–Perot laser amplifiers
- injection current distributed feedback (DFB) laser amplifiers

Salient characteristics of SOA's are:

- high gain (25–30 dB)
- output saturation power in the range of 5 to +13 dBm
- nonlinear distortions
- wide bandwidth
- spectral response in the wavelength regions 0.8, 1.3, and 1.5 μm
- SOAs are made with InGaAsP, and thus they are small, compact semiconductors easily integrable with other semiconductor and optical components
- SOAs may be integrated into arrays
- polarization dependency; thus, they require a polarization-maintaining fiber (polarization sensitivity 0.5–1 dB)
- higher noise figure than EDFAs (higher than 6 dB over 50 nm)
- higher cross talk level than EDFAs due to nonlinear phenomena (four-wave mixing).

Because SOAs are compact solid-state devices, their fast responding nonlinearity may also be employed in wavelength conversion, regeneration, time demultiplexing, clock recovery, and optical signal processing applications.

2.17.2 Rare Earth–Doped Fiber Optical Amplifiers

Optical fiber amplifiers (OFA) are specialized fibers that are heavily doped with one or more rare earth elements. Their purpose is to absorb optical energy from one spectral range and emit optical energy (or fluoresce) in another, especially in the range useful in fiber communications (800–900 or 1,300–1,620 nm). However, each element has its own absorption-emission characteristics; that is, some absorb energy in a single step and some others in multiple steps and emit light in one or more narrow spectral ranges. In fact, depending on how many (energy) steps ions "jump up and/or down" onto higher energy levels to populate the level that eventually is beneficial to fiber amplification, classifies a two-level system, a three-level system, and so on (Fig. 2.48). Since energy is related to optical frequency or wavelength, this also implies that the population of each energy level depends on the actual wavelength. As such, an OFA does not exhibit exactly the same gain for all wavelengths in the amplification spectral range. This defines the degree of *gain flatness* of an OFA. In subsequent sections we will see that this is an important issue for consideration and that the non-flatness must to be compensated for with special filters.

Unfortunately, there is no single element that can be used in OFAs to cover the complete fiber communications spectrum. For instance, an element absorbs (optical) energy to reach an energy level and emits energy not within the spectrum of interest. Or, it reaches an energy level but the excited atom does not remain there for a sufficiently long time, and statistically the energy level is not populated enough and is quickly depleted, making it of little use as an optical amplifier.

To clarify this, consider the metaphor of a reservoir with a source filling it and a sink emptying it. As atoms become excited, they reach the reservoir and remain in it for a while. If in the meantime a photon passes by it, it stimulates some excited atoms that release photons, and these atoms leave the reservoir, becoming available to be excited again. However, if the atoms spontaneously emit photons and leave the reservoir, because by nature they cannot remain in it sufficiently long, the reservoir is quickly emptied, and when a photon passes by, there are no excited ions in the reservoir to be stimulated and thus no amplification for it (Fig. 2.68).

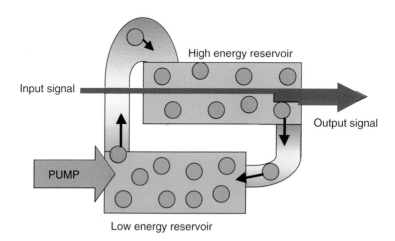

Ions absorb pump energy and are excited to a higher energy reservoir, N_e.

Ions returning to lower energy either by stimulation, N_{st}, or spontaneously, N_{sp}.

Figure 2.68 For sustained amplification, the rate of excitation should be less or equal to the rate of stimulation + the rate of spontaneous emission.

In general, for sustained amplification, the rate of excitation should be less than or equal to the rate of stimulation plus the rate of spontaneous emission:

$$dNe/dt < dNst/dt + dNsp/dt$$

where Ne is the number of electrons excited to a higher energy level, Nst the number of electrons returning to lower energy by stimulation, and Nsp, spontaneously.

From a physics and mathematics point of view, the excitation/stimulation process and the amplification process reduces to a flow problem, particularly to a set of differential rate equations. These equations take into account many significant phenomena that take place during the stimulation and excitation process, as well as fiber propagation phenomena (dispersion, FWM, polarization, etc.). Depending on the boundary conditions and assumption, some phenomena may be neglected if they are deemed negligible contributors and thus simplify the already complex equations.

Thus, in a two level system for example, if n_U and n_L are the number of electrons in the upper and lower energy levels, respectively, the set of partial differential rate equations may be summarized as

$$\eta n_U / \eta t = -[\text{absorption term}]_U + [\text{spontaneous emission term}]_L$$
$$+ [\text{absorption and pump effects term}]_L + [\text{cross-relaxation term}]_U$$

and

$$\eta n_L / \eta t = -[\text{stimulation emission term}]_L - [\text{spontaneous emission term}]_L$$
$$+ [\text{absorption and pump effects term}]_U + [\text{cross-relaxation term}]_L$$

where the subscript U and L at each term indicates effect at the upper or lower level, respectively.

The quantum yield, Φ, is also a measure of the efficiency of a photon at a given wavelength for a given reaction and for a given period of time. This is defined by

$$\Phi = (\text{number of transformed molecules})/(\text{number of absorbed photons})$$

However, the number of absorbed photons, I_a, is not directly proportional to the optical density (OD) at the excitation wavelength but is connected with the relationship:

$$I_a = k \, (1 - 10^{-OD})$$

where k is a constant proportional to incident intensity.

Some of the attractive rare earth elements that are used in DWDM optical fiber amplification are those whose spectral gain matches the spectrum of minimum fiber loss, such as Nd^{3+} and Er^{3+} that emit in the ranges of 1.3 and 1.5 µm, respectively. Besides Er and Nd, other rare earth elements have been used to produce optical fiber amplifiers such as Ho, Te, Th, Tm, Yb, and Pr, or in combination (e.g., Er/Yb), each operating in various spectral bands (Fig. 2.69).

Presently, the overall gain of OFAs is in the range of 30 dB with an output power of approximately 10 mW. Better OFAs (shorter length, more gain, and more power) are expected in the near future.

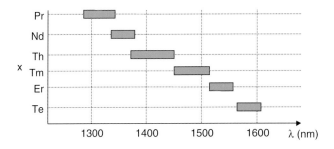

Figure 2.69   xDFA approximate range of amplification.

2.17.2.1 Classification of Optical Fiber Amplifiers

Optical fiber amplifiers (OFA) are classified, similar to electronic amplifiers, as *power amplifiers*, *preamplifiers*, and *line amplifiers*.

Power amplifier: This is an OFA capable to increase the optical power of the modulated photonic source (i.e., the optical transmitted signal). It receives a large signal (from the laser source or the modulator) with a large signal-to-noise ratio and it boosts the signal power to levels about −10 dBm or higher. An optical power amplifier acts like a booster and it is place right after the source (or the modulator) and thus it may be integrated with it.

Preamplifier: This is an OFA with very low noise able to increase a highly attenuated signal to a level that can be detected reliably by an optical detector. Thus, a preamplifier is placed directly before the detector and may be integrated with it.

Line amplifier: This is a low-noise OFA able to amplify an attenuated signal so that it can travel an additional length of fiber. Therefore, the line amplifier must have high gain and very low noise so that it does not degrade the signal-to-noise ratio of an already attenuated signal.

The proper applicability of each OFA type is being recommended by ITU-T in G.662 and G.663 so that nonlinearity, polarization, and other factors that affect the integrity of the channel and the quality of the transmitted signal are minimized. In addition to G.662 and G.663, more ITU standards deal with optical amplifiers, such as G.957 (optical return loss) and G.973 (remotely pumped amplifier).

2.17.2.2 Erbium-Doped Fiber Amplifiers

Among the various OFAs, *erbium-doped fiber amplifiers* (EDFA) have gained popularity in communications, because their spectral emission in the range of 1,530 to 1,565 nm, which is used in DWDM. In fact, erbium ions can be excited by a number of optical frequencies (known as *pumps*) such as 514 nm, 532 nm, 667 nm, 800 nm, 980 nm, and 1,480 nm.

The shortest wavelength, 514 nm, excites erbium ions to the highest possible energy level. From this level, excited electrons drop to one of four intermediate metastable levels, radiating phonons (the acoustical quantum equivalent of photon). From the lowest metastable level, they finally drop to the initial (ground) level emitting photons of a wavelength around 1,550 nm. A similar activity takes place with the remaining excitation wavelengths (however, the number of intermediate metastable levels is decreasing as the wavelength becomes longer). Finally, the longest wavelength, 1,480 nm, excites electrons to the lowest metastable level from which it drops directly to the ground level. Clearly, the shorter the pump wavelength the more the intermediate metastable levels, the more inefficient the pumping mechanism and also the amplifier, as a lot of energy is wasted to generate phonons instead of photons. Thus, the two most convenient excitation wavelengths for EDFAs are 980 and 1,480 nm. What is important is that as photons with wavelengths in the range of 1,530 to 1,565 nm pass through the EDFA, they stimulate the excited erbium atoms to emit photons of the same wavelength with the passing by photons and the result is more photons out than photons in; this is known as *light amplification by stimulated emission.*

When EDFA ions are excited by a 980 nm source, after approximately 1 µs the excited ions fall on the metastable energy level from which, if triggered, they drop to the ground energy level and emit light at the wavelength of the triggering photon. If they are not triggered, then after approximately 10 ms (known as *spontaneous lifetime*), they spontaneously drop from the metastable level emitting light in the range around 1,550 nm (Fig. 2.70). Thus, some of the important parameters in the EDFA gain process are:

- concentration of dopants
- effective area of EDFA fiber
- length of EDFA fiber
- absorption coefficient
- emission coefficient
- power of pump
- power of signal
- relative population of upper states
- lifetime at the upper states
- direction of signal propagation with respect to pump

In communications, the bit period of very high bit rates (Gb/s) is very short (ps) compared with the lifetime (ms), and thus intersymbol interference does not become an issue. However, spontaneous emission adds to the signal noise.

An EDFA amplifier consists of a pump laser (at 980 or 1,480 nm and output power from under 100 mW to about 250 mW), a coupling device; an erbium-doped fiber several meters long (depending on dopant concentration, 70–100 m); and two isolators,

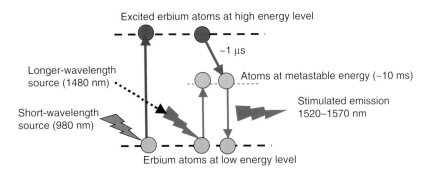

Figure 2.70   Spontaneous emission of erbium (simplified).

one per EDFA end. The pump laser is enclosed in a small package (approx. 20 mm × 15 mm × 8 mm) with a connectorized single-mode fiber pigtail that can be coupled with the EDFA fiber. Pumping can also be done through the cladding of a multimode (EDFA) fiber, a method known as *cladding pumping*; in this case, inexpensive 1 W diode (LED) pumps may be used. The fiber carrying the modulated optical signal is connected with the EDFA via the isolator to suppress light from the EDFA, and the isolator at the far end of the EDFA, suppresses reflections from the outgoing fiber into the EDFA (Fig. 2.71).

EDFAs have found applications in WDM long-haul transport systems. Gain in excess of 50 dB over a spectral range of 80 nm and very low noise characteristics have been demonstrated. A fiber span (of hundreds of kilometers long) consists of fiber segments (tens of kilometers each) where EDFAs are placed at the interconnecting points to restore the attenuated optical signal. Thus, there may be several EDFAs (typically up to 8) along the fiber span. However, three issues become important because EDFAs do not exactly amplify all wavelengths the same: (a) gain flatness, (b) dynamic gain, and (c) low noise.

First, the EDFA gain is not flat over the spectral range (Fig. 2.72). This is addressed with gain flattening optical filters. These are passive in-line filters with low insertion loss, low dispersion, and stable performance over a wide range of temperatures.

Second, the total gain provided by the EDFA is shared by the number of optical channels. Thus, as the number of wavelengths (optical channels) to be amplified

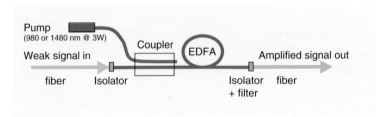

Figure 2.71 An EDFA amplifier consists of an erbium-doped silica fiber, an optical pump, a coupler and isolators at both ends.

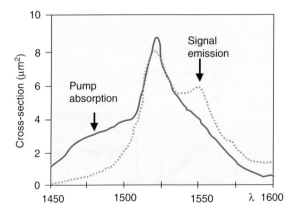

Figure 2.72 Pump absorption and signal emission spectra of EDFA.

increases, the shared gain per channel decreases. This is addressed by using higher gain EDFA amplifiers. This means that either more powerful pump laser or a higher concentration of erbium ions must be used. However, as pump power increases (980 or 1,480 nm), other issues become more critical (laser stabilization becomes cumbersome, longevity of laser device becomes shorter, and the cost of pump increases). Currently, a typical output power of 980 nm laser pump is about 350 mW and of 1,480 nm is about 250 mW; however, laser pumps with more output power are becoming available. Increasing the erbium concentration has its own issues. As ion concentration increases, erbium ions tend to cluster causing the efficiency of the amplifier to drop and dispersion to increase. The clustering effect of erbium is controlled with the introduction of Al atoms; a positive side effect of this is the Er + Al + Ge combination producing a fiber amplifier that now performs over a wider spectral range covering the C-band and L-band. Indeed, new EDFAs (co-doped with Al and Ge) have gain over a wider range than common EDFAs, thus extending the amplifier spectral range (from 1,525 to above 1,615 nm) and supporting more DWDM optical channels (160 wavelength-channels at 50 GHz spacing).

As the gain of an EDFA is shared by all wavelength-channels, the more channels, the less gain per channel. This has an undesirable effect in optical add-dropped multiplexing (OADM). The dropped and added wavelengths continue their travel in different networks that support fewer or more wavelengths (e.g., one supports 40 and the other supports 80). Thus, if each network has its own EDFAs, assuming that they are of the same gain, they amplified their channels more or less. Similarly, assuming that all networks support the same number of channels, there is no guarantee that all EDFAs provide a uniform gain. Thus, after a few optical add-drops in a span, the received wavelengths have different power levels. This is addressed with optical power equalization and by engineering the WDM system.

The third issue is addressed differently. EDFA spontaneous emission introduces noise that degrades the S/N ratio. Moreover, optical noise sources are cumulative; the more the EDFAs, the more the S/N degradation. Thus, one would be inclined to use a stronger optical signal to overcome this. However, near the zero-dispersion wavelength region four-wave mixing become more significant and further degrades the S/N ratio.

Thus, the selection of power (per channel) launched into the fiber becomes a puzzle: amplifier noise restricts the minimum power of the signal, and four-wave mixing limits the maximum power per channel launched into the fiber. This implies that a power level between a lower limit and an upper limit must be selected. To determine the proper power level, many other parameters must be taken into account so that the required quality of the signal is maintained. Some of these parameters are:

- fiber length between amplifiers (in kilometers)
- fiber attenuation (loss) per kilometer
- number of amplifiers in the optical path
- amplifier parameters (gain, noise, chromatic dispersion, bandwidth)
- number of channels (wavelengths) per fiber
- channel width and channel spacing
- receiver (detector) specifications
- transmitter specifications

- dispersion issues
- polarization issues
- nonlinearity issues
- optical component losses and noise (connectors, other devices)
- quality of signal (bit error rate, S/N)
- signal modulation method and bit rate
- many other design parameters

EDFA advantages:

- EDFAs have a high power transfer efficiency from pump to signal (>50%).
- They directly and simultaneously amplify a wide wavelength region over 80 nm (in the region of 1,550 nm), at an output power as high as +37 dBm, with a relatively flat gain (>20 dB), which is suitable to WDM systems. Modified EDFAs can also operate in the L-band.
- The saturation output is greater than 1 mW (10–25 dBm).
- The gain time constant is long (>100 ms) to overcome patterning effects and intermodulation distortions (low noise).
- They are transparent to optical modulation format.
- They have a large dynamic range.
- They have a low noise Figure.
- They are polarization-independent (thus reducing coupling loss to transmission fiber).
- They are suitable for long-haul applications.

EDFA disadvantages:

- They are not small devices (they are kilometer-long fibers) and cannot be integrated with other semiconductor devices.
- EDFAs exhibit amplified spontaneous light emission (ASE). That is, even if no incoming optical signal is present, there is always some output signal as a result of some excited ions in the fiber; this output is termed *spontaneous noise*.
- Other drawbacks are cross talk and gain saturation.

Erbium has also been (experimentally) used to dope solid-state waveguides to produce compact optical amplifier devices, called erbium-doped waveguide amplifier (EDWA). Initial results have been promising as such devices may also integrate couplers and combiners on the same substrate. Using a pump laser at 977 nm at 150 mW, a gain of ~15 dB at a signal at 1,549 nm has been achieved, a saturated power of 9 dB, and a noise figure of 4.2 dB.

2.17.2.3 Praseodymium-Doped Fiber Amplifiers
Praseodymium-doped fluoride fiber amplifiers (PrDFFA, PDFFA, or PDFA) when (Pr^{3+} ions) excited have an energy transition in the 1.3 μm spectral range making them suitable as optical amplifiers in the region 1,280 to 1,340 nm, where EDFAs are not

suitable. This is of interest because a significant part of the optical network is already engineered for this window (1,312 nm). In addition, PDFAs have a high gain ($\sim$30 dB) and a high saturation power (20 dBm).

However, PDFAs require non-silica and uncommon (fluoride) fiber, increased quantum efficiency of the Pr^{3+} ions at the 1.3 μm transition, as well as a high power (up to 300 mW) pump laser at 1017 nm (which is not the popular 980 nm or 1,480 nm). Therefore, PDFA amplifiers have not been widely deployed yet.

Currently, many efforts are made to increase the quantum efficiency, by using low-phonon-energy glass fiber that employs elements such as gallium-lanthanum-sulfide (GLS) and gallium-sulfide-iodide (GSI).

2.17.2.4 Thulium-Doped Fiber Amplifiers

Another type used as a fiber amplifier contains the element thulium (Tm). It is suitable for amplifying optical channels in the region about 1500 nm.

To achieve amplification in the region of interest, Thulium atoms are excited in stages (Fig. 2.73). The pump energy at 1,407 nm excites the ground level atoms to a level higher than $^3F_4$. Thorium atoms drop to the level $^3F_4$, from which they are pumped to a higher level above $^3H_4$. They again drop to the level $^3H_4$, from which they are finally stimulated by photons in the range of 1,440 to 1,520 nm and they drop to the level $^3F_4$, and so on.

In reality, trivalent thulium ions (Tm^{3+}) in fluoride fiber have a complex energy transition diagram and, when excited, can emit in three regions, 800 nm, 1,470 nm, and 2,300 nm. Moreover, the lifetime at the excited level $^3F_4$ is shorter (1.35 ms) than the lifetime at the target lower level $^3H_4$ (9 ms), and thus it is difficult to create a population inversion level at $^3F_4$ to maintain continuous amplification. These obstacles are being worked out, and current results promise another excellent fiber amplifier that can be used in communications.

TmDFA (or TDFA) co-doped with Yb^{3+} have been reported to have a gain well over 10 dB at about 1,480 nm, and a low noise figure of less than 6 dB in this region. The required total pump power (from a Nd^{3+}:YAG laser) at 1,064 nm was about 100 mW.

2.17.2.5 Neodymium-Doped Fiber Amplifiers

Yet another fiber amplifier contains the element neodymium (Nd). Neodymium is an element the ions of which have a multiple absorption and emission spectrum. For

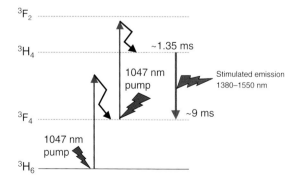

Figure 2.73 Thulium transition energy levels (simplified).

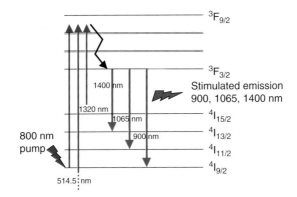

Figure 2.74 Neodymium transition energy levels (simplified).

example, ions may be excited by an 800-nm pump to an intermediate energy level from which they fall to rest at the luminescence level, from which they may be stimulated to emit light at 900 nm, 1,065 nm, and 1,400 nm (Fig. 2.74). Or they may be excited with a 514.5 nm pump to a high energy level, or be excited to the same high energy level from an intermediate level by absorbing 1,320 nm light. With the exception of the 1,400 nm, the 900 and 1,065 nm are not presently popular in DWDM communications.

2.17.2.6 Tellurium-Based Erbium-Doped Fiber Amplifiers
Tellurium-based erbium-doped fiber amplifiers offer the potential of a flat optical band-width in the C- and L-bands, 1,532 to 1,608 nm, thus increasing the potential bandwidth of an erbium-doped optical amplifier to over 110 nm.

2.17.2.7 Amplified Spontaneous Light Emission
As already mentioned, amplified spontaneous light emission (ASE) in fiber amplifica-tion is an issue of concern because it is a serious noise source that must be studied and minimized. The effect of ASE on DWDM signals is illustrated in Figure 2.75.

The generated ASE propagates in both directions of the fiber amplifiers, forward as well as backward (with respect to the pump).

- The backward ASE is mostly intense (highest peak) at the first meters (EDFA) or centimeters (NdDFA) of the fiber amplifier, and its contribution decreases rapidly after a couple of meters. Having an isolator at the beginning of the fiber (i.e.,

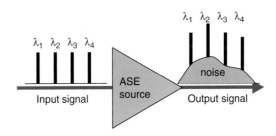

Figure 2.75 ASE noise added by optical fiber amplifier.

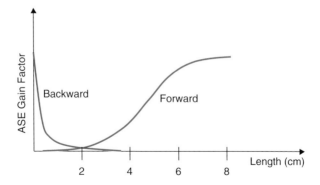

Figure 2.76 Forward and Backward ASE.

where the pump is) will minimize the possibility of having ASE propagating backward in the transmission fiber.

• The forward ASE is not as intense at the beginning of the fiber amplifier. As forward is generated and propagated, there are two countermechanisms, ASE loss and ASE accumulation. The combination of the two yields a monotonically increasing ASE at the end of the few-meters long fiber. This is where a rejection filter should minimize the transfer of ASE from the fiber amplifier to the transmission fiber.

Figure 2.76 captures qualitatively the backward and forward ASE.

2.17.3 Optical Parametric Amplifiers

Optical parametric amplifiers (OPA) capitalize on the property of highly nonlinear optical materials and on four-wave mixing (also a nonlinear phenomenon). When three optical frequencies satisfy the relationship $\omega_3 = 2\omega_1 - \omega_4$, where ω_3 is the signal, ω_1 is the pump and ω_4 is an idle frequency, then, under the right conditions, they are coupled by the four-wave mixing mechanism and energy from the pump (and the idler) passes onto the signal, thus amplifying it (Fig. 2.77).

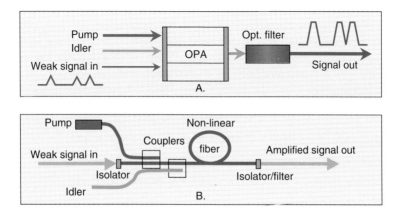

Figure 2.77 Principles of parametric optical amplifiers, A. crystal, B. fiber.

The study of optical parametric amplifiers involves the solution of a set of coupled differential equations of the form

$$\eta A_3 / \eta z = +q A_4 e^{-ikz}$$

$$\eta A_4 / \eta z = -q A_3 e^{-ikz}$$

where A_3 and A_4 is the envelope of ω_3 and ω_4, respectively, q is related to the nonlinearity coefficient of the material γ and to a function δ by $q = (i\gamma + \delta)P_0$ (P_0 is an initial constant power value), $k = \Delta\beta - 2\gamma P_0$, and $\Delta\beta = \beta_3 + \beta_4 - 2\beta_1$, where β_n is the propagation constant of each of the three frequencies.

It has been shown that when a fiber (<2 km long) is made strongly nonlinear, a signal, a pump, and an idler may propagate through it and achieve signal amplification. The gain bandwidth of optical parametric fiber amplifiers can theoretically be in the hundreds of nanometers. The pump power in the fiber is more than 100 mW, and the pump frequency is selected to satisfy the aforementioned relationship (1,480 nm may also be used for amplification in the C-band).

2.17.4 Raman Amplifiers

Consider two light sources propagating within the same medium, one of a short wavelength and the other of a longer wavelength. Because of the nonlinear properties of the medium, even if they are weak, the short-wavelength high-energy ($\sim$500 mW) source (known as pump) excites electrons to a higher energy level. Then, as photons at longer wavelength pass by, they stimulate the excited electrons and cause them to "drop" at an intermediate energy level by releasing photonic energy of a "longer wavelength"; the wavelength of the released photons depends on the wavelength of the pump and the stimulating signal. In general, the photon frequency emitted when an electron falls from an energy level E_{high} to an energy level E_{low} is determined by the general relationship $E = h\nu$. Thus, the emitted frequency is

$$\nu = [E_{high} - E_{low}]/h$$

In this case, the short wavelength source becomes the "pump" transferring energy from it to a modulated weak signal of a longer wavelength. These amplifiers are called *Raman amplifiers*. If the conditions are right, the stimulating optical source and the released photons are of the same wavelength, they join each other, and hence *Raman amplification* is achieved. As the excited atoms "drop" to their initially low (or ground) energy level, they become available for re-excitation and thus the process continues, but with a diminishing effect the farther away from the pump until there is no more amplification (Fig. 2.78). Thus, some of the important parameters in this process are:

- the efficiency of excitation of atoms to the upper level
- the relative population of the upper level (number of populated upper states)
- the lifetime of atoms in the excitation state, or upper state (E_{high})
- the intensity of signal causing stimulation
- the duration of signal or length of the signal pulse

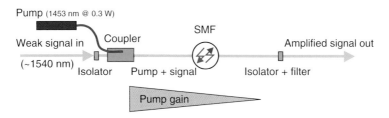

Figure 2.78 Principles of Raman amplification.

From a classical viewpoint and in terms of signal and pump power, the signal power gradient (from which the Raman gain, G_R, may be obtained) is

$$dP_S(z)/dz = \{[g_0/(K A_{\text{eff}})]P_R(z) - \alpha\}P_S(z)\}$$

where $P_S(z)$ is the signal power at point z, $P_R(z)$ is the power of the Raman pump at point z, g_0 is the Raman gain coefficient, α is the fiber attenuation coefficient, K is a factor (set at the value of 2), and A_{eff} is the fiber core effective area.

Assuming that the Raman gain coefficient is linear, solving the differential equation (and integrating from 0 to L), one obtains

$$G_R = \exp\{g_0 P_R(L) L_{\text{eff}}/(2A_{\text{eff}})\}$$

where L_{eff} is the effective length expressed as the integral of $[P_R(z)/P_R(z)]\,dz$ over the fiber length L. L_{eff} is also given as $[1 - \exp(-\alpha L)]/\alpha$, and it expresses the effective fiber length seen by the Raman gain evolution.

In optical transmission systems with more than one wavelength in the same fiber, SRS may result in signal cross talk if the launched power of each channel exceeds a threshold level, thus restricting the per channel power in the fiber. However, for SRS to become a significant cross talk contributor, the transferred energy must also exceed a certain threshold level, which is a function of the fiber medium.

In DWDM transmission, there typically are many wavelengths within a band, such as C or L that require amplification. One implication of Raman gain is that gain is not uniform for all optical channels (wavelengths) in these bands, but it is a function of the wavelength difference between pump and signal. In fact, the Raman gain coefficient increases almost linearly with wavelength difference (or offset), it peaks at 100 nm and then rapidly drops (Fig. 2.79). As a consequence, the best gain performance is at an offset of 100 nm from the pump wavelength. Figure 2.80 illustrates typical Raman amplification over the 35-nm spectral range.

A second implication is that the usable gain bandwidth is narrow, in the range of 20 to 40 nm. Therefore, if a broader band of weak signals require Raman amplification, then more than one pump is needed, each offset by ~40 nm, so that all together can effectively cover the broad spectral band (Fig. 2.81).

However, because of the high power of Raman pumps and spectral spaced position, several issues arise: a gain ripple over the usable band, interpump and interchannel coupling, nonlinearity effects (FWM, parametric gain, modulation instability), and stimulated Brillouin scattering; these issues are depicted in Figure 2.82.

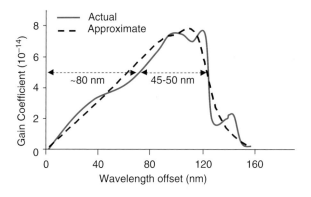

Figure 2.79 Raman gain coefficient vs signal-pump wavelength off-set.

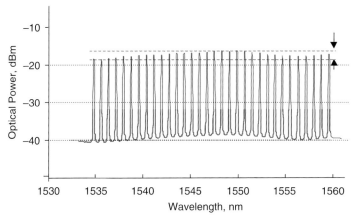

Figure 2.80 Typical Raman amplification over a 35 nm range (notice the peak-to-peak amplitude variation).

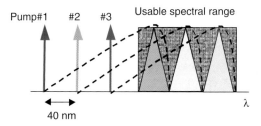

Figure 2.81 Spacing several Raman pumps by ~40 nm, channels in a wider spectral range are amplified.

Mathematically speaking, the gain of Raman amplification of a channel is described by a set of simultaneous (coupled) differential equations and the power gain is a function of fiber distance from the pump, z. Qualitatively, the closer to the pump, the more the excited atoms that contribute to power gain, and exponentially decreasing with distance from the pump. Thus, if the initial signal power is $P_s(0)$, then the signal

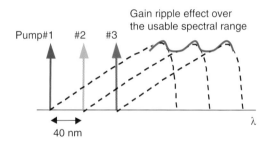

Figure 2.82 Gain ripple effect due to Raman amplification and to pump spacing.

power at point z, $P_s(z)$, as a result of Raman power gain is described by the exponential relationship

$$P_s(z) = P_s(0)\exp\{G_R P_p(z)L_{\text{eff}} - \alpha z\}$$

where

- A_{eff} is the effective core area of the pump
- K is a polarization factor that describes how close the polarization state of the pump is with the signal, ranging from orthogonal to parallel
- $G_R = g_R/A_{\text{eff}}K$ is known as the Raman gain efficiency
- g_R is the Raman gain
- $P_p(z)$ is the pump power
- α is the fiber attenuation coefficient
- L_{eff} is the effective fiber length

For all practical purposes, it suffices to say that to derive this relationship, pump depletion, self-phase modulation, cross-phase modulation, dispersion, fiber loss, fiber effective area, and Raman gain over all channels are explicitly involved in these equations.

In a two-pump system, the power and gain of a second pump is estimated from the power and gain of the first pump according to

$$P_{\text{pump2}} = P_{\text{pump1}}(g_2/g_1)\ \text{mW}$$

where P_{pump1} and g_1 are the first pump power (in mW) and gain (in dB), P_{pump2} and g_2 are the second pump power (in mW) and gain (in dB).

Raman scattering is dominant when the source is broadband, and it may occur equally in both directions in a fiber with respect to the direction of the optical signal, forward or backward.

Raman amplification uses common (non-doped) fibers and takes advantage of their nonlinearity properties in the presence of high pump power; thus Raman scattering is a nonresonant process. Because of this, Raman scattering can provide amplification in the complete useful spectrum 1.3 μm to 1.6 μm.

There are three methods for Raman amplification. One method uses the Raman pump at the receiver and the pump light travels in the opposite direction of the

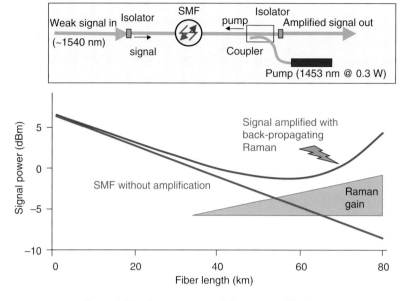

Figure 2.83 Counter-pumped Raman amplification.

signal, toward the source (Fig. 2.83). This is termed a counter-propagating (or counter-pumped) Raman pump. Thus, the optical intensity of the pump is higher at the receiver and weakens at it travels toward the source. This has the advantage of providing more gain where the signal is most attenuated and less gain where the signal is strongest. In this case, and for certain fiber types, the power sum of Raman pump and signal may be greater than 600 mW. Additionally, because the higher-state lifetime of excited atoms (in undoped fiber) is a few femtoseconds, the signal traveling against the excitation evolution (because of the counterpropagating Raman pump) experiences a relativistic longer lifetime that minimizes gain fluctuations; that is, the ultrashort lifetime compared with the much longer signal pulses result in a fluctuation of coupling between signal and pump-excited atoms, and thus an undesirable gain fluctuation.

Moreover, four-wave mixing effects are minimized because of the weak signal. However, because the signal is mixed with noise, the Raman amplification will amplify both the weak signal and the noise together, thus degrading the signal to noise ratio.

The second method uses the Raman pump at the source, and the pump light travels in the same direction with the optical signal, toward the receiver (Fig. 2.74). This is termed *co-propagating* (or co-pumped) *Raman pump*. In this case, the Raman gain boosts the signal to a level that compensates for downstream losses. This method has improved noise characteristics but worse four-wave mixing effects than the counter-propagation method, since both signal and pump are at the outset at maximum strengths. However, the Raman induced noise is independent of the signal power but proportional to bit rate, in contrast to Rayleigh backscattering, which is proportional to the signal power and independent of bit rate. One important observation can be made here. The fiber causes dispersion on both pump and signal. However, the pump wavelength group is shorter than the signal wavelength group. Thus, chromatic dispersion is different at each group, and from an observer's point of view it seems that the one "walks away or off" from the other.

The third method combines both co-propagating and counter-propagating Raman pumps, but now the pumps can be at lower power levels. Thus, the signal is both boosted and amplified.

It should be noticed that the Raman gain as well as the usable gain bandwidth depend on the pump power level. Raman gain (in the range of 4–11 dB) is typically proportional to pump power, but it also depends on the fiber length and on the method (co-pumped or counter-pumped). In addition, the Raman gain is not "flat" over the usable spectrum region, but because of signal–signal interactions and Raman scattering, the Raman gain is lower at shorter wavelengths, monotonically increasing at the longer wavelengths; this is known as Raman gain tilt.

Most important, Raman amplification is applicable over a broad spectrum, from 1,300 to 1,600+ nm, known as *Raman super-continuum*. In this spectrum, over 500 optical channels with 100 GHz spacing (or 1,000 channels with 50 GHz spacing) may be amplified thus enabling a multi-terabit DWDM technology. On the negative side, Raman amplification requires pump lasers with relatively high optical power and thus thermal management; high power also raises safety issues.

Raman amplification is a distributed process and thus it requires several kilometer-long fibers; however, this is not a serious issue as the amplifying fiber is also the transmission fiber, which is long to begin with. On the negative side, however, because Raman amplification requires long fibers, existing noise in the signal is also amplified and more noise is added by the Raman pump, known as relative intensity noise (RIN) and is expressed in dBs. The added RIN noise on the signal, R_S, is caused by fluctuations of the Raman pump and is equal to the ratio of the mean square fluctuation of optical power, $\langle \delta P_S^2 \rangle$, to the square of the mean optical power, $\langle P_S \rangle^2$:

$$R_S = \langle \delta P_S^2 \rangle / \langle P_S \rangle^2$$

Similarly, as the pump induces noise on the signal, the strongly fluctuating (because of its modulation) signal induces noise on the pump. This relative induced noise, R_P, is again expressed by a similar ratio,

$$R_P = \langle \delta P_P^2 \rangle / \langle P_P \rangle^2$$

The RIN, R_S, is expressed in terms of the pump RIN, R_P, and the Raman gain, g_R, dependent term as:

$$R_S = R_P + 20 \log[\ln(g_R)] + 10 \log[D, \Delta\lambda, L, \alpha, v_S, v_g, f_P)$$

where the third term, $10 \log[D, \Delta\lambda, L, \alpha, v_S, v_g, f_P)$, is a function that depends on the pump propagation direction (counter- or co-propagating) expressed in terms of the fiber length, L; dispersion, D; wavelength difference, $\Delta\lambda$; fiber attenuation constant, a; signal velocity, v_S; group velocity of the pump, v_g; and fluctuation of the pump, f_P.

Some observations may be made now, related to co-pumped and counter-pumped Raman methods.

- The RIN induced on the signal is always greater than the RIN on the pump.
- To maintain the RIN on the pump below 30 db than the RIN on the source (assuming that the third term in the above relationship is eliminated), the Raman gain should not be greater than 4.4 db, that is, $20 \log[\ln(g_R)] = 30$ db, or $g_R = \sim 4.5$.

- Counter-propagating averages the noise over the transit length of fiber, thus acting as a low-pass filter with an extinction ratio of 20 db per decade.

- Co-propagating averages the noise transfer because of "walk off." In this case, dispersion acts like a low pass filter with an extinction rate of 20 db per decade.

Although amplified spontaneous emission (ASE) in optical amplification is unavoidable, Raman-ASE is much less than EDFA-ASE. The reason is that Raman is a distributed process that in effect takes place over a long length of fiber (tens of kilometers), as opposed to EDFA amplification that takes place over a shorter span (tens of meters). Thus, an equivalent (lumped) noise figure, F_R, is defined as:

$$F_R = [(R_{ASE}/hf) + 1]/G_R$$

where R_{ASE} is the Raman-ASE density at the end of the fiber, G_R is the Raman on–off gain, h is Planck's constant, and f is the optical frequency (Raman on–off gain is defined as the ratio of signal power when the Raman pump power is on over the signal power when the Raman pump power is off).

In this case, the ASE spectral density, ρ_{ASE}, is

$$\rho_{ASE} = h\nu(G_R F_R - 1)$$

where h is the Planck's constant and n is the frequency.

Additionally, another noise source is the double Rayleigh scattering (DRS), which is proportional to fiber length and therefore significant in Raman amplification. As a consequence, the contribution of DRS noise is limited by lowering the Raman pump power, and thus the Raman gain; thus, the DRS effectively puts a limit on Raman gain per stage.

Some of the most common pump wavelengths that have been used in the C-bands and L-bands are (notice that C and L are partitioned in two sub-bands), Table 2.7.

In addition, for each fiber a figure of merit (FOM) is defined as a function of the effective length of Raman, L_{eff}, the fiber effective area at the pump wavelength, $A_{eff-pump}$, and the Raman gain coefficient, g_R

$$FOM = L_{eff} A_{eff-pump}/g_R$$

Depending on specific fiber type, typical FOMs are approximately 10 and typical effective lengths are approximately 20 km. The largest variability among current fibers is in effective area at the wavelength of the pump, $A_{eff-pump}$, which varies between 40 and 80 μm^2.

Table 2.7 A sample of typical Raman pumps in the C and L-bands

C1: 1429 nm, 250 mW
C2: 1445 nm, 180 mW
L1: 1470 nm, 85 mW
L2: 1491 nm, 195 mW

2.17.5   Synergistic Amplification

In communications, it is common practice to combine different amplification methods to achieve the gain and quality of amplification required. For example, at the output of an optical cross-connect, small SOAs may be used on a per-channel basis to ensure that all channels are at the same ballpark power level. However, after all optical channels are multiplexed, amplification is required to provide enough gain to the DWDM signal to overcome the fiber losses over a fixed length (such as 80 km). Which amplification method is used is a matter of optical transmission engineering, component parameters, and cost.

In communications, it is not uncommon to use a combination of different amplification methods, also known as *hybrid* methods, that synergistically accomplished the goal of signal amplification.

2.17.5.1   EDFA + Raman

EDFA and Raman amplification has its own merits. In certain applications Raman makes more sense than EDFA and vice versa. For educational purposes, currently some of their (approximate) salient characteristics are listed in Table 2.8 (this is a dynamically evolving field that may soon change some of them).

Thus, depending on the application and what must be achieved, EDFA amplification can also be used in conjunction with Raman amplification. In this case, Raman amplification enhances the EDFA amplification and actually extends the fiber distance before regeneration to a total of few thousand kilometers (Fig. 2.84). In fact, since Raman amplification adds very little to noise compared with EDFA, it actually improves the overall signal to noise ratio. Thus, it is not unusual to use an EDFA amplifier (in the direction of the signal) and one or two Raman amplifiers, one co-propagating and the other counter-propagating, for long-reach to achieve sufficient gain and manageable noise. Moreover, in this case, a DCF fiber would also reduce dispersion and noise.

2.17.5.2   OPA + Raman

When fiber optical parametric amplification (OPA) is employed, and under the right conditions (pump power and frequency, and distance of signal), Raman amplification may also be applied. Typically, each amplification mechanism will amplify each wavelength in the band with different gain. In general, this may be undesirable because gain controllability becomes weaker.

2.17.6   Stimulated Brillouin Scattering

Stimulated Brillouin scattering (SBS) is the nonlinear phenomenon by which, in contrast to Raman scattering, a signal causes stimulated emission when a threshold power

Table 2.8   Comparison between EDFAs and Ramans

Characteristic	EDFA	Raman
Gain (dB)	>20	>10
Output power (dBm)	20	<30
(mW)	100	500
Bandwidth (nm)	32	32
Noise figure (dB)	>5	<1
Flatness (dB)	1	1

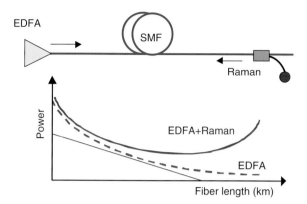

Figure 2.84   Synergistic optical amplification using EDFA and counter-pumped Raman.

level is reached. Stimulated emission takes place in both directions. However, the part that is in the same direction with the signal is scattered by acoustical phonons and the part that is in the opposite direction is guided by the fiber but is downshifted by 11 GHz at 1,550 nm (i.e., it is of shorter wavelength than the signal); this is known as the *Brillouin frequency*. The downshifted SBS signal is also modulated as the original one that caused it. If another optical signal at the downshifted wavelength propagates in the same direction with the SBS generated signal, it will be added to it and crosstalk takes place.

Experimentally, it has been determined that:

- SBS is dominant when the spectral power of the source is high, and
- It abruptly increases when the launched power reaches a threshold value.

Several factors determine the threshold value of launched power. Among them are the fiber material, the pump linewidth, the fiber length, the fiber-core effective cross-section area, and the bit rate of the signal. SBS threshold values for fiber systems are in the range of 5 to 10 mW of launched power (for externally modulated narrow linewidths) and 20 to 30 mW for directly modulated lasers (see ITU-T G.663).

Brillouin scattering, like Raman scattering, restricts the launched power per channel. However, SBS may also be advantageously used in optical amplification, where the backward signal may be the pump and the forward signal the one to be amplified.

2.17.7   Amplification in the Low-Loss Spectral Range

As the photonic signal propagates through the lossy fiber, at certain distances the optical power loss is so considerable that optical amplification is required to reinstate the signal strength and reach its destination after few thousands of kilometers. The fiber low loss region (see Fig. 1.39 and Table 1.8) supports signals in the range of 1,280 to 1,620 nm. Unfortunately, there is no single amplifier that can perform amplification over the entire DWDM spectral band as already discussed. Therefore, this issue is currently addressed by using several optical amplifiers, each performing in a specific sub-band. Based on the spectral performance of optical amplifiers, Figure 2.85 maps the spectral region that each one covers.

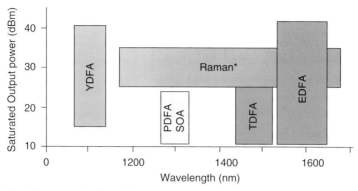

*for a wide range see also Figure 2.81

Figure 2.85 Mapping optical amplification by various amplifiers.

For example, praseodimium-doped fluoride fiber amplifiers (PDFFA) promise an acceptable performance in the S band (1,310 nm). Thorium-doped fiber amplifiers (ThDFA) promise to fill the need of photonic amplification in the 1,350 to 1,450 nm range and thulium-doped fiber amplifiers (TmDFA) in the range of 1,450 to 1,530 nm. In the C-band, erbium-doped fiber amplifiers (EDFA) have been extensively used for optical signal amplification, and erbium + germanium–doped fiber amplifiers promise to extend the C-band to also cover the L-band (1,532–1,608 nm) for multichannel

Table 2.9   Comparison between Raman and OFAs

Characteristics	Raman Amplification	OFA
Amplification	Depends on pump offset	Depends on dopant (Er, Th)
Band gain	25–50 nm per pump	~20 nm
Gain	>10 dB	>20 dB
Gain tilt	Amplifies longer λs more than shorter, but it is adjustable; it may compensate for EDFA gain tilt	Amplifies longer λs more than shorter, but it is fixed
Output power	<30 dBm 500 mW	~20 dBm 100 mW
Noise	ASE, double Raleigh scatter	ASE
Noise figure	<1 dB	>5 dB
Flatness	1 dB	1 dB
Pump l	<100 nm than amplified range	980/1480 nm for erbium
Pump power	~300 mW	~3 W
Saturation power	Depends on power of pump	Depends on dopant and gain; largely homogeneous saturation characteristics
Direction sense	Supports bidirectional signals	Unidirectional
Other	Possible crosstalk among Ochs due to OCh–OCh interaction	
Simplicity	Simpler	More complex

long-reach network applications. Similarly, in the L-band modified tellurium-erbium–doped fluoride fiber amplifiers (Te-EDFA).

Raman amplifiers have made inroads in fiber amplification because they efficiently address the extended spectrum from S to L using a standard single-mode fiber. Other fiber amplifiers better suited in short-wavelength ranges have taken advantage of optical parametric properties of fibers. Table 2.9 provides a comparison between Raman amplification and OFA amplification.

2.18   WAVELENGTH CONVERTERS

Wavelength conversion is a critical function in DWDM systems and networks; it enables optical channels to be (spectrally) reallocated, adding to network flexibility and bandwidth efficiency.

Wavelength conversion may be accomplished by properly managing the nonlinearity properties of heterojunction semiconductor optical amplifiers or of fibers, which otherwise have been deemed undesirable. Such properties are *cross-gain modulation*, *cross-phase modulation*, *four-wave mixing*, and *optical frequency shifting*.

The basic structure of semiconductor wavelength converters is compact and consists of an active layer (a heavily erbium-doped waveguide) sandwiched between a p-layer InP and an n-layer InP (Fig. 2.86).

2.18.1   Cross-Gain Modulation

When high optical power is injected into the active region and the carrier concentration is depleted through stimulated emission, *gain saturation* occurs and the optical gain is reduced. Based on this, consider two wavelengths injected into the active region of an optical amplifier. Wavelength λ_1 is of high power and is on–off keying modulated with binary data, whereas wavelength λ_2, the target signal, is of lesser power and is continuous (Fig. 2.87).

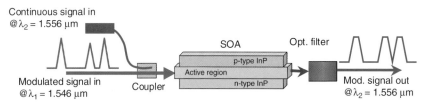

Figure 2.86 The wavelength of a modulated signal may be converted to another using SOA nonlinearity properties.

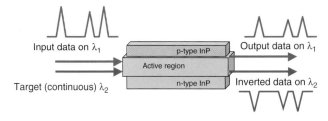

Figure 2.87 Cross-gain modulation transfers inverted data from one wavelength channel to another.

When the input bit in λ_1 is logic "one," the power is high and depletion occurs such that blocks λ_2, hence, λ_2 is at logic "zero." When the bit in λ_1 is logic "zero" (no power), depletion does not occur and λ_2 passes at full power; hence λ_2 is logic "one." Thus, a transfer of inverted data from λ_1 to λ_2 takes place. This method is known as cross-gain modulation (XGM).

2.18.2   Cross-Phase Modulation

The nonlinear properties of certain semiconductor materials lend themselves, in a process similar to cross-gain modulation, to construct a wavelength converter by taking advantage of the phase difference induced on two propagating wavelengths. One wavelength (the signal), λ_1, is modulated and the other (the target), λ_2, is continuous. Consider also that λ_2 is split into two portions, $\lambda_{2,A}$ and $\lambda_{2,B}$ (Fig. 2.88). Portion A is coupled in the nonlinear material and portion B bypasses it. However, as the modulated wavelength λ_1 enters the nonlinear material, it modulates its refractive index. As a result, the continuous "target" wavelength $\lambda_{2,A}$ undergoes phase modulation. At the output of the nonlinear material, a filter rejects λ_1 and lets through only $\lambda_{2\text{-}A}$, which now recombines with $\lambda_{2\text{-}B}$ and through constructive/destructive interference, the two produce a recombined wavelength λ_2, which is modulated as the original signal λ_1 was, and hence wavelength conversion has been accomplished. This method is known as cross-phase modulation (XPM).

2.18.3   Four-Wave Mixing

We have described that four-wave mixing (FWM) is a nonlinearity that generates an undesirable wavelength. However, the generated wavelength can be advantageous if it is produced in a controllable manner. Consider that a modulated wavelength λ_1 is to be converted to another, λ_2. Then λ_1 and two continuous wavelengths, selected for maximum FWM, are injected into a highly nonlinear fiber device. Because of FWM, a fourth wavelength, λ_2, is produced, which is modulated as the λ_1 is. In series to this device, a passband filter rejects all but the newly created wavelength, λ_2.

2.18.4   Optical Frequency Shifting

Optical frequency shifting is based on the nonlinearity property of dispersion-shifted doped fibers that produce a new wavelength when two wavelengths of high power and

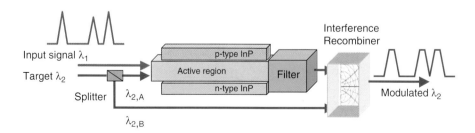

Figure 2.88   Principles of a cross-phase modulating devices.

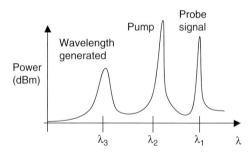

Figure 2.89 When two high power wavelengths are in close proximity and in dispersion-shifted doped fiber, a third wavelength is produced.

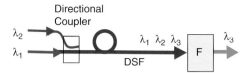

Figure 2.90 At the output of the dispersion-shifted fiber a filter eliminates the probe and pump wavelengths.

in close wavelength proximity interact (in the range of 1,550 nm), as in four-wave mixing.

Thus, by launching into a 10-km dispersion-shifted fiber a modulated wavelength, λ_1, called the *probe signal*, and a continuous power wavelength, λ_2, called the *pump*, a third modulated wavelength, λ_3, is generated (Fig. 2.89).

The newly created wavelength, λ_3, is shifted by an amount equal to the difference between the original wavelength of the signal, λ_1, and the pump, λ_2. At the output of the dispersion-shifted fiber, band pass filters eliminate the probe and the pump wavelengths and allow only the frequency-shifted λ_3 to pass through (Fig. 2.90).

2.19 OPTICAL PHASE-LOCKED LOOPS

An *optical phase-locked loop* (OPLL) is a device that is based on a tunable laser source, a filter, and a photodiode bridge. Its principle of operation is similar to that of

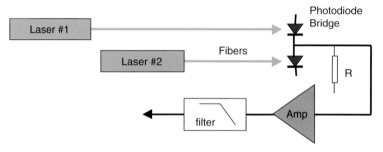

Figure 2.91 An optical phase-locked loop (OPLL) is a device based on a tunable laser source (#2), a photodiode bridge, an electronic amplifier and a filter.

an electronic PLL. Ideally, the frequency from laser #1 ($\cos \omega t$) is in perfect quadrature with that from laser #2 ($\sin \omega t$). A balanced pin–diode bridge detects both frequencies. When the two frequencies are the same, the bridge is balanced at a quiescent state, else, an unbalanced current is amplified and fed back through a low-pass filter to tunable laser #2 to adjust its frequency (Fig. 2.91). Clearly, this arrangement assumes that both incoming light sources are at the same optical power level, and if they are not, a compensating mechanism has been incorporated.

2.20 RING RESONATORS

Consider a fiber ring with its core in close proximity to the transmission fiber, thus forming a coupler with a coupling length L_O and a coupler power loss Γ at the interaction region (Fig. 2.92). The coupler is a $(1 - \Gamma)^{1/2}$ type (this describes the power coupled onto the ring). The ring has a circumference length L and attenuation constant α. Now, consider a lightwave traveling through the transmission fiber. When it reaches the coupler device, it is coupled onto the ring and travels around it. After a complete revolution around the ring, the coupled lightwave returns to the coupler with an attenuation α and a phase-shift $\Phi = \beta L$ that depends on the length ring L and the wavelength λ.

At the coupler, the lightwave from the ring and the lightwave from the transmitting fiber interfere constructively or destructively, depending on which condition is valid, $\Phi = 2\pi N$ or $\Phi = 2\pi(N + \frac{1}{2})$, respectively, where N is an integer.

The frequency difference Δf between the maximum and minimum of the transmitted power is obtained by

$$\Delta f = c/(2 n_{\text{eff}} L)$$

where n_{eff} is the effective refractive index. The effective refractive index in this case is defined as the weighted average of the refractive index of the waveguide and the refractive index of the evanescent substrate.

Ring resonators act like a passband filter with sharp cutoff characteristics and a high *finesse* (reported to be higher than 182).

In another configuration, a fiber is looped to a ring and is spliced to form a directional coupler ring. In this case, the optimum splitting ratio is expressed by

$$(P_2/P_1) = (L_e - k)/k = 1/\{1 + 1/(L_e L_s)\}$$

where k is the coupling coefficient, L_e is the directional coupler excess loss, and L_s is the splice loss.

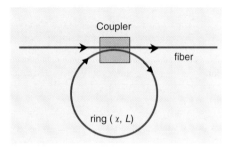

Figure 2.92 Principles of a ring resonator.

2.21   OPTICAL ATTENUATORS

Optical attenuators are devices that, as their name reveals, attenuate or absorb a fixed amount of the optical power of a signal over its complete spectral range. Fixed optical attenuators may be of thin film (polymer) or semiconductor.

A variable optical attenuator (VOA) is an attenuator that can control the amount of attenuation by the application of a voltage. VOAs over a wide attenuation range (1–99%) have an almost linear voltage–attenuation performance curve. VOAs may be polymer, mechanical, thermo-optic, electro-optic, or MEMS.

Currently, there are single VOA and arrayed VOA devices. In DWDM applications, the arrayed devices may be more suitable, as each VOA is used for each optical DWDM channel. At present, however, single VOAs have better performance specifications (Table 2.10; actual specifications may vary by manufacturer).

As technology evolves, arrayed VOAs are expected to be at parity with single VOAs in terms of performance and to be better in terms of cost.

2.22   OPTICAL SIGNAL-TO-NOISE RATIO

We have discussed signal-to-noise ratio and (in optical communication) about *optical signal to noise ratio* (ONSR), as a measure of optical noise with respect to pure optical signal. If the signal would suffer only attenuation and everything else would be perfect, then its diminished power would be easy to deal with. Unfortunately, fiber and component parameters vary in amplitude, spectrally, and temporally, and these variations along with light–matter, light–light, and light–matter–light interactions cause signal disturbances such as, power reduction, dispersion, polarization, unbalanced amplification, on the signal that are manifested as random noise; consequently, OSNR is a complex parameter. Noise is what causes misalignments, jitter, and other disturbances that impact the quality and integrity of the optical signal causing erroneous bits, the rate of which is known as *bit error rate* (BER). Given an OSNR value in dB, a first order approximation empirical formula to calculate the BER for single mode fiber is

$$\log_{10}(\text{BER}) = 10.7 - 1.45(\text{OSNR})$$

Example:
Assume that OSNR = 14.5 dB.
Then $\log_{10}(\text{BER}) = 10.30$, and BER $= 10^{-10.30} \simeq 10^{-10}$

Table 2.10   Comparison between single and arrayed VOAs

Specification	Single VOA	Arrayed VOA
Insertion loss (dB)	0.2	1
Wavelength range (nm)	1530–1565	1525–1600
Dynamic range (dB)	>25	>25
PDL (dB)	<0.1	<0.2
Response time (ms)	~0.3	<10

Noise typically has a Gaussian spectral distribution, but non-Gaussian distributions (Poisson, bursty noise, etc.) may also be present. In communications systems, the OSNR and the bit error rate correlate and thus there are mathematically connected.

Designing an optical system, a system margin should be established, depending on optical (DWDM) transmission system parameters. Such parameters are:

- Bit rate of channel
- Modulation method of channel (RZ, NRZ)
- Target BER
- Transmitter aging margin
- Receiver decision threshold margin
- Receiver cross-talk margin
- Fiber parameters and effects (loss, PMD, dispersion, etc.)
- Optical reflections
- Amplification noise

For example, ultrahigh bit rate optical transmission with FEC and target BER 10^{-16} is projected to an OSNR of 28 dB.

2.22.1   Bit Error Rate

2.22.1.1   Bit Error Rate Contributors

In communications, four contributors that affect the quality of signal are unavoidable: *intersymbol interference* (ISI), *cross-talk*, *noise*, and *bit error rate* (BER), in both electrical and optical transmission.

Bit spreading and sidetones in the propagating optical signal may drift into the next symbol and thus, although two contiguous symbols in the original bit stream might have been "10," they now appear at the receiver as "11." This is known as *intersymbol interference* (ISI) and pertains only to an optical channel.

Bits from one DWDM channel influence bits in another channel (because of nonlinear light–matter–light interactions or because of spectral overlap of optical channels, and although two contiguous symbols in the original bit stream of a channel might have been "10," they now may appear as "11." This is *cross-talk* and it pertains to more than one optical channel in a fiber.

In optical communication, we do not have the additive noise of electromagnetic interference that we have in electrical transmission. However, optical communication is not immune to noise, as optical amplifiers (doped fibers, Raman, and SOA) spontaneously emit photons in the spectral band of optical channels, as well as other nonlinear mechanisms (scattering, and so on), manifested as *optical noise*.

2.22.1.2   Bit Error Rate Probabilities

Bits transmitted by the source and bits arriving at the receiver, because of all possible influences already outlined, may not have the same value; that is, some logic "ones" or "zeros" have been corrupted and are read as logic "zeros" or "ones." In actuality, what takes place is that the threshold of the receiver is set at a certain power value. When the power level of an incoming optical symbol is above the threshold level of the photodetector, a logic "one" is provided, otherwise a logic "zero." The number of erroneous bits over a number of bits transmitted is known as *bit-error-rate* (BER). BER currently cannot be directly measured in the photonic regime. To measure BER, the optical signal is converted to an electrical signal, and the electrical signal is used to measure BER. That is, the BER measurement is an indirect method as the receiver itself adds to the noise of the signal (dark current, shot noise). Errored bits are a reality of transmission that cannot be overlooked, regardless of how well the transmission path has been engineered. Therefore, for efficient BER measurements, specific codes have been embedded in the overhead of the signal at the source, based on a generating polynomial. In fact, this code has error-detection and error-correction capabilities. Thus, the signal consists of the actual client-generated data plus overhead that contains an error detection and error correction code (ECDC), in addition to performance and maintenance, source and destination, and so on. However, the type and size of overhead depends on the type of protocol used (IP, SONET, ATM, etc.).

An errored bit is a random process, and its mathematical treatment is based on stochastic processes and probabilities. In communications, the ratio of detected errored bits, ε, to total bits transmitted, n, is expressed as $P(\varepsilon)$:

$$P(\varepsilon) = \varepsilon/n$$

Typically, the probability $P(\varepsilon)$ is estimated, denoted by $P'(\varepsilon)$. If the sample of bits is very large (almost infinite), then the estimated probability is almost equal to the actual value.

In communications, an upper limit of $P'(\varepsilon)$ is typically set to a specified level γ, such as $\gamma = 10^{-N}$, where N, depending on application, may vary from 8 to 15, and errored bits are calculated over a period to determine the actual error probability, $P(\varepsilon)$; $P(\varepsilon)$ must be equal to or less than $P'(\varepsilon)$. Predicting the acceptable error probability, one resorts to statistical methods and binomial distribution functions. Thus, if p is the probability that a bit will be erroneous, and q is the probability that a bit will not be erroneous (here a good model of the transmission medium is required to determine these probabilities, which in a binomial distribution $p + q = 1$), then the probability that k bit errors will occur in n transmitted bits is expressed by

$$P_n(k) = \{n!/(k!(n-k)!)\}p^k q^{n-k}$$

Similarly, the probability that N or fewer errors will occur in n transmitted bits is expressed by

$$P(\varepsilon <= N) = \sum P_n(k) = \sum[\{n!/(k!(n-k)!)\}p^k q^{n-k}]$$

where the sum is calculated from $k = 0$ to N, and in the case of N or more errors,

$$P(\varepsilon - N) = 1 - P(\varepsilon </= N) = \sum P_n(k) = \sum[\{n!/(k!(n-k)!)\}p^k q^{n-k}],$$

where the sum is calculated from $k = N + 1$ to n.

These equations are simplified if errors are Poisson random, in which case and for n very large (almost infinite), $p^k q^{n-k} = \{(np)^k/k!\}e^{-np}$, and thus

$$\sum P_n(k) = \sum\{(np)^k/k!\}e^{-np}$$

The probability that the actual $P(\varepsilon)$ is better than the acceptable set level γ, is known as the confidence level (CL) expressed in percent (%) and defined as

$$CL = P(\varepsilon > N|\gamma) = 1 - \sum [\{n!/(k!(n-k)!)\} P^k (1-\gamma)^{n-k}]$$

where the sum is calculated from $k = 0$ to N. The last equation can be solved for n, the number of transmitted bits required to be monitored for errors. Clearly, the number n in the unit of time is directly related to a bit rate. Assuming a confidence level of 99%, a BER threshold set at $\gamma = 10^{-10}$, and a bit rate of 2.5 Gb/s, the required number n is 6.64×10^{10} to detect a single error.

A comprehensive treatment of bit error rate analysis is beyond the scope of this book. The point is that predictions can be made so that transmission engineering BER rules can be set (based on an accepted quality of received signal), but the actual BER value must be monitored (because it determines the quality of the transmission medium).

2.22.1.3 Bit Error Rate Monitoring

To monitor the signal quality, one or more techniques may be used such as *termination*, *sampling*, *spectral monitoring*, and *indirect monitoring*.

- The termination technique consists of error-detecting codes (EDC) that have been incorporated into the information bit stream of the source. At the receiver, an EDC code checks the incoming bit stream bit by bit and it finds erroneous bits, which are counted to deduce the actual BER. Error-detecting and error-correcting codes EDCs also have limited correcting capability. Signal termination implies that the optical signal is converted to an electrical signal and therefore, apart the destination terminal, it puts a severe penalty on other nodes in terms of transparency and cost if termination is not required.

- Sampling methods require discrete sampling and a signal analyzer that consists at minimum by a demultiplexer, very low noise detectors, a synchronizer to sample the received signal, and algorithmic discrete signal analysis.

- Spectral monitoring consists of noise level measurements and spectral analysis.

- If no direct signal monitoring is performed (noise, distortion, power spectra, etc.), then the quality of signal depends on the quality of system design. Thus, it is grossly concluded from indirect information (similar to legacy systems) such as system alarms (loss of frame, loss of synchronization, etc.).

2.22.2 BER and Eye Diagram

In transmission, one quick and qualitative measure of the quality and integrity of the electronic signal (since optical has already been converted to electrical) is a superposition of bit periods (marks for "ones" and spaces for "zeros") on an oscilloscope. This superposition is known as "eye diagram." If the signal has little noise and its amplitude is sufficient to be clearly recognized as a "one" or "zero," then the superposition provides an "open eye" (see also Section 2.15.3 for a discussion of error probabilities). Otherwise, the eye is corrupted and "fuzzy" (Fig. 2.93).

Based on the expected eye diagram, decision levels have been determined, such as the sampling point in time, and the threshold levels for logic "one" and logic "zero."

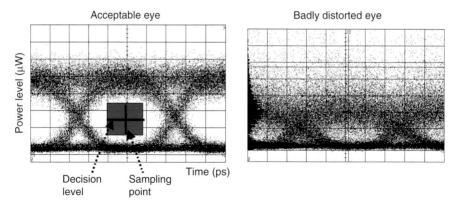

Figure 2.93 Eye diagrams provide a quick and qualitative measure of the quality and integrity of the signal at the receiver (optical has already been converted to electrical).

The *bit error rate* (BER) and the opening of the eye are closely related. However, the eye opening is not an observation of an optical signal but of an electrical signal. Photonic pulses are converted to electrical pulses and thus, as is well known from classical digital sampling, a logic one or a logic zero are decided based on two current thresholds (assuming no jitter) at the half-period of the bit rate, a minimum current threshold for a logic 1, $I_{1,\min}$, and a maximum current threshold for a logic 0, $I_{0,\max}$. Then, the eye opening is defined as

$$E_{\text{eye}} = I_{1,\min} - I_{0,\max}$$

Noise and jitter are random effects, most likely with a Gaussian distribution. If the standard deviation for a logic "one" bit (or mark) is σ_1 and for a logic "zero" bit (or space) is σ_0, there is a measure of signal-to-noise ratio (or quality factor), Q, illustrated in Figure 2.84 and defined as

$$Q = E_{\text{eye}}/\sqrt{|\sigma_0^2 - \sigma_1^2|}$$

Then the BER is defined as

$$\text{BER} = \tfrac{1}{2}\,\text{erfc}\,(Q/\sqrt{2})$$

where erfc is the error function, values of which are provided in tables and sqrt is the square root. If noise is Gaussian, the BER is also expressed as

$$\text{BER} = \{1/[\sqrt{(2\pi Q)}]\}\exp(-Q^2/2)$$

Based on this, a Q-value of 6.1 corresponds to BER $= 10^{-9}$, and a Q-value of 7.2 to BER $= 10^{-12}$.

In addition, based on the expected eye opening, E_{eye}, and the actual average eye opening, E_{avg}, a quantitative penalty ratio is also defined as

$$\text{Penalty} = E_{\text{eye}}/2E_{\text{avg}}$$

In the presence of jitter, an adjustment in these above two threshold values is made with respect to the jitter position, displaced from T/2 by $\Delta\tau$, and then the eye is denoted as $E(\tau)$ (Fig. 2.94). Degradations due to timing include both jitter and static decision time (or temporal sampling point) misalignment.

Figure 2.94 also defines the sum of all contributors responsible for amplitude degradation, ΔA, the maximum peak-to-peak eye, E_{max}, and the eye opening, E_{eye}. Then, the signal degradation is expressed in terms of maximum and open eye as

$$\Delta S/N = 20 \log[E_{max}/E_{eye}]$$

Figure 2.95 outlines the steps required for measuring the penalty from an eye diagram.

Then, $I_{1,min}$ is the minimum current threshold level at the receiver for detecting a logic "one" symbol and $I_{0,max}$ is the maximum level for logic "zero," at the jitter point.

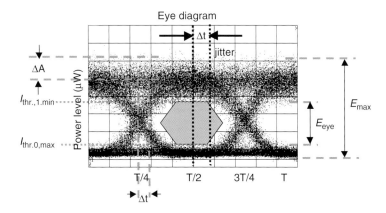

Figure 2.94 Threshold levels (power and jitter) mapped on eye diagram.

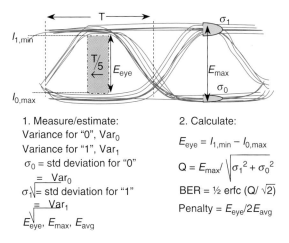

1. Measure/estimate:
Variance for "0", Var_0
Variance for "1", Var_1
σ_0 = std deviation for "0"
$\qquad = \sqrt{Var_0}$
σ_1 = std deviation for "1"
$\qquad = \sqrt{Var_1}$
E_{eye}, E_{max}, E_{avg}

2. Calculate:

$E_{eye} = I_{1,min} - I_{0,max}$

$Q = E_{max}/\sqrt{\sigma_1{}^2 + \sigma_0{}^2}$

BER = ½ erfc (Q/$\sqrt{2}$)

Penalty = $E_{eye}/2E_{avg}$

Figure 2.95 BER and penalty estimation based on eye diagram.

If the *probability* of a single bit to be in error within the unit of time or within an equivalent block of bits is q, the probability of two errors occurring independently within the same block is q^2, of three errors is q^3, and so on.

The BER is directly proportional to the error probability q for single error, q^2 for double, and so on.

For a poor BER $= 10^{-3}$, this means:

- A single error is *most likely* to occur in 1,000 bits in the unit of time
- A double error is 1,000 times *most unlikely* to occur than a single bit error
- A triple error is a 1,000,000 times *most unlikely* to occur than a single bit error, and so on.

A triple error is 1 million times *most unlikely* to occur than a single bit error; this implies an almost never occurring event, and it may be a reasonable assumption at very low bit rates, such as Kbps. However, at extremely high bit rates for which there are many trillions of bits per second (e.g., 10 or 40 Gb/s), this assumption is not true at all.

The eye diagram method has been successfully used in both electrical (legacy) transmission and optical transmission. However, this method depends on a visual observation of the superposition of many marks ("ones") and spaces ("zeros") to yield a quantitative visual observation of how well the "eye is open," and from it to estimate the standard deviations for "one" and for "zero," and the parameters to estimate the BER and OSNR. A more accurate and more complex method is, instead of superimposing the marks and spaces, to count the amplitude of each mark and each space (not all marks and all spaces arrive with the same amplitude). Based on these data, a statistical histogram is formed, which for a large number of marks and spaces provides a better measure of the standard deviation and thus the BER and OSNR of the optical signal. To accomplish this, each incoming pulse is sampled (at the same timing reference point), the samples are stored, and a histogram is formed based on amplitude and frequency of occurrence (Fig. 2.96). In a more elaborate scheme, each incoming pulse is randomly sampled, and assuming that the acquired samples are sufficient, the statistical histogram is obtained. Thus, the histogram technique lends itself to automated BER estimates.

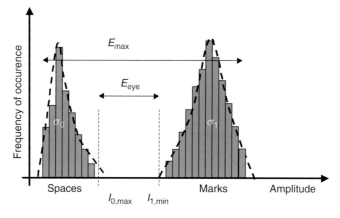

Figure 2.96   BER and penalty estimation based on the histogram diagram.

2.23 NEW MATERIALS AND COMPONENTS

Today, optical components and materials are where electronic transistors were about 30 years ago. Few single transistors were interconnected to make a radio or a television set; one could count the number of transistors in them. Today, because of integration it is impossible to count the transistors of a pocket calculator or an electronic wristwatch with the naked eye.

Today, optical functionality is achieved with single, and in certain cases two or three, optical components. Tomorrow, optical integrated "circuitry" based on new materials, methods and techniques will make it almost impossible to identify each component in the mix and regard it as a "black" box with well-defined input–output functionality.

Here we make an attempt to outline the ongoing research effort and emerging optical technologies that will make this possible. This is extremely difficult to capture because new materials and methods are announced each day or week.

However, new materials will be combined with existing materials with well-known transmission characteristics, some of which (suitable in communications) are tabulated in Table 2.11.

2.23.1 Optical Materials

Artificial new solid-state optical materials with unusual characteristics are currently in the experimental stage. Such characteristics are based on extremely high values of the index of refraction, transmission range, polarization, and switching properties when a varying field is applied. Other properties are based on optical energy absorption

Table 2.11 Transmission range (in μm) for certain materials

Material	Transmission Range (μm)
Al_2O_3	0.2–9
BaF_2	0.29–9.5
CaF_2	0.13–10
CdTe	1.0–25
Cr_2O_3	0.6–5
CsBr	0.35–32
CsI	0.42–40
GaAs	2.0–15
Ge	2.0–14
In_2O_3	0.4–9
KBr	0.26–23
KCl	0.3–16
LiF	0.12–8.5
NaCl	0.23–12
Nd_2O_3	0.4–8
Pr_2O_3	0.3–8
Si	1.2–7
Silica (Fused)	0.25–3.5
SiO_2	0.2–7
TiO_2	0.3–10

and coherent photoluminescence in a wide spectral range that covers the C-bands and L-bands and beyond.

Among them, gallium nitride is a stable semiconductor material that can be used for light-emitting diodes (LED) that emit an intense blue light when electricity is passed through it. These LEDs are expected to find many applications in home, entertainment (DVDs), displays, and communications.

In addition to solid-state materials, researchers are experimenting with organic compounds that absorb one wavelength and emit another (useful in wavelength conversion and memory applications), or they absorb a wavelength and emit it back when it is stimulated (useful in memory applications).

Organic compounds, although not challenge-free (thermal, mechanical, birefringence, etc.) promise easily manufacturable and very inexpensive components (can be molded for mass-production). Some organic compounds can be deposited to virtually any type of material, such as glass, plastic, and treated paper. As an example, consider organic compounds that can be made into an optical *organic thin film* (OTF). Then, when a voltage excites their molecular state, based on fluorescence they emit light of a specific wavelength, a phenomenon known as *exciton*. However, the duration of light emission of such compounds is on the order of many microseconds. Such compound is perylene that emits blue light, coumarin-6 that emits green and other compounds that emit different wavelengths. These compounds have high luminescent efficiency and emit at a wide angle. Organic thin films may find several optoelectronic applications, such as flat thin displays with transparent electrical contacts made of titanium oxides by deposition.

Other organic compounds, such as pentacene, have electrical properties that are suitable for field-effect transistors. Pentacene is a simple molecule made of five connected benzene rings that forms good crystals. They may find several applications in portable devices, communications, electronic identification, and others.

In a different endeavor, organic materials are used to extract compounds that can be used in the optical and semiconductor fields. For example, corn is used to extract compounds that can be turned into plastic films. Rice hull and coconut are rich in silicon dioxide, or silica, which can be used for semiconductors. Silica from the world of plants may also possess other convenient properties.

2.23.2   Hollow Fibers

Photonic crystal fibers (PCF) comprise a new type of fiber that promises improved optical propagation for longer fiber lengths. As described in Chapter 1, PCFs consist of a bundle of microscopic silica tubes, about 1 micrometer in diameter (Fig. 1.66). Such fibers exhibit spectral selectivity, no dispersion, very low loss, and uniform propagation characteristics for all supported wavelengths. Because of these properties, PCFs are expected to find applications not only in fiber transmission but also in components with specialized functionality, including amplifiers and sensors.

2.23.3   Lasers and Receivers

Low-cost lasers are important in all applications. Some researchers are even experimenting with organic compounds to create inexpensive high-density plastic lasers and other components.

High-power tunable inexpensive lasers and dense laser arrays and matrices with narrow linewidth and sufficient optical power for DWDM applications are other noteworthy activities.

A similar activity aims to produce tunable receivers and receiver arrays and matrices at low cost. In this venue, some researchers have succeeded in generating hundreds of wavelength channels with a single laser. In a similar venue, announcements have been made demonstrating dense sources and receivers all integrated on the same substrate, combining mixed technologies for lasers, receivers, and standard CMOS, thus enabling parallel transmission and reception of many fiber links, with an aggregate bandwidth that may be beyond imagination.

2.23.4 Optical Cross-Connects

As the number of wavelengths increases to large numbers, large 1000×1000 optical cross-connecting fabrics, nonblocking, with low loss and fast switching become a challenge. Today, there is a substantial effort to develop high-density devices switching fabrics based on MEMS, bubbles, and other technologies.

In addition, there is ongoing research to develop ultrafast switching devices; these are based on glasses that contain chalcogenides. Chalcogenide glasses (Ge-Se-Te) have an index of refraction 1000 times higher than that of SiO_2 glass, they have an ultrafast response time (they can switch from high nonlinear absorption to low) in less than 1 psec, they have a low linear loss and a low nonlinear loss β, and a high figure of merit (FOM) on the order of 20.

2.23.5 Optical Memories

To date, optical storage, or memory devices, is in the infancy state. However, storage is an important function in signal processing and thus optical memory components are expected to also play their role when in mature state. Consequently, there is substantial ongoing research aimed at the development of new materials, methods, and techniques that will be able to "freeze" light, or at best delay it in a manageable manner so that optical information can be stored and retrieved at some later time.

Another form of optical storage is based on holographic storage in certain electro-holographic nonlinear crystals, known as *paraelectric photorefractive*. These crystals can store many holograms in a latent form as a trapped space charge. When a specific voltage is applied to them, one of the holograms is activated. Ongoing research aims to store a very large number of patterns and to make them rewriteable. In a similar venue, researchers are experimenting with glass doped with samarium and europium elements to produce clusters of fluorescent spots (each dot about 400 nm in diameter) and arranged in layers in the three-dimensional space (each layer about 100 nm apart). Thus, dots correspond to bits, and if millions of bits are stored on each of millions of layers, the potential storage capacity in such material is on the order of many terabits per unit volume.

Photochromicity is not a new application; one may think of it as write once read many (WORM).

Another type of temporary optical storage is the optical delay line. Light slows down as it travels in optically transparent matter by a factor equal to its refractive

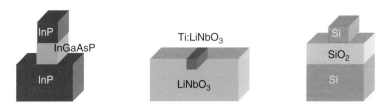

Figure 2.97 Examples of integrated photonic waveguides.

index. For example, a refractive index of 3 will slow down the speed of light by that factor. The principle of delay line is already used in monolithic interferometers.

In summary, judging from the focused effort in compact optical devices that can store a light pulse as long as necessary, would be able to quickly retrieve it, erase it, and rewrite another one is a device of perhaps the very near future. Then, integrating it with other optical components, we will truly see the first optical integrated circuit and perhaps computer.

2.23.6 Optical Integration

Optical device integration is the result of technological evolution (Fig. 2.97). It will not be long before optical devices follow the evolution path of the transistor. A few years ago it was a dream to integrate 1 million transistors into a chip; now this is trivial reality. Thus, combining optical integration and sophisticated packaging devices with complex functionality will perform signal processing in the optical regime.

EXERCISES

1. A Fabry–Perot interferometer has a refractive index $n = 1$. For $m = 1$, what should the spacing be to resonate at 1400 nm?

2. Calculate the finesse of a Fabry–Perot interferometer if the reflectivity is A. $R = 0.9$, and B. $R = 0.3$.

3. The Bragg spacing is 5 times 750 nm. What is the order of the Bragg grating for a wavelength 1500 nm?

4. A Bragg grating has a grating constant $d = 700$ nm. For what wavelength the first order reflection is maximal?

5. A diffraction grating converts optical frequencies. True or false?

6. For $\lambda = 1500$ nm and $d = 3000$ nm, calculate the modes of a grating so that the relationship $|m\lambda/d| < 2$ holds.

7. Consider an XY-LiNbO$_3$ crystal with $n_{TE} = 2.207$ and $n_{TM} = 2.135$ and acoustic speed through the crystal 1737 m/sec in an acousto-optic filter. We want to select an optical wavelength with center at 1.5 μm. Calculate:
   a. the optical wavelength Λ
   b. the RF frequency that should be applied.

8. Is it true or false that an arrayed waveguide grating (AWG) is based on the principle of interferometry?

9. A Mach–Zehnder interferometer receives two coherent light sources, one at wavelength λ_1 and the other at wavelength λ_2. Is it possible to guide each wavelength to a different output?

10. Is it true that an acousto-optic filter (AOF) requires a specific RF signal to operate?

11. Could an LED be classified as a diode device?

12. What is the effect of temperature on the stability of LED devices?

13. Could LEDs be applied in communications, and if so, what would the fiber type be?

14. What are the basic elements of a semiconductor laser?

15. We need to modulate a laser source with the minimum amount of chirping. What type of modulation should we use?

16. Is it true that EDFAs perform best in the region 1350 nm?

17. Name a natural photosensor and two artificial photosensors.

18. What limits the switching speed of a PIN diode?

19. An APD diode has very little gain. True or false?

20. What is the main difference between a regenerator and an optical amplifier?

21. What is the difference between an semiconductor optical amplifier (SOA) and an EDFA?

22. What is amplified spontaneous emission (ASE) and what is spontaneous noise?

23. What is a wavelength converter?

24. What is a wavelength shifter?

25. A wavelength fiber shifter requires two inputs, a probe signal and a pump source. Which one is the continuous source and which one is the modulated source?

26. List five of the most desirable characteristics of optical couplers.

27. What is the fundamental principle on which a ring resonator operates?

28. What is an optical isolator?

29. What is a rotator?

30. A fiber transports a bundle of wavelengths. However, a specific wavelength must be dropped off at a node, whereas the remaining to pass through. Is this possible? If no, why? If yes, how?

31. If a single wavelength can be dropped off and added, could more than one wavelength be dropped off and added? If no, why? If yes, how?

32. From the various optical switches available, which one is the fastest, which one with medium speed, and which one with slow.

REFERENCES

1. S.V. Kartalopoulos, *Introduction to DWDM Technology: Data in a Rainbow*, IEEE Press, New York, 2000.

2. W.L. Wolfe, *Introduction to Infrared System Design*, SPIE Press, 1997.

3. G.J. Zissis, *The Infrared Handbook*, ERIM and SPIE, 1978.

4. S.V. Kartalopoulos, *Fault Detectability in DWDM: Toward Higher Signal Quality and System Reliability*, IEEE Press, New York, 2001.

5. G. Keiser, *Optical Fiber Communications*, McGraw-Hill, New York, 1983.

6. P. Yeh, *Introduction to Photorefractive Nonlinear Optics*, John Wiley & Sons, New York, 1993.

7. S.O. Kasap, *Optoelectronics and Photonics*, Prentice-Hall, Upper Saddle River, NJ, 2001.

8. S.V. Kartalopoulos, What is DWDM?, SPIE OE Reports, no. 203, Nov. 2000, pp. 4 and 12.

9. L. Desmarais, *Applied Electro-Optics*, Prentice-Hall, Englewood Cliffs, NJ, 1999.

10. G.P Agrawal, *Nonlinear Fiber Optics*, 2nd ed., Academic Press, New York, 1995.

11. R. Ramaswami and K.N. Sivarajan, *Optical Networks*, Morgan Kaufmann, San Francisco, CA, 1998.

12. B. Mukherjee, *Optical Communication Networks*, McGraw-Hill, New York, 1997.

13. I.P. Kaminow and T.L. Koch, eds., *Optical Fiber Communications IIIA* and *Optical Fiber Communications IIIB*, Academic Press, New York, 1997.

14. J.C. Palais, *Fiber Optic Communications*, 3rd ed., Prentice-Hall, Englewood Cliffs, NJ, 1992.

15. S. Sudo, ed., *Optical Fiber Amplifiers: Materials, Devices, and Applications*, Artec House, Boston, 1997.

16. K. Nassau, *The Physics and Chemistry of Color*, John Wiley & Sons, New York, 1983.

17. T. Wildi, *Units and Conversion Charts*, 2nd ed., IEEE Press, New York, 1995.

18. D.P. Jablonowski, U.C. Paek, and L.S. Watkins, Optical fiber manufacturing techniques, *AT&T Tech. J.*, vol. 66, issue 1, Jan.–Feb. 1987, pp. 33–44.

19. W.M. Flegal et al., Making single-mode preforms by the MCVD process, *AT&T Tech. J.*, vol. 65, issue 1, Jan.–Feb. 1986, pp. 56–61.

20. C. Palmer, *Diffraction Grating Handbook*, www.thermorgl.com Apr., 2002.

21. J.B. MacChesney, P.B. O'Connor, and H.M. Presby, A new technique for the preparation of low loss and graded index optical fibers, *Proc. IEEE*, vol. 62, 1974, pp. 1278–1279.

22. D. Kalish and L.G. Cohen, Single-mode fiber: From research and development to manufacturing, *AT&T Tech. J.*, vol. 66, issue 1, Jan.–Feb. 1987, pp. 19–32.

23. J.E. Clemens, T.I. Ejim, W.A. Gault, and E.M. Monberg, Bulk III-V compound semiconductor crystal growth, *AT&T Tech. J.*, vol. 68, no. 1, 1989, pp. 29–42.

24. W.D. Johnston, Jr., M.A. DiGiuseppe, and D.P. Wilt, Liquid and vapor phase growth of III-V materials for photonic devices, *AT&T Tech. J.*, vol. 68, no. 1, 1989, pp. 53–63.

25. N.K. Dutta, III-V device technologies for lightwave applications, *AT&T Tech. J.*, vol. 68, no. 1, 1989, pp. 5–18.

26. D.S. Alles and K.J. Brady, Packaging technology for III-V photonic devices and integrated circuits, *AT&T Tech. J.*, vol. 68, no. 1, 1989, pp. 83–92.

27. S-Y. Lin and J.G. Fleming, A three-dimensional optical photonic crystals, *J. Lightwave Technol.*, vol. 17, no. 11, Nov. 1999, pp. 1944–1947.

28. H. Kosaka et al., Superprism phenomena in photonic crystals: Toward microscale lightwave circuits, *J. Lightwave Technol.*, vol. 17, no. 11, Nov. 1999, pp. 2032–2038.

29. J.J. Refi, Optical fibers for optical networking, *Bell Labs Tech. J.*, vol. 4, no. 1, 1999, pp. 246–261.

30. B. Giles and E. Desurvire, Modeling erbium-doped fiber amplifiers, *J. Lightwave Technol.*, vol. 9, Feb. 1991, pp. 271–283.

31. E. Desurvire, *Erbium-Doped Fiber Amplifiers*, Wiley, New York, 1994.

32. A. Saleh, R. Jopson, J. Evankov, and J. Aspen, Modeling of gain in erbium-doped fiber amplifiers, *IEEE Photon. Technol. Lett.*, vol. 2, Oct. 1990, pp. 714–717.

33. O. Leclerc, Optical 3R Regeneration for 40 Gbit/s line-rates and beyond, Technical Digest OFC2002, paper TuN1, pp. 79–81, Mar. 2002.

34. M.L. Nielsen, Experimental demonstration of all-optical 2R regeneration at 10 Gb/s in a novel MMI-SOA based device, Technical Digest OFC 2002, paper TuN2, pp. 81–83, Mar. 2002.

35. H. Dai, O.M. Stafsudd, and B. Dunn, Measurement of the stimulated emission cross-section and fluorescence brnching ratio for Nd^{3+} in $YAlO_3$ crystal, *IEEE J. Quantum Electron.*, vol. 25, Feb. 1989, pp. 144–146.

36. K.O. Hill, Photosensitivity in optical fiber waveguides: From discovery to commercialization, *IEEE J. Select. Top. Quantum Electron.*, vol. 6, no. 6, Nov./Dec. 2000, pp. 1186–1189.

37. M. Matsuhara, K.O. Hill, and A. Watanabe, Optical-waveguide filters: Synthesis, *J. Opt. Soc. Amer.*, vol. 65, 1975, pp. 804–809.

38. S.R. Forrest, Active optoelectronics using thin-film organic semiconductors, *IEEE J. Select. Top. Quantum Electron.*, vol. 6, no. 6, Nov./Dec. 2000, pp. 1072–1083.

39. K.A. Winick and J.E. Roman, Design of corrugated waveguide filters by Fourier transform techniques, *IEEE J. Quantum Electron.*, vol. 26, 1990, pp. 1918–1929.

40. S.V. Kartalopoulos, Temperature self-compensating diffraction-based optical components in DWDM, submitted for publication *Opt. Eng. J.*

41. R. Feced, M.N. Zervas, and M.A. Muriel, An efficient inverse scattering algorithm for the design of non-uniform fiber Bragg gratings, *IEEE J. Quantum Electron.*, vol. 35, 1999, pp. 1105–1115.

42. M.A. Muriel, J. Azana, and A. Carballar, Fiber grating synthesis by use of time-frequency representations, *Opt. Lett.*, vol. 23, 1998, pp. 1526–1528.

43. R.J. Mears, L. Reekie, I.M. Jauncey, and D.N. Payne, Low-noise erbium-doped fiber amplifier operating at 1.54 μm, *Elect. Lett.*, vol. 23, no. 19, Sept. 1987, pp. 1026–1028.

44. E. Desurvire, J.R. Simpson, and P.C. Becker, High-gain erbium-doped traveling-wave fiber amplifiers, *Opt. Lett.*, vol. 12, no. 11, Nov. 1987, pp. 888–890.

45. C.K. Campbell, Applications of surface acoustic and shallow bulk acoustic wave devices, *Proc. IEEE*, vol. 77, no. 10, 1989, pp. 1453–1484.

46. K.-W. Cheung, Acoustooptic tunable filters in narrowband WDM networks: system issues and network applications, *IEEE J. Select. Areas Comm.*, vol. 8, no. 6, Aug. 1990, pp. 1015–1025.

47. D.A. Smith, J.E. Baran, J.J. Johnson, and K.-W. Cheung, Integrated-optic acoustically-tunable filters for WDM networks, *IEEE J. Select. Areas Comm.*, vol. 8, no. 6, Aug. 1990, pp. 1151–1159.

48. S.R. Mallison, Wavelength-selective filters for single-mode fiber WDM systems using Fabry–Perot interferometers, *Appl. Opt.*, vol. 26, 1987, pp. 430–436.

49. N. Takato et al., Silica-based integrated optic Mach–Zehnder multi/demultiplexer family with channel spacing of 0.01–250 nm, *IEEE J. Select. Areas Comm.*, vol. 8, no. 6, Aug. 1990, pp. 1120–1127.

50. R.C. Alferness, Waveguide electro-optic modulators, *IEEE Trans. Microwave Theory Techniques*, MTT-30, 1982, pp. 1121–1137.

51. E. Ackerman, S. Wanuga, D. Kasemset, A. Daryoush, and N. Samant, Maximum dynamic range operation of a microwave external modulation fiber-optic link, *IEEE Trans. Microwave Theory Technology*, vol. 41, pp. 1299–1306, Aug. 1993.

52. U. Cummings and W. Bridges, Bandwidth of linearized electro-optic modulators, *J. Lightwave Technol.*, vol. 16, pp. 1482–1490, Aug. 1998.

53. J. Frangen et al., Integrated optical, acoustically-tunable wavelength filter, Proc. 6th European Conf. Integrated Opt., Paris, SPIE, 1989, post-deadline paper.

54. F. Ouellette, All-fiber for efficient dispersion compensation, *Optics Lett.*, vol. 16, no. 5, Mar. 1991, pp. 303–304.

55. R.M. Measures, A.T. Alavie, M. LeBlanc, S. Huang, M. Ohn, R. Masskant, and D. Graham, Controlled grating chirp for variable optical dispersion compensation, Proceedings, 13th Annual Conference on European Fiber Optic Communications and Networks, Brighton, England, 1995, pp. 38–41.

56. G.D. Boyd and F. Heismann, Tunable acoustooptic reflection filters in LiNbO3 without a Doppler shift, *J. Lightwave Technol.*, vol. 7, Apr. 1989, pp. 625–631.

57. L.G. Kazovsky, Optical signal processing for lightwave communications networks, *IEEE J. Select. Areas Comm.*, vol. 8, no. 6, Aug. 1990, pp. 973–982.

58. A. Yariv, Coupled mode theory for guided wave optics, *IEEE J. Quantum Electron.*, vol. QE-9, 1973, pp. 919–933.

59. H.F. Taylor and A. Yariv, Guided wave optics, *Proc. IEEE*, vol. 62, 1974, p. 1044.

60. D. Sadot and E. Boimovich, Tunable optical filters for dense WDM networks, *IEEE Comm. Mag.*, vol. 36, no. 12, Nov. 1998, pp. 50–55.

61. M. Zirngibl, Multifrequency lasers and applications in WDM networks, *IEEE Comm. Mag.*, vol. 36, no. 12, Nov. 1998, pp. 39–41.

62. F. Tong, Multiwavelength receivers for WDM systems, *IEEE Comm. Mag.*, vol. 36, no. 12, Nov. 1998, pp. 42–49.

63. K.A. McGreer, Arrayed waveguide grating for wavelength routing, *IEEE Comm. Mag.*, vol. 36, no. 12, Nov. 1998, pp. 62–68.

64. A. Iocco, H.G. Limberger, and R.P. Salathe, Bragg grating fast tunable filter, *Electr. Lett.*, vol. 33, no. 25, Dec. 1997, pp. 2147–2148.

65. M.K. Smit and C. van Dam, PHASAR-based WDM-devices: Principles, design and application, *IEEE J. Select. Top. Quantum Electron.*, vol. 2, no. 2, 1996, pp. 236–250.

66. H. Tanobe et al., Temperature insensitive arrayed waveguide gratings on InP substrate, *IEEE Photon Tech. Lett.*, vol. 10, no. 2, 1998, pp. 235–237.

67. D. Nesset, T. Kelly, and D. Marcenac, All-optical wavelength conversion using SOA nonlinearities, *IEEE Comm. Mag.*, vol. 36, no. 12, Nov. 1998, pp. 56–61.

68. Y.K. Chen and C.C. Lee, Fiber bragg grating-based large nonblocking multiwavelength cross-connects, *J. Lightwave Technol.*, vol. 16, no. 10, 1998, pp. 1746–1756.

69. C.R. Doerr, Proposed WDM cross connect using a planar arrangement of waveguide grating routers and phase shifters, *IEEE Photon. Technol. Lett.*, vol. 10, Apr. 1998, pp. 528–530.

70. J.E. Ford, V.A. Aksyuk, D.J. Bishop, and J.A. Walker, Wavelength add/drop switching using tilting micromirrors, *J. Lightwave Technol.*, vol. 17, no. 5, May 1999, pp. 904–911.

71. J.R. Thompson and R. Roy, Multiple four-wave mixing process in an optical fiber, *Optics Lett.*, vol. 16, no. 8, Apr. 1991, pp. 557–559.

72. K. Inoue, Four-wave mixing in an optical fiber in the zero-dispersion wavelength region, *IEEE J. Lightwave Technol.*, vol. LT-10, no. 11, Nov. 1992, pp. 1553–1563.

73. K. Inoue, Suppression of fiber four-wave mixing in multichannel transmission using bire-fringent elements, *IEICE Trans. Comm.*, vol. E76-B, no. 9, Sept. 1993, pp. 1219–1221.

74. K. Inoue, Experimental study on channel crosstalk due to fiber four-wave mixing around the zero-dispersion wavelength, *IEEE J. Lightwave Technol.*, vol. LT-12, no. 6, June 1994, pp. 1023–1028.

75. K. Inoue, Fiber four wave mixing in multi-amplifier systems with nonuniform chromatic dispersion, *IEEE J. Lightwave Technol.*, vol. LT-13, Jan. 1995, pp. 82–93.

76. R.H. Stolen and J.E. Bjorkholm, Parametric amplification and frequency conversion in optical fibers, *IEEE J. Quantum Electron.*, vol. QE-18, no. 7, 1982, pp. 1062–1072.

77. J. Hansryd, P. Andrekson, P.-O. Hedekvist, J. Li, and M. Westlund, Optical Parametric Amplifiers and their Applications, OFC'02, paper TuS1, pp. 123–125, Technical Digest OFC 2002, paper TuS1, Mar. 2002.

78. J.P. Pocholle, J. Raffy, M. Papuchon, and E. Desurvire, Raman and four photon mixing amplification in single mode fibers, *Optical Eng.*, vol. 24, no. 4, 1985, pp. 600–608.

79. A. Evans, Raman Amplification in Broadband WDM Systems, Technical Digest OFC 2001, paper TuF4-1, Mar. 2001.

80. P.M. Krummrich, R.E. Neuhauser, and C. Glingener, Bandwidth limitations of Broadband distributed Raman fiber amplifiers for WDM systems, Technical Digest OFC 2001, paper MI3-1, Mar. 2001.

81. C.R.S. Fludger, V. Handerek, and R.J. Mears, Pump to signal RIN transfer in Raman fiber amplifiers, *IEEE J. Lightwave Technol.*, vol. 19, no. 8, Aug. 2001, pp. 1140–1148.

82. C.R.S. Fludger, V. Handerek, and R.J. Mears, Fundamental noise limits in broadband Raman amplifiers, Technical Digest OFC 2001, paper MA5-1, Mar. 2001.

83. M. Bolshtyansky, J. DeMarco, and P. Wysocki, Flat, Adjustable Hybrid Optical Amplifier for 1610 nm-1640 nm band, Technical Digest OFC 2002, paper ThJ5, pp. 461–462, Mar. 2002.

84. H. Masuda, Review of wideband hybrid amplifier, Technical Digest OFC 2000, paper TuA1, Mar. 2000.

85. C.R. Giles and M. Spector, The wavelength add/drop multiplexer for lightwave commu-nication networks, *Bell Labs Techn. J.*, vol. 4, no. 1, 1999, pp. 207–229.

86. U. Koren et al., Wavelength division multiplexing light sources with integrated quantum well tunable lasers and optical amplification, *Appl. Phys. Lett.*, vol. 54, 1989, pp. 2056–2058.

87. G. Coquin, K.W. Cheung, and M. Choy, Single- and multiple-wavelength operation of acousto-optically tuned lasers at 1.3 microns, *Proc. 11th IEEE Int. Semiconductor Laser Conf.*, Boston, MA, 1988, pp. 130–131.

88. L.A. Coldren, Monolithic tunable diode lasers, *IEEE J. Select. Top. Quantum Electron.*, vol. 6, no. 6, Nov./Dec. 2000, pp. 988–999.

89. M. Yan, J. Chen, W. Jiang, J. Li, J. Chen, and X. Li, Pump depletion induced noise and crosstalk in distributed optical fiber Raman amplifiers, *IEEE Photonics Technol. Lett.*, vol. 13, no. 7, 2001, pp. 651–653.

90. H. Kobrinski and K.W. Cheung, Wavelength-tunable optical filters: Applications and tech-nologies, *IEEE Comm. Mag.*, vol. 27, Oct. 1989, pp. 53–63.

91. S. Suzuki et al., A photonic wavelength-division switching system using tunable laser diode filters, ICC'89 Conference Records, Boston, MA, 1989, paper 23.1.

92. H. Kogelnik, Theory of dielectric waveguides, in *Integrated Optics*, 2nd ed., Chapter 2, T. Tamir, ed., Springer-Verlag, New York, 1979.

93. M.C. Parker and S.D. Walker, Design of arrayed waveguide gratings using hybrid fourier-fresnel transform techniques, *IEEE J. Select. Areas Quantum Electron.*, vol. 5, Sept./Oct. 1999, pp. 1379–1384.

94. C. Dragone, Efficient NXN star couplers using Fourier optics, *J. Lightwave Technol.*, vol. 7, 1989, pp. 479–489.

95. C.M. Ragdale, D. Reid, D.J. Robbins, and J. Buus, Narrowband fiber grating filters, *IEEE J. Select. Areas Comm.*, vol. 8, no. 6, Aug. 1990, pp. 1146–1150.

96. A-R. Bahrampour and M. Mhjoei, Theoretical analysis of spectral hole burning and relaxation oscillation in all-optical gain stabilized multichannel erbium-doped amplifier (EDFA), *IEEE J. Lightwave Technol.*, vol. 19. no. 8, Aug. 2001, pp. 1130–1139.

97. J.P. Gordon and H. Kogelnik, PMD fundamentals: Polarization mode dispersion in optical fibers, *Proc. National Academy of Sciences*, vol. 97, no. 9, pp. 4541–4550, Apr. 25, 2000.

98. C.D. Poole, R.W. Tkach, A.R. Chraplyvy, and D.A. Fishman, Fading in lightwave systems due to polarization-mode dispersion, *IEEE Photon. Technol. Lett.*, vol. 3, pp. 68–70, Jan. 1991.

99. E. Lichtman, Limitations imposed by polarization-dependent gain and loss on all-optical ultralong communications systems, *J. Lightwave Technol.*, vol. 13, pp. 906–913, May 1995.

100. Y. Sun, A.K. Srivastava, J. Zhou, and J.W. Sulhoff, Optical fiber amplifiers for WDM optical networks, *Bell Labs Tech. J.*, vol. 4, no. 1, 1999, pp. 187–206.

101. M.J. Adams, Theory of twin-guide Fabry–Perot laser amplifiers, *IEE Proc.*, vol. 136, no. 5, Oct. 1989, pp. 287–292.

102. G.J. Cannell, A. Robertson, and R. Worthington, Practical realization of a high density diode-coupled wavelength demultiplexer, *IEEE J. Select. Areas Comm.*, vol. 8, no. 6, Aug. 1990, pp. 1141–1145.

103. A.J. Lowery, Computer-aided photonics design, *IEEE Spectrum*, vol. 34, no. 4, Apr. 1997, pp. 26–31.

104. K.S. Giboney, L.A. Aronson, and B.E. Lemoff, The ideal light source for datanets, *IEEE Spectrum*, vol. 35, no. 2, Feb. 1998, pp. 43–53.

105. M.-C. Amann and W. Thulke, Continuously tunable laser diodes: Longitudinal versus transverse tuning scheme, *IEEE J. Select. Areas Comm.*, vol. 8, no. 6, Aug. 1990, pp. 1169–1177.

106. K. Kobayashi and I. Mito, Single frequency and tunable laser diodes, *J. Lightwave Technol.*, vol. 6, Nov. 1988, pp. 1623–1633.

107. L.A. Coldren and S.W. Corzine, Continuously tunable single frequency semiconductor lasers, *IEEE J. Quantum Electron.*, vol. QE-23, June 1987, pp. 903–908.

108. M. Okuda and K. Onaka, Tunability of distributed Bragg reflector laser by modulating refractive index in corrugated waveguide, *Japan J. Appl. Phys.*, vol. 16, 1977, pp. 1501–1502.

109. Y. Kotaki, M. Matsuda, H. Ishikawa, and H. Imai, Tunable DBR laser with wide tuning range, *Electron. Lett.*, vol. 24, Apr. 1988, pp. 503–505.

110. H.A. Haus, *Waves and Fields in Optoelectronics*, Prentice-Hall, Englewood Cliffs, NJ, 1984.

111. S. Adachi, Refractive indices of III-IV compounds: Key properties of InGaAsP relevant to device design, *J. Appl. Phys.*, vol. 53, 1982, pp. 5863–5869.

112. J. Stone and D. Marcuse, Ultrahigh finesse fiber Fabry–Perot interferometers, *J. Lightwave Technol.*, vol. LT-4, no. 4, Apr. 1986, pp. 382–385.

113. A.A.M. Saleh and J. Stone, Two-stage Fabry–Perot filters as demultiplexers in optical FDMA LAN's, *J. Lightwave Technol.*, vol. LT-7, 1989, pp. 323–330.

114. S.R. Mallinson, Wavelength selective filters for single-mode fiber WDM systems using Fabry–Perot interferometers, *Appl. Opt.*, vol. 26, 1987, pp. 430–436.

115. A.M. Hill and D.B. Payne, Linear crosstalk in wavelength division multiplexed optical fiber transmission systems, *J. Lightwave Technol.*, vol. LT-3, 1985, pp. 643–651.

116. G. Hernandez, *Fabry–Perot Interferometers*, Cambridge University Press, Cambridge, UK, 1986.

117. F.J. Leonberger, Applications of guided-wave interferometers, *Laser Focus*, Mar. 1982, pp. 125–129.

118. H. Van de Stadt and J.M. Muller, Multimirror Fabry–Perot interferometers, *J. Optic Soc. Amer. A*, vol. 2, 1985, pp. 1363–1370.

119. P.A. Humblet and W.M. Hamdy, Crosstalk analysis and filter optimization of single- and double-cavity Fabry–Perot filters, *IEEE J. Select. Areas Comm.*, vol. 8, no. 6, Aug. 1990, pp. 1095–1107.

120. K.Y. Eng, M.A. Santoro, T.L. Koch, J. Stone, and W.W. Snell, Star-coupler-based optical cross-connect switch experiments with tunable receivers, *IEEE J. Select. Areas Comm.*, vol. 8, no. 6, Aug. 1990, pp. 1026–1031.

121. H. Toba, K. Oda, K. Nosu, and N. Takato, Factors affecting the design of optical FDM information distribution systems, *IEEE J. Select. Areas Comm.*, vol. 8, no. 6, Aug. 1990, pp. 965–972.

122. H. Onaka et al., 1.1 Tb/s WDM Transmission Over a 150 Km 1.3 zero-dispersion single-mode fiber, OFC'96, San Jose, CA, Feb. 1996, pp. PD19:1–5.

123. A.R. Chraplyvy, Optical power limits in multi-channel wavelength-division-multiplexed system due to stimulated Raman scattering, *Electron. Lett.*, vol. 20, no. 2, Jan. 1984, pp. 58–59.

124. K. Nosu, *Optical FDM Network Technologies*, Artec House, Boston, 1997.

125. M. Cvijetic, *Coherent and Nonlinear Lightwave Communications*, Artec House, Boston, 1996.

126. H. Toba and K. Nosu, Optical frequency division multiplexing system—review of key technologies and applications, *IEICE Trans. Comm.*, vol. E75-B, no. 4, Apr. 1992, pp. 243–255.

127. D. Cotter, Stimulated Brillouin scattering in monomode optical fiber, *J. Opt. Comm.*, vol. 4, 1983, pp. 10–16.

128. P.S. Henry, Lightwave primer, *IEEE J. Quantum Electron.*, vol. QE-21, 1985, pp. 1862–1879.

129. M. Kawasaki, Silica waveguides on silicon and their application to integrated optic components, *Opt. Quantum Electron.*, vol. 22, 1990, pp. 391–416.

130. L. Kazovsky, S. Benedetto, and A. Willner, Optical fiber communication systems, Artec House, Boston, 1996.

131. N.A. Jackman, S.H. Patel, B.P. Mikkelsen, and S.K. Korotky, Optical cross connect for optical networking, *Bell Labs Tech. J.*, vol. 4, no. 1, 1999, pp. 262–281.

132. H. Takahashi et al., Arrayed-waveguide grating for wavelength division multiplexing/demultiplexing with nanometer resolution, *Electron. Lett.*, vol. 26, 1990, pp. 87–88.

133. C. Dragone, T. Straser, G.A. Bogert, L.W. Stulz, and P. Chou, Waveguide grating router with maximally flat channel passband produced by spatial filtering, *Electron. Lett.*, vol. 33, no. 15, July 1997, pp. 1312–1314.

134. J. Minowa and Y. Fujii, Dielectric multilayer thin film filters for WDM transmission, *IEEE J. Lightwave Technol.*, vol. 1, no. 1, 1983, pp. 116–121.

135. W.K. Chen, *Passive and Active Filters*, John Wiley & Sons, New York, 1986.

136. R. Watanabe et al., Optical multi/demultiplexers for single-mode fiber transmission, *IEEE J. Quantum Electron.*, vol. 17, no. 6, 1981, pp. 974–951.

137. Y. Hibino et al., High reliability silica based PLC 1X8 Splitters on Si, *Electron. Lett.*, vol. 30, no. 8, 1994, pp. 640–641.

138. K. Kato et al., Packaging of large-scale integrated optic NXN star couplers, *IEEE Photonics Technol. Lett.*, vol. 4, no. 33, 1993, pp. 348–351.

139. A. Hasegawa and Y. Kodama, Signal transmission by optical solitons in monomode fiber, *IRE Proc.*, vol. 69, 1981, pp. 1145–1150.

140. R. Bullough and P.J. Caudrey, *Solitons*, Springer-Verlag, Berlin, 1980.

141. N. Doran and K. Blow, Solitons in optical communications, *IEEE J. Quantum Electron.*, vol. QE-19, 1983, pp. 1883–1888.

142. L.F. Mollenauer et al., Experimental observation of picosecond pulse narrowing and solitons in optical fibers, *Phys. Rev. Lett.*, vol. 45, 1980, pp. 1095–1096.

143. J.P. Gordon, Theory of soliton self-frequency shift, *Optics Lett.*, vol. 11, 1986, pp. 855–858.

144. H. Rokugawa et al., Wavelength conversion laser diodes application to wavelength-division photonic cross-connect node with multistage configuration, *IEICE Trans. Comm.*, vol. E-75-B, no. 4, 1992, pp. 267–273.

145. O. Ishida and H. Toba, A 1.55-mm lightwave frequency synthesizer, *IEICE Trans. Comm.*, vol. E75-B, no. 4, 1992, pp. 275–280.

146. K. Vilhelmsson, Simultaneous forward and backward Raman scattering in low-attenuation single-mode fibers, *J. Lightwave Technol.*, vol. LT-4, no. 4, 1986, pp. 400–404.

147. H. Kobrinski and K-W. Cheung, Wavelength-tunable optical filters: Applications and technologies, *IEEE Comm. Mag.*, Oct. 1989, pp. 53–63.

148. R. Tewari and K. Thyagarajan, Analysis of tunable single-mode fiber directional couplers using simple and accurate relations, *J. Lightwave Technol.*, vol. LT-4, no. 4, 1986, pp. 386–399.

149. N. Kashima, *Passive Optical Components for Optical Fiber Transmission*, Artec House, Boston, 1995.

150. S. Kawakami, Light propagation along periodic metal-dielectric layers, *Appl. Opt.*, vol. 22, 1983, p. 2426.

151. K. Shiraishi, S. Sugayama, K. Baba, and S. Kawakami, Microisolator, *Appl. Opt.*, vol. 25, 1986, p. 311.

152. K. Shiraishi, S. Sugayama, and S. Kawakami, Fiber Faraday rotator, *Appl. Opt.*, vol. 23, 1984, p. 1103.

153. W. Eickhoff, In-line fiber-optic polarizer, *Electron. Lett.*, vol. 6, 1980, p. 762.

154. T. Hosaka, K. Okamoto, and J. Noda, Single-mode fiber type polarizer, *IEEE J. Quantum Electron.*, vol. QE-18, 1982, p. 1569.

155. R.A. Bergh, H.C. Lefevre, and H.J. Shaw, Single-mode fiber-optic polarizer, *Opt. Lett.*, vol. 5, 1980, p. 479.

156. Palais, J.C., *Fiber Optic Communications*, 3rd ed., Englewood Cliffs, NJ, Prentice-Hall, 1992.

157. M. Francon, *Optique: Formation et Traitement des Images*, Macon & Cie, Paris, 1972.

158. T.G. Robertazzi, ed., *Performance Evaluation of High Speed Switching Fabrics and Networks*, IEEE Press, New York, 1993.

159. Y. Pan, C. Qiao, and Y. Yang, Optical multistage interconnection networks: new challenges and approaches, *IEEE Comm. Mag.*, vol. 37, no. 2, Feb. 1999, pp. 50–56.

160. J.G. Eden, Photochemical processing of semiconductors: New applications for visible and ultraviolet lasers, *IEEE Circuits and Devices Magazine*, vol. 2, no. 1, Jan. 1986, pp. 18–24.

161. R.J. von Gutfeld, Laser-enhanced plating and etching for microelectronic applications, *IEEE Circuits and Devices Magazine*, vol. 2, no. 1, Jan. 1986, pp. 57–60.

162. J. Bokor, A.R. Neureuther, and W.G. Oldham, Advanced lithography for ULSI, *IEEE Circuits and Devices Magazine*, vol. 12, no. 1, Jan. 1996, pp. 11–15.

163. A. Yariv, Quantum well semiconductor lasers are taking over, *IEEE Circuits and Devices Magazine*, vol. 5, no. 6, Nov. 1989, pp. 25–28.

164. J. LaCourse, Laser Primer for Fiber–Optics Users, *IEEE Circuits and Devices Magazine*, vol. 8, no. 2, Mar. 1992, pp. 27–32.

165. D. Botez and L.J. Mawst, Phase-locked laser arrays revisited, *IEEE Circuits and Devices Magazine*, vol. 12, no. 11, Nov. 1996, pp. 25–32.

166. Z.V. Nesterova and I.V. Aleksaandrov, Optical-fiber sources of coherent light, *Sov. J. Opt. Technol.*, vol. 54, no. 3, Mar. 1987, pp. 183–190.

167. B. Hitz, J.J. Ewing, J. Hecht, *Introduction to Laser Technology*, 3rd ed., IEEE Press, New York, 2001.

168. Kenichi Iga, Surface-emitting laser — Its birth and generation of new optoelectronics field, *IEEE J. Select. Top. Quantum Electron.*, vol. 6, no. 6, Nov./Dec. 2000, pp. 1201–1215.

169. J.S. Harris, Tunable long-wavelength vertical-cavity lasers: the engine of next generation optical networks? *IEEE J. Select. Top. Quantum Electron.*, vol. 6, no. 6, Nov./Dec. 2000, pp. 1145–1160.

170. C.J. Chang-Hasnain, Tunable VCSEL, *IEEE J. Select. Top. Quantum Electron.*, vol. 6, no. 6, Nov./Dec. 2000, pp. 978–987.

171. T. Komukai, T. Yamamoto, T. Sugawa, and Y. Miyajima, Upconversion pumped thulium-doped fluoride fiber amplifier and laser operating at 1.47 μm, *IEEE Quantum Electron.*, vol. 31, 1995, pp. 1880–1889.

172. S. Aozasa, T. Sakamoto, T. Kanamori, K. Hoshino, K. Kobayashi, and M. Shimizu, Tn-doped fiber amplifiers for 1470-nm-based WDM signals, *IEEE Photonics Technol. Lett.*, vol. 12, no. 10, Oct. 2000, pp. 1331–1333.

173. G. Eisenstein, Semiconductor optical amplifiers, *IEEE Circuits and Devices Magazine*, vol. 5, no. 4, July 1989, pp. 25–30.

174. C.F. Buhrer, Four waveplate dual tuner for birefringent filters and multiplexers, *Appl. Opt.*, vol. 26, no. 17, Sept. 1987, pp. 3628–3632.

175. J.W. Evans, The birefringent filter, *J. Optic. Soc. Amer.*, vol. 39, 1949, p. 229.

176. H. Hinton, *An Introduction to Photonic Switching Fabrics*, Plenum, New York, 1993.

177. C. Tocci and H.J. Caufield, *Optical Interconnection-Foundations and Applications*, Artec House, Boston, 1994.

178. A. Budman et al., Multi-gigabit optical packet switch for self-routing networks with sub-carrier addressing, *Proc. OFC'92*, paper Tu04, San Jose, CA, Feb. 1992.

179. C.-K. Chan, L.-K. Chen, and K.-W. Cheung, A fast channel-tunable optical transmitter for ultrahigh-speed all-optical time-division multi-access network, *IEEE J. Select. Areas Comm.*, vol. 14, no. 5, June 1996, pp. 1052–1056.

180. K. Padmanabhan and A.N. Netravali, Dilated networks for photonic switching, *IEEE Trans. Communications*, vol. 35, no. 12, Dec. 1987, pp. 1357–65.

181. C. Qiao et al., A time domain approach for avoiding crosstalk in optical blocking multistage interconnection networks, *J. Lightwave Technol.*, vol. 12, no. 10, Oct. 1994, pp. 1854–1862.

182. R.A. Thompson, The dilated slipped banyan switching network architecture for use in an all-optical local-are network, *J. Lightwave Technol.*, vol. 9, no. 12, Dec. 1991, pp. 1780–1787.

183. D. Hunter and D. Smith, New architecture for optical TDM switching, *J. Lightwave Technol.*, vol. 11, no. 3, Mar. 1993, pp. 495–511.

184. E. Nussbaum, Communication network needs and technologies — A place for photonic switching, *IEEE J. Select. Areas Comm.*, vol. 6, no. 7, Aug. 1988, pp. 1036–1043.

185. S.A. Cassidy and P. Yennadhiou, Optimum switching architectures using D-fiber optical space switches, *IEEE J. Select. Areas Comm.*, vol. 6, no. 7, Aug. 1988, pp. 1044–1051.

186. C.J. Smith, Nonblocking photonic switch networks, *IEEE J. Select. Areas Comm.*, vol. 6, no. 7, Aug. 1988, pp. 1052–1062.

187. J.D. Evankow, Jr. and R.A. Thompson, Photonic switching modules designed with laser diode amplifiers, *IEEE J. Select. Areas Comm.*, vol. 6, no. 7, Aug. 1988, pp. 1087–1095.

188. W.D. Johnston, Jr., M.A. DiGiuseppe, and D.P. Wilt, Liquid an vapor phase growth of III-V materials for photonic devices, *AT&T Tech. J.*, vol. 68, no. 1, Jan./Feb. 1989, pp. 53–63.

189. W.G. Dautremont-Smith, R.J. McCoy, and R.H. Burton, Fabrication technologies for III-V compound semiconductor photonic and electronic devices, *AT&T Tech. J.*, vol. 68, no. 1, Jan./Feb. 1989, pp. 64–82.

190. N.K. Dutta, III-V device technologies for lightwave applications, *AT&T Tech. J.*, vol. 68, no. 1, Jan./Feb. 1989, pp. 5–18.

191. K.Y. Eng, A photonic knockout switch for high-speed packet networks, *IEEE J. Select. Areas Comm.*, vol. 6, no. 7, Aug. 1988, pp. 1107–1116.

192. T. Ikegami and H. Kawaguchi, Semiconductor devices in photonic switching, *IEEE J. Select. Areas Comm.*, vol. 6, no. 7, Aug. 1988, pp. 1131–1140.

193. R.I. Macdonald, Terminology for photonic matrix switches, *IEEE J. Select. Areas Comm.*, vol. 6, no. 7, Aug. 1988, pp. 1141–1151.

194. J.V. Wright, S.R. Mallinson, and C.A. Millar, A fiber-based crosspoint switch using high-refractive index interlay materials, *IEEE J. Select. Areas Comm.*, vol. 6, no. 7, Aug. 1988, pp. 1160–1168.

195. J. Skinner and C.H.R. Lane, A low-crosstalk microoptic liquid crystal switch, *IEEE J. Select. Areas Comm.*, vol. 6, no. 7, Aug. 1988, pp. 1178–1185.

196. T. Morioka and M. Saruwatari, Ultrafast all-optical switching utilizing the optical Kerr effect in polarization-maintaining single-mode fibers, *IEEE J. Select. Areas Comm.*, vol. 6, no. 7, Aug. 1988, pp. 1186–1198.

197. H. Inoue, H. Nakamura, K. Morosawa, Y. Sasaki, T. Katsuyama, and N. Chinone, An 8 mm length nonblocking 4 × 4 optical switch array, *IEEE J. Select. Areas Comm.*, vol. 6, no. 7, Aug. 1988, pp. 1262–1266.

198. R. Driggers, P. Cox, and T. Edwards, *An Introduction to Infrared and Electro-Optical Systems*, Artec House, Boston, 1999.

199. R. Marz, *Integrated Optics: Design and Modeling*, Artec House, Boston, 1995.

200. S.V. Kartalopoulos, A plateau of performance? *IEEE Comm. Mag.*, Sept. 1992, pp. 13–14.

201. J. Nellist, *Understanding Telecommunications and Lightwave Systems*, IEEE Press, New York, 1996.

202. W.Y. Zhou and Y. Wu, COFDM: an overview, *IEEE Trans., Broadcasting*, vol. 41, no. 1, Mar. 1995, pp. 1–8.

203. D.J. Bishop and V.A. Aksyuk, Optical MEMS answer high-speed networking requirements, *Electronic Design*, Apr. 5, 1999, pp. 85–92.

204. R. Tewari and K. Thyagarajan, Analysis of tunable single-mode fiber directional couplers using simple and accurate relations, *IEEE J. Lightwave Technol.*, vol. LT-4, no. 4, Apr. 1986, pp. 386–390.

205. N.A. Olsson and J. Hegarty, Noise properties of a Raman amplifier, *IEEE J. Lightwave Technol.*, vol. LT-4, no. 4, Apr. 1986, pp. 396–399.

206. N. Shibata, K. Nosu, K. Iwashita, and Y. Azuma, Transmission limitations due to fiber nonlinearities in optical FDM systems, *IEEE J. Select. Areas Comm.*, vol. 8, no. 6, Aug. 1990, pp. 1068–1077.

207. A. Brauer and P. Dannberg, Polymers for passive and switching waveguide components for optical communication, in *Polymers in Optics: Physics, Chemistry, and Applications*, R.A. Lessard and W.F. Frank, eds., SPIE, Bellingham, WA, 1996, pp. 334–348.

208. L. Eldada and L.W. Shacklette, Advances in polymer integrated optics, *J. Select. Top. Quantum Electron.*, vol. 6, Jan./Feb. 2000, pp. 54–68.

209. J.M. Zavada, Optical modulation in photonic circuits, pp. 61–92, in *Photonic Devices and Systems*, R.C. Hunsperver, ed., Marcel Dekker, New York, 1994.

210. S.V. Kartalopoulos, *Fault Detectability DWDM: Technology Data in a Rainbow*, IEEE Press, New York, 2000.

211. Bell Telephone Laboratories, *Transmission systems for communications, 1982*.

212. N.S. Bergano, F.W. Kerfoot, and C.R. Daqvidson, Margin measurements in optical amplifier systems, *IEEE Photon. Tech. Lett.*, vol. 5, no. 3, pp. 304–306, 1993.

213. M. Schwartz, W.R. Bennett, and S. Stein, *Communications Systems and Techniques*, IEEE Press, New York, 1996.

214. N. Hanik et al., Application of amplitude histograms to monitor performance of optical channels, *Electron. Lett.*, vol. 5, pp. 403–404, 1999.

215. G. Bendelli, C. Cavazzoni, R. Giraldi, and R. Lano, Optical performance monitoring techniques, *Proc. ECOC 2000*, vol. 4, pp. 113–116, 2000.

216. C.M. Weinert, Histogram method for performance monitoring of the optical channel, *Proc. ECOC 2000*, vol. 4, pp. 121–11622, 2000.

217. I. Shake and H. Takara, Transparent and Flexible Performance Monitoring Using Amplitude Histogram Method, *OFC'02 Tech. Digest*, paper TuE1, pp. 19–21, OFC'02, Anaheim, CA, 2002.

218. A. Papoulis, *Probability, Random Variables, and Stochastic Processes*, McGraw-Hill, New York, 1984.

219. M. Schwartz, *Information, Transmission, Modulation, and Noise*, McGraw-Hill, New York, 1970.

220. Abramovitch and Stegun, Handbook of Mathematical Functions, *National Bureau of Standards*, Boulder, CO, 1964.

221. S. Shen and J.C. Palais, Passive single-mode fiber depolarizer, *Appl. Opt.*, vol. 38, Mar. 1999, pp. 1686–1691.

222. S.V. Kartalopoulos, Emerging technologies in communications, *IEEE Comm. Mag.*, Nov. 2001.

STANDARDS

1. American Conference of Governmental Industrial Hygienists (ACGIH), "Threshold Limit Values and Biological Exposure Indices for 2000," American Conference of Governmental Industrial Hygienists, Cincinnati, OH, 2000.

2. American National Standards Institute (ANSI), "Safe use of lasers," ANSI Z136.1-2000 (2000).

3. ANSI/IEEE 812-1984, "Definition of terms relating to fiber Optics."

4. ITU-T Recommendation G.650, "Definition and test methods for the relevant parameters of single-mode fibres," 1996.

5. ITU-T Recommendation G.652 version 4, "Characteristics of a single-mode optical fiber cable," April 1997.

6. ITU-T Recommendation G.653 version 4, "Characteristics of a dispersion-shifted single-mode optical fiber cable," April 1997.

7. ITU-T Recommendation G.654, "Characteristics of a 1550 nm wavelength loss-minimized single-mode optical fibre cable," 1993.

8. ITU-T Recommendation G.655 version 10, "Characteristics of a non-zero dispersion-shifted single-mode optical fiber cable," Octo. 2000.

9. ITU-T Recommendation G.661, "Definition and test methods for the relevant generic parameters of optical fiber amplifiers," Nov. 1996.

10. ITU-T Recommendation G.662, "Generic characteristics of optical fiber amplifier devices and sub-systems," July 1995.

11. ITU-T Recommendation G.663, "Application related aspects of optical fiber amplifier devices and sub-systems," Oct. 1996.

12. ITU-T Recommendation G.671, "Transmission characteristics of passive optical components," Nov. 1996.

13. U.S. Dept of Health and Human Services, Food and Drug Administration, Laser Performance Standard, Title 21, Subchapter J, Part 1040, Washington DC, U.S. Government Printing Office, 1993.

14. Telcordia (previously Bellcore), TR-NWT-233, "Digital cross connect system," Nov. 1992.

15. Telcordia (previously Bellcore), TR-NWT-917, "Regenerator," Oct. 1990.

3

COMMUNICATIONS FUNDAMENTALS

3.1 INTRODUCTION

Communications systems and networks are the subject of a multitude of books, treatises, and other publications. Clearly, the main focus in all these publications is to explain how the communications network works and, in the case of telephony, what occurs from the moment we lift the handset and dial a number to the moment we connect with "the other" end and say "hello," and to the moment a statement arrives at home with telephone charges.

One would think that from the time Alexander Graham Bell made it happen, the network would have undergone very little change; clearly, this is not true. The original communications network, with many wooden poles and copper cables mounted on them (such photos may have been seen in several historical archives or photo shows) could be paralleled with the first manmade, late nineteenth century automobile, which was mounted on the chassis of a horsecart cruising at a (fast then) speed of 15 to 20 kmph.

Today, telephony, e-mail, and other communication services are ubiquitous and are interwoven with our lives; communication with anyone, anytime, or anyplace is as easy as pushing a single button. In fact, a new lifestyle has emerged that puts pressure on the communications network in terms of bandwidth, service quality, service elasticity, reliability, scalability, and affordability. As a consequence, a communications network evolution is in progress, and new technology replaces the old one, yet on a foundation that was set by the architecture of the "old" legacy network. Therefore, it is important to provide a quick overview of this foundation so that as we replace it by better and more potent technology, we maintain certain good and universal qualities.

This chapter contains device specifications for illustrative and educational purposes. Because specifications are continuously changing, no responsibility is assumed for correctness. The reader is encouraged to consult the most current manufacturers' data sheets.

3.2   PULSE CODED MODULATION

Natural sound is an analog signal. As the cords or a membrane vibrate, an acoustic wave is generated, the pressure of which impinges on a *transducer* that converts it to an electrical (current, voltage) signal. This electrical signal is also analog, and it changes value in a continuous manner with respect to time following the changes of the acoustical pressure. At the receiving end, this electrical signal activates the electromagnetic coil of a speaker, another *transducer*, which reproduces an acoustical signal, which in the absence of noise and distortion is similar to the original signal. This is the principle on which telephony is based.

Initially, telephony entailed a few basic functions such as *number dialing*, *ringing*, and *call initiation* (a timed handshake-type protocol), and the signal transmitted over the telephone network was analog. This became known as *plain old telephone service* (POTS). Soon thereafter, the analog signal was sampled 8,000 times per second (following Shannon's theorem), and each sample was converted to an 8-bit binary based on a weighted procedure specifically developed for spoken voice and known as *pulse coded modulation* (PCM). Thus, a continuous binary bit stream of 64,000 bits per second, known as *digital signal level 0* (DS0), was generated (Fig. 3.1). However, in several applications, such as in mobile telephony where bandwidth is at a premium, 64 Kbps per channel in voice applications is uneconomical. Thus, several algorithmic methods have been developed compressing 64 Kbps down to 5.3 Kbps, or even lower. Such compression algorithms are the differential PCM (DPCM), adaptive DPCM (ADPCM), sigma-delta PCM ($\Sigma \Delta$PCM), code-excited linear prediction (CELP), adaptive code excited linear prediction (ACELP), and multirate coder.

Shannon's theorem emanated from studying the minimum acceptable bit rate possible from which the original analog (voice) signal could be faithfully reproduced, even in the presence of noise. This minimum bit rate at a given bit error rate (BER) characterizes the capacity of a digital channel. The bit error rate is mainly dependent on the signal power to noise power ratio. Thus, for an available bandwidth per system,

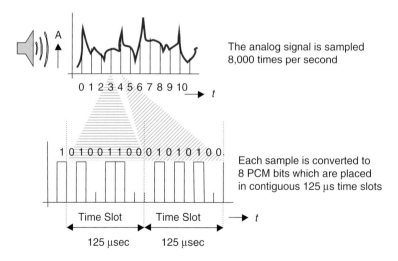

Figure 3.1   Analog to PCM: DS0 rate.

Table 3.1   Delay limits for certain CODECS

CODEC	Standard	Rates	Time
ADPCM	G.726	16, 24, 32, 40 kbps	0.125 μsec
CELP	G.728 LD	16 kbps	2.5 msec
ACELP	G.729 CS	8 kbps	10 msec
Multirate coder	G.723.1	5.3, 6.3 kbps	30 msec

an acceptable BER and a minimum bit rate per channel, there is a channel capacity, which is a matter of effective utilization of the bandwidth.

The circuitry responsible for converting analog electrical signals to PCM and vice versa is known as a *CO*der/*DEC*oder, abbreviated *CODEC*. A CODEC translates each sampled value into a binary representation according to one of two conversion tables. One conversion table, known as the μ-law (mu-law), is used in the United States, and the other, known as the α-law (alpha-law), is used in Europe. In POTS service, the CODEC is found at the service provider equipment, not in the subscriber's telephone set (standardized CODEC specifications are provided in the ITU-T G.711 recommendation).

The reason for the weighted procedure is that voice is almost logarithmic, and thus for efficiency an antilogarithmic weighting system should be used to "linearize" it. However, because of the different conversion tables used in the United States and in Europe, any voice signal transmitted today across the Atlantic must undergo at systems known as gates a μ/α-law conversion before sending the signal from, say, New York to London over the transatlantic link.

Coding and compressing an analog signal to a subrate below 64 Kb/s PCM requires time because of buffering and algorithmic execution, which although very short represents a certain amount of delay (also known as *algorithmic delay*). Since delay is cumulative, standards set limits as a guideline to CODEC manufacturers to minimize *echo* and *talker overlap*. A representative list of standard CODECS and their frame times is given in Table 3.1.

3.3   LOOP ACCESSING METHODS

The access network is that part of the public switched network that connects a *central office* (CO) or *point of presence* (POP) with the *customer premise equipment* (CPE) of subscribers. The traditional transmission medium for analog signals with a frequency content up to 4 KHz (actually up to 3,400 KHz) has been a twisted copper pair cable, which to this day connects most homes with the telephone service provider equipment. This copper network is known as the local *loop plant* or simply the loop plant. Because of U.S. demographics, loops range from a few hundred feet long to more than 18,000 feet (6 km); the longest loops are in rural areas where farmhouses are at a distance from each other. Thus, an inductor (a coil known as a loading coil) had to be placed to bring the analog signal to these distances. In Europe, however, the longest loops are much shorter because farmhouses are not as far apart.

When the transmitted information over the loop is in digital form (i.e., the CODEC is on the subscriber side), the loop is known as a *digital subscriber line* (DSL). However, a digital signal cannot be transmitted over long lengths due to rapid attenuation and (coil) loading; in this case, the twisted pair cable must be conditioned.

When 64 Kbps started being transmitted over the loop, it soon increased The desire for more bandwidth and integrated services beyond telephony and slow-speed data. In fact, the need for multimedia and Internet services has created a need for bit rates as high as several Mbps per user. Thus, a question arose: what would the best transmission medium be so that high bandwidth could be provided over the loop? Clearly, media such as coaxial and fiber-optic cables could quickly solve this problem, but copper twisted pair cable was already in place, and it would be more economical if the same copper cable could be used. Most of the capital investment (or simply cost) is not in the copper cable itself. It is in the installation, maintenance, and plant management, and thus economics became the driving force in developing several high bit rates transmission methods, especially for the last or first mile subscriber access, which accesses 75% of medium or large data customers. For example, cost analysis has shown that 35% is access-related and only 15% is network-related; that is out of proportion. Among these technologics are the digital subscriber line (DSL), the local multipoint distribution service (LMDS), the wireless access, the wireless optical access, the fiber-optic and others; some of these technologies are in deployment, whereas others are in the proposal phase.

3.3.1 xDSL

The traditional transmission medium that connects most homes with the telephone service provider equipment is twisted copper wire pair cable, also known as the local loop plant. This is also the medium that has been used in wiring most existing business buildings; only 5% of buildings are fiber-ready, although this is rapidly changing. The twisted copper medium on the loop plant is meant to support analog signals up to 4 KHz (in fact, up to 3.4 KHz) and in excess of 18,000 feet (5.5 km); that is, telephony and low-speed modems (up to 56 Kb/s).

However, bandwidth demands have changed so that modems at 56 Kb/s fall short of satisfying the Internet bandwidth appetite. With the Internet and perhaps with video services, bandwidth in excess of 1 Mbps is desirable, even if it is not needed 100% of the time and is time-shared with other users.

Hence, we have a dilemma as well as an opportunity: can we develop a technology that can deliver more than 1 Mbps over existing twisted pairs at the sacrifice of some loop length?

A digital technology at 80 Kbps (64 + 16 Kbps) per direction, known as *time compression multiplexing* (TCM) or *circuit switched digital capability* (CSDC), also known as *ping-pong*, was deployed in the early 1980s, but it quickly became obsolete because it did not truly address the imminent bandwidth demand. However, it proved that digital high bit rates over the loop are possible, and soon thereafter the *basic rate integrated services digital network* (BRI) emerged and offered digital rates at 144 Kbps (64 + 64 + 16 Kbps) over twisted pair cable. The loop lines were thus renamed *digital subscriber lines* (DSL).

This DSL technology delivers high bit rates over existing twisted copper pair cable of 144 Kbps, or 1.544 Mbps, and in some cases up to 7 Mbps. However, DSL is deployable only on loops that have no inductors or coils; that is, they are not "Loaded." Coils had been used in traditional telephony of filtering out, or "choke," the high-frequency content above 3.4 KHz of analog signals to reduce noise. However, even without "loaded" loops, high bit rate DSL signals over unshielded twisted pair cables dissipate faster than analog low-frequency signals. Thus, the effective loop distance of DSL signals shortens as the bit rate increases. For example, a DSL signal at 1.5 Mb/s travels as far as several miles, but at 25 Mb/s it travels as far as half a mile.

Thus, xDSL may be deployed in most digital transmission services, including high-speed digital transmission and the Internet. However, xDSL is a technology that requires terminating devices at both the user end and the service provider end to terminate the upstream (user to provider) and downstream (provider to user) digital signals.

Because there are several DSL technologies, DSL is collectively referred to xDSL. The x in the xDSL denotes the particular DSL technology, format, and rate. Thus,

- In **VDSL**, V means very high bit rate.

- In **HDSL**, H means high bit rate.

- In **ADSL**, A means asymmetric bit rate. The downstream bit rate is much higher than the upstream bit rate.

- In **SDSL**, S means symmetric bit rate.

- In **RADSL**, RA means rate-adaptive. RADSL-based systems typically run in auto-rate-adaptive mode or in manual mode to adapt to a variety of bit rates as required by the user.

- In **MSDSL**, MS means multirate symmetric; MSDSL-based systems build on the single pair SDL technology and offer one of many rates, and thus one of many loop lengths. For example, MSDSL on a 24-gauge unloaded copper pair can provide service at 64/128 Kb/s up to 29 Kft (8.9 Km), or 2 Mbps up to 15 Kft (4.5 Km).

Depending on application, the upstream and downstream signals differ; that is, the bit rate is asymmetric, and cable lengths are different. More specifically, for a 24-gauge wire with no repeaters and loading coils:

- *HDSL two pairs*: Downstream bit rate = 2.048 Mb/s, upstream bit rate = 2.048 Mb/s, maximum length of loop = 13,000 feet. Compare with a T1 line that requires two repeaters.

- *HDSL single pair*: Downstream bit rate = 768 Kb/s, upstream bit rate = 768 Kb/s, maximum length of loop = 12,000 feet.

- *ADSL DMT single pair*: Downstream bit rate = 1.5 Mb/s, upstream bit rate = 176 Kb/s, maximum length of loop = 12,000 feet.

- *ADSL CAP single pair*: Downstream bit rate = 6 Mb/s, upstream bit rate = 640 Kb/s, maximum length of loop = 12,000 feet.

- *ADSL CAP single pair*: Downstream bit rate = 1.5 Mb/s, upstream bit rate = 64 Kbps, maximum length of loop = 18,000 feet.

- *ISDN two pairs*: Downstream bit rate = 144 Kb/s, upstream bit rate = 144 Kb/s, maximum loop length = 18,000 feet; 144 Kb/s is ($2 \times 64 + 8$) Kb/s or 2B + D channels.

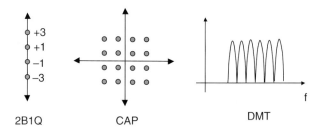

Figure 3.2 Line codes.

Thus, xDSL may be deployed in most access high-speed digital transmission services, including voice, data, and Internet. However, xDSL is a technology that requires specialized modulation and loop conditioning, as well as the same terminating devices at both ends of the loop.

3.3.1.1 Modulation Techniques

An xDSL signal requires modulation. Such modulation techniques are the *two bits to one quartenary* (2B1Q), the *discrete multitone modulation* (DMT), and the *carrierless amplitude phase* (CAP) (Fig. 3.2).

- The **2B1Q** translates the four states of a two-bit binary code into one of the four voltage levels, −3, −1, +1, and +3, hence *two binary, one quartenary*. Its transmitting power is superior to AMI (used in T1 lines at 1.544 Mbps), but its bit rate is limited to 392 Kbps, which is suitable for upstream transmission on the loop. 2B1Q coding is used for BRI signals.

- The **DMT** divides the bandwidth into frequency channels onto which traffic is overlaid; hence *discrete multitone*. With DMT, when a certain (frequency) channel is detected to have inferior transmission characteristics, the traffic is assigned another frequency channel, a technique known as *frequency hopping*. DMT is the official standard of the ANSI T1E1.4 Working Group supporting up to 6 Mbps services (this includes up to four MPEG-1 or a single MPEG-2 compressed video data; MPEG stands for Motion Picture Experts Group).

- **CAP** is a derivative of the quadrature amplitude modulation method (QAM). CAP translates a four-bit code in 1 of 16 voltage-phase points; hence *carrierless amplitude and phase* modulation. One may think of the CAP as a 2B1Q two-dimensional approach, where on the vertical axis is amplitude and the horizontal axis is phase. Its transmitting power is superior to that of AMI and 2B1Q, but its effective bit rate is in the range of 10 to 175 Kbps. Although DMT has been the standard of choice, CAP has been a de facto standard, which by 1996 had dominated (∼97%) all ADSL applications.

Figure 3.3 illustrates the comparative frequency spectra of T1 AMI, CAP T1 HDSL, and 2B1Q HDSL.

3.3.1.2 ADSL

In asymmetric bit rate, the downstream (from the network to the home) bit rate may reach 6.144 Mbps and the upstream (from the home to the network) bit rate may reach

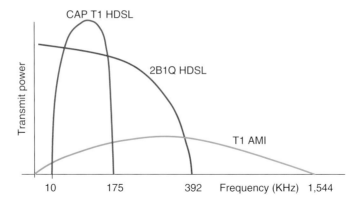

Figure 3.3 Relative transmit power and frequency range for modulation methods.

640 Kbps. Other versions offer a downstream bit rate at 1.5 Mbps and an upstream bit rate at 512 Kbps. This bit rate asymmetry is due to higher bandwidth flow in the downstream direction than in the upstream direction (e.g., more frequent video or picture downloading than uploading).

ADSL has gained more momentum than other xDSL solutions. Telephone companies offer ADSL technology to counterreact coaxial cable companies that offer low-cost data bit rates over cable at 1.5 Mps. ADSL uses DMT (discrete multitone) modulation. However, because of the high bandwidth, several issues become more pronounced at the ADSL transceivers such as dispersion by which higher frequencies propagate faster than slower frequencies, near-end cross talk (NEXT) and far-end cross talk (FEXT). To describe the difference between NEXT and FEXT, one must view the bidirectional loop from the transmitting end to the receiving end. NEXT is the noise generated by the strong transmitted signal on the incoming weak signal, and FEXT is the noise added to an already weak signal by various external influences. Between the two noise components, NEXT is more important and is addressed with equalizers.

ADSL is described in the T1.413 standard, which also partitions the frequency spectrum to 0 to 4 KHz for voice data, 25 to 138 KHz for upstream data, and 200 to 1,100 KHz for downstream data. If echo cancellation is to be used, then the downstream bandwidth may be extended from 138 to 1,100 KHz.

The benefit with ADSL is that twisted pair connects the home with a remote loop carrier system or the central office. However, demographics play an important role here. In the United States, 50% of the loops are less than 2 km, whereas 20% are longer than 5.5 km (18,000 feet). The disadvantage with ADSL is that about half of the loops can be used, those that are less than 3.6 km long and without noise-suppressing coils (loading coils were installed years ago to suppress high-frequency noise, above 4 KHz, to analog signals). The 20% of loops that are longer than 5.5 km from the central office, the signal is severely attenuated and cannot be used. Therefore, more expensive solutions are used, such as a combination of copper for the short reach and fiber for the remainder of the distance.

A rival technology to the latter is HFC (hybrid fiber-coax) by which fiber carries ultra-broadband bandwidth to a head-end (fiber-coax bandwidth distribution terminal) from which coaxial cables carry broadband traffic to clusters of homes.

3.3.2 Other High-Speed Short-Reach Technologies

A number of other short-reach and high bit rate technologies are emerging with copper, fiber and wireless solutions. We mention some as they will impact the access plane-field:

- Bluetooth is a protocol-based wireless technology that interconnects within 10 m distance from the transmitter up to seven devices, such as portable telephones with wireless earphones, PDAs (personal digital assistants), and other devices. It operates in the ISM (industrial, scientific, and medical) unlicensed 2,402–2,483.5 MHz band. In this band, 79 channels have been defined spaced 1 MHz and at 720 Mbps data rate per channel. Each Bluetooth radio is assigned during manufacture a 48-bit unique address. When a device starts communicating (thus becoming the master) with a few more devices, they define a temporary wireless *piconet* that lasts as long as the communication session. Thus, another piconet may exist in the immediate vicinity. To avoid interference from other wireless devices, Bluetooth transmitters hop randomly every 625 μsec to a new frequency (among the 71), unless the transmitted packet is longer than the hop duration. The packet format consists of a 72-bit access code, a 54-bit header, and a maximum of 2,745 bits payload. The master antenna transmits only in the even channels (of the 79), and the slave antenna responds only in the odd time slots, after the master has transmitted to the slave. Devices assume the master role or the slave role at the start of communicating among them; thus, a master in one session may be a slave in another session. The standard defines three error-correction strategies, two FECs (forward error correction) and an automatic retransmit packet scheme. The transmitter operates at one of three power levels, class 1 transmits at about 20 dBm (100 mW), class 2 at about +4 dBm (2.5 mW), and class 3 at about 0 dBm (1 mW); the last two levels are expected to be the most commonly used. The Bluetooth specification may be found at *http://www.bluetooth.com*.
- The IEEE 802.11 is a wireless LAN (WLAN) Ethernet standard, which is targeted for products with RF or infrared interface up to 54 Mb/s and a distance of 100 feet (approximately 30 meters). WLAN operates in the unlicensed 2.4 GHz (2,400–2,483.5 MHz) band and in the 5 GHz band. This band is also known as ISM (industrial, scientific, medical). IEEE 802.11 defines the WLAN medium access control (MAC) and physical (PHY) layers and a transmission bit rate at 11 Mbps over a 100-m distance.
- Ultra-wideband (UWB) is a wireless low-cost technology based on which ultrashort E-M very low power pulses are transmitted at a bit rate up to 1 Gb/s. However, these bits are not transmitted on a single spectral line, but they are spread over a spectrum, a technology known as spread-spectrum. That is, sequential bits are transmitted according to a randomized spectral schedule so that contiguous bits do not reside on the same channel. Because of the spread-spectrum and low power, the UWB signal does not cause noticeable interference. This also implies that the receiver must know the random schedule in order to receive all bits that have been spread over the spectrum. To explain this, assume that there is a spectrum of four frequencies, f1, f2, f3 and f4. Assume also four sequential bits of the code A = 1,011. Now, assume that the four bits are spread over four frequencies according to the schedule f2, f4, f3, f1. In the time domain, this is illustrated as:

Time period:	t1	t2	t3	t4
Bits of code A:	1	0	1	1
Frequency f1:	—	—	—	1
Frequency f2:	1	—	—	—
Frequency f3:	—	—	1	—
Frequency f4:	—	0	—	—

According to this schedule, each frequency is used one-fourth of a four periods time, which means that a frequency may be available to host bits from another UWB channel during the unused periods (indicated by —). In this scenario, two different schedulers may be used to host two independent sequential codes in the same interval. As an example, assume code A = 1,011 with scheduler f2, f4, f3, f1, and code B = 1,101 with scheduler f3, f1, f4, f2. This is illustrated as:

Time period:	t1	t2	t3	t4
Bits of code A:	1	0	1	1
Bits of code B:	1	1	0	1
Frequency f1:	—	1	—	1
Frequency f2:	1	—	—	1
Frequency f3:	1	—	1	—
Frequency f4:	—	0	0	—

Ultra-short E-M pulses have some interesting properties. They propagate through walls and flesh, and they do not interfere with modulated E-M waves such as cellular transmission. Moreover, UWB can be used for bit rates up to 1 Gb/s and for a distance up to 30 feet. Compare this with Bluetooth specified to transmit up to 720 Mb/s to a comparable distance, and 802.11 up to 54 Mb/s to a distance of 100 feet.

A similar technology, which is in the experimental phase, employs ultra-narrow pulses at an effective bit rate of a trillion bits per second and at very short distances. This is potentially useful in imaging applications and thus it is dubbed "The imaging technology."

- The IEEE 100BASE-T, also known as fast Ethernet, has combined fast FDDI technology (100 Mbps) and traditional Ethernet (carrier sense multiple-access/ collision detection or CSMA/CD) technology to enable easy migration from 10 to 100BASE-T.

- The optical IEEE Ethernet 802.3ac standard is designed for efficient 10 Gb/s IP-over-fiber, and it rivals data solutions with similar OC-192/STM-64 bit rates. However, half-duplex is not supported, traditional Ethernet CDMA/CD protocol is not used, and copper solutions are not considered.

- The 1000BASE-T allows for transmission of a balanced digital signal at one Gb/s over category 5 unshielded twisted pair cable (UTP-5) and for 100-m link segments, or over multimode fiber up to 550 m, or over single-mode fiber up to 5 km.

- HomeRF is similar to IEEE 802.11, but it has 1 to 2 Mbps bit rate over a 50-m range. This is designed for wireless communication inside a building.

- Infrared, defined by IrDA (Infrared Data Association), enables line-of-sight infrared connectivity between two devices, such as a PC and a printer, or a PC and a mouse, over a distance of 1 m or less.

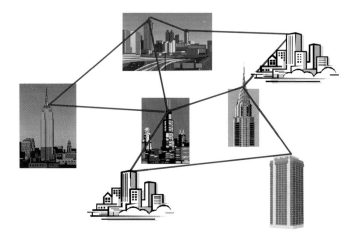

Figure 3.4   Free space optical communications network.

- Free-space optical (FSO) communications systems are designed to provide the last mile gigabit connectivity in urban enterprise applications. FSOs use a modulated laser beam that aims at a receiver positioned at some other building (Fig. 3.4). In fact, the optical principle of this method has roots in the ancient optical communications method, known as Agamemnon's link (1,200 B.C.). This method used a torch to signal a message from one tower to another, which was part of a network of towers. In the United States, although about 5% of the business multilevel buildings are directly connected with the optical network, more than 75% of them are within 1 mile. Thus, positioning a modulated laser beam at the top of a building, which is connected with the fiber network, data from the network can be beamed to another building about 1 mile away with high precision where a receiver is positioned. The receiver can be at the top of the building, on the wall, or even at a specific window for security purposes. The FSO application, however, has few issues to be addressed; dense fog attenuates the beam more than 350 dB/km (on a clear day, there is only 0.5 dB/km), thus making the link unavailable, and depending on the transmitter or the receiver direction, sunlight or other light sources may interfere with the data beam. In this case, worst-case scenarios may be addressed with mesh networks and survivability strategies, as well as worst-case link length of about 1 Km. FSO applications are feasible with laser beams in the spectral range of 860 nm, 1,310 nm, or even in the C-band, and at bit rates of OC-3, OC-12, and 1 GbE. However, as free space laser beam characteristics improve and as commercial demand grows, OC-48 bit rates may also be possible as well as beams consisting of more than one wavelength, thus forming an FSO WDM network.

3.4   TIME DIVISION MULTIPLEXING SYSTEMS

In traditional digital networks, a POTS telephone converts the acoustical signal to an electrical signal. The electrical signal then is transmitted over a pair of copper wires to an Access system where the *CODEC* function is performed. From that point on, the

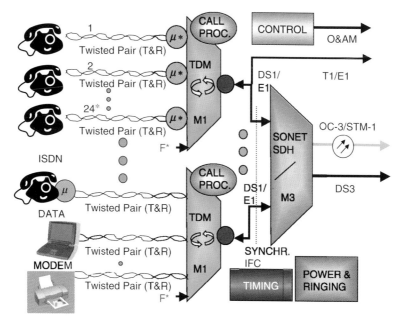

Figure 3.5   A digital subscriber line access multiplexer (DSLAM) system.

signal is transmitted throughout the network and up to the receiving Access system in digital form, and this is what constitutes an *all-digital communications network.* In a different application, such as the basic rate integrated services digital network (B-ISDN or BRI), the telephone apparatus converts the acoustic signal to PCM, which is transmitted to the Access system; hence the CODEC function is embedded in the ISDN phone. BRI uses two 64 Kbps channels, known as channels B, and one 16 Kbps subrate channel, known as channel D, to support a combination of voice services and data services over a single pair of wires. Figure 3.5 illustrates a SONET-enabled access system that provides both POTS services, data (modem), and ISDN in which the CODEC is embedded in the end device (or end station).

In addition to PCM voice, an all-digital network can pass through data (raw digital data, encoded video, encoded sound, and so on). An earlier data service that took advantage of the 64 Kbps channel is the *digital data services* (DDS).

The interface where the 64 Kbps user signal first meets the network is known as the *user-to-network interface* (UNI). At the UNI, signals from many users are synchronized with an 8-KHz system clock. Then, based on a periodic sequential and circular polling scheme known as "round-robin," the signals are sequentially polled, time-compressed (their bit rate is upped), and placed by a time slot interchanger (TSI) in a sequential order that is defined by a protocol (known in the United States as TR-08 and as TR-303). This process is known as *time (slot) division multiplexing* (TDM). At the receiving end, *time division demultiplexing* takes place; each byte in the received TDM signal is extracted and each is distributed to its end terminal.

In the United States, 24 bytes (a byte from 24 different sources) are time division multiplexed. The beginning of the 24-byte sequence is marked with the addition of a single bit, the F-bit, and altogether 24 bytes and the F-bit construct a *DS1 frame*. Thus, in a DS1 frame there are $24 \times 8 + 1 = 193$ bits that are transmitted within 125 μsec or at a bit rate of 1.544 Mbps, known as *digital signal level 1* (*DS1*). The added F-bit constitutes an 8-KHz channel; framing information (4 KHz) and data link functionality (4 KHz or $2 + 2$ KHz), known as the *superframe* or SF (Fs) and as *extended superframe* or ESF (Fe). The complete Fs data link packet consists of 36 bits; it consists of fixed length fields, the frame synchronization, the maintenance switch, the alarm, and the line switch. Thus, a complete Fs packet is extracted from 72 DS1 frames.

The aforementioned time division multiplexer is known as an M1 multiplexer. In the reverse direction, a received DS1 signal is demultiplexed, and the 24 user channels are each decompressed to 64-Kbps channels.

In contrast to the U.S. multiplexing hierarchy, European systems are based on 30 bytes; that is, bytes from 30 different sources are time division multiplexed. To these, one byte for every 15 user time slots (for framing and signaling) is added to yield an E1 (or E11) frame with a total of 32 bytes. The function of the multiplexer is round-robin polling, byte interleaving, and time compression. In the reverse direction, a received E1 signal is demultiplexed, the two channels for framing and signaling are extracted, and the remaining 30 user channels are each decompressed to 64 Kbps. Here, we use the terms *European* and *U.S.* with the understanding that other countries around the world use the same or similar multiplexing schemes.

The DS1 signal is transmitted over a pair of wires (typically a 22-gauge pulp-insulated cable) known as a T1 line; one pair of wires is used for each direction. The traveling electrical signal is attenuated and becomes susceptible to external electromagnetic interferences. As a consequence, the attenuated binary signal may or may not be correctly recovered at the receiver; that is, a "one" may be perceived as a "zero" and vice versa, and hence bit errors may occur. Communications systems at the DS1 level are designed with an error objective of 10^{-6} or better; that is, one bit error or less for each million bits transmitted. To ensure that the strength of the signal is sufficient to travel a long distance, a maximum section loss of 34 dB and assuming a high one's pulse density ($p = 0.7$) with an additional 3 dB margin, high-quality low-noise regenerators are placed every 3,000 feet from users and every 6,000 feet between regenerators to amplify and recondition the binary signal.

When a DS1 regenerator fails, however, it interrupts the service of 24 or 30 users, and thus the maintenance and troubleshooting overhead is increased, which translates into increased operating cost. To reduce maintenance overhead, higher-level multiplexers were designed to up the bit rate over the same pair of wires. Thus, 28 DS1 signals (plus control bits) are multiplexed by a multiplexer (M13) to construct a DS3 signal at a bit rate of 44.736 Mbps.

Similarly, the hierarchy in European communications systems is such that 16 E1s plus 36 bytes are multiplexed to construct an E3 signal at 34.368 Mbps. Table 3.2 captures the variety of bit rates in three major areas of the world.

3.4.1 Access and Pair-Gain Systems

As stated previously (see ADSL), only 50% of the loops are shorter than 2 km (~6,000 feet). As it turned out, connecting a central office (CO) directly with telephones (POTS) that were longer than a few thousand feet afar was a costly solution.

Table 3.2   **SONET/SDH rates**

Signal Designation			Line Rate (Mbps)
SONET	SDH	Optical	
STS-1	STM-0	OC-1	51.84
STS-3	STM-1	OC-3	155.52
STS-12	STM-4	OC-12	622.08
STS-48	STM-16	OC-48	2,488.32
STS-192	STM-64	OC-192	9,953.28
STS-192	STM-256	OC-768	39,813.12

Hence, the *pair-gain* (PG) system was born to allow more economical connectivity with all loop lengths.

In this case, many groups of 24 lines from a CO were connected with a nearby CO-SLC, and the CO-SLC *time division multiplexed* (TDM) all subscriber signals and sent them over 1.5-Mbps cables (T1 lines with repeaters) to a remote SLC (RT-SLC) located in the neighborhood of subscribers; the RT-SLC received the T1 signals, demultiplexed them, converted PCM to analog signals, and sent each analog signal over a TP cable to the subscriber CPE. This was known as *plain old telephone service* (POTS). Figure 3.6 illustrates the pair-gain idea.

To explain this, consider that a CO must be connected with 24 POTS that are found afar (in reality, it may be one of several communications devices, including modems, faxes, etc.). However, instead of doing this, consider that 24 port units from the CO (each port unit connected with a POTS) are multiplexed to a DS1 signal (the DS1 rate is at 8,000 [24 × 64 Kbps + 1 bit] bits per second or 1.544 Mbps); this multiplexing system is known as the central office terminal SLC (COT-PG). Now, consider that a four-wire T1, with repeaters every 6,000 feet to regenerate the signal, connects a demultiplexer at a far distance; this system is known as the remote terminal SLC (RT-PG). The RT-PG receives DS1s and demultiplexes them into 24 DS0s. The DS0s are passed through CODECs, and from there each analog signal is transmitted over a twisted pair to a POTS telephone (or equivalent device), which now is in close

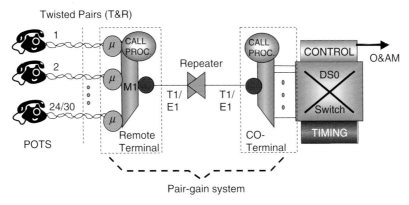

Figure 3.6   A pair-gain system is a cost-effective method to reach communications devices that are at a long distance from the local switch (end office).

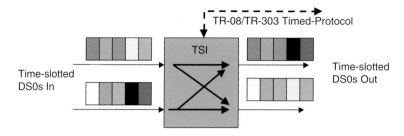

TSI = Time slot interchanger (based on time slot assignment from local switch)

Figure 3.7 DSOs in a pair-gain system are assigned time-slots in the DS1 signal by the local switch executing a TR-08 or TR-303 timed-protocol.

proximity. In the RT to CO upstream direction and during call processing (call initiation and call termination), assigning (or mapping) DSOs onto DS1s is accomplished by executing a timed protocol, the TR-08 or TR-303; based on this protocol, the local switch assigns to each DS0 a time slot onto the DS1 signal, determined by bandwidth availability. A time slot interchange (TSI) function accomplishes the time slot assignment (Fig. 3.7).

Clearly, the preceding description of a SLC access system is very simplistic. In reality, it was designed to handle many DS1 equivalent signals. It included line protection schemes, concentration (some but not all), OC-3 links, call initiation and termination protocols, self-testing and remote testing capabilities, performance, maintenance and alarms, craft interfaces for provisioning and for in-situ testing, and others.

Since the first SLC deployment, SLC access systems evolved to include data services, ISDN, and Internet by replacing appropriately subunits to offer a mix of services (see Fig. 3.4). The digital subscriber line access multiplexer (DSLAM) is an access system that supports both voice services and broadband services to the home (e.g., the Internet). It separates voice signals (POTS) from high-speed data (xDSL, modem); it sends voice signals to a local switch and sends data to a router.

To complete this section, we must explain the term *concentration*. This means that although a SLC access system can establish N subscriber connections with the network, the number of actual subscribers physically connected with the SLC may be twice as many; this represents a 2:1 concentration. The reason for POTS service concentration stems from the statistical fact that not all POTS devices will be off-the-hook all the time but for several minutes on average. As a consequence, if the average number of calls (for a particular day and period of the day) originated during a period of 1 hour is C and if each call has an average duration T, then the average traffic flow A is expressed as

$$A = CT \text{ (calls-unit of time)}$$

The "call-unit of time" may be expressed in "call-hours" or "call-minutes." In the United States, "one hundred call-seconds" (CCS) is equated to one "unit call."

A unit that is frequently used in traffic engineering is the *Erlang*; a subunit is the milli-Erlangs (mE). An Erlang represents a "busy" circuit for an hour. Thus, it provides an indication of the traffic intensity of a system at a given time. For example, if a system consists of 48 circuits and the *Erlang* is 8 "unit-calls," then one should expect 8 of 48 circuits to be "busy" within any given second. As a consequence, an *Erlang* provides an indication of the system traffic utilization as compared to its capacity. Therefore, based on traffic parameters, traffic engineers can determine whether concentration may be advisable. Clearly, these units pertain to traditional telephony where most calls (circuit connections) are on the order of a few minutes and very rarely hours. However, with the relatively new services (such as the Internet), the average connectivity may be on the order of hours. In this case, the concept of traditional traffic engineering can easily be extended to modern networks and services, although the unit of hour now becomes the norm replacing the calls-per-second of telephony.

Example: In a system, for a particular day and period of a day there are on average 340 calls in a given hour, with an average duration of 12 minutes each. Then,

$$A = CT = 340 \times 12 \times 60/100 = 2,448 \text{ CCS}$$

3.4.2 Fiber-to-the-Home Technology

Multimedia (voice, video, high-speed data) and Internet services drive the need for higher bit rates (several Mbps) to the home. Although a huge capital investment has already been made in copper cable (twisted pair, coaxial) and new techniques have been developed (ADSL), it seems that the appetite for more bandwidth keeps increasing. Therefore, to ensure that the loop plant of the future will be and remain bandwidth-scalable, fiber-optic cable is replacing copper wherever possible. Depending on where the fiber is terminated (Fig. 3.8), this technology is known by different names such as:

- Fiber-to-the-home (FTTH) if the fiber reaches the premises of the end user where it is also terminated. At the APOC'01 conference, it was reported that in the summer

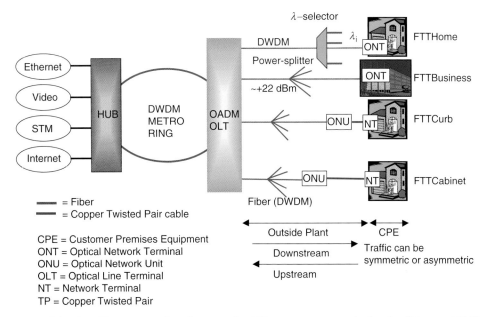

Figure 3.8 The different scenarios of a generalized fiber access system (notice the distance of ONU in the last two scenarios).

of 2,001, FTTH deployment in Japan started with two monthly fee offers, $70 at 100 Mb/s and $40 at 10 Mb/s.

- Fiber-to-the-curb (FTTC) if the fiber is terminated at a "small box" at the curb, where the optical signal is converted to an electrical signal and reaches the home over a twisted copper medium.

- Fiber-to-the-cabinet (FTTCab) if the fiber is terminated at a "community box," where optical signals are converted to electrical signals and are distributed to each home over copper medium, wireless or even a passive optical ring.

- Fiber-to-the-desk (FTTD) if the fiber is terminated directly at the desk or even at the PC. However, the nature of desk or the PC of the future is not known yet.

Thus, the current question that companies try to answer is which of these fiber loop implementations offers the most flexible scalability and best cost-effectiveness so that, once reengineered and replaced, it remains untouched for many years, a concept known as "future-proofing." For the time being, we call this technology FTTx.

Disregarding the specific merits of each possible implementation, the key advantages common to all are:

- FTTx offers flexible bandwidth up to Gb/s to the home.
- FTTx is implementable with passive optical components.
- Fiber can reach communities located far from the central office.
- Fiber takes advantage of the evolving DWDM technology.
- Battery backup is local and thus power consumption is lower.
- Fiber is a reliable and secure medium.
- Fiber may be easily replaced if "new type" needs to replace the old.

Where the fiber is terminated impacts the architecture, engineering, maintenance, and cost structure of the loop plant. Is the fiber all the way up to the home? Or is it up to some point from which the signal continues electrically over copper? And who maintains what? Clearly, these are difficult questions to answer very quickly as, besides engineering and so forth, legislature is also involved in setting policy so that certain rules are applied to protect service providers and subscribers.

If the fiber is terminated at the home, it implies that the premises' terminating equipment (PTE) is able to filter out the particular wavelength destined for this home (if multiple wavelengths are received) and convert the photonic signal to an electrical signal and distribute it over twisted pair throughout the home. In a different configuration, the PTE receives a single wavelength; converts the photonic signal to an electrical signal; disassembles (or demultiplexes) the incoming multiplexed services of video, voice, high-speed and low-speed data; and distributes over twisted pair through the home; the direction from the network to the home is dubbed *downstream*. In the other direction, the *upstream*, the PTE should be able to receive and assemble (or multiplex) a variety of services in one signal, convert to optical (wavelength), and couple it in the fiber. Depending on the complexity of PTE, the number of services it provides, the number of subscribers it serves, and ownership of equipment, the maintenance of PTE equipment may be the responsibility of either the service provider or the subscriber. In yet a different configuration, the signal from the PTE may be broadcasted to the home over low-power wireless, thus eliminating or minimizing the communications wiring throughout the home; this technology, which is known as home communications, enables appliance mobility in the home, but it requires dedicated electronics in each appliance and specialized protocols (Bluetooth is such a technology).

When there is an infrastructure of copper twisted pairs in a neighborhood and it makes no sense to replace it, the fiber-terminating equipment is located at the curb; hence FTTC. In this case, the optical signal destined for the home is filtered out and terminated at the FTTC equipment; each subscriber's signal is converted to a xDSL electrical signal and is transmitted to the home over existing twisted pair.

In contrast to FTTC, in the FTTCab case the fiber is terminated far from the home, at a fiber network interface device, from which the signal may continue over fiber to the home or the curb; otherwise it may be converted to electrical over copper, or it may be broadcasted over wireless to the homes of a neighborhood.

3.4.3 Switching Systems

For switched services, the end customer is connected via the loop to a switching system in the local central office building. This switching system executes call initiation and termination protocols; for example, this is what takes place as soon as the telephone handset is lifted, or placed back on the cradle, and the destination number is dialed up; hence it is known as *dialed-up services*. This is also what takes place when one clicks on the "connect" or "disconnect" button of a modem (the destination number is already programmed in the PC). It also communicates with the next higher up switching system.

In general, a switching system consists of input–output port units, which terminate one of many services (DS0, ISDN, DS1, OC-3, Ethernet, and other packet-based data rates) of the switching fabric and of the system controller. In this system, several functions are performed, including call processing, emulation, performance management, path establishing, maintenance, statistical data recording, and others (Fig. 3.9).

In North America, a hierarchy has been established that distinguishes the switching systems in "end offices" (class 5), "toll centers" (class 4), "primary centers" (class 3), "sectional centers" (class 2), and "regional centers" (class 1) (Fig. 3.10). The switching capacity, complexity, and cost of the switching systems increase as we move toward the regional center. Early switching systems were interconnected with trunk copper cables, but currently they are interconnected with fiber cables. In the U.S. hierarchy there are three principal types of interoffice trunks (see Fig. 3.9): local (interoffice, tandem, and intertandem), toll, and intertoll. All trunk support transmission and signaling (supervision).

Some connectivity examples include:

- A CO-SLC or an end station (such as a telephone) is always connected with an end office (EO).
- An end station (C) requests connectivity with another end station (A) that is serviced by the same EO; the two are connected locally via the same EO.
- An end station (A) requests connectivity with another end station (B) that is serviced by another EO; then they two may be connected via a tandem (TAN) switching office.

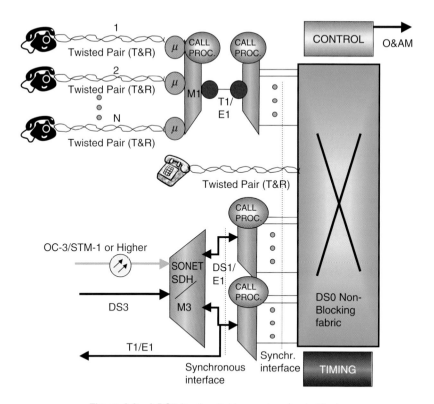

Figure 3.9 A DS0-level switching system (end office).

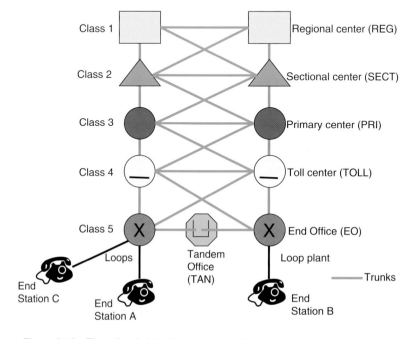

Figure 3.10 The toll switching hierarchy; switching centers, classes and trunks.

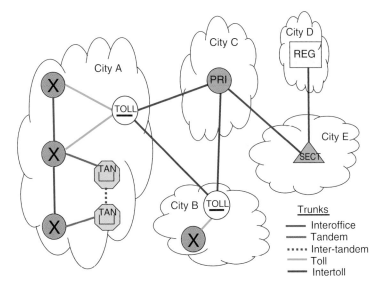

Figure 3.11   Trunk connectivity between cities, based on the U.S. switching hierarchy.

- An end station (A) that requests connectivity with another end station (B) in a multioffice location; this presents several possibilities for trunk interconnectivity.

Figure 3.11 illustrates the types of trunks and trunk interconnectivity between cities.

3.4.4   Digital Cross-Connect Systems

In contrast to switching systems, digital cross-connect systems (DCS) evolved from a need to automate and accelerate patch-cord connectivity for aggregate bandwidth, such as DS1s and DS3s, that had to be routed from one city to another. Based on destination, a switch previously would have sorted all incoming traffic and have aggregated to DS1, DS3, or OC-3/12 signals, which were sent to a DCS. The DCS, based on input–output connectivity tables, had already established a semipermanent input–output connection for each signal. Thus, one DCS with very high aggregate bandwidth (modern optical cross-connects plan for several terabits/sec) provided a cost-effective and complementary function to several switches and a solution to high bandwidth traffic routing. In addition, DCSs provided routing to leased private lines supporting DS1 or higher bandwidth service for banks, stockbrokers, and large corporations.

Digital cross-connects also provided other salient characteristics such as network survivability, service restoration, and signal conditioning. This, in addition to remote provisioning, performance data monitoring, data collection, and data communication to a (remote) network operating system, established DCS as a key communications element in "hub" cities where very large aggregate traffic needed to be managed. You may think of it as a hub airport where passengers deplane either because they have reached their destination (an add-drop function) or because they need to go to other gates and board airplanes with different destinations (a switching function).

Although DCSs were able to receive a variety of services (DS1, OC-3, etc.), the cross-connecting fabric was designed, for simplicity and efficiency, to cross-connect traffics

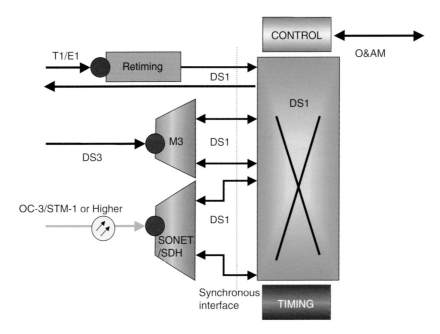

Figure 3.12   A DS1-level cross-connect system.

at a single rate. For example, it would connect DS1s, DS3s, or only OC-3 signals. This implies that cross-connects with a "DS1" fabric would have to disassemble DS3 and OC-3 incoming services to its constituent DS1s, perform the cross-connect function, and then assemble the DS1s back to DS3s and OC-3 (Fig. 3.12). As simple as disassembly, cross-connect, and reassembly may sound, it is not trivial because the embedded overhead at the inputs must be recreated at the outputs (a nightmare in terms of input–output communication that keeps track of performance data as well as other operational data. In certain applications, input–output communication was resolved by adding overhead (tags) on constituent DS1s before entering the cross-connecting fabric and extracting them after exiting the fabric; this practice is also adopted in ATM switching.

3.5   GETTING CONNECTED

Legacy networks were initially designed to carry voice signals from any source to any destination. Imagine an end terminal (a POTS telephone) that must be connected with another terminal at a remote location. The intent to connect is initiated when the calling telephone goes "off-hook"; then a current flow on the loop is detected by an access system, that requests a time slot from the switch. The switch grants the request and assigns a time slot. This process takes a few milliseconds. Then the source end terminal dials the destination number. The switch communicates with the next level switch (using a signaling protocol), and eventually a path over the complete route (known as a circuit) is determined. If the destination device is not used (busy), then a ringing is activated, which is echoed back to the calling device. The complete process takes less than 300 milliseconds. If the destination device is busy, then the calling party hears either a busy signal or silence, as in systems such as ISDN. When the destination device answers to the ringing (by activating its loop), the complete end-to-end circuit becomes active, and from that moment connectivity is established and a timer keeps track of the duration of active service, based on which charges are calculated; this is known as "*switched service*."

Clearly, a digital switching node in this scenario must be able to execute call-processing protocols and dialed number identification and to dynamically change the input–output connectivity of many thousands of channels per second. This is in contrast to digital cross-connecting systems (DCS) that do not establish connectivity on a per-call basis and thus do not execute "call processing." DCSs establish semipermanent connections of high-rate traffic pipes such as DS1s, DS3s, and OC-3s by provisioning; this is known as "*nonswitched*" service.

3.6   DATA SYSTEMS

Legacy synchronous communications networks have efficiently addressed the voice bandwidth needs for many years. However, they have not efficiently addressed the data bandwidth needs in an equitable manner. This means that the primary concerns for voice networks such as *short delays*, extremely *low error rate*, and *high quality of service* did not match the concerns of data networks such as *high data rate* and *low-cost* per bandwidth-unit of time. This mismatch between voice and data stems from fundamental traffic differences between the two. Figure 3.13 illustrates the time variation of data natural bit rate about an average value; in general, the rate peaks about midday.

Short delay over the total end-to-end path is predominantly related to real-time communication, such as real-time or interactive video and real-time voice transmission services. Perhaps many of us have seen or experienced long delay and the level of annoyance while on the phone or watching live broadcasting video (such as the news from a remote country). By and large, it is this annoyance level that dictates short delay

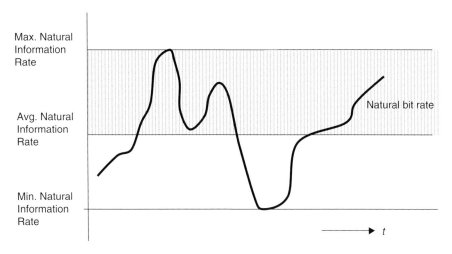

Figure 3.13   Natural bit rate.

in data communications systems and networks; that is, short path delay. To study the path delay, then, one must examine each delay component over the end-to-end path. In general, these components are:

- Delay due to packet length bit rate. This delay is related to time it takes for a packet of n-bits to be transmitted at a rate of X bit/seconds. For example, 1,000 bytes at 1 Gb/s transmission rate will take 1,000 ns = 1 μs to be transmitted. Transmission of the same packet at 1 Mb/s would take 1 ms.

- Delay due to propagation in the medium. Electromagnetic waves and light in free-space travel at the "speed of light," about 30 cm in a nanosecond. Now, for a distance of 1 km, it takes about 3.3 μs.

- Throughput intranode delays. These are delays that depend on the architecture and design of each node, excluding queuing delays.

- Delay due to packet queuing. When a packet is received, it is temporarily stored in a queue, and after some time, it is processed and passed to the next station on the path. This packet may experience delay as short as one packet length, a few packet lengths, and occasionally, if there is congestion, many packet lengths.

- Protocol-dependent and topology-dependent delays. These are delays that depend on the particular network topology and protocol used. For example, although the packet is ready to depart from a node and a request to transmit has been issued, if the transmission medium is already occupied or seized by another node, then the packet may remain in the output queue until the medium becomes available.

As a result, the total path delay is the sum of all delay components on the path. Although the first three components may be well known (as soon as the path is established, in general, the fourth and fifth components may be known only statistically, and this is where statistics, probability, and information theory are involved to define a model that predicts minimal queuing delay based on engineering network and temporal parameters. The last component also requires efficient protocol mechanisms with minimal average delay to seize the transmission medium.

Considering the natural bit rate of different services, the burstiness (rate irregularity over time) of data may be examined by plotting the peak rate versus the average rate and mapping the various services based on their data rate characteristics (Fig. 3.14). For example, data rate due to voice is continuous and, as such, the peak rate is always constant (64 Kb/s), whereas data are bursty (as in Fig. 3.13), with the exception of real-time video. Voice traffic is symmetric and requires low network latency (with zero perceived echo), whereas data are asymmetric and latency is not as critical. Voice is full-duplex, whereas data by and large are half-duplex.

These contrasting needs brought about a data network able to transport chunks of data, up to about 9,000 bytes, known as *packets* or *frames*. Thus, the "data network" now switches at the packet granularity and not at the DSn. Figure 3.15 illustrates the packet formation at irregular time due to their bursty nature of information (Fig. 3.15A), the packet buffering to smooth out burstiness, and cross-connection to provide input–output connectivity (Fig. 3.15B). Note that to smooth out the data rate irregularity, "idle packets" may be inserted to fill time gaps. Clearly, this requires buffers, and the depth of buffer is related to queue depth. Queue depth and bandwidth allocated to queue are related to delay and delay variation (jitter).

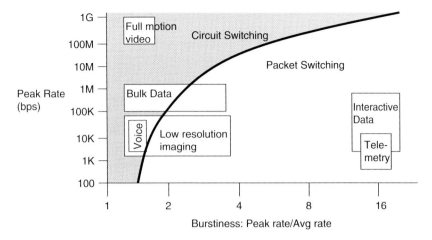

Figure 3.14 Burstiness: Peak versus average rate.

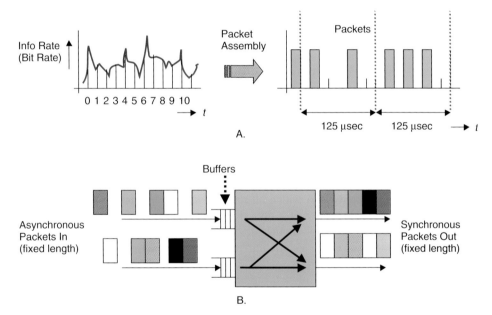

Figure 3.15 A. The formation of fixed-length packets is time-irregular, B. packets are buffered and (in synchronous transmission) time gaps are filled with idle packets to provide a continuous bit flow at the output.

With reference to Figures 3.13 and 3.14, a key observation is made when comparing the natural bit rate and the bandwidth capacity of a node. Typically, nodes (comprised of communications systems or routers) are designed to handle a maximum bandwidth capacity. Mapping the maximum capacity of a node and the natural bit rate of data, one can easily recognize that at certain times the node is underutilized and at certain other times it is overutilized. When the node is underutilized, the system becomes cost-inefficient because potential bandwidth (and thus revenues) is wasted. When it is

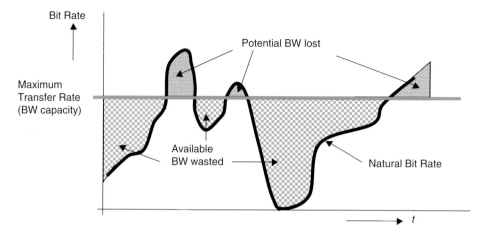

Figure 3.16   Natural bit rate and bandwidth utilization.

overutilized, the system must make a decision and drop the excess capacity, which means lost the opportunity for increased revenues (Fig. 3.16). This dynamic behavior of natural bit rate of data is in contrast to synchronous nodes, where the bandwidth is static and slowly growing linearly, approaching the maximum bandwidth of the node; when it reaches about 95% of its total bandwidth capacity, either a larger node replaces it or a second node is added.

3.6.1   The OSI Model

Data networks comply with a several-layer model, known as the *open system interconnect* (OSI). The lowest layer is the physical (PHY) layer, followed by the data link layer (DLL); the highest layer is the applications layer (APP). Each layer describes the rules and specifications with which all data devices on the network must comply. To manage the latter, each layer of a data device communicates only with the corresponding layer (or peer layer) of another device. Thus, as long as peer layers conform to the same specification, devices can communicate even if they are made by different manufacturers.

The seven layers of the OSI model, top to bottom, and their purpose briefly are:

1. Applications (APP): Provide services to users, such as file transfer protocol (FTP).
2. Presentation: Performs data transformations, such as encryption, compression, and so on.
3. Session: Manages and terminates connections (or sessions) between cooperating applications.
4. Transport: Provides end-to-end error recovery and flow control.
5. Network: Establishes, maintains, and terminates connections; provides independence to upper layers of switching functions.
6. Data link (DL): Provides functions for reliable transfer of data across the physical link. It includes the media-specific access control (MAC) sublayer, which is

responsible for flow control (including collision resolution), data synchronization, and error control.

7. Physical (PHY): Defines the medium of the physical link and the physical inter-connect, the signal format, modulation method, bit rates, electrical levels, jitter and noise limits, and procedural characteristics to establish, maintain, and deac-tivate the physical link. It also includes the physical media attachment (PMA) where encoding (4B/5B or 8B/10B) takes place as well as parallel to/from serial conversion.

Note: The 4B/5B and 8B/10B encoding ensures that there is always a nonzero code in the bit stream over the medium; 4 bits are encoded to 5B and 8 bits to 10, respectively.

Let us assume that we want to send a file from one data device to another. We issue a command "send" and it just happens. But what really happens? How does a layer know how to communicate with another peer layer? Well, this is sim-ply a matter of how the frame is formed as it starts from the highest layer, the applications layer.

At the applications layer, the file is partitioned into smaller chunks of data, and a little overhead is added to each one to identify that this chunk belongs to this layer and to keep track of the sequence of its chunks (Fig. 3.17). This action is known as *fragmentation*. Then this is passed on to the next lower layer, and after data have been compressed or encrypted, a little more overhead is added (Fig. 3.18) and passed to the next lower layer, and so on, to the data link layer, at which point the complete frame has been formed. The process of attaching overhead segments from layer to layer to assemble a complete frame is known as *encapsulation*. The data link layer will initiate the "call" process (or "cease the link"), and if successful, it will pass the frame to the physical layer for transmission.

At the receiving end, the physical layer will receive the frame, it will pass it to the link layer, where the link layer overhead is stripped off the packet and the remaining is passed to the next layer and so on, up to the applications layer. The applications layer will receive all fragments from the originating data device, and it will place them one after the other in the correct order. This is known as *reassembly*.

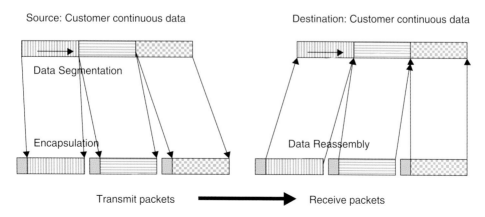

Figure 3.17   Segmentation, encapsulation and reassembly.

OSI Model

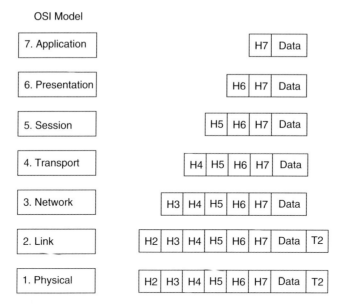

Figure 3.18 OSI model & encapsulation.

3.6.2 Local Area Networks

Data networks that provide interconnectivity among communicating data devices and within a limited area (a building or a campus) are called local area networks (LAN). Data devices that are connected to the *LAN backbone* communicate according to a LAN *communications protocol.*

The first LAN deployment had a limited distance, but soon thereafter LANs were expanded to cover a city and a metropolis, the *metropolitan area network* (MAN), the *wide area network* (WAN), and the *switched multi-megabit data services* (SMDS).

Traffic from one data network to another was brought over via a function known as a *bridge*, and LAN/MAN traffic was *routed* to the communications network so that connectivity between two (or more) remote LANs/MANs was established. Should traffic demand between two LANs/MANs be sustained 24 hours a day and be high enough, then a *dedicated link* between the two would be more efficient, thus establishing a *private data network*, or a *semipermanent link* if the traffic demand level does not justify it.

SMDS is a public MAN service that was developed by Bellcore® (now Telcordia) primarily for LAN interconnections. SMDS is a connectionless technology specified over DS1, DS3, E1, and E3 synchronous carriers. It enables large packet transfers (about 9 Kbytes each but segmented into 53-byte cells) to several destinations using *group addressing*. It also enables data transfer across different LANs. SMDS is based on the *distributed queue dual bus* (DQDB) transport and multiplexing protocol, which is defined in IEEE 802.6.

LAN networks are distinguished as *Ethernet* type or *ring* type. Ethernet LANs are hierarchical, and the transmission rate is at 10 Mbps, 100 Mbps, 1 Gb/s, and recently 10 Gb/s over fiber. IEEE specifies all LAN types in a series of specifications known as 802.n, where n is a number.

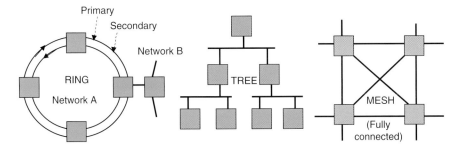

Figure 3.19   Ring, tree and mesh topologies.

3.6.2.1 Ethernet

Ethernet has evolved from the experimenter's workbench to a hierarchical tree topology in an attempt to interconnect several computers (other LAN topologies are the ring and the mesh) (Fig. 3.19). As such, it evolved to a data network characterized by relatively high speed, simple and relatively small distance, easily maintainable, and low cost. Since its objective was not to compete with an existing telephone network, error control, network protection, security, real-time aspects, and quality of service were not of paramount importance. The fundamental difference between the two was its asynchronous (bursty) transmission, which was based on a protocol, and nonsynchronous real-time characteristic. That is, stations on the Ethernet network formed frames (packets) of information, and any station on the network could initiate a frame transfer (according to the Ethernet 802.3 protocol) anytime. "Anytime" implies that there is a finite probability that two or more stations may attempt to initiate frame transfers at the same time, a situation known as *collision*. However, the protocol is smart enough to detect such collisions and resolve them, based on the principle of "equal fairness to all stations"; this is called *carrier sense multiple-access/collision detect* (CSMA/CD). CSMA/CD is one of the fundamental differences between tree (Ethernet) and ring (FDDI) LANs, as the latter is based on priority tokens; each station on a ring LAN is assigned a priority level based on which they can or cannot send a packet.

CSMA/CD was based on simultaneous active listening to traffic on the network by all stations, including the one that is transmitting. If the carrier were absent for at least twice the collision window (a short period that was determined by the propagation delay between two extreme stations on the network), only then could a station start transmitting. If two or more stations started transmitting simultaneously from "listening to the network traffic," they should be able to detect a collision situation and back off. At a random time thereafter, they could start again, but this time one of them would be first (due to randomness). Transmission starts with a preamble signal (a string of zeros and ones); the preamble has a dual purpose; to listen and to wake up and stabilize the clock of the receivers (clocks have an acquisition time to achieve stability). The preamble code is followed by a start-of-frame delimiter, the source and destination ID, and other information, including length of data field, which is followed by data; this concludes with a frame check sequence (Fig. 3.20).

Ethernet Media Designation

IEEE 802.3 has developed a designation for the various Ethernet flavors. For all practical purposes, this designation is

$$n\text{BASE-(phy)}$$

SFD = Start-of-frame delimiter
DA = Destination address
SA = Source address
LLC = Logical link control
PAD = Packet assembler-disassembler
FCS = Frame check sequence
DSAP = Destination service access point
SSAP = Source service access point

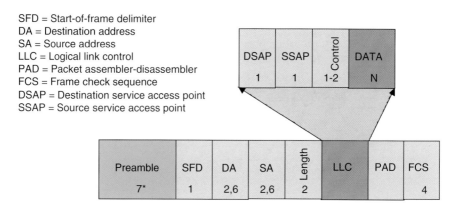

*Numbers indicate bytes

Figure 3.20 Ethernet CSMA/CD frame format.

where *n* is the data rate (but not necessarily the bit rate on the medium), BASE indicates baseband signaling on the channel, and (phy) indicates the nature of the physical medium (e.g., T = twisted pair). Thus, 10BASE-T means 10 Mbps baseband over twisted pair, 10BASE-F means 10 Mbps baseband over fiber, and 1000BASE-T means 1,000 Mbps (or 1 Gb/s) baseband over twisted pair.

1000BASE-T

The IEEE 802.3ab Task Force has worked out a standard, known as 1000BASE-T, commonly known as *Gigabit Ethernet* over copper medium, which allows for transmission of a balanced digital signal at 1 Gigabit per second over four pairs of category 5 unshielded twisted pair cable (UTP-5) and for 100-meter link segments; each pair transmits at 250 Mb/s. It also allows for transmission over multimode fiber and for 550-meter segments, or over single-mode fiber and for 5-km segments.

Although 1000BASE-T makes us think that it is similar to its predecessors, 100BASE-T and 10BASE-T, this is not the case. In fact, 1000BASE-T is substantially different from 100 and 10BASE-T, and only few similarities have been preserved such as:

- It is a connectionless technology.
- It is based on the OSI seven-layer model.
- It transmits variable length frames, complying with 802.3 Ethernet frame format.
- It uses the 8B/10B encoding scheme.
- It cannot guarantee real-time delivery.
- It cannot provide preferential treatment of frames.
- It does not deliver the expected quality of service (QoS) for multimedia services.

1000BASE-T may operate in half-duplex or in full-duplex. In half-duplex, it uses the standard CSMA/CD with a *carrier extension* technique for detecting and resolving collisions; this remains under the responsibility of the MAC sublayer. The MAC sublayer is also made up of two components, the *MAC client* (which receives formatted data from the software application) and the *MAC control* (which controls flow and collision situations). In full-duplex, collision detection is not an issue because collisions do not occur. However, the receiver must cope with echoes, adaptive filtering for channel equalization, near-end cross talk (NEXT), and far-end cross talk (FEXT). The PHY layer includes the PMA sublayer where 8B/10B encoding/decoding and serialization/deserialization (SERDES) take place.

One of the applications of the Gigabit Ethernet is in internetworking switch links (ISL). That is, workstations with data device interfaces at 1, 10, and 100 Mb/s transport the aggregate traffic to another workstation over a 1 Gb/s (1000BASE-T) link.

What's Next?

The race for higher bit rates and low cost is on. Currently, specifications are near completion for a 10 Gigabit Ethernet, and after this? You guessed right—a 40 Gigabit Ethernet. Ethernet will keep pushing the bit rate envelope as long as there is a demand for more bandwidth. And this is where DWDM technology steps in. *DWDM Ethernet* is considered by many to be the final solution.

3.6.2.2 *FDDI*

The fiber distributed data interface II (FDDI-II) is a token ring LAN. It is defined for voice and data over long distances, and it consists of a dual-fiber ring (the primary and the secondary) topology (Fig. 3.21).

FDDI networks are theoretically unbounded in size. However, each station and fiber segment adds to the token delay affecting the throughput and reconfiguration time of the network. Thus, each link can be up to 2 km in length. Based on this, a practical FDDI network can have up to 200 Km total fiber length (both primary and secondary), and it can accommodate more than 500 stations.

The FDDI frame consists of nine fields. These are:

- the preamble field (64 bits)
- the starting delimiter (8 bits)
- the frame control (8 bits)
- the destination address (16 or 48 bits)
- the source address (16 or 48 bits)

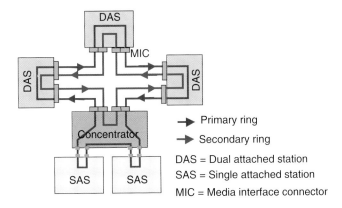

Figure 3.21   The dual-fiber ring FDDI local area network.

- the information (up to 4,500 octets)
- the frame check sequence (32 bits)
- the end delimiter (8 bits)
- the frame status (at least 12 bits or 3 symbols; each symbol consists of 4 bits)

The FDDI station standard consists of four sections, with direct correspondence to the open system interconnect (OSI) layers, with the exception of the SMT:

- the physical layer medium dependent (PMD)
- the physical layer protocol (PHY)
- the medium-specific access control (MAC)
- the station management (SMT)

The FDDI token administration differs from other token ring networks. FDDI uses a timed-token protocol (TTP) that is based on a bidding process to offer both synchronous and asynchronous service to other stations.

FDDI is defined for a data bit rate at 100 Mb/s. However, it uses a coding scheme, known as 4B/5B, according to which every four bits are converted to a 5-bit symbol; this guarantees that all symbols will have a sufficient density of ones, even if the initial code would be 0000. This coding scheme, however, adds 25% overhead, and thus the actual bit rate on the ring is 125 Mb/s.

Each FDDI station is responsible for identifying fault conditions in the network (through link-level bit error rate and light-level monitoring) by transmitting special frames. When a fault is identified, all stations know about it, and the network reconfigures itself so that operation continues.

FDDI has also given rise to a two-connected regular ring-mesh network (RMN) architecture, also known as Manhattan street network (MSN) or Manhattan FDDI (M-FDDI) (Fig. 3.22). This network utilizes distributed control, packet queuing, adaptive routing, flow control, deadlock avoidance, and packet resequencing and exhibits an increased (superior) throughput performance as well as fault and disaster avoidance. As an example, a 64-node RMN network outperforms in throughput a bus network by a factor of 20 to 30, all things being equal. The factor increases in larger networks.

Moreover, the M-FDDI exhibits a superior routeability or packet deliverability from the standpoint of the number of available routes between two nodes in the network. For unidirectional M-FDDI with NXN nodes, the total number of possible routes

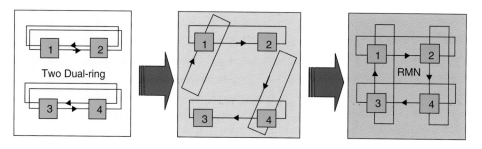

Figure 3.22 Evolution from dual ring to a ring-mesh network.

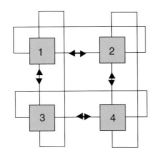

Bidirectional 2 × 2 Ring-Mesh Network

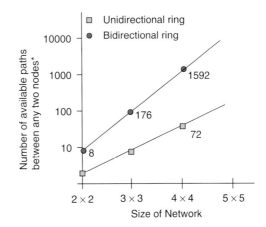

*Certain paths are more optimum than others

Figure 3.23 Routeability of ring-mesh network.

per channel between source and destination, without visiting the same node twice, is estimated to be N!(N − 1). However, in bidirectional RMNs, this number increases rapidly. For example, a 2 × 2 node network has eight possible routes, a 3 × 3 has 176, and a 4 × 4 has 1,592 (Fig. 3.23).

As a sidenote, terrestrial M-FDDI networks are also applicable in multisatellite networks where laser beams are used instead of fiber to form a network of picosatellites (inexpensive satellites about the size of a briefcase) in free space.

3.6.3 Packet Networks

Packet networks are data networks that offer integrated multiple service levels at a quality agreed upon by the service provider and the client based on a service level agreement (SLA). Packet networks perform bandwidth management, buffering (queuing), scheduling, routing and dynamic rerouting, policing, and traffic shaping.

- Bandwidth management consists of functions such as the call admission control, class of service routing, and signaling.
  - CAC is performed per service level.
  - Routing requires knowledge of the complete network topology in terms of available bandwidth per service level. It executes shortest path algorithms (e.g., traveling salesman algorithm), and when the optimum route has been identified, it forms a routing database. Routing also executes scheduling algorithms and simple or complex queuing algorithms, per SLA. Dynamic rerouting may also be performed during service.
- Policing provides a provisioned mechanism at the entry point (edge) of the network to verify and control subscriber traffic parameters in terms of the SLA.
- Traffic shaping is a buffered function that smooths the traffic exiting the system to ensure compliance with the agreed upon profile, and it avoids congestion situations by proper bandwidth management.

Packet networks assemble a number of client data bytes (or octets) into a payload block, attach several overhead bytes to it, and form a packet of some length (measured in octets or bytes). Typically, there are two types of packet networks: those that form a short fixed-length packet and those that form a variable-length packet; packet lengths may vary from 40 to many thousands of octets. In addition, various protocols define the position of the overhead and the meaning of each byte in it. Clearly, packet networks are defined for bursty data, and therefore it is doubtful that they can always meet the real-time requirements of voice and real-time video without substantial signal delays. Delaying a real-time signal (e.g., voice) becomes annoying because the signal must be buffered to form a long (several thousand bytes) packet. However, with adequate network bandwidth capacity and sophisticated protocols voice/video service with acceptable perceived delays cannot be delivered.

In addition to the delay introduced during packet assembly and disassembly, large delays are experienced during the switching process. Packets are buffered, and based on a store-and-forward process, they are switched on a priority basis, according to SLA. Clearly, the more switching elements on the packet path, the higher the overall latency. In a worst-case scenario of extreme congestion, if the total packet rate has exceeded the bandwidth capacity of a node, packets with the lowest priority are the first candidates to be "dropped" and never delivered (see also Fig. 3.13).

SMDS, ATM, frame relay (FR), and Internet protocol (IP) are all packet-based networks; data are partitioned into 53-byte packets (e.g., SMDS and ATM) or into packets of thousands of bytes (e.g., Ethernet, IP). This diversity in packet length stems from the need to have a data network that routes short-packet data and meets, by virtue of low latency, real-time requirements; ATM, for example, can transport voice and data with acceptable (perceived) delay.

Multiple service levels are supported with parallel overlay networks, or with native multiservice technologies like asynchronous transfer mode (ATM).

The overlay is a purpose-built network to support multiservice offer. The supported classes of service by this network are generally four:

- Guaranteed: synchronous, negligible jitter, bounded latency, and low packet loss (such as TDM).

- Predictable: isochronous, minimal oversubscribing (or overbooking), bounded jitter, and bounded latency (such as ATM).

- Shared: moderate oversubscribing, bandwidth aware, low jitter, some latency (such as frame relay — FR).

- Best effort: highly oversubscribed, high jitter, moderate latency (such as IP).

Note: Per GR-253-CORE, jitter is defined as the "*short-term variation*" of a signal's significant instants from their ideal position in time. "Short-term variation" implies some frequency oscillation greater than or equal to a frequency demarcation. In the North American hierarchy (DS1-DS3), the demarcation between jitter and wander is 10 Hz. Jitter network element (NE) criteria (see GR-499-CORE for details) are specified as:

- *Jitter transfer* (per interface category) is defined as the jitter transfer characteristics (limits) of an NE.

- *Jitter tolerance* (per interface category) is defined as the point-to-point amplitude of sinusoidal jitter applied on the OC-N (SONET/SDH) input signal that causes a 1-dB power penalty.

- *Jitter generation* (per interface category) defines the limits of jitter generated by an NE without jitter or wander at its inputs. In communications systems, payload mapping, bit stuffing, and pointer adjustments are sources of jitter.

Typically, these service levels are instantiated over separate networks, each perhaps based on a different technology platform (TDM, FR, ATM, or IP) and from a different service provider, and thus each may be provisioned differently. Thus, guaranteed services may also be an issue.

Multiservices arise from multiple protocol label switching (MPLS) and the differentiated services model (Diffserv).

- *MPLS* is a protocol encapsulation technique, which also includes bandwidth aware routing extensions and path signaling specifications. MPLS enables packet networks to apply ATM traffic engineering principles.

- *Diffserv* provides a model for multiple service levels, utilizing enhanced IP and MPLS protocols to deliver multiservices over an IP backbone network. Based on this model, packets can be classified and dynamically aggregated into provisioned service levels (each with a different QoS).

3.6.4 Frame Relay

Frame relay (FR) is a packet service (Fig. 3.24) that takes advantage of traffic pattern variability and oversubscription to provide a cost-effective data service. At the access points, or user-to-network interface (UNI), circuitry concentrates the packet traffic from a number of users, typically over leased lines (T1/E1). Then the concentrated traffic is switched by means of a Frame relay switch and is put on a common backbone. A number of FR switches are interconnected to form a frame relay network.

3.6.5 ATM

The *asynchronous transfer mode* (ATM) is a standardized technology that enables the convergence of a variety of services, low and very high bandwidth, synchronous and asynchronous transmission, voice and data, real-time and non−real-time, slotted and

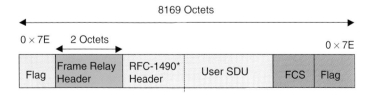

*RFC 1490 specifies encapsulation of multi-protocol data for transmission over Frame Relay
FCS = Frame Check Sequence

Figure 3.24 Frame relay frame format.

packetized, and switched and nonswitched services. In principle, ATM is independent of the transmission medium, wire, wireless, or fiber. Consequently, ATM allows a variety of bit rates, which with sophisticated bandwidth management enables the network to be more efficient and at the same time maintain a *quality of service* that is *custom-suited* to users.

In ATM, asynchronous and bursty information is collected over 48 octets, 5 overhead octets are added and the complete construct of 53 octets is known as a cell (Fig. 3.25). This also means that in ATM a packet from another system (e.g., Internet) that may be several thousand octets long can also be partitioned to form many concatenated cells. This process is known as ATM *emulation*.

The definition of the ATM overhead at the user-to-network interface (UNI) is different from the network-to-network interface (NNI); both cases are illustrated in Figure 3.26.

UNI case: The first 4 bits are used for *generic flow control* (GFC), the following 8 bits are the *virtual path identifier* (VPI), the next 16 bits are the *virtual channel identifier* (VCI), the next 3 bits are the *payload type identifier* (PTI), one bit is the *cell loss priority* (CLP), and the last octet is used for *header error control* (HEC).

NNI case: The first 12 bits are the *virtual path identifier* (VPI), the following 16 bits the *virtual channel identifier* (VCI), the next 3 bits are the *payload type identifier* (PTI), one bit is the *cell loss priority* (CLP), and the last octet is used for *header error control* (HEC).

The ATM functionality is organized in a stack of layers, each layer assigned to its specific functions. All layers deal with *control* and *management* issues. This is known as the *ATM reference model* (Fig. 3.27).

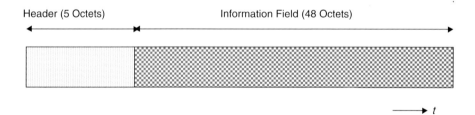

Figure 3.25 53-octet ATM cell format.

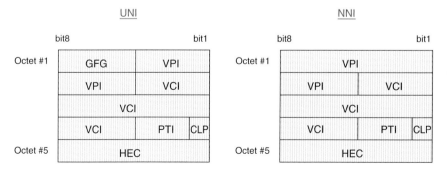

Figure 3.26 ATM cell header — definition of UNI and NNI.

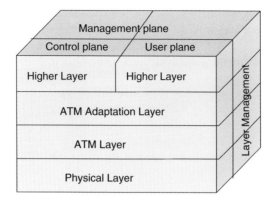

Figure 3.27   ATM cell reference model.

- The *physical layer* layer deals with issues related to physical connectivity of the transmission medium and transmission of the ATM cells.
- The *ATM layer* deals with flow issues of the ATM cells.
- The *ATM adaptation layer* (AAL) deals with the assembly of a continuous data bit stream in ATM cells.
- Above these layers are higher layers and the application layers.

ATM is designed to provide a variety of services:

- *constant bit rate* (CBR)
- *variable bit rate* (VBR)
- *real-time VBR* (rt-VBR)
- *non-real time VBR* (nrt-VBR)
- *available bit rate* (ABR)
- *undefined bit rate* (UBR)

A call is established following a protocol known as call admission control (CAC). Although a path is established during CAC, the physical path may not remain the same for the duration of the call. The actual path (or route) may change based on bandwidth availability and priority of service.

3.6.6   Quality of Service

Quality of service (QoS) pertains to a set of parameters negotiated and agreed upon between the end user and the service provider. However, in order for QoS parameters to have meaning, they must be measurable, negotiable or improvable, controllable, and guaranteed. This implies that QoS parameters have threshold values and lower and upper bounds. Such parameters are bandwidth, latency, packet loss, and jitter.

In ATM networks, QoS relates to cell integrity and cell flow parameters, such as *cell loss*, *cell delay*, and *cell delay variation*. From a node point of view, QoS is closely related to bandwidth (BW) utilized as compared to BW available.

When a connection is established based on a service level agreement (SLA), the user expects that and the service provider promises that the agreed upon QoS parameters will be honored. However, the QoS parameters are closely linked to potential errors. Therefore, it is logical that the "standard" negotiable QoS parameters for a connection be expressed in terms of errors.

Semantic transparency determines the capability of the network to transport information from source to destination with an acceptable error rate. Some of the potential errors are:

- Errors pertaining to transmission are the *bit error rate* (BER) and *packet error rate* (PER).
- Errors pertaining to accuracy are the *cell misinsertion rate* (CMR) and *cell error ratio* (CER).
- Error pertaining to dependability is the *cell loss rate* (CLR).
- Errors pertaining to speed are the *cell transfer delay* (CTD) and *cell delay variation* (CDV).

Finally, QoS defines more detailed parameters, which, although of interest, are beyond the scope of this book. However, we hope that it has become clear that QoS is an important issue and extremely difficult to be implemented in an all-optical DWDM system and network, and this is discussed again in more detail at the end of this book.

3.7 SONET AND SDH

In the 1980s, the deployment of the optical fiber in high-speed, low-cost communications led to the standard *Synchronous Optical NETwork* (SONET) in the United States and the *synchronous digital hierarchy* (SDH) in Europe. Since then, SONET/SDH has by and large established the optical network of choice.

SONET, as well as SDH, is defined for synchronous networks and is a set of standard interfaces in an optical synchronous network elements (NE) that conform to these interfaces. These interfaces define all layers, from the physical layer to the applications layer.

The SONET/SDH network consists of nodes or network elements (NE) that are interconnected with fiber cable. SONET network elements may receive signals from a variety of facilities such as DS1, DS3, ATM, Internet, LAN/MAN/WAN, and of course SONET. They may also receive signals from a variety of network topologies such as rings or trees, for example, LAN at 10 Mbps, 100 Mbps, or higher (Gb/s). However, SONET network elements must have a proper interface to convert (or emulate) the incoming data format into the SONET format.

Although SONET and SDH substantially overlap, they also differ somewhat. Some of the similarities are:

- bit rates and frame format organization
- frame synchronization schemes
- multiplexing and demultiplexing rules
- error control

Some of the major differences are:

- By and large, the definition of overhead bytes is very similar; some variations have been introduced to accommodate differences between U.S. and European communications nodes and networks.
- SDH photonic interface specifies more parameters than SONET does.
- SONET and SDH standards have enough minor differences (technical and linguistic, i.e., terminology) that adds enough complexity (and cost) in their design (HW & SW).

3.7.1   SONET Topologies

SONET technology is predominantly defined for the ring with add-drop topology, also applicable in long-haul point-to-point topology.

The ring topology consists of network elements (NE) interconnected with a dual fiber, the primary fiber and the secondary fiber. One or more NEs on the ring may be assigned the function of communicating with other rings or topologies. When one of the two fibers breaks, the other fiber in the ring is used. This mechanism provides transmission protection and ring restoration capabilities. If both fibers break, then the network reconfigures itself to form a ring using both the primary fiber and the secondary fiber. Thus, the ring topology offers fast path protection. All NEs on the ring include add-drop functionality, similar to add-drop functionality discussed in Chapter 2.

The point-to-point topology provides an "express" source to destination connectivity. However, there typically are add-drop multiplexers in between to either terminate or detour a fraction of the total traffic.

3.7.2   SONET and SDH Rates

SONET and SDH rates are defined in a range from 51.85 Mb/s up to 39,813.12 Mb/s or OC-768 (almost 40 Gb/s); higher rates are under study. In long haul, transporting SONET OC-192 (or SDH STM-64) signals at 10 Gb/s over single-mode fiber is currently a mature technology and the most popular rate. As a result the cost of a 10 Gb/s termination has dropped within 3 to 4 years by almost $4,000. However, as bandwidth demand increases, OC-768 signals at 40 Gb/s over single-mode fiber and for 100 km spans (without amplification) are readily available. At 40 Gb/s, half a million simultaneous telephone conversations can be transmitted.

An electrical SONET signal is known as *synchronous transport signal-level N* (STS-N). The SDH equivalent is known as *synchronous transport module-level N* (STM-N). After its conversion to optical level, it is known as *optical carrier-level N* (OC-N). In SONET, N takes the values 1, 3, 12, 48, 192, and 768, with corresponding bit rates at 51.84, 155.52, 622.08, 2,488.32, 9,953.28, and 39,813.12 Mbps, and in SDH the values 0, 1, 4, 16, 64, and 256 (see Table 3.2). That is, the SONET or SDH bit rates are prefixed, and there is no further bandwidth elasticity whatsoever (this is contrasted with DWDM in Chapters 4 and 5).

3.7.3   SONET and SDH Frames

The smallest SONET frame is visualized as a two-dimensional matrix of 9-row by 90-column bytes; this is known as an *STS-1 frame* (Fig. 3.28), thus containing a total

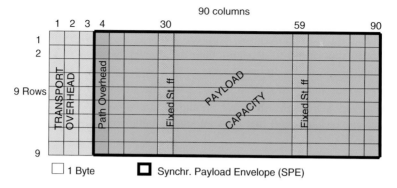

Figure 3.28 SONET STS-1 frame structure.

of 810 bytes. The first 3 columns of the STS-1 frame contain the *transport overhead*, which is overhead pertaining to section and line and the remaining 87 columns. The remaining columns, from column 4 to column 90 (included), contain *path overhead* and *end user data*, known as the *synchronous payload envelope* (SPE). Path overhead information is in column 4 of the STS-1 frame (the first of the SPE). Moreover, two SPE columns (column 30 and 59 of the STS-1) do not contain any information and are known as "fixed stuff." Thus, the actual (end user data) *payload capacity* is 84 columns (or 756 bytes) at an effective 48.384 Mbps bit rate.

STS-1 frames are transmitted consecutively (i.e., when one ends the next one starts). Bytes are transmitted serially, starting with the most significant bit of the byte in column 1 and row 1 and ending with the last byte in row 9 and column 90. At the end of the frame, the process continues with the next frame and so on (Fig. 3.29). A complete STS-1 frame of 6,480 bits is transmitted in 125 μsec. Multiplying 6,480 bits per frame by 8,000 frames per second, one obtains the *OC-1 rate* of 51.84 Mbps.

User payload is mapped in SPE in a hierarchical and organized manner. For example, the SPE is organized such that only one of several sizes of blocks of columns, known as virtual tributaries, may be used (Fig. 3.30). A three-column VT is known as VT1.5, a 4-column as VT2, a six-column as VT3, and a 12-column as VT6.

Clearly, a number of VTs may fit in a SPE. However, VTs are mapped in larger containers known as groups; a SPE fits seven groups each of 12 columns. Thus, in a

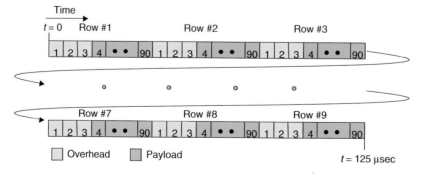

Figure 3.29 SONET STS-1 frame unfolded.

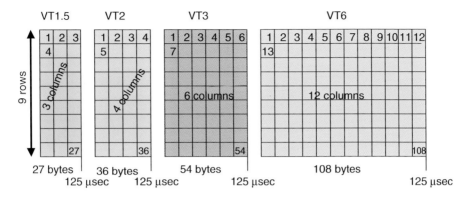

Figure 3.30 Allowable virtual tributaries in SONET.

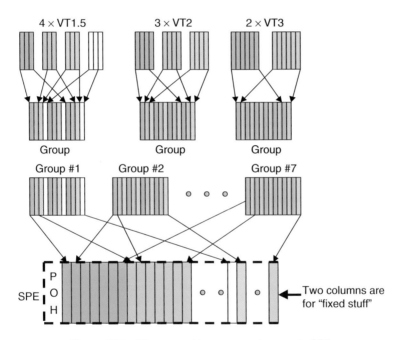

Figure 3.31 VTs mapped in groups and groups in SPE.

group either four VT1.5s, or three VT2s, or two VT3s, or one VT6 fit. Figure 3.31 illustrates the process of mapping of VTs in groups and seven groups in a SPE.

A VT, according to its size, defines a maximum bit rate for a client's payload. For example, a VT1.5 contains 27 bytes transmitted in 125 μsecs, and therefore the bit rate can be up to 1.728 Mb/s. One can easily calculate bit rates for the remaining VTs, as listed in Table 3.3.

SDH does not specify a frame similar to SONET STS-1. However, it specifies a payload container as small as the SONET SPE (Fig. 3.32). The smallest SDH payload container is visualized as a two-dimensional matrix of 9 rows by 87 columns, known as *virtual container-3* (VC-3). The VC-3 contains a column for path overhead, called

Table 3.3 Virtual tributaries and payload rates

VT Type	Columns/VT	Bytes/VT	VT Payload Rate (Mbps)
VT1.5	3	27	1.728
VT2	4	36	2.304
VT3	6	54	3.456
VT6	12	108	6.912

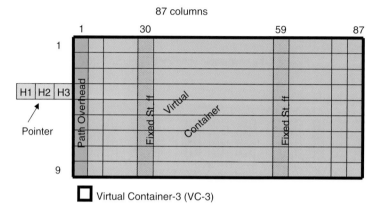

Figure 3.32 SDH AU-3 frame format structure.

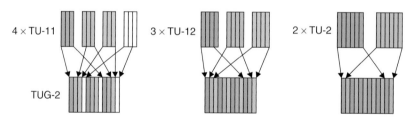

Figure 3.33 SDH TU and TUG structures.

the VC-3 path overhead (VC-3 POH) and two fixed stuff columns. Thus, the actual *payload capacity* in a VC-3 is 84 columns (or 756 bytes), as in the SONET case.

Similar to VTs and groups that are mapped in a SONET SPE, so are AU-3 (administration units) TUGs (tributary unit groups), and TUG TUs (tributary units) mapped in SDH (Fig. 3.33).

At the VC-3 and in the fourth row, three additional bytes are added for the VC-3 pointer (H1, H2, and H3). The end result, VC-3 and pointer, comprise an *administrative unit level-3* (AU-3). When three such AU-3s are byte-multiplexed, the end result is an *administrative unit group* (AUG).

Note: SDH frames contain the same number of bits as their corresponding SONET frames, and they are also transmitted in 125 ms; thus the bit rate is the same (see Table 3.2).

In theory, any type of non-SONET signal may be transformed (or mapped) into SONET following a *hierarchical* process. From a high-level point of view, this process starts with partitioning (or segmenting) the signal and mapping the segments into small containers known as *virtual tributaries* (VT). Once the VTs have been filled with segmented payloads, they are grouped into larger containers that are known as *groups*, and these are mapped in what is called a SONET frame. Many contiguous frames comprise the SONET signal, which is transmitted to an optical transducer, or the optical transmitter, over the OC-N fiber (Fig. 3.34).

In SDH, the same process follows. However, virtual tributaries are called *tributary units* (TU), and the groups are called *tributary unit group* (TUG).

3.7.4 Floating Frames and Pointers

When the end user data are mapped in the SPE, it is not necessarily in phase with the STS-1 frame; that is, the customer equipment and the system clocks are out of phase. To eliminate the phase difference the data should be buffered, but this means additional cost and, more important, more delay. Therefore, the method of a floating SPE and a pointer in the overhead space was adopted. Typically, a floating SPE will cross the boundary of two consecutive frames (Fig. 3.35).

3.7.5 Overhead Definition

As SONET/SDH frames move from node to node, certain operations take place to ensure both deliverability and integrity of the signal. This means that additional

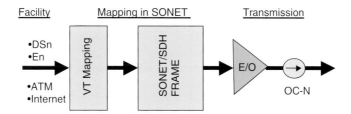

Figure 3.34   SONET hierarchy.

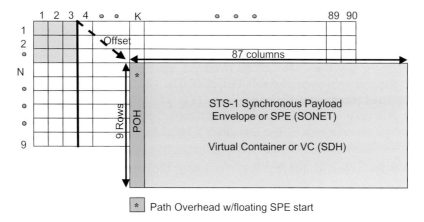

Figure 3.35   SONET STS-1 with floating SPE.

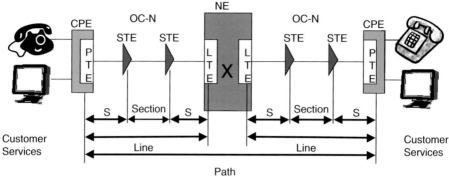

CPE = Customer Premises Equipment
LTE = Line Terminating Equipment
PTE = Path Terminating Equipment
STE = Section Terminating Equipment
NE = Network Element

Figure 3.36 Responsibilities of section, line, and path in SONET.

information (bits), or overhead bits, must be added to customer data for network administration purposes. This is equivalent to a letter packed in a postal bag on which additional information (labels) is added; this bag may also be enclosed in a larger container with more labels on it. This overhead information is *transparent* to the end user.

Overhead has been organized hierarchically into the following three administrative sectional responsibilities (Fig. 3.36):

- The path overhead deals with path terminating equipment (PTE) and is terminated by the receiving PTE.

- The line overhead deals with line terminating equipment (LTE) and is terminated by the receiving LTE.

- The section overhead deals with equipment terminating a physical segment of the transmission facility, such as a segment between two repeaters, or a LTE and a repeater, or a PTE and a repeater, or a LTE and a LTE without repeaters.

3.7.5.1 SONET

In SONET, the first three rows of the overhead space in an STS-1 frame carry synchronization and section overhead information. The very first two bytes of the frame contain a fixed pattern, 0xF628 or in binary 1111 0110 0010 1000, known as A1 and A2 (Fig. 3.37). This pattern is tracked by the receiver to find the beginning of the frame and thus synchronize with it. The remaining 7 bytes in this overhead section are:

- C1 is the STS-1 ID and is defined for each STS-1.

- B1 is used for error monitoring.

- E1 is a 64-Kbps voice communication channel for craft personnel.

- F1 is used by the section.

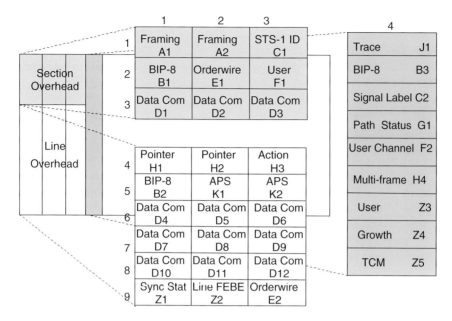

Figure 3.37   STS-1 section, line and path overhead.

- D1 to D3 constitutes a 192-Kbps communication channel between STEs for alarms, maintenance, control, monitoring, administration, and other communication needs.

The remaining rows in the overhead space of an STS-1 frame (rows 4 to 9) carry line overhead information:

- H1 and H2 define the offset between pointer and first payload byte in the SPE space.
- H3 defines an action byte for frequency justification purposes. It contains payload if the justification is negative.
- BIP-8 is used for locating errors.
- K1 and K2 are for automatic protection switching.
- D4 to D12 constitute a 576-Kbps communication channel (also known as DCC) between LTEs for alarms, maintenance, control, operations, administration, monitoring, provisioning (known as OAM&P), and other communication needs.
- Z1 and Z2 are not defined.
- E2 is an express 64 Kbps communications channel between LTEs.

Recently, the terms *SONET-lite* and *SONET-like* have been used in the telecommunications industry. Either of these two terms is an attempt to describe a simplified SONET by removing overhead complexity and relaxing jitter tolerance specifications. This simplification frees overhead bytes (part of the DCC) that can be used for data transport at the expense of interoperability and maintainability that the DCC provide.

3.7.5.2 SDH

In SDH overhead, the first three rows are called the regenerator section overhead (RSOH), the fourth row is called the administrative unit pointer, and the remaining five rows are called the multiplex section overhead (MSOH). The first two bytes of the RSOH contain a fixed pattern, known as A1 and A2 (as in SONET). This pattern, 0xF628 or in binary "1111 0110 0010 1000", marks the start of frame.

3.7.6 Frequency Justification

When the data rate (data to be mapped in SPE) is the same as that of the system clock, the offset due to a phase difference is the same as the previous frame and the alignment of the SPE remains constant. This is known as *no justification*. When the frame rate is less than that of the clock, the alignment of the SPE slips back by a byte. This is known as *positive justification*. When the frame rate of the STS SPE is higher than the transport OH (i.e., NE), the alignment is advanced by a byte. This is known as *negative justification*.

3.7.7 Path Overhead

The first column of the SPE (9 bytes) is dedicated to path overhead information; this overhead is terminated by (path) end equipment (PTE) only. The path overhead has a directional meaning (i.e., from the originating PTE to the terminating PTE).

These bytes are known as J1, B3, C2, G1, F2, H4, Z3, Z4, and Z5.

- J1 verifies the connectivity with the transmitting PTE.
- B3, or BIP-8, is used for error control.
- C2, or signal label, indicates how the SPE was constructed.
- G1, or path status, indicates the status and performance of the terminating PTE.
- F2, or user channel, is allocated for end user communication purposes.
- H4, or multiframe, is a generalized pointer.
- Z3, Z4 and Z5 are reserved for future use.

3.7.8 Maintenance

Maintenance in all communications systems and networks is a complex, comprehensive, and important function that defines criteria to maintain the NE and the network operation at an acceptable performance level. Maintenance in SONET/SDH is particularly important because many of the concepts and mechanisms developed for it are also used in DWDM systems and networks. Therefore, a comprehensive understanding of this subject is helpful in the understanding of DWDM maintenance issues.

In SONET/SDH, maintenance requirements include *alarm surveillance*, *performance monitoring* (PM), testing, and control to perform maintenance tasks such as:

- trouble monitoring and detection
- trouble or repair verification
- trouble sectionalization
- trouble isolation

- testing
- restoration

Alarm surveillance deals with monitoring, detection, and reporting of degraded or abnormal conditions (failure states) in the network. Network element alarm surveillance takes place at different levels: section (STE), line (LTE), STS path (STS PTE), and VT path (VT PTE). A VT PTE contains all the functionality of a STE, LTE, and STS PTE.

Failure states are conditions that require detection. A network element enters a failure state when a failure condition has been detected; it exits a failure state when the failure condition has been corrected. A *failure* is a persistent defect. A *defect* is a limited interruption in the ability of an item to perform a required function, and an *anomaly* is a discrepancy between the actual and desired characteristics of an item, it may or may not affect the ability of an item to perform a required function.

When failure states are detected, an *alarm indication signal* (AIS) is immediately or subsequently constructed and transmitted to the next NE. There are STS path, VT path, and DSn AIS signals. The sequence of AIS events is:

- When a STE receives an invalid signal, it sends downstream an AIS-line alarm.
- When a LTE receives an invalid signal or an AIS-L and it is unable to protect the line, it sends an STS path AIS downstream.
- When a STS PTE receives either an invalid signal or an STS path AIS, it propagates the appropriate AIS downstream.
- When a VT PTE receives either a VT path AIS or an invalid signal, it generates the appropriate AIS downstream.

The response to AIS is a *remote defect indication* (RDI) signal; RDI signals are sent upstream to alert the network and to initiate trunk conditioning. Alarm states and RDI are coordinated between source and sink to restore service. There are STS path, VT path, and DSn RDI signals. These automatic service management processes are initiated and maintained for the duration of the failure.

Performance monitoring (PM) sets the rules for in-service monitoring of the transmission quality. SDH PM is based on counting errored blocks in a second. SONET PM is based on counting code violations in a second.

SONET NE performance monitoring includes:

- detection of transmission degradation
- deviations from performance parameters
- communication with OSs

NEs are required to accumulate a variety of performance monitoring (PM) parameters for a section, line, STS path, or VT path layer entity. A NE should provide the following accumulation and storage registers:

- one current 15-minute
- one current day
- one previous 15 minute

- one previous day
- 31 recent 15-minute

Testing deals with procedures to isolate a failure to a replaceable or repairable entity. This is achieved by:

- maintenance tools in the SONET signal
- test access; nonintrusive/intrusive monitoring
- diagnostics; HW/SW, routine/on-demand
- loopbacks; terminal/facility LB

Moreover, PM parameters at various path layers and parameter registers are defined in SONET/SDH, which, although of interest, are beyond the scope of this book. However, we hope that it has become clear that maintenance (*alarm surveillance* and *performance monitoring*) as defined for SONET/SDH is extremely difficult to be implemented in an all-optical DWDM system and network.

3.7.9 Operations Communications Interface

The requirements for the *SONET operations communication interface* (SOCI) are based on the requirements specified in GR-828-CORE. SOCI utilizes a common set of 7-layer OSI protocol:

- physical layer
- data link layer
- network layer
- transport layer
- session layer
- presentation layer
- applications layer

At the physical (PHY) layer:

- OS/NE: NEs shall support the PHY layer requirements of the TP4/CNLS Protocol Case (GR-828-CORE).
- NE/NE-LAN: The PHY layer shall support a 10BASE-T and 10BASE2 (see GR-253-CORE for standards).
- NE/NE-DCC: The section DCC is a 192-Kbps channel that is carried in section overhead bytes D1, D2, D3 of the first STS-1 in an STS-N signal. Section DCC shall be used as the PHY layer of the message-oriented EOC.

At the data link (DL) layer:

- OS/NE: NEs shall support the DL layer requirements of the TP4/CNLS Protocol Case.
- NE/NE-LAN: Media access control (MAC) carrier sense multiple access/collision detection (CSMA/CD), logical link control (LLC) class 1, type 1, and LSAP (0xFE) shall be as specified by standards.

- NE/NE-DCC: The data link layer protocol shall be based on link access protocol D-channel (LAPD) as specified by standards. Both unacknowledged information transfer service (UITS) and acknowledged information transfer service (AITS) shall be supported. The SAPI value shall be preassigned and shall be settable locally or remotely by an OS (see GR-253-CORE for standards).

At the network layer:

- OS/NE & NE/NE: TP4 runs over the connectionless network layer protocol (CLNP).
- NE/NE-LAN & DCC: The network layer protocol for DCCs and LANs shall be CLNP as specified in ISO 8473, and subnetwork dependant convergence function (SNDCF) as specified by same (1988, Add 3). The ISO 8473 category 3 QoS shall be supported.

At the transport network layer:

- OS/NE & NE/NE: Class 4 of ISO 8073 (Add 2, TP4) shall be supported.

At the session layer:

- OS/NE & NE/NE: The ISO session layer shall be supported.

At the presentation layer:

- OS/NE & NE/NE: The ISO presentation layer shall be supported.

At the applications layer:
ACSE: The *application control service element* shall be supported.

- ROSE/CMISE: SONET NEs shall support
  ○ Real-time operation system element/common management information service element (ROSE/CMISE) as specified by GR-828-CORE.
  ○ The TMN application context, defined in CCITT M3100 Section 10, shall be used.
- FTAM: SONET NEs shall support file transfer and access method (FTAM) when file-oriented applications are supported.
- TL1: SONET NEs, on an interim basis, may support TL1.

3.7.10 Interworking

Based on supported protocols and messages, there are several interworking cases between OSs and NEs in SONET/SDH:

- TL1/X.25[OS]-TL1/OSI [SONET]
  ○ SONET LAN interworking: TL1 messages are sent between OS and a SONET NE using an intrasite LAN.

- ○ SONET DCC Interworking: TL1 messages are sent between OS and a SONET NE using a DCC network.

- ○ SONET LAN and DCC Interworking: TL1 messages are sent between OS and a SONET NE using a DCC network and an intrasite LAN.

- TL1/X.25[OS]-CMISE/OSI[SONET]

  - ○ SONET LAN and/or DCC interworking: TL1 messages are sent by OSs and CMISE messages are sent by NEs.

3.7.11   Next-Generation SONET

Next-generation SONET is a simplified modification (of the existing SONET) to support provisioning of multiservices, Ethernet, ATM, and frame relay in a cost-effective manner. Be it so, it still conforms to the same bit rates, structure, and switching for VT and protection. Because it supports multiservices, a separate circuit and different switching fabric type are required for each service type.

Currently, some vendors associate next-generation SONET with the multiservice provisioning platform (MSPP), and others define each one differently. As soon as a standard is defined, we will know for sure what the commonalities are. The key point here is that there is a serious effort to define a next-generation simplified version of the existing SONET to address a multiplicity of services in a more cost-effective manner.

3.8   INTERNET

The Internet technology evolved over a few decades, even though it has been commercially deployed at an explosive rate within the last few years. This technology emerged from a need to transfer data files over the communications network inexpensively, and yet it was built on a foundation that did not require switched services (so that connectivity was not charged based on a long-distance call basis). This was made possible with the Internet protocol (IP), which does not establish over the network a fixed (switched) path, which is continuously dedicated during the session. Instead, it assembles packets and by a store-and-forward process takes advantage of available bandwidth resources and delivers the packets over one or more dynamically changing routes. Doing so, there is no guarantee that all packets would arrive at their destination in the same order they were generated (what would the end result have been if these packets belonged to one picture?). Therefore, for efficient transmission of packets, all data devices on the network were assigned an individual address; special devices kept lists of device addresses; and the packet included the source and the destination address, as well as a packet sequence number, among other overhead information. Figure 3.38 illustrates on a high level how data have been partitioned and additional overhead bytes added based on the seven-layer OSI model.

Based on this, the Internet (described in RFC791) specification, is a connectionless technology, which is developed to provide a best-effort delivery, but it does not guarantee delivery of a packet or a timely delivery of it. Perhaps many have experienced overt delays and delivery suspension halfway through downloading. Nevertheless, the Internet still provides an economical delivery system of data, and this is why it has reached all businesses and most homes globally. In addition, Internet software is included

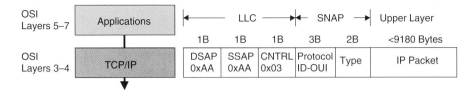

Figure 3.38   Internet protocol and OSI layers.

(almost free) with every personal computer, and other promotional offers (free services and discounts on purchases) have done a remarkably stimulating job.

The sophistication of IP is continuously evolving (each version is designated by a subscript number, as in IP_{v6}, meaning IP version 6) to offer more sophisticated services, such as restoration and real-time aspects so that voice and real-time compressed video may be transmitted over the Internet network; for this, routing information no longer relies on only a single source but it can be obtained from different sources, including multiple protocols. However, since all sources are not equal, there is a *trust rate* assigned to each. Clearly, the most sophisticated source will have the highest trust rate, such as a *directly connected interface* or a *manually entered static routing*, and the least sophisticated source, such as an *internal border gateway protocol*, will have the lowest trust rate.

It is not surprising that the highest trusted rate source starts to look very similar to traditional communications practices. As a consequence, encapsulated Internet has been deployed in "several forms" in the optical network, such as, for example "Internet over SONET," "Internet over ATM over SONET," and so on, and there also is work to define a standard optical-Internet, which, although it sounds like SONET (maintaining SONET bit rates of 10 and 40 Gb/s), it is not. In this venue, optical-Internet will offer QoS and SLA attributes comparable to those of ATM and frame relay. Moreover, the plan is to define virtual private lines (VPL), offering customers service flexibility, granularity, scalability, shared access, point-to-multipoint, customized bit rates, and easy service migration.

In the following two sections, we mention two evolving Internet technologies, voice over the Internet and fax over the Internet. We do not discuss other technologies such as wireless Internet and so on.

3.8.1   Voice over IP

Voice communication has been the centerpiece business of traditional synchronous transport networks. Because of the huge business opportunity and economic benefit, AT&T, NTT, Siemens, Alcatel, and the like grew to empire-size companies, occa-sionally employing up to 1 million people. However, because of the opportunity and prosperity, basic research brought about the transistor and the computer, the radar, space travel, and so forth.

One of the paramount rules in telephony is pristine service. Service should be of the highest quality and available, even under disaster conditions, during a hurricane, during an electric power outage or blackout, or even when the telephone device was dropped on the floor. In fact, one of the tests that AT&T would perform was to ensure that its telephone devices would still be operational if the set fell from the table onto a concrete floor. However, this is changing.

With the advent of the Internet and its economic benefit, there is a serious effort to include phone service over the Internet. However, the current Internet specification, when drafted, did not have in mind real-time full-duplex service offerings, such as real-time telephony, despite the wishful thinking of many. However, this by no means implies that a future improved Internet cannot offer reliable and acceptable quality telephony or that it cannot offer half-duplex voice services, such as voice messaging and so on. It all depends on the protocol(s), the bandwidth, and the network. In this section, we examine the key challenges that can make this happen.

First, the Internet network must be telephony-aware; that is, it must exhibit a technological sophistication by which,

- Overall delays and network latency are minimized to an acceptable level, comparable to that of the traditional network.

- Lost packets should be compensated for and the rate of packet loss should remain below a threshold level commensurable with speech sample loss or burst error rate.

- The service must be reliable under extreme conditions, network and environmental, complying with the quality of service (QoS) subscribed to.

- The network should be managed in compliance with the American National Standards Institute, ANSI.1, with signaling network-management protocol (SNMP) V1 syntax, and other real-time protocols (RTP).

- It addresses synchronization, clock as well as jitter issues. The traditional network operates on a clock that is derived from an 8-KHz global master clock of extreme accuracy. Routers operate on their own local clock.

- It addresses echo cancellation. Echo is caused by signal reflections back to the speaker's ear. It becomes a significant problem when overall (round-trip) echo exceeds 50 msec.

- It addresses talker overlap. This is caused when one-way delay exceeds 250 msecs and when one talker steps on the other talker's speech.

- Voice compression algorithms with almost zero conversion delay to optimize bandwidth resource utilization.

- It forms "short" packets with almost zero insertion delay (the amount of buffer delay required to form packets).

- Call initiation and termination procedures, emulating call admission control or traditional telephony-signaling such as off-hook, on-hook, ringing, busy, and so on.

- Although an Internet telephone may be required, the telephone must be operable under extreme conditions.

3.8.2   Fax over IP (FoIP)

As a page is scanned, intonations on the scanned paper are encoded in a digital form; thus, fax data in their original form are digital. However, traditional fax machines convert the digital information into analog signals to transmit it over the public switched transport network (PSTN) using "switched services." This analog signal is again encoded to 64 Kb/s channel, thus committing a relatively disproportionate bandwidth in both directions (even if only one direction is fully used). In fact, the peak rate for a fax transmission is 14.4 Kb/s in one direction. Thus, fax would be more efficient if it were sent in pure digital form end-to-end over a unidirectional path, and packet networks (ATM, FR, IP) support this.

Two methods have been used to send fax: real-time and store-and-forward. The difference between these two methods lies in the actual time of delivery and the method of confirmation. In real-time, a fax is transmitted to the destination as soon as the send button is pressed. In store-and-forward, the contents of a document may be entered in memory, a timer is set, and the fax is sent later when the network transmission rates are lower. Clearly, these two methods correspond to two different urgency and priority levels. In fact, timing is an important issue in FoIP networks; excessive delay in FoIP may cause the timing to be skewed and result in loss of call, which impact QoS (ITU recommends that the FoIP protocol compensates for the loss of a fixed timing of messages so that the T.30 protocol operates without error).

As fax can be transmitted using switched services, fax can also be sent over other packet networks. In this respect, the Frame Relay Forum has defined a real-time protocol for the transmission of fax over frame relay (FoFR). ITU has defined the T.37 recommendation for store-and-forward FoIP and the T.38 for real-time FoIP. Furthermore, T.38 is selected for H.323.

3.8.3 ATM over SONET

There are three options to transport ATM traffic over SONET/SDH: *embedded* ATM transport, *hybrid* ATM transport, and *pure* ATM transport.

In embedded ATM over SONET, ATM cells are mapped in the SONET/SDH payload of an STS/STM frame, and the switching SONET/SDH network elements (NE) route a STS/STM. Clearly, these NEs require SONET/SDH traffic management only as ATM is embedded in the payload (Fig. 3.39; see also Fig. 3.40). However, in this case, the SONET payload is modified (Table 3.4).

In hybrid ATM transport, SDH/SONET (VT) traffic and ATM traffic are combined in the same SONET/SDH bearer over SONET/SDH tributaries. However, the network elements have visibility of the ATM cells. Network elements separate the SONET/SDH traffic from the ATM and route each one to corresponding switching fabric. After the two different traffics have been switched, they may be recombined to form a hybrid payload. Clearly, such network elements require both SONET/SDH and ATM traffic management.

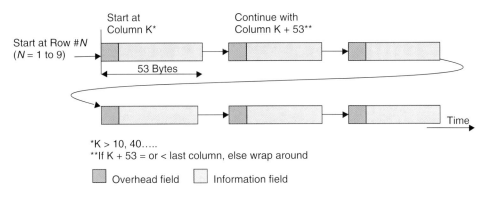

Figure 3.39 ATM over SONET cell mapping in SONET.

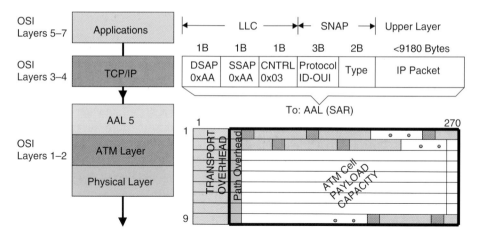

Figure 3.40 Mapping internet protocol over ATM.

Table 3.4 ATM over SONET overhead definition

OH Bytes	Coding	Definition
A1, A2	11110110,00101000	Framing bytes
C1	000000001-000000010-000000011	STS-1 Identifiers
B1	BIP-8	Section error monitoring (previous STS-3c)
B2	BIP-24 (STS-3c)	Line error monitoring
H1 (1–4)	0110 (norm), 1001 (act)	New data flag (change of pointer indication)
H1-H2 (7–16)	0000000000-1100001110	Pointer value (set to 1s for AIS)
H1*, H2*	10010011,11111111	Concatenation indication (set to 1s for AIS)
H3		pointer action (freq. Justification)
K2 (6–8)	111.110, any non-110 value	Line AIS, Line RDI, removal of line RDI
3rd Z2 byte (2–8)	B2 Error count	Line FEBE
J1		STS path trace
B3	BIP-8	Path error monitoring (previous SPE)
C2	00010011	Path signal level indicator
G1 (1–4)	B3 Error count	path FEBE
G1 (5)	0 or 1	Path RDI (also used to indicate loss of cell delin.)

*Defined at the UNI.

In pure ATM transport, all STS/STM traffic from a tributary is *circuit-emulated* into ATM cells. This is the reverse case of SONET/SDH over ATM. All circuit-emulated and pure ATM cells are then carried as ATM cells. Clearly, such NEs require only ATM traffic management.

For purposes of ATM mapping description, consider that ATM cells (5 bytes overhead and 48 bytes payload) arrive in a sequential order and that the first byte of a cell is aligned with the Kth column byte of the Nth row in the SONET PC. Note that the Kth column byte cannot be in the overhead space of the SONET frame (Fig. 3.31).

In SDH, ATM cells are also mapped contiguously row-wise in C11, C12, C3, or C4 containers. When the container transport capacity does not meet the ATM bandwidth, perhaps because the ATM bit rate is higher that the bandwidth of these containers, the ATM bandwidth may be split and use virtual or continuous concatenation.

3.8.4   IP over SONET

When IP packets reach the SONET network, a process should take place so that IP packets look like meaningful and recognizable payload to SONET. There are two ways to do this. The first is a two-step process; the other is more direct.

1. Partition IP packets (see Fig. 3.16) and convert in ATM cells; then map ATM cells in SONET (Fig. 3.40). Mapping ATM in SONET is discussed in the next section.

2. Directly write IP packets in the SONET payload and over contiguous SONET frames.

Clearly, in the first method, IP packets can be switched by SONET as well as by ATM switching systems. In the second method, they can be switched only by SONET. The North Carolina Network Initiative has adopted this method. The efficiency of each method depends on the actual route and the networks the IP packets cross.

Each case, however, has its own complexities; the destination of the IP packet must be read and translated in the destination code of ATM cells, and in either case using SONET procedures to set up the path.

3.9   OPTICAL NETWORKS

The classification "optical networks" is a misnomer. What it really means is that the interconnecting links of nodes that form a network are fiber, not copper or radio. Today there are no pure optical nodes (not yet), and thus current networks should be called "almost optical networks" or "first approximation optical networks." Nevertheless, this early title, even if not correct, provided the motivational springboard to research and industry to keep trying for more "optical" networks than before. Of course, the benefits of the fiber-network were soon realized, and it was not an accident that the industry funded a (double-digit) percentage of its profits in the research and development of optical components and better fiber.

The early deployment of fiber was point-to-point interconnecting links. In the mid-1980s the bit rate was low (by our standards). ODL-50 devices, for example, were 50-Mb/s optical transceivers. Soon thereafter, electronic switching systems with optical interfaces were developed based on nonstandard interfaces but were quickly withdrawn from the market because at the same time new optical standard interfaces emerged, the SONET in the United States and SDH in Europe. SONET/SDH standards have described synchronous transport of information based on dual optical rings that were proven to be reliable, real-time, and able to meet most of the communications needs in the late 1980s and 1990s, and thus they became ubiquitous. However, they were costly and did not meet the newly emerged needs in inexpensive data transport, which caused the Internet to boom.

Optical transport networks have been classified based on the link length as long-haul applicable to optical transport networks (>100 km), medium-haul applicable to metropolitan networks (<100 km), and short-haul applicable to access (<20 km). Each one is designed with different switching capacity, complexity, and bit rate on the medium, and each has its own cost structure; clearly, all that increases from short haul to long haul.

The specification of optical networks defined the best convenient optical carrier frequency, 1,310 nm, over standard single-mode fiber (SSMF), and a bandwidth scalability that came in fixed increments. For example, the SONET rates, OC-3, OC-12, and so on, were specific bit rates that could not be violated. Of course, this is one of the assurances for internetworking and vendor compatibility. One cannot imagine what a network would be if bit rates were chosen on the basis of convenience. However, this scalability provided an upper bound to transported bandwidth per fiber, which at the time were 10 Gb/s and now are 40 Gb/s. Further scalability was accomplished by utilizing two or more fibers, thus multiplying the total bandwidth. The model of adding fibers to increase the transportable bandwidth was good as long as it was one fiber or only a few fibers. The late 1990s, however, deemed this model insufficient. Because of an explosive bandwidth demand, optical networking companies were racing to install more fiber around the globe at a speculative projection that by "tomorrow" it might not be enough. Clearly, this frenzy required huge investments and presented an engineering nightmare. Thus, a new optical technology evolved and was known as DWDM.

3.10   WHAT IS A DWDM SYSTEM AND NETWORK?

Wavelength division multiplexing (WDM) is an optical technology that has opened up the fiber to more than one wavelength. Dense WDM (DWDM) is a technology with a potential number of wavelengths of more than 1,000 coupled into a fiber. According to this technology, many modulated wavelengths are coupled in the same fiber to increase the aggregate bandwidth per fiber. As an example, 40 wavelengths at 40 Gb/s each and in the same fiber raise the aggregate bandwidth to 1.6 Tb/s; this is 1.6 trillion bits in 1 second.

Several optical components have contributed to the realization of DWDM technology (see Chapter 2), including:

- Optical fiber with superior optical transmission performance over the wavelength spectrum of 1.3 nm and 1.55 nm, and fiber over the complete spectrum from 1.3 to 1.6 nm.

- Optical amplifiers over a wide range of spectrum to boost the optical signals, thus eliminating regenerators; this includes solid-state, doped fibers, and Raman amplifiers.

- Integrated solid-state optical components, such as filters, lasers, modulators, and others.

- Efficient solid-state cool lasers at high power levels for signal sources and pumps.

- Optical multiplexers and demultiplexers.
- Tunable devices (filters, lasers) for dynamic wavelength selectability.
- Optical add-drop multiplexers (OADM).
- Optical cross-connect (OXC) components, implemented with a variety of technologies and at a variety of sizes and switching speeds.
- Optical low-loss, small and smart connectors.
- Novel optical materials.
- New optical techniques to self-correct, modulate, equalize, and shape optical pulses, and to process optical information.

In DWDM, each optical channel represents a bit stream that is carried over a different modulated wavelength (λ_i). In principle, different DWDM channels may carry different bit rates and different services (e.g., voice, data, video, IP, ATM, SONET, etc.). As such, DWDM technology is application-transparent because wavelengths do not know or care about the type of payload and service provided. Think of DWDM as a track transporting color-coded boxes with no knowledge of the contents of each box; all it knows is where each colored box should be delivered. Thus, DWDM finds applications in ultrahigh bandwidth long haul, in very high speed metropolitan or innercity networks, at the edge of other networks (SONET, IP, ATM), as well as in the neighborhood (e.g., FTTH, FTTC). DWDM is also expected to become a low-cost technology in many other applications such as wireless (mobile) and fiber-to-the-desktop PC (FTTPC). Thus, it is not surprising that since the introduction of DWDM in 1997, the DWDM market grew from 1.7 billion at a compound annual growth rate of 84% over a period of four years, and that whereas the number of DWDM system-level vendors was 15 in 1999, it doubled to 30 in just one year. What will the market level be in the next five year? All analysts predict a skyrocketing market. And in my (biased) opinion, DWDM is "the optical solution" to a network with scalable bandwidth. Besides communications, DWDM technology will find a myriad of other applications such as parallel computation, medicine, photochemistry, space and remote sensing, entertainment, biochemistry, home appliances, toys, and many others.

So what is a DWDM network and system? This is the subject of the next two chapters.

EXERCISES

1. The DS0 bit rate is 64 kilobits per second. Explain why it is so.

2. Could we transmit violin music with high fidelity at 64 Kb/s? Explain why.

3. The DS3 rate is 44.736 Mb/s. How many DS0s are in a DS3 signal?

4. Consider a DS1 signal. This is the result of polling 24 DS0 signals, placing each in one of the 24 time slots in the DS1 signal, 8 bits each, and adding a framing bit. Consider that from the 24 potential DS0s, statistically only 16 at a time contain actual user data. Calculate the bit rate of the DS1 signal.

5. An Ethernet LAN operates based on the token ring method for collision detection. True or False?

6. An FDDI network is a local area network that support two fiber rings. True or False?

7. How long does it take to transmit:

   a. a DS-1 frame in a SONET frame?

   b. a DS-3 frame in a SONET frame?

8. We have user data in the following configurations: 3 VT1.5s, 4 VT3s, and 1 VT6 to be mapped in OC-1. How could they be mapped in the SPE?

9. A VT1.5 consists of 3 columns and 9 rows. How long does it take to transmit a VT1.5 in a:

   a. STS-1?

   b. STS-3?

10. Frequency justification is used in SONET to compensate for slight frequency differences between the network element and the incoming payload. True or False?

11. By voice over IP it is meant that voice is transmitted first and then IP. True or False?

12. By IP over SONET it is meant that SONET frames are transmitted over the Internet network. True or False?

REFERENCES

Books and Papers

1. S.V. Kartalopoulos, Emerging technologies at the dawn of the millennium, *IEEE Comm. Mag.*, vol. 39. no 11, Nov. 2001, pp. 22–26.
2. S.V. Kartalopoulos, Elastic bandwidth, *IEEE Circuits Devices Mag.*, vol. 18, no. 1, Jan. 2002, pp. 8–13.
3. C. Bisdikian, An overview of the Bluetooth wireless technology, *IEEE Comm. Mag.*, vol. 39, no. 12, Dec. 2001, pp. 86–94.
4. S.V. Kartalopoulos, *Understanding SONET/SDH and ATM Networks*, IEEE Press, New York, 1999.
5. S.V. Kartalopoulos, *Introduction to DWDM Technology: Data in a Rainbow*, IEEE Press, New York, 2000.
6. S.V. Kartalopoulos, *Fault Detectability in DWDM: Toward Higher Signal Quality and System Reliability*, IEEE Press, New York, 2001.
7. J.A.C. Bingham, Multicarrier modulation for data transmission: an idea whose time has come, *IEEE Comm. Mag.*, vol. 28, no. 5, May 1990, pp. 5–14.
8. E.B. Carne, *Telecommunications Primer*, Prentice-Hall PTR, 1995.
9. N. Dagdeviren, et al., Global networking with ISDN, *IEEE Comm. Mag.*, June 1994, pp. 26–32.
10. J.R. Freer, *Computer Communications and Networks*, IEEE Press, New York, 1996.
11. R. Handel and M.N. Huber, *Integrated Broadband Network*, Addison Wesley, 1991.
12. G. Hawley, ADSL data: the next generation, *Telephony*, Aug. 12, 1996, pp. 24–29.

13. R.D. Gitlin, J.F. Hayes, and S.B. Weinstein, *Data Communications Principles*, Plenum, New York, 1992.

14. G.H. Im and J.J. Werner, Bandwidth-efficient digital transmission over unshielded twisted pair wiring, *IEEE J. Select. Areas Comm.*, vol. 13, no. 9, Dec. 1995, pp. 1643–1655.

15. R.E. Matick, *Transmission Lines for Digital and Communication Networks*, IEEE Press, New York, 1995.

16. S.V. Kartalopoulos, Global multi-satellite networks, Proceedings of IEEE ICC'97, June 1997, Montreal, Canada.

17. S.V. Kartalopoulos, "Temporal Fuzziness in Communications Systems", WCCI'94, ICNN, Orlando, FLA, July 2, 1994

18. S.V. Kartalopoulos, "A Manhattan Fiber Distributed Data Interface Architecture", Globecom'90, San Diego, December 2–5, 1990.

19. S.V. Kartalopoulos, "A Manhattan Street Network with Loop Architecture", U.S. Patent No. 5,289,467, 1994.

20. S.V. Kartalopoulos, "Disaster Avoidance in the Manhattan Fiber Distributed Data Interface Network", Globecom'93, Houston, TX, December 2, 1993.

21. S.V. Kartalopoulos, A time compression multiplexing system for a circuit switched digital capability, *IEEE Trans. Comm.*, vol. Com-30, no. 9, Sept. 1982, pp. 2046–2052.

22. S.V. Kartalopoulos, "A Loop Access System for a Circuit Switched Digital Capability", ISSLS'82., Toronto, Canada, Sept. 20–24, 1982.

23. S.V. Kartalopoulos, A Plateau of Performance? (guest editorial), *IEEE Comm. Mag.*, Sept. 1992, pp. 13–14.

24. S.V. Kartalopoulos, "Signal Processing and Implementation of Motion Detection Neurons in Optical Pathways", Globecom'90, San Diego, Dec. 2–5, 1990.

25. S.V. Kartalopoulos, "Micro-computers in Real-Time Processing of Information", 23rd Midwest Symposium on Circuits and Systems", Toledo, OH, Aug 4–5, 1980.

26. S.V. Kartalopoulos, *Understanding Neural Networks and Fuzzy Logic*, IEEE Press, New York, 1995.

27. K. Maxwell, Asymmetric digital subscriber line: interim technology for the next forty years, *IEEE Comm. Mag.*, Oct. 1996, pp. 100–106.

28. W. Goralski, *ADSL and DSL Technologies*, McGraw-Hill, New York, 1998.

29. Members of the Technical Staff, *Transmission Systems for Communications*, Bell Telephone Laboratories, 1982.

30. J. Nellist, *Understanding Telecommunications and Lightwave Systems*, IEEE Press, New York, 1996.

31. B. Petri and D. Schwetje, Narrowband ISDN and broadband ISDN service and network interworking, *IEEE Comm. Mag.*, June 1996, pp. 84–89.

32. S.U.H. Qureshi, Adaptive equalization, *Proc. IEEE*, vol. 73, no. 9, Sept. 1985, pp. 1349–1386.

33. W.D. Reeve, *Subscriber Loop Signaling and Transmission Handbook*, IEEE Press, New York, 1995.

34. W. Stallings, *Local Networks: An Introduction*, Macmillan Publishing Co., New York, 1987.

35. D.G. Cunningham and W.G. Lane, *Gigabit Ethernet Networking*, Macmillan Technical Publishing, 1999.

36. J.C. Collins, J. Dunn, P. Emer, and M. Johnson, Data express, gigabit junction with the next-generation Internet, *IEEE Spectrum*, pp. 18–25, February 1999.

STANDARDS

1. ADSL Forum TR-001, "ADSL forum system reference model," 1996.

2. ANSI/IEEE 812-1984, "Definition of terms relating to fiber optics."

3. CCITT Recommendation I.371, "Traffic control and resource management in B-ISDN."

4. IEEE 802.1 to 802.6, Standards on local area networks.

5. IEEE 802.3ab, 1000BASET.

6. IEEE/ANSI Std 802.4, "Token ring access method," 1985.

7. IEEE/ANSI Std 802.2, "Token-passing bus access method," 1985.

8. ITU-T Recommendation G.701, "Vocabulary of digital transmission and multiplexing, and pulse code modulation (PCM) terms," 1993.

9. ITU-T Recommendation G.702, "Digital hierarchy bit rates," 1988.

10. ITU-T Recommendation G.704, "Synchronous frame structures used at 1544, 6312, 2048, 8488 and 44736 Kbps hierarchical levels," 1995.

11. ITU-T Recommendation G.711, "Pulse code modulation (PCM) of voice frequencies," 1988.

12. ITU-T Recommendation G.726, "40, 32, 24, 16 Kbps adaptive differential pulse code modulation (ADPCM)," 1990.

13. ITU-T Recommendation G.731, "Primary PCM multiplex equipment for voice frequencies," 1988.

14. ITU-T Recommendation G.732, "Characteristics of primary PCM multiplex equipment operating at 2048 Kbps," 1988.

15. ITU-T Recommendation G.733, "Characteristics of primary PCM multiplex equipment operating at 1544 Kbps," 1988.

16. ITU-T Recommendation G.734, "Characteristics of synchronous digital multiplex equipment operating at 1544 Kbps," 1988.

17. ITU-T Recommendation G.736, "Characteristics of synchronous digital multiplex equipment operating at 2048 Kbps," 1993.

18. ITU-T Recommendation G.741, "General considerations on second order multiplex equipments," 1988.

19. ITU-T Recommendation G.805, "General functional architecture of transport networks," Nov. 1995.

20. ITU-T Recommendation I.113, "Vocabulary of terms for broadband aspects of ISDN."

21. ITU-T Recommendation I.121, "Broadband aspects of ISDN."

22. ITU-T Recommendation I.211, "B-ISDN service aspects."

23. ITU-T Recommendation I.311, "B-ISDN general network aspects."

24. ITU-T Recommendation I.321, "B-ISDN protocol reference model and its application."

25. ITU-T Recommendation I.327, "B-ISDN network functional requirements."

26. ITU-T Recommendation I.371, "Traffic control and congestion control in B-ISDN."

27. ITU-T Recommendation I.413, "B-ISDN user–network interface."

28. ITU-T Recommendation I.432, "B-ISDN user–network interface—physical layer specification."

29. ITU-T Recommendation I.580, "General arrangements for interworking between B-ISDN and 64 Kb/s based ISDN," Dec. 1994.

30. ITU-T Recommendation I.610, "OAM principles of B-ISDN access."

31. ITU-T Recommendation Q.931, "ISDN UNI layer 3 specification for basic call control," 1993.

32. Telcordia,* GR-1110-CORE, "Broadband switching system (BSS) generic requirements," 1995.

33. Telcordia, GR-1111-CORE, "Broadband access signaling (BAS) generic requirements," 1995.

34. Telcordia, GR-1112-CORE, "Broadband ISDN UNI and NNI physical criteria generic criteria," 1994.

35. Telcordia, TA-NWT-077, "Digital channel banks—requirements for dataport channel unit functions," April 1986.

36. Telcordia, TA-NWT-418, "Generic reliability requirements."

37. Telcordia, TA-NWT-1042, "Ring information model," 1992.

38. Telcordia, TA-NWT-1250, "File transfer," 1992.

39. Telcordia, TR-NWT-233, "Digital cross connect system," Nov. 1992.

40. Telcordia, TR-NWT-499, "Transport systems generic requirements (TSGR): common requirements," issue 5, Dec. 1993.

41. Telcordia, TR-NWT-782, "Switch trunk interface," Oct. 1992.

42. Telcordia, TR-NWT-917, "Regenerator," Oct. 1990.

43. Telcordia, TR-NWT-1042, "Ring information model," 1992.

44. Telcordia, TR-TSY-303, "Digital loop carrier system," Oct. 1989.

45. Telcordia, TR-TSY-496, "Add-drop multiplexer," May 1992.

46. *www.bluetooth.com*

47. *www.irda.org*

48. *www.adsl.org*

* (previously known as Belcore documents)

DWDM SYSTEMS

4.1 INTRODUCTION

To resolve bandwidth exhaustion and enable multiple services over the same network, more than one wavelength has been multiplexed in the same fiber using dense wavelength division multiplexing (DWDM) technology. DWDM potentially allows for an aggregate traffic of many terabits per second per fiber. Since nodes terminate several such fibers, the total pass-through bandwidth can be in the multiterabit range. However, to accomplish this efficiently, DWDM systems require specialized optical functionality such as massive, dynamic, and fast cross-connect fabrics; tunable lasers and filters; low-noise and high-sensitivity receivers; optical pulse compressors; optical equalizers, low-noise and wide-band optical amplifiers; fast and low-noise optical sensors; optical "smart" connectors; and so on.

Current DWDM systems use optical channels the wavelength of which is determined according to ITU-T defined grid. The many wavelengths in the same fiber provide versatility and flexibility of both service and bandwidth. Consider a wavelength as being a colored thread connecting two points, perhaps hundreds of kilometers apart. And many such threads are used to make a string, the equivalent of a fiber. In this scenario, because there are many wavelengths (channels) in a fiber, each channel may transport a different type of traffic, such as SONET/SDH over one channel, ATM over another channel, and perhaps TDM voice or Internet over another channel, and each one potentially at different bit rate, OC-N (OC-3 to OC-768) or Gigabit Ethernet. Currently, no other system or network can accomplish that.

As DWDM systems become more "optical," many traditional limitations are lifted to provide a truly scalable, dynamically reconfigurable, and future-proof system and network with optimum efficiency and bandwidth utilization. Present limitations are imposed only by the current state of the art of optical technology and by embedded

This chapter contains device specifications for illustrative and educational purposes. Because specifications are continuously changing, no responsibility is assumed for correctness. The reader is encouraged to consult the most recent versions of standards and most current manufacturers' data sheets.

traditional technology. Thus, in the next-generation and the next-after-next generation DWDMs, one wavelength (or optical channel) will carry traffic at a well-established bit rate and another at a rate to be defined (by emerging needs and demands); wavelength assignment will be dynamic (this also implies wavelength conversion); and bandwidth will be completely scalable and tradable, enabling both wholesale and bandwidth sharing so that more than one service or end user can share the same wavelength. The latter will enable far better bandwidth utilization, particularly when four end users may request up to 10 G/s each. The driver for this flexibility is the class of service, an entirely different approach to traditional services. Class of service implies that service providers and clients have the flexibility to offer and select, respectively, a service in one of many quality flavors. For example, the best quality service guarantees high reliability and bandwidth availability. The lowest quality service ensures "best effort" in both reliability and bandwidth availability, lowest cost of service, and therefore no guarantees. A service between the two ensures reliability of service and meeting minimum compliance quality levels (minimum bandwidth, jitter, delay, and noise) but no guarantees of meeting maximum levels unless bandwidth is available. Some call these classes "platinum," "gold," and "silver"; some "guaranteed," "differentiated," and "simple"; and some others give different names. Clearly, no matter what they are called, cost escalates from the silver to platinum, and quality of service is very important to all services.

Despite the technological evolution that facilitates the design of DWDM systems, the system designer still has to address many key challenges: How many wavelengths in a single fiber and at what bit rates each? How to engineer and budget the optical (end-to-end) path in a dynamically reconfigurable network? How are wavelengths monitored, managed, and provisioned? How many different types of client payload? How can the system be robust and deliver reliably uninterrupted services at the expected quality? What are the most efficient algorithms and protocols? How long can the fiber span be with or without amplification? What type of optical amplifiers can be used to meet gain and noise requirements? How can the system meet functionality density, cost, and performance objectives for the services it is designed for? And, how do the system interfaces comply with international standards and meet interoperability and internetworking specifications?

4.2   DWDM NETWORK TOPOLOGIES-REVIEW

To describe some aspects of DWDM system complexity, we must elaborate on some key network topologies. The most well known topologies are the point-to-point, the ring (single and dual), the fully connected mesh and star. In addition, there are subtopologies such as the ladder and point-to-point with add-drop.

The performance of each network topology depends on many factors. Among them: number of nodes, elasticity, seamless evolution, maximum traffic capacity, service restoration capability, fault resiliency, real-time aspects of transported traffic, versatility of supported traffic types, reliability, bandwidth management efficiency, number of fiber links between nodes, maintainability, reconfigurability, scalability, economics, trends and market preference, and so on. The ring topology may currently be preferred only because of familiarization with the already embedded SONET/SDH ring network, and the mesh (fully connected) topology because of superior survivability.

The point-to-point DWDM topology is a transport technology that enables aggregate traffic with few or many wavelengths over a single fiber (see Chapter 1, Figure 1.1). In this case and for short distances (a few kilometers), few wavelengths (16 to 40) at low bit rate each (1.25 Gb/s, 2.5 Gb/s and up to 10 Gb/s) and multimode fiber may be used. For long distances (hundreds of kilometers), many wavelengths (80–160 or more) at high bit rate each (10–40 Gb/s or higher) each are multiplexed in a fiber. Optical add-drop multiplexing typically is not an option and because of the insertion loss, fiber loss, and other phenomena that degrade the optical signal (see Chapter 2) amplification, equalization, and pulse-shapers are used. Optical amplification (depending on fiber and amplifiers) is every 60 to 80 kilometers, as is dispersion compensation. In addition, supervisory signals that transport data for performance, control, provisioning, maintenance, and administration for each channel may be in-band (embedded in the optical channel) or out of band (using a separate channel).

Another point-to-point application but for very short-distance (up to a few hundred meters) converts a serial bit stream in parallel and transmits over a (parallel) fiber bundle at a rate per fiber kGbps/N, where k is the serial bit rate and N is the number of fibers in the bundle (Fig. 4.1).

Parallel transport takes advantage of low cost when laser-arrays and photodetector-arrays are integrated on the same substrate. In this case, even though a moderate bit rate per laser is used, a high aggregate bit rate is achieved (Fig. 4.2). We examine the parallel transport and other derivatives more in subsequent sections of this chapter (see parallel λ-bus).

The ring topology comes in many flavors, depending on size (circumference) of the ring, the number of nodes it supports and the types of services. It may be a small ring (a few kilometers circumference) that supports up to 16 passive OADM nodes (Fig. 4.3). In this case, the number of wavelengths is at minimum 16 (one per OADM node and perhaps some more for protection), the bit rate per wavelength may be up to 10 Gb/s, and there is an additional supervisory channel shared by all nodes at a bit rate between 2 and 10 or perhaps 100 Mb/s. Such rings have one of the ring nodes designated as a hub. The hub in this case performs some additional duties such as flow control and management; it provides connectivity to other networks and connectivity from one node to another on the same ring, and it sources and terminates the supervisory

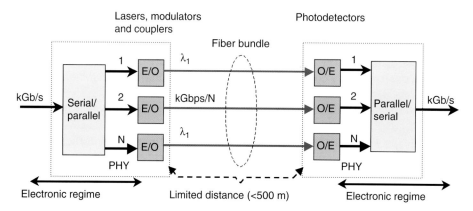

Figure 4.1 Parallel transport of high bandwidth over short distances.

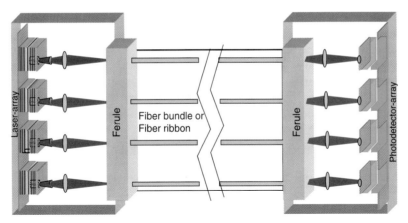

Figure 4.2 Laser and photodetector arrays make the serial to parallel transmission economically feasible in many short-haul applications.

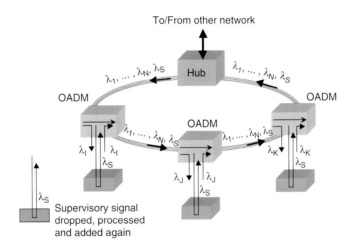

Figure 4.3 A ring topology with add-drop multiplexers and supervisory channel.

channel. In some cases, the hub receives a wavelength from a node and converts it to another wavelength. This is also known as *broadcast and select.*

The ring also may be large (several tens or even hundreds of kilometers in circumference) supporting several (32 or more) active OADM nodes, each dropping and adding one or more wavelengths. In this case, the number of wavelengths is at minimum 32 and at maximum NX32 (N per OADM node). In such case, wavelengths may be remotely programmable; the ring is protected (i.e., this is a dual ring); the signal requires amplification, equalization, and pulse-shaping; and there are one or more supervisory channels that are either shared by all nodes, or each node has its own dedicated supervisory channel, or some other strategy.

In general, the supervisory channel carries performance, control, provisioning, maintenance, and administration data to and from each node. Here, four supervisory channel strategies are described, *addressable packets, shared packets, channelized packets*, and *hybrid packets.*

In *addressable packets*, the supervisory data are mapped in a packet addressing a node on the ring. Nodes read the destination address in each incoming packet. The node that is addressed terminates it and sources a new packet which is added on to the ring (see Fig. 4.3). Packets not addressed to a node are not terminated; they are multiplexed into the main WDM stream heading to the next node.

In *shared packets*, the packet has been partitioned into sections, and each section corresponds only to a node. Thus, each node terminates its own section, buffers the other sections unaltered, rewrites its own section, and re-sources the complete packet to the next node. Thus, all nodes may be addressed at once with the same packet minimizing latency.

In the *channelized* case, each node has its own dedicated supervisory channel (wavelength); the wavelength is dropped, terminated, re-sourced, and multiplexed in the main DWDM stream. This is the fastest method to communicate with a node, but it uses spectral resources (wavelength) for each node. However, it may be applicable in high-performance systems where real-time supervisory data at high rate is very critical.

In the *hybrid* case, it may be any two of the above methods combined. For instance, it may be addressable and shared, addressable and channelized, or shared and channelized.

Which of the preceding supervisory strategies is most suitable depends on the type of services supported, the performance parameters of the network, protocol efficiency, node complexity, and economics.

A special case of a physical ring is that of a fully connected mesh topology or a star topology (Fig. 4.4). These cases result in different supervisory strategies.

We have made reference to nodes based on terminology that stems from traditional communications networks. In data networks, the term *node* is replaced by the term *router*. For simplicity, it really does not matter which term is used, since modern DWDM networks transport a mix of traffic, TDM (DSn, SONET/SDH), ATM, and IP, thanks to convergence, transparency of service, and the evolving network. In DWDM applications, a router that provides IP connectivity; performs DSn or OC-n grooming, optical multiplexing, and optical cross-connection; and provides real-time

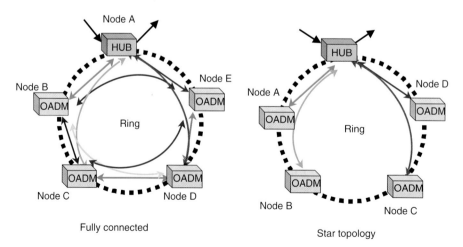

Figure 4.4 Mapping a fully connected mesh and a star topology onto a physical ring topology with add-drop multiplexers.

quality of services (QoS) starts looking like a traditional node. Similarly, a traditional node that provides packet-like connectivity, with priority based on bandwidth availability, and service level agreement (SLA), starts looking like a traditional router. Therefore, although nodes and routers may differ conceptually, we do not discriminate between the two.

4.3 DWDM SYSTEMS AND NETWORK LAYERS

DWDM systems are applicable to many network types and network layers. They are applicable to long-haul optical transport networks (OTN), backbone networks, large Metropolitan (Metro) networks, medium and small local area networks and access networks that eventually connect with the home or office (FTTH, FTTC, etc.). Therefore, DWDM systems, depending on applicability, have different design and specification challenges. Figure 4.5 captures the layered networks and illustrates the applicability of each, indicating the level of complexity in terms of bit rates, wavelength capacity, and physical size.

4.3.1 DWDM and Standards

In WDM networks, depending on the number of nodes and optical channel (wavelength) specifications, a system is termed DWDM (dense WDM) if many wavelengths are used (above 40 and based on the ITU-T grid) and CWDM (coarse WDM) if few wavelengths are used (8–32); the number of channels is related to channel spacing, which along with other factors (power of laser and SMF or MMF), impact performance and cost.

DWDM technology is evolving and therefore issues associated with it are also evolving. Standards bodies, such as ITU-T, are issuing recommendations (e.g., G.709 for optical transport networks) and are working toward drafting new ones. In the meantime, manufacturers offer systems with semiprivate solutions to meet market demands, which can be retrofitted to meet forthcoming standards. As a consequence, network management, as well as reliability, switching time, latency, and quality of service, may differ from vendor to vendor. Some manufacturers also use a supervisory channel for OAM&P (typically at 1,310 nm or at about 1,500 nm), but wavelength, bit rate, and protocol may not be common.

Dynamic wavelength assignment and wavelength protection are issues awaiting solutions. Current systems support fixed wavelength assignment per node, but automatic and remote provisioning is highly desirable.

Finally, degradation or fault detection, localization, and remedial actions, although defined for optical networks with a single wavelength per fiber, have not been addressed in DWDM networks. Fault detection and localization in DWDM systems and networks require specialized monitoring devices and critical diagnostic functions at different levels that affect the quality of signal and service. These are on the component, module, and unit levels. Detected degradations or failures generate messages and/or alarm signals, based on which correlation may provide an early warning of an upcoming critical failure. Then, fault-case scenarios activate testing and fast remedial action so that service is provided virtually uninterrupted.

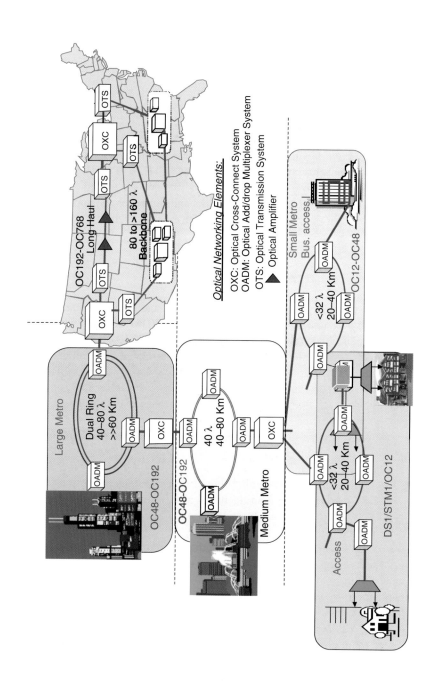

Figure 4.5 DWDM systems are applicable in all network layers; access, Metro, large Metro, and long haul/backbone optical transport network.

As many standards are still on the drafting board, the reader is encouraged to consult relevant standards documents and their amendments, if any, before embarking on actual engineering and design work.

4.3.2 Domains or Functions

DWDM systems consist of communication nodes that receive a multiplicity of continuous and synchronous data streams of multiplexed optical channels, which are not synchronized; they terminate, pass through, or add-drop channels, as described in Chapter 1. Such systems consist of well-established functions, which are typically referred to as *domains* such as transmitting and receiving, amplification, timing, provisioning, signal conditioning, cross-connectivity, multiplexing and demultiplexing.

4.3.3 System Partitioning and Remoting

The aforementioned functions or domains may not represent physical entities. Physical entities or units consist of printed circuit boards that may contain one or more functions, such as, for example, optical receiving and transmitting, timing, power amplification, cross-connecting, and so on. In general, the partitioning and consolidation of functions on physical entities does not have strict rules but it is a logical outcome based on cost, power, heat dissipation, physical dimensions, component size, and backplane interconnectivity. Thus, partitioning may culminate in one or many physical units that necessitate grouping (collocation of several units with similar functionality). For large systems the physical partitioning may be so complex that units are organized into subgroups, whereby each subgroup has its own power supply, timing unit, and controller comprising a shelf. Then, several shelves may comprise a bay, and several bays may comprise the "system" or node (Fig. 4.6). In large systems, a shelf may house the main system controller, the optical amplifiers, or the cross-connecting fabric.

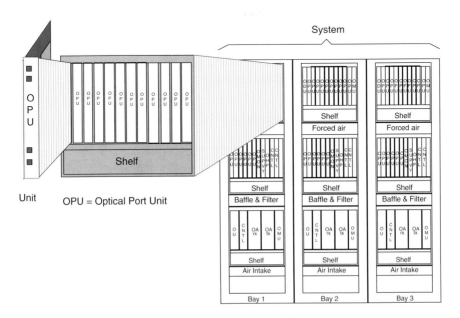

Figure 4.6 Large optical systems consist of units, shelves and bays (unit arrangement is imaginary).

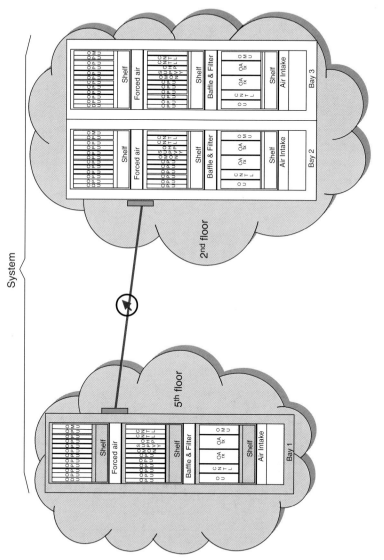

Figure 4.7 The concept of "remoting" a large multibay system.

In certain cases, because of floor space limitation, it is not uncommon to have bays of a system located on different parts of a floor or in different floors of a building, thus requiring *point-to-point* interconnectivity that may be up to 1 kilometer long (but preferably under 200 m); this practice is known as "*remoting*" (Fig. 4.7). When bays are adjacent to each other, interconnecting cables are on the order of a few meters, and the physical cable plant as well as the transmission driving capability and latency are manageable. Remoting, however, creates another challenge that requires different solutions, as described in Section 4.2 (see Fig. 4.2).

4.4   KEY BUILDING BLOCKS OF A DWDM SYSTEM

The functional domains outlined in the previous section comprise the key functional building blocks of any communications system; domain consolidation depends on actual implementation. As such, purely optical DWDM systems (those that do not convert the optical signal to an electrical signal) consist of physical units that perform the following major functions:

- optical transmitting (output ports)
- optical receiving (input ports)
- optical (pre- and/or post-) amplification
- optical demultiplexing and multiplexing
- signal conditioning (power equalization, pulse compression, depolarization, dispersion compensation)
- wavelength conversion
- optical cross-connecting
- optical monitoring (power and spectral)
- optical interconnecting (connectors, fibers, waveguides, optical backplanes)

In addition, some major systems perform functionality in the electrical regime, such as control and system provisioning. Thus, the current definition of an "all-optical" system is not exactly "optical" in all aspects, but the term *all-optical* is limited to the path of the client data-bearing signal as it passes through the system entirely in the photonic regime, whereas all other ancillary functions are in the electrical regime. As a consequence, signal performance monitoring is not easily performed in current all-optical systems, and particularly error detection and correction; error detection may be performed electrically, but it is not very useful if optical correction cannot be performed. Obviously, this presents a challenge and future optical technology will address this as well.

To summarize, the key building blocks from a system point of view (depending on system and layer, some functions may not be applicable) are:

- input ports [postamplification, equalization, compensation, wavelength conversion, supervisory channel termination, photodetection (at the path termination)]
- output ports (laser sourcing and modulation (at the path source), booster amplification, equalization)

- optical converters
- timing units (optical clock extraction and optical retiming)
- switching (amplification, switching fabric, drivers, equalization)
- multiplexing (filtering, amplification, multiplexing, equalization)
- demultiplexing (filtering, polarization, amplification, demultiplexing, equalization)
- controller
- program store and database
- drivers
- display (LED, LCD, status, alarms, equipage, neighborhood, ambient conditions)
- power (sensing, distribution)
- cooling fans and air intake
- fuse panel
- connector panel and cable ducting
- cable drawer
- other (depending on system architecture partitioning)

4.4.1 Transmitters and Receivers

In DWDM systems, the main function of the transmitter is to source a modulated optical signal complying with a set of specifications (as specified by standards and application), a list of which is (those with an asterisk are, in addition, specific to tunable transmitters):

- sourced maximum output optical power
- center wavelength(s), compliant to ITU-T grid
- spectral line-width of optical channel
- optical channel separation (spectral distance from adjacent channels)
- center frequency drift limits
- wander and jitter variability and allowed limits
- bit rate accuracy and drift limits
- modulation and modulation depth
- accuracy of new acquired center wavelength*
- spectral range of tunable transmitter*
- dynamic response or (wavelength) acquisition time*
- state of polarization
- TE/TM mode of photonic beam
- beam profile and uniformity
- signal to noise ratio
- floor noise
- source dependency on bias
- source dependency on temperature

The actual values in this list depend on the application the transmitter is designed for. For example, the bit rate may be as low as several Mb/s or as high as 40 Gb/s. The signal modulation may be nonreturn to zero (NRZ) or return to zero (RZ); the latter may also be 50% RZ or 33% RZ. The output optical power may be specified for short fiber lengths or for long fiber lengths (in all cases, sources must comply with eye safety specifications). Center frequency may be based on a C-band 80-λ grid, on a 40-λ grid, or on a 160-λ C + L-band grid, and for different fiber types (such as SSMF, DSF, and MMF).

The main function of the receiver is to detect and respond to a modulated photonic signal with a predetermined level of accuracy, which is measured in bit error rate. The modulated photonic signal has traveled through the fiber and many components so that when it arrives at the photodetector it is already degraded in power, spectral, and noise content. When fiber is many kilometers long, the incident light at the receiver is very weak due to signal attenuation, and a logic "one" contains photons counted in single digit; the minimum number of photons required for a receiver to recognize a logic "one" is known as the *quantum limit*.

At minimum, a receiver consists of an optical preamplifier (optional); a polarization filter (optional); a power equalizer; a focusing lens (preferred); an efficient, fast-responding, and low-noise photodetector; an electronic low pass filter; a circuit that extracts the clock from the incoming signal and determines the time and threshold level for sampling (in on–off keying demodulation); and other components needed to demodulate the signal.

In DWDM systems, after the preamplifier, polarizer, and power equalizer, an optical wavelength demultiplexer separates the wavelengths, and each is directed to its receiver either via an optical waveguide, by a short fiber, or directly. Thus, the key characteristics of the DWDM receiver are:

- receiver sensitivity
- optical preamplifier spectral response
- optical preamplifier gain and gain flatness
- optical preamplifier noise
- demultiplexer polarization effects
- power equalization spectral range and flatness
- demultiplexer insertion loss
- waveguide, connector, and splices insertion loss
- waveguide polarization effects
- detector technology (e.g., APD, PIN)
- detector minimum threshold optical power, min-max threshold level (one-zero) at a given BER (e.g., less than 10^{-12})
- detector quantum efficiency
- detector dependency on polarization
- detector temporal responsivity, max-min bit rate
- detector spectral responsivity per wavelength, λ_0
- detector wavelength discrimination
- detector polarization dependency

- detector shot noise
- detector dependency on bias
- detector dependency on jitter
- detector dependency on temperature
- low-pass filtering characteristics
- receiver clock sensitivity on one's density
- demodulation method
- clock sensitivity

From the transmitter launched power in the fiber (Tx) and the receiver sensitivity (Rs), the maximum allowable loss is calculated (Loss_{max}):

$$\text{Loss}_{\text{max}} = Tx - Rs \ (\text{dB})$$

For example, if $Tx = 0$ dBm and $Rs = -20$ dBm, then $\text{Loss}_{\text{max}} = 0 - (-20) = 20$ dB; remember that we can subtract dBms yielding a difference in dBs (Chapter 2). The maximum allowable loss helps determine the optical path span, the required amplification gain, and the needed compensation.

4.4.1.1 Modulation and Demodulation of the Optical Signal

Modulation is the action of temporally altering one or more of the parameters of the photonic signal. In optical communications, these parameters are phase, frequency, and amplitude of an optical carrier or wavelength. When the phase is modulated, the method is called *phase-shift keying* (PSK); when the frequency is modulated, it is called *frequency-shift keying* (FSK); and when the amplitude is modulated, it is called *amplitude-shift keying* (ASK). The latter case includes the *intensity modulation with direct detection* (IM/DD) and the on–off keying (OOK) modulation method.

In optical communications, the modulation method plays a key role in:

- optical power coupled into the fiber
- bit rate limits
- dispersion limits
- fiber span limit
- linear and nonlinear contributing effects
- overall signal-to-noise ratio and BER
- reliability of signal detection and receiver penalty

Coherent heterodyne and *homodyne* detection techniques were initially developed for radio communications. In optical transmission, the term *coherent* indicates that another light source is used as the local oscillator at the receiver; optical coherent methods improve receiver sensitivity by approximately 20 dB, allowing longer fibers to be used (by an additional 100 Km at 1.55 μm). In addition, using IM/DD the channel spacing is on the order of 100 GHz; with coherent techniques it can be as small as 1 to 10 GHz. A metric of good line coders (for 10 Gb/s) is an acceptable eye diagram at the

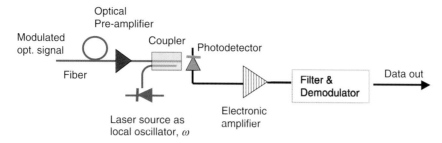

Figure 4.8 Coherent detection requires a low-noise local oscillator with narrow linewidth comparable to or better than the incoming optical signal.

receiver (see Chapter 2) such that the uncertainty of the state (1 or 0) of the received bits is less than 1 bit per second per Hertz (<1 b/s/Hz). Optical communications systems are designed with error rates (as specified in ITU-T standards) at less than 10^{-12} BER.

Coherent detection of an incoming modulated signal uses a local oscillator (i.e., a light source of a frequency in the vicinity of the transmitted source), which must have a narrow spectral (line) width comparable to that of the source (Fig. 4.8). In addition, the local oscillator must have low noise characteristics; otherwise the spontaneously emitted light adds to noise and the method is not practical. Therefore, amplitude of the local oscillator in coherent receiver design is important. In the case of IM/DD, the incoming signal is directly coupled into the detector, thus eliminating the coupler and the local oscillator.

4.4.1.2 Line Coding Techniques

Several coding techniques have been proposed for optical communications: the on–off keying (OOK), the frequency shift keying (FSK), and the phase shift keying (PSK). Currently, the most popular technique is the OOK with return to zero (RZ) or with nonreturn to zero (NRZ).

On-Off Keying. This is a modulation method according to which a logic "one" is manifested by the presence of light; similarly, logic "zero" is manifested by the absence of light. When the logic "one" is lighted for the full period ($T = 1/f$), this OOK is termed *nonreturn to zero* (NRZ), and when for a fraction of the period (such as $\frac{1}{3}$ or $\frac{1}{2}$), it is termed *return to zero* (RZ) (Fig. 4.9).

The OOK can be used in coherent detection or in IM/DD detection. However, coherent detection requires constant phase. As a consequence, the laser source cannot be directly modulated because this may shift the signal phase. Therefore, in this case, the signal amplitude is modulated externally with a titanium-diffused $LiNbO_3$ waveguide in a Mach–Zehnder configuration or with a semiconductor directional coupler based on electroabsorption multiquantum-well (MQW) properties and structures. Conversely, IM/DD detection does not require constant phase, and thus phase shift is unimportant (however, direct laser modulation may also alter the spectral content of the source).

Phase Shift Keying. This method modulates the phase of a light beam (the carrier) at the transitions between logic "zero" and logic "one"; that is, it shifts the phase by

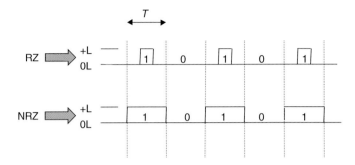

Figure 4.9 OOK RZ and NRZ optical coding.

180 degrees while the frequency and amplitude of the signal remain constant during all bits, thus appearing as a continuous light wave. For multilevel PSK, the change may be in increments of 45 degrees (8-levels). PSK is a coherent technique.

PSK is implemented by passing the light beam through a device that operates on the principle that, when a voltage is applied to it, its refractive index changes; this is known as *electrorefraction modulation* (ERM). Such devices are made with electro-optic crystals, such as $LiNbO_3$, with proper orientation. The phase difference is expressed by:

$$\delta\phi = (2\pi/\lambda)(\delta n)L_m$$

where the index change δn is proportional to applied voltage, V, and L_m is the length over which the index changes by the applied voltage (Fig. 4.10).

Frequency-Shift Keying. This method modulates the frequency ω of a light beam (the carrier) at the transitions between logic "zero" and logic "one"; that is, it shifts the frequency while the amplitude of the signal remain constant during all bits. At the transitions, the frequency changes by Δf, $f + \Delta f$ for logic "1," and $f - \Delta f$ for logic "0." Thus, FSK is a coherent two-state (on–off) FM technique. Typical frequency changes are about 1 GHz.

The total bandwidth of a FSK signal is approximated to $2\Delta f + 2B$, where B is the bit rate and Δf is the frequency deviation.

- When the deviation is large, $\Delta f \gg B$, the bandwidth approaches $2\Delta f$, and this case is known as *wideband-FSK*.

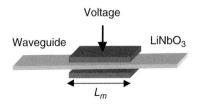

Figure 4.10 PSK modulator: a varying voltage modulates the refractive index of its electro-refractive element and thus the phase of coherent light passing through it.

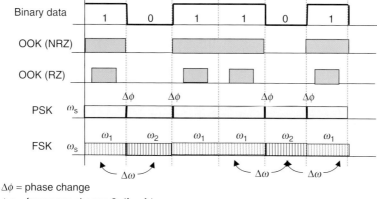

Δφ = phase change
Δω = frequency change 2π|f₁ − f₂|

Figure 4.11 Optical modulation methods.

- When the deviation is narrow, $\Delta f \ll B$, the bandwidth approaches 2B, and this case is known as *narrowband-FSK*.

A *frequency modulation index* (FMI), defined by $\Delta f/B = \beta_{FM}$, distinguishes the two cases; wideband-FSK has an FMI $\beta_{FM} \gg 1$ and narrowband-FSK has an FMI $\beta_{FM} \ll 1$.

FSK is achieved with electroacoustic Bragg modulators or with DFB semiconductor lasers that shift their operating frequency by 1 GHz when the operating current changes by a mere 1 mA. The small current change required for FSK is viewed positively because it causes a small variation on the optical output power of the laser beam. Thus, DFB semiconductor lasers make very good and fast coherent FSK sources with high modulation efficiency. Figure 4.11 summarizes all shift keying modulation methods.

4.4.1.3 Line Decoding Techniques

Optical decoding entails detecting the optical signal and retrieving binary coded information (or demodulate) from the received modulated lightwave, based on one of the three coding techniques:

- detect optical amplitude level if amplitude shift keying (ASK or OOK) is used
- detect phase change (from 0° to 180°) if binary PSK is used
- detect frequency change (from $\omega - \Delta\omega$ to $\omega + \Delta\omega$) if FSK is used

The employed technique clearly impacts the receiver and demodulator design complexity, but it primarily affects the quality of the received signal and the fiber span.

OOK RZ and NRZ Demodulators. On−off keying demodulators use receivers that directly detect incident photons. The number of incident photons in the time domain generates an electrical signal with similar amplitude fluctuation, plus some electrical noise added by the photodetector. When the optical signal has been converted to an electrical signal, amplitude high-frequency fluctuation (and noise) is low-pass filtered. In addition, the signal is sampled at the rate of the expected incoming bit rate by a local phase-locked loop to minimize jitter and signal level uncertainty. Thus, the number of incident photons is interpreted as logic "1" when it is above a threshold level and as logic "0" when it is below that level (see Fig. 2.90). However, there are instances when the incident amplitude is ambiguous due to excessive noise and jitter (manifested by a corrupted eye diagram), and an erroneous 1 or 0 may be produced.

OOK modulation/demodulation may be return to zero (RZ) or nonreturn to zero (NRZ), see Figure 4.15. It should be noted that a NRZ signal provides photons for the full duration of the bit period, whereas a RZ signal for a percentage of the period. Popular percentages are 33%, 40%, and 50%. The NRZ or RZ modulation, and the percent, is particularly important in ultrahigh bit rates such as 10 or 40 Gb/s. For example, a 50% OOK 40 Gb/s signal has logic "1" illuminated for 12.5 ps, whereas a 33% for 8.25 ps, that is a reduction by 34%. All other things being equal, this reduction is significant in the amount of received power and thus in the received bit error rate. However, if the path is engineered and budgeted correctly, the RZ peak power is higher, provides better noise isolation, and thus improves the overall optical signal-to-noise ratio.

PSK and FSK Demodulators. PSK and FSK demodulation is based on coherent detection; that is, in addition to the received optical signal from the fiber, one or two local (optical) oscillators are required to interferometrically interact with the received optical signal and convert it to OOK.

The received PSK modulated optical signal, ω_S, is mixed coherently with a locally generated laser light, ω_{LO}, and because both are of the same frequency, they interact interferometrically (Fig. 4.12), so that when both frequencies are in phase, there is constructive contribution, and when they are not in phase, destructive, and thus (ideally) an on–off keying signal is generated. Since the accuracy of this method depends on the phase variation of the signal, phase stability and low noise are very critical.

The basic principle of a simplified homodyne FSK demodulator is shown in Figure 4.13.

The received FSK modulated optical signal, ω_S, is passed through a narrow-band optical filter tuned to pass the frequency $\omega_1 = \omega + \Delta\omega$. Thus, whenever this frequency

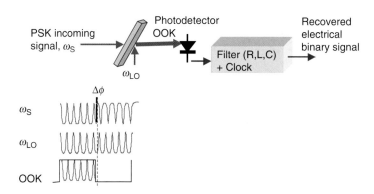

Figure 4.12 Principles of a homodyne PSK demodulator.

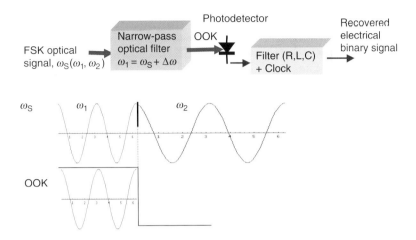

Figure 4.13 A simplified FSK demodulator.

only passes the filter, the frequency ω_2 is rejected and the outcome is equivalent to an OOK modulated signal. Since the accuracy of this method depends on the frequency variation of the signal, no frequency shift (high frequency stability) and low optical noise are very critical.

4.4.2 Optical Amplifiers and Regenerators

4.4.2.1 Amplifiers
In Chapter 2 (Section 2.17), we described the physics and technology of optical amplification. Amplification is required to overcome signal losses in the fiber and other components (depending on application and fiber, span loss is in the range of 23 to 15 dB). The key three types of optical amplifiers were the fiber (OFA), the Raman, and the semiconductor (SOA). Each of them has distinct benefits and limitations so that no one type by itself is currently suitable for all applications and for the complete spectrum from 1,250 to 1,650 nm (see Figs. 2.66 and 2.81). As such, each amplifier must be evaluated on its own merits and should be applied where it makes more sense in technical and cost terms.

OFAs (EDFA, YEDFA, TDFA, etc.) and have been suitable and largely been deployed in fiber networks. There is a continuous effort to improve them in terms of increased gain, bandwidth, and functionality. However, although YEDFAs (yttrium-erbium doped fiber amplifiers) have extended the EDFA range in the C-band and the L-band, they still have a limited range (1,530–1,620 nm). Table 4.1 lists the optical channels (frequency and wavelength) in the extended L-band. Thus, EDFA or YEDFA is optimized for power restoration with minimal added noise of the depleted optical signal in the 1,550-nm wavelength band.

EDFAs are applicable as booster optical amplifiers in DWDM and CATV, as low-noise (5 dB typical) low power consumption (<3.5 W) compact optical preamplifiers in optical cross-connects and in metropolitan networks. EDFA preamplifiers have a relatively small package size (approximately $7 \times 9 \times 1.2$ cm^3) so that they can be installed on a board. The complete package includes the pump laser, couplers, isolators, filters,

Table 4.1   Extended L-band optical channels (ITU reference frequency 193.1 THz)

Frequency (THz)	Wavelength (nm)	Frequency (THz)	Wavelength (nm)	Frequency (THz)	Wavelength (nm)	Frequency (THz)	Wavelength (nm)
192.950	1,553.731	191.250	1,567.542	189.600	1,581.184	187.950	1,595.065
192.850	1,554.537	191.200	1,567.952	189.550	1,581.601	187.900	1,595.489
192.800	1,554.940	191.150	1,568.362	189.500	1,582.018	187.850	1,595.914
192.750	1,555.343	191.100	1,568.773	189.450	1,582.436	187.800	1,596.339
192.700	1,555.747	191.050	1,569.183	189.400	1,582.854	187.750	1,596.764
192.650	1,556.151	191.000	1,569.594	189.350	1,583.271	187.700	1,597.189
192.600	1,556.555	190.950	1,570.005	189.300	1,583.690	187.650	1,597.615
192.550	1,556.959	190.900	1,570.416	189.250	1,584.108	187.600	1,598.041
192.500	1,557.363	190.850	1,570.828	189.200	1,584.527	187.550	1,598.467
192.450	1,557.768	190.800	1,571.239	189.150	1,584.946	187.500	1,598.893
192.400	1,558.173	190.750	1,571.651	189.100	1,585.365	187.450	1,599.320
192.350	1,558.578	190.700	1,572.063	189.050	1,585.784	187.400	1,599.746
192.300	1,558.983	190.650	1,572.476	189.000	1,586.203	187.350	1,600.173
192.250	1,559.389	190.600	1,572.888	188.950	1,586.623	187.300	1,600.600
192.200	1,559.794	190.550	1,573.301	188.900	1,587.043	187.250	1,601.028
192.150	1,560.200	190.500	1,573.714	188.850	1,587.463	187.200	1,601.455
192.100	1,560.606	190.450	1,574.127	188.800	1,587.884	187.150	1,601.883
192.050	1,561.013	190.400	1,574.540	188.750	1,588.304	187.100	1,602.311
192.000	1,561.419	190.350	1,574.954	188.700	1,588.725	187.050	1,602.740
191.950	1,561.826	190.300	1,575.368	188.650	1,589.146	187.000	1,603.168
191.900	1,562.233	190.250	1,575.782	188.600	1,589.568	186.950	1,603.597
191.850	1,562.640	190.200	1,576.196	188.550	1,589.989	186.900	1,604.026
191.800	1,563.047	190.150	1,576.610	188.500	1,590.411	186.850	1,604.455
191.750	1,563.455	190.100	1,577.025	188.450	1,590.833	186.800	1,604.885
191.700	1,563.863	190.050	1,577.440	188.400	1,591.255	186.750	1,605.314
191.650	1,564.271	190.000	1,577.855	188.350	1,591.678	186.700	1,605.744
191.600	1,564.679	189.950	1,578.270	188.300	1,592.100	186.650	1,606.174
191.550	1,565.087	189.900	1,578.686	188.250	1,592.523	186.600	1,606.605
191.500	1,565.496	189.850	1,579.102	188.200	1,592.946	186.550	1,607.035
191.450	1,565.905	189.800	1,579.518	188.150	1,593.369	186.500	1,607.466
191.400	1,566.314	189.750	1,579.934	188.100	1,593.793	186.400	1,608.329
191.350	1,566.723	189.700	1,580.350	188.050	1,594.217		
191.300	1,567.133	189.650	1,580.767	188.000	1,594.641		

doped fiber, and multiplexers. As amplifier technology evolves, level of integration and functionality will increase and package size will decrease, increasing performance and reducing the cost of the system.

As optical fiber with very low OH-content becomes available, the complete window 1,250 nm to 1,650 nm will soon be available in DWDM networks. Therefore, it is logical that other solutions must be used to complement YEDFAs. Such amplifiers are the Raman amplifier and parametric fiber amplifiers.

Raman amplification is deployed solely in fiber networks and at repeater sites. It also has been deployed in conjunction with EDFA/YEDFAs to improve transmission performance. That is, to enhance gain flatness and improve the optical signal to noise ratio. These improvements reduce the need for dynamic gain equalization and enable higher channel density, faster transmission bit rates (10 and 40 Gb/s), and better gain response and hence longer distance between regeneration sites. However, the OFA

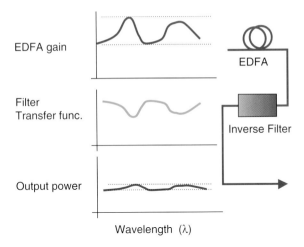

Figure 4.14 Inverse filters reduce EDFAs gain ripple.

gain is not flat over the amplified spectral range. Excessive OFA gain ripple may be reduced with inverse filters (filters with transfer function compensating for EDFA gain) (Fig. 4.14).

Similar to EDFAs, Raman amplifiers are compact devices. The Raman pump may also be incorporated into the EDFA package, when both a preamplifier EDFA and a Raman amplifier are used in synergy (see Section 2.17). A Raman amplifier package also contains pumps, taps, isolators, couplers, thin-film filters, and combiners.

Because Raman amplification evolves over the existing single-mode fiber used for transmission, the Raman amplifier gain varies with fiber type (from about 15 to 23 dB). For example, although the gain may be 20 dB in one fiber type of manufacturer X, it may be 15 dB in another type of manufacturer Y. As discussed in Chapter 2, Raman amplification may also have pump(s) in co-propagating, counter-propagating, or amphi-propagating (both) directions with respect to the signal.

During the propagation of pump-light an amplification evolution takes place as well as other nonlinear effects. We separate them into two groups, those related to gain and those that degrade the quality of the signal manifested by added noise.

First, there are at least three mechanisms that take place during this evolution: signal loss, amplifier gain, and pump loss ($\sim$0.05 dB/km higher than signal loss). As such, the amplifier gain is not uniform along the fiber span but it is stronger at the input to the span (in the copropagating case) or at the output of the span and going backwards (counterpropagating) (Fig. 4.15).

Second, because the pump light is strong (compare hundreds of mW of the pump with few mW of the signal), the signal is subject to nonlinearities due to Raman pump as well as to noise sources. Noise and increased nonlinearity need to be minimized for optimum optical signal-to-noise ratio (OSNR). In either case, fiber amplifiers should not have an SBS threshold less than 3 dBm.

The nonlinearity for a Raman-pumped fiber span is provided by the integral

$$\Phi_{NL}^{Raman} = \int_0^L \gamma P(z)\, dz$$

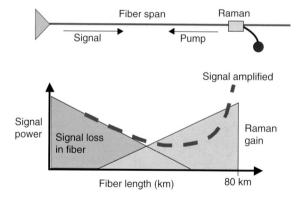

Figure 4.15   Counter-propagating Raman amplification.

The nonlinearity for the unpumped span is:

$$\Phi_{NL}^{Unpumped} = \int_0^L \gamma e^{-az}\, dz = P_{in}(1 - e^{-az})/\alpha$$

where $P(z)$ is the Raman power evolution function, a is the loss, γ is a function of the signal power, and L is the length of the span.

From these two relationships, the ratio of nonlinearity increase due to Raman pumping is

$$\Phi_{NL}^{Increase} = \Phi_{NL}^{Raman}/\Phi_{NL}^{Unpumped}$$

The noise sources are mainly due to broadband spontaneous Raman scattering noise and narrow-band double (in both directions) Rayleigh scattering noise (Fig. 4.16).

Similarly, if the span loss is L_f, then the noise figure of the fiber span (without pump) is defined as

$$NF_{unpumped} = 1/L_f$$

Then, the noise figure for the Raman pumped fiber span is:

$$NF = [P_{noise}/(h\nu\Delta\nu G_R L_f)] + 1/(G_R L_f)$$

where h is Planck's constant, ν is the frequency, P_{noise} is the noise power in the electrical filter bandwidth (here we assume that the signal has been received and converted to electrical), and G_R is the Raman gain.

Based on these two noise figures, an improvement noise figure is calculated from

$$NF_{improvement} = NF - NF_{unpumped}$$

As also discussed in Chapter 2, several Raman pumps are used to amplify a wider spectral range. In this case, the above relationships become more complex and a gain

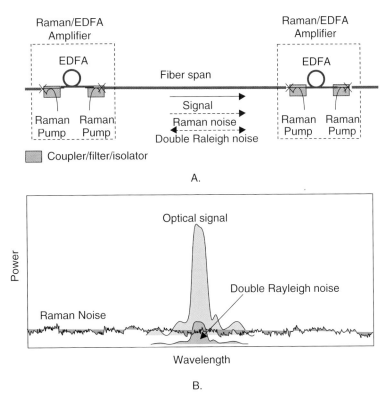

Figure 4.16 A. Model of Raman Noise and Double Rayleigh Scattering, and B. their contributions to the optical signal.

ripple effect must be considered (see Fig. 2.78), with a typical average variation of 0.1 to 0.5 dB. When Raman and EDFA are used in synergy, both Raman ripple and EDFA ripple may be designed so that an almost flat gain is realized. Figure 4.17 illustrates the flat gain region in the C-band for various channel densities.

Based on the preceding, Raman amplification and EDFA amplification are not as straightforward but require many parameters to be considered to calculate the optimum strengths of forward and backward pumping for an amplifier with the desired net gain and optimum noise characteristics. However, which parameters should be considered most greatly depend on application and engineering rules. For example, Raman scattering noise is independent of signal power but is proportional to bit rate (the Raman noise bandwidth at 10 Gb/s in SMF is ~12.5 GHz) in contrast to Rayleigh double scattering, which is proportional to signal power and independent of bit rate.

Table 4.2 provides a qualitative comparison between the EDFA and Raman amplifiers.

SOAs have not been as popular in power amplification as EDFA and Raman amplifiers because of lower gain, nonlinear phenomena, and channel cross-talk (here we should distinguish between interchannel and intrachannel cross-talk, the latter being more dominant). However, SOAs present an excellent match with materials that are used for many optical solid-state devices. Therefore, as the level of optical integration increases, SOAs will play a key role in post- and preamplification. For example,

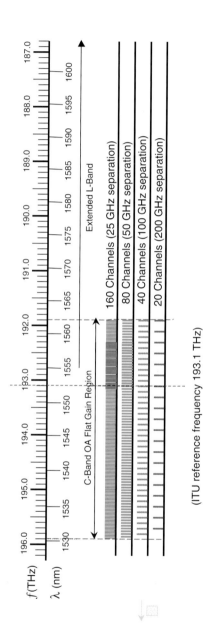

Figure 4.17 Optical amplifier flat gain region in C-band.

316

Table 4.2 Qualitative comparison between Raman and OFAs

Characteristic	Raman	OFA
Amplification band	depends on pump offset	depends on dopant (Er, Y, Th)
Gain BW	20–50 nm per pump	~90 nm (extended range)
Flat gain BW	15–20 nm	
Gain tilt	amplify longer λs more than shorter (but is adjustable)	amplify longer λs more than shorter (fixed)
Noise	Raman scatter, double Raleigh	ASE
Pump wavelength	by 100 nm shorter than amplified signal range	980/1,480 nm for Erbium
Pump power	<300 mW	~3 W
Saturation power	~power of pump	depends on dopant and gain; largely homogeneous saturation characteristics
Direction sense	Supports bidirectional signals	Unidirectional
Other	Potential cross-talk among OChs; other nonlinearities	Potential cross-talk; hole burning
Simplicity	simpler (no specialty fiber needed)	more complex (EDFA needed)

SOAs may be integrated with laser pumps, filters, and optical waveguides to produce compact, small, and inexpensive amplifiers, the power of which may then be boosted with EDFA and/or Raman amplifiers. Or they can be similarly integrated with receivers and demodulators. In addition, SOAs may be the main amplifier in coarse WDM applications such as access and small metropolitan networks.

4.4.2.2 Regenerators

The role of regenerators is to recondition the received weak optical signal; remove noise, jitter and distortions; and amplify the signal (Fig. 4.18). However, this function is good for a maximum fiber span, and therefore it must repeat itself, hence repeaters (Fig. 4.19). Nevertheless, noise is cumulative, and therefore the number of repeaters in a path may be very large. Currently, the common practice (based on amplifiers, fiber, and other parameters) is to have up to seven or eight repeaters in a path of about 4,000 km (see Fig. 4.5). Regenerators that perform reshaping, retiming, and amplification (reconditioning) are known as 3R regenerators. Currently, however, 3R

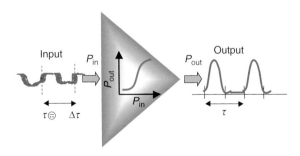

Figure 4.18 Model of an optical regenerator.

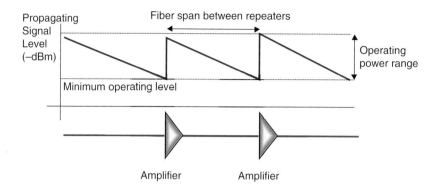

Figure 4.19 Signal regeneration action.

regenerators are opaque, and if they also include functions such as add-drop, performance monitoring, and wavelength translators, they are known as transponders.

Because of maintenance and cost aspects of opaque regenerators and transponders, the trend is that they be all-optical (transparent). Thus, a simple EDFA and Raman amplification stage (including isolation and filters) that simultaneously amplifies many channels is known as a 1R regenerator (i.e., retiming and reshaping are not included). However, sophisticated techniques using nonlinear fibers have demonstrated that 2R all-optical (amplification and reshaping) is feasible as well as cost-effective. If 2R optical solutions include coherent optical oscillators for retiming, then 3R is also feasible; ongoing work will soon bring forth 3R cost-effective solutions.

Since DWDM regenerators pass through an enormous amount of data, it is desirable that they be redundant; that is, they are duplicated so that when one regenerator degrades or fails, the other continues to provide uninterrupted regeneration functionality. In general, a regenerator consists of three stages: a preamplifier (with proper isolators, couplers, power monitors, and filtering); an equalizer (where an add-drop multiplexer may also be included); and a booster amplifier with filtering and isolation (Fig. 4.20). Clearly, other configurations may also be used. For example, the preamplifier may consist of a Raman-pumped DCF followed by an EDFA or Raman booster amplifier so that both amplification and pulse compression due to dispersion, reshaping, and amplification are accomplished.

In addition to EDFA and Raman, regeneration may also be achieved using the nonlinearity properties of SOAs (such as cross-phase modulation) in a Mach–Zehnder interferometric arrangement (see Chapter 2, optical amplifiers) and using dispersion shifted fiber (DSF). Current research has demonstrated that 2R as well as 3R regeneration is possible for 10, 40, and 80 Gb/s signals and for optical paths exceeding 10,000 km (using multiple regenerators in cascade), thus promising compact devices that may revolutionize the regeneration process in optical DWDM transmission.

4.4.3 Dispersion Compensating Solutions

4.4.3.1 Chromatic Dispersion Compensators

We have discussed (in Chapter 2) at least two components that compensate for dispersion, the chirped fiber Bragg grating and the chromatic dispersion compensating

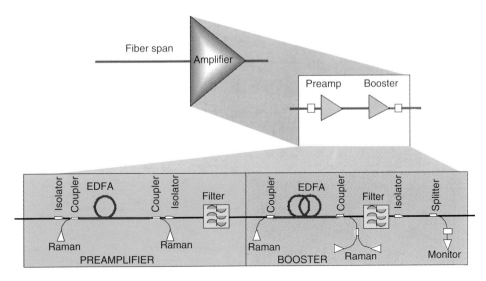

Figure 4.20 A look inside a possible regenerator (redundancy is not shown).

fiber (DCF). DCFs have been designed with a relatively large core effective area (about 20 mm^2) and such that shorter wavelengths travel slower than longer (that is, the opposite of single mode fiber) thus having a negative dispersion (a typical value is −100 ps/nm-km). However, DCFs have also more fiber loss (about 0.5 dB/km). Therefore, although DCFs compress the widening of a pulse, they also cause signal loss that must be compensated for with amplifiers (Fig. 4.21); a 5-km DCF may cause 2.5-dB losses.

Based on this, dispersion compensating modules (DCM) have been engineered that are used in systems and/or in regenerators to help increase the span of fiber (Fig. 4.22).

It is typical that DCMs use Raman pumps in DCFs to both compensate for dispersion and amplify the signal. In this case, Raman amplification and DCF fiber loss counteract. The net DCM gain is obtained by adding the desired Raman gain at the output of the DCM plus the internal DCM losses, and if more that one pump is used, plus a

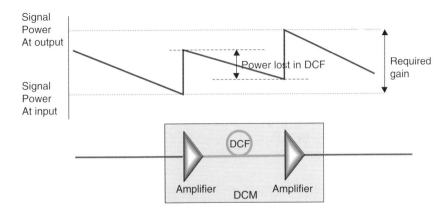

Figure 4.21 Dispersion compensation fiber and amplification action.

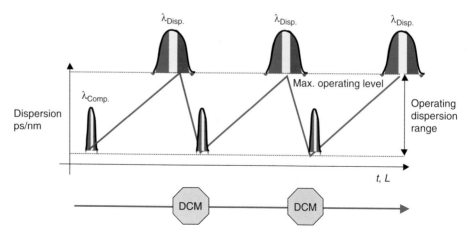

Figure 4.22 Dispersion compensation action.

margin to compensate for Raman ripple and perhaps an equalizer. The net gain then is estimated from

$$\text{Net DCM gain} = \text{desired R} - \text{gain} + \text{internal DCM losses} + \text{margin (dB)}$$

For example, if a desired Raman gain is 6 dB (calculated based on fiber type, span, power launched in the fiber, and receiver sensitivity), the internal DCM losses are 10 dB (this accounts for DCF and splices and connector losses), and the margin is set at 2 dB, then

$$\text{Net DCM gain} = 6 + 10 + 2 = 18 \text{ dB}$$

Although every effort is made to match DCM's negative dispersion slope with the chromatic dispersion slope as much as possible, in reality DCMs do not reduce dispersion to exactly zero but there is always a small amount of dispersion at the output of a DCM. This becomes particularly significant in fiber paths with several DCMs because residual dispersion is cumulative and puts a limit on the number of DCMs in the path (Fig. 4.23). In addition, the uniformity of dispersion compensation is expressed by normalizing the DCM's dispersion slope at a wavelength selected at about the middle of DCM's spectral range. Thus, based on the normalized compensation, the compensation variability of other wavelengths in the spectral range is expressed as a percent (e.g., 95% or 105%); plotting the compensation variability per wavelength, a relative dispersion slope (RDS) is defined.

Another limiting factor in dispersion is long paths with optical add-drop multiplexers (OADM). The reason is that the dispersion characteristics of a dropped signal and an added are not the same. Figure 4.24 illustrates the latter point for the best and worst cases.

4.4.3.2 Polarization Mode Dispersion Compensators

As described in Chapter 1, polarization mode dispersion (PMD) is the polarization dependency of each wavelength in a "chromatic" signal (the spectral content) due

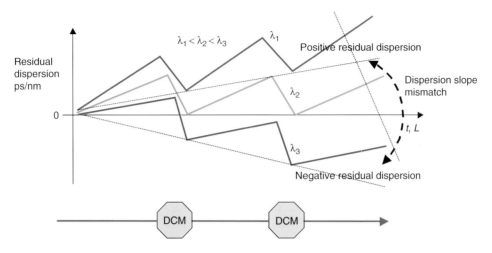

Figure 4.23   Residual dispersion in a path with DCMs.

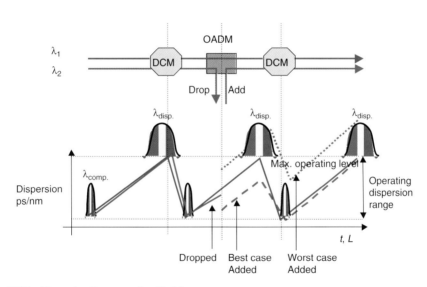

DCM = Dispersion Compensating Module

$\lambda_{comp.}$ = compensated

$\lambda_{disp.}$ = dispersed

Figure 4.24   Dispersion compensation & OADM.

mainly to chemical and geometry imperfections of the fiber core. Although polarization change is very small, as the signal travels along the fiber, the change is cumulative and may become significant. For example, if a fiber has a PMD coefficient equal to $0.12 \text{ ps}/\sqrt{\text{km}}$, it takes 100 km fiber to raise PMD to 10 times that (i.e., only 1.2 ps). However, for 1,000 km fiber length, the cumulative PMD is high at

38 ps. If we compare these numbers with the period of a 40 Gb/s pulse (i.e., 25 ps), the need for PMDC is clear: PMDC is unimportant for 100 km but is very important for 1,000 km.

As a consequence, PMD is a contributor that for short distances (<500 km) and for low bit rates (<10 Gb/s) is insignificant as compared to chromatic dispersion (~0.5 ps/nm-km). Therefore, in such cases, polarization mode dispersion compensation (PMDC) is not contemplated. However, at very long fiber lengths and bit rates at or exceeding 40 Gb/s, PMD becomes significant; even the fiber temperature may become significant, and thence whether the fiber is underground or aerial. In this case, PMDC is included in the design of dispersion compensating modules.

PMDC is accomplished by using strongly polarized fiber that in practice "over-shadows" the polarization states of the signal. PMDC modules still have a residual PMD, which should not be more than half ps and a PDL of more than a tenth of a dB.

4.4.4 Optical Gain Equalizers

In DWDM transmission, optical gain equalization is required because the DWDM signals eventually become unequal in power. This is because the gain characteristic of amplifiers and filters is not flat, because optical cross-connects do not have the same loss characteristics for all channels, or because dispersion is not the same for all channels (see Fig. 4.23), and so on. In addition, as dropping and adding wavelengths takes place, the wavelengths added most likely will not have the same amplitude as those passing through. The end result is that all DWDM channels in the fiber do not arrive at the same optical strength at the receiver. Optical gain equalization improves the signal-to-noise ratio, and thus it enhances the performance of optical amplifiers and allows for longer fiber spans between amplifiers. Therefore, gain equalization is a key function in long-haul applications.

Optical gain equalizers monitor each wavelength channel and selectively make amplitude adjustments on each channel to flatten the optical power spectrum within a fraction of a decibel. They may be static or dynamic.

Static equalizers consist of filters with specific gain profile that counteract the gain variability of channels in the DWDM mix. Such static equalizers, although inexpensive, are applicable to networks that are not expected to (substantially) change.

As system and/or network scalability may alter the gain level, dynamic equalization is able to adjust to this changing environment. A dynamic gain equalizer is an opto-electronic feedback control sub-system that incorporates several components. Among them are an optical demultiplexer and multiplexer, power splitters, per channel variable optical attenuators (VOA), per channel optical power measuring mechanism, and a microprocessor which according to an algorithm performs per channel real-time gain management and VOA adjustments. Based on this, the DWDM signal is demultiplexed, each signal is monitored and adjusted for gain with the VOA, and then all signals are multiplexed again. Clearly, the key component in this method is the transfer function and accuracy of variable attenuators and how well they integrate with the mux/demux. Variable attenuators may be solid state or variable intensity filters; either technology requires voltage to control attenuation. Figure 4.25 illustrates a regenerator with dispersion compensation and gain equalization modules.

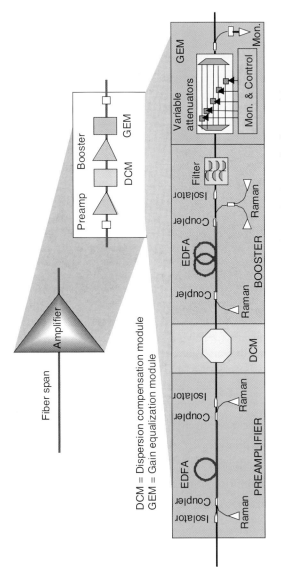

Fiber span

Amplifier

DCM = Dispersion compensation module
GEM = Gain equalization module

Preamp Booster

DCM GEM

PREAMPLIFIER

Raman
Coupler
Isolator
EDFA

Coupler
Isolator
Raman

DCM

BOOSTER

Raman
Coupler
EDFA
Coupler
Isolator
Raman
Filter

GEM

Variable attenuators

Mon. & Control

Mon.

Figure 4.25 A regenerator with dispersion compensation and gain equalization modules.

323

The salient characteristics of controllable or dynamic GEMs are:

- attenuation range
- attenuation resolution
- voltage-attenuation linearity range
- accuracy
- drift over time
- spectral range
- spectral resolution and SR uniformity over spectral range
- PDL and PDL uniformity over spectral range
- PMD and PMD uniformity over spectral range
- insertion loss and IL uniformity over spectral range
- return loss
- maximum input power
- temperature sensitivity
- power dissipation
- physical size

These devices continue to evolve, improve and become more compact and accurate.

4.4.5 Optical Wavelength Translators

Optical wavelength translators receive a signal at wavelength X, they may or may not restore it (2R or 3R), and they translate it to wavelength Y following the recommended ITU grid. This function is very desirable for several reasons:

- to avoid hole burning wavelengths
- to avoid low amplification spectral spots
- to avoid channels with excessive cross-talk
- to avoid channels with high noise content
- to optimize bandwidth (rerouting traffic)
- service survivability (rerouting traffic)

Optical wavelength translators take advantage of the nonlinearity of solid-state devices when they are pumped with a higher power wavelength, which becomes the target wavelength (see Chapter 2).

One significant issue in wavelength translation is wavelength management. If, for example, nodes in a network start changing one wavelength to another, then how this translation is administered so that nodes on the optical path "know" how to route each wavelength? Clearly, there should be an in-band or out-of-band signaling that notifies all nodes on the path of an imminent wavelength translation. However, if notification is in-band, it means that the signal must be terminated by an opaque node.

If out-of-band, then only the supervisory channels must be terminated. All-optical nodes use the out-of-band method as only one or two optical channels need be terminated and not all.

4.4.6 Timing

In communications systems, timing implies the following functions:

- clock extraction from the incoming signal
- jitter or wander removal by passing the serial signal through an elastic store
- retiming the signal at the output with a clock accuracy according to standards, typically ± 20 ppm (parts per million)

Opaque systems extract the clock at and after the photodetector, and based on this and an elastic store buffer they time the (bits of a) signal after converting the optical signal to electrical. At the output, they retime the outgoing signal by virtue of modulation (modulating the laser directly or the modulator after the laser). The clock for retiming can be either a standard reference clock that is provided externally (one active and one standby or alternate), known as Building Information Timing Supply (BITS). In the absence of BITS, clock can be derived (extracted) from an incoming signal (such as an OC-N in SONET or a DS1 in STM or in SONET) (Fig. 4.26).

Timing accuracy is not arbitrary but is defined by standards. In the United States, the primary timing reference source (PRS) is an atomic clock of the highest accuracy (it can miss one tick in 10^{11} or it can slip 2.523 ticks in a year). This clock is referred to as stratum 1, and it is distributed to many geographic areas from which networks and their nodes are synchronized. Subsequent to stratum 1, there are clocks derived from it and thus of lesser accuracy. Depending on the network layer, networks and their nodes must comply with the accuracy of one of the strata (Table 4.3). Typically, the external timing reference to a node is from a BITS clock of stratum 3 or better.

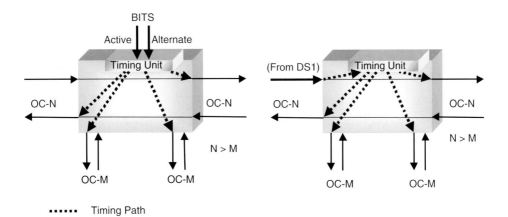

Figure 4.26 Node receiving BITS timing, and node extracting timing from incoming signal.

Table 4.3 Stratum levels

Stratum	Min Accuracy	Slip Rate	System Example
1	10^{-11}	2.523/yr	Primary Ref. Source (PRS)
2	1.6^{-8}	11.06/day	4ESS/5ESS
3	4.6^{-6}	132.48/hr	5ESS/DCS
4	3.2^{-5}	15.36/min	COT/Digital PBX

Timing extraction from the all-optical signal is not currently simple, unless a small part of the optical power of the incoming signal is split off from which clock is extracted as in opaque systems. Similarly, retiming of an all-optical signal is not trivial. Thus, current all-optical commercial systems (nodes, regenerators) do not provide the retiming function but they merely perform amplification and reshaping (dispersion compression), or 2R. However, there are coherent methods under development that promise to soon add the third R to the 2R functionality. These methods are based on fiber loops of fixed delay and circumference, as well as on SOAs with nonlinearity, a pulsed pump and interference methods (see Chapter 2).

4.4.6.1 Optical Phase-Locked Loops

An *optical phase-locked loop* (OPLL) is a method that extracts timing of the optical signal in the optical regime; it is based on a tunable laser source, a filter, and a photodiode bridge and its principle of operation is similar to that of electronic PLLs. For example, consider two optical signals of the same frequency and rms amplitude, one is the frequency of data signal and the other is generated by a local tunable laser source. Each optical frequency impinges on a photodiode of a balanced bridge. If the two optical frequencies are in perfect quadrature (i.e., one is described by $\cos \omega t$ and the other by $\sin \omega t$) and the two frequencies are the same, then the bridge is balanced at a quiescent state. If the two frequencies are not the same, then an unbalanced current is created, amplified, and fed back through a low-pass filter to adjust the frequency of the local laser. Clearly, this arrangement assumes that both light sources (incoming and locally generated) have the same frequency and optical power level. These are two good assumptions as the incoming signal may have drifted in frequency, been dispersed (chromatic and PMD), and been attenuated. These require compensation that complicates the OPLL. However, integration soon will resolve these issues and will make the OPLL a commercially available component.

4.4.6.2 Ultrafast Optical Pattern Recognition

One of the key functions in ultrafast ultrahigh bandwidth systems is real-time pattern recognition. By pattern recognition it is meant recognize and locate the start of frame pattern (SONET, ATM, IP) which is in the overhead or header field. To achieve this, pattern synchronization and knowledge of the location of the sought pattern in the header is required. At bit rates of 10 or 40 Gb/s, ultrafast digital electronic circuitry with picosecond switching capability is challenging, and pattern recognition in the optical regime has not been cost-effectively implemented yet. Here, we describe two methods, an optoelectronic able to locate and transform byte patterns (AR-CAM), and an all-optical pattern detector (OPD) based on weighted optical splitters able to locate the "start of frame" pattern.

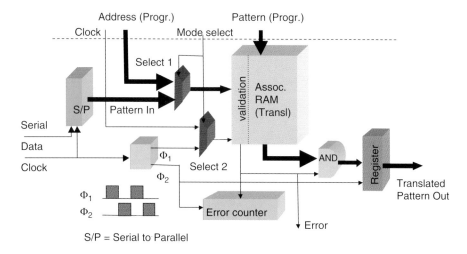

Figure 4.27   Architecture of an associative RAM-based CAM (AR-CAM).

AR-CAM. This is an ultrafast electronic "recognizer" circuitry limited to a clock cir-cuitry and a simple shift register to capture a byte or a word in real time and convert it from serial to parallel. Doing so, it reduces the recognition speed by 8 or 16 and thus the "recognizer" can operate a little slower (in the nsec than the psec regime).

This device, known as *associative RAM-based content addressable memory* (AR-CAM), utilizes fast random access memory (RAM) devices as content addressable taking advantage of the fast access cycle of RAMs (less than 4 nsec) and their low cost. This simple approach has demonstrated pattern recognition and translation at Giga-pattern/sec cost-effectively in SONET, ATM, IP, and other applications (Fig. 4.27).

OPD. This method requires several splitters positioned in series and equidistant on a fiber that carries a single optical channel (Fig. 4.28). The separation of each splitter is such that the travel time of the optical signal from one to the next matches the period of the bit rate (at 10 Gb/s the separation is less than 2 cm). Each splitter removes a small fraction of the optical signal in such a way that all fractions are concurrently multiplexed and detected by a PIN photosensor. The output of the photosensor will provide the highest current level when all bits in the pattern are "one," thus establishing the start of frame (SoF) in the time domain; the assumption is that the SoF is always all "ones." Since the frame is synchronous by nature, other patterns that emulate the SoF will be detected, but they also will be rejected because they are by nature nonperiodic (this is the same argument in all pattern recognizers in communications systems, optical or electronic).

4.4.7   Optical Switching

The optical switching function may consist of a single unit, a module of several units, or even one or two shelves. Depending on the aggregate bandwidth through the switching function, optical switching modules may be simplex (single unprotected switching) or

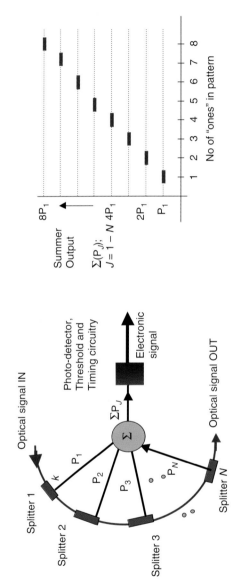

Figure 4.28 All-optical pattern detector and output level.

duplex (one active module and one standby module). Large nodes with aggregate bandwidths in the hundreds of gigabits are clearly "duplex" nodes.

What technology the switching fabric is made of depends on the wavelength capacity (that determines the bandwidth of the system) and the required switching speed (see Chapter 2). Thus, one of the key issues for large switching fabrics is optical interconnectivity as many fibers come in, an equal number of fibers go out, and more fibers are used to drop, add, and interconnect a duplex fabric; in short, a high-density interconnect that presents a challenge in cabling and system physical design. However, as the density of optical channels in fiber increases and as optical backplanes will emerge in the near future, fiber cabling is expected to become less of a challenge.

One of the applications of optical switches is found in *optical add-drop multiplexers* (OADM). In this application, the OADM selectively removes (drops) a wavelength from the west direction, it drops it in the south direction to another node or network, it receives from the south direction the same wavelength with different data content, and adds it in the east direction (see also Chapter 2, Section 2.11 and Figures 2.43 and 2.44).

4.4.8 Control Architectures and Controllers

In this section, we examine the various architectures of the controller function. Thus, the main controller for large nodes is always duplex (an active controller and a standby controller), the shelf controller may be simplex or duplex, and the unit controller is always simplex. Similarly, the processing power, power dissipation, number of interfaces, and physical size of the main controller is much more than the controller of a lower level. For example, a unit controller may consist of a microprocessor/microcontroller at few MHz and few mW supporting one interface port, and a main controller may be at the THz level, consuming several watts and supporting many interface ports.

Depending on node bandwidth capacity and architecture philosophy, the control architecture may be centralized, distributed, or hierarchical.

4.4.8.1 *Centralized Control*

Centralized control is more pervasive in small systems. In this case, the star control architecture is used where a central controller polls several peripheral units (Fig. 4.29). The peripheral units may have a local controller (typically a microprocessor), or they may have a stack of registers, a multiplexer, and an interface driver. The bit rate between the central controller and the peripheral units depends on the number of units polled and on the real-time requirements of the system. Typically, it is a standard Ethernet rate, 10/100Base-T and does not exceed the 1 GbE.

4.4.8.2 *Distributed Control*

Distributed control is more suitable to a mesh LAN that collectively executes a function (such as parallel processing, route finding, neighborhood discovery, automatic restoration, and shelf-healing). In this case, each node requires knowledge of the node type and performance parameters of all nodes in the network (Fig. 4.30). One or two (for redundancy) nodes in the mesh network have been assigned the responsibility to communicate with the network operating system for provisioning and performance

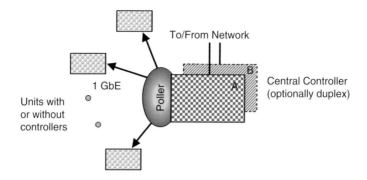

Figure 4.29 A typical centralized control architecture.

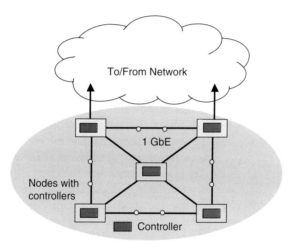

Figure 4.30 A typical distributed control architecture.

monitoring. The control channel is either embedded in the information channel or is carried in a supervisory optical channel at a rate under 100 Mb/s.

4.4.8.3 Hierarchical Control

In large systems, functional units are partitioned into logical groups with a hierarchical structure for system scalability and growability, fast provisioning, efficient performance monitoring, effective fault management, and fast protection. In such systems, each unit may have its own local microcontroller (if required), each group has its own shelf controller that may be duplex or simplex, and a main system controller (typically duplex) that communicates with all shelf controllers and with the network. Communication interfaces among the layered-structured controllers takes place over a separate Ethernet link, with a tree or ring topology and using either a standard protocol or a modified standard protocol to meet special system needs; however, modified standard interfaces come at a premium as new devices must be designed and manufactured (and not low-cost off-the-shelf (OTS)). Typically, the bit rate between system and shelf controllers is

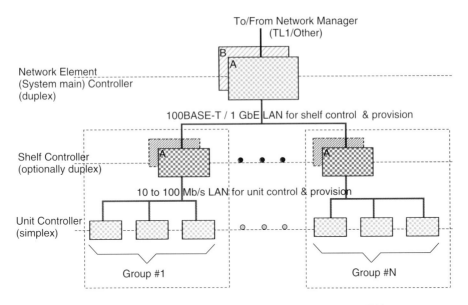

Figure 4.31   A typical hierarchical control architecture for a large DWDM system.

high (1 GbE) and the bit rate between shelf and unit controllers is low (10–100 Mb/s); Figure 4.31 depicts a control hierarchical architecture.

4.4.8.4   Software Domains

Regardless of control architecture, there is an "unseen" layer of software architecture that works in concert with the hardware. Software is organized into domains, each corresponding to a major system function (domain), and manages performance, equipment self-discovery and provisioning, faults, equipment protection, power, cross-connection, synchronization, transmission protection; it also executes communications protocols, both internal and external. The software strategy may be distributed or centralized. Distributed software implies that each unit executes one or more appropriate domains and process collected raw data pertaining to performance, fault, statistics, and so on, the may exchange some high-level information and all together encompass the system software control; this case is more suitable in the distributed control architecture. Centralized software implies that performance, fault, statistical and so on raw data are sent, by various distributed and specialized agents that reside on each functional unit, to a main (or master) software where processing (filtering, correlation, and action) takes place. This architecture is most suitable for distributed control.

Systems/nodes are designed with different requirements and specifications, the complexity of which depends on supported service(s), network architecture, topology and layer (see previous Chapter), and engineering specifications determined by standards. As an example, the switching fabric may be small or large; it may be relatively slow (msec) or very fast (µsec or faster); it may be simple (16 × 16) or complex (1,000 × 1,000); it may cross-connect OC-Ns (e.g., OC-3 at 155.52 Mb/s), or DS-Ns (e.g., DS1 at 1.5 Mb/s or DS0 at 64 Kb/s), or it may cross-connect packets (e.g., Frame Relay, ATM, IP). In data systems, the ports (input and output) are very similar, the controller is similar in functionality but different in terms of protocols as well as performance and O&AM requirements and switching is achieved with a large (memory) buffer. Moreover, the cross-connecting fabric may be static or dynamic, it may be simplex (a single fabric) or duplex (a duplicated fabric) and it may be blocking or nonblocking. Although a simplex fabric provides lower cost of operation, it should be highly reliable with fewer expected mean failures; simplex fabrics are used in low to medium capacity systems. Duplex fabrics are more complex and they are designed such that when one fabric fails the other continues service without interruption; duplex fabrics are used in medium and high capacity systems that require high reliability of service (some examples are systems that cross-connect stock market data, airport traffic control, and so on). In general, blocking was used in legacy statistical switches engineered to handle an average traffic without service interruption; however, the bandwidth per service was in the order of DS3 rates. In DWDM optical systems where the order is more than 100 times that, blocking is highly undesirable. However, in dynamically wavelength configurable DWDM networks, blocking may have merit in the sense that as wavelengths are switched from one fiber to another, under certain circumstances this may not be possible.

As another example, a system may execute a "call processing" (TDM, telephony) or a "call admission control" (ATM) algorithm according to which a connection is established (in connectionless architectures such as IP the path establishing mechanism is distributed). For example, each time a telephone handset is lifted and a number is dialed, a call initiation timed-protocol is executed (e.g., TR-08, TR-303, and SS7). Similarly, in certain local area networks when a request to transmit is sent a timed-protocol may be executed; timed-protocols are those that execute message requests and responses the interval of which is timed. In "connection-full" network architectures, systems that execute such protocols are typically at the "edge" of the network, that is, at the point where the communications network receives subscriber requests and where routing decisions as well as service level agreement (SLA) verifications are made. In "connection-less" network architectures with distributed control, each node in the network executes an input-output connecting algorithm individually to establish a path between origin and destination; in this case, all nodes on the path are involved in this process and this is one of the reasons that such networks cannot match the real-time aspects of the "connection" network. Thus, the complexity of each node/system depends on many factors; among them the type(s) of supported services, bandwidth capacity, number of ports, real-time requirements, and which network (layer) the system belongs to.

In the following sections, we look into some variations of DWDM system architectures, their complexities, and related issues. In particular, we describe the architecture of a Metro-node and of a point-to-point long haul-node and their issues. This description by no means should be interpreted as a detailed guideline for system design, as such guidelines do not publicly exist, but as a foundation that enhances understanding and on which system developers and others can build. A complete description would require a lengthy engineering specification compliant to many standards and recommendations that is far beyond the scope of this book.

4.4.9 Interfaces

A node supports several types of interfaces. Apart from the client–signal interfaces, such as SONET, ATM, IP, and so on, there are internal interfaces between bays, shelves, and units for control and other functions. Similarly, there are external interfaces between the node and the network for operations, administration, management, and protection (OAM&P).

4.4.9.1 External Interfaces

The traditional or legacy network (Chapter 3) was designed for switched-voice traffic and was based on copper loops and a network optimized to process calls. However, this network is evolving to offer integrated access, transport, and multiservices (including switching of voice) at a huge aggregate bandwidth.

Networks are composed of a wide variety of NEs from different vendors. NEs are transmission distribution systems, switching systems, access systems, and the like. This is also known as the NE layer. Each network of NEs is complex and is accompanied by its own element management system (EMS). The EMS manages the elements that comprise the network. This is known as the EMS layer. The communication protocol between NEs in the multivendor network and its corresponding EMS varies. It may be proprietary or standard, such as TL1, signaling network management protocol (SNMP), common management information service element (CMISE), and so on. Conversely, the NE–specific EMSs communicate via an open, standard, northbound interface to a higher-level network management system (NMS) (Fig. 4.32).

NMSs manage the network and systems for capacity, congestion, diversity, and so on. This functionality is known as the *network management layer*. Above that is the *service management layer* (SML) that is responsible for service quality, cost, and so on. Above the NML is the *business management layer* (BML), which is responsible for market share, and so on. This hierarchical management responsibility is known as the telecommunications management network (TMN) five-layer structure (Fig. 4.33). Thus, the TMN is a system that consolidates functionality related to network resource

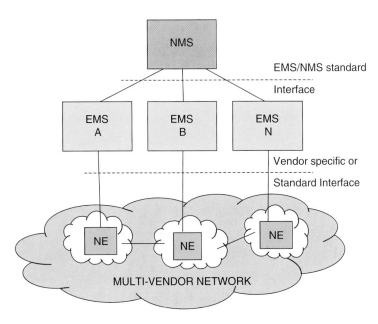

Figure 4.32   A multivendor network is connected with the NMS via EMSs.

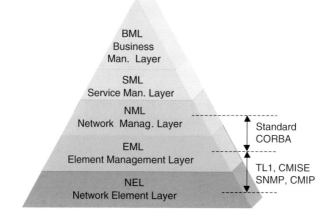

Figure 4.33 The TMN five layering structure and typical interfaces.

management, monitoring, and controlling and ensures the consistent performance of network and services.

The most representative external interface agents between network elements (NEs) and the element management system (EMS) are:

- TL1: transport language 1 sends filtered alarms to a network fault management system. It is also a bidirectional interface for flow-through provisioning from a network management layer (NML) system. TL1 has been traditionally preferred by competitive local exchange carriers) CLECs.

- ODBC: open database connectivity sends bulk data transfer to either an EMS report generator or to external analysis and reporting application. It is also an interface for flow-through provisioning from an NML system.

- SNMP: simple network management protocol is for less complex NE–EMS systems to send faults (traps) to an NML fault management system. It is also a bidirectional interface for flow-through provisioning from an NML system. SNMP does not define network topology nor network auto-discovery. It is a specification of an application layer protocol (ALP) and a management information model (MIM) intended for TCP/IP, but it also supports IP, ATM, FR, ISDN, SMDS LAN (Ethernet, FDDI) and other protocols, and therefore it is currently preferred by Internet service providers (ISP).

- Q3/CMISE: common management information service element is a bidirectional common object request broker architecture (CORBA) interface to send filtered alarms to an NML fault management system and to enable flow-through provisioning from an NML. However, CORBA is a general object distribution framework, and not network management protocol, and it consists of an object request broker (that is, a shared library or middleware), servers and objects.

- CMIP: common management information protocol is used by EMSs to communicate with their NEs.

- Native protocols: these are proprietary protocols used by NEs and their corresponding EMSs.

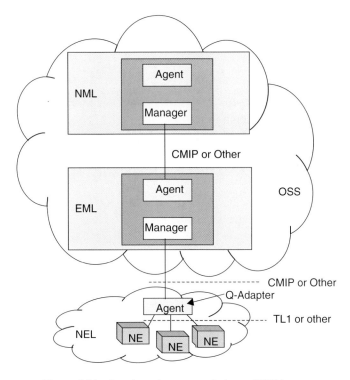

Figure 4.34 Agents and managers between TMN layers.

This large variety of agents may be accommodated within a TMN framework by one of several ways. One is to use a mediation device known as a Q-adapter; A Q-adapter takes a message from a management application and translates it into a language an agent application understands. In turn, the Q-adapter translates alarms and reports from the agent back to the manager (Fig. 4.34).

In the preceding discussion, we have avoided focusing on the management aspects of the various infrastructure layers, such as an IP, ATM, SONET, and so on, and the multilayered infrastructure of, for example, IP over ATM over SONET over optical. Specific networks have specific requirements that deserve to be treated in their own details and standards, which beyond the scope of this section. However, the network management system has the same hierarchical structure, and if, for example, there are ATM elements to be managed, additional parameters would be monitored (QoS, VBR, ABR, CBR, cell rate loss, etc.) to ensure that the network complies with the service level agreement (SLA). We should, however, conclude that there is a great deal of effort to consolidate as much as possible this protocol mosaic, and many manufacturers have developed network management solutions that claim to provide an open platform that easily interfaces with different protocols so that they become transparent to the applications layer.

4.4.9.2 *Internal Interfaces*

Internal interfaces provide the communications link between bays, shelves, and units and their controllers. The type of information exchanged over such links is related to:

- performance parameters and quality metrics
- fault or degradation indication
- alarms
- provisioning at startup
- dynamic provisioning
- automatic discovery of components
- automatic discovery of units and unit type
- testing
- statistical data
- data store
- others, as design requirements demand

The choice of the internal interface, custom versus standard and off-the-shelf (OTS), depends on the system designer. However, this choice is not arbitrary but it is carefully made after examining the cost-performance of standard and available versus custom-designed (proprietary?). The preference is to use a standard interface such as a Gigabit Ethernet (GbE) between the main control and the shelf controllers, scaled down between shelf and unit controllers. However, the communications link between components on the same unit or within a module (a small cluster of units) may be customized to meet specific needs of the node. Typically, customized interfaces are used where standard OTS interfaces do not satisfy the design requirements of the system. In general, customized interfaces on the unit level are implemented with either ASICs or FPGAs.

All communications systems provide a craft interface (through a RJ-45 connector) used by technical personnel to "enter" the management command space of the system using a terminal (such as a portable computer with a GUI interface), known as craft interface termination (CIT). Such commands are useful to initiate system tests on the unit and shelf level and on various signal levels. Via the CIT, technical personnel can also download software upgrades from remote locations using SNMS/CIT file transfer protocol (FTP) or to manually provision various units.

4.4.9.3 Network Management

A telecommunications network consists of resources such as access systems, switching systems, cross-connects, and so on. In TMN these resources are referred to as network elements (NEs). TMN is a standard way to manage a telecommunications network, and it enables communication between operations support systems (OSS) and NEs.

In the previous section we described the five telecommunications management network (TMN) layers:

- the network element layer (NEL)
- the element management layer (EML)
- the network management layer (NML)
- the service management layer (SML), and
- the business management layer (BML)

The TMN model provides a hierarchical approach to network management and segregates the management responsibilities. This makes it possible to use different operating systems, different databases, and different programming languages. The TMN enables telecommunication service providers to achieve interconnectivity and communication across operating systems and telecommunications networks. The TMN is represented by several building blocks:

- The OS performs operations system functions, including monitoring and controlling; the OS can also provide some of the mediation, Q-adoption, and WS functions.

- The MD performs mediation between local TMN interfaces and the OS information model.

- The QA translates between TMN and non-TMN interfaces. For example, a TL1 Q-adapter translates between a TL1 ASCII message and the CMIP, the TMN interface protocol.

- The NE has a standard TMN interface and it contains manageable information that is monitored and controlled by an OS.

- The WS performs workstation functions. WSs translate information between TMN format and a GUI (graphical user interface) displayable format.

- The DCN represents OSI layers 1 to 3 and is the communication network within a TMN.

ITU-T has partitioned the general management functionality offered by systems into five key areas, Fault, Configuration, Accounting, Performance, and Security, known by the acronym FCAPS. FCAPS is not the responsibility of a specific layer of the TMN architecture but portions of FCAPS functionality are performed at different layers. For example, as part of fault management, the EML logs is detail each discrete alarm or event. It then filters this information (it abstracts) and forwards it to an NMS (at the NML layer) that performs alarm correlation across multiple nodes and technologies and root-cause analysis. In addition to fault management, there are configuration, performance, security, and accounting.

The three lower levels of the TMN model describe how a network's NEs are managed by their corresponding EMS and how EMSs are managed by an NMS. It is important to notice that each NE in their network communicates with their respective EMS. Similarly, one EMS is deployed for a group of NEs of the same type. EMSs control and manage all aspects of their domain and ensure maximum usage of available resources. From the detailed knowledge about the NEs and the network, the EMS abstracts relevant aspects, which communicates via a northbound interface to NML. Adjacent TMN layers interface to provide communications between applications. The TMN M.3010 document allows for the use of multiple protocols and thus open standards such as SNMP and CORBA. The TMN model has been effectively used to represent graphically complex relationships within network-management architectures.

The EMS plays a key role in maintaining both NEs and transmission facilities. It is the primary repository of detailed history of NE-specific faults, QoS, events, technicians' actions, and performance data. The EMS model includes service provisioning, service assurance, EMS and NE operations support, and automation enabling. Some of the tasks of an EMS are:

- Installing the NE (load parameters, auto-discover the NE equipment, establish and verify connectivity).

- Collection of data used to determine whether the service provided matches subscribers' usage characteristics and to forecast demand.

- Provisioning and planning capacity (auto-discover NE components, provide inventory information and information on available capacity).

- Upgrading the NE (auto-discover new equipment, download software upgrades, maintain concurrency between EMS and NE software and hardware releases.

- Protecting NEs and EMS database integrity (back up and restore databases, monitor loss of NE–EMS connectivity, resynchronize database when connectivity is lost).

- Service assurance to ensure that the purchased service is provisioned as agreed and delivered. This includes network maintenance and restoration and network monitoring and control.

- Periodic collection of quality metrics to characterize the performance of network resources and discover degradation trends.

- Fault management support to ensure that service remains available and at the agreed QoS. This involves the proactive monitoring of network resources to detect degradations and faults, performance, and utilization parameters.

- QoS assurance to ensure that the quality metrics characterizing the network performance remain within the agreed limits.

- Service usage to measure subscriber usage of the resources for billing. It applies only to those NEs that provide a chargeable function, such as connection and call setup.

The NML has three primary functions: fault management and root-cause analysis, integrated end-to-end service provisioning of multivendor and multitechnology networks, and integration between the EML and the SML.

- Service provisioning encompasses tasks such as equipment installation, capacity planning, capacity provisioning, and NE database integrity upgrading and protecting.

NML, SML, and BML perform high-level management processes, such as network inventory, development and planning, network configuration, and network provisioning.

- Inventory management keeps a detail record of all NE resources in the subnetwork; locations, types of equipment, model numbers, serial numbers, versions, installation dates, and more.

- Configuration management performs gross control of subnetwork resources, topologies, and redundancies. It includes the installation and turn-up of new equipment resources, the assignment of resources to trunk routes or service areas, and network protection switching. It may also include the partitioning of resources into virtual private networks (VPNs).

- Provisioning involves the creation of specific connections or the enabling of specific subnetwork features, including QoS, which are assigned to a specific subscriber for an agreed period.

4.5 WAVELENGTH MANAGEMENT STRATEGY

In current DWDM systems, each wavelength is used as a separate channel and thus, the wavelength assignment may be fixed over the complete path (end-to-end) in the network, even if the path is defined over several subnetworks, each managed by a different network (domain) operator (Fig. 4.35). As a side note, the interface between two domains is known as optical network-to-network interface (ONNI) and in optical transport networks (OTN) is known as interdomain interface (IrDI); the interface between two nodes within the same domain is known as intradomain interface (IaDI). This interface defines the communication interface requirements for interoperability and internetworking.

To examine what this means, let us consider an opaque system with two fibers in, f_{IN1} and f_{IN2}, two fibers out, f_{OUT1} and f_{OUT1}, two wavelengths per fiber λ_{11}, λ_{12}, λ_{21}, and λ_{22}, multiplexers and demultiplexers and a 4×4 switching matrix, where $\lambda_{11} = \lambda_{21}$ and $\lambda_{12} = \lambda_{22}$. Now, we consider two distinct cases.

Case A. We want to switch λ_{11} from f_{IN1} to f_{OUT1}, λ_{12} from f_{IN1} to f_{OUT2}, λ_{21} from f_{IN2} to f_{OUT1}, and λ_{22} from f_{IN2} to f_{OUT2}. This is a simple case for which there is no wavelength conflict; that is, two same wavelengths are not switched to the same output fiber, Figure 4.36.

Case B. We want to switch λ_{11} from f_{IN1} to f_{OUT1}, λ_{12} from f_{IN1} to f_{OUT2}, λ_{21} from f_{IN2} to f_{OUT2}, and λ_{22} from f_{IN2} to f_{OUT1}. This is a typical case for which there is wavelength conflict; that is, two same wavelengths are switched on the same output fiber (for example, λ_{11} and λ_{22}) (Fig. 4.37). Thus, in order to avoid wavelength conflict, wavelength converters must be used. In Figure 4.37, the wavelength converters (WCn) have been placed at the output of the switching fabric. However, their actual location is a design choice and it depends on the switching technology of the fabric. For example, wavelength converters may be located internal to the fabric, at the outputs (as shown) or at both the input and at the output of the fabric.

In the case of fixed wavelength assignment over the complete optical path (Figure 4.35) each node on the path has been provisioned of the input–output–wavelength association. That is, the node "knows" where a wavelength comes from (input) and where it goes to (output). However, in the case of wavelength conversion (or translation), how does the next node on the optical path "know" where the converted wavelength comes from and where it is destined to? And, what if the next node needs to convert the already converted wavelength to another? Figure 4.38 illustrates N signals converted from one wavelength to another as they travel through and are switched by three nodes. Therefore, in DWDM networks the issue of wavelength management arises for the first time, since it was not encountered in legacy single-wavelength optical (such as SONET) or nonoptical systems and networks. In fact, in dynamically wavelength configurable DWDM networks, wavelength blocking may occur as wavelengths are

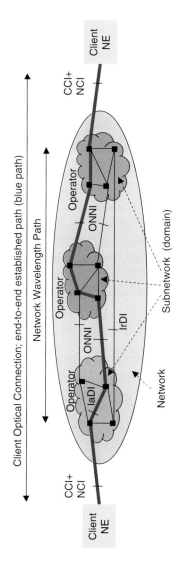

Figure 4.35 An optical path across several subnetwork domains. Each optical link of the path has the same wavelength (shown in blue).

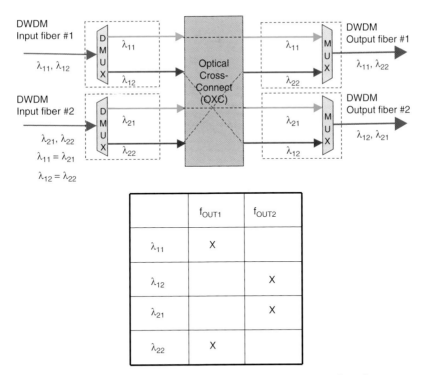

Figure 4.36 DWDM cross-connect and connectivity table; Case A.

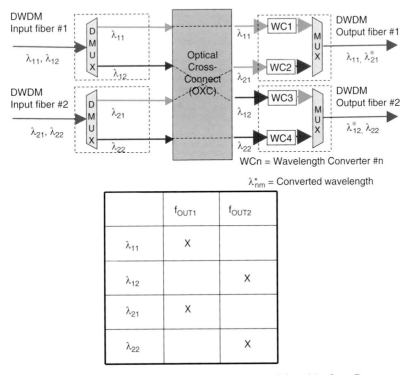

Figure 4.37 DWDM cross-connect and connectivity table; Case B.

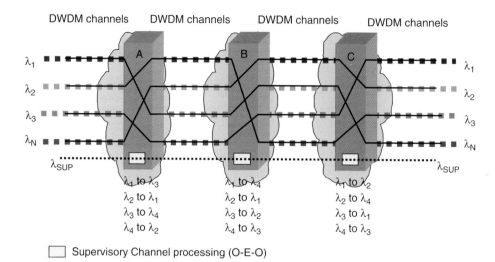

Figure 4.38   DWDM channels arriving from a fiber at one wavelength are switched to other fibers as they pass through concatenated cross-connects with converted wavelength. The supervisory channel λ_{SUP} remains on the same designated fiber.

switched from one fiber to another. To study this, assume K fibers per switching node and N channels (wavelengths) per fiber, each channel lit (or transporting information). Then, there are NXK wavelengths to be switched. In general, there are engineering rules that prescribe the maximum number of wavelengths to be switched from fiber to fiber, such as 50-50. That is, 50% of the channels will pass through express and 50% can be switched. In such case, the problem reduces to switching $N \times K/2$ or $N^* \times K$, where $N^* = N/2$; that is, in principle not different that before. Therefore, assuming that N^* wavelengths from one fiber were switched to another fiber(s) implies that $(N - N^*)$ channels are available to be filled from other fibers. However, there are $(K - 1) \times N^*$ potential wavelengths contending for the same wavelength space $(N - N^*)$, where $(N - N^*)$ is much smaller than $(K - 1) \times N^*$. Clearly, this is a wavelength contention situation where blocking may occur. In this case, one studies the probability that $(K - 1) \times N^*$ channels may have the same destination. If the probability is such that $P > (N - N^*)$ channels require to be switched on the same fiber with the same destination, then two things may occur: drop the excess wavelengths above $(N - N^*)$, a very undesirable case, or pass onto the fiber $(N - N^*)$ channels and the remaining on other fibers following a separate path and perhaps switched by another station in the ingress direction. If the next station is not successful, then perhaps the one after the next station may be able to switch channels to the correct destination fiber, and so on. Thus, now the number of stations on the path gets involved in this exercise.

Clearly, wavelength translations do not present a technological issue when switches are opaque as all optical signals (wavelengths) are converted to electrical; the system keeps connectivity tables with source and destination identification (ID) codes as well as wavelength values for each incoming signal. In this case, each node on the path "reads" the destination ID and "knows" where to switch to or route the optical signal, assign a wavelength and multiplex many signals in the fiber. However, all-optical nodes are not currently able to optically "read" ID codes off the optical signal without imposing a penalty on the optical signal. This is predominantly addressed with two different strategies, (centralized) network wavelength management and distributed management.

In the centralized case, a network wavelength management function provisions each node with *wavelength assignments* establishing semi-static cross-connectivity over a selected path. Thus, the network wavelength manager "knows" at any time all possible wavelength conversions on a path, whereby each link of the path may have a different wavelength, Figure 4.39. This case depends on a centralized database and algorithm that finds the optimum shortest and bandwidth efficient path with the fewer wavelength conversions. Its speed however depends on how fast a path can be established; that is, how fast it can communicate with all nodes, and how fast each node can be provisioned. Clearly, this case implies that all communications interfaces with the various domains are compatible.

In the distributed case, there is an additional optical channel that is common to all nodes and over which messages are exchanged. These messages convey input–output–wavelength associations. Thus, optimization of wavelength reassignment is left to each node to execute. This optical channel is also used to communicate from node-to-node additional information. This is known as *supervisory channel* (SUPV). The *supervisory channel* is terminated and sourced by each node (see Fig. 4.38), is multiplexed with the client data channels in the same fiber but it has a relatively lower bit rate than data channels (under Gb/s compared with over 2.5 Gb/s), and it may be outside the spectral range of data channels. In addition, it may or may not be protected; supervisory channel protection may be on the same fiber (two independent wavelengths in the same fiber) or it may be on two fibers (two same wavelengths in two different fiber).

The supervisory channel conveys messages from node to node very fast and thus it allows for *dynamic system reconfigurability*. The reconfigurability speed is bounded only by the switching speed of the fabric, by the acquisition time of wavelength converters and other tunable components in the path (such as filters, lasers, etc.), and by time required to communicate the message to the control unit and back (latency) and by the processing time.

Dynamic system reconfigurability is required for many reasons, such as system and *network upgrades* and *service restoration*.

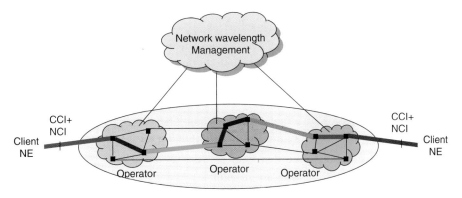

Figure 4.39 An optical path across several subnetwork domains. Each optical link may have different wavelength.

Network upgrades entail downloading new software versions and new system configurations. During network upgrades it is preferable that service is not affected.

Because of component degradation/failure, fiber cuts, excessive additive noise due to nonlinear phenomena, spectral noise, optical power loss, amplification gain drifts and so on, service may be degraded or even lost. Therefore, in order to continue uninterrupted service, systems and networks are architected and designed for service restoration. Service restoration may be on several levels, on the channel, on the fiber, on the node level, and on the network level, and each at various degrees of significance.

Service restoration on the channel level implies that a single wavelength has been degraded or lost affecting all traffic transported by the affected channel. A channel may be affected either by the degradation or by the failure of a single component, by excessive induced noise, or by excessive power loss of the optical signal. Service restoration is the action to either remove the affecting cause or to move the channel from one wavelength to another.

Service restoration on the fiber level implies that all wavelengths in a fiber are affected either because of a fiber cut or because of component failure that affects all channels. Service restoration is the action to move all channels from one fiber to another.

Service restoration on the node level implies that traffic on all fibers at a node are affected because of node failure. Service restoration is the action to move all traffic to other nodes bypassing the faulty node.

Service restoration on the network level implies that many nodes in a network have failed; this is also termed *disaster* failure. Service restoration is the action to move all traffic to other parts of the network bypassing the faulty nodes.

The mechanisms for these four levels may be summarized as follows:

- Service restoration on the channel level:
  a. set BER threshold per channel (according to engineering rules).
  b. monitor BER of incoming signals.
  c. correlate excessive BER of channels and determine if they belong to different fibers or to adjacent channels in same fiber.
  d. if in the same fiber, then adjust amplifier/equalizer taps or hop to another wavelength, if supported, by sending supervisory messages backward.
- Service restoration on the fiber level:
  a. set power threshold level of each channel to two threshold levels; one minimum indicating power/no-power and another to higher level indicating good or marginal. If BER is used, the good/marginal level may be eliminated.
  b. monitor power of incoming signals.
  c. if power is lost on all channels of the same fiber, then there is a fiber cut, or a key component on the link has failed affecting all channels.
  d. Important question: does this fiber support the supervisory channel? If yes, switch to protection supervisory channel.
- Service restoration on the node level:
  a. monitor power of outgoing signals.

   b. If outgoing signals have failed but the incoming signals have not, there is a faulty node. The declaration of a faulty node is made if the failure persists after a switch to protection port has been attempted.

   c. Previous node in the network reroutes traffic such that the faulty node is bypassed. This depends on the survivability strategy supported by the network.

- Service restoration on the network level:

   a. similar to the previous case, but now many nodes fail.

   b. nodes in the network synergistically reroute traffic such that the faulty nodes are bypassed. In this case, low priority traffic may be dropped supporting high priority traffic only. This depends on the disaster avoidance strategy supported by the network and whether nodes belong to the same domain.

However, one issue that must be kept in mind is that, as one wavelength changes to another and new routes are assigned, the optical power budget of the optical path for a particular signal may change, and therefore amplification, dispersion compensation, and equalization become more significant to maintain the quality of signal and the quality of service at the agreed upon levels.

4.6 EQUIPMENT SENSING STRATEGY

In large communications system, unit auto-discovery is particularly important when units are "hot-inserted," that is, when the system is already powered-up and operational. In fact, "hot-insertion" is a requirement for many communications systems; units are inserted in the system either during *system population* or during unit replacement. Therefore, it is also required that as soon a unit is inserted in the system, the system automatically identifies the unit; that is, it "reads" the type, model number, serial number, manufacturing date, etc. of this unit. This action is known as "*auto-discovery*," and the identification data of each unit is known as *unit inventory*.

The auto-discovery procedure starts as soon as the inserted unit comes in electrical contact with the system or as soon as it breaks contact with it. Upon unit contact or disconnect, the system controller is automatically notified (or interrupted).

There are several methods to achieve auto-discovery. The *polling method* requires that the system controller polls periodically all units in the system and discovers if one has been removed or newly inserted. The *tone method* requires that a newly inserted unit in the system transmit a synthesized tone to an equipment administration unit. The polling requires control resources, which in many cases are not affordable. The tome method requires additional hardware resources that add to the design complexity of the system.

A third and simpler method that has been extensively used is by *electrical contact*. According to this, a unit connector pin is allocated, which upon electrical contact with the system backplane it grounds a wire that is connected with an interrupt input of the processor. This wire corresponds to a set of coordinates of the system, known as *slot identification*, where each coordinate set (bay number, shelf number, group number and unit or slot number) has a representation in the processor equipment management registers. Upon interrupt, the processor locates the unit based on the coordinates of the grounded wire and it communicates with the unit over the controller interface using an Ethernet protocol as described previously; the unit contains all required information about it in a nonerasable memory. Similarly, when a unit is removed from the system, it disconnects the wire and it interrupts the controller. One of the drawbacks of this method is that backplane connector pins may be at a premium. However, manufacturers have addressed this issue and have developed solutions to minimize the number of required pins.

4.7 FAULT DETECTION AND REPORTING STRATEGY

Faults at different levels of the traditional optical network have been thoroughly studied. Fault monitoring, detection, triggers, actions, reporting, and restoration scenarios have been defined in standards (e.g., STM, SONET/SDH, and ATM).

However, as the multiwavelength optical transport network (DWDM-OTN) becomes "all-photonic" and with ever-increasing bit rates, the photonic physical layer fault strategy must be reviewed and updated. Because of the huge amount of data rate passing a node, faults should be detected as soon as they occur (within nanoseconds) and should be restored or isolated within less than a millisecond, and when equipment fails (such as a unit) and must be replaced, unit protection should be incorporated into the system design to allow for uninterrupted service and for the craft personnel to replace the failed unit, which may require hours.

The evolution of the DWDM-OTN is predicated on the *transport layer functionality* to the (physical) optical layer and to a *maintenance strategy*. Thus, a need arises to:

- study the degradation and failure mechanisms of optical components
- study the effect of optical component degradation and failures on the client signal
- classify degradations and failures according to impact on the client signal
- investigate optical component failure detection mechanisms
- investigate degradation and failure alarms and reporting mechanisms
- investigate degradation and failure restoration strategies
- investigate correlation of symptoms to probabilistically deduce a possible degradation or failure
- work out possible timing issues (time to declare failure, time to fix failure, etc.)
- work out communication mechanisms of degradations or failures to neighboring nodes, and to network operating system
- work out possible signal overhead (OH) not currently addressed and node responsibility pertaining to OH monitoring
- develop a complete set of OA&M features for the optical layer
- work out error detecting and correcting mechanisms for end to end signal integrity
- work out signal, node, and network security issues that may impact the quality of signal and service
- quantify the required fault coverage per service level agreement (SLA) and develop fault detection and recover mechanisms assuring the SLA
- work out standards

This list pertains to the optical layer. Indeed, this is the layer that impacts the clients signal mostly. Higher layers are not "optical" but they are rather electronic or software. However, this does not mean that they are less important, as they may also cause failures that impact the client signal or service. As an example, a corrupted database may also corrupt SLA, it may mis-switch a path or it may provision the transmitter or receiver wrongly. Nevertheless, these failures are well understood, and countermeasures have already been developed to minimize their probability.

From a network layer perspective, fault detection takes place within an administrative domain. In it, the signal integrity is monitored by the node at its inputs and is compared with an expected value. In general, fault detection, testing, and restoration are preferred to be service nonintrusive. Currently, nonintrusive testing in the optical regime is difficult; however, the level of development activity in optical sensors increases and this will not be the case in the near future. Typically, the received optical signal is monitored for:

- power level
- noise content (bit error rate, optical signal-to-noise ratio)
- wavelength accuracy
- polarization state
- linewidth

4.7.1   Fault Detection on the Network Level

When a failure condition is detected, it is communicated to the network management entity responsible within that domain. It is also communicated to the neighboring nodes to inhibit them from false failure detection and reporting. For example, when a node experiences a failure that impacts the client signal, all nodes downstream of the path may experience the same failure.

The network management entity initiates remote testing, fault correlation, fault locating, isolation, and restoration or protection procedures. The node will execute all service restoration actions and communicate the results to management. As a consequence, architecting an effective DWDM transport network requires that many critical factors be considered, such as:

- multiwavelength optical transmission engineering so that influences due to nonlinearities, dispersion, wavelength–wavelength interactions, and OADM do not adversely affect the link/path power budget
- signal and service survivability on both single and multiwavelength levels; this ensures that a single wavelength or many wavelengths may be affected by degradation or fault of a component or a fiber cut (which affects all channels in it)
- interoperability so that as the optical signal is transported from one provider domain to another monitoring the same signal parameters and with the same accuracy, and having the same or equivalent detection and restoration capabilities
- payload transparency so that clients use the same network for a variety of payload types

4.7.2   Fault Detection Identifiers

From an end-to-end perspective, the signal carries overhead information. This is included by the source end terminal to communicate with the destination end terminal. The client does not "see" this overhead. Some of this overhead is:

- Trace identifier (TI) to verify that the signal is transported to the correct destination. This is particularly important in DWDM, as the signal may have changed from one wavelength to another (see Fig. 4.36).

- Forward defect indicator (FDI) conveys failure information to nodes downstream. This may be used to suppress false fault alarms by the downstream nodes. In DWDM and in "all-optical" networks, the FDI is difficult to use in the signal overhead of optical signals because "all-optical" nodes cannot read overhead. In this case, the FDI is carried by the supervisory signal, which is terminated and re-sourced by each node.

- Backward defect indicator (BDI) is a response by the end terminal acknowledging notification of the fault condition; it is used in conjunction with FDI. Like the FDI, this overhead is carried by the supervisory signal.

- End-to-end communications channel is included in the overhead for end-to-end testing and troubleshooting and path integrity verification.

- Loop-back at different levels for fiber span, between node links, and various path segments are not currently supported in the signal overhead of "all-optical" networks. However, this information is conveyed in the supervisory channel as well as the results of each test.

4.7.3   Overhead, Data, and Error Correction: The Digital Wrapper

The SONET frame consists of two fields, one that contains overhead and one that contains client data (see Chapter 3). The SONET overhead is also partitioned into section, line and path related overhead data. In the overhead, there are bytes, which provide a mechanism for error control. Error control implies that a number of errored bits in the signal are detected, E_d, and a number of errored bits are corrected, E_c; typically, $E_c < E_d$. However, the error control achieved with few bytes in the SONET overhead first does not provide a sufficiently powerful correction or a very fast corrective mechanism, which is required by ultrahigh bit rate optical signals and particularly DWDM signals. In ultrafast DWDM signals (10 to 40 Gb/s), there is a strong relationship of the optical signal to noise ratio (OSNR) with bit-error-rate (BER) and the received optical power, or the optical penalty at the receiver (see Chapter 2). In general, the more degraded the OSNR, the more the penalty and thus the higher the BER. As a consequence, the fiber span between transmitter and receiver (without signal restoration in between) must be shorter to support the expected quality of signal and quality of service. For example, OSNR increases by approximately 5 dB each time the bit rate quadruples; for example, at 2.5 Gb/s OSNR is approximately 10×10^{-10} dB, at 10 Gb/s is approximately 15×10^{-10} dB, and at 40 Gb/s is approximately 20×10^{-10} dB. This clearly affects the receiver sensitivity, which at 2.5 Gb/s is below -40 dBm, and at 40 Gb/s puts a penalty by more than 10 dBm. As a result, the transmitter requirements are also affected from below 5 dB (at 2.5 Gb/s) to approximately 10 dB (at 40 Gb/s).

However, in many long-haul applications it is desirable that the fiber span be as long as possible. To ensure that the quality of signal at the receiver will be at the expected level, a strong error correction code is added, which, by virtue of correcting the number of errors in the signal, effectively allows for longer fiber. Such strong error correction code is the forward error (detection and) correction, or FEC. Such FECs have been used extensively in submarine applications (see, e.g., ITU-T recommendation G.975, *"Forward Error Correction for Submarine Systems,"* November 1996). As an example, the TAT-14 transatlantic submarine cable network launched in September 1998 (by a consortium of more than 50 telecommunications companies) links the United States to Denmark, France, Germany, the Netherlands, and the United Kingdom. Such multimillion or more than billion dollar projects are designed to meet the exponential growth in transatlantic traffic due primarily to fast-expanding demand for data, Internet, and multimedia services.

Table 4.4 illustrates the performance of an FEC by listing some BER values before and after FEC. A poor signal with BER at 10^{-4} has been FEC-improved to a high-quality signal with BER 2×10^{-13} (communications systems require a minimum of 10^{-12}).

The structure of an error detecting and error correcting code based on a Reed–Solomon error correction code is illustrated in Figure 4.40. This code is annotated as

Table 4.4   BER before and after FEC

FEC Performance	
BER before FEC	BER after FEC
10^{-3}	5.0×10^{-5}
10^{-4}	2.0×10^{-13}
10^{-5}	6.3×10^{-24}
10^{-6}	6.4×10^{-33}
10^{-7}	1.0×10^{-40}

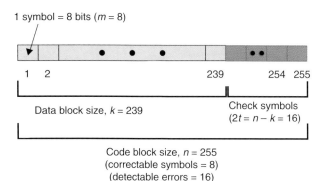

Figure 4.40 Example of a RS(255,239,17) Reed–Solomon error correction code n/k; ($n = 255$, $k = 239$ and $2t + 1 = 17$).

RS(255,239,17), where the numbers in parentheses indicate that the total length is 255 bytes, 139 of which are data. This code is able to detect 16 errors and correct 8 errors.

In optical transport networks (long-haul), the fundamental philosophy of SONET protocol frame has been adopted but with a more powerful protocol suitable for ultra-high data rates, known as *digital wrapper*. The power of the digital wrapper lies in a forward error correction (FEC), tandem connection (TC) functions, path level protection, and higher bandwidth communication channels in the sense of per overhead byte.

The basis of the per optical channel frame of the multiwavelength optical transport network is on three blocks; a (1 byte) block of overhead for operations, administration, and maintenance for the optical channel, a 238-byte block of data (the optical channel payload envelope) in which the client-formatted payload is mapped (SONET, ATM, IP, etc.), and of a separate 16-byte block that contains the FEC code (Fig. 4.41). This 255-byte comprises a *digital wrapper subframe*. Although this subframe with FEC greatly improves the BER, it also adds bandwidth by approximately 7%.

This digital wrapper requires no processing pointers (like SONET); it is format-independent; all payload types are acceptable (SONET, IP < FR ATM, etc., even types not defined yet), it supports the ITU-T optical channel OAM functions (see ITU-T recommendation G.872); and it supports end-to-end performance monitoring required for native data services and lease wavelength applications. It also has a constant bit rate, which implies that the client payload must fit into the optical channel payload envelope.

On the positive side, 16 subframes define a basic frame called an *optical transport unit* (OTU) (Fig. 4.42), and four basic frames define a superframe so that the digital wrapper may evolve to accommodate network bandwidth elasticity, and scalability (see ITU-T recommendation G.709).

Like SONET/SDH, transmission of the OTU requires that long sequences of "1"s or "0"s be avoided. The latter is ensured only if a suitable scrambler is used. According to ITU G.709, "the operation of the scrambler shall be functionally identical to that of a frame synchronous scrambler of sequence length 65,535," and that "the generating polynomial shall be $1 + x + x3 + x12 + x16$." Thus, the probability of data emulating the scrambler and generating a long string of "0"s or "1"s, although finite, is negligible. Scrambling is performed after FEC has been calculated and inserted in the OTU signal (Fig. 4.43). The OTU frame consists of only 4,080 bytes, which is much smaller than 65,535. This implies that the scrambler is reset after the last byte of the frame.

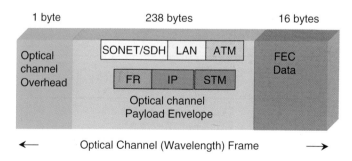

Figure 4.41 The basis of the optical channel digital wrapper.

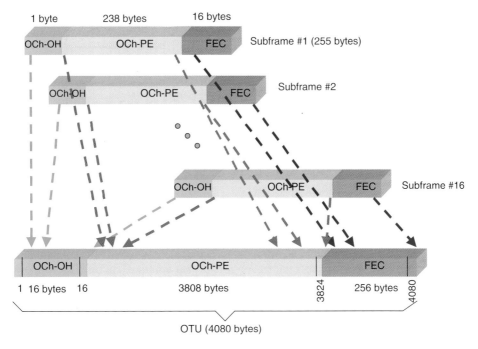

Figure 4.42 The optical transport unit consists of 16 byte-interleaved subframes.

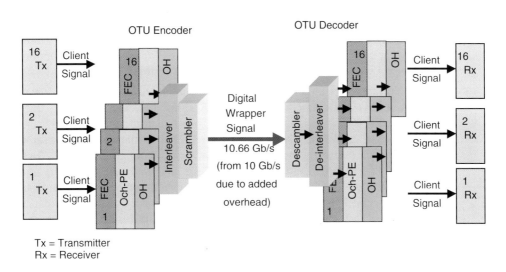

Tx = Transmitter
Rx = Receiver

Figure 4.43 OTU basic sequence of events at the transmitter and receiver sides.

The digital wrapper defines three sublayers: the path, the tandem connection, and the section. The overhead in an optical channel (OCh) basic digital wrapper frame provides sublayer features for all three, section (OCh-S), tandem connection (OCh-TC), and path (OCh-P) (Fig. 4.44).

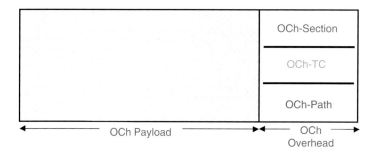

Figure 4.44 Definition of sublayers in the basic optical channel (OCh) frame structure.

For example:

- The OCh-S section sublayer processes associated functions include features for framing, FEC, performance monitoring, and data communication. The supported FEC code is a nonbinary Reed–Solomon (255,239) systematic linear cyclic block code that operates on bytes (or symbols). It detects up to 16 errored symbols and it corrects up to 8 errored bits. A count of FEC-corrected errored bits and a count of uncorrectable errored blocks are communicated to the network manager. To execute FEC, an OTU is de-interleaved into 16 subframes and the FEC is operated on each subframe and over all bytes (1 to 255). The FEC is calculated over all bytes from 1 to 239, and the result is added in bytes 240 to 255 (see Fig. 4.37). In addition, the signal label (SL) is used to verify that the client signal is compatible with the equipment to which it is connected. To illustrate the FEC benefit, consider a signal with an optical signal-to-noise ratio of 22 dB corresponding to a BER of 10^{-5}. When the signal is FEC corrected (this implies that the digital wrapper is used) it has a BER better than 10^{-16}.

- The OCh-TC includes features for tandem connection management (ID, FDI/BDI, SDM/BQI, TCM) and data communication. A single byte contains a TC trace code 0x00-0xFF is also supported. A mismatch between the incoming and outgoing trace byte causes an alarm, which is reported to the network operator. Operators, too, can set outgoing trace bytes and read incoming trace bytes. Tandem connection APS applies in a similar APS for path (see next item). The trail trace (ID) provides the ability to verify connectivity through connection functions (such as, patch panels, OADM, optical cross-connect). The forward and backward defect indications (FDI/BDI) provide the ability to localize faults and enable single-ended maintenance. The tandem connection maintenance (TCM) maintains a channel through an entire subnetwork that does not include the OCh termination elements.

- The OCh-P includes features for optical channel ID, automatic protection switching (APS), fault indicators (FDI/BDI), signal quality monitoring and backward quality indication (SQM/BQI), and data communication. The path APS provides end-to-end wavelength protection; service and path protection can be in different sub-networks or in different service provider domains. However, current optical line systems protect the optical multiplex section layer (that is, when all wavelengths fail due to fiber cut) and there is no protection for one or more wavelengths, although certain system topologies (for example, ring with optical add-drop multiplexer) support protection on the wavelength level but based on proprietary protocols. The SQM/BQI provides the capability to isolate sources of degraded performance and verify quality of service.

4.8   POWER STRATEGY

Communications systems are typically powered by -48 V DC power supply. This power is then down- (and/or up-) converted to 5, 3.2, or other voltages, as electronic and optical components require. However, because the reliability of system also depends on supplied power, the powering plan is redundant (duplex), that is, two independent -48 V feeders supply power to the system, one in active mode and the other in standby mode, but one supplies power to the shelf. Power sensors detect the power status (or "health") of each feeder. When the sensors detect that the supplied voltage is below a threshold voltage (typically at -39.25 ± 0.25 V and for longer than 100 msec), they cause a feeder switch in a manner that generates no power transients that may cause a disruptive effect on transmission or excessive electromagnetic interference (EMI). This is resolved easily with power filters per feeder. Similarly, the sensors should not cause a switch to a restored feeder unless the (feeder's) voltage is greater by 0.25 V than the voltage it caused a switch to stand by or shut down.

In addition, there must be overvoltage protection on both active and standby feeders. This is resolved with circuit breakers. Depending on the circuit breaker distribution strategy throughout the system, the breakers may be slow-blow and they should be able to handle the maximum allowable voltage and current they are designed for indefinitely. In one distribution, there may be a main feeder slow blow (60 ms) breaker (at the power feed to the system), a shelf slow blow (50 ms) breaker (at the power feed to the shelf), and a fast blow breaker on the unit. Other configurations depend on the size and complexity of the system; for example, small systems (shelf-size) may have a single breaker.

A key design in the power detection strategy is not to power the sensors by the power feeder they monitor. Another key design is to allocate the same pins across the backplane should be assigned for power and ground and they should be isolated from low-voltage signals. In addition, backplane pins must be sequenced so that power and ground are applied first and then the signals.

When the active feeder fails (because of under- or overvoltage) and power is switched to the standby feeder, an alarm signal should be generated to alert the system administrator (craft and software). It also is desirable that technical personnel be able to see which of the two feeders supplies power; this visual indication is achieved LEDs on the front panel of the system. All critical components on the power plant (fuses, sensors, power switching, etc.) must be monitored and cause a message to be sent to the shelf/system controller.

Finally, it is important that the ground architecture of the system be robust to avoid ground loops, which may increase EMI. To also avoid electrostatic discharge (ESD), the front panels should be supplied with ground connectors that the personnel can use when handling circuit packs in the system.

4.9 DWDM SYSTEMS BY NETWORK LAYER

In Section 4.3, we described the various layers of the optical communications network and the various DWDM systems in each layer. In this section, we focus on each individual DWDM system, their characteristics and complexities. In particular, we describe point-to-point systems (long-, medium-, and short-haul); large cross-connect systems, optical drop and add multiplexers (single, multiple, and dynamic wavelengths); metropolitan or Metro systems (large, medium, and small), and access systems and first/last mile access.

4.9.1 Point-to-Point Systems

4.9.1.1 Long-Haul Optical Systems

Point-to-point (PtP) long-haul (LH) optical systems are designed to interconnect two distant megalopolises (intercontinental) (see upper right part of Fig. 4.5) or continents (transoceanic) and to handle a huge amount of aggregated traffic; such PtP systems are also known as *ultra-long haul* (ULH) or *ultra long-reach* (ULR). ULH systems are already in deployment in transoceanic applications, and the globe has already been wrapped around several times (Fig. 4.45).

The desired characteristics of a PtP-LH system are to:

- Support cost-effectively and reliably a large number of optical channels (wavelengths) per fiber (80, or 160, projected to 1,000)

- Support one of the highest bit rates per optical channel (10 Gb/s, or 40 Gb/s, projected to 160 Gb/s) and RZ or NRZ modulation (and perhaps solitons)

- Support protocol transparency (transport simultaneously SONET, IP, ATM, GbE, and others), and

- Transport traffic over a distance between end points in excess of 4,000 km

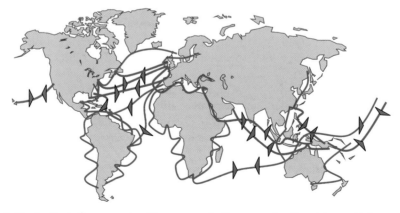

Figure 4.45 An illustrative example of trans-oceanic fiber wrapping the globe and interconnecting every country (an actual picture would have many more fibers).

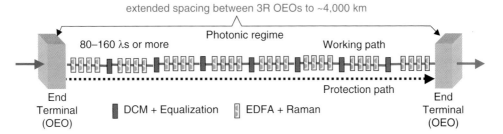

Figure 4.46 All optical amplification (EDFA + Raman) and dispersion compensation modules (DCM) enable the optical signal to reach ultra long distances (~4,000 km) between end terminals.

The optical path between end points is optimized for the minimum possible number of optical amplifiers and optical signal conditioners (chromatic and polarization dispersion compensation), and transponder systems (3R-OEO) are only at each end of the optical path (Fig. 4.46).

The key functions of a transponder system are reshaping, retiming, and restoring (amplification), hence 3R. Currently, 3R transponders convert the optical signal to an electrical signal and back to an optical signal (OEO); as such, they are also known as *optically opaque*. When the signal is converted to electrical, opaque 3R transponders will:

- "clean up" the signal from noise (cumulative ASE noise from OFAs), wander and jitter.
- restore its amplitude from fiber loss, component insertion loss and nonlinear effects.
- restore its pulse spectral shape induced from fiber chromatic and polarization dispersion.

In addition, while the signal is in the electrical regime, OEOs perform signal performance monitoring and wavelength conversion/interchange, and perhaps some traffic shedding or grooming, aggregation, and desegregation.

However, current 3R-OEO implementations are at a cost premium and therefore cost-effective all-optical 3R solutions are preferred. To meet the required LH characteristics, several ramification methods are used for optical amplification (SOA, EDFA, and Raman), dispersion (chromatic and polarization) compensation, channel equalization, and noise filtering.

The design aspects of LH systems comply with ITU-T standards (e.g., G.691) that provide parameters and values for optical interfaces of single-channel long-haul systems. Some of the key components at the outputs of LH systems are:

- high quality, high reliability and high-stability lasers (over short and long time) with ultrafast modulators and excellent isolation.
- optical amplifiers to boost the DWDM signal for transmission on the optical fiber.
- EDFAs and Raman copropagating pumps.

- multiplexers combine wavelengths for transmission on a common optical fiber. They also combine supervisory channels.
- optical monitors to monitor the parameters of the outgoing signal.
- modulators.

and at the inputs:

- Preamplifiers and Raman counterpropagating pumps.
- Dispersion compensating modules to provide bulk compensation. Compensation requires knowledge of the types of fibers on the path. Ideally, a high-quality fiber with low dispersion and low PMD (<0.1 ps/$\sqrt{\text{km}}$) is desirable. Nevertheless, because in reality the optical path may consist of different fiber types a common sense margin ($\sim$1 to 2 dB) is incorporated in the calculations; this also depends on modulation method, span length, number of spans, line amplifiers and the overall tolerance on differential group delay.
- Demultiplexers that separate the DWDM signal into individual channels, including the supervisory channels.
- Highly sensitive and very low-noise receivers and demodulators with stable and adaptive thresholds. This also includes a cross talk margin ($\sim$0.5 dB). In addition, depending on bit rate, the optical signal to noise ratio needs to be better than 20 dB and the BER better than 10^{-16}.
- Optical monitors to monitor the parameters of the incoming signal.

Because of the huge aggregated bandwidth that each PtP-LH system handles over a single fiber, high reliability and service protection are required. The protection strategy may be one of three: 1 + 1, 1:1, or 1:N.

The 1 + 1 protection strategy requires two identical but separate paths that connect the two end terminals, and each end-terminal feeds the same traffic in the two separate fiber paths (Fig. 4.47). At the other end point, the system monitors the integrity of the received signals on both incoming traffics and selects the traffic from the path with

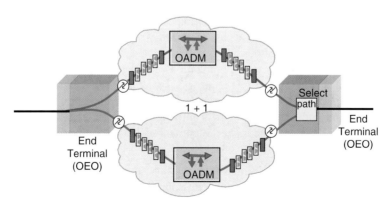

Figure 4.47 To increase service protection, traffic is fed simultaneously in two separate fiber paths and the receiving node selects the best path; this is known as 1 + 1 protection.

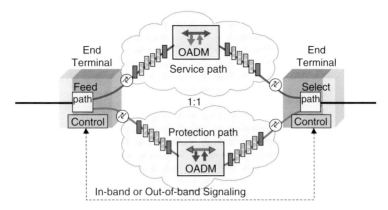

Figure 4.48 High priority traffic is transported over the service path and low priority over the protection path. If the service path is at fault, high priority traffic switched onto protection and low priority is dropped; this is known as 1:1 protection. 1:1 protection requires fast and reliable supervisory channel for signaling.

the best performance. This implies that these systems have redundant fabrics, and they have fast monitors to reliably compare the health of one path with another. Clearly, this protection strategy relies on the healthy operation of the receiving node, but it commits resources. However, it does not rely on supervisory messaging between two nodes, it selects a path autonomously and thus it is the fastest; therefore, it is suitable to highly reliable long-haul transmission.

The 1:1 is another protection strategy (Fig. 4.48). Connectivity between two nodes is established over a single path (the servicing path), and although a second path (the protection path) is committed, data do not flow over it; in fact, the protection path also may be used to transport low-priority data. In the 1:1 case, the integrity of the signal is monitored and performance messages are sent between the two connected nodes over the supervisory channel. If the performance of the servicing path is degraded below an acceptable threshold level, then the sending node sends messages to the receiving node to switch to the latter path and feeds data into the protection path; if the protection path was transporting low-priority data, then they are dropped. This strategy is slower than the $1 + 1$, does not commit the same resources, and is more suitable to medium- and short-haul transmission.

The 1:N protection strategy is similar to 1:1 with the exception that for N servicing paths there is only one path committed. In this case, when one of the N paths experiences severe degradation, its traffic is passed over the protection path. Clearly, this case assumes that no two paths will be severely degraded.

Finally, in PtP-LH transmission, optical add-drop is limited to a small percentage of traffic, and perhaps using dedicated wavelengths. In this case, the end point systems are provisioned to put add-drop traffic on wavelengths that will be dropped and added by intermediate OADMs.

4.9.1.2 *Medium-Haul and Short-Haul Optical Systems*

Medium-haul DWDM systems, also known as *intermediate reach* (IR) systems, are very similar to LH systems. However, because the path length is much shorter than 4,000 km (1,000–1,500 km), system requirements and certain design parameters are relaxed to fit the particular business model. For example, they are engineered for more add-drops than the LH, the bit rate per optical channel can be the highest possible (shorter spans can accommodate higher bit rates), and optical amplification may be less cumbersome. In addition, the protection strategy can be 1:1 instead of $1 + 1$ (this requires half the network resources but complicates the protection protocol).

Short-haul systems, also known as *short reach* (SR) systems and *very short reach* (VSR) systems, are much simpler than medium-haul systems because the path distance is on the order of 500 km (SR) or shorter (VSR). They have several add-drops on the path; the total aggregate bandwidth is large; and, like the MH, they require advanced wavelength and bandwidth management. Standards have been developed specifically for this case such as, ITU-T G.691 Short Haul S-64.2 b and Telcordia GR-1377-CORE Intermediate Reach IR-2.

In general, manufacturers design systems that can be flexible and growable. That is, they offer platforms that can be customized to meet the needs of specific applications; starting with a minimal system configuration, grow as needed by adding more units (circuit packs) in a shelf, add more shelves in a bay, and add more bays; use input and output ports (transceivers) that fit the specific application; use custom-suited software for provisioning, protocols and management, and so on. Thus, based on a generic platform, the specific application determines the final system complexity.

4.9.1.3 Linear Optical Add-Drop Cross-Connecting Systems

Long-haul or medium/short-haul nodes become more cost-effective when they are able to add-drop traffic. Add-drop nodes, also known as add-drop multiplexers (ADM), are known in DWDM systems as optical add-drop multiplexer (OADM) nodes. In long haul, it is not unusual to have several OADMs in a concatenated (or linear) configuration whereby each OADM drops and adds traffic to or from a local network (Fig. 4.49). This is known as "point-to-point with linear OADM" topology.

4.9.2 Large Optical Cross-Connect Systems

Large (in fabric capacity) optical cross-connect systems consist of nodes of a geographically large mesh network, or *backbone*.

Backbone networks are intelligent optical networks (ION) that consist of relatively few but very large bandwidth nodes that are interconnected in a mesh topology (in fact, what makes the network intelligent are its nodes, protocols, and network management). Each node has a very large optical cross-connecting fabric (larger than $1,000 \times 1,000$

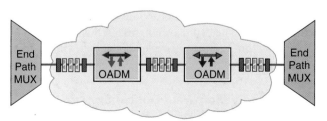

Figure 4.49 Point-to-point linear optical add-drop multiplexer topology allows traffic to be dropped and added between two end points of a path.

wavelengths); the number of wavelengths per fiber ranges from 80 to 160 (or more); the bit rate per optical channel is 10 Gb/s or 40 Gb/s (projected to 160 Gb/s); and each system may terminate several fibers, depending on switching fabric capacity and network survivability strategy. Large optical cross-connect systems transport aggregated traffic from Metro and other networks from node to node in the backbone.

In mesh topology where links between nodes become long (hundreds of kilometers), they appear to have a localized point-to-point topology (see Fig. 4.5, upper right section). In transoceanic applications, the topology is predominantly point-to-point, possibly with a few add-drops. However, submarine DWDM networks may also have a ring or star topology to provide service to a cluster of islands. Realistically, long-haul and backbone networks have a hybrid topology where add-drops are used for traffic distribution, service restoration, and disaster avoidance.

The protection strategy of backbone mesh networks depends on large optical cross-connect (OXC) systems with fast rerouting algorithms. When traffic from a fiber is lost due to a severe fault, the fault is detected and part of the remedial action is to quickly find alternate routes for interrupted service.

Although large electronic cross-connect (EXC) systems with optical inputs/outputs (I/O) and SONET rates have been in use for several years, all-optical cross-connect (OXC) systems surpass them on many counts. OXCs are proving themselves on technology, performance, power consumption, and physical size. As an example, the physical size of large OXCs compared with that of EXCs is twice as small (6 to 7 bays vs. 10 to 14), and the power consumption of large OXCs compared with EXCs is at least three to four times lower (10 to 14 kW vs. 40 to 45 kW). Figure 4.50 depicts a possible system architecture based on current optical technology, and Figure 4.51 the

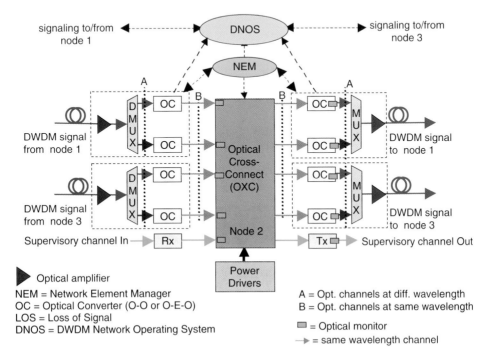

Figure 4.50 A typical DWDM optical cross-connect architecture based on current technology.

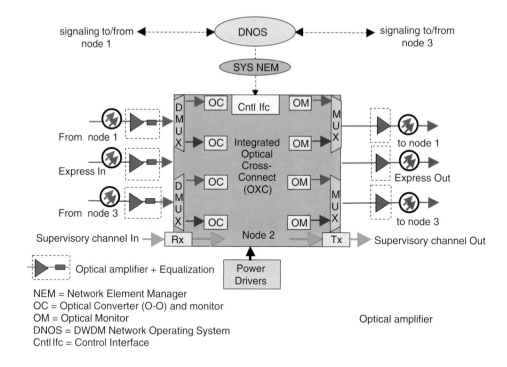

Figure 4.51   An advanced DWDM optical cross-connect architecture.

same system with advanced photonic technology. In addition, they have all the features of an EXC and many desirable features that EXCs do not have, such as (the ones in bold are specific to OXCs):

- optical traffic transparency
- protocol transparency by virtue of DWDM
- capacity
- managed wavelength services (in conjunction with intelligent network management)
- bulk amplification of many channels by virtue of DWDM
- **protection**
- service restoration at different grades: platinum (less than 50 ms, 1 + 1 optical protection), gold (1–2 min, optical channel shared protection ring — OCh/Spring), silver (within day or faster with preplanned restoration routes), and bronze (preemptable service layer restoration)
- service restoration by virtue of DWDM
- bit rate independence (2.5, 10, 40 Gb/s) by virtue of DWDM
- protocol independence by virtue of DWDM
- compliance with standards related to signal input/output (ITU-T, Telcordia, etc.)
- compliance with electrical and physical design standards (NEBS, MEBS, ETSI, UL, CE, etc.)

- scalability by virtue of DWDM
- reliability
- wavelength management by virtue of DWDM
- high density (single stage) cross-connect fabric (more than $1,000 \times 1,000$)
- cross-connect fabric transparent to payload format and bit rate
- redundancy
- $1 + 1$ protection for restoration
- new signal format with FEC
- security
- optical 2R, and 3R to be available soon

Currently, the only function OXCs do not perform is overhead termination and switching on the packet or frame granularity as this requires optical synchronization on the bit/byte level, which has not been implemented yet, although optical solutions have been proposed.

4.9.3 DWDM Metro Systems

DWDM Metro systems consist of network nodes of a physical fiber ring topology (see Fig. 4.3). Connectivity between nodes is achieved via wavelengths (see Section 4.2) so that the logical topology may be a star, a mesh, or purely a ring (see Fig. 4.4).

Depending on the protection strategy, the ring may be single, dual, or quad. Typically, small Metro nodes support a single-fiber ring topology; medium Metro nodes support a two-fiber (dual) ring topology, where one is used for service and the other is used for protection, and large Metro nodes support a four-fiber (quad) ring topology, where two are used for service and the other two are used for protection.

Metro networks have a single-fiber ring if service protection is not an issue or if there is bidirectional traffic; dual-fiber ring if service protection on the optical layer (wavelength) is important; quad if there are two dual rings, one pair for service and one pair for protection. The more aggregate bandwidth on the ring, the more complex the protection method, and the more complex the optical add-drop multiplexer and the node on the ring. In addition, at least two of the nodes on the ring (one a single-fiber ring) are designated as hubs (the second hub is for additional network reliability and protection). Hubs provide connectivity with other similar or dissimilar networks as well as remote access to ring nodes, wavelength management and provisioning via the supervisory channel, as well as node functionality.

In general, a hub accepts various (electrical) payloads (TCP/IP, ATM, STM, LAN, etc.) destined to one or more of its nodes on the ring. Each payload type (channel) is either mapped in another format (e.g., IP over SONET) or sent in its natural form to its corresponding physical interface. From there it is transported over an assigned wavelength, which is multiplexed along with others in the fiber ring. The requirement, complexity, and reliability of the hub are proportional to that of the Metro network.

Different Metro networks cover different geographic areas; they have different aggregate bandwidth, performance requirements, service offerings, and complexity and cost structure. That is, Metros are versatile, they offer managed wavelength services and address a wide range in the applications space, and therefore Metro growth

Table 4.5   Attributes of long haul and Metro systems

Attribute	Long Haul System	Metro System
Distribution	PtP, OADM,	Physical ring,
	Point to multipoint	OADM, logical PtP and multipoint
Performance mgt	BER/FEC/	BER/FEC/
	supervisory channel	supervisory channel
Provisioning time	Seconds	Seconds
Protection	$1 + 1$	Quad/dual ring, optional
Service transparency	yes	yes
Service or BW on demand	yes	yes
Shared wavelength	yes	no
Separate wavelength	yes	yes
QoSignal support	yes	yes
QoS support	yes	yes
SLA granularity	hour	hour
Service differentiation	yes	yes

has been impressive at an almost exponential rate ($\sim x^{1.2}$) per year. Because of this expected growth, most large communications design houses as well as scores of new startups have announced Metro applications and products, which are classified as large, medium, and small Metro. Clearly, large or medium Metro systems and long-haul systems address different needs and services, apart from the common need to transport traffic between two points. The desirable attributes of managed wavelength services offered by Metro and LH systems are listed in Table 4.5.

A DWDM Metro node may be thought of as consisting of two sections, an optical add-drop multiplexer and a system attached to it, which may be either all-optical or opaque; this system manages the optical bandwidth and terminates or re-sources the supervisory channel (see Fig. 4.3). In practice, these two parts have been consolidated into one node system, unless the OADM is a single and fixed wavelength for access applications (then the OADM may be a separate entity).

The OADM consists of an optical demultiplexer and an optical multiplexer based on one of the technologies described in Chapter 2, the channel capacity of which depends on the number of wavelengths supported by the ring; thus, it may be as simple as 1:6 or as complex as 1:40. It also consists of a switching fabric, which may be as simple as a 2×2 cross-connect or as complex as a 40×40 or higher, depending on the path protection strategy (none, $1 + 1$, 1:1, 1:N, etc.). The technology of the cross-connect is again one of those described in Chapter 2.

In addition to the optical add-drop multiplexer, there are one or more bidirectional transceivers (at minimum one for a single unidirectional ring, two for a dual ring and four for a quad ring), optionally optical (wavelength) converters to convert the customer-supplied wavelength to the wavelength supported by the ring (typically, a 1,310 nm to a C-band wavelength), filters, connectors and splices and perhaps polarizers, SOAs, and other components. The optical gain and loss of these components determine the power budget (and the driving capability) of the node and its complexity.

Typical EDFA specifications for long-haul applications are listed in Table 4.6.

Table 4.6 Typical EDFA specifications

Parameter	Value
Gain (dB)	>20
Noise figure (dB)	<5
Power (dBm)	>20*
Gain flatness (dB)	~5
Polarization-dependent gain (dB)	0.1
Cross talk (dB)	Very low
Power consumption (W)	~30

*Preamplifier power is about 10–15 dB.

4.9.3.1 Large Metro Systems

Large DWDM Metro systems are nodes of a quad ring topology. They support 40 to 80 or more wavelengths per fiber, each wavelength at a bit rate of 10 or 40 Gb/s. Such rings cover a large geographic area (greater than 1,000 km in circumference) and interconnect several large cities (Fig. 4.52).

Optical amplification is as complex as that of a backbone or long-haul network, based on OFAs and Raman with dispersion and polarization compensation, including optical equalization; amplifiers are able to support the optical signal for fiber spans

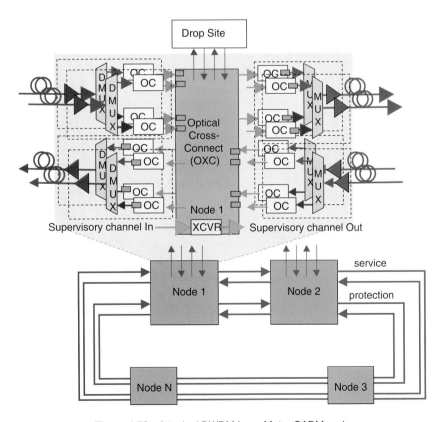

Figure 4.52 A typical DWDM large Metro OADM node.

in excess of 200 km. Thus, the basic architecture and specifications of a large Metro system (node) is not much different from that of the mesh network node.

Large Metro systems are able to drop and add a high percentage of the traffic on the ring and to reroute traffic when a service-affecting fault is detected. Thus, they drop and add multiple wavelengths per node, and nodes are remotely and dynamically provisioned and they support wavelength assignment. This obviously impacts the size of the optical cross-connect as well as the technology used.

Large Metro nodes provide bandwidth management, grooming, and bridging functionality [i.e., connectivity with other networks (backbone, other Metros, access, etc.)]. However, as more nodes on the ring interconnect with other rings or networks, the large ring Metro starts looking more like a mesh network or a medium-size backbone.

OAM&P functionality in Metro applications is provided by an additional optical channel (or two for protection) that may be either in the 1,300s nm band or in the low 1,500s nm or in both. The supervisory channel is terminated and re-sourced at each node.

Large nodes are key participants in the service survivability strategy. The level of survivability depends on network fault management, which impacts fault detection strategy, optical cross-connect design complexity, as well as supervisory channel and protocol responsivity. To demonstrate how this impacts the Metro node design, consider the case of a single fault on the working (or service) dual ring. In one scheme, traffic flows on both dual rings simultaneously, and thus, as soon as the fault is detected, the protection ring becomes the working ring (Fig. 4.53A). This scheme, however, uses only one dual ring at a time, committing the bandwidth resources of a dual ring. In another scheme, the working ring is still the same by the largest part of the network, and only the failed ring is bypassed by cross-connecting traffic over to the protection ring; the protection dual ring is used for lower SLA grade, and via loopbacks (LB), service may also continue on the protection ring, but some traffic shedding may also take place (Fig. 4.53B). In a third scheme, both service and protection rings are used for traffic but not at full capacity. Then, using loopbacks on the working ring, service continues to the degree possible and excess traffic is passed onto the protection ring (Fig. 4.53C); some shedding of low-grade traffic may also take place.

On rare occasion, a dual fiber fault may take place (e.g., disaster or when both rings are collocated in the same cable). In this case, the loopback capability of large Metro systems has the ability to bypass the faulty region (Fig. 4.53D).

As seen in Figure 4.52, the design rules of a Metro system may vary; the larger the system, the more aggregate bandwidth it carries and the more important the service protection. Along with the added design complexity in the optical cross-connect, consider amplification, compensation, equalization, provisioning, mechanical, power, heat, and many other issues that all impact the system's complexity.

4.9.3.2 Medium and Small Metro Systems

Medium Metro systems have 40 wavelengths at a bit rate (per wavelength) from 2.5 Gb/s to 10 Gb/s, with channel separation of 100 nm. They are applicable to a geographic area that covers a region of about 500 km in circumference or a regional area with several multilevel buildings (such as skyscrapers in large cities). Amplification is based on less complex OFAs and Raman amplifiers. Dispersion compensation may not be required, but equalization may be needed, and amplifiers are able to support the signal for fiber spans on the order of 100 to 200 km. Such Metro systems

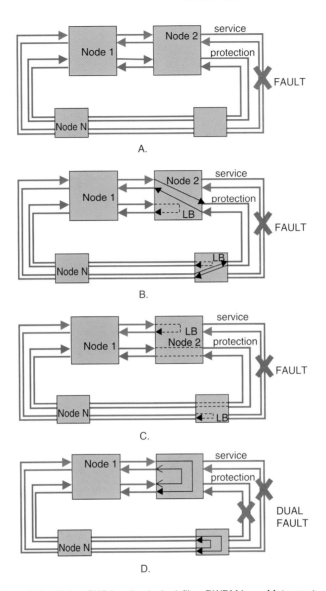

Figure 4.53 Using OXC loopbacks in 4-fiber DWDM large Metro systems.

are also applicable to enterprise (business) networks with fewer nodes that provide a multiplicity of services and support a variety of traffic types (TDM, SONET/SDH, ATM, IP, etc.). In many respects, medium Metro systems are reduced-capability large Metro systems; in fact, some vendors may offer Metro systems that, depending on configuration, may be applicable either to large Metro networks or to medium Metro networks.

Small Metro systems have fewer than 40 wavelengths, each at a bit rate (per wavelength) of up to 2.5 Gb/s, with channel separation of 200 nm. Because of this, they are also known as coarse-WDM (CWDM) Metro systems. CDWMs are applicable to small geographic areas of up to 100 km in circumference with few multilevel buildings, large

Table 4.7 Metro system requirements

Parameter	Value
Gain (dB)	>10
Noise figure (dB)	<8
Power (dBm)	>10
Gain flatness (dB)	~1
Polarization dependence gain (dB)	<1
Cross talk (dB)	Low to medium
Power consumption (W)	~5

Table 4.8 Laser and receiver Metro requirements

Parameter	Value
Laser @ 2.5 Gb/s (dBm)	$\sim+3^{\dagger*}$
Laser @ 10 Gb/s (dBm)	0
Receiver sensitivity (dBm)	-23^{**}

†Depends on technology, λ, modulation, and manufacturer.
*Laser power is between 10 dBm and -2 dBm.
**Receiver sensitivity is between -18 dBm and -32 dBm.

campuses, or several residential neighborhoods. Amplification is simple and compact based on SOAs (and, depending on application and requirements, perhaps on OFAs) so that amplifiers can support the signal for fiber spans of less than 80 km Typically, the transmitter has 0 dBm output power and the receiver is a PIN-type photodetector preferably with no clock and retiming. Because of the small number of wavelengths, CWDMs support few nodes (8–32), and therefore the channel assignment for each node on the ring may be fixed. As a consequence, the optical add-drop multiplexer in each node has a compact, reliable, and simple passive optical technology, such as passive Bragg gratings, rotators, filters, and so on.

Typically, Metro systems with SOA amplification have the requirements listed in Table 4.7.

Similarly, the laser and receiver requirements for Metros are given in Table 4.8.

CWDM demands very inexpensive systems. However, the paramount features of CWDM systems are small physical size, easy maintenance, robustness, and low cost. As simple as these features may seem, in practice they require as few components as possible (no elaborate amplifiers and cross-connects), integration of optical functionality, quality low-cost transmitters and receivers, optical components (filters, connectors, splices, etc.) with very low insertion loss and very small margins. In this case, every tenth of a dB loss counts. A minimal configuration of a simple DWDM OADM node with dual ring Metro is illustrated in Figure 4.54.

4.9.4 Access DWDM Systems and First/Last Mile

DWDM systems are also applicable to access networks (FTTx), as described in Chapter 3. In this case, the DWDM access system is connected to a small or medium access Metro OADM (Fig. 4.55). In this case, the access system receives the drop,

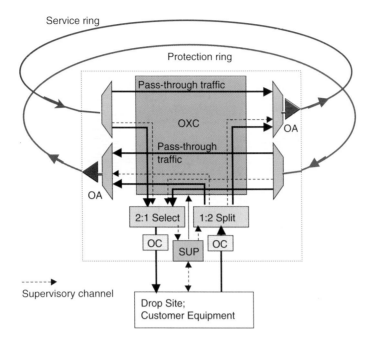

Figure 4.54 A minimal DWDM 2-fiber OADM Metro node.

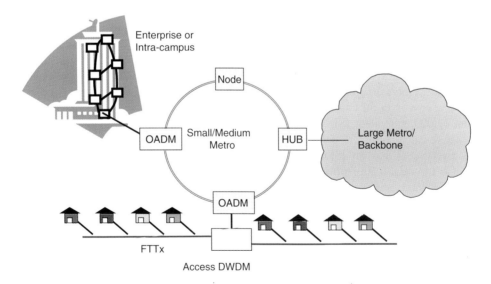

Figure 4.55 An access DWDM OADM node.

and it demultiplexes the signal of the drop to lower bit rates, which are then fed into multimode fibers to feed FTTx plants. Thus, if the drop is 2.5 Gb/s and the rate at each wavelength in the multimode fiber is DS3, the number of wavelengths is about 40 plus some additional for maintenance; similarly, if OC-3 rates are used, then the number of wavelengths is about 20 plus maintenance channels. Multimode fiber on the access site

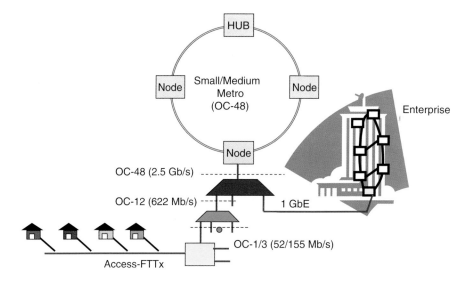

Figure 4.56   A minimal DWDM OADM Metro node.

is preferred because the access fiber length is short. In addition, transmitters (lasers) and receivers are inexpensive and coarse; dispersion and polarization compensation is not required (because of fiber short lengths); and optical amplification, if needed, is achieved with low-cost SOAs. Moreover, optical components made with special plastics, polymers, and glasses are applicable for cost-reduction purposes.

If we assume that one wavelength at 2.5 Gb/s is dropped off at an access node and that each home site requires 288 Kb/s (i.e., equivalent to two ISDN lines), then more than 8,600 homes can be serviced at the same time. For an average of 3 persons per home, a 2.5 Gb/s drop can service a community of more than 25,000 people. Similarly, if the access is in an enterprise environment, then a 2.5 Gb/s drop can service more than 17,000 equivalent ISDN lines, or two 1 GbE.

These calculations are conservative because not every home requires 288 Kb/s and not every desk has an ISDN line. However, it demonstrates two key points: first, 2.5 Gb/s in access is plenty of bandwidth to satisfy the home of the present and of the future; second, access nodes must satisfy a multiplicity of needs simultaneously, such as access to the home and small enterprises, and thus they demultiplex the 2.5 Gb/s to smaller rates, from DS1 to OC-12, and to 1 GbE (Fig. 4.56).

Table 4.9 lists the desired characteristics of long-haul, Metro, and access networks.

4.10   PROTECTED AND UNPROTECTED SYSTEMS

In Section 4.9, we described protection in many occasions. We have described how high bandwidth capacity long-haul and large Metro networks are using the 1 + 1 protection scheme, whereas networks of lesser bandwidth capacity use 1:1 or even 1:N protection.

1 + 1 protection (see Fig. 4.42) sends the same traffic simultaneously over two separate paths. It is up to the receiving end, based on transmission performance metrics, to decide which of the two paths will be accepted. As performance metrics on the

Table 4.9   Characteristics of long-haul, Metro, and access networks

Characteristics	Long-Haul	Metro	Access
Span (transmission distance)	400 to 4000 km	100–1000 km	<20 km
Fiber topology	PtP/Mesh	Mesh/ring	Ring/linear
Fiber type	NDSF/SMF	NDSF/SMF	MMF/SMF?
OCh density	Very high (>160)	Medium (40?)	Coarse–medium
OCh granularity	50 nm (25 nm?)	100 nm	200–400 nm
Aggregate BW capacity	Several Tbps	<Tbps	<10 Gbps
Traffic topology	Linear/mesh	Ring/hub	Linear
Protection strategy	Rerouting (mesh) 1:1/1 + 1 (PtP)	Fiber/Service prot., Single/dual/quad ring	Service protection 1:1/1 + 1 trunk side
Scalability	Up bit rate/λ Add more λs	Up bit rate/λ? Add more λs	Fixed; Add λs (?)
System availability	Very high	Very high–high	High
System reliability	Very high	Very high	Medium–high
System maintainability	Very fast and remote	Fast and remote	Medium and remote
Resiliency to failures	Very high	Very high	High
FEC required	Yes for long paths	?	No
Supervisory Chl. for OAM&P	Yea	Yes	No
Signal amplification	OFAs, Raman	SOA preferred	No; (SOA for RT?)
Required compensation	Yes; DC, PDC	No	No
Switching speed	Very fast	Medium or fixed	Slow
Power consumption	Medium to high	Medium to low	Low
Level of integration	High	Medium	Medium–low
Cost	High	Low	Very low
NE size	1 to few bays	Small (few shelves)	Very small (shelf)

PtP = point-to-point   RT = remote terminal
DC = dispersion compensation   FEC = forward error correction
PDC = polarization dispersion compensation   SOA = semiconductor opt. amplifier

selected path fall short, the receiving end autonomously switches to the other path. Typical performance metrics are BER before and after FEC, signal power level, loss of signal, and others. This protection scheme is highly reliable and fast, but it requires twice the network resources.

1:1 protection has two possible paths between source and destination. However, the source determines which of the two paths will be used for traffic, and it is up to the destination to determine the degradation of performance metrics, in which case it communicates over a separate channel with the source to initiate a path switch. This protection scheme is slower and requires protocol coordination and execution between source and destination, but it does not commit twice the network resources.

In addition to protection on the network level, there is protection on the system level. For example, 1 + 1 protection of the switching fabric implies that there are two units that in parallel pass traffic but only the output of one is selected, based on performance parameters, such as optical power level and wavelength accuracy. When the working unit degrades, the output selector autonomously switches to the other unit; similarly, with the system or shelf controller.

1:N protection on the system level is used predominantly on the input–output ports. In this case, although the system requires N working ports, an additional protection port is included. As soon as any of the N ports degrades or has a fault, the protection port

Table 4.10   Requirements of protection schemes

Protection	Unit
1 + 1	Controller (system/shelf)
	High capacity and fast switching fabric
	High bandwidth transceiver (2.5, 10, 40 Gb/s)
1:1	Medium capacity transceiver (<2.5 Gb/s)
	Medium capacity switching fabric
1:N	Medium to low transceivers
0:N	Protected ring, protected point-to-point
No protection	Low bandwidth data systems requiring craft intervention

replaces it automatically (under system control). The 1:N protection scheme implies that all N ports are of the same type. However, when the N ports are in groups of k types, then k protection ports may be included (one per group), in which case it is termed k:N. When $k = 0$, the 0:N implies that there is no protection on the system level; however, this does not imply that there is no protection against line fault. That is, if one of the trunks is at fault, for example, then there is a mechanism that switches to another protection line (as already discussed in the case of ring protection). The applicability of the various protection schemes on the system level are listed in Table 4.10.

4.11   ENGINEERING DWDM SYSTEMS

Engineering a DWDM system begins with a market investigation to understand the business opportunities and how the "to be built" system fits the communications market and the business portfolio. There are two golden rules to be met (that market research experts know well) for the success of new product: the "to be built" system must differ from any other product on the market, and it must offer a measurable benefit to the customer that no other previous product offers; that is, it has found a niche in the communications equipment space offering a solution to a known problem. When these rules are met, a tedious iterative process begins that involves the interplay of cost/benefit modeling, engineering, and market interaction. When this interplay is fine-tuned, the design process begins.

4.11.1   Parameters That Influence Optical Design

In this section, we do not address the market differentiator or the potential market opportunities present at different network layers, but we focus only on the engineering process that impacts the design of a DWDM system and the quality of signal and service. First, however, we examine the key parameters that influence the design of a DWDM system and a network. These are:

- system aggregate bandwidth capacity
- channel capacity per fiber
- operating band (C, L, etc.) and ITU-T nominal center frequencies (wavelengths)
- channel granularity; channel spacing or separation and channel width
- channel bit rate and modulation (% RZ, NRZ, soliton, etc.)
- multichannel frequency stabilization
- channel performance (BER limits)
- channel allowable dispersion (chromatic, polarization)
- signal polarization states and polarization strategies
- power launched in fiber
- power received (receiver sensitivity)
- system/network application (Metro, LH, small, large, access-type, etc.)
- OSNR level at the receiver
- differential group delay (DGD)
- performance management capability
- redundancy strategy (controller, optical cross-connect)
- I/O port protection scheme (1 + 1, 1:N, etc.)
- control architecture (hierarchical, other)
- interboard communications and communication protocol (100 GbE, 1 GbE, etc.)
- fault detector strategy (location and type of sensors for power, wavelength, polarization, etc.)
- fault/degradation management strategy (monitoring, detection, correlation, alarm, provisioning, isolation and recovery)
- supervisory channels strategy and protocols
- optical amplification strategy (SOA, FOA, RAMAN, hybrid)
- number of fiber spans
- length of span between amplifiers
- fiber type(s) used as the transmission medium
- worst-case optical power budget per path
- optical loss and power budget across system I/Os
- aggregate bandwidth management
- supported transport services (synchronous, asynchronous, multiservices)
- signal format (SONET, ATM, IP, digital wrapper)
- communications standards compliance
- connectivity with network management system and communications protocols (TL1, etc.)
- configuration strategy (remote, local, manual)
- system protection and survivability strategies
- service protection plan for uninterrupted service offering
- system scalability and flexibility (non−service-affecting)

- system provisioning and upgrades (connectivity tables, laser parameters, configuration, etc.), remote and local (CIT)
- wavelength management (wavelength converters)
- physical size, physical partitioning of functions and system collocation.
- physical and environmental standards compliance (NEBS, ETSI, etc.)
- powering plant (power feeders, converters, indicators, fuses, voltages, etc.)
- cabling plant
- smart connectorization for protection (automatic laser shut-down upon disconnect, power-up upon contact)
- heat management
- system reliability
- system security
- visual indicators
- interoperability; compatibility with optical parameters, transmission and transport protocols, survivability strategy and management
- interdomain compatibility

4.11.2   ITU-T Recommended Frequencies

ITU-T G.692 (as of October 1998 has recommended 81 channels (wavelengths) in the C-band starting from 1,528.77 nm and incrementing in multiples of 50 GHz (or 0.39 nm). According to this, the first center frequency is at 196.10 THz (or 1,528.77 nm), and decrementing by 50 GHz (or incrementing by 0.39 nm), all center frequencies (wavelengths) are calculated. Thus, the first of the 81 channels in the C-band is at frequency 196.10 GHz or wavelength 1,528.77 nm, the second channel is at frequency 196.05 GHz or wavelength 1,529.16 nm, and so on, and the last frequency is at 192.10 GHz or wavelength 1,560.61 nm. However, the reference frequency is 193.1 Thz. As DWDM technology evolves and a wider spectrum becomes usable, more channels are included.

For channel spacing of 100 GHz, the center frequencies of the channels are those that start with the first channel in the table and continue every other one, and similarly, for channel spacing of 200 GHz or 400 GHz.

4.11.3   Channel Capacity, Width, and Spacing

The number of channels, the channel selection (center frequency), and the frequency width of each channel, as well as the channel separation, are important parameters in DWDM system design. Channel separation should allow for a frequency deviation (~2 GHz) caused by frequency drifts in the laser, filter and amplifier devices and thus to avoid interchannel interference.

4.11.4   Channel Bit Rate and Modulation

The bit rate of channel and the modulation technique are parameters that determine the limits of channel width and channel separation, as well as channel performance (e.g., BER, cross-talk, etc.). Dispersion and dispersion management as well as noise induced by amplifiers and by other sources should also be considered because they

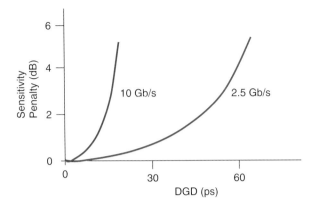

Figure 4.57   Impact of DGD on receiver for 2.5 and 10 Gb/s (put in engineering systems).

affect the signal-to-noise ratio and thus the signal integrity. In addition, the differential group delay has a limiting effect on the bit rate by means of the receiver sensitivity (Fig. 4.57).

4.11.5   Multichannel Frequency Stabilization

In DWDM systems with optical filters, filter detuning, or frequency offset from the center frequency, takes place. As detuning increases, interference with neighboring channels, optical cross talk, and insertion loss increase.

4.11.6   BER and Channel Performance

The bit error rate (BER) is a performance metric specified in standards. DWDM systems should be designed such that the signal integrity is maintained at the expected levels. The BER depends on interchannel interference, optical power level at the receiver with respect to the sensitivity of the receiver, modulation technique, and other noise sources (externally coupled noise, jitter, nonlinear phenomena, etc.).

4.11.7   Channel Dispersion

Fiber dispersion (chromatic and PMD) causes optical pulse widening. As dispersion increases, so does intersymbol interference and cross-talk (which affects signal integrity) and received power decreases (that impacts receiver sensitivity).

4.11.8   Power Launched

The *maximum allowable power per channel* launched in the fiber, or the transmitted power, the receiver sensitivity, and the fiber loss between the two are the starting points for power calculations to ensure that the optical signal arrives at the receiver with enough power to be detected with an expected bit error rate objective (e.g., BER = 10^{-12}). However, the maximum allowable power per channel cannot be arbitrary because of nonlinear phenomena and safety reasons.

4.11.9 Optical Amplification and Compensation

Optical signal losses should be carefully budgeted, and optical amplification (SOA, OFA, Raman) should be used appropriately to restore the intensity of the optical signal (if needed). Concatenated optical amplification introduces cumulative ASE noise. Similarly, dispersion compensation may be required at high bit rates and long fiber spans. However, both amplifications and compensation introduce cumulative effects in ASE noise and in residual dispersion, as well as dispersion slope.

4.11.10 The Fiber-Medium and Limitations

There are a number of limitations imposed on optical transmission by the fiber medium; linear and nonlinear effects such as fiber attenuation, chromatic dispersion, PMD, Kerr effect, FWM, SBS, and so on, that all contribute to degradation of optical signal and thus system performance. For a fixed length of fiber, the only variable that can be manipulated to lower the nonlinear contribution is the optical power. However, when lowering the optical power, the bit rate should be lowered to maintain transmission at the expected bit error rate. In general, the parameters specific to fibers are listed in Table 4.11.

4.11.11 Optical Power Budget

Optical power budget of a path involves calculating all optical signal losses caused by every component in the optical path between transmitter and receiver (couplers, filters, cross-connects, connectors, splices, mux/demux, fiber, optical patch panels, etc.). It also involves power degradations due to linear and nonlinear effects resulting from the light–matter–light interaction, including noise sources. The main objective of the budget is to ensure that the power of the optical signal at the receiver is greater than the sensitivity of the receiver.

Table 4.11   Parameters specific to fibers

Fiber type (MMF, SMF, DCF, pigtail, etc.)
Geometry variation over length (core, cladding)
Core effective area
Refractive index distribution (core, cladding)
Ion concentration (and chemical consistency)
Dielectric constant, ε
Propagation constant, β
Dependence on temperature (ε, β)
Forward attenuation coefficient
Backward attenuation coefficient (if asymmetric)
Core circular uniformity (min-max and avg variation
   over length)
Birefringence
Stress parameters
Polarization mode dispersion
Polarization-dependent loss (PDL)
Dispersion (modal, chromatic, and material)
Dispersion flatness over spectral range
Zero-dispersion wavelength
Cutoff wavelength

Power gain and loss (in dB) are additive, and thus the power budget reduces to straightforward addition or subtraction. Typically, the power of the optical signal to be launched into fiber is at 0 dB. Then, the dB loss of each lossy item in the path is subtracted from it, and the gain for optical amplifiers is added to it. In Chapter 1, we discussed the decibel unit and the precautions to be taken when adding or subtracting dBs and dBms. The net power is then compared with the receiver sensitivity. Typically, a net power margin of several dBs is desirable.

$$(\text{Margin}) = (\text{Transmitter output power}) - (\text{Receiver sensitivity}) - \left(\sum \text{losses}\right), (\text{dB})$$

As an example, the total loss in a path is calculated by the sum

$$\sum L_n + \sum \alpha_s + \sum \alpha_c + \sum L_{N-L} + \sum G_n$$

where Ln represents the loss of each fiber segment, α_s is the mean splice loss, α_c is the mean loss of line connectors, $\sum L_{N-L}$ is the sum of power degradations due to nonlinear effects, including noise sources (a rather involved sum), and $\sum Gn$ is the sum of gain.

In short, for a given transmitter output power and receiver sensitivity, the power budget determines the path length between transmitter and signal regeneration, as well as the bit rate. For example, at OC-12 rate for transmitter output 0 dBm and receiver sensitivity −35 dBm, the fiber length (for SMF) is determined to be 64 km without amplification. Similarly, at OC-48 and receiver sensitivity of −29 dBm, the fiber length is determined to be 51 km; for fibers with improved transmission characteristics, these lengths are calculated longer.

4.11.12   Power Budget Calculations by Example

In this section, we focus further on the optical power budget of the path, as this is a very critical engineering function for all-optical communications systems and networks.

The optical power budget involves everything that is on the path of the optical signal:

- optical connectivity (connectors, splices, patch panels)
- transmitter power and receiver sensitivity
- amplification strategy, the number of amplifiers in the path
- length of each span
- length of the path
- received quality of signal (expected BER and OSNR)
- number of channels and granularity, and more
- linearities and nonlinearities (dispersion, FWM, etc.)
- and many more

There are several factors that affect the signal power level due to loss along an optical path, some obvious and some rather hidden. One hidden source lies in fiber-to-fiber connectivity because of one or more mismatches:

- connecting different fiber types

- fiber characteristics (polarization, birefringence, etc.) mismatch

- angular misalignment

- core diameter mismatch

- lateral offset

- numerical aperture mismatch

- concentricity mismatch

- core ellipticity mismatch

- excessive distance (gap) between fibers

- temperature variation along the fiber (part is underground and part is aerial)

Another hidden source of optical power loss is reflections at the end-face of a fiber, also known as *Fresnel reflections*. Reflections traveling toward the source may cause noise and thus increase the BER. Reflections are reduced by treating the fiber ends with AR coatings, angled finished faces, and ferrules with a small radius. The reflected optical power in a fiber is expressed as part of the reflection loss, or the reduction of reflected energy compared with transmitted energy. Treated fiber has a return loss in the range of -30 to -60 dB, and if the fiber face is angled finished -60 dB.

Although component specifications vary from manufacturer to manufacturer, Table 4.12 lists the approximate loss values used in our examples (actual values should be consulted from manufacturers' specification data sheets).

Example #1: Consider an optical module, the diagram of which is shown in Figure 4.58. Calculate the total input to output insertion loss (IL) if each monitoring device (Mon) subtracts 0.6 dB; consult Table 4.12 for connector losses.

(Answer: 15.0 dB)

Table 4.12 Loss (dB) for various passive components

Component	Value (Units)
Fiber (SMF)	0.1 (dB/km)
Fiber connector	0.4 (dB)
Multifiber connector	0.5 (dB)
Patch connector	>0.5 (dB)
Splice	0.2 (dB)
Optical mux (OMux)	<1 (dB/channel)
Optical demux (ODemux)	<1 (dB/channel)
OXC (through)	0.5 (dB)
OXC (drop)	<2 (dB)
Splitter	<3 (dB)
Tap	0.2 (dB)
2:1 selector	<3 (dB)
Filter	0.5 (dB)
Other component	Consult data sheets

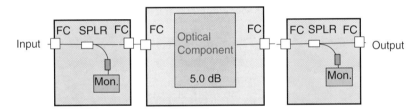

Mon. = monitoring device

SPLR = splitter

SPLC = splice

FC = fiber connector

Calculations:
IL = 6 × FC + 2 × SPLRs + 2 × SPLC + 2 × Mon. + 1 × OptComp
= 6 × 0.4 + 2 × 3 + 2 × 0.2 + 2 × 0.6 + 5 = 15.0 dB

Figure 4.58   Example of IL calculations of an optical module.

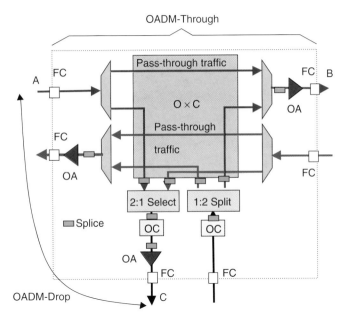

Calculations:
A.   IL(A => B) = 2 × FC + OMux + O × C(through) + ODemux + 1 SPLC − OA
= 2 × 0.4 + 1 + 0.5 + 1 + 0.2 − 6 = −2.5 dB
B.   IL(A => C) = 2 × FC + OMux + O × C(drop) + 3 × SPLC + Select + OC − OA
= 2 × 0.4 + 1 + 2 + 3 × 0.2 + 3 + 1 − 6 = 2.4 dB

Figure 4.59   Example of IL calculations of an OADM.

Example #2: Consider an OADM module, the diagram of which is shown in Figure 4.59. Calculate the IL per channel for

a. the OADM-through

b. the OADM-drop side

The gain of the OA is 6 dB and for the wavelength converter (OC) is 1 dB. Consult Table 4.12 for connector losses.

(Answer: a. −2.5 dB, b. 2.4 dB)

Example #3: The optical output at a transmitter is 0 dB. The receiver sensitivity (for a given bit rate per channel and BER) is −40 dB. Calculate the maximum fiber span on the basis of loss only.

(Answer: for 40 dB total loss and for a fiber with 0.1 dB/km, the total span is 400 km)

Example #4: For the example #3, and for 400 km span, if the fiber PMD coefficient is 0.2 ps/$\sqrt{\text{km}}$, based on PMD calculations only and without PMD compensation, could the highest bit rate be 40 Gb/s?

(Answer: $0.15 \times \sqrt{400} = 4.0$ ps; this corresponds to a bit rate $\gg 40$ Gb/s, so the answer is yes)

Example #5: For the example #4, considering both PMD and chromatic dispersion at 0.5 ps/nm-km,

a. What the highest maximum bit rate would be without compensation?

b. How much compensation would be required to transmit at 40 Gb/s?

(Answer: a. $0.2 \times \sqrt{400} + 0.5 \times 400 = 204$ ps; this corresponds to a bit rate 5 Gb/s; b. 40 Gb/s has a period of 25 ps. The required compensation should be such that 204 is reduced to 25 or less, thus 180 ps total)

Example #6: For the example #5, considering a DCF with a coefficient of -100 ps/nm-km and ignoring DCF fiber loss, how many kilometers of DCF should be used?

(Answer: $180/100 = 1.8$ km)

Example #7: Single-mode power loss calculations for a DWDM optical link (the following is an approximate example of power loss calculations over an optical link and for 40 optical channels).

Fiber used:	Standard SMF
Fiber loss:	0.1 dB/km
Chromatic Dispersion:	0.5 ps/nm-km
PMD:	0.12 ps/$\sqrt{\text{km}}$
Total fiber span length:	80 km
Number of OChs:	40 in C-band
Channel separation:	100 nm
Transmitter wavelength accuracy:	f $\pm$ 20 nm
Transmitter output power, P_T:	0 dB
Bit rate:	10 Gbps
Detector type:	APD
Maximum receive signal/OCh:	−20 dBm

Receiver power sensitivity, P_R:	-33 dBm @ 10^{-9} BER
Opt. Mux/Demux through IL:	7 dB
Opt. Mux/Demux drop IL:	8 dB
Amplification gain:	0 dB
Number of fiber connectors in path:	4
Number of fiber splices in path:	10
Number of expected future splices (margin):	4
Margin due to degradations:	2 dB

Calculations:

1. Transmitter output power:		0 dBm	
2. Receiver sensitivity (@10^{-9} BER):	P_R	-33.0 dBm	
3. Total fiber system gain (#1-#2):	G		33 dB
4. Dispersion loss (@10^{-9} BER):	P_D	1.0 dB	
Miscellaneous losses:	P_{Misc}	0.4 dB	
5. Connector losses (4@0.5 dB each):	L_C	2.0 dB	
6. Splice losses (10@0.2 dB each):	L_S	2.0 dB	
7. Margin for future 4 repair splices:	M_R	0.8 dB	
8. Margin for WDM upgrades:	M_{WDM}	3.0 dB	
9. Maximum allowable fiber loss: (#3-#4-#5-#6-#7-#8-#9)	L		23.8 dB
10. Total loss due to fiber:	L_F	8.0 dB	
11. Margin due to degradations	P_{Margin}	2.0 dB	
12. Received power level: (#1-#10-#11-#12)	R	-33.8 dBm	

Conclusions

The received power level (-33.8 dBM) is within the receiver sensitivity (-35 dBm @ 10^{-9} BER), with only 1.2 dB additional margin left. Consequently, no pre-amplification or attenuation at the receiver is required. In addition, the total dispersion per channel is a little over 40 ps, and thus at 10 Gb/s (100 ps period), no dispersion compensation is required. However, if this fiber span is to be concatenated with more similar spans to construct a longer path, dispersion compensation of 60 to 80 ps will be required at least every other amplification stage (or every 160 km) and for 6 to 8 spans.

Example #8: Calculate the fiber span from the optical power budget.

Consider the following parameters:

Transmitter launched power = Tx
N connectors each with IL = Lconn
K splices each with IL = Lsplice
Tap loss for monitoring = Lmon
Receiver sensitivity = Rxsens
Fiber Loss coefficient = α dB/km
Margin of 3 dB, or otherwise specified

Then the maximum loss between transmitter and receiver is

$$\text{Max. loss} = \text{Lspan} + \text{NLconn} + \text{KLsplice} + \text{Lmon}$$

The maximum allowable loss is then

$$\text{Max. allowable loss} = \text{Max. loss} + \text{margin}$$

The fiber span loss Lspan is:

$$\text{Lspan} = \text{Tx} - \text{Rxsens} - \text{margin} - \text{NLconn} - \text{KLsplice} - \text{Lmon}$$

From this and the fiber loss coefficient α (dB/km), the fiber span is calculated:

$$\text{Fiber span} = \text{Lspan}/\alpha \ (\text{km})$$

Example #9: Channel capacity supported by linear optical fiber systems and networks

Before fiber-optic systems were in use, Shannon developed a mathematical theory that related the channel capacity with the signal-to-noise (S/N) ratio. His celebrated relationship has been used extensively in all communications fields, electrical, optical, and wireless:

$$\text{Channel capacity} = \log_2(1 + \text{S/N})$$

Using a typical value of S/N = 40 dB, a channel capacity of 13 bits/s-Hz is obtained (notice that the logarithm is base-2). Although this number at first glance looks small, note that it is per Hertz; that is, the channel capacity 13 b/s is multiplied by a giganumber of 10^9 in a GHz system, and by 10^{12} in a THz system. Today, the highest commercially available bit rate of 40 Gb/s represents only a small fraction of b/s-Hz.

Note, however, that the above relationship and theory consider a linear transmission medium. In reality, and particularly in DWDM systems, one must consider nonlinear optical fiber and related phenomena. Then the channel capacity is mathematically more involved because it requires solution of the nonlinear Shrödinger equation, signal and noise powers have a statistical distribution (such as Gaussian, Poisson, or other), nonlinear phenomena must be included (such as Kerr effect, polarization effects), photon–photon interactions (such as four-wave mixing, etc.), dispersion effects as well as the multispan fiber path. Then this case proves that Shannon's theoretical treatment provides the first order of magnitude solution to channel capacity, which in most applications is more than adequate because bit rates are not very high and there is not a high density of optical channels (access, Metro, short-haul), and it is applicable only to the very dense and ultrahigh bit rate systems and networks.

Example #10: Number of optical channels supported in a fiber network

1. Determine the conditions that N optical channels in a WDM system over a bandwidth spectrum B(λ) expressed in nm. Consider that for a bit rate of B Gb/s, 2B GHz of bandwidth is needed for encoding (this determines the channel width) and that for low cross-talk, (as a rule of thumb), a channel spacing of 6B GHz is required.

For a center frequency λ, and from the identity

$$\Delta f = c\Delta\lambda/\lambda^2$$

the bandwidth range (in terms of frequency) is:

$$\Delta f = B(f) = B(\lambda)c/\lambda^2$$

Now, the bandwidth required over all N channels is:

$$B_{\text{req}} = 2BN + 6B(N-1)$$

Assuming that B_{req} is equal to or less than $B(f)$, then

$$N = (B_{\text{req}} + 6B)/8B$$

Clearly, if B_{req} is greater than $B(f)$, then the accommodated number of channels can be smaller.

2. For the previous example, calculate the maximum number of channels that fit in Δf.

   For a bandwidth Δf and for the same assumptions, the maximum number of channels is calculated by

$$N = (\Delta f + 6B)/8B$$

3. For the previous example, consider that the channel spacing is fixed to C_S and that the channel width to C_W. How many channels can fit in bandwidth Δf?

   From

$$\Delta f = (C_W)N + C_S(N-1)$$

   one obtains

$$N = (\Delta f + C_S)/(C_W + C_S)$$

EXERCISES

1. The digital cross-connect executes a "call processing protocol" to establish input–output connectivity (5 points). True or False?

2. A switch is a dynamic cross-connecting machine. An electronic switch is designed such that it can switch both synchronous and asynchronous traffic. True or False?

3. A purely optical cross-connecting fabric is limited by the:

   a. type of traffic   True or False?

   b. signal bit rate   True or False?

4. Explain what we mean by "*remoting.*"

5. A hybrid node has eight quad-OC-12 input–output units and a maximum cross-connect capacity = 50 Gb/s. We forecast an increase in bandwidth demand, and we would like to upgrade the node to handle 50% more input–output capacity, yet maintain a 15% margin of cross-connect capacity. What you would recommend:

a. upgrade the input–output units

b. Increase the switching bandwidth capacity

c. Both

d. Do nothing

6. Consider the optical node of problem 5. It consists of four shelves; two shelves are allocated for the eight input–output units, controllers, and a timing unit; one shelf for the cross-connecting fabric, drivers, and controller; and the fourth shelf for power feed, craft access, alarm display, and test units. What type of controller would you recommend (simplex or duplex) for each shelf?

7. The 1 + 1 protection requires two identical but separate paths that connect the two end-terminals; each end-terminal feeds the same traffic in the two separate fiber paths. True or False?

8. Backbone systems are mostly applicable in networks that connect nodes separated by a maximum of 100 km. True or False?

REFERENCES

1. S.V. Kartalopoulos, *Introduction to DWDM Technology: Data in a Rainbow*, IEEE Press, New York, 2000.

2. S.V. Kartalopoulos, *Understanding SONET/SDH and ATM: Communications Networks for the Next Millennium*, IEEE Press, New York, 1999.

3. J.C. Palais, *Fiber Optic Communications*, 3rd ed., Englewood Cliffs, NJ., Prentice-Hall, 1992.

4. B. Furht, *Handbook of Internet and Multimedia: Systems and Applications*, IEEE Press, New York, 1999.

5. L.G. Raman, *Fundamentals of Telecommunications Network Management*, IEEE Press, New York, 1999.

6. I.P. Kaminow and T.L. Koch, eds., *Optical Fiber Communications IIIA* and *Optical Fiber Communications IIIB*, Academic Press, 1997.

7. R.A. Linke, Optical heterodyne communications systems, *IEEE Comm. Mag.*, Oct. 1989, pp. 36–41.

8. R.A. Linke and A.H. Gnauck, High-capacity coherent lightwave systems, *J. Lightwave Technol.*, vol. 6, no. 11, 1988, pp. 1750–1769.

9. R.E. Slusher and B. Yurke, Squeezed light for coherent communications, *J. Lightwave Technol.*, vol. 8, no. 3, 1990, pp. 466–477.

10. T. Wildi, *Units and Conversion Charts*, IEEE Press, New York, 1991.

11. J. Nellist, *Understanding Telecommunications and Lightwave Systems*, IEEE Press, New York, 1996.

12. A. Borella, G. Cancellieri, and F. Chiaraluce, *Wavelength Division Multiple Access Optical Networks*, Artec House, Boston, 1998.

13. B.T. Doshi, S. Dravida, P. Harshavardhana, O. Hauser, and Y. Wang, Optical network design and restoration, *Bell Labs Tech. J.*, vol. 4, no. 1, 1999, pp. 58–84.

14. S. Chatterjee and S. Pawlowski, All-optical networks, *Comm. of the ACM*, vol. 47, no. 6, June 1999, pp. 74–83.

15. S.V. Kartalopoulos, A Manhattan Fiber Distributed Data Interface Architecture, *Globecom'90*, San Diego (December 2–5, 1990).

16. S.V. Kartalopoulos, Disaster Avoidance in the Manhattan Fiber Distributed Data Interface Network, *Globecom'93*, Houston, TX, December 2, 1993.

17. Y. Chen, M.T. Fatehi, H.J. LaRoche, J.Z. Larsen, and B.L. Nelson, Metro optical networking, *Bell Labs Tech. J.*, vol. 4, no. 1, 1999, pp. 163–186.

18. D.B. Buchholz et al., Broadband fiber access: A fiber-to-the-customer access architecture, *Bell Labs Tech. J.*, vol. 4, no. 1, 1999, pp. 282–299.

19. G.C. Wilson et al., FiberVista: An FTTH or FTTC System Delivering Broadband Data and CATV Services, *Bell Labs Tech. J.*, vol. 4, no. 1, 1999, pp. 300–322.

20. M. Berger et al., Pan-European optical networking using wavelength division multiplexing, *IEEE Comm. Mag.*, vol. 35, no. 4, 1997, pp. 82–88.

21. D. Cotter, J.K. Lcek, and D.D. Marcenac, Ultra-high-bit-rate networking: From the transcontinental backbone to the desktop, *IEEE Comm. Mag.*, vol. 35, no. 4, 1997, pp. 90–96.

22. E. Traupman, P. O'Connell, G. Minnis, M. Jadoul, and H. Mario, The evolution of the existing infrastructure, *IEEE Comm. Mag.*, vol. 37, no. 6, 1999, pp. 134–139.

23. A.G. Malis, Reconstructing transmission networks using ATM and DWDM, *IEEE Comm. Mag.*, vol. 37, no. 6, 1999, pp. 140–145.

24. H. Toba and K. Nosu, Optical frequency division multiplexing systems: Review of key technologies and applications, *IEICE Trans. Commun.*, vol. E75, no. 4, Apr. 1992, pp. 243–255.

25. O.E. DeLange, Wide-band optical communication systems: Part II-frequency-division-multiplexing, *Proc. IEEE*, vol. 58, no. 10, 1970, pp. 1683–1690.

26. D.K. Hunter et al., WASPNET: A wavelength switched packet network, *IEEE Comm. Mag.*, vol. 37, no. 3, March 1999, pp. 120–129.

27. A. Asthana et al., Towards a Gigabit IP Router, *J. High-Speed Networks*, vol. 1, no. 4, 1992.

28. M.A. Marsan, A. Bianco, E. Leonardi, A. Morabito, and F. Neri, All-Optical WDM Multi-Rings with Differentiated QoS, *IEEE Communications Magazine*, vol 37, no 2, Feb. 1999, pp. 58–66.

29. M.A. Marsan et al., Daisy: a Scalable All-Optical Packet Network with Multi-Fiber Ring Topology, *Computer Networks and ISDN Systems*, vol. 30, 1998, pp. 1065–82.

30. I. Gidon and Y. Ofek, MetaRing — a full-duplex ring with fairness and spatial reuse, *IEEE Trans. Communications*, vol. 41, no. 1, Jan. 1993, pp. 110–20.

31. J.M. Simmons et al., Optical crossconnects of reduced complexity for WDM networks with bidirectional symmetry, *IEEE Photonics Technology Letters*, vol. 10, no. 6, June 1998, pp. 819–821.

32. E.A. De Souza et al., Wavelength-division multiplexing with femtosecond pulses, *Optics Letters*, vol. 20, no. 10, 1995, pp. 1166–1168.

33. E. Modiano, WDM-based packet network, *IEEE Comm. Magazine*, vol. 37, no. 3, March 1999, pp. 130–135.

34. R. Glance, K. Pollock, C.A. Burrus, B.L. Kasper, G. Eisenstein, and L.W. Stulz, Densely spaced WDM coherent optical star network, *Electron. Lett.*, vol. 23, no. 17, 1987, pp. 875–876.

35. N. Takato et al., 128-channel polarization-insensitive frequency-selection-switch using high-silica waveguides on Si, *IEEE Photon. Technol. Lett.*, vol. 2, no. 6, 1990, pp. 441–443.

36. Y.-K.M. Lin, D. Spears, and M. Yin, Fiber-based local access network architectures, *IEEE Comm. Mag.*, Oct. 1989, pp. 64–73.

37. A. McGuire, *Architectural Models for Supervisory and Maintenance Aspects of Optical Transport Networks*, ICC'97 Workshop on WDM Network Management and Control, Montreal, Quebec Canada (8 June 1997).

38. E. Goldstein, *The Case for Opaque Multiwavelength Lightwave Networks*, ICC'97 Workshop on WDM Network Management and Control, Montreal, Quebec Canada (8 June 1997).

39. M. Garnot et al., Dimensioning and optimization of the wavelength-division-multiplexed optical layer of future transport networks, Proceedings IEEE ICC'98, Atlanta, Georgia, June 7–11, 1998, pp. 202–206.

40. P. Black and T. Meng, A 1-Gb/s four-state sliding block Viterbi decoder, *IEEE JSSC*, vol. 32, no. 6, June 1997, pp. 797–805.

41. D. Edforrs et al., An introduction to orthogonal frequency-division multiplexing, *http://www.tde.lth.se/home/oes/publications.html*.

42. S.V. Kartalopoulos, An associative RAM-based CAM and its application to broad-band communications systems, *IEEE Trans. Neural Networks*, vol. 9, no. 5, 1998, pp. 1036–1041.

43. S.V. Kartalopoulos, Ultra-fast pattern recognition in broadband communications systems, *ISPACS'98 Conference Proceedings*, Melbourne, Australia, November 1998.

44. R.E. Matick, *Transmission Lines for Digital and Communication Networks*, IEEE Press, New York, 1995.

45. Members of the Technical Staff, *Transmission Systems for Communications*, Bell Telephone Laboratories, New York, 1982.

46. S.U.H. Qureshi, Adaptive equalization, *Proc. IEEE*, vol. 73, no. 9, Sept. 1985, pp. 1349–1386.

47. S.V. Kartalopoulos, All fiber-optic pattern recognition and D-to-A converter, submitted for publication to Opt. Eng. Jl.

48. S.V. Kartalopoulos, Emerging technologies at the dawn of the millennium, *IEEE Comm. Mag.*, Nov. 2001, vol. 39, no. 11, pp. 22–26.

49. S.V. Kartalopoulos, A plateau of performance? *IEEE Comm. Mag.*, Sept. 1992, pp. 13–14.

50. C.E. Shannon, A mathematical theory of communication, *Bell Syst. Tech. J.*, pp. 379–423, 623–656, 1948.

51. J. Tang, The Shannon channel capacity of dispersion-free nonlinear optical fiber transmission, *J. Lightwave Technol.*, vol. 19, no. 8, pp. 1104–1109, Aug. 2001.

52. W.Y. Zhou and Y. Wu, COFDM: An overview, *IEEE Trans. Broadcasting*, vol. 41, no. 1, Mar. 1995, pp. 1–8.

53. S.V. Kartalopoulos, Elastic bandwidth, *IEEE Circuits Devices Mag.*, vol. 18, no. 1, Jan. 2002, pp. 8–13.

54. S.V. Kartalopoulos, Surviving a disaster, *IEEE Comm. Mag.*, vol. 40, no. 7, pp. 124–126, July 2002.

STANDARDS

1. ANSI/IEEE 812-1984, "Definition of terms relating to fiber optics."

2. ANSI T1X1.5/99-002, *A Proposal for Providing Channel-Associated Optical Channel Overhead in the OTN*, Lucent Technologies (Jan. 1999), *http://www.t1.org/index/0816.htm*.

3. ANSI T1X1.5/99-003, *A Proposal Implementation for a Digital "Wrapper" for OCh Overhead*, Lucent Technologies (January 1999), *http://www.t1.org/index/0816.htm*.

4. ANSI T1X1.5/99-004, *Optical Channel Overhead Carried on the Optical Supervisory Channel*, Lucent Technologies (January 1999), *http://www.t1.org/index/0816.htm*.

5. ANSI T1X1.5/99-060, *Draft Rec. G.871 version 1.4* (Oct. 1998).

6. IEC Publication 825-1, "Safety of laser products — Part 1: Equipment classification, requirements and user's guide."

7. IEC Publication 825-2, "Safety of laser products — Part 2: Safety of optical fibre communication systems."

8. IEC Publication 1280-2-1, "Fibre optic communication subsystem basic test procedures; Part 2: Test procedures for digital systems; Section 1 — Receiver sensitivity and overload measurement."

9. IEC Publication 1280-2-2, "Fibre optic communication subsystem basic test procedures; Part 2: Test procedures for digital systems; Section 2 — Optical eye pattern, waveform and extinction ratio measurement."

10. IEEE 802.3ab, 1000BaseT.

11. IEEE 802.1 to 802.6, Local Area Networks.

12. Internet study group: *http://www.internet2.edu*.

13. ITU-T Recommendation G.650, "Definition and test methods for the relevant parameters of single-mode fibres," 1996.

14. ITU-T Recommendation G.652, "Characteristics of a single-mode optical fiber cable," April 1997.

15. ITU-T Recommendation G.653, "Characteristics of a dispersion-shifted single-mode optical fiber cable," April 1997.

16. ITU-T Recommendation G.655, "Characteristics of a nonzero dispersion-shifted single-mode optical fiber cable," Oct. 1996.

17. ITU-T Recommendation G.661, "Definition and test methods for the relevant generic parameters of optical fiber amplifiers," Nov. 1996.

18. ITU-T Recommendation G.662, "Generic characteristics of optical fiber amplifier devices and sub-systems," July 1995.

19. ITU-T Recommendation G.663, "Application related aspects of optical fiber amplifier devices and sub-systems," Oct. 1996.

20. ITU-T Draft Recommendation G.664, "General automatic power shut-down procedure for optical transport systems," Oct. 1998.

21. ITU-T Recommendation G.671, "Transmission characteristics of passive optical components," Nov. 1996.

22. ITU-T Recommendation G.681, "Functional characteristics of interoffice and long-haul line systems using optical amplifiers, including optical multiplexers," June 1986.

23. ITU-T recommendation G.691 "Optical interfaces for single channel STM-64, STM-256 systems and other SDH systems with optical amplifiers," 2000.

24. ITU-T draft Recommendation G.692 (ex Gsaf), "Optical interfaces for multichannel systems with optical amplifiers," Oct. 1998.

25. ITU-T Recommendation G.702, "Digital hierarchy bit rates," 1988.

26. ITU-T Recommendation G.707, "Network node interface for the synchronous digital hierarchy," 1996.

27. ITU-T Draft Rec. G.709, "Network node interface for the optical transport network (OTN)," Oct. 1998.

28. ITU-T Recommendation G.741, "General considerations on second order multiplex equipments," 1988.

29. ITU-T Draft Rec. G.798, "Characteristics of optical transport networks (OTN) equipment functional blocks," Oct. 1998.

30. ITU-T Rec. G.805, "Generic functional architecture of transport networks," Oct. 1998.

31. ITU-T G.825, "The control and wander within digital networks which are based on the synchronous digital hierarchy (SDH)."

32. ITU-T Draft Rec. G.871, Framework for optical networking recommendations," Oct. 1998.

33. ITU-T Recommendation G.872, "Architecture of optical transport networks," Feb. 1999.

34. ITU-T Draft Rec. G.873, "Optical transport network requirements," Oct. 1998.

35. ITU-T Draft Rec. G.874, "Management aspects of the optical transport network element," Oct. 1998.

36. ITU-T Draft Rec. G.875, "Optical transport network management information model for the network element view," Oct. 1998.

37. ITU-T Recommendation G.911, "Parameters and calculation methodologies for reliability and availability of fibre optic systems," 1993.

38. ITU-T Recommendation G.955, "Digital line systems based on the 1,544 kbit/s and the 2,048 kbit/s hierarchy on optical fibre cables," 1993.

39. ITU-T Recommendation G.957, "Optical interfaces for equipments and systems relating to the synchronous digital hierarchy," 1995.

40. ITU-T Recommendation G.958, "Digital line systems based on the synchronous digital hierarchy for use on optical fibre cables," 1994.

41. ITU-T Draft Rec. G.959, "Optical networking physical layer interfaces," Feb. 1999.

42. ITU-T G.975, "Forward error correction for submarine systems," Nov. 1996.

43. Telcordia (formerly Bellcore) GR-253, "Synchronous optical network (SONET) transport systems: common generic criteria," issue 2, Dec. 1995.

44. Telcordia (formerly Bellcore), TR-NWT-233, "Digital cross connect system," Nov. 1992.

45. Telcordia (formerly Bellcore) TR-NWT-499, "Transport systems generic requirements (TSGR): common requirements," issue 5, Dec. 1993.

46. Telcordia (formerly Bellcore), TR-NWT-917, "Regenerator," Oct. 1990.

47. Telcordia (formerly Bellcore) GR-1209-CORE, "Generic requirements for fiber optic branching components," issue 2, Feb. 1998.

48. Telcordia (formerly Bellcore) GR-1377, "SONET OC-192 transport systems generic criteria," issue 3, Aug. 1996.

49. W. Simpson, "PPP over SONET/SDH," IETF RFC 1619, May 1994.

5

DWDM NETWORKS

5.1 INTRODUCTION

The evolving optical network with the introduction of DWDM has whetted the appetite for bandwidth and offering new multiservices differentiating from traditional ones. As an example, a streaming MP3 channel requires 200 Kb/s, high-quality videoconferencing requires 3 Mb/s, and two-channel DVD-quality streaming video requires 10 to 14 Mb/s. As already presented in previous chapters, DWDM systems need careful design to offer in an optimum and reliable manner the required services of today and of tomorrow in a single optical network with multiple services. These systems are interconnected into a well-managed transparent network, which is remotely provisioned and quickly reconfigured, easily maintained, cost-effective, and quickly restored (<50 ms). This optical network will not consist of multiple devices each providing support for specific network functions such as IP routing, or layer 2 switching, and so on, as the current network does, but is more intelligent, more robust, and yet flexible and scalable, more resilient, and fault-tolerant and it delivers services in the most expedient manner possible with end-to-end service provisioning.

The DWDM network offers the capability to support both already established traditional services and new differentiating services such as real-time multicast, streaming video, e-commerce, virtual and virtual private networks (VPNs). This is very attractive because it also means that overlay networks converge to a single and more potent optical network. However, an optical network that supports converged services demands that certain practices of the data network such as quality of service (QoS), and "best effort" transport be revised. This revision requires:

- protocols to support QoS such as IP differentiated services (DiffServ)
- protocols to support traffic engineering with dynamic connections in the packet/cell-based network such as multiprotocol label switching (MPLS)

This chapter contains device specifications for illustrative and educational purposes. Because specifications are continuously changing, no responsibility is assumed for correctness. The reader is encouraged to consult the most recent versions of standards and most current manufacturers' data sheets.

388

- protocols to support bandwidth as well as wavelength management with dynamic connections at the optical layer such as multiprotocol lambda (wavelength) switching (MPλS)
- fast, transparent, and multiservice optical switches
- interoperation of both optical core and edge network elements
- dynamic optical signaling
- advanced network management systems
- security

As the number of wavelengths per fiber increases, as the bit rate per wavelength increases, and as new services requiring more bandwidth are offered, core services come closer to the edge. This also brings fiber closer to the edge and closer to the home or office. As a consequence, the number of network layers becomes smaller, and the edge network elements must be able to support a large variety of protocols and bit rates, be scalable with a finer granularity of bandwidth traffic, be easily provisioned, reliable, available, fault-tolerant, restored and it must be intelligent as well. This will enable provision of reliable services not only on the wavelength level but also on a smaller granularity ranging from DS1/E1 to GbE over *optical virtual private networks* (OVPN). The OVPN will operate across multiple managed wavelengths and networks as one network that can be dynamically configured and support numerous applications, appearing to the end-customer as a VPN completely protocol- and bit rate-independent. This network will also enable bandwidth trading and reselling (bandwidth on demand), multiservices, and service transparency with various *service level agreements* (SLA).

We have discussed SLA in previous chapters and we will discuss it again. In particular, SLA metrics pertain to:

- information rate
- network availability (this is not exactly the same with network downtime)
- latency
- performance-level parameters
- quality of service
- time to report
- time to respond
- compensation
- on-time provisioning

To ensure that these SLA metrics are met, both the system and the network are responsible for continuously monitoring the optical signal(s), network traffic, and continuous continuously perform tests on the network.

Although new fiber networks are currently in deployment and planned to meet the projected exploding traffic needs, DWDM networks require additional efficiency requirements that are related to demographics, communications customs, peoples' habits and trends, economic profiles, and embedded network technology that influence the future network.

5.1.1 Multiprotocol Label Switching

Multiprotocol label switching (MPLS) *protocol* emerged from a need to provide the ability to support any type of traffic on a large IP network, thus minimizing the limitations of different routing protocols, transport layers and addressing schemes, and reduce routing costs. It also provides traffic engineering with dynamic connections in the packet/cell-based (and IP) network.

Underlying the MPLS framework is the ability to separately determine the best route and forward traffic. The latter is accomplished by using simple look-up tables to define or discover a specified *label-switched path* (LSP) over the IP network and comply with traffic engineering constraints. These constraints include bandwidth, acceptable network resources, and a quality of service specified by a service level agreement (SLA). This label-switched path is known as a *tunnel*.

When a tunnel is specified, the same label is assigned at the head end of all IP packets with the same destination prefix, the label is encapsulated in a labeled envelope and sent into the tunnel (Fig. 5.1). Thus, *tunnels* are explicit routes over which aggregate traffic flows are mapped based on traffic conditions and availability of network resources. As a result, traffic management is simplified and traffic congestion is minimized (by channeling traffic around the congestion point). Channeling traffic between customer sites and using explicit routing establishes a virtual private network (VPN). MPLS enhances the ability of a VPN to establish, maintain, and guarantee QoS and cost of service (CoS) for a label-switched path (LSP).

QoS, which is well defined in ATM technology, provides the ability to manage network traffic bandwidth, congestion, and latency. To ensure QoS, the characteristics of the path end-to-end require attention; these include network architecture, security, survivability, management, devices, technologies, protocols, *user to network interfaces* (UNI), *network to network interfaces* (NNI), interoperability, scalability, and feature-rich services supported by the elements in the network.

In MPLS, multiple hierarchies of tunnels can be established between core multiservice switch/routers over an optical network, thus simplifying the physical network to a "service agnostic" network and providing IP/MPLS ATM/QoS-like services over the optical core beyond the current "best effort."

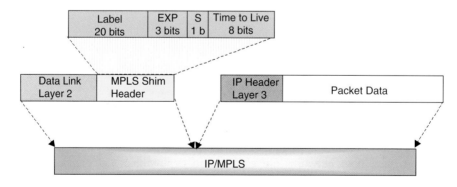

EXP = Experimental bit

Figure 5.1 IP/MPLS encapsulation.

MPLS allows traffic to be directly switched through IP routers by applying a layer-2 label to the IP (layer-3) frame as it enters the edge of the MPLS-aware network eliminating the traditional IP packet store, read IP packet header first and then forward the IP packet to the next hop, and repeat it again. As the label is applied and the path (route) is identified (via signaling), the forwarding hardware on the path is provisioned with predefined traffic engineering parameters to guarantee levels of traffic bandwidth, delay variation, and control congestion. When the data begin to flow, the network devices monitor and report the performance parameters and actual level of resources being utilized at each interface. In addition, the information flow is transparent to higher protocol levels, and thus the network appears to unauthorized individuals to be inherently secure.

As a result, the applied label corresponds to an established path through the network, between point A and point B, by signaling and network path configuration; in many respects, a dynamically configured and switched private path, hence LSP. Thence the obvious question:

MPLS label switching involves the following components:

- The *traffic engineering policy* (TEP) at the user interface is responsible for selecting the traffic path complying with the applied constraints.
- *The Internet gateway protocol* (IGP) is responsible for implementing the routing protocol.
- The *signaling component* is responsible for executing the signaling to establish a path (tunnel).
- The *data-forwarding component* is responsible for the IP/MPLS packet routing.

Since the MPLS-aware network requires signaling and dynamic provisioning, how is this network different from the optical transport network? The answer is not much! In fact, this is the central point that enforces the argument that the next-generation optical (DWDM) communications network facilitates convergence of services and consolidation of network overlays so that IP, TDM, SONET/SDH, and so on, are all supported by the same network; at the same time, it allows for route engineering using pre-agreed upon CoS and QoS parameters. However, this network has elements with specialized functionality such that the full MPLS protocol with all extensions does not run on each *label edge-router* (LER) or on each *label switch-router* (LSR) within an MPLS-aware network. An LER or LSR requires only supporting MPLS-explicit routing functionality. Thus, as the fiber-optic communications network evolves, so too will MPLS. In fact, the next-generation MPLS to allow for configuring nonpacket devices, in addition to packet, is already emerging and is known as generalized MPLS (GMPLS), previously known as MPλS, where λ stands for wavelength (implying WDM applicability). A wealth of information may be found in *http://www.mplsrc.com* and *http://www.gmpls.org*.

5.1.2 MPλS

Multiprotocol lambda (wavelength) *protocol switching* enables dynamic connectivity at the optical layer; that is, the optical network supports signaling standards and is supported by dynamic optical switches and/or routers and wavelength converters so that, based on demand and traffic flow, it has the intelligence to set up and take down lambda connections and cope with network availability issues. It also copes with congestion situations by discovering new physical paths. The signaling standards are being specified by the *optical domain service interconnect* (ODSI), Optical Internetworking Forum (OIF), and *Internet Engineering Task Force* (IETF).

5.1.3 DiffServ, IntServ, and MPLS

Differentiated services (DiffServ) involves marking the packets within a flow with a tag indicating the requested QoS treatment on a *per hop* (link) *basis* (PHB). DiffServ defines standardized traffic classes and delay; queue depth and bandwidth allocated to queue are related to delay and delay variation (jitter). Thus, DiffServ edge routers perform service classification, shaping, metering, scheduling, and tag marking.

PHBs are forward provisionable over the path (or tunnel). As a consequence, PHBs are easily defaulted to predefined treatments for IP precedence values (RFC 1812 and RFC 791), and thus DiffServ is considered scalable [DiffServ codepoints (DSCP) are defined in RFC 2474]. Both DCP and IP precedence are derived from the IPv4 header. However, DiffServ does not guarantee end-to-end QoS, and ingress points on the flow do not know of congestion conditions (and thus congestion management is not as straightforward).

As opposed to DiffServ, Internet Services (IntServ) is a connection-oriented service. IntServ programs edge routers with microflows to maintain QoS SLAs between user/client and application/server, thus providing end-to-end service guarantees. Although the connection-oriented nature of MPLS tunnels flows into LSPs, IntServ desegregates IP traffic into microflows.

At the boundary between customer edge and provider edge, the microflows terminate at the provider edge router, where packets are marked with DSCPs that match the QoS requirements. The DSCP-marked packets are sent to the Internet core, where *provider core routers* (PCR) classify them and inject them into MPLS LSPs that meet the DSCP QoS requirements. Thus, all three services, IntServ, DiffServ, and MPLS, meet at the Internet core.

5.1.4 Optical Virtual Path Network

The term *virtual path network* (VPN) denotes a logical end-to-end path (or route) across a multivendor network rather than the actual physical path of a single-vendor network, thus acting as a private network but without the high cost of leased private lines; hence the term *virtual*. Similarly, the term *optical virtual path network* (OVPN) denotes a VPN, but now the path is over a multivendor optical network acting as a dedicated wavelength path.

5.1.5 Network Layers and Protection

DWDM is applicable not only to all network topologies but also to all network layers (see Fig. 4.5), from the ultra-long-haul and backbone to enterprise and residential networks. As a consequence, DWDM networks, depending on topology and layer, have different complexities and challenges to meet. In countries with large communications networks, the number of layer and/or nomenclature may differ somewhat. For example, China plans for an aggressive four-layer (fiber) network, whereby layer 1 is known as *interprovince* (this is equivalent to a backbone network) with MSPRing signaling and with peak traffic greater than 130 Gb/s; layer 2 is known as *intraprovince* (this is a large metro ring network); layer 3 is known as *junction* (this is an interconnected multiring/mesh network) and layer 4 is known as *access*.

Network layers are associated with network architectures because network complexity, number of optical channels, and bit rate per channel (i.e., the aggregate bandwidth per fiber) for each layer are different. In addition, networks at different layers are associated with different protection or restoration schemes. A ring topology scheme is known as a shared protection ring (SPRing) and as a multiplexed-shared protection ring (MSPRing) (see Section 5.2).

There are several steps in network protection and restoration: network/service monitoring, network notification, network alarming, and protection action. Based on network architecture, protection and restoration schemes may also differ: 1 + 1, 1:1, dual-ended, bidirectional, and distributed restoration architectures. Some do not require signaling channels (such as 1 + 1), and some do require signaling (dual-ended, bidirectional, and distributed restoration). In the aforementioned China example both two-fiber and four-fiber MSPring with 1 + 1 protection are planned. There is protection at different network levels: path, line, section, and service. Path protection is an end-to-end network responsibility that entails the discovery of a different end-to-end path. Line protection is the responsibility of line-terminating equipment to find another route (using cross-connecting facilities) to bypass a fault. Section protection is also the responsibility of section-terminating equipment to find another route (using cross-connecting facilities) to bypass a fault. In SONET/SDH, protection (notification, alarming, and action) is accomplished with embedded in the signal (in-band) signaling channels such as automatic protection switching (APS) is defined in the associated overhead (K1/K2) bytes for section layer protection and (K3/K4) bytes for VC layer protection. In OTN, this is not accomplished with in-band channels but with out-of-band channels; that is, signaling channels are now embedded in the supervisory channel. Only end-to-end optical path protection and restoration may be possible with in-band channels because this is where the optical signal is terminated; an all-optical network does not terminate a client's optical signal, only the supervisory signal. In OTN, the multiplex and transmission sections are protected using the supervisory channel (see Section 5.2).

5.1.6   The Evolving Telecommunications Management Network

The evolving DWDM network will support integration of multiservices at various levels. Edge metropolitan networks (Metro) will support TDM, SONET/SDH, ATM, IP/MPLS, FR, and Ethernet. They also will support interoperability, scalability, service protection, and future-proofing, as well as new standards that are under development. This necessitates self-managing network elements with simplified yet sophisticated network management, service management, and fault management capabilities. In all, this culminates in telecommunications management network (TMN) architecture with fewer levels as the result of functionality distribution.

As a quick review, network management encompasses the following traditional functions:

- Performance management
  — Performance parameters monitoring
  — Performance parameters storing and reporting

- Fault management
  — Thresholds for degradation or failure declaration
  — Failure localization, isolation, testing, and restoration
  — Failure reporting and statistical data buildup
  — Alarm surveillance
- Configuration management
  — Memory update, database query
  — Database backup and database restoration
- Security management
  — Data and system integrity
  — System/resource access control
- Accounting management
  — PVC and/or SVC accounting
- Interim local management interface (ILMI); (per ATM forum: UNI)
  — ILMI protocol and traffic requirements

With this as reference, the TMN architecture evolves in a direction such that:

- Network management functionality moves to the network element.
- Connection management is handled by network elements in a distributed manner. This allows for fast connection setup and tear-down as well as fast restoration.
- Network elements have knowledge of topology and network autodiscovery capability. Such elements comprise a neural-like adaptive network with self-learning capabilities.
- It provides service transparency, and thus fewer interfaces to simplify handoffs and latency between different systems. Only the end-to-end (client-defined) service must be provisioned by a local terminal. As a consequence, the element management function becomes an archive of performance monitoring and provisioning data, and a function for alarm, inventory management, and software management.
- It provides self-planning and switched broadband connections to individual network devices.
- It provides a single interface point for concentration.
- It can be simplex or duplex for survivability, reliability, and availability purposes.
- It simplifies the human–machine interaction, and
- It is cost-efficient.

5.2 THE OPTICAL TRANSPORT NETWORK

As the network was becoming too complex and complicated with overlays, the communications industry found itself needing to simplify the network The evolution of the optical network into a multiwavelength scalable, future-proof network (DWDM), as well as the accumulated experience of previous optical synchronous protocols such as

SONET/SDH and asynchronous such as ATM, IP, FR, Ethernet, and so on, provided the stimulus to redefine the synchronous optical network into the *optical transport network* (OTN), which at the optical layer will be reconfigurable, quickly restorable (a few 100 ms), provisionable, easily maintainable, flexible, survivable, and transparent where cost-efficiency permits. As a result, the ITU-T and other standards bodies got to work coming out with recommendations defining interfaces, payload format, transport unit format, and functional architectures that are described in several documents such as G.709, G.805, G.872, and so on.

In OTN, many (simplified) terms have been adopted from SONET/SDH but they now have an "O" to signify the term *optical*; for example, ONNI means optical transport network node interface, and so on. Moreover, forming a frame consisting of payload and overhead in a matrix arrangement, in principle is done as in SONET/SDH. Thus, it is this author's opinion that a good understanding of SONET/SDH facilitates the understanding of OTN specification. Because the OTN specification cannot be covered in detail in one section, the interested reader is encouraged to study the aforementioned ITU-T OTN-related recommendation and (if any) amendments.

OTN specifies two different network interfaces, the *interdomain interface* (IrDI) and the *intradomain interface* (IaDI). The IrDI defines the frame format between two domain networks (each domain belongs to or is administered by a different vendor). The IaDI defines the frame format between two nodes or network elements within the same domain network. In addition, the OTN defines the various sections of the transportable frame, such as the payload structure, the overhead structure, the multiplexing hierarchy, and the transportable frame in a DWDM group of optical channels. In SONET/SDH there was only one optical channel (wavelength) per fiber; because in DWDM there are many optical channels per fiber, an additional subscript is needed to distinguish a particular optical channel in a DWDM group of channels.

An OTN frame, known as an *optical transport unit* (OTU), consists of client data payload and added overhead. An OTU is organized into a matrix of 4 rows and 4080 columns, where each element in the 4×4080 matrix is a (8-bit) byte.

The 4×4080 OTU is subdivided into two areas. The first 3824 columns comprise the *optical channel data unit-k* (ODU-k), and the last 256 columns comprise the *forward error correction* (FEC) code. If the FEC is not implemented, these 256 columns are stuffed with "zeros."

The ODU consists of (Fig. 5.2):

- the frame alignment and OTU-k overhead in the first 14 bytes of the first row
- the ODU overhead area in bytes 1 to 14 of rows two to four)
- the optical payload overhead (OPU-k OH) in columns 15 and 16, and
- the client payload area (OPU-k) in columns 17 to 3824

A DWDM transportable group of OTN frames consists of a number of optical channels (wavelengths) plus one or more supervisory channels, which are all optically multiplexed in a single fiber; a simplified version is illustrated in Figure 5.3 (see also Figs. 4.38, 4.39, and 4.40). Thus, a transportable fully formatted group of frames in which each optical channel (wavelength) is modulated by an OTU is called an *optical transport module-n* (OTM-n). The sequence of events in the formation of the OTM-n signal from data to a transportable DWDM signal is as follows:

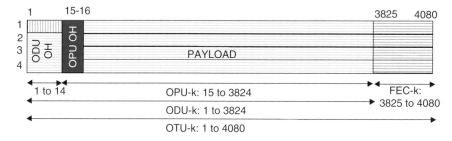

Figure 5.2 OTN transport unit structure.

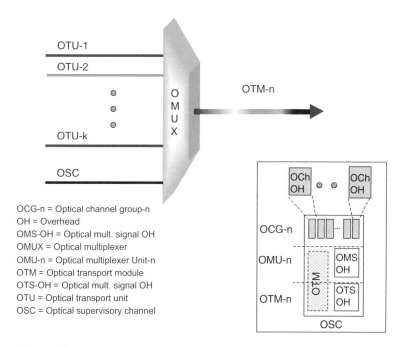

Figure 5.3 As several OTUs comprise an OTM-n, the OSC channel is formed.

- Client data are mapped in the payload area and OPU overhead is added to form the OPU-k subframe.

- ODU overhead is added to OPU-k to form the ODU-k subframe.

- OTU overhead is added to ODU-k to form the OTU-k frame.

- The OTU-k is associated with an OCh and OCh overhead data for the particular OTU-k is formed; this overhead is mapped in an OTM overhead signal (OOS) supervisory channel, which is outside the DWDM amplifier range.

- The OCh modulates an optical channel carrier (OCC), that is, a wavelength.

- OCCs are optically multiplexed into an *optical channel group* (OCG) and multiplexer overhead data is formed; this overhead is also mapped in the OTM Overhead Signal (OOS) supervisory channel.

- OCG overhead is formed and is mapped in the OOS; the OCG is transported via the optical transport module (OTM), as well as the OOS but over a separate optical supervisory channel (OSC).

A consequence of the separate optical supervisory channel is that the channel carrying payload and the channel carrying supervisory overhead may fail independently. However, G.872 dictates that both the payload carrying the OTU channel and the OSC channel should be supervised independently; thus, OSC failures "shall not initiate consequent actions on the payload" channel. A further consequence of this is that failures of the OTU or OSC require separate and independent forward defect indications (FDI) mechanisms, one for the payload (FDI-P) and one for the OSC (FDI-S).

Currently, three ODU rates are defined, ODU1 = 2.488320 Gb/s, ODU2 = 9.953280 Gb/s, and ODU3 = 39.813120 Gb/s, $\pm$20 ppm; the corresponding ODUk nominal rates are OTU1 = 2.666057143 Gb/s, OTU2 = 10.709225316 Gb/s, and OTU3 = 43.018413559 Gb/s; these rates reflect an approximate 7% bit rate increase due to the FEC addition. Thus, the period of each OTUk is 48.9710 μs (OTU1), 12.1910 μs (OTU2), and 3.0350 μs (OTU3).

5.3   DWDM NETWORK TOPOLOGIES AND RESTORATION STRATEGIES

The most well-known network topologies are the ring, star, all-connected mesh, and point-to-point. In addition, there are subtopologies such as the ladder and point-to-point with add-drop. In an end-to-end network, a client signal travels from a small access network, and as it is "packed" with other client signals, to increasingly larger networks, and depending on its destination, it may eventually reach a backbone or an ultra-long-haul point to point network (Fig. 5.4; see also Fig. 4.5).

What has just been described is the *main goal of any communications network*, that is, to deliver a client's signal to its destination with the acceptable integrity. Anything else is nothing more but added complexity to ensure that the main goal is preserved. However, one cannot lose sight of the fact that there is a finite natural lifespan for every component that makes up a system and a network, including fiber links, and also that there are inadvertent causes of failures (such as breaking a fiber). Hence, in a large and complex network with millions of components and millions of variables subject to change, the network must be architected and designed to be resilient and to maintain its main goal, that is, continue to provide acceptable quality of service regardless of degradations and faults. Clearly, this requires network architectures and systems with embedded countermeasures that automatically detect faults and are able to work around them, either autonomously (and reporting the event to the network manager), or by quickly reporting the condition to the network manager. Similarly, DWDM systems should include critical diagnostic functions at different level, component, module and unit, to monitor the integrity of functionality and provide alarm signals and/or early warning messages if any of the functions is not performing as expected.

Another important aspect is how fast a network restores service. The total interval from fault detection to service restoration should be short so that service is perceived uninterrupted (in SONET/SDH this interval has been set to 50 ms). However, in high-bandwidth networks, even a short interval may seem too long if one considers higher than a Tb/s per fiber DWDM aggregate traffic. For example, at one Tb/s aggregate

398

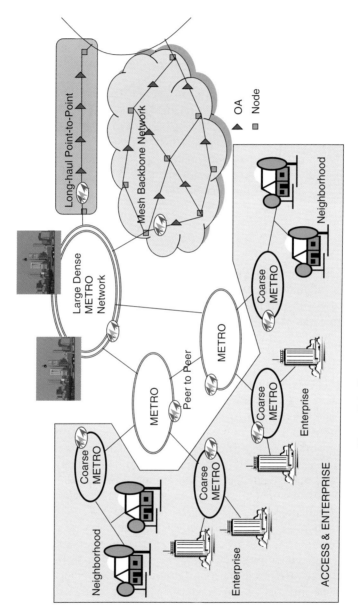

Figure 5.4 From access to increasingly larger networks.

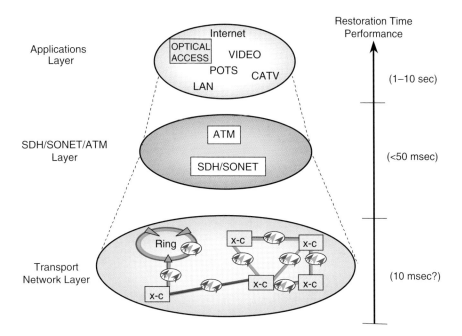

Figure 5.5   Restoration time in layered networks.

traffic (such as in backbone or ultra-long-haul), 50 ms interruption corresponds to 50 billion bits lost. However, at one Gb/s (such as in small metro and access), 50 ms interruption corresponds to 50 million bits lost. Therefore, restoration time performance need not be the same for all network layers (Fig. 5.5).

As such, expedient service restoration is an extremely important aspect of any network architecture, particularly DWDM, which deals not only with fiber and node degradation/faults but also with optical channels degradation/faults, either due to hard faults (laser, detector) or due to linear and nonlinear interchannel interaction (see Chapters 1 and 2). In DWDM, even degradation may be significant, particularly at ultrahigh bit rates; DWDM channels at 40 Gb/s when degraded beyond an acceptable level should require restoration. Therefore, service protection in DWDM encompasses the following key functions and features:

- comprehensive degradation/fault monitoring
- efficient and accurate degradation/fault detection, correlation, and localization
- a reporting mechanism to a fault manager
- efficient and reliable signaling to notify other downstream and upstream nodes
- efficient routing algorithm and bandwidth management
- network architecture with fast restoration schemes
- efficiently provisionable nodes
- network with built-in overcapacity
- efficient and well-balanced inter- and intranetworking interfaces

Similarly, the performance of each network topology depends on many factors. Among them are:

- number of nodes
- network scalability, elasticity, and flexibility
- seamless evolution
- maximum traffic capacity
- service restoration and disaster avoidance capability
- quality of service and cost of service
- real-time aspects of supported traffic
- variability of supported traffic
- reliability
- network resilience
- network response and agility
- number of fiber links between nodes
- trends and market preference (e.g., ring may be preferred because of familiarization with SONET/SDH embedded networks, or mesh may be preferred because of better survivability capability).

DWDM started with a point-to-point topology with the main goal to increase the transported bandwidth per fiber. However, it was soon recognized that DWDM provides a cost-effective solution to other topologies, such as point-to-point with several add-drops, ring, and mesh. With the exception of the point-to-point topologies, a star and a fully connected mesh topology may also be mapped onto a DWDM physical fiber ring topology (see Fig. 4.4). Thus, *fiber ring topology* is a generic term because DWDM different rings have different requirements and complexities. For example, a DWDM ring may be a small single-fiber ring with few wavelengths, a medium size two fiber bidirectional shelf healing ring (BSHR/2), or a large four-fiber bidirectional shelf healing ring (BSHR/4). Such ring diversity deploys nodes with different requirements and complexities. Nodes may be single OADM, multiple-wavelength OADM, or statically or dynamically reconfigurable. They may or may not require optical amplification, dispersion compensation, and so on, as we already have presented in previous chapters. Moreover, DWDM is applicable to mesh networks, networks that typically cover a large geographic area with high cross-connecting capacity nodes.

Any of these topologies provide protection and restoration capabilities. These are on the link level, on the channel level, on the client payload level, on the multiplex level, and so on. ITU-T (G.872) specifies identifiers in the frame overhead for optical channel operation, administration, and management (OCh-OAM) that are used to localize faults, isolate faults, and provide a mechanism for automatic protection switching:

- *Trail trace* (OCh-ID) is used to verify connectivity through OADMs, optical cross-connects, fiber patch panels, and so on.
- *Signal label* (OCh-SL) is used to verify that the client signal is compatible with the equipment.

- *Per channel automatic protection switching* (OCh-APS) is used for OCh shared protection rings (OCh/SPRINGs) and OCh trail protection.

- *Forward and backward defect indication* (OCh-FDI/BDI) is used to localize faults and to enable single-ended maintenance.

- *Per channel signal quality monitoring and backward quality indication* (OCh-SQM/BQI) are used to verify quality of service and as an instrument to isolate sources of degraded performance.

- *Per channel tandem connection maintenance* (OCh-TCM) is used to maintain a channel through an entire subnetwork that does not include the OCh termination elements.

5.3.1 Point-to-Point Topology

The *point-to-point* (PtP) topology establishes connectivity between two users. In a strict sense, it consists of two transceivers and an optical link or path between them; hence its name. The principles of topology have been illustrated in Figure 1.1. Point-to-point topology is applicable in a range of fiber lengths, from a few hundred meters to many thousands of kilometers. However, these two extremes address different applications and require an entirely different engineering effort and cost structure. Therefore, PtP networks are distinguished in short-haul or SH (a few kilometers long), medium-haul or MH (a few tens of kilometers long), long-haul or LH (a few hundreds of kilometers long), and ultra-long-haul or ULH (a few thousands of kilometers). In addition, there is the very short-haul (a few hundreds if meters) and ultra-short-haul for distances of a few meters or even a few decimeters.

Applications for short-distance PtP have been illustrated and described (see Fig. 2.58, Section 2.13.2.10, and Section 4.3.3). In DWDM optical communications systems, the PtP network is usually of the medium to ultra-long-haul type, and because of the long distance and economics of the PtP DWDM path, the highest possible aggregate bandwidth is squeezed into the fiber. Thus, the ULH PtP DWDM topology interconnects continents (transoceanic optical connectivity) and distant intercontinental metropolises, and therefore it requires state-of-the-art photonic technology, optical amplification, dispersion compensation, and equalization, among others (see Chapter 2). Thus, ULH PtP DWDM is the topology that truly fuels the race for higher bit rate per optical channel (40 Gb/s and above), higher optical channel density per fiber (channel spacing below 50 nm) and more wavelengths per fiber (160 and above), longer links between optical amplifiers, and fiber with superior transmission characteristics.

ULH PtP DWDM becomes more economical when intermediate stations with intelligent optical add-drop capability (i.e., with optical switching) are placed between the two end points, as illustrated in Figure 4.36. However, intelligence requires signaling and perhaps a switching protocol, as defined by ITU-T (G.841) for multiplex-section/shared protection ring (MS/SPRing).

However, one of the challenges of a linear LH and ULH PtP DWDM network is restoration, as each component on the path is likely to fail; every component is associated with a real and finite probability of *failure-in-time* (FIT). Based on this, and considering that in a ULH PtP DWDM network between two end points there are many hundreds or thousands of components increasing the probability for failure from miniscule to substantial, one recognizes that such networks must have built-in countermeasure strategies to detect and avoid or bypass faults. Such a strategy is redundancy (i.e., dual amplifiers that work in parallel). Then, detector devices monitor the signal and component integrity, identify severe degradations and/or faults, and, based on a plan of action, select the healthy device in a timely fashion (Fig. 5.6).

Clearly, the strategy illustrated in Figure 5.6 addresses the bypassing of a faulty optical amplifier. However, it does not address how to bypass a faulty (broken) fiber link. This is a network architecture issue resolved with path diversity. For instance, assume that there are two separate paths, as illustrated in Figure 4.44. Then, it is the responsibility of the end terminals and network manager to locate the fiber fault and to identify an alternate path. This process may be tedious and time-consuming, or fast responding with a pre-provisioned "switch to protection" path. For example, consider the network of Figure 5.7 of a chain of nodes in a LH DWDM network; there are two separate fiber links between nodes for protection. In this case, traffic capacity C1 is termed *through traffic*, and switching nodes SW11, SW12, and SW13 are termed *transit nodes* for traffic C1; SW12 is also an optical add-drop node for traffic capacity C2.

In the nonblocking case, the performance of the network depends on system and network engineering rules; such rules may be up to 40% of traffic for add-drop and up to 60% for transit; use through-traffic capacity for high priority as needed and fill the remainder capacity for low-priority traffic. Uneven percent may stem from an anticipated quality of service variability (based on SLA) allowing low-priority traffic to be "killed" if high-priority service restoration is needed or when traffic utilization exceeds a 90% threshold (10–15% margin is a good rule). Thus, if we assume, for example, that on fiber A, traffic C1 consists of 80% highest priority and 10% low priority, and on fiber B traffic C2 consists of 10% high priority and 80% low, then a fault on fiber A will result in a bandwidth reallocation of 80% C1 on fiber B, plus 10% high priority C2 and optionally up to 10% low priority (from C1 or C2) on fiber B (Fig. 5.6B). A fault on fiber B, however, will maintain traffic C1 through and on fiber A, but the high-priority 10% C2 traffic is now switched on fiber A (Fig. 5.6C).

In this service restoration scenario there is another issue that we did not address, namely, the wavelengths on fiber A and fiber B. Clearly, when traffic from fiber A is switched onto fiber B, or vice versa, wavelength management becomes very critical. In this case, either the spectrum has been subdivided so that wavelength "collisions"

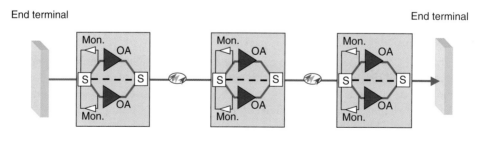

OA = Optical amplifier
Mon. = Monitoring device
S = Selecting device

Figure 5.6 Point to point topology with redundant line-amplifiers.

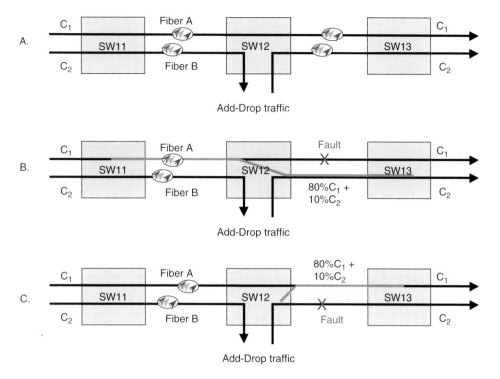

Figure 5.7   Nonblocking switch capacity considerations.

do not occur or there are wavelength converters in every switch that in some complex manner rearrange the traffic in the spectrum space; with current technology, the latter is too complex and requires monumental spectrum administration.

5.3.2   Ring Topology

The ring topology was inspired by the local area FDDI network, which consists of two counter-rotating fiber rings (see Fig. 3.21). In FDDI, a fiber fault was self-detected at the physical optical input of the first station (node) after the fault (this makes two nodes, one at each side of the fault). Then, the detected fault was automatically bypassed by the neighboring nodes by optically connecting the primary ring to the secondary ring at the physical layer (the MIC), a FDDI process known as *self-healing* (Fig. 5.8).

5.3.2.1   Single-Fiber Unidirectional Rings

Single-fiber unidirectional ring (1F) DWDM networks are not protected from faults if the fault is on the fiber, such as a break. However, if the fault is on the transmitter or receiver, then some protection is possible. For example, consider a fiber ring with nodes having $1 + 1$ or 1:N transmitter–receiver protection. Then, as soon as a fault is detected on the working transmitter, the node switches to the protection transmitter. This scenario is better suited for 1:1 protection, it does not require many additional resources, but it requires automatic protection protocol over a supervisory channel. In a different scenario, each node may transmit on two different wavelengths, one as the working wavelength and the other as the protection wavelength. As soon as the

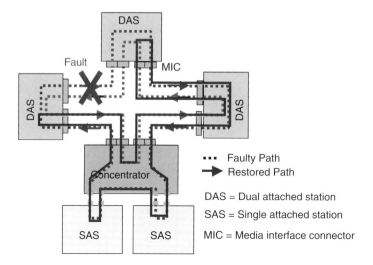

Figure 5.8 Self-healing strategy of the FDDI dual-fiber counter-rotating ring.

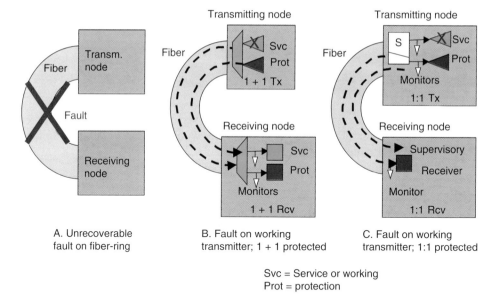

Figure 5.9 Protection schemes for a unidirectional single fiber ring.

working transmitter is at fault, the receiving node detects it and selects the protection wavelength. This scenario is better suited for $1 + 1$ protection, it requires twice the resources, but switching protection is automatic and does not require protocol over a supervisory channel (Fig. 5.9).

5.3.2.2 Single-Fiber Bidirectional Rings

Single-fiber bidirectional rings may be protected if each node on the ring has the capability of looping back all optical channels (wavelengths). In one scenario, half

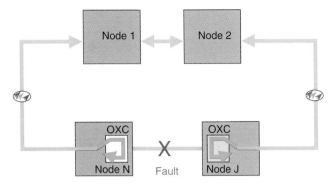

Figure 5.10 Protection schemes for a bidirectional single fiber ring; the OXC must be capable to loop back all optical channels (wavelengths).

of the wavelengths are used as working (or service) channels and the other half as protection. This scenario provides protection on the fiber as well as on the channel level, but it requires twice the resources. In another scenario, all channels are used in one direction, and when a faulty channel is identified, it is looped back. This scenario provides protection on the fiber as well as on the channel level, but it assumes that photonic components are bidirectional, that transceiver cross talk is extremely low, and that the same wavelength can be used in either direction in the fiber (Fig. 5.10). Single-fiber rings are applicable to coarse WDM Metro with 8 to 16 wavelengths, each modulated at 622 Mb/s or Gb/s, and they provide an inexpensive solution to small Metro such as enterprise intrabuilding and small campus with a periphery of several kilometers.

5.3.2.3 Two-Fiber Rings

Two-fiber (2F) rings provide a simpler and more straightforward $1 + 1$ protection scheme than single-fiber rings (see Fig. 4.49). This is also known as a unidirectional path-switching ring $1 + 1$ (UPSR $1 + 1$) and is very similar to FDDI (see Fig. 5.8). However, they require two fibers and separate transceivers per direction, as well as a protected supervisory channel. Because of their advanced protection features, these rings are suitable for small and medium Metro applications; depending on application, they have 8 to 32 wavelengths, each modulated at 1 or 2.5 Gb/s, and a periphery up to 80 Km, or more if amplification is used.

5.3.2.4 Four-Fiber Rings

Four-fiber (4F) rings are bidirectional path-switching rings (BPSR/4) with a $1 + 1$ protection scheme (see Figs. 4.47 and 4.48). BPSR/4 $1 + 1$ rings consist of two dual counter-rotating fibers. As such, they require two pairs of fibers, one pair for working (or service) and another pair for protection. They also require protected supervisory channels per pair. In certain applications, when the working pair is used, the protection pair may also be used for low-priority traffic. When a fiber is at fault, the fault may be bypassed as in the 2F case by reconfiguring the pair with the faulty fiber, as in the FDDI case; in this case, the other pair continues providing service as it did before the fault occurred. In a different scenario, traffic from the working pair is switched to the protection pair; in this case, low-priority traffic is dropped, in whole or in part to free needed bandwidth on the protection pair for high-priority traffic. In a third scenario, a combined protection strategy may be followed.

Four-fiber rings are suitable for large Metro applications with 40 wavelengths, each modulated at 2.5 or 10 Gb/s and, depending on amplification strategy, a periphery of 400 to 1000 Km, or perhaps more.

In these schemes, we have not discussed the protection scenarios when wavelength converters are deployed. Wavelength conversion adds another dimension to protection and restoration as a failed optical channel (or wavelength) may be forced to hop to another channel (wavelength). However, this scenario requires supervisory channel intelligence to notify the receiving end as well as all passing nodes that wavelength conversion has taken place and what the new wavelength is.

5.3.2.5 *Ring-to-Ring Protection*
In addition to protecting the working fiber or optical channel in a ring network, there is the case of protecting the fiber and/or optical channel when two peer ring networks are interconnected. If the two ring networks are interconnected with a single link, it is obvious that this link is not well protected. However, in typical cases, the two rings are connected with two links. That is, two or more nodes have been designated as hub-nodes and thus the ring-to-ring link appears as $1 + 1$ protected (Fig. 5.11). This protection scheme is sufficiently fast (~60 ms), but requires overcapacity, so that one ring can carry traffic of two rings and it requires maintenance messages between the two rings.

5.3.2.6 *Multi-Ring Shared Protection*
The multi-ring shared protection topology is a special case that consists of several adjacent rings in a pseudo-mesh architecture in which some or all links are shared by neighboring rings (Fig. 5.12). This network permits utilization of the same fiber resources by more than one ring. For example, ring W shares the fiber link AC with ring X and shares the fiber link CD with ring Y, but each in a different direction of traffic flow. This implies that optical transmission in single-fiber links is bidirectional. In this case, when a fault occurs, nodes are provisioned to bypass the faulty link and include the shared protection ring; the direction of traffic flow is maintained.

5.3.3 Mesh Topology

Although the OTN network addresses all topologies, it puts more emphasis on the mesh topology. This is because backbone networks have a mesh topology and current

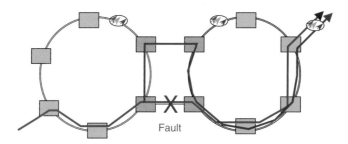

Figure 5.11 Ring-to-ring protection schemes; two ring nodes are hub nodes.

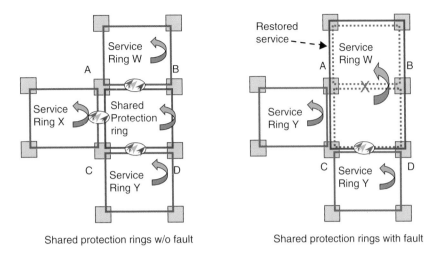

Figure 5.12   Principles of shared protection rings.

SONET/SDH standards do not address mesh restoration. In addition, because the point-to-point topology includes more and more add-drops, the network starts to resemble more and more a mesh network. As a result, mesh network deployments to date use proprietary solutions.

Mesh restoration takes advantage of optical cross-connects (see Figs. 4.34, 4.35, 4.36, and 4.46), which have the ability to connect optical channels from any input to any output. This provides the ability to intelligently and automatically reroute one optical channel or many optical channels around a fault in the network. However, this intelligence is gained with intelligently distributed monitors (degradation/fault detectors) in each node and with fast signaling and efficient protocols that trigger appropriate actions for expedient service restoration; in this case, restoration is achieved by updating the topology either with algorithms or with preplanned routes. Thus, the restoration scheme can be fast (50 ms or less) and can facilitate efficient bandwidth management (minimal loss of low-priority traffic), fast provisioning, and good capacity planning assurance for continuous and uninterrupted service.

In general, protection is required on the fiber level as well as on the optical channel level. In addition, it is required on the section, link, or multiplex section, and on the path section. Protection may be accomplished using 1 + 1 or 1:1 or 1:N schemes, as already described. The protection scheme may be centralized (one entity decides what the protection action will be) or it may be distributed (many nodes collectively figure out what the protection action will be). Moreover, protection may be algorithmically decided upon the fault detection, or it may be precalculated, or it may be partially precalculated and the final protection route is determined by performing minimal calculations based on the current state of certain variables. The more precalculations made and the fewer last-minute calculations required, the faster the restoration scheme. Clearly, the network efficiency to determine a protection route depends on the network architecture and features outlined in the beginning of this section.

As an elementary exercise in precalculating the various routes in a mesh network, consider the one in Figure 5.13A. Then, the various possible routes between two points are classified based on a number of parameters in the path. In traditional optical

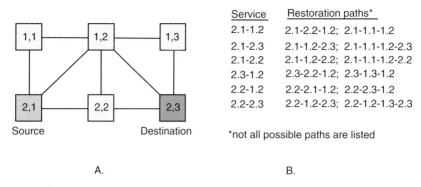

Service	Restoration paths*
2.1-1.2	2.1-2.2-1.2; 2.1-1.1-1.2
2.1-2.3	2.1-1.2-2.3; 2.1-1.1-1.2-2.3
2.1-2.2	2.1-1.2-2.2; 2.1-1.1-1.2-2.2
2.3-1.2	2.3-2.2-1.2; 2.3-1.3-1.2
2.2-1.2	2.2-2.1-1.2; 2.2-2.3-1.2
2.2-2.3	2.2-1.2-2.3; 2.2-1.2-1.3-2.3

*not all possible paths are listed

A. B.

Figure 5.13 A. Mesh network and, B. pre-calculated paths.

networks, the various paths would easily be found based on the number of nodes (or hops) and length of links. Thus, for the network in question, a table could be constructed (Fig. 5.13B).

Based on this table, assume now that the serviced path is from node (2.1) to node (2.2) to node (2.3), and that a link fault occurs between the two nodes (2.1) and (2.2). For this link there are three possible precalculated paths, A: (2.1) to (1.2) to (2.3); B: (2.1) to (1.1) to (1.2) to (2.3); and C: (2.1) to (1.1) to (1.2) to (1.3) to (2.3). However, if path A is available, it is preferred since it has fewer hops than path B or path C. Assuming that path A is available, signaling initiates an orderly cross-connecting activity in each node of the new path and transmission resumes. Figure 5.14 illustrates the sequential and logical actions necessary from fault detection to switching to protection path and reestablish service; such a sequential logical order of actions is also known as a *case scenario*.

This case scenario was simplified to demonstrate the fundamental principles and steps necessary for service protection. Clearly, in DWDM networks, a comprehensive

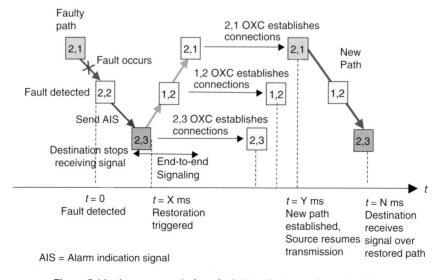

Figure 5.14 A case scenario from fault detection to service restoration.

scenario involves many variables that must be considered (see Chapters 1 and 2) when a new path is selected, such as:

- channel bit rate on the link (bit rate compatibility?)
- density of optical channels (wavelengths) on the link (spacing, channel width)
- available bandwidth on the link (channels reserved?)
- available wavelengths on the link (is wavelength contention imminent? is λ-conversion supported?)
- type of fiber on the link (does fiber support wavelength efficiently?)
- optical power of channels to be rerouted compared with that of channels already on the link (is equalization required? is equalization supported?)
- spectral and polarization issues (power and density of total number of channels, linearity and nonlinearity effects, holes, and so on).

Thus, if every variable is considered and is associated with a weighting (penalty) factor, taking into account QoS, BER, OCh delivery, a cost factor, and a latency factor, in addition to link length, number of hops, wavelength density, and so on, then the network of Figure 5.13 may look entirely different from an optical channel perspective. For example, if the network would have a weighing factor associated with each path as shown in Figure 5.15, then based on it a path evaluation would reveal that the path that normally looked shorter and more attractive may be not, and the one that looked longer and less attractive may be better. In the figure, numbers on links are normalized penalty factors; their value is artificial to illustrate the point in question — the smaller the sum over a path, the less the penalty and the path is better preferred. In practical networks, the penalty factor on each link changes as parameters change, and therefore a periodic reevaluation may be necessary.

Mesh networks, in general, have superior survivability and restoration efficiencies, protect against link and against node failures, and are sufficiently fast (~50 ms) by virtue of precalculated connectivity maps. On the negative side, they require overcapacity but it is variable considering that there are different priorities and grades of service. Overall, mesh networks have the ability to add a node as needed and thus they are truly scalable.

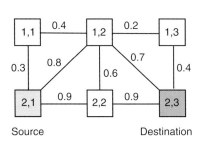

Path	Weighed sum	Preference
2.1-2.2-2.3	1.8	4
2.1-1.2-2.3	1.5	3
2.1-1.1-1.2-2.3	1.5	3
2.1-1.2-1.3-2.3	1.4	2
2.1-1.2-2.2-2.3	2.3	7
2.1-2.2-1.2-2.3	2.2	6
2.1-2.2-1.2-1.3-2.3	2.1	5
2.1-1.1-1.2-1.3-2.3	1.3	1
2.1-1.1-1.2-2.2-2.3	2.2	6

A.   B.

Figure 5.15   A. DWDM mesh network with weighed links and, B. Path evaluation.

5.3.4   Ring-Mesh Networks

A subcategory of the mesh network is the ring-mesh network. The ring-mesh network consists of two orthogonal sets of parallel rings (see Fig. 3.23). The routeability of the ring-mesh networks is exceptionally flexible, as already shown in Figure 3.24, where a mere 4 × 4 node network has 1,592 available paths between any two nodes and without crossing the same node twice. Large ring-mesh networks have distributed control and thus exceptional disaster avoidance features.

5.4   DISPERSION MANAGEMENT

In DWDM transmission, as an optical channel travels through the fiber and optical components, it undergoes dispersion. As already discussed, for fixed fiber length dispersion put a limit on the data rate. This is because as dispersion increases, intersymbol interference increases, bit error rate increases and the signal power decreases, impacting the quality of the signal and manifested by closed eye diagram, increased bit error rate, and receiver penalty. In fact, dispersion is a highly nonlinear relationship, following almost a square power. For example, although the fiber length limit due to chromatic dispersion is at 2.5 Gb/s near 1000 Km, at 10 Gb/s it is about 16 times less than that, and at 40 Gb/s it is about 16 times less again. Similarly, polarization dispersion follows a highly nonlinear relationship, although not as critical as the chromatic dispersion. PMD at 2.5 Gb/s is not critical, at 10 Gb/s it puts a limit at about 400 to 600 Km, and at 40 Gb/s 16 times less than that.

Dispersion management is a transmission engineering activity that based on the fiber parameters and on spectral content of the signal, it determines if dispersion compensation is needed, and if it does, at what intervals of the optical path. As discussed in Chapters 1 and 4, dispersion and data rate are closely related; the significance of dispersion for a given fiber length increases exponentially, almost as the square with the data rate. Thus, whereas at 10 Gb/s dispersion compensation is every several hundreds of kilometers, at 40 Gb/s, it is every few tens of kilometers. The total dispersion of a channel is calculated taking into account many parameters: fiber dispersion coefficient, zero dispersion wavelength, fiber length, density of optical channels, data rate, nonlinearities, polarization states, modulation scheme, and so on. Only then, dispersion management can be engineered properly and efficiently.

As discussed in Chapters 1 and 4 (Section 4.4.3), chromatic dispersion compensation may be achieved by several technologies; one uses dispersion compensating fibers (DCF), another uses chirped in-fiber Bragg gratings, and another uses *dispersion compensating waveguides* (DCW). Each technology has its own merits and demerits.

Regardless of technology deployed, there are also other components needed to achieve dispersion compensation; the design of a dispersion compensator consists of a compact subunit known as *dispersion-compensating module* (DCM). As DCMs compensate each channel for dispersion, in actuality they improve the BER of the received signals, thus allowing for longer fiber spans (see Fig. 4.21), but, as also discussed in Chapters 1 and 4, residual dispersion due to dispersion slope mismatch is still a concern (see Fig. 4.22) that DCMs do not eliminate.

Polarization-mode dispersion becomes significant at rates starting with 40 Gb/s and above, and thus, PMD compensation may also be required in LH and ULH. However, PMD compensation is a complex process and currently is costly. Since PMD depends largely on the geometry of the core (noncircular), PMD is minimized by using new and better fiber with a circular core over the entire length in order to maintain the polarization state of the signal unchanged; some solution may also use strong polarization fibers to force the signal to travel at only the polarization state of the fiber.

To summarize, based on data rate, receiver sensitivity, and expected BER, the maximum expected dispersion, $D_{exp\text{-}max}$, for acceptable BER is calculated. Then, based on fiber dispersion coefficient, other components on the optical path, and a margin, a fiber length, Lmax, is calculated with an estimated dispersion, D_{est}, equal to or less than $D_{exp\text{-}max}$. At that length, a DCM is placed that ideally restores the signal to its initial nondispersion state. However, considering that DCMs have a nominal compensating efficiency of 90%, DCMs should then be selected with a value overcompensating by 10%, or the fiber length is shortened accordingly compensating for the DCM 10% inefficiency.

This strategy works well in point-to-point transmission. If optical add-drop multiplexing is deployed, however, then dispersion management becomes more tedious because the added wavelength may already have a dispersion that is close to its limit (see Fig. 4.23).

In summary, dispersion management encompasses dispersion measuring techniques for fiber spans between DCMs and also at the end of the fiber path to measure and compensate for the total residual compensation. As the data rate per optical channel increases above 10 Gb/s, dispersion management per wavelength becomes more critical. In fact, a performance–cost analysis must be executed to evaluate the cost-efficiency benefit of data rate increase, based on the fact that as the data rate increases, more DCMs must be placed in shorter intervals adding to cost and maintenance. In that case, high-efficiency (>90%), passive (maintenance-free), compact (integrated and small footprint), and low-cost DCMs will allow one to increase the data rate without any compromise.

Fiber maintenance is very costly, in transoceanic DWDM transmission, and thus DCMs are not easy to deploy. In this case, dispersion compensation as well as dispersion-slope compensation are achieved by having in the same cable two types of fibers, a nondispersion-shifted fibers (NDSF) and a negative dispersion or *inverse dispersion fiber* (IDF). The NDSF has an effective area of 100 μm^2 (large to accommodate higher optical power without damage), positive dispersion and dispersion slope. The IDF has a negative dispersion coefficient and negative dispersion slope. The two fibers have been engineered so that their absolute specifications match, and when they are connected in series, the dispersions (positive and negative) as well as dispersion slopes cancel each other. However, an issue with large effective areas is that the cutoff wavelength increases to longer wavelengths that are above 1300 nm. This may be unfortunate for transmission at 1310 nm, but in current DWDM applications the operating wavelengths are above 1500 nm in the C-bands and L-bands.

5.5 BANDWIDTH MANAGEMENT

Bandwidth management is a function required by all systems and networks, voice or data, small or large, so that a client's data are delivered with the agreed upon quality. As traffic becomes more elastic, the aggregate bandwidth keeps growing, and as faults and severe degradations occur on nodes, fiber links, and optical channels, traffic management becomes more important and additional requirements are added to increase efficiency.

5.5.1 Wavelength Management

In DWDM systems and networks where each wavelength is used as a separate channel, it is reasonable to consider the *failure in time* (FIT) of the various optical components such as transmitters, receivers, amplifiers, and so on. In fact, manufacturers provide FIT and other reliability data for all components. When a component fails, it is considered to be a hard failure and should be easily detected. However, in addition to hard failures, there may be severe degradations that impact the quality of signal so that an optical channel performs below an acceptable level (e.g., BER $< 10^{-9}$), and yet they may not be detected. Although monitoring for degradations is more complex, certain severe degradation mechanisms are as important as hard failures. In such a case, when the quality of optical signal becomes unacceptable, the channel should be dynamically switched to a protection wavelength in the same fiber or in another fiber.

In Section 5.3, we discussed a number of network topologies and protection strategies that are necessitated because of potential failures, such as fiber breaks or faulty nodes. The same argument also holds for one or more optical channels. For example, switching traffic from service fiber to protection fiber (as discussed in Section 5.3) may be restated as switching optical channel(s) from service fiber to protection fiber (see, e.g., Figs. 5.7, 5.12, and 5.15).

In traditional single-wavelength networks, wavelength collision clearly has not been an issue since the optical channel was only one (at 1,310 nm). Thus, moving this channel from one fiber to another was a straightforward operation as long as a protection fiber was available. In DWDM, where one system in one domain (for which a network provider may use 40-wavelength/fiber systems) is interconnected with a system in another domain (for which another network provider may use systems having a different number of wavelengths/fiber), and with optical add-drop multiplexing that may add-drop wavelengths from another yet network provider moving a specific wavelength from one fiber to another is not as straightforward. In fact, this may lead to a new possible situation that we term *wavelength collision*. Figure 5.16 illustrates a mesh network requiring wavelength conversion to avoid wavelength collision. Such systems and networks have several attractive attributes:

- optical channels allow for format and bit rate independence flexibility
- wavelength conversion minimizes stranded (available) capacity
- optical channels are wavelength-independent
- systems support easy access to optical layer
- support multivendor environment
- support scalability and upgradability
- support fast fault detection and fault localization
- support real-time communication and QoS

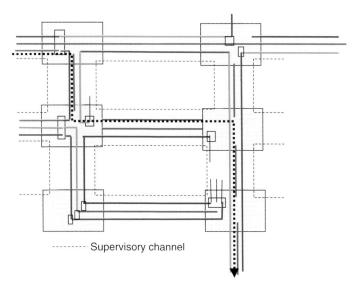

------- Supervisory channel

Figure 5.16   A DWDM mesh network with wavelength management (the dotted line path is illustrative of the wavelength conversions).

Here we define *wavelength collision* as the action by which one optical channel associated with a particular wavelength is switched from fiber A to fiber B, where in fiber B the same wavelength is already in use; this definition is extendable to more than one wavelength.

Wavelength collision is a DWDM reality, particularly in all-optical systems and networks that are operating on the same band (C and/or L) and with the same channel spacing and density. As a result, wavelength management becomes as important as bandwidth management for uninterrupted flow of information, service protection, and service reliability.

With current technology, wavelength management can be addressed with appropriate out-of-band signaling and with wavelength converters and tunable devices. In addition, it may be addressed by reserving "protection" wavelengths to be used for "moving" a channel from one wavelength to another, as in "wavelength hopping." In this scheme, however, the acquisition time of wavelength converters is very critical for seamless and uninterrupted service. As technology evolves, it also will be possible to have in-band signaling, and thus wavelength hopping or wavelength conversion will be executed reasonably fast.

Currently, wavelength management is a real concern, and a great deal of standards activity is under way to establish recommendations and a great deal of research and development to manufacture tunable devices that cover a wide range, from transmitters and receivers, to filters and wavelength converters (see Chapter 2).

5.5.2   Traffic Management

Traffic management has a different task compared with bandwidth management. Typical nodes have many inputs and outputs, and each input or output may support one or more services with different quality of service specifications and at a different bit rate.

Thus, traffic management ensures that incoming traffic is monitored and properly connected and that its quality level is maintained. To accomplish this, traffic must be policed. Traffic policing requires continuous monitoring for compliance with agreed upon traffic parameters, as well as monitoring for connection parameter violations and user's equipment malfunctioning, a function known in ATM as *connection monitoring*.

Nodes of different network layers manage traffic at a different level of complexity. For example, a backbone node manages presorted traffic but at very high bit rates, as compared with small Metro hub-nodes that do not receive moderate bit rates but a very diverse traffic.

The ATM Forum and ITU-T have defined parameters to maintain the agreed upon traffic QoS. It also has defined algorithms for policing the traffic at the user–network interface (UNI), for both *constant bit rate* (CBR) and *variable bit rate* (VBR). This algorithm is known as the *generic cell rate algorithm* (GCRA). The GCRA is implemented with the continuous-state *leaky bucket* and is based on two parameters, the *increment* (I) and the *limit* (L). The I parameter affects the cell rate; the L parameter affects the cell burst.

The parameters utilized in ATM for traffic management are: *peak cell rate* (PCR) for *constant bit rate* (CBR) and *variable bit rate* (VBR) connections, *sustainable cell rate* (SCR) for VBR connections, and *maximum burst size* (MBS) for VBR connections. These parameters are provided by the user during the connection admission control (CAC) at UNI. In addition, there is the *burst tolerance* (BT) parameter, which puts a restriction on the additional traffic above the SCR before it is tagged excessive traffic.

Although wavelength and traffic management are different, in DWDM, there is a close link between the two, and both traffic management and wavelength management should work hand-in-hand.

5.5.3 Congestion Management

When a network fault occurs or unpredictable statistical fluctuations of traffic flow take place, traffic is rerouted to avoid the fault. When this takes place, there is a finite probability that the aggregate bandwidth through a node or link in the network reaches the maximum capacity that it was designed for and quality of service cannot be guaranteed. This establishes a congestion condition that is manifested by either a node overload, bandwidth lost, or even a network crash. In general, congestion management is defined as a network element state unable to meet the negotiated network performance objectives (QoS) for the already established connections. As such, congestion management is a concern that is always addressed very seriously. This is attested to by a number of congestion management mechanisms that have been recommended for various types of service, such as TDM, ATM, SONET/SDH, IP, and so on.

Congestion management becomes more critical in DWDM networks because nodes, optical links, or optical signal(s) also may severely degrade or fail, but in this case, the size of transported bandwidth is mind-boggling. Therefore, traffic rerouting due to faults must be executed not only expediently but also efficiently; otherwise the bandwidth loss will be in many gigabits or terabits. As a result, congestion management must consider the type of fault (because each fault influences bandwidth flow at a different level), types of services supported by the network (because each traffic type has different requirements), network topology (because each topology has different service survivability merits), size of network (in both bandwidth capacity and number of nodes), internetworking (because the overall path may cross several network-provider domains, each consisting of nodes with different system capabilities).

Congestion is studied with flow equations, which are linear differential equations with fluctuating boundary conditions reflecting the fluctuation of traffic over time. However, congestion management is not an independent operation. It is also closely linked with neighborhood discovery (so that each node "knows" the capabilities and bandwidth availabilities of all other nodes in the network domain to which it belongs; this also implies distributed control and proper signaling), with fault management (so that it "knows" the health state of its neighboring nodes), wavelength management (because this is also related to bandwidth supported by a node, bit rate, and number of optical channels per fiber). Therefore, the congestion equations must include terms that reflect the contribution of dependencies.

5.6   FIBER SPAN BETWEEN TRANSMITTER AND RECEIVER

The fiber span between transmitter and receiver is one of the most important calculations in optical networks of any topology. The fiber span is determined based on transmission parameters, optical component parameters on the transmission path, and expected quality of signal at the receiver. Here we outline the calculation of the fiber span with an example. Consider the following parameters:

- Tx = laser launched power
- Lconn = N connector insertion loss; assume N connectors on the path
- Lsplice = K splice insertion loss; assume K splices on the path
- Lmon = Tap monitoring loss
- Lmsc = Miscellaneous insertion losses (filters, cross-connect, and so on)
- Ldegr = signal degradation due to liner and nonlinear interactions between wavelengths
- Rsens = Receiver sensitivity
- Margin = Assume a typical margin of 3 dB, or as specified
- a = fiber loss coefficient (dB/km)

Based on these parameters, the maximum loss between transmitter and receiver is

$$\text{Maximum loss} = \text{Lspan} + \text{NLconn} + \text{KLsplice} + \text{Lmon} + \text{Lmisc} + \text{Ldegr}$$

Similarly, the maximum allowable loss is

$$\text{Maximum allowable loss} = \text{Maximum loss} + \text{Margin}$$

Then, the fiber span loss Lspan is

$$\text{Lspan} = \text{Tx} - \text{Rsens} - [\text{Maximum allowable loss}] \ (\text{dB})$$

From the latter and the fiber loss coefficient a, the fiber span is calculated

$$\text{Fiber span} = \text{Lspan}/a \ (\text{km})$$

Amplification gain is not included in these calculations. The need for amplification and the amount of gain is determined if the fiber span is fixed and the calculated Rsens falls short of the expected value. Then, the amplification is included to adjust the calculations so that the calculated Rsens has the expected value. However, when amplification is included, there are several parameters to be considered. Among them are the loss due to the amplifier component, Lampl; amplification gain per channel, g; amplifier spectral band efficiency; insertion losses of components required for the inclusion of the amplifier (couplers, filters, and so on); and the ASE noise component added to the signal. In all, calculations of the fiber span with signal amplification are certainly more involved because they also depend on the type of amplification (OFA, Raman, SOA). In this case, the gain evolution of EDFAs and Raman amplifiers as well as optical add-drops in the fiber span may also be considered.

5.7 FAULT MANAGEMENT

Fault management entails the functions fault monitoring, detection, reporting, isolation, and restoration/recovery or avoidance. However, fault management in DWDM systems and networks is more involved; DWDM fault management must monitor, in addition to hard faults on the link, node, unit, and component levels, severe degradations of optical signals that are caused not only because of some component degradation but also because of physics (i.e., light–matter–light and light–light interactions). Consequently, the fault monitors are more complex, the reporting mechanisms are more comprehensive, the fault correlation is more convoluted, the signaling and protocols are more complex, the fault avoidance is more cumbersome, and the recovery time is more stringent.

The complexity of fault management is influenced by network topology. For example, point-to-point topology deals with faults on a linear path as compared with mesh topology where the path is not linear; each node on the mesh is interconnected with other adjacent nodes, so finding an alternate route is much more complex. Fault management is also influenced by the network layer. For example, fault recovery has different requirements in a high bandwidth backbone than in a low bandwidth small Metro network.

Therefore, some of the key questions are:

- What are the proper optical monitors and algorithms to conclusively determine the type of degradation/fault?
- How fast can the detector(s) determine the faulty condition?
- How fast is the fault reported and how fast is a decision made regarding the remedial action(s)?
- How long does it take from the moment a service-affecting fault is determined to the moment the fault is recovered and/or service is restored?
- How simple (and cost-efficient) is the fault management process over a large network?

Concerning fault detection time (how fast a fault is detected and declared) and restoration time (how fast the fault is recovered or service is reestablished), DWDM systems and networks must be as good as or better than that of SONET/SDH because of the very high aggregate bandwidth. Currently, the restoration time for SONET/SDH is set at 50 ms, and the fault detection is set at 100 μs (0.1 ms). As a point of reference, restoration and fault detection in IP is on the order of seconds.

5.8 NETWORK SECURITY

Network security is a term that gains more importance each day. The expert's malevolent genius has proven that computer systems can be penetrated without authorization and destroy vital data and in many ways incapacitate the proper operation of nodes and networks. Similarly, electronic virus can be broadcasted to network nodes, they are written in their computer memories and as they are executed they cause the computer to behave erratically, or "crash."

Similarly, unauthorized access also may isolate a signal and transmit it to a different destination. Thus, there are two aspects to network security: security pertaining to the proper system performance and security pertaining to signal proper routing and performance.

With respect to signal security, the solution is relatively easy. The optical signal is not split or copied in a node, and the signal therefore does not reach the node-computer and be routed over the network management path to an unauthorized user. Nevertheless, this does not mean that if the node-computer is "unauthorized" accessed the connectivity tables may change and reroute a signal to another destination. In this case, a well-scrambled signal at the source is almost useless to an unauthorized destination.

With respect to system security, and as compared with signal security, it is perceived more likely to happen. However, modern systems require complex accessing codes that can dynamically change, and systems can detect unauthorized accessing attempts and report them to a network security function that automatically can trace the unauthorized caller and set an alarm.

Tapping a fiber that interconnects two nodes may also be a form of direct intrusion that should not be discounted. However, tapping a fiber is not as simple as tapping a copper wire, and signal security can be provided by sophisticated multidimensional scrambling codes that for all practical purposes are unbreakable so that even if the fiber is tapped, the signal is incomprehensible and useless to the intruder.

5.9 DWDM NETWORK ISSUES

In this and previous chapters, we have presented several solutions pertaining to DWDM systems and networks. The reader may think that all problems have been solved and that optical DWDM technology is mature. This is not true. DWDM technology is a potent technology that penetrates, and it eventually will replace the existing communications network, based on current plans by many communications companies and countries. In the meantime, in parallel to current research to improve DWDM technology, there are several issues to be addressed, such as interoperability and internetworking, performance monitoring in the optical regime, and network future-proofing.

5.9.1 Interoperability and Internetworking

As different DWDM vendors design systems applicable to DWDM networks with
fundamental differences in protocol, signaling, intradomain interfaces, interdomain
interfaces, and wavelength subsets (even though they comply with the ITU-T standard wavelength map), interoperability and internetworking become very difficult. For
example, one country decides to operate in the L-band and another in the C-band.
Connecting these two systems or networks is comparable to two persons speaking
two different languages and trying to understand each other without an interpreter. Or
consider one system using 40 channels in the C-band and another system using all
80 channels in the C-band. Or, consider one network defining quality of service in
one way, and another network defining it in another way. And in such cases, consider
the signal over the optical path transversing such networks! This has been recognized
and the standards body is working on a number of these issues that have been either
published as recommendations (such as ITU-T G.709), the Optical Domain Service
Interconnect (ODSI) Coalition with the goal of developing a framework of protocols
and technical internetworking recommendations, the IETF for developing a Common
Open Policy Service (COPS) policy provisioning protocol for interworking with the
ODSI framework, and others.

5.9.2 Optical Performance Monitoring

Performance monitoring is a critical function performed at the input of each signal
at each node if the signal is in the electronic regime. However, today, there is no
solution for performance monitoring in the optical regime, although research on this
subject continues and possible solutions have been proposed. Therefore, performance
monitoring and error correction are limited to opaque systems that are strategically
positioned at the edge of network domains (Fig. 5.17).

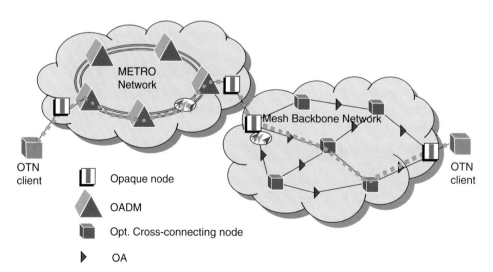

Figure 5.17 Opaque nodes at the edges of all-optical DWDM networks perform PM and EDC
functionality.

5.9.3 Network Future-Proofing

As DWDM systems and networks evolve, how can the capital investment made be secured in a way that the system or network can grow to meet increasing traffic demands by simple upgrades? This is a serious concern of every network and service provider, as well as every system vendor. Systems are currently designed to be modular in both hardware and software. Hardware modularity provides flexibility to replace, upgrade, or retrofit units and shelves, as discussed in Chapter 4. Software modularity provides the flexibility to upgrade software modules (or objects) that are related to control, management, protocol, and/or provisioning. Software modularity also provides the flexibility of upgrading remotely, in contrast to hardware modularity, which requires replacing a unit in situ by personnel.

5.9.4 Wavelength Sharing

Imagine that a wavelength is modulated at 10 Gb/s. Also imagine that a client needs half the bandwidth of this channel (i.e., 5 Gb/s) and other clients need 1 Gb/s. In electronic systems this is not an issue as time division multiplexing (VT multiplexing in SONET/SDH) or packet time sharing (IP, ATM, FR) can accomplish this. However, if the signal is already in the optical regime (and assuming all-optical nodes), currently it is not possible to optically multiplex more than one channel in one (although research and proposal have been made in this area). When research in optical time sharing (or optical time division multiplexing — OTDM) will provide a robust and cost-effective solution, OTDM will allow true bandwidth flexibility and scalability, as well as transmission at the highest possible bit rate and optically multiplex several subrate signals and grow bandwidth without having to replace and provision transceiver units.

5.9.5 IP/SONET over DWDM

A substantial effort has been made to transmit a traffic type directly over an optical DWDM channel. What this truly means is that an optical DWDM source (laser) is modulated with IP or Ethernet or SONET traffic. Having oversimplified this issue, one would ask the trivial question: What's the big deal? The issue is not really whether the source can be modulated with any of these traffic types. The main reason is that at 10 Gb/s all these traffic types are synchronous, and thus the clock rate and density of "ones" in the signal is maintained; that is, if there is no ATM or IP packet to transmit, a "dummy" packet is transmitted to keep the receiver clock active and to keep the photodetector from "thinking" that there is a fiber break in the absence of light for even a short period. The key issue is if IP, for example, supports the functionality required (signaling, protocols, etc.) for quality of service, service survivability, and network reliability and survivability. This has been recognized by the various standards bodies (IETF), and significant progress has been made in this direction.

5.9.6 Maintenance

Maintenance is a network function responsible for maintaining the NE and the network operation at an acceptable performance. This is accomplished by defining a set of criteria.

In SONET, the maintenance issue has been addressed and a number of maintenance requirements have been defined, including *alarm surveillance* (AS), *performance monitoring* (PM), and control features to perform maintenance tasks:

- trouble monitoring and detection
- trouble or repair verification
- trouble sectionalization
- trouble isolation
- testing
- restoration

Alarm surveillance deals with the monitoring, detection, and reporting of degraded or abnormal conditions (failure conditions) in the network. When a failure condition is detected, a NE enters a failure state, and a NE exits a failure state when the failure condition has been corrected. When a failure state is detected, AIS signals are constructed and transmitted to the next NE. The response to AIS is a *remote defect indication* (RDI) signal.

Some of the failure indications in SONET/SDH are:

- Loss of signal (LOS); when there is no light pulses for 100 msec. If less than 2.3 msec, then no LOS. If more than 2.5 secs, then the NE sends an alarm message to OS.

- Loss of frame (LOF); when a Severely Error Frame (SEF) persists for >3 msec then the NE sends a message to OS (when at least 4 consecutive frames have incorrect framing patterns).

- Loss of pointer (LOP); such as out of range, wrong nondata found (NDF), and other failures related with the pointer processing mechanism. Report to OS.

- Equipment failures; a. Service affecting (SA), b. Nonservice affecting (NSA) Classified as: Critical, Major, Minor. Report to OS.

- Loss of synchronization; Loss of primary or secondary timing reference. Send message with cause to OS (LOS, LOF, OOF, etc.).

- Automatic protection switch (APS) troubles.

- DCC failures; Hardware or failure to carry DCC. Action: switch to standby DCC. Report to OS.

- Signal label mismatch; This is related to SPS or virtual tributary (VT) signal label. Two defects are defined: Payload Label Mismatch (PLM) and Unequipped (ENEQ). Monitor C2 for STS Signal Labels and for STS Payload Label Mismatch (PLM-P). Monitor V5 (b5-b7) for VT Payload Label Mismatch and VT Path Unequipped.

- Alarm indication signal (AIS); It alerts the downstream equipment that a defect or failure has been detected. AIS-L for Line, AIS-P for Path, AIS-V for VT Path.

- Remote alarm indication (RAI); It alerts the upstream equipment of a downstream failure. Two types: remote defect indication (RDI) and remote failure indication (RFI);

- Payload defect indication (PDI); It alerts the downstream equipment that there is a defect in one or more of its embedded payloads.

- Trunk conditioning; Supported by SONET byte-synchronous VT mapping and no DS0 termination functions

- LOS, LOF and LOP cause AIS alarm signals on all three levels, AIS-L for Line, AIS-P for Path, AIS-V for VT Path.

Performance Monitoring (PM) sets the rules for in-service monitoring of the transmission quality. Performance monitoring is based on counting errored blocks in second or counting code violations in a second.

SONET NE performance monitoring includes:

- detection of transmission degradation

- deviations of performance parameters

- communication with OSs

SONET network elements NEs are required to accumulate a variety of PM parameters for a section, line, STS path, or VT path layer entity. PM information stored in registers is:

- current period

- previous period

- recent period

- threshold

Notice that most of the maintenance concepts are borrowed from legacy systems, particularly SONET/SDH and ATM. However, these concepts do not completely fulfill the needs of DWDM networks.

5.9.7 DWDM Network Management

By network managing we mean all the functions required to provision and monitor the performance and health status of the complete DWDM network (of a network provider) from a remote central place. It is important that such network management be simple (with a small number of managing elements and simple unified protocols), fast, comprehensive, and cost-effective. Faults should be quickly detected and remedied, and traffic should be quickly and optimally balanced over the network to minimize path latency and congestion. Bandwidth should be dynamically provisioned over the optimum route to offer cost-effective bandwidth on-demand services. Finally, the network should be remotely provisioned and upgraded.

5.10 WIRELESS DWDM NETWORKS

What are wireless WDM networks? This may sound like an oxymoron, as WDM technology has been applied to optical transmission. However, none of the words in the acronym specify "optical." In fact, in a strict definition, "wavelength division multiplexing" may also define a waveguide supporting many wavelengths in the microwave band.

Thus, if we go a step beyond and remove the boundary conditions that a waveguide imposes by virtue of a light beam, then we may have many wavelengths propagating in space, which also belong to a dense band of frequencies.

In that respect, wireless WDM is explained as follows:

1. Transmitting multiple wavelengths in space whereby each wavelength establishes a specific communications channel; this may be mobile wireless (station is stationary and target end devices may be mobile), or stationary wireless (both stations and target devices are stationary or mobile but within a limited range).

2. Converting many wireless channels in optical wavelengths that are optically multiplexed and transmitted over DWDM fiber from one station to another.

3. Transmitting in free space an optical beam that consists of many wavelengths, each wavelength constituting a channel, an extension of a single wavelength transmission of free space optical transmission (see also Section 3.3.2 and Fig. 3.4).

EXERCISES

1. The optical interface between two networks providers is known as ONNI.
   a. True
   b. False

2. MPLS is a protocol designed by the Internet Engineering Task Force (IETF) with the objective to increase IP data throughput efficiency.
   a. True
   b. False

3. A backbone network has few wavelengths per fiber, low operating bit rates, and short fiber links.
   a. True
   b. False

4. For a fixed fiber span, dispersion compensation improves the BER of a signal.
   a. True
   b. False

5. A fiber link is engineered for an error probability 10^{-10}. For a signal at 1 Gb/s, calculate the average period a single error occurs.

6. A good forward error correcting code effectively increases the fiber link distance between amplifiers.
   a. True
   b. False

7. In $1 + 1$ protection, the client signal is fed in two paths simultaneously although the receiving node selects the signal from one only.
   a. True
   b. False

8. In 1:1 protection, a node communicates with each adjacent node over a separate link to perform switch to protection.
   a. True
   b. False

REFERENCES

1. S.V. Kartalopoulos, *Introduction to DWDM Technology: Data in a Rainbow*, IEEE Press, New York, 2000.

2. S.V. Kartalopoulos, *Fault Detectability in DWDM: Towards Higher Signal Quality and Network Reliability*, IEEE Press, New York, 2001.

3. S.V. Kartalopoulos, Emerging technologies at the dawn of the millennium, *IEEE Comm. Mag.*, vol. 39, no. 11, pp. 22–26, Nov. 2001.

4. S.V. Kartalopoulos, DWDM: Shaping the future communications network, *IEEE Circuits & Devices Mag.*, Jan./Feb. 2002.

5. S.V. Kartalopoulos, What is DWDM? *SPIE Electro-Optic News*, Nov. 2000.

6. S.V. Kartalopoulos, *Understanding SONET/SDH and ATM: Communications Networks for the Next Millennium*, IEEE Press, New York, 1999.

7. H. Yoshimura, K.-I. Sato, and N. Takachio, Future photonic transport networks based on WDM technologies, *IEEE Comm. Mag.*, vol. 37, no. 2, Feb. 1999, pp. 74–81.

8. R. Ramaswami and K.N. Sivarajan, *Optical Networks*, Morgan Kaufmann Publishers, San Francisco, CA, 1998.

9. B. Mukherjee, *Optical Communication Networks*, McGraw-Hill, New York, 1997.

10. K. Sato, *Advances in Transport Network Technologies — Photonic Networks, ATM and SDH*, Artec, 1996.

11. T.-H. Wu, *Fiber Network Service Survivability*, Artec House, Boston, 1992.

12. Y. Miyao and H. Saito, Optimal design and evaluation of survivable WDM transport networks, *IEEE J. Select. Areas Comm.*, vol. 16, no. 7, pp. 1190–1198, Sept. 1998.

13. B. Van Caenegen, W. Van Parys, F. De Turck, and P.M. Demeester, Dimensioning of survivable WDM networks, *IEEE J. Select. Areas Comm.*, vol. 16, no. 7, pp. 1146–1157, Sept. 1998.

14. S.V. Kartalopoulos, A plateau of performance? *IEEE Comm. Mag.*, vol. 30, no. 9, Sept. 1992, pp. 13–14.

15. E. Karasan and E. Ayanoglu, Performance of WDM transport networks, *IEEE J. Select. Areas Comm.*, vol. 16, no. 7, pp. 1081–1096, Sept. 1998.

16. J. Nellist, *Understanding telecommunications and lightwave systems*, IEEE Press, New York, 1996.

17. B. Furht, *Handbook of internet and multimedia: Systems and applications*, IEEE Press, New York, 1999.

18. Internet study group: *http://www.internet2.edu*

19. L.G. Raman, *Fundamentals of Telecommunications Network Management*, IEEE Press, New York, 1999.

20. J.C. Palais, *Fiber Optic Communications*, 3rd ed., Englewood Cliffs, NJ, Prentice-Hall, 1992.

21. A. Borella, G. Cancellieri, and F. Chiaraluce, *Wavelength Division Multiple Access Optical Networks*, Artec House, Boston, 1998.

22. B.T. Doshi, S. Dravida, P. Harshavardhana, O. Hauser, and Y. Wang, Optical network design and restoration, *Bell Labs Tech. J.*, vol. 4, no. 1, 1999, pp. 58–84.

23. S. Chatterjee and S. Pawlowski, All-optical networks, *Comm. ACM*, vol. 47, no. 6, June 1999, pp. 74–83.

24. M.A. Marsan, A. Bianco, E. Leonardi, A. Morabito, and F. Neri, All-optical WDM multi-rings with differentiated QoS, *IEEE Comm. Mag.*, vol. 37, no. 2, Feb. 1999, pp. 58–66.

25. M.A. Marsan et al., Daisy: A scalable all-optical packet network with multi-fiber ring topology, *Computer Networks and ISDN Systems*, vol. 30, 1998, pp. 1065–1082.

26. S.V. Kartalopoulos, A Manhattan fiber distributed data interface architecture, *Globecom'90*, San Diego, Dec. 2–5, 1990.

27. S.V. Kartalopoulos, Disaster avoidance in the Manhattan fiber distributed data interface network, *Globecom'93*, Houston, TX, Dec. 2, 1993.

28. Y. Chen, M.T. Fatehi, H.J. LaRoche, J.Z. Larsen, and B.L. Nelson, Metro optical networking, *Bell Labs Tech. J.*, vol. 4, no. 1, 1999, pp. 163–186.

29. A.R. Chraplyvy, High-capacity lightwave transmission experiments, *Bell Labs Tech. J.*, vol. 4, no. 1, 1999, pp. 230–245.

30. S.V. Kartalopoulos, The λ-bus in ultra-fast DWDM systems, TBP.

31. S.V. Kartalopoulos, "Synchronization Techniques Ultra-fast DWDM Systems: The λ-bus", TBP.

32. S.V. Kartalopoulos, "Add-Drop with Ultra-fast DWDM/λ-bus", TBP.

33. S.V. Kartalopoulos, Increasing bandwidth capacity in DWDM/λ-bus systems, TBP.

34. S.V. Kartalopoulos, Cryptographic techniques with ultra-fast DWDM/λ-bus systems, TBP.

35. D.B. Buchholz et al., Broadband fiber access: A fiber-to-the-customer access architecture, *Bell Labs Tech. J.*, vol. 4, no. 1, 1999, pp. 282–299.

36. G.C. Wilson et al., FiberVista: An FTTH to FTTC system delivering broadband data and CATV services, *Bell Labs Tech. J.*, vol. 4, no. 1, 1999, pp. 300–322.

37. M. Berger et al., Pan-European optical networking using wavelength division multiplexing, *IEEE Comm. Mag.*, vol. 35, no. 4, 1997, pp. 82–88.

38. B. Fabianek, K. Fitchew, S. Myken, and A. Houghton, Optical network research and development in European community programs: From RACE to ACTS, *IEEE Comm. Mag.*, vol. 35, no. 4, 1997, pp. 50–56.

39. D. Cotter, J.K. Lcek, and D.D. Marcenac, Ultra-high-bit-rate networking: From the transcontinental backbone to the desktop, *IEEE Comm. Mag.*, vol. 35, no. 4, 1997, pp. 90–96.

40. S.F. Midkiff, Fiber optic backbone boosts local-area networks, *IEEE Circuits Devices Mag.*, vol. 8, no. 1, Jan. 1992, pp. 17–21.

41. E. Traupman, P. O'Connell, G. Minnis, M. Jadoul, and H. Mario, The evolution of the existing infrastructure, *IEEE Comm. Mag.*, vol. 37, no. 6, 1999, pp. 134–139.

42. A.G. Malis, Reconstructing transmission networks using ATM and DWDM, *IEEE Comm. Mag.*, vol. 37, no. 6, 1999, pp. 140–145.

43. R.K. Snelling, Bringing fiber to the home, *IEEE Circuits Devices Mag.*, vol. 7, no. 1, Jan. 1991, pp. 23–25.

44. H. Toba and K. Nosu, Optical frequency division multiplexing systems: Review of key technologies and applications, *IEICE Trans. Comm.*, vol. E75, no. 4, Apr. 1992, pp. 243–255.

45. O.E. DeLange, Wide-band optical communication systems: Part II — Frequency-division-multiplexing, *Proc. IEEE*, vol. 58, no. 10, 1970, pp. 1683–1690.

46. A. McGuire, *Architectural Models for Supervisory and Maintenance Aspects of Optical Transport Networks*, ICC'97 Workshop on WDM Network Management and Control, Montreal, Quebec, Canada, June 1997.

47. E. Goldstein, *The Case for Opaque Multiwavelength Lightwave Networks*, ICC'97 Workshop on WDM Network Management and Control, Montreal, Quebec, Canada, June 1997.

48. D.K. Hunter et al., WASPNET: A wavelength switched packet network, *IEEE Comm. Mag.*, vol. 37, no. 3, March 1999, pp. 120–129.

49. D. Banerjee, J. Frank, and B. Mukherjee, Passive optical network architecture based on waveguide grating routers, *IEEE J. Select. Areas Comm.*, vol. 16, no. 7, pp. 1040–1050, Sept. 1998.

50. E. Modiano, WDM-based packet network, *IEEE Comm. Mag.*, vol. 37, no. 3, March 1999, pp. 130–135.

51. R. Glance, K. Pollock, C.A. Burrus, B.L. Kasper, G. Eisenstein, and L.W. Stulz, Densely spaced WDM coherent optical star network, *Electron. Lett.*, vol. 23, no. 17, 1987, pp. 875–876.

52. N. Takato et al., 128-channel polarization-insensitive frequency-selection-switch using high-silica waveguides on Si, *IEEE Photon. Technol. Lett.*, vol. 2, no. 6, 1990, pp. 441–443.

53. Y.-K.M. Lin, D. Spears, and M. Yin, Fiber-based local access network architectures, *IEEE Comm. Mag.*, Oct. 1989, pp. 64–73.

54. R.A. Linke, Optical heterodyne communications systems, *IEEE Comm. Mag.*, Oct. 1989, pp. 36–41.

55. A.E. Willner, Mining the optical bandwidth for a terabit per second, *IEEE Spectrum*, April 1997, pp. 32–41.

56. S.V. Kartalopoulos, *Understanding Neural Networks and Fuzzy Logic*, IEEE Press, New York, 1995.

57. Members of the Technical Staff, *Transmission Systems for Communications*, Bell Telephone Laboratories, 1982.

STANDARDS

1. ANSI/IEEE 812-1984, "Definition of terms relating to fiber optics."

2. IEC Publication 825-1, "Safety of laser products—Part 1: Equipment classification, requirements and user's guide."

3. IEC Publication 825-2, "Safety of laser products—Part 2: Safety of optical fibre communication systems."

4. IEC Publication 1280-2-1, "Fibre optic communication subsystem basic test procedures; Part 2: Test procedures for digital systems; Section 1—Receiver sensitivity and overload measurement."

5. IEC Publication 1280-2-2, "Fibre optic communication subsystem basic test procedures; Part 2: Test procedures for digital systems; Section 2—Optical eye pattern, waveform and extinction ratio measurement."

6. ITU-T D.68 (4/15), "Re-categorization of study items and proposed overhead channel realization for optical layers," K. Oguchi, NTT, Geneva, 7–18, April 1997.

7. ITU-T Recommendation G.650, "Definition and test methods for the relevant parameters of single-mode fibres," 1996.

8. ITU-T Recommendation G.652 version 4, "Characteristics of a single-mode optical fiber cable," April 1997.

9. ITU-T Recommendation G.653 version 4, "Characteristics of a dispersion-shifted single-mode optical fiber cable," April 1997.

10. ITU-T Recommendation G.655 version 10, "Characteristics of a non-zero dispersion-shifted single-mode optical fiber cable," Oct. 1996.

11. ITU-T Recommendation G.661, "Definition and test methods for the relevant generic parameters of optical fiber amplifiers," Nov. 1996.

12. ITU-T Recommendation G.662, "Generic characteristics of optical fiber amplifier devices and sub-systems," July 1995.

13. ITU-T Recommendation G.663, "Application related aspects of optical fiber amplifier devices and sub-systems," Oct. 1996.

14. ITU-T Draft Recommendation G.664, "General automatic power shut-down procedure for optical transport systems," Oct. 1998.

15. ITU-T Recommendation G.681, "Functional characteristics of interoffice and long-haul line systems using optical amplifiers, including optical multiplexers," June 1986.

16. ITU-T Draft Rec. G.691, "Optical interfaces for single channel SDH systems with optical amplifiers, and STM-64 systems," Oct. 1998.

17. ITU-T Draft Rec. G.692, "Optical interfaces for multi-channel systems with optical amplifiers," Oct. 1998.

18. ITU-T Recommendation G.707, "Network node interface for the synchronous digital hierarchy," 1996.

19. ITU-T Draft Rec. G.709, "Network node interface for the optical transport network (OTN)," Oct. 1998.

20. ITU-T Draft Rec. G.798, "Characteristics of optical transport networks (OTN) equipment functional blocks," Oct. 1998.

21. ITU-T Rec. G.805, "Generic functional architecture of transport networks," Oct. 1998.

22. ITU-T Rec. Q.831, "Specifications of signalling system No. 7–Q3 interface," Oct. 1997.

23. ITU-T Recommendation G.841, "Types and characteristics of SDH network protection architectures," 1996.

24. ITU-T Draft Rec. G.871, "Framework for optical networking recommendations," Oct. 1998.

25. ITU-T Recommendation G.872, "Architecture of optical transport networks," 1999.

26. ITU-T Draft Rec. G.873, "Optical transport network requirements," Oct. 1998.

27. ITU-T Draft Rec. G.874, "Management aspects of the optical transport network element," Oct. 1998.

28. ITU-T Draft Rec. G.875, "Optical transport network management information model for the network element view," Oct. 1998.

29. ITU-T Recommendation G.911, "Parameters and calculation methodologies for reliability and availability of fibre optic systems," 1993.

30. ITU-T Recommendation G.957, "Optical interfaces for equipments and systems relating to the synchronous digital hierarchy," 1995.

31. ITU-T Recommendation G.958, "Digital line systems based on the synchronous digital hierarchy for use on optical fibre cables," 1994.

32. ITU-T Draft Rec. G.959, "Optical networking physical layer interfaces," Feb. 1999.

33. *http://www.itu.int/ITU-T/index.html*

34. W. Simpson, "PPP over SONET/SDH," IETF RFC 1619, May 1994.

35. Telcordia (previously Bellcore) GR-253, "Synchronous optical network (SONET) transport systems: Common generic criteria," issue 2, Dec. 1995.

36. Telcordia (previously Bellcore) GR-1377, "SONET OC-192 transport systems generic criteria," issue 3, Aug. 1996.

37. Telcordia (previously Bellcore), TR-NWT-233, "Digital cross connect system," Nov. 1992.

38. Telcordia (previously Bellcore), TR-NWT-917, "Regenerator," Oct. 1990.

6

EMERGING TECHNOLOGIES

6.1 INTRODUCTION

As the previous millennium has set and the new one is rising, we find ourselves on an explosive technology curve. In the communications systems of the 1990s, the aggregate bandwidth per transmission medium per kilometer was a daring gigabit per second; these days we speak of terabits per second, which is 1000 times higher, and in a decade or two it will be 1000 times this. Only our imagination can capture and science fiction describe the achievements of the coming decades as did *"From the Earth to the Moon"* (by Jules Verne) and wireless communicators in popular cartoons. Thus, from a tempoparochial viewpoint, this explosive technological progress makes us believe that our millennium will be the greatest of all, and this can be said for virtually all technological sectors. Although no one truly knows what the future holds, the only fact is that *"today is yesterday's future, and tomorrow's past."*

This technological progress depends on several emerging technologies that must become (commercially) available. In this chapter we look in the foreseeable-future emerging technologies that are expected to redefine communications services for voice, slow and fast data, and real-time image. Communications services however that are truly global and portable at any time, any place, by anyone and by any (communicating) thing.

6.2 EMERGING TECHNOLOGIES

In this section, we outline certain emerging technologies that in one way or another impact communications, specifically theory and materials, communications components, systems and networks, intelligent homes, intelligent transportation, and intelligent powering systems. Other disciplines also impact communications such as computing, computer communications, testing techniques (particularly in the optical regime), manufacturing techniques and others, which have been implicitly mentioned in this outline. Figure 6.1 encapsulates the current activity on certain optical technologies

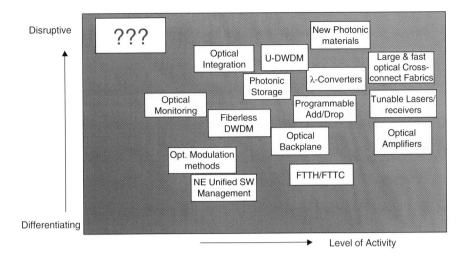

Figure 6.1   Emerging optical technologies applicable to DWDM.

that promise to even disrupt our lifestyles. By definition, differentiation is that technology that improves and simplifies lifestyles, whereas *disruption* is that technology that changes lifestyles.

6.2.1   Theory and New Materials

New photonic materials are emerging with powerful properties and functionality that will lead to microscopic components with powerful properties applicable to communications, remote sensing, medicine, instrumentation, computation, image processing, and so on.

More specifically:

- The true nature of light, beyond its classical model, is under scrutiny to gain a better understanding of it and its interaction with new photonic materials. Some of the questions raised are: Can we "freeze-stop" light and release it in a controllable manner? If light is both E-M radiation and particle, (beyond the classical model) where does it reside in the electron? What really propels light?

- The crystal-like optical properties of synthetic materials and artificially made photonic crystals are a subject long awaiting exploration. Research is under way to model artificial structures and better understand their photonic, electrical and magnetic properties.

- Nanowires and nanodevices: Integration of many devices requires massive interconnect technology. Research is on several fronts, such as placing chips side-by-side or stacked-up like a cube with many interconnecting points between them. One of the contemplated technologies interconnects chips with nanowires, grown on the surface like whiskers between chip layers having a wire density in the millions per square centimeter. Such technology will enable miniaturization of many optical devices as well as devices that will find wide applicability.

- New polymers have demonstrated superconducting properties at elevated temperature and photopolymers have displayed several interesting photonic properties.

Research is under way to better understand and explain the underlying physics. How can a tiny insect generate intense light visible from great distances using miniscule brain control voltages? Can we emulate these organic materials?

- Complex monolithic integration of optical components will increase optical functionality per bandwidth and per volume unit, and decrease cost.

- Reliable and low-cost nanomachines will find a broad range of applications.

- Intelligent photosensitive fabrics will find a broad range of uses, including fashion and entertainment. Such fabrics will be self-powered and will have interwoven sensors and smart antennas for short-range wireless communication.

- Ultrafast computing at the "speed of light" will enable optical signal processing never before imagined. Based on quantum mechanical principles and on neuronal synaptic communication, novel mathematical algorithms will emerge that will unleash the power of computing.

6.2.2 Communications Components, Systems, and Networks

Today, communications provide the exchange of information on a global scale and at the "speed of light." From one end device to another, the signal travels a path changing from electric, to electromagnetic and optical, over land, air, and space, and optical fiber. However, many technological bottlenecks must be resolved. Messages such as "no circuit available for the country you call" or "sorry, the line is busy" should be a thing of the past.

- Fast, wide spectral-range and low-cost tunable components operating at high bit rates ($\gg$10 Gb/s) are on the way to revolutionize the design practices of communications systems and networks.

- Accurate wavelength converters, along with tunable components will make possible an all-optical network with dynamic wavelength assignment.

- New low-cost pump lasers (tunable or fixed) with adjustable power level, and high-energy couplers and isolators will enhance optical fiber amplifier solutions (e.g., OFAs, and Raman) and extend the distance between source and receiver.

- Semiconductor-based optical amplifiers and wavelength converters (fixed and tunable) will become more reliable, accurate, cost-effective, and will be integrated with other optical components.

- New fibers optimized for spectrally flat and low dispersion and extended linear behavior, combined with dispersion compensating fibers and techniques, will also increase the fiber span to super-long reach, driving the cost per Gb/s down.

- An emerging new class of fiber waveguide structures that promise increased functionality is currently in the experimental or development stage. These fibers will have cladding modified with non-silica material such as photonic crystal fibers. Or they will have localized modifications such as gratings and perhaps integrated couplers. Or they will have cladding with thin-film filters for thermal, electrical or magnetoresistive actuation. Modified cladding will enable optical attenuation variability, dispersion and/or polarization controllability, simplified optical add-drop multiplexing, tunable filtering, compact equalization control, and tunable optical fiber amplification.

- Intelligent compensating optical techniques combined with new fibers and low cost amplification will increase the fiber span to super-long reach allowing for more aggregate bandwidth and new services.

- Ultra high wavelength density in a single fiber, modulated at many Gb/s will by far exceed the currently available 160 λs, approaching 500 or even 1000 in medium- and long-reach applications. Moderate wavelength densities will also be deployed in short-reach and medium Metro applications, but the bit rate will be, depending on application, from 2.5 to 10 Gb/s per optical channel (larger Metros will scale up to 40 Gb/s per channel). In very-short-reach applications (such as residential), the bit rate will scale down from few Mbps to 1 (and in some cases 10) Gb/s per subscriber allowing for multimedia interactive services.

- Short-reach applications will require very inexpensive optical add-drop multiplexers and other optical components as well as bandwidth distribution systems. Plastics/polymers, integrated passive optical and electronic components will be key technologies to achieve this.

- A truly unified communication standard (an extension of true "convergence") with a common well-defined management and operating system will simplify the system and network, opening many markets.

- An elastic ultra-broadband network capable of supporting extreme traffic diversity, with inherent quality of service assurance and real-time aspects, will stimulate a wealth of communications services.

- A widely available and interoperable global wireless communication network with global number mobility (via optical, terrestrial, submarine, and satellite routes), a truly single portable number, will greatly facilitate communication (person-to-person and machine-to-person). This will increase bandwidth demand and will spawn novel services not imagined before.

- Global wireless services will require self-reconfigured wireless devices for voice, slow and high-speed data applications (including the next-generation Internet).

- Self-reconfigured wireless devices will require smart, integrated, adaptive antennas combined with sophisticated algorithms to offer beam-forming capability, dynamic channel assignment, frequency reuse, interference avoidance, and space–time diversity for fixed or moving terminals.

- The ultra-broadband network will be a truly Intelligent Optical Network for many traffic models featuring ultra-high-capacity, high reliability, survivability, and distributed control. However, the near-term "all-optical" network will be "cost-conscious," combining a pragmatic mix of photonics and high-speed electronics with a swift and continuous displacement of electronic functionality by photonic functionality, as innovation, manufacturability and cost permit.

- Simple nodes with various degrees of intelligence, depending on traffic capacity and capabilities, will characterize this fiber-based network. Some of the high-end node characteristics will be:
  - ✓ Photonic processing
  - ✓ Optical DWDM signals modulated at bit rates above 40 Gb/s and perhaps higher than 100 Gb/s (160 Gb/s?).
  - ✓ The ability to switch photonic signals intelligently with simple cost-efficient implementation. Switching speeds, depending on application, will vary from

μsec to below nsec. Similarly, the size of switching fabric will vary from 40 to more than 1000 inputs and outputs.

✓ Overall, the network will exhibit some degree of "neural network" architecture with "collective intelligence." Such a network will be able to perform neighborhood-discovery, self-organization, traffic and routing optimization, as well as disaster avoidance, based on algorithms that take into consideration link/path optical loss and real-time traffic requirements.

• Low-cost photonic (passive and active) components will allow for wider deployment of fiber to the curb or home, as well as fiber (LAN) to the PC. However, in several applications the race for the first or the last mile will be rampant between fiber, high-speed wired, and optical-wireless.

• The physical size and cost per node will be measured per cubic foot and per Gb/s.

• A simple common-sense operating system will emerge to facilitate network management, record keeping, and billing.

6.2.3   Intelligent Homes

Imagine walking into your home, tired after a long day at the office. A gentle voice is welcoming you, the lights turn on automatically at a soothing intensity and the hue is adjusted to relax you, the food is ready in the oven, a complete list of all bills paid is on a screen, and your pet has been fed and is content. You need to purchase new shoes, but after a long day you do not feel like going to the market. With your voice, you activate a flat screen on your wall and describe the style and color you like, even in fuzzy terms if you are not sure. Shoes from various shoestores are displayed in three dimensions, and they are virtually fit to your foot while the quality, price, and availability are displayed on the screen. You select the model that satisfies you, and the order is placed and confirmed. Is this a dream? Perhaps, but it is a dream that is becoming reality because:

• Limited range optical local area networks with emerging smart protocols and (wireless or wired) communications interfaces to the outside plant and enables the future home to become intelligent.

• The intelligent home will include:

✓ Smart appliances with wireless or wired communications interfaces and control, with internet, e-mail and/or voice recognition

✓ Smart sensors (wireless, infrared, electromagnetic, photonic) for movement detection and analysis and with intelligent signal processing for security and intrusion control and alarm

✓ Intelligent voice recognition for voice command, communication as well as security and validation

✓ Smart sensors that remotely detect temperature and other vital signs for medical diagnosis

✓ A multiplexed entertainment center, activated upon voice command and/or behavioral pattern analysis

✓ Flat screens incorporated into the wall as well as into wearable glasses

✓ Low-power high-efficiency interior lighting and window electropolarizing shades with eye-soothing spectral radiation and intensity control

✓ Smart software with neuronal and fuzzy logic and simulation capabilities

✓ Windows that can automatically will filter and adjust the amount of light

✓ Automatic climate control with self-cleaning and sterilizing air and surfaces

- New materials for photoelectric power generation will also be critical in the home of the next decade. Intelligent power distribution systems will harvest solar power and add commercial power only upon demand.

6.2.4 Intelligent Transportation

Each new day finds the roads more congested. New highways are planned, and by the time they are in service, congestion is again at its peak. Cities and roads were initially planned for a much smaller population and vehicle traffic density. Many of these cities grew to become megalopolises, adding to congestion of people and vehicles. As the density of vehicles increases, so do the casualties of traffic that cost an enormous amount of money each day. To facilitate traffic and safety, new technologies are emerging.

- Mass transportation between cities will be rapid; rapid trains have already been deployed and are in use for some time. Such transportation requires elevated (floating) cars that ride on a cushion of air, yet maintain controllability of motion. Among the technologies that will enable this is superconductivity and supermagnets as well as advanced propulsion technology.

- Mass and rapid transportation will offer the "feel" of the office. During travel, passengers will continue their productive work and be able to communicate (voice and fast data) with the office.

- A transportation network will be required with intelligent and fast communications protocols among vehicles and between vehicles and with main control. Intelligent vehicles will be monitoring their performance parameters and communicate them to other vehicles and to main control. At any moment, the position, performance parameters and other data of each vehicle in the network (speed, load, performance, fuel level, etc.) will be known to main control as well as to all other vehicles in the network to optimize traffic.

- Road networks will be intelligent. Congestion spots will be monitored and will be communicated to a central control as well as to other vehicles on the road-network. Alternate paths will be sought and will be recommended bypassing congestion spots.

- Vehicles will have intelligent sensors and they will communicate with the highway monitoring service. Along with global positioning systems, vehicles will be able to navigate in traffic and avoid collision.

- Vehicles will be able to navigate in a manual or in an autonomous mode.

- Vehicles will be able to sense the state of the driver and/or passengers and communicate with them.

- Vehicles will be energy-efficient, able to switch from one energy type to another or to enter an energy conservation mode when in traffic.

- New cost-effective, lighter, and durable materials, better than fiberglass and plastics, will emerge to increase safety and decrease energy consumption.
- The vehicle of the future will be optimized according to type of transportation as well as for comfort, for short as well as for long-distance travel. Some pioneering examples of such vehicles are already in use, and some recommendations for modular vehicles have been made.
- Roads with improved synthetic pavement and cars with advanced wheel technology will increase safety, riding comfort, and cruising speed. When constructed properly, such roads will also decrease maintenance costs.

6.2.5 Intelligent Powering Systems

Recently, many experienced power interruptions due to power shortage. One may wonder, with all advanced technology available how can these happen in this millennium? The near future we will experience:

- New photochemical and electrochemical methods that will enable alternate powering methods amalgamated into intelligent powering systems.
- Alternate powering technologies will be integrated and advanced power management software will determine which type of energy, or combination of energies, will be used for cost efficiency and uninterrupted service.
- Intelligent power distribution networks will automatically sense and balance loads, so that areas in greater need will "borrow" power from areas with less need.

And the list of emerging technologies may go on and on as new methods and materials are explored as the economy permits.

6.3 CURRENT RESEARCH

However, research in photonic technology continues which is expected to find direct applicability in DWDM systems. In this section we look into some current research (see also Fig. 6.1). The objective is to eventually have an all-optical and intelligent network that will monitor the quality of signal and service in the photonic regime, and traditional performance monitoring and error-detection and correction (EDC) will take place at the two ends of the path (and if it is needed) (Fig. 6.2).

6.3.1 Advanced Lasers

There are three major activities: in laser development low-cost high-density matrix lasers, high-quality tunable lasers, and laser arrays with narrow spectral line and sufficient optical power, as well as high-power pump lasers. Low-cost lasers, some made with organic compounds, are critical in many applications. High-quality tunable lasers are critical in all-optical networks with optimized bandwidth and wavelength management, with dynamic reconfiguration, and in optical cross-connects.

Another activity is to make lasers with nanometer dimensions, known as *nanolasers*. This activity stems from an effort to grow nanowires needed in massive interconnect of very small devices, that is a wire density in the millions per square cm.

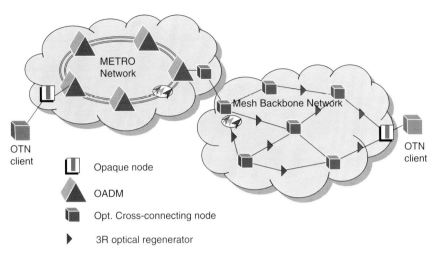

Figure 6.2 In a true all-optical DWDM network, end-to-end performance monitoring and EDC is performed at the edges of the path whereas network nodes monitor QoS intelligently.

Nanolasers will miniaturize many optical devices which at low power will provide critical functionality in many systems. Thus the applicability of nanolasers includes communications, medicine, biotechnology, analytic chemistry, optical computing, storage, displays, optical connectivity, and consumer products.

6.3.2   Artificial Optical Materials

Artificial new solid-state optical materials exhibit unusual characteristics based on very high values of the refractive index. A recent revision of theory assumes a negative refractive index, which, if proven correct, will open new horizons. Other properties are based on optical energy absorption and coherent photoluminescence in a wide spectral range that covers the C-bands and L-bands and beyond.

In this area of research, gallium nitride is a stable semiconductor material with which light-emitting diodes (LED) emitting an intense blue light can be made when electricity is passed through it. These LEDs are expected to find many applications in home entertainment (DVDs), displays, and communications.

Certain organic compounds absorb one wavelength and emit another (useful in wavelength conversion and memory applications), or they can absorb a wavelength and emit it back when they are stimulated (memory applications). Such organic compounds are perylene, coumarin-6, and others. Organic compounds, such as pentacene, have electrical properties suitable for field-effect transistors. Organic thin films (OTF) may also find several optoelectronic applications, such as flat thin displays.

6.3.3   Optical Cross-Connect

As the number of wavelengths increases to densities approaching 1000×1000, low-loss, nonblocking and fast-switching optical cross-connecting technologies are a challenge. Today, there is substantial effort in this direction, and currently there are at least a dozen or more different technologies, each claiming benefits that the other technology does not have.

However, all currently available high-density technologies are relatively very slow (μs to ms) compared with the actual bit period (ps). Research on chalcogenide glasses (Ge-Se-Te) with a refractive index 1000 times higher than SiO_2 glass exhibit switching time in less than 1 psec, low linear loss, low nonlinear loss β, and a high figure of merit (FOM), on the order of 20.

6.3.4 Optical Memories and Variable Delay Lines

Optical delay lines consist of fiber cut at lengths that, based on travel time of light in the fiber medium, can delay light by a fixed amount of time. For example, a waveguide with a refractive index of 1000 would also slow down the speed of light by 1000. This principle is already used in monolithic interferometers and is based on the propagation principles of light in matter. However, optical devices based on quantum principles could store a light pulse (photons) for as long as it is needed and release it when it is stimulated. Such devices would be truly optical memories storing light pulses in a similar manner as electronic pulses are stored in RAM.

6.3.5 Nonintrusive Optical Sensors

Nonintrusive optical sensors are key components in fault management and proper operation of both system and network; "nonintrusive" means that these sensors do not disturb the optical signal. The optical signal must be monitored for power, noise, "eye" closure (enough power to be detected by the receiver), wavelength, and linewidth. In general, nonintrusive optical monitoring reduces the amount of optoelectronics, reduces latency, increases reliability, but reduces the optical power of the signal, and therefore optical power restoration may also be required; however, if the amount of power is miniscule, this may not be as important because it may be part of the margin included in the power budget.

6.4 CONCLUSION

In this chapter, we have made some predictions of a small sample of emerging technologies particularly focused on communications. We have not addressed other technologies (such as biotechnologies) that may also contribute to communications or benefit from them, nor have we addressed the financial stimulus, which may accelerate or decelerate emergence.

The likelihood that these emerging technologies will be available within the next decade (some earlier than others) is very high. Unfortunately, beyond that point any prediction can only be classified as "imaginative."

Predicting emerging and disruptive technologies is an educated extrapolation of current advancements and a guarded look into a crystal ball, which sparks both imagination and inventiveness.

REFERENCES

1. S.V. Kartalopoulos, Elastic bandwidth, *IEEE Circuits Devices Mag.*, vol. 18, no. 1, pp. 8–13, Jan. 2002.

2. S.V. Kartalopoulos, Emerging technologies at the dawn of the millennium, *IEEE Comm. Mag.*, vol. 39, no. 11, pp. 22–26, Nov. 2001.

3. S.V. Kartalopoulos, DWDM: shaping the future communications network, *IEEE Circuits Devices Mag.*, Jan./Feb., 2002.

4. S.V. Kartalopoulos, A plateau of performance? *IEEE Comm. Mag.*, vol. 30, no. 9, pp. 13–14, Sept. 1992.

5. S.V. Kartalopoulos, *Introduction to DWDM Technology: Data in a Rainbow*, IEEE Press, New York, 2000.

6. S.V. Kartalopoulos, *Fault Detectability in DWDM: Toward Higher Signal Quality and System Reliability*, IEEE Press, New York, 2001.

7. S.V. Kartalopoulos, What is DWDM? *SPIE Electro-Optic News*, Nov. 2000.

8. H. Yoshimura, K.-I. Sato, and N. Takachio, Future photonic transport networks based on WDM technologies, *IEEE Comm. Mag.*, vol. 37, no. 2, Feb. 1999, pp. 74–81.

9. S.V. Kartalopoulos, *Understanding SONET/SDH and ATM: Communications Networks for the Next Millennium*, IEEE Press, New York, 1999.

10. E. Traupman, P. O'Connell, G. Minnis, M. Jadoul, and H. Mario, The evolution of the existing infrastructure, *IEEE Comm. Mag.*, vol. 37, no. 6, 1999, pp. 134–139.

11. S.V. Kartalopoulos, Ultra-fast Pattern Recognition in Broadband Communications Systems, *ISPACS'98 Conference Proceedings*, Melbourne, Australia, Nov. 1998.

12. S.V. Kartalopoulos, Cryptographic Techniques with Ultra-fast DWDM/λ-bus Systems, TBP to be published.

13. Y. Pan, C. Qiao, and Y. Yang, Optical multistage interconnection networks: new challenges and approaches, *IEEE Comm. Mag.*, vol. 37, no. 2, Feb. 1999, pp. 50–56.

14. N. Takachio and S. Ohteru, Scale of WDM transport network using different types of fibers, *IEEE JSAC*, vol. 16, no. 7, 1998, pp. 1320–1326.

15. A.E. Willner, Mining the optical bandwidth for a terabit per second, *IEEE Spectrum*, April 1997, pp. 32–41.

16. S.V. Kartalopoulos, *Understanding Neural Networks and Fuzzy Logic*, IEEE Press, New York, 1995.

STANDARDS

1. ANSI/IEEE 812-1984, "Definition of terms relating to fiber optics."

2. IEC Publication 825-1, "Safety of laser products—Part 1: Equipment classification, requirements and user's guide."

3. IEC Publication 825-2, "Safety of laser products—Part 2: Safety of optical fiber communication systems."

4. ITU-T Recommendation G.652 version 4, "Characteristics of a single-mode optical fiber cable," April 1997.

5. ITU-T Recommendation G.653 version 4, "Characteristics of a dispersion-shifted single-mode optical fiber cable," April 1997.

6. ITU-T Draft Recommendation G.664, "General automatic power shut-down procedure for optical transport systems," Oct. 1998.

7. ITU-T Recommendation G.681, "Functional characteristics of interoffice and long-haul line systems using optical amplifiers, including optical multiplexers," June 1986.

8. ITU-T Draft Rec. G.692, "Optical interfaces for multi-channel systems with optical amplifiers," Oct. 1998.

9. ITU-T Draft Rec. G.709, "Network node interface for the optical transport network (OTN)," Oct. 1998.

10. ITU-T Draft Rec. G.798, "Characteristics of optical transport networks (OTN) equipment functional blocks," Oct. 1998.

11. ITU-T Rec. G.805, "Generic functional architecture of transport networks," Oct. 1998.

12. ITU-T Draft Rec. G.871, "Framework for optical networking recommendations," Oct. 1998.

13. ITU-T Recommendation G.872, "Architecture of optical transport networks," 1999.

14. ITU-T Draft Rec. G.873, "Optical transport network requirements," Oct. 1998.

15. ITU-T Draft Rec. G.874, "Management aspects of the optical transport network element," Oct. 1998.

16. ITU-T Draft Rec. G.875, "Optical transport network management information model for the network element view," Oct. 1998.

17. ITU-T Recommendation G.957, "Optical interfaces for equipments and systems relating to the synchronous digital hierarchy," 1995.

18. ITU-T Draft Rec. G.959, "Optical networking physical layer interfaces," Feb. 1999.

19. *http://www.itu.int/ITU-T/index.html*

ANSWERS TO EXERCISES

ANSWERS TO CHAPTER 1

1. 3 mm.

2. What really changes is the wavelength.

3. 333

4. 7.8 eV

5. No. Free space has $n = 1$, and everything else has n greater than 1.

6. No. However, theoretically speaking, n is a material variable, and if in opto-electronic equations n is allowed to be negative, then some interesting properties come out. Based on this, some researchers think that there are some specially made materials that may exhibit negative n.

7. a. Yes, there would be a reflected ray.

   b. Yes, there would be a refractive ray, and the refractive angle would be zero.

8. Due to refraction, the bottom appears to be closer to the surface and thus its actual depth is more than 3.5 feet.

9. The index of refraction depends on the wavelength. Thus, the propagation is different for each wavelength. Since the pulse is almost monochromatic, each wavelength travels at a slightly different speed. Thus, the spectral envelope of the pulse, the group, will move at a different velocity than each wavelength component. Hence, the phase is faster than the group velocity.

10. See the figure for answer to problem 10.

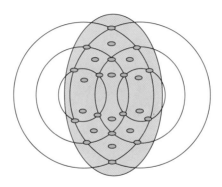

11. No. Based on the electromagnetic nature of photons and general relativity, a photon will propagate in (linear) free space and in a straight path forever. However, it is possible that a photon may be confined, or "trapped," in a space of strong fields (some researchers have claimed recently that they have accomplished to "freeze" photons in matter; this remains to be confirmed).

12. Although a photon has mass, it also behaves like a wave. Thus, capturing a photon is not like grabbing in space a moving ball and closing it in a box. It is merely captured by means of an atom that is raised to a higher energy level and the added energy is later released in the form of a photon. When a photon interacts with an atom, it may either be absorbed by it, it may cause it to release more photons, or it may be deflected by it.

13. The fringe density increases. One of the reasons that photolithography requires very short wavelengths, beyond UV.

14. The speed of pulses in the fiber is $v = c/n = 3 \times 10^{10}$ cm/s/1.5 $= 2 \times 10^{10}$ cm/s. The travel time throughout the fiber is $t = L/v = 10^5$ cm/2×10^{10} cm/s $= 5 \times 10^6$ ps. The period of each bit is 1/10 GHz $= 100$ ps. Thus, the fiber bit capacity is 5×10^6 ps/100 ps $= 50,000$ bits.

15. NA $= \pi(1.48^2 - 1.46^2) = 0.242487$, and $\Theta_{NA} = \sin^{-1}(NA) = 14.03°$.

16. The total fiber length is 60 km. Thus, the total attenuation is $60 \times 0.1 = 6$ dB. The total loss due to connectors, two at the ends and two interconnecting is, $4 \times 0.1 = 0.4$ dB. Thus, the total power loss over the link is $6 + 0.4$ dB $= 6.4$ dB.

17. The 3 mW (0.003 watts) signal corresponds to about 5 dBm and a gain of 8 to 9 dB. Hence the amplified power is 3 mW $\times 8 = 24$ mW, which corresponds to 14 dBm. Alternatively, using only dBs and dBms, the calculation would be 5 dBm $+ 9$ dB $= 14$ dBm. Mathematically, the calculations are:

$$10 \, Log(3 \times 10^{-3})/(10^{-3}) + 10Log(8) = 10Log(3 \times 8) = 10Log(24) = 14 \text{ dBm}$$

18. 5 dBm correspond to 3 mW and 9 dBm to 8 mW. Thus, the total combined power is $3 + 8 = 11$ mW, which is calculated to $10\log(11 \text{ mW}) = \sim 10.5$ dBm, which obviously is not the erroneous answer of 14 dBm.

19. **a.** λ_B moves faster than λ_A.

   b. λ_C moves faster than λ_D.

   c. λ_A moves about the same with λ_D.

   d. See Figure for answer to problem 19.

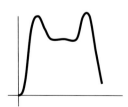

ANSWERS TO CHAPTER 2

1. For the relationship that satisfies the values $\lambda = (2\,dn)/m$ for the *resonant wavelengths* of a Fabry–Perot resonator the distance d is calculated:

$$d = \lambda m/2n = 1400/2 \text{ nm} = 700 \text{ nm}.$$

2. The finesse is estimated by the relationship $F = (\pi R)/[2(1 - R)]$.

   a. For $R = 0.9$: $F = (3.14 \times 0.9)/[2(1 - 0.9)] = 14.13$

   b. For $R = 0.3$: $F = (3.14 \times 0.3)/[2(1 - 0.2)] = 2.35$

3. 750 nm is half the wavelength of 1500 nm. Thus, the Bragg grating is fifth order for this wavelength.

4. For $n = 1$ (first order) and for $d = 700$ nm, $\lambda_B = 2d/n = 2(700/1) = 1400$ nm.

5. False.

6. $\lambda/d = 1500/3000 = 0.5$. Thus, m has the absolute values 1, 2, 3, and 4.

7. **a.** $\Lambda = 21$ μm.

   b. $f = 177$ MHz

8. True.

9. Yes.

10. True.

11. Yes. An LED is a special diode that emits light.

12. As temperature rises, the LED spectrum shifts and its intensity decreases.

13. Yes. They are suitable in multimode fiber applications.

14. At minimum they are an active region (where stimulated emission takes place), an optical waveguide (to limit light in a single direction), and optical feedback (a cavity in which light bounces back and forth for gain and filtering purposes).

15. Chirping is minimized if external modulation is used.

16. False. They perform best in the 1550-nm region.

17. Natural: *rods* and *cones* of the eye retina. Artificial: semiconductor PIN and APD.

18. The capacitance of the reversed biased PIN photodiode is a limiting factor to its response (and switching speed).

19. False. It has a high gain.

20. A regenerator converts the optical signal to an electrical signal, it conditions and amplifies the electrical signal and then it converts the electrical signal in an optical signal. An optical amplifier amplifies an attenuated optical signal directly.

21. A SOA is a semiconductor laser-type device that requires electrical current to excite its electron-hole pairs. An EDFA is an erbium-doped fiber that requires another exciting source of light, known as the pump.

22. In EDFAs, even if no incoming signal is present, there is always some output signal as a result of some excited ions in the fiber; this output is known as amplified spontaneous emission and is spontaneous noise.

23. A wavelength converter is an optical or semiconductor device that receives a signal at one wavelength and converts it into another.

24. A wavelength shifter is a dispersion-shifted fiber device in which a pump and a data signal, at different wavelengths, interact to produce a third modulated signal at a wavelength approximately equal to the lower wavelength shifted by the difference of the pump and signal wavelengths.

25. The probe signal is modulated and the pump source is continuous.

26. High isolation, low coupling power loss, no signal reflectivity no signal absorption, and no through phase shift.

27. Interferometry. Two waves, one from the ring and one from the fiber, encounter each other and, depending on their phase, interfere constructively or destructively at the coupler.

28. An optical isolator is a device that transmits optical power (of a band of wavelengths) in one direction more than in the other direction.

29. It is a device that is based on the property of certain materials to rotate the polarization of a wave by an angle.

30. Yes. It is possible with an optical add-drop multiplexer.

31. Yes. With reference to Figure 2.44, conceptually as many wavelengths may be dropped off and added by using an equal number of 2×2 switches.

32. The fastest, on the order of nanoseconds, are semiconductor-based switching devices, such as the $LiNbO_3$. Acousto-optic and MEM devices are on the order of microseconds, and thermo-optic devices are on the order of milliseconds.

ANSWERS TO CHAPTER 3

1. 8,000 samples per second. Each sample converted to 8 bits PCM results to 64,000 bits per second or 64 Kb/s.

2. No. We could not transmit violin music with high fidelity. There are two good reasons. First, violin music has an approximate high frequency of 20 KHz. Therefore, for high fidelity, the sampling should be 40,000 per second. Second, 8 bit-PCM was designed for voice, not for high-frequency content music; this would require a different CODEC than μ-law/α-law.

3. There are 24 DS0s in a DS1 signal, and 28 DS1s in a DS3 signal. Thus, there are $24 \times 28 = 672$ DS0s.

4. A DS1 signal is always at 1.544 Mb/s regardless of how many DS0s contain actual data.

5. False. An Ethernet LAN operates on the CSMA/CD collision detection.

6. True. FDDI is a dual fiber ring LAN.

7. a. 125 μsec.; **b.** 125 μsec.

8. Three VT1.5s with data and 1 VT without data in one group, three with data VT3s in one group and 1 VT with data +2 VT3s without in another group, and 1 VT6 in another group; that is, a total of four groups, leaving three more groups unused.

9. a and b. Any VT is transmitted in any STS-N within 125 μsec.

10. True

11. False. Voice over IP means that voice PCM is encapsulated in the IP payload and transmitted over the asynchronous and connectionless network, as opposed to the synchronous TDM network.

12. False. On the contrary, it means that IP packets are encapsulated in the SONET payload and then transmitted over the synchronous SONET network.

ANSWERS TO CHAPTER 4

1. Digital cross-connects do not execute a connection protocol; they are provisioned.

2. A typical dynamic switch that executes a call processing protocol is designed to switch synchronous signals. In a different implementation, it may be possible to switch asynchronous signals (e.g., ATM) provided there are buffers at the inputs to smooth out the incoming rate, in which case the switching fabric becomes synchronous.

3. a. False; **b.** False;

4. Remoting means that bays of a multibay system are located in different parts of a building but are connected with a communication link.

5. Eight quad-OC-12 require approximately 8×2.5 Gb/s $= 20$ Gb/s. A 50% increase will increase it to 30 Gb/s, which is below $50 - 15\% \times 50$ Gb/s $= 42.5$ Gb/s. Thus:

    a. An upgrade of the input–output units is required, as the system permits (either by adding more units or upgrade some units to octal, if possible).

    b. No switching bandwidth capacity increase is required

6. The controller for each input–output shelf could be simplex or duplex; for the cross-connecting switching fabric should be duplex; and for the fourth shelf a simplex controller.

7. True.

8. False. Backbone systems are designed for links that are several hundreds of kilometers.

ANSWERS TO CHAPTER 5

1. True.

2. True.

3. False.

4. True.

5. $1/(10^9 \times 10^{-10}) = 10$ seconds.

6. True.

7. True.

8. True.

ACRONYMS

10BaseT	10 Mbps over Twisted Pair
100BaseT	100 Mbps over Twisted Pair
1000BaseT	1000 Mbps over Twisted Pair
2B1Q	Two Bits to One Quaternary
3-D	Three-dimensional
3R	Reamplification, Reshaping, and Retiming
8B/10B	Eight Bit to Ten Bit coding
AAL	ATM Adaptation Layer
ABR	Available Bit Rate
ACELP	Adaptive Code Excited Linear Prediction
ACGIH	American Conference of Governmental Industrial Hygienists
ACTS	Advanced Communications Technology and Services
ADC	Analog to Digital Conversion
ADM	Add-Drop Multiplexer
ADPCM	Adaptive Differential Pulse Code Modulation
ADSL	Asymmetric Digital Subscriber Line
AFM	Atomic Force Microscope
AIS	Alarm Indication Signal
Al	Aluminum
ALP	Application Layer Protocol
AM	Administration Module; Amplitude Modulation
AMI	Alternate Mark Inversion
AN	Access Node
ANSI	American National Standards Institute
AON	All Optical Network
AOTF	Acousto-Optic Tunable Filter
AP	Access Point; Adjunct Processor
APC	Adaptive Predictive Coding
APD	Avalanche Photo-Detector; Access Procedure-D channel
APDU	Application Protocol Data Unit; Authentic Protocol Data Unit
APON	ATM-based broadband PON
APS	Automatic Protection Switching
APSD	Automatic power laser shutdown
AR	Antireflecting coating
ARM	Access Resource Management

ARPA	Advanced Research Project Agency
As	Arsenic
ASE	Amplified Spontaneous Emission; Application Service Element
ASIC	Application-Specific Integrated Circuit
ASK	Amplitude Shift Keying
ATM	Asynchronous Transfer Mode
AU	Administrative Unit
AUG	Administrative Unit Group
AWG	Array Waveguide Grating
BB	Broadband
BCD	Binary Coded Decimal; Blocked-Calls-Delayed
BDI	Backwards Defect Indication
BEI	Backward Error Indication
BER	Bit Error Rate; Basic Encoding Rules
BISDN	Broadband Integrated Services Digital Network
BIP	Bit Interleaved Parity
BIP-8	Bit Interleaved Parity 8 field
BITS	Building Information Timing Supply
BML	Business Management Layer
Bps	Bits per second
BPSR	Bidirectional Path-Switching Ring
BRI	Basic Rate Interface
BSHR	Bidirectional Shelf Healing Ring
BSHR/2	2 fiber Bidirectional Shelf Healing Ring
BSHR/4	4 fiber Bidirectional Shelf Healing Ring
C-n	Container-level n; n = 11, 12, 2, 3, or 4
CAC	Connection Admission Control
CAM	Content Addressable Memory; Computer Aided Manufacture
CAP	Carrierless Amplitude Phase; Competitive Access Provider
CBR	Constant Bit Rate
CC	Composite Clock
CCC	Clear Channel Capability
CCITT	Consultative Committee International Telegraph and Telephone (renamed ITU)
CCS	One hundred call-seconds
CDC	Chromatic Dispersion Coefficient
CDMA	Code Division Multiple Access
CD-ROM	Compact Disk — Read Only Memory
CELP	Code Excited Linear Prediction
CEPT-n	Conference of European Posts and Telecommunications-level n (see E1)
CIT	Craft Interface Terminal
CLASS	Custom Local Area Signaling Services
CLEC	Competitive Local Exchange Carrier
CLP	Cell Loss Priority
CLR	Cell Loss Rate

CM	Communications Module; Connection Management; Connection Monitoring
CMI	Coded Mark Inversion
CMIP	Common Management Information Protocol
CMISE	Common Management Information Service Element
CMIS/P	Common Management Information Service/Protocol
CMT	Coupled-Mode Theory
CNM	Customer Network Management
CNTRL	Control
CO	Central Office
CODEC	COder-DECoder
COP	Connection Oriented Protocol
COPS	Common Open Policy Service
CORBA	Common Object Request Broker Architecture
CoS	Class of Service; Cost of Service
COT	Central Office Terminal
COTS	Commercial Off-the-Shelf technology/equipment
CP	Customer Premises; Control Point; Connection Point; Communications Processor
CPE	Customer Premises Equipment
CPN	Calling Party's Number; Customer Premises Network
CPRING	Client Protection Ring
CPWDM	Chirped-Pulse Wavelength-Division Multiplexing
CRC	Cyclic Redundancy Check
CS	Convergence Sublayer
CS-PDU	Convergence Sublayer-PDU
CSA	Carrier Serving Area
CSDC	Circuit Switched Digital Capability
CSES	Consecutive Severely Errored Seconds
CSMF	Conventional Single Mode Fiber
CSMD/CD	Carrier Sense Multiple Access/Collision Detection
CTD	Cell Transfer Delay
CU	Channel Unit
CW	Continuous Wave
CWDM	Coarse Wavelength Division Multiplexer
dB	Decibel
dBm	Decibel with 1 mWatt reference level
DBR	Distributed Bragg Reflector
DC	Direct Current
DCB	Digital Channel Bank
DCC	Data Country Code; Data Communication Channel; Digital Clear Channel
DCE	Data Circuit-terminating Equipment
DCF	Dispersion Compensation Fiber; Distributed Coordination Function
DCM	Dispersion-Compensating Module
DCN	Data Communications Network
DCS	Digital Cross-connect System

DCW	Dispersion Compensating Waveguide
DDD	Direct Distance Dialing
DDS	Digital Data Service
DFB	Distributed Feedback
DFCF	Dispersion-Flattened Compensated Fiber
DFF	Dispersion-Flattened Fiber
DFI	Domain Format Identifier
DGD	Differential Group Delay
DiffServ	Differentiated Services
DIP	Dual In-line Package
DL	Data Link
DLC	Digital Loop Carrier
DMT	Discrete Multitone modulation
DPBX	Digital PBX
DPCM	Differential Pulse Code Modulation
DPDU	Data link PDU
DPE	Distributed Processing Environment
DPSK	Differential PSK
DQDB	Distributed Queue Dual Bus
DR	Digital Radio; Dynamical Routing
DRI	Dual Ring Interface
DSAP	Destination Service Access Point
DSCF	Dispersion-Shift Compensated Fiber; Dispersion-Slope Compensated Fiber
DSCP	DiffServ codepoints
DSF	Dispersion Shifted Fiber
DSL	Digital Subscriber Line
DSLAM	Digital Subscriber Line Access Multiplexer
DS-n	Digital Signal level n; n = 0, 1, 2, 3
DS-SMF	Dispersion Shifted Single Mode Fiber
DSP	Domain Specific Part; Digital Signal Processor
DSU	Data Service Unit
DSX-n	Digital Signal Crossconnect point for DS-n signals
DTE	Data Terminal Equipment
DTF	Dielectric Thin Film
DTMF	Dual-Tone Multi-Frequency
DTS	Digital Termination Service
DWDM	Dense Wavelength Division Multiplexing
DXC	Digital Cross Connect
DXC 4/4	DXC with a maximum VC-4 interface and VC-4 cross-connecting fabric
DXI	Data Exchange Interface
E	Extraordinary ray
E1	A wideband digital facility at 2.048 Mbps, aka CEPT-1
E3	A broadband digital facility at 34.368 Mbps, aka CEPT-3
E4	A broadband digital facility at 139.264 Mbps, aka CEPT-4
EBC	Errored Block Count

EBCDIC	Extended Binary Coded Decimal Interchange Code
EC	Echo Canceller; Embedded Channel
ECC	Embedded Communication Channel
ECDC	Error Detection and Correction Code
ECMA	European Association for Standardizing Information and Comm. Systems
ECSA	Exchange Carriers Standards Association
EDC	Error Detection Code
EDCC	Error Detection and Correction Code
EDFA	Erbium-Doped Fiber Amplifier
EFI	Errored Frame Indicator
EFS	Error Free Second
EIA/TIA	Electronics Industry Association/Telecommunications Industry Association
EIR	Excess Information Rate; Equipment Identity Register
ELAN	Emulated LAN
EM	Element Manager; Electro-Magnetic
EMAC	European, Middle East, and Africa Market Awareness and Education Committee
EMC	Electromagnetic Compatibility
EMI	Electromagnetic Interference
EML	Element Management Layer
EMS	Element Management System
E-n	European signal level n (n = 1, 2, 3 and 4)
E/O	Electrical to Optical
ERM	Electro-refraction modulation
ER–LSP	Explicitly Routed Label-Switched Path
ES	Error Seconds
ESCON	Enterprise Systems Connectivity
ESF	Extended Super-Frame format
ESR	Errored Seconds Ratio
ETRI	Electronics and Telecommunications Research Institute
ETSI	European Telecommunications Standardization Institute
EX	Extinction Ratio
EXC	Electronic cross-connect
EXP	Experimental
F	Fluoride
FAS	Frame Alignment Signal; Fiber Array Switch
FBG	Fiber Bragg Grating
FBS	Fiber Bundle Switch
FCAPS	Fault, Configuration, Accounting, Performance, and Security
FCC	Federal Communications Commission
FDDI	Fiber Distributed Data Interface
FDI	Feeder Distribution Interface; Forward Defect Indicator
FDI-P	Forward Defect Indicator–Payload
FDI-S	Forward Defect Indicator-OSC
FDM	Frequency Division Multiplexing

FDMA	Frequency Division Multiple Access
FEC	Forward Error Correction; Forward Equivalency Class
FER	Frame Error Rate
FET	Field Effect Transistor
FEXT	Far End Cross-Talk
FFT	Fast Fourier Transforms
FFTS	Fiber Feeder Transport System
FH	Frequency Hopping
FHD	Flame Hydrolysis Deposition
FHSS	Frequency Hopped Spread Spectrum
FIT	Failure-In-Time
FITL	Fiber In The Loop
FM	Frequency Modulation
FMI	Frequency Modulation Index
FOA	First Office Application
FoFR	Fax-over-frame relay
FoIP	Fax-over-IP
FOT	Fiber Optic Terminal
FOTS	Fiber Optic Transmission System
FPGA	Field Programmable Gate Array
FPI	Fabry–Perot Interferometer
FPM	Four Photon Mixing
FPS	Fast Packet Switching
FR	Frame Relay
FRAD	Frame Relay Assembler/Disassembler
FRAMES	Future Radio wideband Multiple access System
FSK	Frequency Shift Keying
FSO	Free space optical communications systems
FSR	Free Spectral Range
FTAM	File Transfer and Access Method
FTP	File Transfer Protocol
FTTB	Fiber To The Building
FTTC	Fiber To The Curb
FTTCab	Fiber To The Cabinet
FTTD	Fiber To The Desk
FTTH	Fiber To The Home
FTTO	Fiber To The Office
FTTT	Fiber To The Town
FWHM	Full Width at Half Maximum
FWM	Four Wave Mixing
FX	Foreign Exchange
FXC	Fiber Cross-connect
Ga	Gallium
GbE	Gigabit Ethernet
Gbps	Gigabits per second = 1,000 Mbps
GEF	Gain Equalization Filter
GFC	Generic Flow Control

Ghz	Gigahertz (10^9 Hz)
GNE	Gateway Network Element
GoS	Grade of Service
GRIN	Graded Index fiber
GUI	Graphical User Interface
GVD	Group Velocity Dispersion
HDLC	High-level Data Link Control
HDX	Half-Duplex
HEC	Header Error Control
HFC	Hybrid Fiber Coax
HIPERLAN	High Performance Radio Local Area Network
HIPPI	High Performance Parallel Interface
HPF	High Pass Filter
HTML	Hyper-Text Markup Language
HTTP	Hypertext Transfer Protocol
IaDI	Intra-Domain Interface
IANA	Internet Assigned Number Authority
IBS	Ion Beam Spattering
IBSS	Independent Basic Service Set
IC	Integrated Circuit; Interference Canceller
ICC	Interstate Commerce Commission
ICCF	Interchange Carrier Compatibility Forum
ICI	Inter-Carrier Interference; Inter-Carrier Interface
ICIP	Inter-Carrier Interface Protocol
ID	Identifier
IDF	Inverse Dispersion Fiber
IDI	Initial Domain Identifier
IDL	Interface Definition Language
IDLC	Integrated Digital Loop Carrier
IDSL	ISDN DSL
IEC	Interstate Electrotechnical Commission
IEEE	Institute of Electrical and Electronics Engineers
IETF	Internet Engineering Task Force
IFFT	Inverse Fast Fourier Transforms
IGP	Internet Gateway Protocol
ILEC	Incumbent Local Exchange Carrier
ILMI	Interim Local Management Interface
IM	Intensity Modulation; Inverse Multiplexer; Intelligent Multiplexer
IM/DD	Intensity Modulation with Direct Detection
IMS	Information Management System
In	Indium
IN	Intelligent Network
IntServ	Internet Services
IOF	Inter Office Framework
ION	Intelligent Optical Networks
IP	Internet Protocol; Intelligent Peripheral

IPng	Internet Protocol next generation
IPv6	Internet Protocol version 6
IPX	Inter-network Packet Exchange
IR	Infrared; Intermediate Reach
IrDA	Infrared Data Association
IrDI	Inter-Domain Interface
ISA	Industry Standard Architecture
ISDN	Integrated Services Digital Network
ISI	Inter-Symbol Interference
ISM	Intelligent or Integrated Synchronous Multiplexer
ISO	International Standards Organization
ISOC	Internet Society
ISP	Internet Service Provider
ITSP	Internet Telephony Service Provider
ITO	Indium Tin Oxide
ITU	International Telecommunications Union
ITU-D	ITU Development Sector
ITU-R	ITU Radio-communications Sector
ITU-T	ITU Telecommunications standardization Sector
IW	Inter-Working
IWF	Inter-Working Function
IWU	Inter-Working Unit
IXC	Inter-exchange Carrier
JIDM	Joint Inter Domain Management group
JIT	Jitter Transfer Function
JTC1	Joint Technical Committee 1 (ISO/IEC)
Kbps	Kilobits per second = 1,000 bps
KLTN	Potassium lithium-tantalate niobate
LA	Line Amplifier
LAC	Link Access Control
LAN	Local Area Network
LANE	Local Area Network Emulation
LAPD	Link Access Protocol for the D Channel
LAPF	Link Access Protocol for Frame Relay
LASER	Light Amplification by Stimulated Emission or Radiation
LATA	Local Access and Transport Area
LB	Loop Back
LBO	Line Build-Out
LC	Link Connection
LCFPI	Liquid crystal Fabry-Perot Interferometer
LD	Laser Diode; Long Distance
LEC	Local Exchange Carrier
LED	Light-Emitting Diode
LER	Label Edge-Router
LH	Long Haul

LiNbO$_3$	Lithium Niobate
LLC	Logical Link Control
LMDS	Local Multipoint Distribution Service
LO	Low Order
LOF	Loss Of Frame
LOH	Line Overhead
LOM	Loss Of Multiframe
LOP	Loss Of Pointer
LOS	Loss Of Signal; Loss Of Synchronization
LPC	Linear Prediction Coding
LPF	Low Pass Filter
LSB	Least Significant Bit
LSO	Local Serving Office
LSP	Label-Switched Path
LSR	Label Switch-Router
LSS	Loss of Sequence Synchronization
LSSU	Link Status Signaling Unit
LTE	Line Termination Equipment
LU	Logical Unit
LVC	Low order Virtual Container
M1	Level 1 Multiplexer
M12	Level 1-to-2 Multiplexer
M2	Level 2 Multiplexer
M23	Level 2-to-3 Multiplexer
M13	Level 1-to-3 Multiplexer
MAC	Media-specific Access Control
MAN	Metropolitan Area Network
Mbps	Megabits per second (1000 Kbps)
MBS	Maximum Burst Rate
MCN	Management Communications Network
MCVD	Modified Chemical Vapor Deposition
MEMS	Micro-Electro-Mechanical System
MF	Mediation Function; Matching Filter
MFL	Multi-Frequency Laser
MH	Medium haul
Mhz	Megahertz (10^6 Hertz)
MI	Management Information; Michelson Interferometer; Modulation instability
MIB	Management Information Base
MII	Ministry of the (China) Information Industry
MIM	Management Information Model
MOCVD	Metal Organic Chemical Vapor Deposition
MONET	Multiwavelength Optical NETworking
MPE	Maximum Permissible Exposure
MPEG	Motion Picture Experts Group
MPLS	multiprotocol Label Switching
MPλS	Multiprotocol lambda (wavelength) switching

MQW	Multiple Quantum Well
MQWL	Multiple Quantum Well Laser
MS-AIS	Multiplex Section AIS
MSB	Most Significant Bit
MSDSL	Multirate SDSL
msec	milliseconds
μsec	microseconds
MSN	Manhattan Street Network
MSO	Multiple Service Operator
MSOH	Multiplexer Section Overhead
MSP	Multiplex Section Protection
MTBF	Mean Time Between Failure
MUX	Multiplexer
mW	milliWatts
MZI	Mach–Zehnder
MZI	Mach–Zehnder Interferometer
MZF	Mach–Zehnder filters
NAP	Network Access Provider
NASA	National Aeronautics and Space Administration (USA)
NC	Network Connection
Nd	Neodymium
NE	Network Element
NEBS	Network Equipment Building System
NEF	Network Element Function
NEL	Network Element Layer
NEXT	Near End Cross Talk
NF	Noise Figure
NGI	Next Generation Internet
NIC	Network Interface Card
NIST	National Institute for Standards and Testing
NIU	Network Interface Unit
nm	nanometer
NML	Network Management Layer
NMS	Network Management System
NNI	Network to Network Interface; Network node interface
NOLM	Nonlinear Optical Loop Mirror
NRM	Network Resource Management
NRL	Naval Research Laboratory (USA)
NRZ	Non Return to Zero
ns	nanosecond
NSA	National Security Agency (USA)
NSN	Network Service Node
NSP	Network Service Provider
NT	Network Termination
NTSC	National Television Standards Committee
NTU	Network Termination Unit

NZDF	Non-Zero Dispersion (shifted) Fiber
NZSMF	Non-Zero dispersion Single Mode Fiber
O	Ordinary ray
OA	Optical Amplifier
OAM	Operations, Administration and Management
OADM	Optical ADM
OAMP	OAM and Provisioning Services
OAR	Optically Amplified Receiver
OAS	Optical Amplifier Section
OAT	Optically Amplified Transmitter
OC	Optical Carrier
OCC	Optical Channel Carrier
OCDM	Optical Code Division Multiplexing
OCG	Optical Channel Group; Optical Carrier Group
OCh	Optical Channel
OCI	Open Connection Indication
OC-n	Optical Carrier level n (n = 1, 3, 12, 48, 192)
ODBC	Open Database Connectivity
ODL	Optical Data Link
ODMA	Open Distributed Management Architecture
ODP	Optical Diverse Protection; Open Distributed Processing
ODSI	Optical Domain Service Interconnect
ODU	Optical Demultiplex Unit; Optical Data Unit
ODUk	Optical Channel Data Unit-k
O-E	Optical to Electrical conversion
OEIC	Opto-Electronic Integrated Circuit
OEM	Original Equipment Manufacturer
OFA	Optical Fiber Amplifier
OFDM	Optical Frequency-Division Multiplexing; Orthogonal Frequency-Division Multiplexing
OFS	Optical Fiber System
OH	Overhead; Hydroxile
OLA	Optical Limiting Amplifier
OLC	Optical Loop Carrier
OLE	Object Linking and Embedding
OLED	Organic Light Emitting Diodes
OLS	Optical Line System
OLTM	Optical Line Terminating Multiplexer
OLTS	Optical Loss Test Set
OMA	Object Management Architecture
OMAP	Operations, Maintenance, and Administration Part
OMS	Optical Multiplex System; Optical Multiplex Section
OMS-OH	Optical multiplex section overhead
OMU	Optical Multiplex Unix
ONNI	Optical Network Node Interface
ONTC	Optical Networks Technology Consortium

ONU	Optical Network Unit
OOF	Out Of Frame
OOK	On-Off Keying
OOS	OTM Overhead Signal; Out Of Synchronization
OPLDS	Optical Power Loss Detection System
OPLL	Optical Phase-Locked Loop
OPM	Optical Protection Module
OPS	Optical Protection Switch
OPU	Optical Payload Unit
OPUk	Optical Channel Payload Unit-k
ORL	Optical Return Loss
OS	Operating System
OSA	Optical Spectrum Analyzer
OSC	Optical Supervisory Channel
OSF	Operating System Function
OSI	Open System Interconnect
OSI-RM	Open System Interconnect Reference Model
OSNR	Optical Signal-to-Noise Ratio
OSS	Operations Support System
OTDM	Optical Time Division Multiplexing
OTDR	Optical Time Domain Reflectometer
OTE	Optical Terminating Equipment
OTF	Organic Thin Film
OTM	Optical Transport Module
OTN	Optical Transport Network
OTS	Optical Transmission Section; Off-the-self
OTS-OH	Optical transmission section overhead
OTU	Optical Transport Unit
OTUk	Optical Channel Transport Unit-k
OUI	Organization Unit Identifier
OVPN	Optical Virtual Private Network
OXC	Optical Cross-Connect
P	Phosphorus
PACS	Personal Access Communications System
PAD	Packet Assembler and Disassembler
PAM	Pulse Amplitude Modulation
PBS	Polarization Beam Splitter
PBX	Private Branch Exchange
PC	Payload Container; Protection Channel; Personal Computer
PCM	Pulse Coded Modulation
PCR	Provider Core Routers
PCS	Personal Communication Services
PCF	Photonic crystal fiber
PD	Photodiode; Propagation Delay
PDC	Passive Dispersion Compensation
PDFA	Praseodymium Doped Fiber Amplifier

PDH	Plesiochronous Digital Hierarchy
PDL	Polarization Dependent Loss
PDN	Packet Data Network; Passive Distribution System
PDG	Polarization-Dependent Gain
PDU	Protocol Data Unit
PE	Payload Envelope
PG	Pair gain system
PHASARS	Phased-array gratings
PHB	Per hop (link) basis
PHY	Physical Layer
PIC	Photonic Integrated Circuit
PIN	Positive Intrinsic Negative photodiode
PLC	Planar Lightwave Circuit
PLCP	Physical Layer Convergence Protocol
PLL	Phase-Locked Loop
PM	Performance Monitoring; Path Monitoring
PMC	Polarization mode coupling
PMI	Payload Missing Indication
PMD	Polarization Mode Dispersion; Physical Medium Dependant
PMDC	Polarization mode dispersion compensation
PMMA	Poly-Methyl-Meth-Acrylate
PN	Pseudo-random Numerical sequence
PNNI	Private NNI
POH	Path Overhead
PON	Passive Optical Network
POP	Point Of Presence
POTS	Plain Old Telephone Service
PP	Pointer Processing
ppm	parts per million
PPP	Point-to-Point Protocol
PRC	Primary Reference Clock
PRI	Primary Rate Interface
PRS	Primary Reference Source
PS	Protection Switching
PSI	Payload Structure Identifier
PSIM	Phase-shifting interferometric microscope
PSK	Phase Shift Keying
PSP	Principal States of Polarization
PSTN	Public Switched Telephone Network
PT	Payload Type
PTE	Path Terminating Equipment
ptp	peak-to-peak
PTT	Postal Telephone and Telegraph ministries
PVC	Permanent Virtual Circuit
PVP	Permanent Virtual Path
QAM	Quadrature Amplitude Modulation
QoS	Quality of Service; Quality of Signal

QPSK	Quadrature PSK; Quartenary PSK; Quadriphase PSK
QWL	Quantum well lasers
RACE	Research of Advanced Communications technologies in Europe
RADSL	Rate Adaptive DSL
RAM	Random Access Memory
RBOC	Regional Bell Operating Company
RDI	Remote Defect Indicator, formerly FERF; aka yellow alarm.
REI	Remote Error Indicator
RF	Radio Frequency
RFI	Remote Failure Indication; Radio Frequency Interference
RM	Resource Management
RMN	Ring-mesh network
RMS	Root Mean Square
ROM	Read Only Memory
ROSE	Remote Operation Service Element
RS	Reed-Solomon
RSM	Remote Switch Module
RSOH	Regenerator Section Overhead
RSTE	Regenerator Section Terminating Equipment
RSU	Remote Switch Unit
RSVP	Resource reSerVation setup Protocol
RT	Remote Terminal
RTT	Round Trip Time; Radio Transmission Technology
RTU	Remote Termination Unit
RZ	Return to Zero
SAP	Service Access Point
SAR	Segmentation And Re-assembly
SBS	Stimulated Brillouin Scattering amplifiers
SCR	Sustainable Cell Rate
SDH	Synchronous Digital Hierarchy
SDLC	Synchronous Data Link Control protocol
$\Sigma\Delta$PCM	Sigma-Delta PCM
SDSL	Symmetric DSL
SDU	Service Data Unit
SEED	Self Electro-optic Effect Device
SF	Signal Fail; Super-Frame; Spreading Factor; Single Frequency
SH	Short haul
SHR	Self-Healing Ring
SI	Step Index
SIP	SMDS Interface protocol; Series In-line Package
SIR	Signal-to-Interference Ratio
SL	Signal label; Submarine Lightwave
SLA	Service Level Agreement
SLC	Synchronous Line Carrier
SLM	Synchronous Line Multiplexer
SM	Switching Module

SMASE	System Management Application Service Element
SMDS	Switched Multi-megabit Digital Services
SMF	Single Mode Fiber; Service Management Function
SML	Service Management Layer
SMN	SONET Management Network; SDH Management Network
SMS	SDH Management Sub-network
SMSR	Single Mode Suppression Ratio
SN	Sequence Number; Service Node
SNA	Systems Network Architecture
SNAP	Sub-Net Access Protocol
SNC/Ne	Sub-Network Connection Protection/intrusive end-to-end monitoring
SNC/Ns	Sub-Network Connection Protection/nonintrusive sublayer monitoring
SNCP	Sub-Network Connection Protection
SNI	Service Node Interface; Subscriber to Network Interface; SMDS Network Interface
SNMP	Simple Network Management Protocol
SNMS	Sub-Network Management System
SNP	Sequence Number Protection
SNR	Signal to Noise Ratio
SOA	Semiconductor Optical Amplifier
SoF	Start of frame
SOH	Section Over Head
SOHO	Small Office/Home Office
SONET	Synchronous Optical Network
SP	Switching Point
SPDU	Session Protocol Data Unit
SPE	Synchronous Payload Envelope
SPM	Self Phase Modulation
SPRING	Shared Protection Ring
SQM/BQI	Signal quality monitoring and backward quality indication
SR	Short reach; Software Radio; Symbol Rate
SRS	Stimulated Raman Scattering
SS7	Signaling System #7
SSAP	Source Service Access Point; Session Service Access Point (ISO)
SS-CDMA	Spread Spectrum CDMA
SSMF	Standard Single Mode Fiber
STE	Section Terminating Equipment; Switching Terminal Exchange
STM-n	Synchronous Transport Module level n (n = 1, 4, 16, 64)
STP	Shielded Twisted Pair; Signal Transfer Point
STS	Synchronous Transport Signal; Space-Time-Space switch
SVC	Switched Virtual Circuit
SWC	Service Wire Center
T1	A digital carrier facility used to transmit a DS1 signal at 1.544 Mbps
T3	A digital carrier facility used to transmit a DS3 signal at 45 Mbps
TA	Terminal Adapter
Tbps	Terabits per second = 1,000 Gbps

TC	Tandem Connection
TCP	Transmission Control Protocol
TCM	Tandem Connection Maintenance
TCAM	TeleCommunications Access Method
TCAP	Transaction Capabilities Part
TCM	Tandem Connection Monitoring; Trellis Code Modulation
TCP	Transmission Control Protocol; Trail Connection Point
TCP/IP	Transmission Control Protocol/Internet Protocol
TDM	Time Division Multiplexing
TDMA	Time Division Multiple Access
TE	Terminal Equipment; Trans-Electric
TEC	Thermo-Electric Cooler
Te-EDFA	Tellurium-EDFA
TEI	Terminal Endpoint Identifier
TEP	Traffic Engineering Policy
TE–RSVP	Traffic Engineering Resource Reservation Protocol
tFWM	Temporal FWM
Thz	Tera-hertz (1000 Ghz)
TI	Trace identifier
TIA	Telecommunications Industry Association
TIM	Trace Identifier Mismatch
TINA	Telecommunications Information Networking Architecture consortium
TL1	Transport language 1
TLV	Threshold limit values
TM	Traffic Management; Terminal Multiplexer; Trans-Magnetic
TMM	Transmission Monitoring Machine
TMN	Telecommunications Management Network
TOH	Transport OverHead (SOH + LOH)
ToS	Type of Service
TP	Twisted Pair; Transport layer Protocol
TPC	Transmit Power Control
T&R	Tip and Ring
TS	Time Stamp; Time Slot
TSI	Time Slot Interchanger
TTA	Telecommunications Technology Association
TU	Tributary Unit
TU-n	Tributary Unit level n; n = 11, 12, 2, or 3
TUG-n	Tributary Unit Group n; n = 2 or 3
UBR	Unspecified Bit Rate
UCAID	University Corporation for Advanced Internet Development
UDC	Universal Digital Channel
UDP	User Datagram Protocol
UI	Unit Interval
ULH	Ultra long haul
ULR	Ultra long-reach
UNEQ	Unequipped

UNI	User to Network Interface
UPC	Usage Parameter Control
UPSR	Unidirectional Path Switch Ring
URL	Uniform Resource Locator
USART	Universal Synchronous/Asynchronous Receiver Transmitter
USF	(dispersion) Unshifted Single-mode Fiber
USHR	Unidirectional Shelf-Healing Ring
USTIA	United States Telecommunications Industry Association
UTP	Unshielded Twisted Pair
UV	Ultra-violet

VBR	Variable Bit Rate
VC	Virtual Channel
VC-n	Virtual Container level n (n = 2, 3, 4, 11, or 12)
VC-n-Mc	Virtual Container level n, M concatenated Virtual Containers
VCC	VC Connection
VCI	Virtual Circuit Identifier
VCSEL	Vertical-Cavity Surface-Emitting Laser
VDSL	Very-high-bit rate DSL
VF	Voice Frequency
VHF	Very High Frequency
VLAN	Virtual LAN
VLSI	Very Large Scale Integration
VOA	Variable Optical Attenuator
VOD	Video On Demand
VoIP	Voice over IP
VP	Virtual Path
VPC	VP Connection
VPI	Virtual Path Identifier
VPN	Virtual Private Network
VSR	Very short reach
VT	Virtual Tributary
VTAM	Virtual Telecommunications Access Method
VTOA	Voice Telephone Over ATM

WADM	Wavelength Add-Drop Multiplexer
WAN	Wide Area Network
WATS	Wide Area Telephone Service
WATM	Wireless ATM
W-CDMA	Wideband DS-CDMA
W-DCS	Wideband Digital Cross-connect System
WDM	Wavelength Division Multiplexing
WGR	Waveguide Grating Router
WIS	Wavelength Independent Switch
WIXC	Wavelength Interchanging Cross-connect
WLAN	Wireless LAN
WPON	WDM PON
WSC	Wavelength Selective Coupler

WSS	Wavelength Selective Switch
WSXC	Wavelength Selective Cross-Connect
X.25	Packet switching international standard
xDSL	any-DSL
XML	Extensible Markup Language
XOR	Exclusive OR logic function
XPM	Cross-Phase Modulation
YIG	Yttrium Iron Garnet
ZBTSI	Zero Byte TSI

Channel dispersion, dense wavelength division multiplexing systems (DWDM) systems, 373

Channel interleavers, dense wavelength division multiplexing (DWDM) systems, optical multiplexers/demultiplexers, 134–135

Channelized nodes, dense wavelength division multiplexing (DWDM) systems, 298

Channel splitters, dense wavelength division multiplexing (DWDM) systems, optical multiplexers/demultiplexers, 134–135

Chirped fiber Bragg gratings, properties, 114

Chirped-pulse amplification (CPA), laser properties, 161

Chirped-pulse wavelength-division multiplexing (CPWDM), laser properties, 160–161

Chromatic compression, chirped fiber Bragg gratings, 114

Chromatic dispersion
compensation, 64–65
dense wavelength division multiplexing (DWDM) systems, compensators, 318–320
ITU-T standards, 59–60
single-mode calculations, 64

Circuit switched digital capability (CSDC), xDSL, 238

Circular polarization, optical components, 26–29

Circulators, dense wavelength division multiplexing systems (DWDM) systems, 130–132

Cladding
dense wavelength division multiplexing (DWDM) systems, laser properties, 153–155
fiber optic transmission, 41

Coarse-WDM metro system, dense wavelength division multiplexing (DWDM) systems, 365–366

CODEC circuitry
all-digital communications network, 245
pulse-coded modulation, 237

Code-excited linear prediction algorithm (CELP), pulse-coded modulation, 236–237

Coherence, degree of, laser beams, 168–169

Coherent heterodyne/homodyne detection techniques, dense wavelength division multiplexing (DWDM), optical modulation/demodulation, 306–307

Coherent lights sources, dense wavelength division multiplexing (DWDM) systems, 149

Collinear acousto-optic tunable optical filters (AOTF), properties, 123–124

Collision, ethernet systems, 261–262

Collision length, soliton systems, 81–82

Common management information service element (CMISE), dense wavelength division multiplexing (DWDM) systems, 333–335

Communications systems
connection technology, 254–255
data systems, 255–270
ATM, 267–269
ethernet, 261–265
frame relay, 267
local area networks, 260–265
OSI model, 258–260
packet networks, 265–267
quality of service (QoS) parameters, 269–270
DWDM system and network, 288–289
emerging technologies, 430–432
internet, 282–287
ATM over SONET, 285–287
Fax over IP (FoIP), 284–285
IP over SONET, 287
voice over IP, 283–284
loop accessing methods, 237–244
high-speed short-reach technologies, 242–244
xDSL, 238–241
optical networks, 287–288
pulse coded modulation, 236–237
SONET and SDH, 270–282
floating frames and pointers, 275
frames, 271–275
frequency justification, 278
interworking, 281–282
maintenance, 278–280
next-generation systems, 282
operations communications interface (SOCI), 280–281
overhead definition, 275–278
path overhead, 278
rates, 271
topologies, 271
time division multiplexing systems, 244–254
access and pair-gain systems, 246–249
digital cross-connect systems, 253–254
fiber-to-home technology, 249–251
switching systems, 251–253

Composite refractive indices, fiber optic transmission, 44

Concentration, time division multiplexing, access and pair-gain systems, 248–249

Congestion management, dense wavelength division multiplexing (DWDM) networks, 414–415

ABOUT THE AUTHOR

Stamatios V. Kartalopoulos is currently the president and CTO of PhotonExperts, a consultancy on advanced optical technology and optical communications. He is also a Williams Professor in Telecommunications Networking at the University of Oklahoma. Previously, he was with the Advanced Optical Networking Organization of Lucent Technologies, Bell Labs Innovation. Dr. Kartalopoulos holds a B.Sc. in physics, a graduate diploma in electronics, and a M.Sc. and Ph.D. in electrical engineering.

Dr. Kartalopoulos' responsibilities have been in DWDM technology and networks, scaleable protocols for DWDM metro applications, in SONET/SDH and ATM architectures, ATM payload mapping over SONET/SDH, controller architectures, high-efficiency scalable protocols, digital cross-connects, switching systems, local area networks, transmission and access systems, complex VLSls, neural networks and fuzzy logic, and microprocessor-based real-time architectures. In addition to his technical expertise in systems and networks, he had led and managed focus teams in technical marketing and customer service with responsibility in both Europe and the United States. His most recent activities have been in the definition of Optical Transport Network Overhead (OTN-OH), in the definition of DWDM technology and fault detectability of optical platforms, in the survivability of optical networks, and in the definition of the supervisory channel protocol for WDM metro applications.

Dr. Kartalopoulos has published four books, *Fault Detectability in DWDM: Toward Higher Signal Quality & System Reliability* (IEEE Press, 2001), *Introduction to DWDM Technology: Data in a Reinbow* (IEEE Press, 2000), *Understanding SONET/SDH and ATM: Communications Networks for the Next Millennium* (IEEE Press, 1999), and *Understanding Neural Networks and Fuzzy Logic: Basic Concepts and Applications* (IEEE Press, 1996). He has also contributed chapters to other books and has been a guest editor of *IEEE Communications Magazine*, as well as editor in chief of a technical in-house publication. Also, he has published more than 40 scientific articles.

Dr. Kartalopoulos has been awarded 12 patents, and has submitted six more applications in optical communications. Having been an IEEE Distinguished Lecturer, he has lectured on DWDM technology, on SONET/SDH, on ATM, on Neural Networks, and on Fuzzy Logic at international conferences of IEEE and SPIE as well as in academic forums. He is a member of IEEE (the editor in chief of the IEEE Press Board, past vice president, and committee chair), of Sigma XI, and of Etta Kappa Nu. He has received the President Award, the Award of Excellence, and numerous certificates of appreciation.